Out of the Night

Richard Julius Herman Krebs writing as
JAN VALTIN

Author Richard Julius Herman Krebs (1905–1951), alias Jan Valtin, in 1950.

OUT OF THE NIGHT

Jan Valtin

Cover © 2020 by Steve W. Chadde. All rights reserved.
Printed in the United States of America.

AN ORCHARD INNOVATIONS BOOK
ISBN 9781951682262

Out of the Night was originally published in 1941 by Alliance Book Corporation, New York. Jan Valtin, also author of *Children of Yesterday,* is the pseudonym of Richard Julius Herman Krebs.

CONTENTS

Book One
THEY CALLED IT DAWN

1. LUMPENHUND 3
2. SAILOR'S WAY 14
3. I STRIKE OUT 26
4. SMUGGLING FOR THE COMINTERN 36
5. "DID YOU EVER KILL A MAN?" 45
6. SCAPEGOATS ON THE BARRICADES 57
7. RED VAGABONDAGE 70
8. PASSAGE TO CONSPIRACY 82
9. I ATTACK THE PACIFIC 93
10. THE ROAD TO LENINGRAD 104
11. COURIER TO THE ORIENT 115
12. FROM SHANGHAI TO SAN QUENTIN 125

Book Two
THE DANCE OF DARKNESS

13. NEW WEAPONS 143
14. THE INFALLIBLES 154
15. FIRELEI 166
16. FIRELEI MAKES HER DECISION 178
17. BETWEEN THE HAMMER AND THE ANVIL 191
18. SOVIET SKIPPER 205
19. IMPOTENT AND OMNIPOTENT 218

20. THE MAN HUNTERS	228
21. STALIN OVER THE SEVEN SEAS	241
22. INSPECTOR-GENERAL FOR ENGLAND	252
23. HOW WE ENGINEERED MUTINIES	266
24. THE SWASTIKA CASTS ITS SHADOW	275
25. SCANDINAVIAN INTERLUDE	287

BOOK THREE

THE NIGHT OF LONG KNIVES

26. STORM SIGNALS	301
27. IN THE HURRICANE	313
28. DEAD MEN ON FURLOUGH	326
29. IN THE LANDS OF TWILIGHT	340
30. WEST OF THE RHINE	359
31. "DEATH IS EASY"	373
32. CAPTURED	387
33. THE GESTAPO QUESTIONS ME	402
34. HELL	425
35. I SIGN A CONFESSION	445
36. OF COMRADES AND THE HEADSMAN	458
37. MAN-CAGE MAGIC	471
38. MY BATTLE FOR "MEIN KAMPF"	492
39. DARK DUEL	511
40. I JOIN THE GESTAPO	524
41. FREEMAN ON A LEASH	539
42. ABDUCTED	553
43. FLIGHT	570
WHO'S WHO	585

BOOK ONE

THEY CALLED IT DAWN

2

Chapter One

LUMPENHUND

I am a German by birth. But the years of my childhood were scattered over places as far apart as the Rhine and the Yangtze-kiang. My voyage began at the point where the Rhine suddenly sweeps westward to bite its course through the mountains before it curves north again to flow, broad and swift, past the Lorelei and the towers of Cologne. One day in 1904 my mother, then on the way from Genoa to Rotterdam to join her husband, who had come in from the sea, felt that her time was near at hand. She interrupted her journey and went to the home of people who knew her, in a little town near Mainz. There she gave birth to her first son. And before I was one month old, she carried me aboard a steamer, bound down the Rhine to Rotterdam.

My father had spent most of his life at sea. But despite his roamings, he had the devotion of a wanderer for the land of his birth, a devotion which I did not learn to share. During the decade preceding the World War my father was attached to the nautical inspection service of the North German Lloyd, in the Orient and in Italy; it was a shore job which allowed him to take his family from port to port at Company expense. One result of this nomadism was that by the time I was fourteen I spoke, aside from my native language, fragments of Chinese and Malay, and had a smattering of Swedish, English, Italian and the indomitable Pidgin-English of the waterfront. Another upshot was that I acquired early a consciousness of inferiority toward boys who had had the privilege of experiencing their boyhood in one country. In the face of the challenging bigotry of those who had taken root—"This is my country; it is the best country,"—I felt a certain sad instability. I retaliated by regarding with a childish contempt the healthy manifestations of nationalism.

Invincible wanderlust was another result of our life on the waterfronts. I ran off on hot afternoons to explore the harbors and to watch maneuvering ships and toiling stevedores. I knew the smells of godowns and of ships' holds; when the wind stood right I could distinguish the aroma of jute or copra or tropical woods a quarter of a mile away from the wharves. I liked to read books of exploration and bold voyaging. I never played at being a soldier. I was either a skipper, a boss of longshoremen or a pirate. I liked to sail the little boat I had when I was twelve through squally weather in the estuaries of the rivers Weser and Elbe. I had my proudest moment when the master carpenter at the boatyard pointed me out to a colleague with the words, "That curly-head, he sails like the devil."

My father rarely spoke of his adventurous past of which tattooings of anchors, barques, and exotic wenches with enormous hips on his arms and body, as well as ponderous silver decorations bearing the Chinese dragon and the Persian lion, gave an inkling. Like most German craftsmen of the period, he was conservatively class conscious. He belonged to the Social Democratic Party, was a loyal trade-unionist, and considered the Kaiser as a superfluous clown. He was militant in a quiet way, yet capable of sudden eruptions of temper, and he firmly believed in a just and beautiful socialist future.

My courageous and deeply religious mother had a dream of her own: a house on some hill, with a garden and a sprinkling of birches around, a friendly anchorage to which her four sons, all of whom were destined to follow the sea, would flock for a holiday after every completed voyage. She was a native of Schonen, the southernmost province of Sweden, and she shared the natural hospitality and a respectful love for all growing things which seem to be the characteristics of the Swedish.

The first school I attended was the German school of Buenos Aires. I remained there but a little over a year, and my memory of it is vague. Two years at a British school in Singapore followed. It was here, in an atmosphere of equatorial heat and British world domination, that I first became aware, shamefacedly, of the vast gulf which separated me, the child of a worker, from the sons and daughters of colonial officials and the white merchants of the East. I had no access to their parties, and the bourgeois arrogance of their parents made them shun the humble home of my family. We had but two Chinese servants, while they had fifteen and twenty. Because my father saw no harm in my association with the offspring of his industrious Eurasian aides, the little "imperialist" snobs of my class coined a nickname for me which even made some of the grown-ups smile. It was Lumpenhund, which means "ragged dog." I was awkward and too big for my age. The teacher, a genteel but slightly battered Englishwoman, suspected, I fear, that her discriminations against her only proletarian pupil and her genuflections before the sires of the well-to-do escaped my attention.

In 1913 my father was transferred to a temporary job in Hongkong, and later the same year he was called to supervise the outfitting of newly-bought ships in Yokohama and Batavia. In all these travels his family went with him—traveling second or third class on chance steamers of the North German Lloyd. I well remember the officious deck steward of the liner Kleist who hustled me from the promenade deck to a deck considerably nearer the waterline.

"Sei nicht traurig," my father had consoled me. *"Wir sind nun eimnal Menschen der zweiten Klasse."*

People of the second class! The family grew larger from year to year. A sister was born in Hongkong. Another aboard a ship between Suez and Colombo. A brother was born in Singapore; it was he who later became an officer in the Nazi air force to find his death through an act of communist sabotage in 1938.

The year 1914 saw us in Genoa, Italy, where the company needed an expert on stowage to help the agent in charge in the dispatching of the so-called "macaroni liners," the huge ships of the *Berlin* type engaged in carrying vast numbers of Italian emigrants and harvest hands to New York and the South American wheat and beef metropoles. It was in Genoa that the War overtook us. German shipping came to a standstill.

We continued to live in Genoa until Italy declared war on Germany in the following year. The intervening nine months savored of a protracted nightmare. They taught me what mass hatred and chauvinism in its ugliest forms could be. Every news kiosk was plastered with pamphlets and posters showing German soldiers nailing children to tables by their tongues, or tearing out the tongues of beautiful young women. I could not go into the harbor, which held for me a fascination I am at a loss to explain, without being assaulted and trounced by bands of Italian hoodlums. On the way to and from school, and even in the garden adjoining our cottage on the slope of the Righi, I and other boys suspected of being German, were bombarded with stones and manure of mules, beaten with sticks, spitten into our faces and hounded even through the broken windowpanes of our homes. I had little respect for Italian boys as fighters. Banded together and armed with solid clubs, six Austrian, Swiss or German boys could easily, I believed, put ten times their number of youthful *salita* wolves to flight.

Had my father called these Italian super-patriots traitors and *Schweinehunde,* I could have understood the situation and sung the Hohenzollern anthem; but he fervently condemned this war. Because he believed in an active socialist internationalism and workers' solidarity above and beyond the borders of nations, he also condemned the socialist leaders of Germany when they declared a social truce and voted for war credits in August, 1914. All this left me puzzled, frightened, distrustful, and somewhat mutinous against the might-is-right slogans of the time.

When Italy finally declared war, my father, to avoid imprisonment as a naval reservist, had disappeared toward the northern frontier together with scattered groups of compatriots. An official in a flaming uniform entered our home and demanded that we leave Italian soil within twelve hours, taking only such belongings as we could carry. Abandoning by far the larger portion of our possessions, mother and children boarded the Milano express and crossed the Alps into Germany overnight. We entered the Fatherland like refugees from abroad. After all, to the older of us children Germany was like an alien land.

Beginning with the third year of the War we lived in Bremen. My father served in the Imperial fleet. His first assignment had been aboard a Heligoland patrol boat; now his post was in the forward torpedo room of the battleship *Thueringen,* stationed at Wilhelmshaven and for periods at the Kiel naval base. My mother fought incredibly hard to keep her brood alive on the meager allowance allotted to families of men in the service. I wore clothes made of paper, my shoes were made of wood, in summer I went barefoot, and our staple food consisted of turnips and dismal bread, with potatoes rare and horse meat a luxury. They were years in which we came to know the meaning of steady hunger, and in the winters, of fierce cold. We collected beech-nuts in the woods to have oil, and acorns to have coffee. Like a pack of wolves we boys would prowl at the edges of the estates and the fields and the army depots, stealing wood, potatoes and tinned food, and scavenging for precious coal in the vicinity of factories and railroad yards.

Repeatedly I was caught by an elderly forest-keeper or gendarme. Since I saw nothing wrong in such petty depredations, I arrived at a point where I regarded everyone who wore a badge of authority as an overbearing foe.

In school my marks were below the average. The haphazard training I had received at the foreign schools did not enable me to meet the rigid requirements of the German educational system. My teacher, a man named Schlueter, had lost both his sons in France, whereupon his wife had killed herself with gas. He reacted to his own misery by beginning and ending his days at school with most brutal beatings of his pupils. At the slightest provocation he used to haul them across his desk, in front of a class of fifty, and flog them with a cane until they were unconscious. I became his frequent victim because my personal heroes were neither Bismarck nor Ludendorff, but Magellan, Captain Cook, and J. F. Cooper's "Red Rover"—foreigners all as, indeed, I was myself.

This teacher would pound into our heads the famous catchword "Hold out!—Hold through!—Hold your tongues!" and tell us that the British blockade was to blame for the plight of all Germans. But my father, and other sailors, home on furlough with a load of filched sugar and *Kommisbrot*, blamed the Kaiser and the munition makers. With the sons of other rebellious workers I sat in secret cellar gatherings and sang:

> *Death to hangmen, kings and traitors,*
> *Give the masses bread!*
> *Forward! 'Tis the people's slogan:*
> *Free we'll be—or dead.*

In September, 1918, when I was almost fourteen, an older friend who was a journeyman to a master chimney sweep brought me into one of the youth groups of the Independent Socialists. These groups, which already used the name of Spartakus Jugend, were, I was told, illegally organized by young revolutionists from Berlin.

A scraggy band of child rebels, we met secretly in attics, in abandoned houses an3 even on roofs. We were taught by men who claimed they were deserters from the navy to hate the rich, to tell the poor that they must rise in a body and fight, to disrupt patriotic school meetings with itching powder and stink bombs which were given to us packed in candy boxes, and to sabotage the war chest collections of old metal parts, bottles and felt hats which were conducted through the schools. This we did, and more, acting out of our own zealous initiative. We drew caricatures of the Kaiser hanging from a gallows and passed them furtively from hand to hand. We gave articulation to our contempt for established authority by hurling dead rats through the open window's of police stations.

From my father and other sailors, when they came home for a monthly two-day leave, we heard much of what was going on in the fleet. Mutiny brewed. The men, crammed into narrow quarters a thousand and more on a single ship and ridden by hunger, hated the officers for their arrogance and the champagne and butter they consumed. The *Kulies* of the Fleet wanted more than an end to the war; they talked of revenge for all the degradations of the past. On several ships secret action committees of the sailors and stokers had been elected. The latrines in the shipyards became the centers for clandestine revolutionary meetings. Desertions increased; sailors sold their uniforms and decamped inshore. Several ringleaders from the warships had been court-martialed and executed by Imperial firing squads.

Not a week passed that we did not have a deserter staying overnight in our dingy apartment. Usually they left at dawn, clad in civilian rags, on their way to Berlin or Munich and on to Saxony and Silesia. Most of them brought service pistols into the houses of .workers. My mother abhorred arms. But I knew that several families in the same tenement had firearms hidden away in the basement, under floor boards, in window casings, and stove pipes. People were silent and sullen. No one in our block or the next believed that the end of the war was near.

Once a sailor returning from Petrograd was our guest. Tall, gaunt, to my eyes a rather adventurous figure, he stood in a corner of the living room and told about the victory of the Bolsheviki and the first workers' government in the world. He drank great quantities of bad, black, unsugared coffee, and talked until he was hoarse. The room was full of people. They kept on coming and going. They asked questions, shook their heads, argued, and many eyes shone. When it was time to go to sleep he became afraid to stay; someone might have informed the police, he thought. I led him to the family of a friend on the other side of the river. This sailor slunk into a doorway or into a side street whenever he saw a police man under the street lights ahead. In the end I was a little disgusted. I had a fairly low opinion of policemen. For two long hours we trudged through the night, the sailor and I, without exchanging a word.

Toward the end of October, 1918, my father wrote that the High Seas Fleet had received orders for a final attack against England. No secret was made of it. The officers, he reported in his blunt fashion, reveled all night. They spoke of the death-ride of the Fleet. Rumor had it that the Fleet was under orders to go down in battle to save the honor of the generation that built it. "Their honor is not our honor," my father wrote.

Two days later the Fleet was under way. The people in Bremen were more surly than ever.

Then came stirring news. Mutiny in the Kaiser's fleet! Young sons of the bourgeoisie who had been sporting sailors' caps now left them at home. I saw women who laughed and wept because they had their men in the Fleet. From windows and doors and in front of the food stores sounded the anxious voices: "Will the Fleet sail out? . . . No, the Fleet must not sail! It's murder! Finish the war!" Youngsters in the streets yelled, "Hurrah."

Details filtered through. Aboard the *Thueringen* the mutineers had seized the ship. They had dropped the anchors, smashed the lights and disarmed the officers.

A shout went up: "Down with the Kaiser! Down with the war! We want peace!"

Passing men shook their heads and said the penalty for mutiny was death. A deserter from a mine sweeping flotilla carried further news. The battleship *Helgoland* had followed the example of the *Thueringen*. The stokers had doused the fires and killed the steam.

The Fleet did not sail. The Fleet returned to port.

Five hundred and eighty mutineers from the *Thueringen* and the *Helgoland*, among them my father, were arrested and jammed into cells in the ships.

At home we spent two dreary nights. My mother prayed. The younger children shivered in their beds. There was no coal and no food. I remember wondering why I could not get excited over the possibility that my father would have to face the firing squad. The arrest of the mutineers, however, was only an incident. With help from outside they smashed the doors, stormed the ships, and took control. The officers gave way. Aboard the *Helgoland* a chunky young stoker yanked down the Kaiser's flag and hauled the red flag to the masthead. By November 7 the whole Fleet was in revolt.

That night I saw the mutinous sailors roll into Bremen on caravans of commandeered trucks—red flags and machine guns mounted on the trucks. Thousands milled in the streets. Often the trucks stopped and the sailors sang and roared for free passage. The workers cheered particularly a short, burly young man in grimy blue. The man swung his carbine over his head to return the salute. He was the stoker who had hoisted the first red flag over the Fleet. His name was Ernst Wollweber.

In front of the railway station I saw a man lose his life. He was an officer in field gray who came out of the station the minute it was surrounded, and was seized by the mutineers. He was slow in giving up his arms and epaulettes. He made no more than a motion to draw his pistol when they were on top of him. Rifle butts flew through the air above him. Fascinated, I watched from a little way off. Then the sailors turned away to saunter back to their trucks. I had seen dead people before. But death by violence and the fury that accompanied it were something new. The officer did not move. I marveled how easily a man could be killed.

I rode away on my bicycle. I fevered with a strange sense of power. I did not know that it was part of the mass intoxication which, like the chunky stoker from the *Helgoland*, had risen from the depths to take charge of minds and events. Not far from Hillmann's Hotel a band of civilians was trouncing a policeman who tried to forbid them to ride on the outside of a tramcar.

I circled toward the Brill, a square in the western center of the town. From there on I had to push my bicycle through the throngs. The population was in the streets. From all sides masses of humanity, a sea of swinging, pushing bodies and distorted faces was moving toward the center of the town. Many of the workers were armed with guns, with bayonets, with hammers. I felt then, and later, that the sight of armed workers sets off a roar in the blood of those who sympathize with the marchers. Singing hoarsely was a sprawling band of demonstrating convicts freed by a truckload of sailors from Oslebshausen prison. Most of them wore soldiers' greatcoats over their prison garb. But the true symbol of this revolution, which was really naught but a revolt, were neither the armed workers nor the singing convicts—but the mutineers from the Fleet with their reversed hatbands and carbines slung over their shoulders, butts up and barrels down.

The City Hall of Bremen fell without real fighting. No one rose to defend the toppling Empire. The masses did not want bloodshed, not even revenge; they were war-weary and now they were determined to stop the spook. Late that night tens of thousands of workers filled the marketplace. Among them was a sprinkling of soldiers and the inevitable sailors from the warships.

At the foot of the Roland statue a frightened old woman crouched. "Ach, du lieber GGott," she wailed piercingly. "What is all this? What's the world coming to?" A huge-framed young worker who gave intermittent bellows of triumph and whom I had followed from the Brill, grasped the old woman's shoulders. He laughed resoundingly. "Revolution," he rumbled. "Revolution, madam."

Speaker followed speaker in proclaiming the new epoch from the balcony of the City Hall; a lanky soldier, a representative of a newly elected workers' council, a large-bodied official of the Social Democratic Party, and in between the thick-set ringleader of naval mutineers, Ernst Wollweber.

Wollweber hurled his words like rocks into the masses.

"We stripped the Kaiser of his boots," he ended. "Now let us finish off the capitalists. Long live the German Soviet Republic!"

The masses responded. They roared until it seemed their faces would burst. The compulsion was irresistible. I roared with them. The upsurge spread from the coast to the south, with sailors as the spearhead of revolt. The Prussian government gave way. Bavaria was proclaimed a republic. In Hamburg, traditionally the reddest town of Germany, Soviets came to power. The Kaiser bolted to Holland, and two days later the Armistice was signed.

I did not see my father again. I was told that he had been elected to the revolutionary workers' and soldiers' council of Emden. Later my father went to Berlin. The Independent Socialists sent him to Brunswick. Meanwhile I spent the better part of each day on my bicycle, running errands for a sailors' committee which had established headquarters in the Weser Shipyards. I did not understand the quarrels between the various workers' parties, but I easily acquired the contempt with which the former mutineers regarded the moderate politicians. Each day in Bremen saw demonstrations and counter-demonstrations of rival proletarian blocs. A semblance of unity came to pass only when the field gray troops flooded back from the front, still under the command of their old officers. I was among the multitude who met the returning regiments 75 and 213 on the north-western fringe of the city. The soldiers were silent and plastered with mud. The officers had their swords drawn and they answered the shouting masses with sneers and threats.

"We're going to clean up here," was their threat.

Once in the city, the soldiers from the front were surrounded by revolutionary sailors and shipyard workers entrenched in machine gun nests on roofs and balconies. The troops were trapped; everyone expected a massacre. However, they were disarmed and disbanded without bloodshed. A few days later the first signs of the existence of newly formed nationalist bands were in evidence. Posters shouted from the walls, "Destroy the November Criminals." Squads of workers tore them off. Tired horses, abandoned by the troops, were butchered at night in the streets by flocks of determined women.

In January, 1919, disunity led to open battle. The Ebert-Scheidemann-Noske forces, right-wing socialists, enlisted the aid of nationalist divisions under the command of officers from the Western Front to head off the attempts of the Spartakus Bund to seize power. Hundreds died in the streets of Berlin. Karl Liebknecht and the heroic woman who shared his leadership, Rosa Luxemburg, were murdered by a camarilla of such officers. Rosa was torn to pieces and flung into a canal, and the monarchist rabble rejoiced in a new song which began:

"A corpse floats in the Landwehr Canal..."

In Bremen the sailors were still optimistic. As one of them put it, "As long as we have a machine gun, a loaf of munition bread and a liverwurst, we have no cause for worry." There was street fighting in Munich, in Hamburg, in Silesia. In Bremen the moderates were shoved aside. Soviets ruled the city, and proclaimed it an independent republic.

On January 20 came the news that my father had died in a hospital in Wolfenbuettel. That gave me a fearful shock. My mother, almost out of her mind with grief, left at once for Brunswick. The younger children were left in charge of a neighbor. On January 22 my youngest brother, five years old, was found dead in his bed. No one saw him die.

Since the middle of November, 1918, I had ceased going to school. The Young Spartakus group to which I belonged was quite active. Each morning we went to the Red House on the left bank of the Weser and got packs of leaflets from the secretary of a fierce hunchback who had somehow come to power in the councils of the revolutionary sailors. The leaflets we distributed in the harbor, at the factory gates, and in suburban tenement districts.

In the first days of January, 1919, the Spartakus Bund constituted itself as the Communist Party of Germany, but we had taken such pride in the old name of our organization that we did not call ourselves Young Communists, but Young Spartacists. On January 27, on the Kaiser's birthday, sailors with red armbands organized us boys into squads of twenty. All day we spent in breaking up the Kaiser Day meetings arranged by the principals of *gymnasiums* and high schools. We armed ourselves with clubs and stones and burst in on the meetings. We tore the Imperial flags from the pulpits and subdued the singing of *"Heil Dir im Siegerkranz"* with the German version of the Marseillaise. The teachers did not dare to interfere with our rowdyism. The better-dressed and better-fed boys we drove out into the streets.

Came February. The tragedy that had been enacted in Berlin— the crushing of fighting revolutionary minorities by the young *Reichswehr* under the command of War Minister Gustav Noske, a social democrat—was repeated in many outlying cities. Rumors spread in our ranks that Berlin was sending reactionary troops to suppress the Soviets in Bremen. On February 3, people clustered around posters announcing that General Gerstenberg's division was approaching the city from the south. All revolutionary workers were called to arms. The sons of the bourgeoisie evacuated the city. In long drawn-out columns they raced away on skates over the frozen moorland to join the onmarching troops.

The somewhat less than three hundred members of the Young Spartakus League were mobilized to serve as messengers and dispatch riders. Many of us were supplied with new bicycles which had been taken from the stores. The Revolutionary Defense Committee used boys and girls as couriers because youngsters were less likely to be suspected and halted by advancing Noske troops. All through the day I watched sailors and workers place field cannon on covered spots along the river front and machine guns on strategic housetops. Spartacist detachments were marching toward the outskirts of the city. Most of the marchers were young, under twenty. They were all badly clad. Some wore rags in place of boots. They had their rifles slung butt-end up over their shoulders and their hands buried in their pockets. Their faces were pale, and blue with the cold.

The night from February 3 to February 4 I did not go home. A mixture of self-destructive defiance and hectic fatalism, a mood that sprang from the tireless little horde of sailors, seemed to dominate all of us, old and young. I heard men talk of annihilating the counter-revolution. They could not fool me; I knew what was in their minds. They themselves faced annihilation and they realized it, but their fever and their self-respect and their sensitivity toward ridicule did not permit them to give up a position already as good as lost. I half slept through that night on the ground floor of the Stock Exchange building.

The large hall was cluttered with young men and a few young women. Scores of bicycles leaned against the walls. Firearms were stacked near the doors. On heaps of straw people snored or conversed in whispers. Big pots of bad coffee steamed on kerosene stoves. It was still dark when we were roused. Several sailors ran among us, leaping over the debris, kicking the sleepers right and left, and shouting.

"All up! *Reise! Reise!* The Noske guards are coming!"

On Market Square the undersized hunchback, a huge sailor, and a young man with spectacles were issuing orders. From the left bank of the river drifted the thump of artillery and the hard chatter of machine guns. With five other boys I was ordered to proceed to the central savings bank on Kaiser Street. We were to serve as dispatch riders between the bank and the Weser Shipyards in the west.

•••

Three of our courier group deserted at once. I doubt that their motive was fear. They simply went off to get closer glimpses of the battle. All that day curious mobs were dodging around street corners, undeterred by bullets whining past their ears. Two times during the forenoon I made the journey between the bank and the shipyard with a scrawled report of the comrade in charge of defending the entrance of Kaiser Street, a thoroughfare that led from the river to the central railway station. At that time the western portion of the town was still outside the zone of fighting. Barricaded stores, shattered windows, patches of pavement torn up and heaped to form barricades were landmarks all along the route. There seemed nothing more to do after the second trip. Since I had never been inside of a bank I proceeded to explore the building. Not a window was intact. Doors had been broken. Desks, chairs, filing cabinets and rugs were piled up against the windows, ready to be hurled on the heads of attackers in the street below. At some of the windows snipers were at work. No one stopped me; any spy of the counter forces could have walked into the building to reconnoiter the forces of the defenders. Finally I came to rest in a large room on the top floor. From Hein Rode, a sailor with whom I was acquainted, and from what I saw, I gained an understanding of the rudiments of the most bitter form of combat— house-to-house fighting in the streets.

There was a machine gun firing from the largest window. Two sailors and a youth about my own age served it. By this time the whole city reverberated with the sounds of battle.

Snipers fired at soldiers crawling over distant housetops. The field pieces along the river roared intermittently. The vicious hammering of machine guns was continuous. Men were shooting from speeding lorries and from doorways. Several houses were afire. Down in the Brill inquisitive pedestrians ran for their lives. Fragments of rock and much glass littered the streets. Then came prolonged explosions of such violence that the building rocked as if under an earthquake.

"A direct hit?" I asked excitedly.

"Mines," Hein Rode said calmly. "They're using mine-throwers."

Advancing along the Meter Strasse, the Noske guards were nearing the left side of the river. I saw them leap from doorway to doorway, while others came simultaneously across the roofs and garden fringes. From half a mile off they looked like animated toy soldiers; in reality they were veterans of the Western Front. The thumping of the mines increased. The southern bridge-head of the Kaiser bridge swarmed suddenly with field-gray shapes under steel helmets.

At the window the machine gun jammed. A sailor turned and said, "Hang on now, the comrades are blowing up the bridges."

An instant later he cursed: "*Verdammt,* why don't they blow up that bridge?"

There was a lull in the firing. The Noske guards stormed the bridge. As they ran, they shouted. And abruptly the machine guns opened in merciless bursts. I saw many soldiers fall. Death was commonplace. That day it evoked in me no other emotion than would a fascinating show. An instant later we all ran from the building in a panic. The thunder of exploding hand-grenades was less than two hundred yards away. Shells exploding in the air ripped chunks of rock out of the towers of the cathedral. A dispatch rider coming from the direction of the marketplace roared something about armored cars.

Angry shouts went up. "The bridges are taken!" There was no sign of discouragement. But there was a hideous confusion. A rumor spread that Knief, the revolutionary teacher, and Fraczunkovitz, the hunchback, had escaped by plane.

"Better get going," Rode advised me. "Save your skin."

I mounted my bicycle and rode away, unaware at first of the direction I was taking. Dead men sprawled grotesquely here and there, and in many places the snow was splotched with blood. I reached the moat, a natural line of defense encircling the inner city. It too had been deserted. Red Guards were retreating to the railway station. Several times I was stopped by Noske Guards, but seeing that despite my height I was only a child, they let me proceed. Everywhere lorries loaded with soldiers in field gray advanced slowly. I fled the town, following a detachment of retreating mutineers. After three days of wandering I reached Hamburg.

From the railway station I wrote a postcard to my mother to assure her that I was alive. She wired me what little money she managed to scrape up. Next day she arrived in Hamburg, looking like a ghost.

"I don't want to go back," I told her. "I'm going to sea."

For a long while she was silent. Only her patient gray eyes widened and filled with fathomless sadness. Finally she said, "But our country has no ships. They were all taken by the British."

"I shall sign on as deck boy under some foreign flag," I replied. In the following days my mother sold the remnants of family silver she had brought with her, and bought me oilskins, seaboots, blankets and a few other necessities. She also gave me a small Bible, and she arranged with Wolfert, a shipping master with crafty blue eyes in a drinker's face, that I could live at his boarding house until he had procured me a ship.

When the train moved out of the Hamburg station I saw her standing at the window, frail, shabby, sad and invincibly loyal. "Fair winds," she called to me. "May God be with you."

Chapter Two

SAILOR'S WAY

It was springtime in Hamburg. I wanted a ship, a job at sea, and a chance to work myself up to a captain's rank. For weeks I haunted the waterfront, but the great seaport was a sleeping giant. Except for coastal trade and a few food ships from America, the Hamburg harbor was dead. The British blockade was still in force, although it was months after the signing of the Armistice. It was springtime in Versailles, too, where the peace that was to haunt the world was being perfected.

I would awake hungry, and was still hungry when I went to sleep. Hunger wiped out the lines between adolescents and full-grown men. A sack of flour was worth more than a human life. When a fruit cart of a peasant from Vierlanden was turned over in the street and a middle-aged man tried to shoulder me aside in the scramble for the winter apples, what else was there to do but to stand up and hit him in the face? I was in my fifteenth year.

I took part in the plundering of a wholesale fish store in Altona. Tons of fish were dumped on the cobblestones, and people grabbed the fish and ran. When a policeman interfered, what else was there to do but to slam a ten-pound codfish into his face? When for a fish or a piece of leather cut out of a stolen transmission belt, a boy could have the body of a girl not older than himself or be instructed in lewd practices by a soldier's widow turned prostitute, what meaning was there in all the pratings of the need for law and order and a decent life?

When one is thrown adrift in a polluted stream, with no dry land in sight, what escape is there? I took no active part in the political riots of this Hamburg spring, but my heart was with the revolutionary workers, perhaps because it was their side which always lost in the end. Whenever I saw a policeman level his rifle against a civilian, I felt the same hatred as at the sight of a teamster cruelly mistreating his emaciated horse. Each day armed workers skirmished with the police. Night after night the sounds of desultory firing echoed over the city. Yet the news that a trawler loaded with flounders or herring was steaming up the river moved the people more than stumbling against a dead man in the gutter, or encountering a lorry piled high with crude coffins, or coming upon a barricade manned by a few determined-looking youths.

I hunted for food and work. But the struggle to conquer and defend power seemed the essence of life. In the Grenzfass, a large beer hall in the St. Pauli district, I heard and met for the first time Herrmann Knueffgen, an incarnation of all the political adventurers of our century. Surrounded by a singularly well-knit assortment of revolutionary toughs, Knueffgen radiated an atmosphere of indestructible aplomb. Of medium height, slight of build, with a mop of almost colorless hair, his pale eyes gleaming with reckless deviltry, he was no more than twenty-two or -three at the time. Early that morning, at the head of his *Rollkommando,* he had successfully raided a basement arsenal of the *Buergerwehr,* a counterrevolutionary organization of armed citizens. Knueffgen made a speech. The hall was full of workless dockers.

"The rich must die so that the poor may live," he cried. There was a thunder of cheers. The sailor's Messianic fervor fired my imagination, yet there was nothing bloodthirsty about him as there was about many others who had risen from the depths. Shortly after this stirring meeting in the Grenzfass, Knueffgen embarked on an enterprise that made him the idol of waterfront radicals the world over. A delegation of the Communist Party of Germany was scheduled to go to Moscow at a time when Russia was closed to the West by the civil war. Herrmann Knueffgen was commissioned to bring this delegation to Moscow dead or alive. He stowed himself and the delegates away in the fishtank of an outbound trawler. Once at sea, he emerged with a revolver in each hand, imprisoned the captain and the crew of ten, and took possession of the vessel which he then navigated around the North Cape to Murmansk. The delegation arrived in Moscow to confer with Lenin, and Knueffgen, upon his return to Germany, was convicted and jailed for piracy on the high seas. No prison, however, could hold him long.

The faithful shipping master Wolfert, through his acquaintance with former sailship masters, at last found me a ship. One morning, half drunk as usual and bullying his frightened wife, he thrust a letter into my hands and shouted at me to report to the Shipowners' Association for duty aboard the former Africa liner *Lucy Woerman.* As if by sudden magic, I was signed on as ordinary seaman and the following day I packed my canvas bag and went aboard. The ship hulked gray and mournful at her wharf, her flanks covered with creeping rust. The thought of being able to make my living on the good clean sea made me weep with joy.

The ship was bound for South America. She was loaded with crews who were to man and bring home the large fleet of German vessels marooned in the ports of Chile and Peru during the war. Desperately anxious to leave the hunger-ridden Fatherland, thousands schemed and bribed to get a berth aboard the *Lucy Woerman.* Scores of the nearly four hundred who were signed had been among the mutineers of the Imperial navy; scores of others had never been aboard a ship before; once at sea none manifested the slightest intention of bringing German ships back home, or of ever returning to Germany.

The ship was infested with stowaways. Three boatloads of them were returned to shore off Cuxhaven. Before the red rock of Heligoland was abeam, five prostitutes were discovered in the boatswain's locker, and three other young women, who proved to be the wives of former storekeepers, among the crew. All of them were transferred to homebound fishermen. But many others, found later, remained aboard.

Soon after the Cornwall capes had slipped out of sight astern and the Lucy Woermm bucked westward over the Atlantic rollers, gambling centers and even a brothel set up in business in messrooms and cabins overnight. Tattooing booths, bands of musicians, instructors in English and Spanish and jiu-jitsu began to flourish. Spartacists, anarchists and self-styled missionaries launched discussion circles. Gangs of hoodlums assaulted and robbed the more prosperous voyagers. One old man was found with his throat cut. Another elderly man put on holiday clothes and at sunrise jumped into the ocean.

The ship's officers, reinforced by a few loyal mariners of the prewar school, barricaded themselves on the bridge and in the engine room. Elsewhere conditions bordering on madness reigned. A Pirate's Club sprang up, announcing as its purpose seizure of the ship for a journey to the South Seas. Off the Azores, however, such leadership as there could be fell to a man named Herrmann Kruse.

Kruse, an old member of the Spartakus Bund, called a general meeting of his followers aboard the *Lucy Woerman* and emerged as the head of a newly elected ship Soviet. He formed a ship Tcheka, and by sheer terror subdued all independent marauders in our midst. Kruse, about twenty-five years old, was blond, bearish, quick-tempered, and had a flair for oratory. He brought some order out of the confusion and now he demanded control of the ship. The skipper armed his officers with pistols for the meeting with Kruse's Soviet. By way of retaliation Kruse's strong-arm squads seized all available provisions and began a hunger blockade against the bridge and the engine room. Most of the time the steam was kept low, and at times the ship wallowed helplessly without steam at all. In sight of the green shore of Jamaica a passing oil tanker, apparently suspecting trouble aboard the *Lucy Woerman*, signaled.

"Can I give you assistance?"

"Thank you. I have a cargo of lunatics," our skipper answered.

But the officers succeeded, despite all difficulties, in bringing the vessel to Colon. One faction on board planned to scuttle the ship in the Panama Canal, to desert, and to walk through the jungles to Mexico or the United States. Herrmann Kruse and his guerrillas, armed with clubs and belaying pins, opposed this. Kruse's plan was to allow the *Lucy* to pass through the Canal, then to overpower the officers. After that, we were to steam for the Galapagos Islands, establish a Soviet Republic, and ask Moscow for protection, supplies and women.

Opposing factions shrieked their protest. "Kruse wants to be a dictator! Down with Galapagos! We land right here!" Little did the American authorities at Colon suspect what a mess was passing into the Canal. In defiance of Kruse, "debarkation squads" were hastily formed as we steamed through the Canal. The rush to reach a shore that looked inviting from a little way off was contagious. As a matter of course, I joined one of the squads.

We packed our belongings, put on life preservers, and lined up along the rail for the plunge. The captain shouted from the bridge for us to desist, but he was greeted with laughter. Group after group heaved their bundles overboard and jumped after them. The Canal waters were soon dotted with swimming men.

I, too, jumped. I felt the water rush upward, smooth and warm, and then I swam for dear life, pushing with all my strength to get away from the deadly propeller. Several of my fellow-deserters were cut to shreds. The shore was much farther away than it had seemed from the ship. Close behind me, as I swam, struggled a middle-aged shoemaker. *"Das ist schoen,"* he kept saying to encourage me, "now, ho! for America!"

Together we finally reached the muddy bank and ran for the green cover less than fifty yards away. The ground was soggy, and the underbrush dense. But we pushed forward. Soon we came on four other deserters, and the six of us proceeded in single file, carrying our water-soaked bundles and streaming with perspiration. Our leader was a stoker who had once served on Amazon River steamboats. Sometimes the underbrush was so thick that we could not penetrate it; at other times we were confronted with swamps which seemed to stretch out for miles. Once in a while the Amazon River stoker climbed a tree to look around. All he could report was jungle all around, a few hills, and steamers passing in the Canal. The passing steamers looked as if they were threading their way through the treetops.

After walking in circles for four or five hours, we struck a lake. We tried to skirt the shore of the lake, but soon ran into swamps. The Amazon River stoker cursed almost without interruption. The shoemaker chattered happily. He told us he had all the tools of his trade in the bundle he carried, and he looked forward to a prosperous existence in some American city. Suddenly our leader halted.

"Look—a railroad," he exclaimed.

Ahead of us was a railroad embankment, neat, compact, dry.

Someone said: "Let's stay here and dry out our bundles. When they're dry, they'll be easier to carry." We all agreed.

We opened our bundles and spread the wet things over the tracks: shirts, pants, papers, tobacco. The stoker sent one man a hundred yards in each direction to watch for oncoming trains. We stripped off our clothes and spread them out to dry. The second youngest of our group, who had been a metal worker's apprentice, had found some wild bananas.

We munched bananas and relaxed in the sun. Our hopes rose. The shoemaker wanted to ride the next train into Panama City. He was anxious to start himself in business without loss of time. The stoker spoke of a foreman's job in a vast banana plantation.

It was agreed that the men who stood guard on both sides of the tracks should whistle when a train approached. But when a train came from the Atlantic side, the guard did not whistle. Naked, his pants and shirt jammed under his arm, he came running toward us down the tracks. Behind him rumbled the train.

It was too late to save our things. Our leader yelled, "All hands take cover."

We dived into the jungle. The train ran over our belongings. Then it stopped. Men in khaki uniforms jumped from the train, and began to comb the jungle.

We separated. I crawled through broad-leaved bushes, moving on hands and knees, and when I rose I confronted a grinning soldier.

"Come on," he said, grasping my shoulders. "You can't run around here with no clothes on."

He led me to the train. All my companions had been caught. I put on a shirt which had been cut under the armpits by the train, and a pair of trousers which had but one leg. My comrades did not look much better. We were herded into the train and taken to a station. From there we were marched to a police post. The Americans treated us hospitably. They fed us and plied us with cigarettes.

Before nightfall we were all loaded into a motor launch and returned to the *Lucy,* which was anchored in Panama Bay. The ship weighed anchor and shaped a course down the west coast of South America, calling at Callao and ports to the south. The majority of the men on the *Lucy Woerman* refused to man the ships for the voyage home. There were strikes, arrests by the Chilean police, jail breaks. Herrmann Kruse became known all along the Nitrate Coast as the "Commissar from Hamburg."

I deserted the ship at Antofagasta. Seven months I lingered on the Chile coast. Here I found a freedom I had not known in Europe. The world of political strife, of cold and hunger, seemed as distant as Saturn. Employers and officials asked neither for references nor for papers of identification. I worked in a rigger's gang engaged in refitting a number of old sailing vessels in the roadsteads of Antofagasta and Iquique, and thus acquired a working knowledge of old-fashioned seamanship and of Spanish. After that job gave out, a labor agent of Antofagasta recruited me for the Chuqui copper mines high up in the barren Andes. My work was that of a splicer of wire cables and my pay was high beyond all expectation—ten pesos a day, for good splicers were rare. Life in the mining camps was rough, particularly after paydays when gambling bouts frequently ended in a flash of knives. Much of the bestiality was due to the absence of women; all but the hardiest prostitutes from the coast shunned the trade with the rabble of the Chuqui mines. Many of my fellow workers had been more or less forcibly conscripted from the jails of the larger towns; they were of many nationalities, a hard-working, hard-drinking, unruly crew. The vision of a Chilean girl, Carmencita, with whom I had become friendly, drew me back to the coast. I arrived in Antofagasta on a copper train, with more than three hundred pesos in my pockets, only to find that Carmencita had become the companion of a jobless Norwegian second mate.

I traveled south as a deck passenger aboard a slow coastwise steamer, and after a few aimless days in Valparaiso, I decided to visit the nearby capital,

Santiago de Chile. Here I found work in a candle factory under a domineering British foreman. It was inside work which I detested heartily. In a café I met a young American who had come from Argentina and spoke enthusiastically about the lusty life in Buenos Aires. Next day I threw up my job of packing candles and bought a trans-Andean railway ticket to Buenos Aires. I arrived in the La Plata metropolis with two pesos and sixty centavos. Mounted *carabineros* were rounding up beachcombers in large batches, belying Buenos Aires' reputation as the ideal haven for castaways from all the world. After three days of dodging the energetic *carabineros,* I signed on as a fullfledged sailor aboard the barque *Tiljuca*, a supply ship for the Norwegian and British whaling bases' on the Antarctic island of South Georgia, and manned entirely by Russians and Germans. Toughened as I was, compared with the toughness of the *Tiljuca* tars, I was a mere infant. One of them ate his salt pork, seasoned with tobacco, raw. Another answered a letter from his mother, imploring him to come home after so many years, by writing that he would come home as soon as he had found someone rich enough to be killed for his money. They gloried in their toughness. Thoroughly soaked with vino tinto, none of them hesitated to rob an itinerant hawker or to rape an immigrant girl come aboard to beg food, but all of them showed an almost sentimental affection for the *Tiljuca's* mongrel dog and the forecastle canary. Perhaps only that combination of life on the Buenos Aires Boca and on the forbidding Antarctic seas is able to produce such types. One four months' voyage to the bleak island of South Georgia killed off my ambition to become an Antarctic whaler. I left the *Tiljuca* on her return to Buenos Aires for trampship journeys under the flags of Britain, Norway and Greece which landed me in the fall of 1921 in the negro quarter of Galveston, Texas. I was seventeen.

The black folk were friendly to me. An elderly master painter treated me as if I had been his son until, by a stroke of luck, I found a berth on what, I believe, was the finest and largest sailing ship afloat at that time. It was the *Magdalene Vinnen,* a four-masted barque, which eventually brought me back to Chile.

One of my shipmates had broken a leg off Tierra del Fuego. The captain of our ship refused to have the injured man transferred to a hospital. There was a near mutiny on board in which I had a hand. To avoid arrest by the Chilean harbor police I deserted at night in the captain's gig and repaired to familiar haunts in Antofagasta. Christmas Eve of 1922 found me celebrating with other stranded sailors on the green lawns of Plaza Colon, toasting Mrs. Bready, the chesty female shipping master of Nitrate Coast, who generously had supplied a keg of wine. For a fee of six pounds sterling Mrs. Bready found me a berth aboard an ancient barque, the *Obotrita,* Captain Dietrich, bound with nitrate around Cape Horn to Hull, England. I paid off in Hull in the early spring of 1923. From there I bought passage to Hamburg.

I came home to study navigation, with the intention of obtaining an officer's ticket. But the minute I set foot on German soil, I found myself sucked back into a whirlpool of hate and distress even more fierce than the one I had left. I found that my family, my mother and the three younger children, stripped by the cyclonic inflation, badly needed what little money I had.

I saw an aged woman standing at a curb, burning thousand-mark bills, and cackling at the silently watching crowd.

"What's the matter with the woman?" I asked a bystander.

"The matter?" the man said. "She's crazy." And he added: "The country needs a good revolution."

I walked away. The country was sick. During my years at sea, which had almost made me forget the old hates, my country had had no peace. In 1920, the militarists under Kapp had struck at the Weimar Republic. Ministers of the Republic had been assassinated. In 1921, armed insurrections in Saxony and Thuringia had been crushed without mercy. In January, 1923, French and Belgian armies had invaded the Ruhr to enforce payment of war reparations. Separatist bands rioted in the Rhineland. Inflation stalked the land with giant strides. Foreign scavengers descended upon Germany in droves, exchanging for a pittance the products of native toil. Prices leaped ahead of wages in a mad dance.

Between the city of Hamburg and its great harbor flows the river Elbe. I was at the ferry landing when the thousands of dockers returned from work. The dockers were met by their wives and daughters who seized their day's pay and rushed to the nearest stores to buy food because next day this money would be worthless.

On the ferry landing stood a squad of customs officials and harbor police. Each worker, before he was allowed to pass, was searched for contraband by the officers. One worker had concealed under his coat a small bag of flour he had taken from some ship's hold.

A policeman held the bag with flour aloft.

"You are under arrest," he said.

"I took this flour from a broken bag," the worker protested. "It was spilled into the hold anyway."

The officer snapped: "I know all about your broken bags. You fellows rip open the bags with your hooks. Come on, now."

He took the worker by the sleeve to lead him away.

The worker tore himself free. "Give me back my flour," he demanded. "It's mine!"

Two other policemen stepped up and tried to put handcuffs on the worker. A scuffle ensued. Another stevedore stepped in. "You fat-necked parasites," he roared at the policemen. "Let my friend go. Give him his flour back."

"Nothing doing. Keep moving."

Other dockers joined the struggling group. The policemen drew their rubber truncheons, formed a skirmish line, drove the workers back from the wharf. A worker, young and lean, with the five-point star, the emblem of the Communist Party, on his blue cap, sprang on a bitt and shouted:

"Down with the police. Down with the lackeys of capitalism. Throw them into the harbor!"

That night, on my way to the dingy room I had rented in a tenement in the waterfront district, I was accosted by two women. One was about forty, the other barely over sixteen.

The older woman tugged at my sleeve and said, "You have a good face. Please help us."

They were refugees from the Rhineland. The older woman's husband had been a member of a sabotage brigade against the French. He had helped blow up a railway line to prevent shipment of German coal to France. He had been arrested, convicted to twelve years of penal servitude by a military court, and had been carried off into France. His family had been told to leave the zone of occupation within twelve hours. Their house and their garden were seized. They had wandered for weeks, pushed on from town to town by unwilling authorities. The older woman was terribly emaciated.

"It's bitter cold," she said. "Please give us a place to sleep."

"I have only a small, cold room," I explained.

The woman's eyes lit up. "We can sleep on the floor," she said. "We are thankful just to have a roof over the head."

I hesitated. I thought of giving her some money, but then I remembered that the stores were closed, that the hotels demanded foreign currency, that the money would be useless. It was German money.

"All right," I said. "You can come with me."

I took them to my room and we had a supper of tea and black bread.

The woman said: "My daughter can sleep with you in the bed and I will sleep on the floor."

I was not astonished. In their home town they had been respectable people. But it was the custom all over the land, in the degeneration of post-war years, that refugee girls had to peddle their bodies for bread and a place to sleep.

I looked at the girl.

"I am not afraid," the girl said. "I've had to do it before."

I said no. I thought of their man languishing in some distant French prison. He had blown up a railway. In such times, it seemed to me, the best thing one could do would be to blow up the whole world. I told the women to use the bed. Then I walked down to the street. There a group of young workers were busy pasting posters on the walls.

"Communism alone brings national and social freedom," the posters said.

"Can I help you?" I asked.

The leader of the group brought his face close to mine. He seemed satisfied.

"Sure," he said.

For two hours I helped the young workers put up posters. Often we climbed on one another's shoulders to place the posters so high that they could not be torn off. Very little was said. Three of us worked, and two stood at the corners watching for police. Twice police patrols surprised us. They came running, swinging their clubs. But we ran faster and escaped.

"Some day," the leader of the Young Communist group said, "we won't run.

We'll have guns and fight them on the barricades. Ten dead policemen for every dead worker."

His eyes blazed hate.

"Blood must flow," said another.

We parted. All night I walked aimlessly through cold streets. Near the Stemschanze Station I passed a house in front of which stood an ambulance. Attendants carried an old woman out of the house. The old woman was dead.

"She has hanged herself," someone said. "Hanged herself with a piece of wire."

"Why?"

"She had a pension, but her month's pension couldn't buy her a box of matches."

A man standing nearby spat vigorously.

"The poor grow poorer and the rich grow richer," he growled.

"Good night," I said, moving on.

The man raised his right fist. "Red front!" he bellowed.

In the gray of early dawn I found myself in an outlying section where long streets were lined with drab one-family houses which resembled one another like so many eggs in a box. In front of the stores, at the street corners, women began to line up. They shivered in the cold and counted the paper in their hands. They counted hundreds of thousands, millions. They were determined to be first to spend this money when the stores opened.

As it grew lighter I came to a house where a town official argued heatedly with a housewife. The housewife looked unhappy. She had her arm tightly around the shoulder of a boy about ten. At the curb stood a truck. Two sinewy truckmen were waiting. I stopped and listened to the argument.

The woman could not pay her rent. The official showed her a warrant of eviction. Every day there were mass evictions. To attract the least attention, they were carried through in the early morning hours.

"We shall transport your belongings to the city storage," the official said. He pushed the woman aside and entered the house, and the two truckmen followed him.

A minute later they began loading the furniture into the truck. A passing man who carried a big bundle of newspapers under his arm halted and asked the woman: "An eviction?"

The woman nodded. "I don't know where we shall go now," she said dejectedly.

"I'll call up the Red Self-Help," the man said.

He placed his newspapers on the sidewalk and ran to the nearest store. Then he sauntered back and told the truckmen: "You can't drive away with this woman's furniture."

The woman waited nervously. In less than ten minutes the truck was loaded and the truckmen were tightening the ropes around their load. At this moment a column of roughly-clad men swept around the corner on bicycles. All of them had the red five-pointed star on blue caps.

The truckmen, seeing the raiders approach, stood aside. The official came running out of the house. The man with the newspapers pounced on the official and started beating him. The others leaped from their bicycles, cut the ropes on the truck. Each of them seized a piece of furniture and carried it back into the house. Two minutes later the truck drove away, empty, and the official had fled. People gathered. The men of the Red Self-Help formed a picket line in front of the house. Others marched along the street, shouting in chorus:

"Refuse to pay rent to the landlords!"

"Form Red Self-Help squads in every block!"

"Only Communism gives you freedom and bread!"

Slowly I walked from the scene. Three blocks away I saw a lorry loaded with green-uniformed Security Police speed past me down the street.

I wanted to ship out to get away, to go back to the far seas. I made the rounds of the British and Scandinavian shipping masters. They had no ship for me. Their offices were besieged by stranded foreign seamen.

"Our nationals come first," they told me. "You'd better go and sign aboard a German ship."

I went down to the riverfront, to the central shipping office of the Shipowners' Association. I walked through a filthy backyard and up a flight of iron steps. The shipping office was a dark, gloomy hall. Thousands of men lounged in the backyard and in the hall. All seamen out of a job.

I went to one of the barred windows and threw in my papers. The clerk looked at them, shoved them back.

"What do you want?"

"I want to register for a berth," I said.

"On deck?"

"On deck, yes."

"I can't register you."

"Why not?"

"All your discharges show foreign service."

"Want me to starve to death?"

"No; you can apply for a dole."

"To hell with your dole. I want a ship."

"Can't give you a ship. You've sailed on .foreigners. You've paid no taxes in Germany. I can't give you a ship, I tell you."

"Listen! I'm a sailor. I'm a German. This is a German shipping office. I'm willing to work. Any ship. Anywhere."

"Aw, get out!"

At this instant a broad-shouldered man with bronzed features, who had stood in the crowd around the windows, shoved me aside.

"Come on, partner," he said to the clerk, "register this fellow. An equal deal to everybody."

"I can't," protested the clerk, "that's against the regulations."

"Damn your regulations. If you don't register this man, he can't even get a dole."

"Who are you anyhow?"

"Never mind that," said the man, "I'm a stoker. And I tell you this man will be registered."

"Getting tough?"

"You bet your teeth."

"Hah, beat it."

The stoker thrust his sun-blackened head close to the bars. "Listen, Bonze," he growled, "do you know what'll happen if you don't register this comrade?"

"What?"

"I'll get a hundred men to take those benches and smash up the place. Smash your cocoanut, too, for that matter."

"I'll call the police."

"You've called them many times. That won't save this new partition. Remember how we smashed the other one? Touch that telephone and we'll dance with you."

The clerk did not touch the telephone. He went into a private office and returned with the director. The director looked like a walrus. His name was Captain Brahms. When he spoke, he thundered as if he was shouting through a megaphone.

"What's all the noise about?" he thundered.

"This man must be registered," demanded the stoker.

"Is he your brother?"

"Don't try to be funny."

"Oh, it's you," barked the walrus, "what's your name?"

"You won't get it," said the stoker truculently.

"Are you not the hellion who brought a gang with stinkbombs in here a week ago? You're ripe for arrest."

"Go ahead, you old crook."

"Are you inciting riot?"

"Sure," said the stoker, "we're tired of your special lists for boys who come with recommendations and bribes. We're tired of rotting on your blacklists."

"There are no blacklists," shouted Captain Brahms.

By that time hundreds of men stood packed around the window. Loud calls burst from the charivari of voices.

"Down with the politician!" ... "Pull off his beard!" ... "Beat him!"

"Register this man!" the stoker roared.

Captain Brahms walked calmly to a telephone. He called the

Eight or ten men had seized one of the heavy benches and used it as a ramming pole. The clerks fortified themselves behind their desks which they hastily pushed together. Outside, from the yard, rocks hurtled through the windows.

The stoker roared: "Down with the special lists! Abolish secret placement! We're years ashore and can't get a ship! Down with the hunger regime!"

After two blows the partition splintered. A score of sailors raised havoc with furniture and files. Others pounced on the clerks who defended themselves with broken-off chair legs. Captain Brahms crawled under a table. The broad-shouldered stoker pounded the captain's hindquarters with both fists. The thousands in the hall and down in the yard milled about, laughing, shouting, cursing. In the center of the hall a group of fifty men stood massed, yelling in chorus: "Hunger! Hunger! We want a ship!"

A high-pitched scream came from the yard.

"*Ueberfallkommando!*"

Police. Sirens pierced the air. Three large trucks full of men in green uniforms clashed to a halt. Before they had stopped, a hundred policemen leaped to the pavement. They drew their rubber truncheons while they ran. They pitched into the crowds, dealing vicious blows left and right. Those who resisted were handcuffed and led to the trucks. A voice roared:

"*Arbeitermoerder!*" Murderers!

A policeman had lost his footing on the stairs. Four, five seamen were on top of him, hitting, kicking, robbing him of his truncheon and pistol. In the yard a young policeman ran to the shelter of a doorway. He drew his pistol and took careful aim. An instant later a youngster in a gray sweater spun around and pitched on his face. There was a thousandfold howl of rage.

"Murderers!"

"Re-mem-ber ... the police chief is a socialist!"

"Down with the socialist traitors!"

Suddenly all policemen had pistols in their hands. They were nervous and badly scared. Voices barked:

"*Strasse frei! Es wird geschossen!*"

Men ran away in all directions, often trampling one another underfoot. Women, appearing from nowhere, shouted abuse. Others threw garbage cans from windows at pursuing policemen. Half-stunned, I made my way to the Cathedral of St. Michael. Beside me walked an old mariner. He was serene, as if nothing had happened.

"Even if they had registered you," he said, "you'd have waited all of two years for your turn to ship out."

"They killed a man up there," I said.

"That's all right, you'll get used to that... Let's have a beer."

Chapter Three

I STRIKE OUT

I wandered about aimlessly, thinking what to do. Shall I run away from this diseased country? Or shall I join the forces which are actively attacking the wrongs that made my blood rebel? One road tempted me with the free and happy countries I had seen during my seafaring years. The other filled me with the fervor and the high expectations of revolutionary youth. I felt a strangulating loneliness. I yearned for a place where I could belong.

In a waterfront tavern I studied the Shipping News. There was a steamer of the Roland Line leaving at five for Panama and Valparaiso. The very names of those ports conjured up before me vistas of high coast-lines, of warmth and abundance, of laughing brown-eyed girls, and of jobs under foreign flags or in the copper mines, of jobs with decent wages and with promise for the future.

I decided to go. With the last of my money I filled a satchel with food—biscuits, sardines, corned beef and a bottle of water, and crossed the river to the India Docks.

The steamer was loaded. The longshoremen were closing the hatches, and the deckhands were busy lowering the derricks. In an unguarded moment I slipped aboard and ran forward to hide. I climbed into the chain locker, closing the manhole above me. The bulkheads were damp and rusty. Beneath me tons of ponderous chain were curled up like iron snakes. A smell of mud and bilge water filled the place.

I heard the siren roar, muffled commands, the loud tramping of many feet, the rumbling of winches. Then the whole ship vibrated as the engines began to turn over. We were outbound. In two or three days the ship would have cleared the English Channel and I could come on deck and report myself as a stowaway to the captain.

Somewhere in the river estuary the steamer ran into a fog. I knew it by the roar of the siren which came at steady two-minute intervals. Three, four times the siren roared. The vibration in the bulkheads ceased. The engines were stopped.

I heard the patter of feet on the forecastle head. It was followed by the clashing sound of metal striking metal. Someone was working on the windlass directly above my head. Suddenly I realized: the fog was too dense for the ship to proceed and the pilot had decided to anchor until the weather cleared. They'd drop the anchor and the chain beneath me would rush upward, tons of iron banging upward through the chain locker and I would be smashed to shreds in the darkness below.

A clear voice rang above me: "All clear anchor!"

Faintly, a rumbling voice came from the bridge—"Forty-five fathoms. Stand by to let go!"

"Help!" I yelled. "Hold anchor! Man below! Help, help!"

The clear voice above me said: "God Almighty."

The next instant I had unfastened the manhole and scrambled out of the chain locker. A young officer came rushing down from the forecastle head.

Seeing me, he shouted: "Any more of you bums down there?"

"No."

He ran back on the deck. "All clear!"

A command from the bridge: "Let go anchor."

The anchor thundered to the bottom. All around was soupy fog. From near and far sounded the sirens of other ships groping in the fog. My knees trembled as the officer led me up to the bridge. "Stowaway, sir," he reported to the skipper.

Late at night I was taken ashore in the pilot's launch. I spent the night in a dank police station in Cuxhaven. Next day a cold-eyed police judge sentenced me to seven days in jail for trespassing on the property of the Roland Line.

I served the seven days in the Hamburg city jail. The jail was overcrowded with workers of all ages caught stealing on the wharves, in railroad yards and warehouses, or surprised by police in the act of plundering food stores.

Among my fellow prisoners was a communist agitator, a thin young man whose name was Willy Zcympanski. A fanatic fire burned in his gray eyes. Seeing my eagerness, he singled me out for special attention. His explosive enthusiasm was contagious. The clear sincerity of his devotion thrilled me. More and more I became convinced that dedication to the revolution was the only worthwhile thing in life.

"With us a man can find awareness of his own strength," Zcympanski said. "He is no longer a homeless cur. A man is born to fight."

His influence upon me was so strong that I gripped his shoulder.

"Great battles are in the offing," he continued. "The Party must prepare the armed rising. This time we won't be losers. Soviet Germany and Soviet Russia will be invincible together. Then we'll reach out—France, China, America, the whole world. No nobler aim is possible. To achieve it, no sacrifice can be too great."

On the morning of the fourth day Zcympanski was called out. He went to trial for having organized communist nuclei among the police. Before he went he gave me a message for his sister, who worked at the Hamburg telephone exchange. The message, in code, was written on a piece of toilet paper. He also gave me a ragged little book, urging me to pass it on before my release. It was the Communist Manifesto.

I did not see Zcympanski again until 1932. By then he had become one of the most efficient operatives of the Foreign Division of the G.P.U. Loyal to the last, he committed suicide in a Nazi prison in 1937.

When I was released, a police officer ordered me to leave Hamburg immediately. "We want no vagrants in this town," he said.

"Who, indeed," I thought, "is making vagrants out of us?"

I went to see Zcympanski's sister. She was a handsome blonde of twenty-five, tall and intelligent. Her name was Erika. Immediately she invited me to the first hot bath I had had in weeks. The fact that I had brought her a message from her brother made her regard me as a comrade. The sound of the word comrade, coming from her lips, made my blood leap. She told me I could stay at her apartment as long as I liked. Her warm, yet practical simplicity aroused my trust and admiration. I found in her a trait which is characteristic of many honest revolutionists: a fundamental kindliness and compassion side by side with a cruel disregard for the lives of all who actively opposed the interests of the revolution. On the walls were a portrait of Lenin and the picture of a young mother nursing her child.

"Do you like to read?" she asked me.

I nodded. Beneath the pictures low shelves were crowded with books.

"Revolution is a science," she smiled. "Without sound theory, action is nonsense."

I read hungrily. When I did not read, I prepared a frugal meal over the tiny gas range, and then I slept. After three days of it, I craved motion. The Communist Party had called the unemployed masses to a demonstration which was to take place that night. I decided to be there.

It was clear from the start that among the thousands who assembled in the belt of suburbs there were many who were determined that the demonstration should not be a peaceful affair. These were the trained Party members. They came with short pieces of lead pipe in their belts and stones bulging in their pockets. They did not hide their intention of coming to grips with the police.

Torches cast flickering lights over the swelling crowds. A whistle shrilled and the crowds began to move forward behind gray-uniformed military detachments of the Party. Red flags were unrolled, and the workers' bands began to play the *Internationale*.

Toward nine o'clock the demonstrations from the outskirts converged. We were now skirting the inner city. All streets leading toward the center were blocked by police. Searchlights fingering over hundreds of crimson flags; sudden fanfares, and the gleaming reflections of torches on steel helmets imparted a strong macabre effect to the whole. And suddenly, after a muffled and manifold repeated command, the head of the demonstration swung toward the banned ground of the inner city.

Immediately the police pitched in. The pace of the masses slowed down. Men in the gray uniforms of the Red Front League pressed forward to assault and break up the police phalanx into small isolated groups. Then twittering sounds pierced the night. Flying squads of the police, emerging from side streets where they had been lurking, drove wedges into the flanks of the demonstration.

"Dissolve! Clear the streets!"

It was impossible to follow that order. Tumult ensued. Rocks flew. Clubs cracked. Throngs ran from pursuing policemen, only to reassemble and return to the fray as soon as their pursuers had turned for a sally in another direction. I found to my astonishment that, in the excitement of a street battle, a blow across the face with a rubber truncheon did not cow a man's fighting spirit, but lashed it to a bright flame. The intimidating psychological effect which police uniforms usually have on a nondescript mass of rioters vanishes when the rioters discover that even a well-armed policeman is no match for a score of bare fists at close quarters. At times I saw young workers with the red five-pointed star on their caps jab their pocket knives into the legs of police horses. Invariably the horses reared and bolted.

In the end, we were scattered. The battlefield was littered with caps, torn clothing, broken glass, police helmets. With a horde of several hundred men and women I wandered toward the Aussenalster, a residential section of the well-to-do. The flags had disappeared. The bandsmen, to save their instruments, had long since gone home. A ragged, wild-eyed assembly of scarecrows, we roved up and down the broad, clean residential streets, yelling in unison.

"Hunger! Hunger!"

Lights were switched off, shades rattled down, doors were locked as we approached. A single howl out of a hundred throats plunged whole blocks into darkness. Once in a while a police truck sped around a corner, siren yelling, and cursing men leaped to the pavement amid the screaming of brakes. Instead of bread we got beatings. After all, it was what we had asked for.

Toward midnight we parted, tired, bruised, and hoarse from shouting. I turned up the collar of my coat, for it was bitingly cold. I had lost my cap in the brawling. My overcoat was in a pawnshop. As I passed the railway station, a young woman walked beside me. She was older than I; twenty-eight, perhaps.

"Going home?" I asked.

"Home," she said ... ' that dank hole ..."

For a while we walked side by side, saying nothing. She buried her hands in her armpits and whistled a song. Then she said:

"Let's sleep together.'

"No."

"Why not? You are a comrade, *nicht wahr?*"

"Yes," I said absently

"So come," she urged, and her voice sagged into a plaintive wail as she continued: "I need a man. I'm so goddam alone. I have not slept with a man for ages."

"I like you, but I can't."

"Listen, I'm good in bed."

"I have a girl to go to," I explained.

She nodded. "I have one, too," she said.

"A girl?"

"Yes, a little girl. I wish, by Christ, she'd been born dead."

Two days after taking part in the hunger demonstration, in the second week of May, 1923, I joined the Communist Party. Early in the morning I went to the Red House in Hamburg.

A short, wiry man with strong eyebrows and a salient jaw received me, and asked a few pointed questions. It developed that he had known my father during the wartime underground work of the Spartacists in the Fleet. Considering me a very fit and reliable recruit, he signed me up at once.

"We have very little time to train and choose our cadres," he said. "We believe in pushing young blood to the fore. We believe in youth, bold, disciplined youth."

"I shan't disappoint you," I replied.

"Remember, a campaign is not a matter of leaflets and meetings, but of action, action and more action. Action means strikes. Mass strikes are the prelude to armed insurrection. We must bring conditions to a revolutionary boiling point, with any and all means at our command. Is that clear to you?"

"Very clear," I answered.

"All right," he went on, "you'll work in the maritime section. Comrade Walter handles that. You know that Germany is an industrial country dependent on industrial exports and raw material imports. So shipping is a jugular vein of German capitalism. Should we succeed in making harbors and ships into fortresses of the Communist Party—we've got that jugular vein in our grip. We can break it and the bourgeoisie will bleed to death. You'll report to Comrade Walter."

Albert Walter was a thick-set, jovial, highly energetic Bolshevik of international caliber, and the undisputed chieftain of communist activities along the German seaboard. Bronzed, barrel-chested, he had a massive forehead, mobile features, and his small brown eyes seemed always on the alert. He was in his late thirties, and had lived for fifteen years the life of a professional seaman.

After his release he made his way to Moscow where Lenin made him a political commissar in the Baltic fleet. In 1922, the Comintern chiefs, considering Walter their most able man in marine affairs, assigned him to head the International Propaganda and Action Committee of Transport Workers (IPAC-Transport). The communists being entrenched more solidly in Hamburg than in any other great seaport, Hamburg became the center for Comintern enterprises in the all-important marine industry.

Albert Walter ordered me to join one of the communist "activist" brigades in the harbor of Hamburg. Each month about a thousand ships entered this port, for the bulk of German exports and imports went through the docks of Hamburg. In the river basins along the Elbe flew the flags of every maritime nation on earth.

Each morning the harbor "activists" gathered on various concentration points along the waterfront. There the leader of each brigade assigned his men to certain docks and ships, and supplied them with leaflets and pamphlets, and with the slogans of the day. So armed, we slipped into the harbor and boarded the ships and set out to win over their crews. Most ships were guarded by officers or company watchmen, and a wide range of dodges and tricks had to be employed to board the ships in spite of the guards. Often we swarmed aboard over the hawsers. At times we slunk aboard disguised as hawkers of neckties or as laundrymen. We distributed our leaflets, sold newspapers and pamphlets, launched discussions, and endeavored to enlist the young militants among the crews in the Communist Party.

Our immediate aim was to arouse discontent among the seamen, discontent against rations, wages and ship's discipline. Wherever a crew was receptive to our agitation, we went on to form an action committee on the ship to prepare for coming strikes, or to build up the Party unit among the men, or to pick particularly able individuals for courier service and other confidential work.

Returning ashore at the end of the day, each "activist" wrote a detailed report on the ships he had visited that day. At headquarters these reports were copied and filed. These shipping files contained detailed data on practically every ship in the merchant service, permitting Albert Walter and his aides to obtain at any time an accurate picture of available forces before deciding on any major action. This system, known as the "Hamburg method," was later adopted by communist waterfront organizations on all continents.

I pitched into Party work with a high fervor. Nothing mattered outside the communist offensive. From early morning, when the stevedores went to work, until the ships' crews went ashore at nightfall, I went from ship to ship, from wharf to wharf, in fulfillment of Party duty. And in the evenings there were meetings and discussion circles and political courses to attend which rarely broke up before midnight. I had no thought of clothes, amusements or girls. I felt myself a living wheel in the Party machine. I grew leaner, harder, and was supremely happy.

Among the innovations which I introduced was a method of work whereby the most active communists on each ship pledged themselves to engage in propaganda drives among the crews of other German ships in foreign ports of call. At one of the next conferences of the "activist" brigades I gave a detailed report of my experiments which met with acclaim. Up to then I had been classed as an agitator; I was now accepted as an organizer. The proposal of Albert Walter that I was to take charge of all Party work aboard the Hamburg-America Line vessels was accepted. Some fifty ships manned by more than two thousand seamen came into the category. That night I was so elated I could not sleep! All night I made plans—I thought of the fifty ships as my ships. Such responsibility was sweet.

I was on the way to become a professional revolutionist, in accordance with Lenin's conceptions. I learned well the Party principle that the heart of the Comintern and its affiliated Parties must consist of an inner organization of men and women whose one and only aim in life is to work for the revolution; who are ready for any personal sacrifice the Party should demand, who are pledged to unreserved obedience to their Central Committee and utmost unity of aims.

I was class-conscious because class-consciousness had been a family tradition. I was proud to be a worker and I despised the bourgeois. My attitude to conventional respectability was a derisive one. I had a keen one-sided sense of justice which carried me away into an insane hatred of those I thought responsible for mass suffering and oppression. Policemen were enemies. God was a lie, invented by the rich to make the poor be content with their yoke, and only cowards resorted to prayer. Every employer was a hyena in human form, malevolent, eternally gluttonous, disloyal and pitiless. I believed that a man who fought alone could never win; men must stand together and fight together and make life better for all engaged in useful work. They must struggle with every means at their disposal, shying no lawless deed as long as it would further the cause, giving no quarter until the revolution had triumphed.

Already in June it became clear that decisive revolutionary events were impending. The breathtaking collapse of currency, the rapid disintegration of the anti-communist trade unions, the growing demoralization of the middle class and the spontaneous influx of large numbers of desperate and rebellious young workers into the ranks of the Communist Party were unmistakable signals of the coming tempest. Moscow had given a mandate to Karl Radek, the Comintern's most clever—and most cynical—propagandist, to direct from Berlin the political campaign for a communist seizure of power. The order of the day called for transformation of sporadic strikes into a general strike, which in turn was to be the prelude to armed insurrection. An emissary of Radek, an ascetic-looking, fair-haired Russian named Kommissarenko, outlined the plans in a meeting of all communist forces in the harbor of Hamburg.

A few of the older communists objected. "But the masses are not ready," they said. "They'll stand aside and leave us to fight alone."

Kommissarenko's reply came like the crack of a whip: "Once we strike out, the masses will follow. The masses must make the revolution—but we will lead it!"

The young elements carried the day. We cheered the Russian. We were prepared to go ahead with a blind religious elan.

Came the day when all the action committees of the waterfront met in a secret session. Ernst Thaelmann, who was then the chief of the Hamburg organization, spoke: "Let nothing deter us. The actions of a determined minority will rouse the fighting spirit of the masses. Stop ships by force when their crew refuses to strike. Board the ships and kill the steam. The Party is with you with every ounce of its strength. With the seamen in action, the workers of other industries will follow—the dockers, the shipyard hands, the railwaymen. Above all, we must teach the masses that there is no substitute for strike and armed rising in the struggle for power."

I did not sleep that night. Between eleven and three my brigade was busy painting strike slogans in six-foot letters on the sides of ships and quays. In groups of four men we went out in commandeered rowboats, with strips of burlap wrapped around the oars to muffle the sounds of rowing, and slipped from ship to ship, from wharf to wharf, smearing in white and red paint the words: "Strike for the right to live decently. Strike! Strike!" On some ships this slogan reached almost from bow to stern.

In the dark of the night, across the oily harbor water, we could see other boats move stealthily along the sides of sleeping ships. My companions in the boat were Ilja Weiss, a bold, sinewy Hungarian; Hans Wonneberger, a broad-framed sailor; and a boy from the Young Communist League. Weiss led the expedition; Wonneberger and I painted with brushes tied to broom sticks; the young communist bailed the water out of the leaking boat.

While painting in the Hansa Docks, we were surprised by a launch of harbor police. Caught in the beam of a searchlight we rowed madly toward a ladder at the end of the wharf. The young communist swarmed up the ladder with catlike agility. I followed close behind. Just then the police launch came alongside and a young officer leaped into our boat, shouting:

"Ha, rioters. *Halt!* You are under arrest!"

I scrambled up the wharf. Hans Wonneberger dived into the harbor and swam away in the night.

Ilja Weiss snarled: "Take this!"

He crashed a pail half filled with red lead squarely into the officer's face. The officer gasped for air, then fell. Weiss lunged up the ladder.

"Red Front triumphs," he yelled.

The men in the police launch started shooting. We ran away in the shadows of a long freight shed and heard the bullets ricochet from the corrugated iron walls.

"Close shave," chuckled Weiss.

"Where's Comrade Wonneberger?" I panted.

"Never mind him. He swims like a fish."

Two minutes later the twittering siren of a police car sounded ahead. We ran into the shed and crawled into a stack of concrete sewer pipes. When all was quiet, we returned to the city on separate routes.

Ilja Weiss is today the secretary of the International Club in Odessa, wanted by most European police departments. Hans Wonneberger made the mistake of falling in love with a girl who turned out to be a secret agent of the Nazi Party in 1932. He was abducted by the G.P.U. to Novorossisk, and has since disappeared in Soviet Russia.

At seven in the morning all Party forces entered the harbor. The gates and the ferry landings were guarded by police. Communist military units engaged the police to allow the mass of agitators to penetrate the harbor from all sides. We overran the gangway guards and told the seamen to strike or to suffer a strikebreaker's fate. Other "activist" units were working in a similar fashion among the dockers' gangs. An officer who confronted the group of Ilja Weiss with a pistol in his hand was thrown into the harbor. Columns of striking seamen and unemployed workers mobilized by the Party boarded the ships to chase recalcitrant crews ashore by main force. Trade union officials who advised moderation were beaten up.

By noon the wide reaches of the harbor resembled a battlefield. Communists reinforced by a few hundred strikers waged a hand to hand battle with seamen who refused to heed the communist order. On three wharves we cut the mooring lines of ships, setting the vessels adrift in the hope that they would collide and block the channel to navigation. Mobile police squads descended to join the affray and to make arrests. Trucks filled with prisoners rumbled toward the jails. Steamers which had been boarded by special sabotage units whose task was to douse the fires in the stokehold roared their sirens for police assistance. By three o'clock forty ships lay paralyzed, but the police slowly succeeded in pressing us out of the harbor. Police barricaded the entrances. At the Elbe tunnel stood a machine gun and a sign: "Stop—he who proceeds will be shot."

Most of the seamen who had followed the communist slogans had lost their berths, and many were in jail. No one thought of criticizing the communist doctrine that no strike, even if the strikers wind up out of a job or in jail, must be regarded as a defeat. Strike is training for civil war; so every strike, no matter how it ends, is a political triumph for the Party.

Even before our wild June action in the harbor of Hamburg had been brought to its conclusion, I was summoned to a secret meeting. The majority of the lesser-known waterfront agitators were present. After we had been pledged to silence, one of Thaelmann's aides issued instructions that all communist sailors in the meeting should inform the Shipowners' Association of their willingness to man the steamers which had been tied up by the strike.

Murmurs of surprise and indignation ran through the audience. I was deeply shocked by this crafty and dishonest maneuver. That very morning we had led two newly arrived ships' crews into the strike. Albert Walter's propaganda squads had distributed the crimson leaflets which told the seamen: "No steam for the engines! No work on deck! STRIKE!"

A rebellious shout came from a comrade behind me:

"We are no strikebreakers!"

The Party officer was unperturbed. He waited patiently until our protests had subsided. Then he spoke.

"Comrades," he explained, "what the Party demands of you is not blacklegging. What the Party demands is your co-operation in a tactical maneuver which is bound to carry Bolshevism more solidly into the merchant marine. The strike will not continue for long. Shall we give the ship-owning sharks a chance to retaliate by excluding communists from the crews of their ships? Shall we permit the ships to sail without availing ourselves of an opportunity to make each ship a fortress of the Communist Party? . . . We must take advantage of today to strengthen our positions for the battles of tomorrow. We are not a crowd of deaf-mutes. We are communists. Party discipline demands that you follow the Party command."

It was dirty business, we knew. It was like stabbing a knife into the back of our fellow-workers, the sailors and stokers who had trusted our leadership and followed our strike call.

To us, communists, loyalty to the Party, however, came before loyalty to the proletariat. While the action committees still issued manifestos exhorting the seamen to continue to strike, ships stealthily manned by communists steamed seaward at dawn.

Chapter Four

SMUGGLING FOR THE COMINTERN

One evening, toward the end of June, Albert Walter requested me to meet him at ten in the Café Rheingold in St. Pauli, amusement district of Hamburg.

"It has to do with a strictly conspirative matter," he warned me. "I know you can be trusted."

At the Rheingold, over a glass of *Niersteiner,* Walter introduced me to a man called Hugo, an inconspicuous young man with a sharp nose, steady eyes and somewhat oblique manner. He wanted exact information about the number of reliable communists aboard Hamburg-America Line steamers on the North Atlantic run. I told him that the Party had strong positions on four of these ships; one of them, the *Westphalia,* was due to leave in a few days. Hugo was pleased. He confided that three comrades whose lives were endangered had to be smuggled to America aboard the *Westphalia.*

Hugo's full name, I later learned, was Hugo Marx. He was the resident agent of the G.P.U. in Hamburg. Next morning he took me to the apartment where the three fugitive comrades were hidden. They were mere boys, and two of them were rather drunk. All of them were overjoyed when they heard that a way had been found to ship them to New York.

After Hugo departed, they began to talk. It was with amazement that I learned that they had been the leaders of one of the holdup gangs which the underground section of the Party—the *Apparat*—had organized to carry out payroll robberies, a practice originated in Tsarist Russia by Joseph Stalin to fill empty Party coffers. At the head of a band of fifteen communists they had held up and robbed the payroll of the municipal gas works of Berlin-Charlottenburg in January, 1923, and a few weeks later they had seized another payroll in a factory at Berlin-Spandau. Their technique was simple. Masked and armed with revolvers, they had invaded the respective offices with the words: "In the name of the revolution—hands up!" Their loot they delivered to the military section of the Party in Berlin. Then one of their gang had broken down, and would not carry on. Threatened with death by his comrades, he turned informer for the Berlin police.

"Why don't you go to Russia?" I demanded.

The three knew no answer. "Hugo said we must go to America," one of them blurted out.

"Why don't they go to Russia?" I asked Hugo Marx at our next meeting.

"They are known to the police," the G.P.U. agent replied. "We cannot incriminate the Soviet Government."

There may have been other reasons for sending the fugitives to New York. It is not customary to ask questions regarding internal Party matters. A night later I had three of our militants from the *Westphalia* come ashore. Each of them received twenty-five dollars from Hugo Marx for smuggling the three youngsters aboard their ship, and to supply them with food during the voyage. Hugo sent a courier with a supply of women's clothing. Disguised as girls and escorted by the seamen, the three fugitives boarded the ship at night and were safely hidden in a space formed by large crates in hold number one. They reached New York harbor undetected, were duly smuggled ashore, and disappeared. Their names were Emil Bergeman, Paul Gorisch, and Paul Eyck.

There is an epilogue to the Odyssey of these youths. Abandoned by the Party, they eventually returned to Germany after long and aimless wanderings. Captured by the police and brought to trial years later, each was sentenced to fifteen years' imprisonment. The Party did not even organize a campaign in their defense.

Less than a week after the hapless brigands had clandestinely left Germany, Hugo Marx requested me to release a number of my best men on Hamburg-America Line ships from all official Party work. I flatly refused. The men he wanted to have at his disposal were the backbone of our organizational network on the North Atlantic. Hugo Marx did not quarrel with me; he quietly went to Party headquarters and complained about my stubbornness. A few hours later a messenger from headquarters summoned me into the presence of Ernst Thaelmann, then the Party chief in Hamburg. Thaelmann had been a transport worker in his youth. He was a burly, thick-faced man, blunt of manner, and a victim of the habit of pounding table-tops with his sledgehammer fists. Rudely, he asked me if I knew the meaning of the word sabotage.

"Yes," I said timidly, overawed by the nearness of one of the strongest figures in the German Communist Party.

"What you do looks to me like sabotage," he growled. "Why do you refuse to co-operate with Comrade Hugo?"

The outcome of it was that I promised to follow all of Hugo's directions. I did not know the power wielded by the G.P.U. in Party affairs; I had not yet realized that the G.P.U. was completely in charge of the *Apparat*—vital subterranean section of the Party machine; and that it safeguarded itself by the crude and effective method of intimidating even its most lowly assistants.

When I stepped out of Thaelmann's office, I found Hugo Marx waiting for me. He gave me a thin smile. We boarded a taxi and rode to the Dammtor Station. At a corner table, we joined a swarthy, middle-aged, elegantly dressed man. He gave his name as Meyer. With gnashing teeth I surrendered to him and Hugo Marx a list of about thirty communist seamen in the North and South American trade. "Meyer" busily made notes. He looked more like a Levantine merchant than a German Bolshevik. During the following weeks, in addition to the usual Harbor propaganda, Hugo Marx and "Meyer" contacted me each time a German vessel had returned to Hamburg from New York or Buenos Aires. I was instructed to escort individually the selected communists among their crews to a basement beer hall on the waterfront where they were interviewed by "Meyer." I was not permitted to be present at these interviews. Invariably I received next day a brief note and a ten-dollar bill; the note ordered me to shun in future all contacts with the respective seamen.

For many months the nature of "Meyer's" schemes remained a deep mystery as far as I was concerned. Most of the sailors who had been transferred to the G.P.U. organization were older Party members than I. They kept their secret well. Only some years later, in 1926, after I had myself advanced into the inner circles of the *Apparat*, did Hugo Marx solve the mystery for me. The communist seamen whom I had surrendered to "Meyer" were employed in a large scale man-smuggling enterprise created by the Party and the G.P.U. to acquire funds for the purchase of arms and ammunition from Belgium. Prospective emigrants from Germany and the East European countries had been lured to Hamburg by promises of cheap transportation to the United States and the Argentine, with no questions asked. "Meyer" had established several boarding houses in Hamburg where the emigrants were fed and housed for one dollar a day while waiting for a suitable ship. Three officials of the Hamburg-America Line had been bribed by "Meyer" to sign up the emigrants as regular members of the crews of outgoing ships. The communists aboard these ships then assisted the illicit immigrants to desert their ships in New York or Buenos Aires. The fee exacted from each of the voyagers ranged from fifty to a hundred dollars. They made the crossing as potwashers, kitchen helpers, coalheavers or ordinary seamen until an investigation started by an officer aboard the *Cap Polonio*—one of the largest German passenger liners—threatened a scandal. In November, 1923, this traffic in human contraband was stopped by an order from Moscow. "Meyer," whose real name was John Bomos, attempted to carry on the smuggling business for his private profit. The G.P.U. ordered him to pack up and go to the Soviet Union. Bomos-Meyer refused. He was then denounced to the German police. He and ten of his collaborators were seized and sent to jail.

The Party ordered me to take a sailor's berth aboard the steamer *Fredenhagen*, a Baltic tramp trading between Bremen, Hamburg and the ports of Finland. Before this ship left port, I was summoned to Party headquarters. With me were several of my shipmates. Similar calls were sent to groups of communists from other ships.

In a dingy little office on a top floor we found a sleek communist from Berlin, a hard-headed ex-marine engineer and trusted lieutenant of, Albert Walter, and the inevitable Hugo Marx. We crowded into the office until we stood packed together like herrings in a barrel. The ex-engineer opened the session with a resounding grunt.

"For a while you boys will become rum-runners," he announced.

I thought at first that he was joking. He explained that much money could be made in smuggling hard drinks to countries where liquor was banned, and that the Party was at financial ebb tide and therefore in need of all the money that could be raked together. One responsible comrade was appointed for each ship. I became the leader of the *Fredenhagen* unit. Our assignment was to buy large quantities of rum, whisky and cognac free of duty in the free-port zone, and to sell this contraband in the ports of Finland. The selling was to be accomplished through specially created agencies in Helsinki and other ports. Among the ships represented at this conference were, besides the *Fredenhagen*, the steamers *Pleskow, Amisia, Fortuna, Bolheim*, several ships in the Swedish ore trade, and others which were in the North Atlantic service. We were in high spirits; the adventurous flavor of our assignment made us forget that we were actually strikebreakers. The ex-engineer unwrapped a shoe box filled with million mark bills, and Hugo Marx carefully noted down the amounts allotted to each ship.

I chose to believe that the money we raised by serving the Party as alcohol smugglers would be used for the purchase of arms and ammunition. Already it was an open secret in our midst that Soviet officers had been sent from Moscow to act as technical advisers, and that military preparations for the expected armed rising were well under way.

Through a ship-chandler's runner who was a Party member I bought eight hundred bottles of assorted liquors. To do this a customs certificate was necessary. I obtained a certificate for eight bottles of cognac. At Party headquarters this certificate was forged by Hugo Marx who added two zeros to the eight. The contraband was brought aboard at night. For hours we were busy burying the eight hundred bottles in the bunkers under tons of coal.

Four days later our ship entered the harbor of Helsinki. From there the *Fredenhagen* proceeded to Viborg and Kotka, other ports on the south coast of Finland. In each of these ports, as soon as the steamer had come to a rest, a dozen Finnish customs officials came aboard to search the ship. The customs law, however, permitted each member of the crew to have one bottle of hard drink for personal use in his cabin. So, as the Finnish customs men crawled through every corner of the ship—but never taking the trouble to dig up the coal in the bunkers—they were offered a gratuitous drink in each cabin they entered. They were not averse to drink. By the time they had finished ransacking the ship for contraband, most of them were well loaded with spirits. When they departed, they left behind a routine guard or two.

Invariably, during the night the two customs guards were lured to a carousal below decks by communist seamen appointed to this duty. Then I went ashore to the address given me by the sleek communist from Berlin. I found a small office in a conservative building in Helsinki near the Park where military bands give concerts during the summer months. The sign on the door read:

"Koskinen & Niminen." This firm was in reality a Finnish Comintern organization camouflaged as a restaurant supply firm. Ironically the words "Export—Import" had been added to the sign.

A husky young woman sat in the office. She spoke Swedish.

I gave her the watchword: "The pneumonia medicines are here."

"That's good," she said. "What ship? How many?"

"Ship *Fredenhagen*; eight hundred bottles," I answered.

She telephoned. After a while she informed me, "Return to your ship, comrade. Friend Koskinen is mobilizing the customers. They'll be streaming in on you all night."

I went back aboard. Two hours later our "customers" arrived, whole swarms of them at a time. Men and women, thirsty stevedores and well-to-do citizens, waiters, bell-boys, chambermaids, prostitutes and others of more opulent aspect. They paid from sixty to a hundred Finmarks for each bottle. A Finmark had gold value. Having bought the liquor with German paper money, our profits exceeded 3,000 per cent. Each bottle brought more than thirty times its original price. While the customs men amused themselves below with drink and enterprising waterfront wenches, the Party unit did a thriving business. By daybreak approximately six hundred bottles had been sold. The proceeds, I calculated, were the equivalent of three machine guns at Belgian wholesale prices. The rest of our stock we sold in Viborg and Kotka, where branch offices of "Koskinen & Niminen" had been established.

This smuggling business in behalf of the Party was not always transacted without friction. Non-communist members of the *Fredenhagen's* crew had formed their own private smuggling-rings. Even the captain, the mates, the engineers—all dealt in contraband because the wages they earned would not even pay the rent for their homes after the voyage was completed.

The rival syndicates aboard were in fierce competition with one another. They began by going into the bunkers at night and dumping all the coal they could shovel atop of our stores so that we were unable to reach them when the customers came. We answered by digging up the bottles of our competitors, emptying them of their contents and filling them with water or tea. More than one sturdy Finlander came raging aboard, as often as not with a dagger in his hands, after he had discovered that what he had bought as rum turned out to be cold tea. In the end, the communist group prevailed. Out at sea, at night, we destroyed or heaved overboard the remaining contraband of our rivals, and put guards armed with crowbars over our own.

We left Finnish waters without serious mishap, homeward bound. An emissary of the Party awaited me on the locks as the *Fredenhagen* passed into the Kiel Canal. I handed bur smuggling profits to the Party courier.

My ship went to Bremen. Before she left on her next voyage, I had aboard, again through Party funds, almost two thousand bottles of three-star cognac for "Koskinen & Niminen." Each round trip to Finland lasted three weeks. Each trip the volume of our contraband increased. On the third trip not only the bunkers, but also the lifeboats, the bilges, the fore peak and even the spare water tanks were crammed with bottles, all carefully wrapped in burlap. The success of our previous enterprises had made our chiefs cast prudence to the winds.

The Central Committee of the small illegal Communist Party of Finland under Nillo Virtanen mobilized the larger part of its organization in Helsinki to take this record consignment off the *Fredenhagen*. About a hundred men and women boarded the steamer, and left it with bottles packed into sacks or strapped around their waists. Three such expeditions were made in the course of a single night. In the early hours of the morning, the leader of the Finn transport column asked me:

"How many bottles have you got left?"

"Plenty," I said. "Better have them off the ship by daybreak."

I realized that the "unloading" had been so conspicuous that it would endanger us to keep the rest of our contraband aboard for another day. The harbor seemed suddenly well-manned with customs men.

The Finn growled in disgust: "Whoever heard of financing a revolution by selling booze!"

I explained that the German Communist Party, by using dozens of ships, had made a good fortune out of such smuggling enterprises. It meant rifles and hand-grenades for quite a number of proletarian companies. And doubtless, I hinted, the Communist Party of Finland was making a fair profit as well.

The Finn agreed. He sent a boy to reconnoiter the location of customs patrols on nearby docks, then armed five local communists with five bottles each, and told them to run athwart of the customs officials to detract their attention from what was going on aboard the *Fredenhagen*.

The five did their job well. We heard them run, the customs men in pursuit. There came the sound of bottles being splintered on the cobbles. Meanwhile, the Helsinki comrades emerged from freight sheds and with the aid of every communist in the *Fredenhagen*'s crew managed to get the remaining bottles ashore. I went to the office of "Koskinen & Niminen" to wait for the money which belonged to the German Party.

I waited fully nine hours. The *Fredenhagen* steamed for Viborg —without me. In the afternoon a Finn came barging into the office, spitting and cursing.

"Where's my money?" I demanded.

"Money, hell!" he ranted. "Do you know what your precious master Bolsheviks are responsible for? I'll tell you! The whole Communist Party of Helsinki is stone-drunk."

This was not what I had expected. I told the Finnish comrade that the cognac had been the property of the Communist Party of Germany, and, therefore, the property of the Comintern. Moscow would not like it.

Most Finns are of a type that is hard to rouse, but when their tempers burst into open flame things are apt to burst asunder. I feared this Finn would go berserk. *"Satana,"* he said with a ferocious twist of his lips. "I have no money. Get out of here." This was followed by a cataract of Finnish of which I did not understand a word. And then: "I regret you're so husky. I'd lynch you —you merchant!"

I fled. From opposite doorways I watched the entrance of the house in which the office of "Koskinen & Niminen" was located. At nightfall Koskinen himself entered the building. I ran across the street and stopped him on the stairway. He was a portly, mild-mannered man whose whole body winced when I grasped his shoulder from behind.

He said nervously, "Why do you bother me?"

"At least give me enough money to take a train to Viborg," I demanded.

He handed me a hundred Finmark note. "We are dissolving our firm," he said. "There have been some arrests. You must notify our friends in Hamburg. They must never, never forget that Finland is a fascist country."

I raced to the station, cursing my own carelessness and the monumental thirst of the Finns. I boarded the east-bound train and arrived in Viborg in time to catch my steamer, the *Fredenhagen*. After four days I was discharged in Bremen. No reasons for my discharge were given. I hastened to Hamburg to report to Walter and Hugo Marx. They had already a complete report of what had occurred at Helsinki. News of the fiasco had left them unperturbed.

In September the Party began to organize its able-bodied members into military companies of one hundred men each—*Hundertschaften*. There were eleven such companies in Hamburg, and several hundred of them in all the Reich. Each formation consisted of five detachments of twenty men. Each Sunday the hundreds marched out for military training in lonely stretches of forest or heath. Young Soviet Russian officers, most of whom spoke German, directed the training. Five or six such officers operated in the Hamburg area. They had come to Germany in the guise of sailors aboard Soviet vessels, and "activists" from Albert Walter's corps had smuggled them ashore at night. Under assumed names, using false German passports, they had their quarters in the homes of Party members. Their chief in Hamburg was a short, gruff, square-headed Russian who called himself Otto Marquardt, nominally an official of the Soviet Trade Mission in Hamburg.

I was detailed to the seventh proletarian company of the Hamburg area. This formation, chiefly composed of seamen, proudly called itself the "Red Marines," and Thaelmann considered it one of the best shock-brigades along the North Sea Coast. In the intervals between week-end maneuvers in the heath south-west of Hamburg, I was singled out for service in the courier corps of the Hamburg organization. At first I thought this service rather dull, because it was simply a matter of relaying messages between the known leaders and their Russian military advisers, men like Otto Marquardt, who took good care not to be seen in the company of German communists well known to the police. But the weekly trips to Kiel, Luebeck, Cuxhaven and Bremen, and two journeys to Berlin, gave me an insight into the doings of an underground élite whose existence I had barely suspected.

Outstanding in this political underworld was the figure of Johnny Dettmer, whose reckless daring could well measure up with that of the pirate heroes of my boyhood. Dettmer was a blond, blue-eyed giant of twenty-four, quick-tempered, clever, and with the strength and agility of a panther. He was one of those honest political desperadoes who are invaluable fighters in riot and upheaval, but who invariably come to grief once orderly conditions have been established. It was Ernst Wollweber, one of the Comintern chieftains, who remarked to me in later years of Comrade Dettmer, "We need men like

Johnny to win the fracas, but after the revolution we've got to shoot them."

In the early fall of 1923, Johnny Dettmer was a gun runner for the Red Hundreds of northern Germany. Otto Marquardt and an unnamed superior of Hugo Marx sent him to Kolberg, a small town on the Baltic between Stettin and Danzig. There, in a tavern, he met a youthful Soviet officer and a German communist named Lukowitz. I came to know Lukowitz well. He was a grizzled, slow-moving man, a former tugboat captain who later became one of the Party chiefs in the Luebeck district. Scattered in third-rate hotels in Kolberg were about a dozen other communists of Dettmer's caliber. All of them had had seafaring experience. Lukowitz sometimes took them out to sea in three motor launches which had been purchased by the Comintern—seemingly to no purpose at all. The three launches—*Liese, Anita,* and *Sturmvogel*—were staunch old boats, built of oak, thirty-six to forty feet in length, fitted with old gasoline motors and capable of making seven knots in friendly weather. (I saw the boats in 1930. Reconditioned, they were then used by the Comintern bureau in Danzig for the smuggling of communist literature to Poland, where the Party was illegal, by way of the lower Vistula and the port of Gdynia.)

Johnny Dettmer and his comrades loafed in Kolberg for a week, justifying their presence by appearing to be interested in the purchase of a boat. Then a courier from Berlin brought a message for the Soviet agent in Kolberg. The Russian summoned Lukowitz. Lukowitz rounded up his waiting crew and between them they manned the three launches, knowing that at last something was afoot.

They left the Kolberg fish pier at daybreak, keeping a steady north-northwest course. Dettmer was aboard the *Anita,* Lukowitz on the *Sturmvogel.* Offshore they spread out so as not to attract the attention of passing craft.

It is fifty-five miles from Kolberg to the southern tip of Bornholm. With the high shores of the island in sight, they cut their motors, brought sea-anchors out and drifted, a lookout man on duty on each boat.

They waited until eleven at night, watching the lights of passing westbound steamers. At eleven a steamer which had crawled up slowly from the east flashed a signal after it had reached a spot five miles south of the southern extreme of the island. The signal was the letter L—dot-dash-dot-dot, repeated at intervals until Lukowitz answered with similar flashes. Then the steamer turned south and the launches followed until they were out of sight of Bornholm.

The steamer was a small trampship. It showed no flag, but all knew that it was a Soviet vessel. As the launches approached, sailors lowered a grating covered with canvas to screen the steamer's name. The launches made fast alongside, and Lukowitz spoke a few words with a man who leaned over the steamer's rail Heavy bundles tied up in pieces of tarpaulin were lowered into the launches. Each bundle contained ten obsolete rifles which had once belonged to the Tsarist army. Then came small barrels full of cartridges buried in flour. Three hundred rifles were transshipped in less than an hour, and after a curt salute the launches drew away from the steamer's side. The launches waited until the Soviet ship had disappeared in the night, heading toward the Kiel Canal and a legitimate port of call.

Lukowitz instructed his crews: "Should the coast patrol stop us —over the side with the stuff."

All next day they drifted, pretending to fish. In the following night the launches ran shoreward. They landed their contraband at a point between Kolberg and a fishing village called Deep. There was a cluster of huts and a shallow channel running a little distance inshore. A truck was waiting beside a heap of rotting fish. They loaded the arms and ammunition into the truck, and covered the whole with rotting fish. The truck, manned by two taciturn youngsters, departed as soon as it had been loaded, heading toward the highway of Stettin.

Johnny told me this story in Low German, his native tongue, which he was in the habit of using. Low German has a tough and earthy flavor, and nuances of rollicking disrespect impossible to translate. As it is, Johnny is beyond bearing me a grudge for doing insufficient honor to his beloved waterside dialect, for, in 1934, his head came off under the Nazi ax.

Chapter Five

"DID YOU EVER KILL A MAN?"

I entered upon my duties as a courier for the underground organization of the Party at the end of September. My first trip was from Hamburg to Berlin. I was instructed to deliver a sealed letter to an address at 104 Moeckernstrasse. There, in a cozy apartment, I was received by a voluptuous-looking olive-skinned young woman. I recognized that she was Russian from the way she spoke German. Her name, I learned subsequently, was Maria Schipora. But the message which I carried from Otto Marquardt was not for her. It was for Hugo Eberlein, a member of the Central Committee of the Party, who was then in charge of communist contacts in the German army and navy.

Maria Schipora served me benedictine while I waited for Eberlein. She kept on urging me to drink. After three or four drinks, I began to fear that this Russian woman might be a spy for the police. I rose and said brusquely: "I do not like this. Who are you? What's your business?"

She leaned forward over the table and laughed.

"You came to meet Comrade Eberlein?" she asked.

"Yes."

"Who sent you?"

I refused to answer.

"I know Marquardt well," she said. "We've worked together for years."

I realized then that Maria Schipora was on the payroll of the G.P.U. We quickly became friends. I harbored admiration for communists engaged in international work. She spoke simply. And she was swift and avid. Her lips were full and red. She grasped my hair and kissed me.

"Comrade Eberlein always comes late," she said.

Eberlein did not come that day. Instead a tall, gloomy ascetic-looking man, in his early thirties, arrived, and I handed the Hamburg letter to him. The stranger immediately began plying me with questions about the excellent intelligence service which the North German Lloyd, the Hamburg-America Line and other shipping companies had established in the fringes of communist waterfront organizations. I gave him what little information I had. When the woman, who listened attentively, mentioned the caller's name, Felix Neumann, I was electrified. When the functionaries of the Red Hundreds spoke of Neumann, it was in whispers. He was the head of a new organization of T-units, terror groups, the skeleton staff of a future German Tcheka. He told me to stay in Berlin until the next day because he wanted me to take to Otto Marquardt some material which would not be ready before morning. He then asked me about my Party work. I told him that I preferred assignments which called for more action than shuttling between towns as a courier.

"Did you ever kill a man?" Neumann asked abruptly.

"No," I said.

"Well, then, how would you do it?"

"I'd shoot him."

Neumann grinned gloomily. "Wrong," he said. "If you shoot at a man and only wound him, what then? He'll go to the hospital and tell the police all about it, is that right?"

Maria Schipora interjected: "Usually a man is shot at night. At night it's dark. In the dark one can't see."

"Besides, shooting makes noise," added Neumann.

"How would you do it?" I asked.

"Always make sure that he's dead," Neumann explained with characteristic cold-bloodedness. "The safest way is to make him unconscious by blows on the head, then to cut his veins with a razor. If you do that, you're sure he'll be dead."

I did not know what to make of it. Was he in earnest? Did he merely want to test my nerves? Was he joking? At that time I did not know the answer. It came to me in fragments, piece by piece, wiping away the doubts. Felix Neumann had spoken in dead earnest.

I spent the night at the Moeckernstrasse apartment. Maria Schipora made a simple supper and, while we ate, we talked about the political mood of the workers and about the strategy of street-fighting. Maria told of an interview she had had with a Kremlin agent, a Tartar by origin, who called himself August Kleine, but whom Brandler, the German Party chief, had nicknamed "the man from Turkestan." Felix Neumann told of an arms buyer for the Party named Grenz who had skipped with $5,000 he had received from the Soviet embassy. They then talked of the tasks of the T-units to keep the Party clean from spies, and of murder.

Late at night five other people arrived, two girls and three men, among whom was a powerful six-footer with slightly Jewish features, Edgar Andree. I took an instinctive liking to him from the beginning. We became staunch friends, and the friendship lasted until he, too, died at the hands of Hitler's headsmen. The two girls were Eva and Lu, both members of the T-units. Eva—small, dark, catlike, was Neumann's mistress. Lu, whose name was Luise Schneller, was angular and hardboiled; she related that Ruth Fischer, a Party leader, had approached her with the request that a T-unit should give her colleague and rival, the "fat Brandler," a terrific beating. Ruth Fischer had even supplied Lu with the addresses of Brandler's secret meeting places. For me this was the first intimation of the existence of fierce jealousy and rivalry among leaders whose word was law for the rank and file.

Long after midnight the talk shifted to the strategy of the coming insurrection, which was to begin with a rising in the provinces and end with a march on Berlin. Partisan corps were being organized all around the capital, a task which lay in the hands of Edgar Andree and his aides. The two of his aides who were present, Gromulat and Bozenhard, looked capable enough; their idea was to emulate on a large scale the exploits of Max Hoelz, the communist Robin Hood of 1921, who since then had been condemned to prison for life. The hours slipped by, and the men and the girls talked and talked as only communists of that wild and irresponsible period could talk when they were among themselves. They were as preoccupied with their own importance and their revolutionary tasks as children are with new and engrossing toys. I listened as if under a spell. After all, compared with the tight-lipped conspirators of a later decade, we were like children partaking of a heady wine.

Finally, halfway between midnight and dawn, Felix Neumann rose and said dramatically: "Children, I want to sleep."

The apartment of Maria Schipora seemed to be a camping place for a great number of functionaries passing through Berlin on illegal missions. Each of those present drew blankets from a stack in a closet. Felix Neumann and Eva had a room of their own. So had Maria. The rest slept on couches and on the rug.

Quite openly Maria said to me: "We two sleep together."

I was a bit embarrassed by Edgar Andree's quizzical glance and by his remark, "Maria, can't you get enough *Reichswehr* officers to keep you content?"

"Bah," Maria snapped, adding in a soft voice: "Comrade Edgar, there is nothing better than good, clean youth."

Turning to me, she said half-angrily, "Don't mind these old troopers. Don't you think there is a reason for my letting you stay here?"

Felix Neumann woke me at eight. He had already been outside to telephone. Andree and his assistants had departed, and Eva and Lu were making ready to leave.

In the morning light Neumann's hollow face was gray. "Snatch your coffee in a restaurant," he said crisply. "A friend wants to see you."

We rode in a taxi to a little hotel in Neukoelln. In a dingy front room of the hotel a man clad in pajamas rose from the bed when we entered. Scattered on the bed and the floor were the morning newspapers.

"This is the comrade from Hamburg," Neumann said.

Dark, strong eyes sized me up. The man in pajamas was about thirty-three years old; his body was strong and lithe, his fair hair tousled, and his sharply-cut face had an expression of unsmiling, wide-awake determination. He looked like a Russian or a Lett. He asked me how our units in Hamburg were armed, how the training progressed, and if the rank and file had confidence in their leadership. He made short-hand notes of the things I told him, and observed that he thought it necessary at times to inform himself of the opinions of the comrades at the bottom. He then instructed me to take two parcels to Hamburg, one for Otto Marquardt, the other for a young lady named Anja Daul. Both packages would be handed to me at the station before I boarded the Hamburg express.

"Do you need money?" he asked me suddenly.

"No," I answered, though I was nearly penniless.

"We might need you," the man said quietly.

Neumann and I were bidden to wait in the room until the other had dressed and departed. When he had gone, I asked Neumann why we had not been allowed to leave first.

"A precaution," Neumann replied. "This is an important comrade. He never sleeps twice in the same place."

"Who is he?"

"General Wolf. Did you ever hear of the Kronstadt rising against the Bolsheviki? Well, General Wolf is the man who crushed it."

Maria Schipora saw me off at the station. She brought the two packages. They were rather bulky bundles, but light for their size.

"Now what's that?" I gasped.

"Soiled towels," she laughed, her liquid eyes twinkling. "Have them washed and send them back."

Each bundle of towels contained a sealed parcel of cigar-box size. I do not know what the boxes contained. One I delivered to Otto Marquardt, the other to Anja Daul who lived with her sister in a two-room place on a short street called Venusberg. Both Daul girls were smartly dressed, young, blonde, uncommunicative, and both wore short bobs. Also, both were Russian, and members of the Hamburg T-units. Both were caught and sent to prison in 1925.

The situation in Hamburg was tense. Two police officers had been murdered, and Ernst Thaelmann had sought cover by going underground. Each day the Party organized the plundering of food stores and raids on transports carrying food. These plunderings were mass affairs, provoked to test the militancy of the mass of unorganized workers.

After a few days of minor activities with the Red Marines, I was again sent to Berlin to deliver a slender envelope to the man I had come to know as General Wolf. The letter was glued to the skin of my back by Marquardt's elephantine secretary, a good-natured but efficient girl known as Fat Grete. She was working in the office of the Soviet Trade Mission, and was destined to become one of the most trusted female veterans in the movement.

Maria Schipora, lissome, bright-eyed and elegantly dressed, met me at the station in Berlin. In a cab we rode to the Melanchthon Strasse, got out and walked to a restaurant where Maria told me to wait. After a short while, she returned with a sedate young man who introduced himself as Karl. Karl escorted me to another restaurant several blocks away, and in the lavatory he loosened the letter from the skin of my back. At a table near the door General

Wolf and a soft, pale-faced man were having coffee. I sat down at the table and slipped the letter to General Wolf. He pocketed it without reading.

"Neumann will see you soon in Hamburg," General Wolf said.

Immediately he and the pale-faced man left. As before, I was told to wait.

For a full half-hour Karl and I sat at the table, staring at each other without a word. The mysterious comings and goings of General Wolf and his friends intrigued me considerably. His pale-faced companion I later recognized as Fritz Heckert who, in 1923, directed the Comintern courier system between Berlin and Moscow; a communist of international importance and a Reichstag member for many years, he perished in Moscow, during the great purge.

Maria Schipora was waiting for me in the street. She had, it seemed, much money to spend. For some time we rode about Berlin in a cab, then had dinner in Café Bauer, and after dark she invited me to her apartment. Again she treated me to benedictine, and was violently amorous, whispering now and then how sweet and easy life could be if one only had money. At first I was puzzled by her behavior, and then I began to develop a strong distrust of her. "What's her game?" I asked myself.

"You act like a bourgeois," I told her. She laughed lazily. "Wouldn't you? It's nice to make money." She went on: "All this political nonsense makes me sick! It's hopeless, anyway. Should someone come to you and say: 'Here are a thousand goldmarks if you do me a little favor,'—would you do it?"

"Do what?"

"Oh, sell interesting items to some people."

"Which people?"

She drew up her knees and clasped her arms around them.

"Hugo Stinnes, for example," she drawled. "Or General von Seeckt. Why not?"

For a moment I was stupefied. I pushed her away and made a grab for my hat and coat. Hugo Stinnes, the industrialist, owned half of Germany's mines, ships, factories. Von Seeckt was the creator and commander of the *Reichswehr*, the real power behind the government of the Republic. Maria Schipora had turned her back. She was observing me in a mirror. She gave a giddy little laugh.

"Please stay," she said. "I was joking."

I took the first train to Hamburg, and was naive enough to rush to Party headquarters to contact Hugo Marx. The ground burned under my feet. Something had to be done with Maria Schipora. I found Hugo Marx, and reported my discovery of a traitor in the party *Apparat*.

Hugo Marx grinned. "That's all right," he said.

Nothing happened. Maria Schipora was no spy. She had tested me, in her own way, under orders from Felix Neumann.

During the following days Felix Neumann was in Hamburg. I met him in the home of Erika Zcympanski which had become for me a refuge for rare free hours. She had given me a duplicate key to her apartment. I was free to use her books and to eat anything I found in her larder. As soon as I came, Neumann motioned her to leave. When we were alone, he showed me a mimeographed circular letter. The headline read: 'Kill spies and provocateurs."

"Do you agree with that?" he demanded.

Without hesitation I said, "Of course."

"We are going to use you for special work," he said. He drew a sheet of notepaper from his pocket and put it on the table. Then he handed me a pencil. "Sign this."

Typewritten on the paper was the following text:

"I herewith admit my participation in the robbery on the bookmaking establishment in Bremen, Bahnhofstrasse."

Neumann noted my surprise.

"A formality," he said.

"But I don't even know of such a robbery," I protested.

"Just the same, anyone who's active in the T-units must sign such a declaration. As I said—a formality. We must be sure of our men. Sign." He fairly rapped it out.

I thought Felix Neumann was mad. I saw no sense in this transaction. I refused to sign it.

"Very well," he said with an air of finality. "We're through with you. We've been mistaken." His eyes grew dull in his cadaverous face.

I hastened to Albert Walter's office. He had acquired a four-story building in the Rothesoodstrasse, near the waterfront, which now served as headquarters for his harbor brigades. The place buzzed with activity. Men from the docks and the ships were shouldering in and out. I told him of Neumann's proposition and proposed at the same time that he, Walter, should find a way to relieve me of further courier duties and put me back to work on the waterfront where I felt I belonged.

Albert Walter gave his volcanic temperament free reign.

"That Neumann is a bloody jackass," he raged. "Tell him to go to the devil. Never mind, I'll tell him." He went on wishing the plague on "all the little Tchekists in Berlin." When he calmed down, he wrote a curt note to Otto Marquardt. "Tell that infernal Neumann to leave my men alone," the note said. Turning to me, Albert Walter concluded, "Take this to Marquardt. He is a sensible man."

Felix Neumann was quick to denounce Albert Walter for his peremptory refusal to release me for duties in the T-units of General Wolf. But Walter knew well how solid a reputation he enjoyed in the Kremlin. He wrote to Moscow, referring to Felix Neumann as a "lunatic." And Moscow backed Walter because the burly old sailor was the most capable man it had to lead its campaigns in the harbors and on the ships. I did not know at the time how lucky I was to return to the Red Marines instead of blundering into the fold of Maria Schipora, Felix Neumann and their clique. For the gloomy Neumann, whose thought and talk revolved around murder, was suddenly arrested. To save his own skin, he betrayed the whole officer corps of the T-units—the German Tcheka—into the hands of the Reich police. Some months later General Wolf himself was captured and charged with murder.

General Wolf had been sent to Germany by the Soviet Government to handle the military end of the planned insurrection. He arrived in Berlin bearing a false Norwegian passport. Soon afterwards a wide network of Red Hundreds and T-units came into existence. He maintained three private apartments in Berlin, one in Dresden, one in Hamburg and another one in the Soviet Embassy in Berlin. In Hamburg, he was known as Herrman, in Berlin as Helmuth or General Wolf, in Dresden as Goresoski, in the Soviet army as Gorev, and upon his arrest he gave his name as Peter Alexander Skoblevski, under which he made history, too.

Felix Neumann went to work for Skoblevski as liaison agent between the military high command of the Party and the Soviet legation in Berlin. On one occasion he drew $35,000 in American currency on order from Skoblevski; on another occasion, $50,000 for the account of "the man from Turkestan." These sums were spent on arms and propaganda.

Felix Neumann was, nevertheless, promoted to the leadership of the T-units. Skoblevski gave Neumann $5,000 to recruit new members for this *Apparat*, and to put the terrorists to work. The revolutionary committee demanded the assassination of General von Seeckt, head of the *Reichswehr*, on the eve of the insurrection. This, they hoped, would disorganize the army and lash the revolutionary hopes to a frenzy. None other than Zinoviev himself, the President of the Comintern, wrote in a manifesto, "General von Seeckt is the German Kolchak, the greatest danger for the workers," while he described Adolf Hitler, who was then preparing his Munich Putsch, as "a ridiculous petit bourgeois."

Felix Neumann at once put the War Ministry under surveillance to gather information about the movements and habits of von Seeckt. He also telephoned the general's *aide-de-camp*, presenting himself as a seller of French military secrets, and asked for a private interview. Neumann's plan was to have General von Seeckt murdered in his own office. But the head of the *Reichswehr* refused to fall into this trap.

Meanwhile Skoblevski's agents had discovered that the general went riding horseback in the Berlin Tiergarten each morning. Felix Neumann bought a quantity of an edition of the *Berline Illustrierte,* which contained von Seeckt's picture. He had the pictures cut out and distributed to the members of the Berlin T-units. For three days in succession the *Reichswehr* chief was followed during his morning rides by G.P.U. agents on horseback, while other terrorists lurked behind trees along the route. Von Seeckt, however, was accompanied on his rides by a group of *Reichswehr* officers, all of them armed to the teeth. Finally a seventeen-year-old girl, Anny Gerber, the mistress of one of the Tchekists, was assigned by Felix Neumann to cultivate a love affair with one of General von Seeckt's orderlies or stablemen. The plan was to hide a Tchekist on the grounds of the general's official villa, and to shoot him off his horse before his fellow officers could join him. The girl was frightened, and Felix Neumann threatened to have her killed if she did not follow orders. Anny succeeded in finding a lover among the general's men, but, it seems, she fell in love with him herself. General von Seeckt was warned, and stopped riding. And Skoblevski decreed the assassination of Anny Gerber.

A stormy session between Neumann and Skoblevski followed. Felix Neumann feared that he might be discharged for incompetence. To be discharged meant to be killed. He later admitted before a high court of the German Republic that he had feared for his own life. The G.P.U. never allows those who know too many secrets to retire. The session ended with a command by Skoblevski: "Von Seeckt must die within three days!"

So a last attempt was made in December, 1923. General von Seeckt had gone to Weimar, but when he returned to Berlin, G.P.U. men were waiting for him in the main hall of the Anhalter Bahnhof, among them Felix Neumann himself. All were armed with new Ortgies pistols.

Von Seeckt sensed trouble. He waited in his train until the arrival of the guards he had summoned. Surrounded by officials and station detectives, he swept through the station to the waiting automobile of the War Ministry. After the decisive defeat of the German Communist Party in the following weeks, Karl Radek, through Brandler, ordered that the plans to kill von Seeckt be dropped.

Other prominent personalities whose death warrant Skoblevski had issued were Hugo Stinnes, Germany's richest man, and Privy Councillor Borsig, the head of the German steel trust. Felix Neumann was put in charge of both undertakings. Tchekists shadowed Stinnes and invaded his residence at the Hotel Esplanade in Berlin. Felix Neumann's men also closed in on Borsig's villa in Tegel, a fashionable suburb. A strike of the steel workers was in progress; the Party chiefs hoped that Borsig's death would raise the strike to a more violent, revolutionary pitch. This time no shooting was to be done. Skoblevski suggested poisoning. From a mysterious source he obtained glass tubes containing typhus and cholera germs. These he entrusted to Felix Neumann. They were to be used in individual murders, and also against army and police officers in case of the outbreak of civil war. Neumann selected a special group from among his agents to procure rabbits and conduct experiments with the germs. Attempts to kill Stinnes and Borsig failed. The steel strike ended in defeat. But the glass tubes were found by the police, and became major exhibits in the Tcheka trial in Leipzig.

Weeks of maneuvering to take the lives of leading figures did not detract the *T-Apparat* from its chief task—counter-espionage and the silencing of police spies in the communist organizations. The death-list included a certain Wetzel, head of the communist unit in the textile workers' union; Police Commissioner Schlotter, in charge of the anti-communist drive in southern Germany, and others. But what proved to be the undoing of Skoblevski and his secret division was the assassination of one Rausch in Berlin. Rausch was a member of the Party and also an undercover agent of the Berlin political police, and in touch with the Hitler movement.

Suspicion first fell on Rausch through the alertness of Hugo Marx in Hamburg. About the middle of October, a motor lorry loaded with rifles and handgrenades, on its way from Stettin to communist Hundreds of the Weser country in the west, was held up by fascist detachments on the highway between Luebeck and Hamburg. Two of Skoblevski's German assistants, in charge of the arms consignment, put up a resistance and were killed. The fascists, reputedly former members of the Iron Division and the Free Corps of Captain Ehrhardt, made off with the heavily loaded lorry to haunts on Junker estates in Mecklenburg or Pomerania. Only a spy in Skoblevski's own *Apparat* could have betrayed this transport of guns and grenades to the nationalist *Feme* organizations.

Hugo Marx, assigned to investigate, reported that Rausch might be the informer. "The more a man engaged in conspirative work talks of violence and bloodshed," Marx observed, "the more likely is he to be in the pay of the police." Hugo Marx's suspicions were soon verified. The police raided two communist basement arsenals in Berlin. A bomb factory, also in a Berlin cellar, was likewise raided. Members of the T-units, who returned to Berlin after they had bombed a few government buildings in Hanover, were arrested at the station. These arrests and raids were traced to Rausch by one of Skoblevski's female counter-spies, and Felix Neumann received instructions to put Rausch out of the way.

Three attempts were made, one with the help of a girl from Maria Schipora's group, the second in the lavatory of a brothel where Neumann had posted Tchekists armed with razors, and the third in Rausch's own home. Felix Neumann himself, with the snarl, "Take this, you bastard!" emptied his pistol into Rausch's groin.

Felix Neumann was too excited to follow the advice he had given me a few weeks earlier. He did not use a razor to slash his victim's throat. Still alive, Rausch was rushed to the St. Lazarus hospital in Berlin.

The court records in Leipzig have it that Skoblevski, hearing that Rausch was not dead, had blurted out: "That's not the way. The man must die!"

Rausch died. Felix Neumann fell into the hands of the police. At once the G.P.U. got busy trying to bribe a prison physician to order Neumann's transfer to an insane asylum, but to no avail. Felix Neumann was broken by the political police. Skoblevski and fourteen other Tchekists were arrested and charged with treason and murder.

Most of the captured terrorists gave way under a year of police pressure. But Skoblevski himself admitted nothing. He maintained stubbornly that he was a Russian student stranded in Germany, that his arrest was a mistake, that he had never set eyes on any of the other men in custody. The trial before the Supreme Court of Leipzig lasted nine weeks. Felix Neumann, Skoblevski and a third G.P.U. man were condemned to death. The others received long terms in prison. Between two court hearings an attempt was made in prison to assassinate Felix Neumann, the traitor. He was struck on the head, but escaped.

Before the Leipzig trial began, a silent drive was inaugurated by Felix Dzerjinsky, founder of the Tcheka and supreme chief of the G.P.U in Soviet Russia, to liberate General Skoblevski. As his tool Dzerjinsky chose the twenty-one-year-old but unscrupulous Heinz Neumann, who was the son of a wealthy Berlin grain dealer. Heinz Neumann, later a member of the Reichstag and one of the most talented agents of the Comintern, acted in 1923 as liaison man between the G.P.U. and the Comintern headquarters in Moscow and the German Communist Party. It is the same Heinz Neumann who was to emerge in later years as a close friend of Stalin and to gain the reputation of the "Butcher of Canton" in the Chinese civil war.

Three young Germans who had come to Moscow in 1923 under the auspices of Berlin Party headquarters were invited to drinking bouts by Heinz Neumann. One of the three, Dr. Carl Kindermann, betrayed homosexual tendencies. This, and a few critical remarks about the conditions in the Soviet Union, gave Heinz Neumann a pretext to denounce the three to the G.P.U. They were arrested and charged with having been sent to Russia by the secret fascist organization "Consul" to assassinate leading Soviet officials. Month after month, the three German radicals languished in the Lubianka dungeons in Moscow, and the German press made a big stir about them, demanding their release.

At this stage the G.P.U. began secret negotiations with the German Ministry of Justice, offering to exchange their German prisoners for Skoblevski. The German government refused. Skoblevski had been sentenced to die. The G.P.U. answered by bringing the three Germans before the highest military tribunal in Moscow. It was the first of the so-called show trials. Carl Kindermann stood up and denounced the G.P.U. in open court. Felix Dzerjinsky himself, Kindermann reported, had bargained with him to obtain a "confession." Another of the accused, the student von Dithmar, followed Kindermann's example. The third, the student Wolscht, had been broken down and made a deal with the G.P.U. while in prison. He had become a member of the Bolshevik Party during his confinement in the Lubianka, and now, while on trial, he praised the Soviet policies and implicated himself and his comrades. All three were condemned to be shot as spies.

Still the German government refused to exchange Skoblevski. Whereupon the G.P.U. arrested a number of German consular officials and their wives, accusing them of anti-Soviet conspiracies. At the same time, the negotiations to free Skoblevski were renewed.

Skoblevski was not executed. In September, 1926, he was exchanged for eleven German prisoners of the G.P.U. Carl Kindermann and von Dithmar were freed. Wolscht, who had "confessed," died in the Lubianka prison in Moscow, according to a Soviet announcement. As for the lesser Tchekists who had been sentenced in Leipzig, the Party abandoned them to their fate.

There is a sequel to this chapter. In 1937, I was questioned about General Skoblevski by the director of the Foreign Division of the Gestapo, *Regierungsrat* Schreckenbach. I then learned that Skoblevski, under the name of Gorev, had become a Soviet military adviser to the Loyalist armies in Spain.

"May I see a photograph of this Gorev-Skoblevski?" I asked.

"There is none," was the reply. "The police records of him were stolen in 1927."

...

General Skoblevski, however, was never put on trial to answer for the thousands of lives sacrificed in the adventurous uprisings which he had organized in Germany during 1923. On October 16 of that year Otto Marquardt appointed me leader of a detachment of twenty men of the Red Marines. Six of these twenty were armed with old Russian carbines, five had new automatic pistols of Belgian make, four had old revolvers of various caliber, the rest were armed with knives and clubs. Between us we possessed six rejuvenated German World War hand-grenades of the egg-shape type. The oldest in my group was twenty-seven years old, the second oldest twenty-three and the youngest sixteen, a husky riveter's apprentice. On October 19, I took my detachment aboard a train bound for Bremen. We got off at Buchholz and had maneuver practice in a nearby forest; a footpath was a city street, selected rocks represented tenements, and fallen trees served as barricades. We agreed on certain signals for assault, for co-operation in ambush, for retreat and for scattering. Then we marched to Hamburg, following the railway, taking sharp note of the terrain on both sides. On October 21, each man bought a quart of kerosene for the purpose, if need be, of setting buildings, barricades, or police lorries afire. On the same day Hugo Marx gave me a detailed plan of Police Post 42 in Hamburg-Eimsbuettel, and I took five of my comrades to the Eimsbuettel district to study all details and approaches of the station at close range. In doing this,

I was as serious as any earnest young skipper who shaped the first course of the first ship under his command. We did not think of ourselves; we thought of our duty to prepare the great breakthrough into a better future.

How strong were we really? Every comrade asked that question; few could answer it. Our leaders maintained that the majority of the German workers stood behind the Communist Party. They always talked that way on the eve of a major blow, so as to inspire confidence among those of their followers who were willing to throw away their lives.

For weeks Moscow's decision as to the general uprising had hung in the balance. Courier after courier arrived in Berlin from

Moscow, bearing message after message. Moscow ordered revolution, countermanded the order, and restored it. In Berlin, the Central Committee of the Party, under Karl Radek, was undecided. Our leaders were immersed in factional squabbles, confused by conflicting commands from the Kremlin, while the Party couriers waited to carry to the Red Hundreds in the provinces the signal to go ahead. The story has been told by Walter Zeutschel, an active participant in the events.

When the Social Democratic Party refused to join the planned communist revolt, Ernst Thaelmann, in a rage, dispatched the couriers with the order for the rising. This exploded like a bomb. The other members of the Central Committee leaped from their seats and stared at each other in bewilderment. Brandler was first to regain his composure. He sent his men out to stop the couriers. But the courier for Hamburg had already started. Brandler's messenger rushed to the station.

"Too late," he was told. "There goes the train."

For a while the messenger stared at the tail lights of the train which rolled toward Hamburg. Then he went home.

Chapter Six

SCAPEGOATS ON THE BARRICADES

In October, 1923, the day's wage of a docker in the harbor of Hamburg was seventeen billion marks.

On the night of October 22 all detachment leaders in Hamburg were summoned to a house on Valentinskamp. There were about sixty men present, denoting that our armed communist forces in the district numbered roughly 1,200. Otto Marquardt and his secretary, the elephantine Grete, were present. So were two young Russian officers. But none of them spoke; listening, they hovered in a corner where the light was dimmest. The final instructions were issued by one of Ernst Thaelmann's aides. There was no enthusiasm. A spirit of silent resignation permeated our meeting. The air was stifling and full of smoke. The faces of the sentries at the door were taut and pale. But we were determined to triumph or to die for the revolution. The meeting broke up with a muffled shout, "Forward! Long live Soviet Germany!"

In a tenement around the corner the detachment couriers, their bicycles parked in a rear courtyard, were waiting. I found my courier, the riveter's apprentice, in a kitchen, eating a large meal of boiled potatoes and margarine. I ordered him to mobilize my group—Detachment Two of the Red Marines—and to tell the men to assemble outside of the suburban town of Harburg at a certain point on the Hamburg-Bremen railway line at twelve-thirty sharp. The rifles were to be left with a Party member in Eimsbuettel, to be called for later. The boy clattered downstairs, still munching.

Then I took the local train to Harburg, a journey of twenty minutes. The night was dark, windy, but not cold. I felt so hot that I loosened the woolen scarf I wore around my neck and unbuttoned my windbreaker. The Harburg organization had assembled a lot of stolen bicycles in a vacant store a couple of blocks from the station. Here the front door was locked, there were no lights, but a side-door, opening on an alley, was open. Comrades were stationed at the corners to warn against occasional policemen. I received a bicycle and crossed the outskirts. Once out on the highway, I extinguished the light, and followed the railway line until a cluster of long low sheds popped out of the night. A few lanterns drew small circles of yellow light. On a siding stood a few empty freight cars. This was our point of assembly. A dark figure leaped suddenly on the highway and raised an arm.

In the shadows of the empty freight cars huddled a group of local communists. None of them had firearms. By midnight sixteen men from my detachment had arrived. Half an hour later two stragglers from another detachment appeared. They had lost their way or misunderstood their directions. Both of them had Belgian pistols. At 12:45 I said: "Let's go."

We surrounded the sheds and overpowered two elderly watchmen. We locked them into a small toolshed. Their guns, small Mausers, were taken by two local militants. A long freight train approached, and we lay still until it had passed. Then each man did the job he had previously been appointed to do. We had a high degree of beginner's luck. Two men cut the telegraph wires. Four, with saws and an ax from the toolshed, felled nearby trees. Another group toiled to dislocate ties and rails. The local communists banded together and pushed a freight car from the siding to the main line of trains bound for Hamburg. Trees, timbers, debris and rocks were heaped on the line. The purpose of this action was to prevent police and troop reinforcements to roll unhindered into Hamburg once the authorities had given the alarm. A lone field policeman who blundered into our midst was immediately disarmed.

In the small hours of morning the city lay quiet. We assembled in the blackness of a small park. Two couriers brought our six rifles from their hiding-place. They were distributed to those who had had rifle experience in previous encounters. We were now twenty-seven strong, including two girls who carried iodine, bandages, scissors and clubs. No one spoke an unnecessary word. Our task was to raid Police Post 42.

We proceeded in two single files, one on each side of the street, hugging the houses. From a public telephone booth I called the police station.

"Come quickly," I telephoned. "There are three burglars here in a luggage shop." I gave an address on the far side of the Eimsbuettel district. That would draw part of the police force away from the post.

I directed my detachment to halt a block away from the station. Like ghosts we vanished into the doorways. I sent a youngster ahead to enter the station. He was to ask the police officer in charge to telephone for a doctor—because of a premature birth somewhere in the district. The young comrade soon returned to report that five policemen were in the station. Three of them had hung their gun belts on hooks in the wall, and were playing cards. I was tempted to attack that very moment, but I held back.

The signal for the insurrection came like a thunderclap. It came in the form of three-men groups who were smashing the street lights. With a feeling as if my skin was shriveling up and going off in all directions, I put two fingers into my mouth and whistled.

From two sides we closed in. That instant I wished I were far away, out at sea on some ship; others later told me that they had the same sensation. But each of us was ashamed to stand back. We rushed at the station building, intent to kill before we ourselves would be killed. It was no bloodless assault. Someone behind me, crazy with excitement, fired his pistol into the air and yelled. That warned the policemen. A window was thrown open. The light in the station went out. The guns barked, blotting out thought.

I saw two of my comrades fall. For a while one of them whimpered like a dog that had been ran over. Against the wall of a short hallway, flanked by two guard-rooms, stood two policemen. Stilettos of yellow fire leaped from their hands. Close to the door a young stevedore in a patched gray sweater pulled the release of a hand-grenade. "Stand off," he said hoarsely. Then he counted, yelled: "Twenty-one ... Twenty ..." Six or seven of us crouched on both sides of the entrance. The grenade roared, and the hallway was free. We sprang forward with the roar of the explosion still in our ears.

Smoke filled the inside of the station. From the floor a policeman was still firing. The stevedore crushed his face with a kick of his heavy boot. Another policeman had the side of his neck torn away; he was bleeding to death under a table. Someone switched on the lights. The three remaining policemen were cornered, their arms raised high.

The stevedore raged: "Shoot them. Kill the whole murderous lot!"

I stopped him. The Party command had ordered us to keep prisoners as hostages. We shackled the policemen together with their own handcuffs. Outside the station a crowd shouted for arms. Men and boys came running from all directions, and a few women from the communist ambulance service. We found a dozen rifles and thirty rounds of ammunition for each, and an equal number of service pistols. There were also some first-aid kits and a machine gun. A middle-aged worker stepped forward when I asked who could use a machine gun. He pulled out his Party book, and said he had served in the war. I gave him the machine gun, and called for volunteers in the crowd to help him mount it on the roof of a house from which three important streets could be dominated. The girls from the ambulance service carried our wounded away. Throughout the city the Party had established first-aid stations in the apartments of sympathizers.

By this time a squad from another Red Hundred, composed of older men, took over the captured station. Others tore up the pavement and erected a barricade; timbers, garbage cans, old furniture obstructed the street. Cursing dispatch-riders lugged their bicycles over the obstructions. The sounds of distant rifle fire filled the night. Within that hour nearly a score of other police posts were stormed by communist detachments in the districts of Hamm, Horn, Barmbeck and elsewhere.

I have often been asked: "What are the thoughts and feelings of a thousand men who set out to conquer a city of more than a million in one onslaught?" The answer is that at first they plunge ahead in a delirium of self-destruction. They cannot believe that they will win, but they would rather die than admit this to themselves. But after their initial success they become, in a way, rational, and their self-confidence grows to monstrous proportions. There was neither fear nor hesitation in our minds. What we did, we felt, was good and right. We did not think of ourselves. We did not anticipate private material gain. We were fanatics prepared to give all, and ask nothing for ourselves. We despised the hoodlums who took advantage of darkness and confusion to loot and maraud for individual profit and pleasure.

A band of such hoodlums was looting a number of stores. A squad of communists gave them battle. The goods in the stores were now the property of the working class, and looting had become a crime. From an apartment in the rear of a store came piercing cries for help. Three or four men from my column forced their way into the apartment. After a while they returned and reported: Two plunderers had surprised a girl in her bed. One of them had grasped the girl's wrists and the other raped her. My comrades had yanked the two into the now empty store.

"You made them cold, I hope?" I said. I heard no shots.

"With bayonets," one of the comrades answered.

We advanced, keeping close to the houses. There was no time to lose. It was still dark, and the surprise element is greatest in the hours before dawn. We moved toward the center of Hamburg. Other columns, I knew, were doing the same from all surrounding points.

Despite the dead and wounded we had lost, my group was stronger now. Clusters of volunteers followed the spearhead. Many streets swarmed with people. Party agitators endeavored to draw people into the streets and to keep them there. Skoblevski's instructors had made it clear to us that it was important to have crowded streets when fighting took place. Nothing will rouse the wrath of the population so much as police firing into unarmed masses. At intersections, small groups of partisans collected kerosene in garbage cans and heaps of old rags; their task was to stop police lorries with sudden barricades of fire.

At daybreak we met resistance. A strong force of Security Police had entrenched around a small railway bridge, behind nearby trees and in adjoining houses. Their carbines cracked.

"Disperse! To the roofs!"

We dived into the houses on both sides. Doors splintered under carbine butts, and tenants in pajamas and nightshirts fled toward the cellars. Men crouched in windows, on the balconies, on the roofs. As if by common consent, the communist units held their fire. It was the prelude to what Soviet officers had taught us was the "bottling up" maneuver.

The police did not walk into the trap. We settled down to an hour of sniping. The machine guns of the police blasted away at anything that moved in the street. We tried to work ourselves toward the enemy by advancing over the roofs, but we lacked the ropes and ladders necessary to do this with success. A few reckless communists who straddled window sills to take better aim were quickly hit. One roared and spread out his arm, and plunged down from a height of five stories. Lying half in a doorway was a small child, stone-dead.

From the roof of a tenement a hundred yards away came a ringing voice.

"Don't give up. Hang on!" the voice shouted. "Reinforcements are on the way."

Communists were marching into Hamburg from all outlying communities. Then came two shrill whistles—the signal for assault. From my perch in an attic window I saw the snipers disappear from other roofs. Voices yelled: "Storm!" I leaped down four flights of stairs into a hallway already crowded with armed partisans. Perhaps one in five had a rifle, one in four a pistol, and the rest carried hammers and spiked clubs.

The signal for assault sounded again.

I and a few others pushed out into the street. Instantly, the screech of whining lead drove us back into the house. The sidewalks were littered with dead and wounded. Gray, fire-spitting things moved forward. Armored cars.

We had been taught how to fight armored cars. Here and there handgrenades were thrown out of doorways and low windows. Only one of them exploded. The others were dead. The armored cars continued to advance, raking the street. A youth carrying a bottle in each hand darted out of a house, and ran up to the first car. He smashed both bottles against the car, and then was dead. An older man, a bristly-faced scarecrow, now lunged toward the armored car. In the moment of his death he threw a bundle of burning rags on the back of the gray thing. This man—I can never forget him. He was the most pathetic hero of the Hamburg rising. The armored car was enveloped in flame and smoke, and the faster it moved, the brighter the flames became. At the end of the block it stopped. But two others continued, machine guns spitting.

By now I was, with many others, in the street. Police counterattacked in the shelter of armored cars. A low barricade of cobblestones at the end of the street stopped them. From a window, a solitary figure took potshots at civilians and policemen who attempted to clear away the obstacle. Before waves of attacking police we scattered into side streets. We retreated, scuttling from doorway to doorway, shooting before we ran. Of my detachment, the Red Marines, I saw nothing more. Around me, men I had never seen before, were shooting and yelling. And then we all ran, each man for himself, each man abruptly aware, it seemed, of the paramount task of saving his own skin.

Retreat is the death of any insurrection. What had begun as a concerted assault ended in a desperate defense, in equally desperate but short-lived attacks, and a guerrilla warfare which knew no leaders except those who took charge of haphazardly assembled groups before they were smashed and dispersed a few minutes later.

At Hamburgerstrasse and Bomes Road, in the north-east of the city, following the sound of heavy firing, I found a series of well-constructed barricades. No one seemed to be in command. But in the cover of piled-up benches, trees and stones, and from behind overturned carts and automobiles, members of the Red Hundreds gave battle to police. Others were sniping from windows and roofs of houses which flanked the barricades. In a courtyard, a woman distributed bread and liverwurst. Here was well-organized resistance. I was relieved, and asked for news.

"More police posts have been taken in the Borgfelde and the Uhlenhort districts," I was told.

"And the harbor?"

The harbor was decisive.

"The whole harbor is on strike."

Toward noon, the police brought mortars and mine-throwers into action. We crawled a little way back, and when the thunder and the smoke cleared away, our barricades were wrecked and police pushed forward in the rear of armored cars. There was a lull in the firing.

"Drop your arms," a policeman barked. *"Haende hoch!"*

He was shot on the spot. A group of communists advanced to meet the police. Ahead of them they shoved three captured police officers. Nevertheless, the police opened fire. One of the prisoners was instantly killed. The two others ran toward the police. A communist sprang from a doorway, tripped one of the escaping officers and shot him through the back of the head.

Again we retreated, fighting for each house. At dusk I found myself with two comrades on the roof of a garage, holding off a police patrol firing from windows on the opposite side of the street. Our fronts had broken up. All forces were scattered. Sounds of shooting came from all directions. A block down the street a group of Red Guards carrying wounded comrades was taken prisoner.

I was glad when it grew dark. One of the men on the garage roof was hit. The other jumped to the street and ran screaming into the arms of the police. I slid down into a backyard and entered the back door of the next house. It was a restaurant. I rushed through the restaurant, left it by the front door, and crossed into another street. The street was empty. I ran into a house and knocked at the door of an apartment.

A white-haired woman with a kind, wrinkled face opened the door. She looked at the pistol in my hand.

"What do you wish?" she asked serenely.

"Let me in."

"Better wash yourself," the woman said.

I did. She gave me coffee and bread and butter. My clothes were badly torn. The woman gave me an old overcoat.

"Take it," she said. "I've kept it eight years now, ever since my husband died."

I put on the overcoat. It was too small, but it was all right.

"I'm going to leave my arms here," I said.

"Yes, leave them here," the woman agreed, adding: "I shall throw them away the first chance I get."

"What happened today in the center of the city?"

"I know only little. Armed bands tried to loot the big stores while the fighting went on in the suburbs."

"Did you see a newspaper?"

"No," she said nervously. "You must go away now."

I went into the street. Posters on the walls ordered all citizens to leave the streets by eleven o'clock. Barbed-wire barricades, guarded by steel-helmeted police, blocked important intersections. At several points I was stopped and searched by police patrols.

"Leave me alone," I said. "I come from work. I want to go home."

"Why is your face burned?"

"There was a fire in the house."

"Well, don't go west," a policeman advised. "Hell is loose in Barmbeck."

I could still hear the sounds of rifle fire interspersed with heavier explosions. I wondered what the Party was doing in Berlin, in Saxony, in Silesia, elsewhere. Like my comrades, I took it for granted that the Red Hundreds had gone into battle all over Germany.

Avoiding the patrols, I made my way westward. I walked for hours. On the edge of the great proletarian district of Barmbeck, the bedlam of battle was louder than ever. Police trucks full of prisoners rumbled by. The prisoners sat on the floors of the trucks, their arms raised high. Police were shooting from the houses, from armored cars, from behind sandbags piled up in the street. I circled northward around the fighting zone. The streets were quieter. Stores showed light, and there was even music in a few small cafes. There were young workingmen and girls who held each other close and laughed. I entered a café for a glass of beer. People drew away from me, and were suddenly silent.

"What's the matter with you?" I asked.

They gave no answer. I hated them. The noises of slaughter less than a mile away were in the room. I drank the beer. When I went out, I slammed the door and the glass panel splintered. Cautiously I approached the zone of fighting.

I hailed a man who passed on a bicycle. I was not mistaken; he was a courier.

"How's the situation?"

"Bad."

The *Reichswehr* command had decreed the death penalty for disobedience to the authorities. It was rumored that the German navy was steaming for Hamburg. More than nine hundred communist partisans had been arrested during the fighting. The police recaptured most of their stations, after driving out the defenders with gas and mines.

"Let me ride with you," I said.

"Can't—I must be off."

A thought burned in my brain: "If the insurrection in other parts of the country has failed, we in Hamburg are lost." The masses, idle in strike, were not willing to fill the gaps of our ranks. The communist vanguard fought. The masses were passive. Perhaps the workers really did not want a revolution? I brushed the doubts aside. A skirmish line blocked the street ahead.

"Halt! Where to?"

"Red Marines."

A sentry held a flashlight into my face. "Pass," he said.

The vicinity of Pestalozzi Street was an armed communist camp.

On the sidewalks columns were re-formed and received their orders. In the van of a couple of hundred silent marchers, I saw Johnny Dettmer, the gun-runner of previous months. Almost all the men seemed well armed. At another spot, raiding parties were formed to attack the harbor. Special squads formed by men of Hugo Marx's *Apparat* were on the way to offer their services as volunteers to the police, to plant themselves in our enemy's camp. The police, it was known, were organizing a Buergherwehr, an auxiliary force of anti-communist citizens. Everyone I saw was going somewhere or doing something. The din of rifles and machine guns, flaring up, diminishing at times, but always loud and disturbing, was only a few hundred yards to the south. Knots of men slept in doorways; they looked at first glance like heaps of corpses. On a corner, shouting violently at a group of dispatch-riders, I saw the short, compact figure of Herrman Fischer, the chief of the first Red Hundred.

"What do you want me to do?" I said.

"Do? Let's see—Red Marines are off to Geesthacht. Go there tonight. You'll be four hundred strong. Get hold of the dynamite factory before morning."

"Can you get me a gun?"

Herrman Fischer laughed. "Disarm a policeman," he said, "and you'll have a gun."

Units of five were assembled for the night march to Geesthacht, an industrial suburb on the right bank of the Elbe. The idea of seizing a dynamite factory animated even the most hungry and weary. Soon we were on the way in small groups, and unarmed, because we had to pass the districts controlled by troops and police.

Without serious mishap we slipped through. One of the bridges which crosses a ship canal running parallel to the river is called the Kornhaus Bridge, and it was for this point that we were heading through a maze of crooked old streets. We came upon two policemen patrolling a little square in front of a church. They had carbines, pistols, bayonets, rubber truncheons, and they wore steel helmets.

Three men are necessary to disarm a policeman—two to hold his arms, the third to cut away his Sam Browne with a sharp knife. In the shadow's of a side street we waited until the officers had passed. Then we pounced on them. Now our group was armed.

We stripped the policemen of their uniforms and told them to run for it or be shot. They ran. The uniforms we took with us.

A little further on, the street was blocked by a barbed-wire entanglement. We ran for cover, suspecting a trap. Nothing happened. The boldest in our group, a scraggy boilermaker, crept forward to investigate. The barricade was unmanned. On its other side an automobile without lights had stopped, and a man was trying to pull part of the entanglement aside. The boilermaker's guffaw echoed in the silent street.

"Come on," he said. "These are profiteers."

The rest of us hastened up to the group on the other side of the barbed wire. The occupants of the car were a pudgy, middle-aged man and a young woman in a fur coat. Between them, with a firm grip on the man's collar, stood the boilermaker.

"Look at these beauties," he said. "Motorcar, fur coat and all."

Here, we thought, was a true profiteer. We made the man take off his topcoat and his pants. The woman we forced to surrender her fur coat and her shoes. She was calm, but her escort shivered like a leaf. He pulled out a wallet and offered to buy back his pants.

"Sure," the boilermaker said. He took the wallet, pulled out a wad of bills, tore them in half and threw them into the night. "So much for your money," he snarled. "Now run or we'll hang you to a lantern.'

The woman walked off on her toes. The man followed her, lurching from side to side as if drunk. We pushed the car into the barbed wire, and overturned it.

We occupied the boat-landing beneath the Kornhaus Bridge and waited. A tall blue-eyed youngster from another unit had donned one of the police uniforms and had gone to the Baumwall a half mile away to hire a water taxi, a *Barkasse*. We posted a sentry up street to warn us should police approach. Armed platoons on motor trucks passed twice. Each time we darted into the public comfort station beneath the quay. Finally the peaceful chugging of a motor told us that a launch was coming along the canal. It drew alongside the landing. The young communist in police uniform held his pistol pressed against the spine of the launch captain. The launch was about forty feet long, with a small cabin in front of the wheel. We crowded into the cabin. Those who found no room lay down flat in the bottom of the *Barkasse*. So, with only the steersman and the uniformed comrade visible from the quays, the launch passed through the end of the canal, veered into the broad river and continued upstream. Nearly twenty men were aboard the launch. About four o'clock in the morning we landed on a grassy embankment off Geesthacht. Again we waited, crouched close to the ground, while the boilermaker slipped away to scout for the points of assembly.

The silence was oppressive. We were too far from Hamburg to hear the sounds of shooting. Presently two girls, muffled to their ears, arrived.

"This way, comrades,' they whispered.

They led us to an abandoned factory. The windows were covered with sacking. Armed guards were on duty behind a breastwork of empty oil drums and piled-up earth. A few girls and women had set up field kitchens with oil stoves. Pea soup and tea in tin bowls were served to all newcomers. Many were too tired to eat; they fell asleep with the spoons in their hands. The dark, bare halls of the factory teemed with activity. Only necessary words were spoken. Squads armed with picks and shovels went out and others returned. Regular trenches were being dug on both sides of the two main highways leading from Hamburg to Geesthacht.

Dawn came dull and gray. We lined up in front of the factory walls for last instructions from the detachment commanders. The instructions were simple enough—seizure of the railway station, the arsenal, the dynamite factory; arming of the Geesthacht workers and a renewed advance on Hamburg. The final admonition was: "Let no wounded fall into the hands of the police. On to victory!"

In the chill morning we attacked. The trenches crossing the highways were well manned to prevent the penetration of police or troops from Hamburg. We advanced in four columns, each with its own important objective. I was assigned to the force which was to raid the dynamite factory; exhausted as I was, I did my duty as a good soldier of the revolution.

Small assault groups went ahead to disrupt the communication lines of the defenders, and to test the strongest points in the defense of the main buildings. We had planned a surprise coup, but it wras we who were surprised. The resistance was fierce. Soon rifles cracked from the windows of workers' dwellings and from the roof on the rambling factory. We gained ground slowly through backyards and gardens, and worked ourselves through many of the small one-family houses that skirted the factory area. An armored lorry was stopped with two hand-grenades. By the time our squad faced the factory gates, half of our number had fallen in the fire.

The day turned into a nightmare. I saw a girl from the communist first-aid columns who had followed us to tend the wounded. Her mouth and chin were half torn away by a slug, and she was still whimpering. We did not take the dynamite factory. We were pressed back into the trenches which followed the crest of a low hill, and there we held out until the afternoon.

Airplanes droned overhead, dropping leaflets first, and then blazing away with machine guns. "Surrender," the leaflets said. "Resistance is useless." That I knew, and so did every other man in the trench. But we had no thought of surrender. We would fight until we were dead. Mortars thundered and threw sheets of rock and mud on our heads. And then came a new, dreaded noise: the juicy hammering of heavy machine guns. Terrified shrieking followed.

"The navy! The navy!"

We had believed in the revolutionary tradition of the navy. We had hoped that our propagandists would cause a naval revolt when the order was given to shoot on workers. We were mistaken. We saw the blue uniforms ran, throw themselves to the ground, rise and run again. They were sailors from a destroyer flotilla that had slipped upriver early in the morning.

Here and there a communist threw away his gun and ran. More followed, and then we all abandoned our arms and ran. We ran like hunted hares in all directions. The "hurrahs" of the sailors sounded menacing and hollow as they charged with bayonets fixed.

Fleeing communists asked one another: "Where do we concentrate? Where is the command?"

"Don't know," was the invariable answer. "Get a breathing spell, and keep on fighting till we know what's happened in Berlin."

Berlin? Berlin was calm. A message from Zinoviev had postponed the revolution. Every third member of the Hamburg Party machine was either dead or wounded or in jail.

But the Party is like an animal with seven lives. After our rout in Geesthacht, I was hidden with three others in the home of a partisan when a Party courier, combing through the houses of sympathizers, brought orders from Otto Alarquardt's staff to assemble in the suburb of Ahrensburg. We headed toward Hamburg, each man alone. Some went by boat, some followed by rails, and others trudged along the roads. Many were arrested by police patrols on the way.

On Thursday, the third day of the rising, shooting continued all through the night, single shots, and now and then, a strong fusillade or a burst of machine gun fire.

Off a street called Wandbecker Chaussee I found a worker who had been shot through the stomach. He groaned at regular intervals, and after each groan, he bit into the barrel of his Russian carbine. Passers-by made a cautious circle around the fallen man and hurried on. I picked him up and carried him around a corner, in the hope of finding a friendly house. I had never been in this section of the city before. I dragged the wounded man into a gap between two houses and tried to speak to him to find out who he was. He could not answer. Like all of us, he had left his identification papers at home. I fell asleep behind three garbage cans, and when I awoke toward the morning, the worker was dead. I dragged the corpse back to the street, and propped him against a wall so that a cruising ambulance could find him. Then I took his rifle; only two cartridges were left.

Ahrensburg, just outside Hamburg on the railroad to Luebeck, was mainly in the hands of Red Hundreds. Headquarters was the railway station. Men slept on the stone floor and others trampled over them without heed. A stocky man was in charge, and a mad plan was afoot.

The plan was to seize the central railroad station of Hamburg, which had a commanding position. Eight important thoroughfares ended at the station. Spies had been sent to find out the strength of police and troops guarding the terminal. The stocky man wanted to fill a local train with armed men, run it into Hamburg, and overwhelm the station. A new consignment of Russian rifles had arrived from Luebeck.

"Once you're inside, massacre every uniform you see," the stocky man said.

A thin communist with a meek face and a drooping mouth protested. "Do you want to murder us all?" he cried. "Go tell Thaelmann and Brandler and Lenin to storm the damned station themselves."

The stocky man pushed the defeatist against a door.

"Hold still, my boy," he murmured.

In a flash he drew his pistol and shot the thin man through the head.

A murmur went up and a few "Bravos." Many of us crashed our rifles to the floor. I was sick of it, and so were others. For a minute it seemed that comrade would murder comrade.

"We're through," someone said.

The argument stopped when a scout arrived from the Hamburg station. He reported two hundred policemen hidden in the waiting rooms. New posters in the city squares had the caption: "Persons bearing arms against the government are subject to the death penalty."

Resistance had become a farce. We had no leaders. Demoralization took its course. Isolated rebel units, still fighting out of sheer stubbornness and, perhaps, a craving for revenge, retreated along the Luebeck road. The vast majority, broken, bedraggled, disgusted, sauntered away, each man leaving the next to shift for himself.

"What did we get out of it?" one of my companions asked.

"I don't know," I said.

"I wish I knew," the other mumbled forlornly.

A skirmish line of policemen bore down the street.

"We'd better separate," I proposed.

"All right."

We parted. I felt as if I should never be happy again or enthusiastic about anything as long as I lived. So much bloodshed and suffering! It made a man want to turn his face to the clouds and roar, so great was the pain. For what? When I entered the Café Bunte Kuh in St. Pauli above which I had rented a shabby little room, someone pointed me out to a police patrol. There was no chance to flee. The people were hostile. Even the prostitutes mocked me. "To the gallows with him," one of them repeatedly chanted, swinging an empty beerglass. A policeman held me in a grip that threatened to break my arm. So I was led to the police post on the Davidstrasse.

The small jail was overcrowded. The cells were packed with arrested men, and new arrivals were herded into the guard rooms which were so crowded that men stood on each other's feet. The usual organized rowdyism of a band of communists in jail found no response in this gathering. A dismal stench filled the place, faces were surly or stoic, and except for the ribaldry of a few intoxicated sailors, men spoke in whispers. After a wretched hour I was called out and pushed aboard an open truck together with many other prisoners. On the rear end of the truck, his carbine across his knees, sat a policeman. We sat on the floor boards, hands raised above our heads, while the truck sped toward the headquarters of the Security Police.

The policeman on the rear end of the lorry was young, and his face was gaunt and sunken from lack of sleep. On the way, the prisoner next to him, a gorilla of a man, lashed out at the guard with both feet. Both pitched to the pavement. The truck stopped, its siren twittering for aid. A policeman jumped down from the front seat, his pistol drawn.

"Nobody move," he commanded.

The next instant he began to shoot. We tumbled off the lorry in a welter of arms and legs, and sprinted away in all directions. The street in which the truck had stopped was long and straight and narrow, but to the left lay the ancient section of Hamburg, a labyrinth of alleys, crooked passages and crumbling houses. The denizens of the *Gaengeviertel*—the alley quarter—prostitutes, pimps, criminals and down-and-outers of every description, hated the police and helped the hunted.

I emerged after dark. That night I spent in the apartment of Erika Zcympanski. Other fugitives were there, two wounded, and all utterly exhausted. We slept on the floor like dead men. Erika, after a sleepless night, was as good-looking and practical as ever. She had summoned a communist physician to treat the wounded. The touch of her firm, cool hand as it stroked over a face hot with fever and crusted with dirt, was like a fairy tale come true. Blood and filth could not affect her. Those who could, departed after a bath and a breakfast of coffee, butter and rolls. The morning papers reported that four hundred dead and wounded had been counted in hospitals and morgues; one-third of the known casualties were policemen. An unknown number of communist casualties were still hidden away in the homes of partisans.

"The police will be after me," I told Erika. "I must get away."

"Where will you go?"

"I'm going back to sea."

"Never forget the cause you fought for," she said. "You can keep up contact with the Party through me."

I left Hamburg in the afternoon. On a corner people were scrutinizing a new bill which showed the figure one followed by twelve zeros—a thousand billion marks on one piece of paper. Life on the streets was orderly and quiet. The churchbells rang for the burial of the dead.

Eleven days I was on the road, wandering toward the Rhine. I begged food from peasant women and slept in barns. I crossed the river Weser at Minden and entered Holland at night over the frontier town of Gronau. The next night, curled up in a meadow, I almost froze to death. But the following day, in the town of Arnhem, I saw a barge captain loading his craft with new red bricks. I asked him if I could help.

"Yes," he replied.

I helped him to load the barge, and for this he granted me a slow passage down the north arm of the Rhine to Rotterdam.

Chapter Seven

RED VAGABONDAGE

In the Norwegian sailors' home in Rotterdam I wrote a letter to Erika Zcympanski, asking her to inform the Party of my whereabouts. It was my plan to stay in Rotterdam until instructions arrived. The Comintern, I knew, had its organizations in every civilized country, and I felt it did not matter whether I was in Germany or not so long as I remained loyal and willing to serve the cause. Though stunned by the Hamburg horrors, my faith was intact. The movement to which I belonged was international; the doctrine that no worker has a fatherland was firmly rooted in my mind, and it was with open defiance and ill-concealed pride that I told myself: "You have not lost your fatherland. You never had a fatherland. You are an internationalist who has but a single task—to help put the capitalists and their henchmen into the grave all over the world."

From the sailors' home I went to the offices of the Communist Party to ask for aid as a refugee from Germany, and to put myself at the disposal of the local organization. The red-cheeked, sleepy-eyed Dutch Bolshevik who received me, glanced slowly around his disorderly office and said:

"Well, you'll have to wait until we inquire about you from the German Party."

Exasperated, I cried: "The Party in Germany is outlawed."

"We can do nothing for you if you have no mandate from your Party," the Dutchman said.

"Just give me an address where I can sleep and eat for a couple of days."

"We are no charitable institution," the Dutchman said.

Angry, on the verge of tears, I left him.

Later that day a detective picked me up and took me to a little jail which gave me the impression of being a detention place for assorted alien beachcombers. I had clambered into the fishtank of a discharged trawler to pick up left-overs which I intended to cook over a fire built by bums in a nearby freight car, when the detective leaned over the coaming and told me to come along.

I had no papers to prove my identity, and refused to give my name to the policemen who questioned me. I feared they would bring me to the border and surrender me to the German police.

"I got drunk and lost my ship in Antwerp," I told them. "So I came to Rotterdam to find me another ship."

They gave me a pound of excellent bread, a hunk of cheese and coffee. Before it got dark a gendarme called, and I was told to go with him. He brought me to a train. No other travelers were in the compartment. The gendarme sat in a corner by the door which he barricaded by keeping his feet on the opposite seat. Soon the train began to move.

"Where are we going?' I asked.

"You are going where you came from," the gendarme said.

I almost blundered. "Germany?" I wanted to ask I rose to open the window.

"Keep it closed," my guard advised. "It's cold." Patting his belt, he added: "Don't try to run away. If you run, I must shoot at you."

"Well, where are we going?"

"To Belgium."

I was relieved. The gendarme gave me a guilder. I was grateful. He never smiled. He had curiously tender eyes in a harsh-featured face, and he began to ask me about the life on ships. It seemed that he liked the sea, but he liked more a warm stove in the evening. At a small station he led me out of the train. The lights were frosty. The night was dark and raw. I shivered in the cold. Despite my six-foot frame, I felt weak and worn-out. The gendarme obtained for me a glass of rum and hot water from a fat girl in the waiting room.

"We are near the frontier," he said, pointing out of the window. "Yonder is Belgium."

A young border patrolman wrapped in a thick woolen shawl and a camel-hair coat, was waiting for us. The gendarme yawned and shook my hand, and the border guard grabbed my arm and led me out into the night. By-and-by the weather cleared, the stars shone, and a howling wind blew across the flat country.

We trudged over fields and waded through shallow ditches.

Thrice the border guard sat down in the shelter of barns to smoke a cigarette. While he smoked, he forced me to lie face to the ground. When we neared the strip of no-man's-land, we began to crawl on our hands and knees. Behind a thin barrier of brushes we paused.

My escort pointed into the gloom ahead.

"Go straight that way," he whispered, "one hundred meters, and you will be in Belgium. There are no patrols. Belgian patrols like to make fires. Now go and keep on going, and don't ever come back to Holland."

"All right," I said.

"Remember, one year in jail if you come back."

"I remember."

I bent my body toward the ground and ran forward. The wet grass made sucking sounds under my feet. A hundred yards away I halted, and turned to yell insults at the border guard.

"Keep quiet, you *smerlapp,*" he answered. "Keep going!"

Early in the morning I stopped at a farmhouse and asked a clean-looking woman for permission to wash under the pump.

"Poor fellow," she said. "Have they pushed you over the border?"

"Yes," I said.

"Many come that way. Pushed here, pushed there, all the time."

She gave me a piece of coarse soap and a towel. After that I had a breakfast of beans and bacon. I helped the woman to wring out a mountain of laundry until a farm helper harnessed the horse to get firewood from the nearest town. I went with him. The town was Esschen, only a few miles due north of Antwerp. I helped the farm-hand to load his cart and then I struck out on a shiny highway leading south.

The waterfront of Antwerp is the home of many outcasts. It is more international than Shanghai; it is the most international waterfront in the world. It was like a tonic to find myself in the pandemonium of harbor noises, docks and wharves cluttered with foreign freight, of seafaring sounds and smells. In the endless line of drinking places, Lascars and Norwegians guzzled away shoulder on shoulder, and a few francs and meal were to be had for the asking. In the Chrystal Palace and all its satellites around the *Steen*, naked women of all types pranced in tap-rooms full of noise and smoke and roistering men from the ships. And Antwerp was at that time one of the toughest places in Europe in which to find an outbound berth; seven thousand men were on the beach, and battalions of bums besieged every ship as soon as it was moored.

I spent the first night in the common sleeping quarters of the Salvation Army, after obliging its dormitory *baas* with a prayer. Early the second night, bent on some form of deviltry to 'shake off the bothersome shadows of blood spilled in Hamburg, I met Mariette.

She was standing behind a window, which reached down to street level, and smiled at me as I entered the short, crooked street. She neither jerked her head nor beckoned with her arm as did the buxom Flemish girls in adjoining houses. She smiled and I stopped.

Small and trim, she had luminous coal-black eyes. The lights in the room drew her outline sharply. I went inside, into a cloud of perfume and tropical heat. There were some palms in pots, a thick rug, a massive radio, a couch as large as a lifeboat, and pictures on the walls. The girl was draped in white silk. Her bare feet stuck in white sandals studded with colored beads. The grime of Antwerp was blotted out. Immediately she drew the curtains.

"Hello," she said.

"Hello," I replied. "What's your name?"

"Mariette."

"You are French?"

"I am from Marseilles."

She slipped her hand under my coat and wriggled close. She was taut and warm.

"Maybe you like me?"

"I have no money," I said.

"Such tales to tell," she laughed. "You're one of the nicest boys I touched."

"You lie."

"Listen, I never lie! You've smiling eyes. How old are you?"

"Twenty."

"I'm thirty," she said, teeth flashing. "The *Meisjes* in the next house are twenty-two and twenty-three. Cows who will stink at thirty. It comes because I take very good care. See, I have skin like silk; a little bit yellow, but it is like silk."

She prattled on like running water.

"Look here, Mariette," I told her, "I have no money. Not one copper."

"That's bad."

"If you hadn't smiled, I wouldn't have come in," I explained. She leaned back and laughed.

"I know how it is," she said. "Tell me, what can I do with you if you have not one copper?"

"You can call a policeman," I answered.

"You are crazy. I never call policemen."

For a short while she eyed me curiously. Then she said: "It is bad business to waste time on a boy who hasn't a copper. But listen, I know a man who pays me much money. He says his wife makes him sick. I can call him to come here, and he can sit behind this door and look. He'll do nothing; just sit and look. You pay not one copper. He pays. All right?"

"No."

"Why not?" She shrugged her firm shoulders. "If you have no copper, why not make money *facilement?*"

"I'll visit you a lot when I have money," I promised.

"*Pouf!* Where you from?"

"Hamburg."

"From Hamburg and no copper, hah?"

"I ran away from the police."

"Why?"

"I helped to try to make a revolution."

Her attitude changed abruptly. "Tell me about it," she said. I did.

We had been sitting on the couch. Mariette rose and brought me a glass of wine.

"I give you a little money," she said.

"Why should you give me money?"

She watched me drink the wine. Her answer astonished me. "Were I a man, I'd be a revolutionist," she said slowly. "But a woman, what can she do? People give me plenty money because I am a nice whore. I don't care. I like revolution. When a revolutionist comes to me, I help him."

We became friends and talked. Prostitutes I had known before had been covering their bedraggled existence with a sheen of irresponsibility, and one or two of them had been stupidly vile. Mariette's outstanding mark was a certain level-headed self-reliance. She told me about her life. She had followed her profession for thirteen years. A Greek brought her into the business. She insisted that she had entered the house willingly; that was in Marseilles, when she was seventeen. "The Greek, he told to all his friends, 'Come, I have a girl who sleep with no man before.' Oh, la! They gave me no rest. Up the stairs, down the stairs, all the time. Then somebody made me sick. . . . But today, if a man is sick, I can see quick. I say, 'Go!' Is he drunk or mad, I take knife. I put the knife against his belly and say, 'Go!' So he goes."

Mariette went on to explain that she felt herself responsible for the welfare of her sailor friends. "When a sailor love me one time, he comes back for more each time his ship is in port. Every morning I look in the paper. I see the names of the ships that have come. I know: this man will come tonight, and this one and that one. Fifteen, twenty, sometimes more. They are friends. When one does not come, I am sad. I ask: What is it? Is he sick? Is he dead? Is he married?"

I asked her if she knew some foreign revolutionists in Antwerp. "I know Bandura," she said. "You meet him?"

"No."

"Maybe his real name is not Bandura," she explained. "We call him Bandura, though. He's always looking for revolutionists to help him."

Inside of me something became alert.

"What does Bandura do?" I inquired.

Mariette drew her knees up to her chin, and put both hands against her temples.

"He makes trouble," she said. "I buy him overcoat and shoes; sometimes he makes me afraid. He sends other men to me and makes me hide them from police. Police come around many times and ask, 'Where is man from Riga? Where is little Chinaman? Where is big Pole?' I laugh. Bandura, he only interested in trouble."

"Maybe I'm from the police. How'd you know?" I interjected. "Maybe some day you will be my sweetheart," she said.

"The hell I will."

"And when you're a policeman and want to go away, I shall tell you: Come, take me one time more. Then I take the knife and— alas! you are a man no more, and then I say: Now go!"

"Well, I'm no policeman," I said.

"I know that."

"I want to meet Bandura."

"Sure." She paused and then said: "Soon it is nine. My friends will come from the ships. Now you must go."

About five the next afternoon I met Bandura in Mariette's den. He looked the part of a tight-lipped, picturesque brigand, a big-boned, starved-looking man with angular Slavic features. He wore brogans, a reeking old overcoat and a smeary sixpence cap from under which protruded the fringes of matted yellow hair turning gray. He sat on the extreme edge of a chair, peering at me as I came in and said, "Good you come."

We talked. The simplicity and ability of the man impressed me from the start. I answered many searching questions. Bandura was a Ukrainian anarchist who carried on an independent war against all shipowners whose vessels traded in ports in which Bandura happened to be at the moment. He worked for no organization and recognized no authority except the right of the underdog to help himself. His collaborators, he maintained, were proletarians of every creed, and nondescripts with a vein for rebellion.

Bandura was the typical representative of those itinerant waterfront revolutionists I have since met in every port of call. One and all, they were fugitives from the political police of their own lands. Few had passports. Thus deprived of all chance to obtain a lasting refuge and steady work, they vagabonded from one country to the next, often voluntarily, more often hounded as dangerous undesirables.

"I hope you are no mutton thief," Bandura said to me.

"What are mutton thieves?"

"Fellows who come with sample cases full of programs, big theories, big plans. Fellows who scram in danger. Heels in a cloud of dust. Fellows who want ham and eggs every morning."

"Then I'm no mutton thief," I said.

"You'll have to prove it," Bandura retorted. "Show us by picking a ship where the chow is rotten. Follow her around from port to port and make the crew raise Cain till the chow gets good. For action we need no politicians; we need 'activists' "

"How can a man get a ship in Antwerp?" I demanded. "Antwerp is bad. But there are other ports. Best chance is England. Alien seamen can't stay in England, so foreign ships are hard up for men in British ports, since Englishmen won't work for less than eight-pound-ten."

"I'll go to England," I said.

"Go to Liverpool. Liverpool is best."

Throughout our conference Mariette was curled up on her couch, listening with apparent interest, but never saying a word. When I was about to depart, Bandura stopped me. "I go first," he said. "I go first and come last." Before he went, Mariette sprang up, took off his cap, and kissed him lightly on the forehead.

I lived and worked with Bandura's band for several days. They had their quarters in garrets above various small waterside saloons. The saloon owners, Greeks, Germans, Estonians, and even a Hindu, tolerated Bandura's "activists" because they brought a lot of seamen with money to spend into the premises. We spent the day in the harbor, visiting ships, arguing with crew members, distributing a small action paper written and printed by Bandura in English, German, and Swedish. Bandura had a remarkable aptitude for languages, but his orthography was atrocious. Nevertheless, the paper had punch. It appeared, as stated under the title, "when needed." Its name was *Our* Rudder.

Came the day when Bandura informed me that he had a ship for me to go to Liverpool. The ship, a British weekly steamer, was to sail from Ghent. In the night and in a pouring rain, a young Lett and I started out on the highway to Ghent. Toward morning, a half-tipsy businessman on his way to the Kortryck cotton exchange invited us to ride in his car, and two hours later he dropped us near the imposing old castle of the Counts of Flandres in the heart of the town.

The following night I was on my way to Liverpool in the coal-bunker of a little weekly tramp. Lying on sacks spread over the coal, a packet of sandwiches as a pillow, I counted the beams overhead and the raindrops which came through a crack in the bunker hatch. Hardly out of the canal, which connects Ghent with the North Sea, I was discovered by a trimmer who entered the bunker with a smoking kerosene lamp. I gave the trimmer ten of the sixteen shillings in silver from Bandura's treasury. He agreed to say nothing. For the ten shillings he supplied me with a blanket and food—on British weekly boats seamen buy and prepare their own provisions—and kept me informed of the vessel's progress along the coasts of England and Wales. North of Bristol Channel we ran into fog; the plaintive yells of the siren continued until we reached the Mersey after a scant four-day voyage. I dug down into the coal during the customs examination, and when that was over, I scrubbed myself off in the stokehold, dousing pails of hot water over my head.

The working class quarters of English cities are the most dreary in the world. The harbor gates are well guarded. By eleven o'clock, the whole city seems to be asleep except for staggering homeward-bounders and a few querulous whisky-Marys. I heartily disliked my new surroundings. Illegal shipping masters demanded four pounds in advance for an illegal berth on a Greek or Baltic tramp-ship. Two nights I slept in a boarding house for West Indian negroes, which was run by a toothless hag who charged ninepence per bed and night. I obtained meals during my cruises through the docks by washing dishes for ships' cooks. By chance I fell in with crew members from a German steamer who told me that their ship was due to leave for the West Coast of North America.

The seamen with whom I spoke were, like most German seamen at that time, communist sympathizers. They supplied me with the remnants of a *paillasse* and with it I climbed into the starboard coalbunker, and from there through a manhole in the after-bulkhead into hold number three. The cargo was pig iron. I put the ragged mattress on the pig iron and went to sleep. The thunder of winches on deck awakened me. "High tide," I told myself. The ship was on her way.

After a few hours, someone hailed me from the bunker.

"All is clear—you can come out."

I crawled back into the bunker and out on deck. It was dusk. We had cleared the river, the pilot had gone, the land dropped down, and the clean horizon of the sea rose high. I went to the forecastle. The iron stove glowed red. I ate a good meal, answered questions, asked for news from Germany, and was content. Life seemed so infinitely sweet and rich.

After breakfast the following morning, I bathed and shaved, put on whatever clean clothes the comrades could spare, and went amidships to report myself to the captain.

The ship's name was *Eleonore,* home port Hamburg, and she had been resurrected from a boneyard by an enterprising Jewish merchant named Regendanz, whose initial was painted in white on the withered green of the funnel. It turned out that Captain Walter, a stout, mild-mannered, white-haired man, with a huge head, had known my father well. He treated me with the utmost kindness. He was too pensive and gentle a man to deal with the rabid radicalism of his crew.

"And in America," he asked me, "you intend to run away?"

"Yes," I admitted.

"I can't blame you," he said sadly. "Germany is going to the dogs."

Without turning his head, he wiped a tear from his eye.

Among the *Eleonore's* crew were men who had taken part in the wild voyage of the *Lucy Woerman*. Before leaving Hamburg, they had formed a syndicate of sailors and stokers, and laid in a contraband cargo of liquor which they hoped to sell in the United States at a great profit. They drank it themselves instead. In the Caribbean, the engine room personnel became thoroughly drunk. The blazing sun and the heat reflected by the iron decks did the rest. Quarrels broke out, knives flashed, and a coalheaver tottering away from a pursuer who was swinging a knife, went clear over the rail.

The ship was stopped and the drunken comrades of the coal-heaver fought some more in the attempt to man and lower a boat. When they were stopped, they became raving mad. The watch on deck, aided by volunteers from the watches below and led by the chief mate, a former submarine commander, overpowered the drunken stokers. It was an ugly job. Each man, and most of them were naked in the grim sunlight, had to be stunned by blows and then tied to ringbolts on the hatch-coamings and drenched with cold water. Meanwhile a sailor whose name was Ronaikal swam out to the man who had fallen overboard. He dragged him to the ship's side and both were hauled aboard with bowlines. The coal-heaver was dead.

For me this was a lucky break. I signed the ship's articles and became a regular crew member in the drowned man's place. I became a coalheaver, carting coal in a wheelbarrow from the reserve bunkers to the fires on the watch from twelve to four. So, when the *Eleonore* steamed into San Pedro harbor two weeks later, the immigration officers had no reason to detain me as a stowaway.

I was jubilant to be back in America. Here a man could roam over a whole continent without being accosted by a border guard.

I deserted ship the first night in San Pedro, slept in a Mexican colony of shacks known as "Happy Valley," and in the morning I walked into the nearest lumber yard and asked the foreman for a job. He hired me on the spot at five dollars a day.

Ten days I worked in the lumber yard. Half of my earnings I sent to Bandura. The following five days, I worked in a sardine cannery in Wilmington. Then I was discharged, having been caught lugging a case of canned sardines to the I.W.W. hall where traveling delegates slept on crude benches. I had a high admiration for these ingenious and resolute invaders who traveled a thousand miles on freight trains with nothing more than a red card and a dollar or two. A few days I worked in Los Angeles as a dishwasher. Then, with a young hobo from Iowa, I loafed through the orange plantations toward the town of San Bernardino, sleeping in the bungalow of a man who had the obsession that his mission was to build a church. For a bed and breakfast I promised him to collect a ton of stones for his church. We struck a bargain; but he happened to be a homosexual. The bargain ended with the builder of churches yelling for help, with sudden flight as my lot. In the San Bernardino mountains, I leaped aboard the first freight train that toiled slowly up an incline. It carried me across a most dismal stretch of desert and at a village called Barstow I was obliged to get off. I was promptly arrested by a cheerful ruffian with a gun in his holster and a badge on his chest. He told me to choose between going to jail for vagrancy or going to work on a bridge construction job in the desert. I chose the job, and the deputy sheriff drove me to a railway camp.

"Ho, Mr. Robinson," he called. "Here's a stiff who wants to work."

I went to work. I carried cement sacks on my shoulder, from a shed to a greedy concrete mixer, at a run, ten hours a day at fifty cents an hour, with an angry sun beating down from a cloudless sky. Cement mixing with sweat entered my pores and hardened. I shivered through a cold night in a boxcar crowded with Mexican fellow-workers. In the morning, the deputy sheriff came around to see if I was still there. The second night I pretended to go to sleep, but slipped out into the night when all was quiet. The stars shone brilliantly. The yellow mountains loomed in the moonlight. Without regrets, I abandoned two days' pay and boarded the first freight toward the coast. It was a cattle train. While I clung precariously to the lattice work of the cars, the wheels thundering beneath me and striking showers of sparks, I felt the tongues of cattle inside run over my hands and wrists. I managed to climb to the roof of the car and there I fell asleep. When I awoke, it was daylight and the train had stopped. A man stood above me, prodding me with his foot.

"Got a gun on you?"

"No."

"Get up. Raise your arms."

He searched me. Then he ordered me to climb down and walk ahead of him to a station house. I asked the man who he was. "I'm a special officer of the Southern Pacific Railroads," he said. Then I asked him to let me go. He demanded a dollar. I gave him the dollar and he commanded me to get out of town.

"What town is this?"

"San Berdoo," he said.

A man in a big blue car offered me a ride. I accepted. He was a cameraman who had traveled far and wide. He drove at breakneck speed. When I got out of his car, stiff-legged and tired, I stood in front of the William Fox Studios in Hollywood.

In a cafeteria on one of the boulevards a fat man was looking for pirates. I told him I was a sailor. Deeply bronzed, without a haircut for many weeks, and wearing only dungarees and a blue shirt with its sleeves cut off, I looked fit enough for a pirate. The fat man hired me at seven dollars a day, for two days.

In the early morning I and a horde of other dark-haired and sun-scorched men were loaded into comfortable trucks and taken to the San Pedro waterfront where three imitations of old galleons were moored to a wharf. We boarded the galleons and were towed out toward Catalina Island. Those among us who were not dark enough were painted brown. Some, half naked and in chains, became galley slaves; others, armed with swords, axes and knives, became pirates. Directors, assistants, cameramen rushed about and snapped directions. The stars, Milton Sills among them, came in motorboats. The day went by in filming a battle at sea. Ships were rammed, boarding parties flew at each other's throats, whips cracked over the backs of the rovers, men pitched overboard, and slaves ran amok. Between the scenes everybody drank lemonade and played dice for dimes and quarters. This went on until the sun stood low. The second day passed in similar ways. The galley slaves who had been painted brown were warned not to wash or bathe overnight.

During one of the intervals, between two spurious battles, I ran into Romaikal, my former shipmate who had fished the drowned coalheaver out of the Caribbean. He seemed quite prosperous. His alertness and perseverance, together with his fine physique and a quick mental grasp of things, had carried him to an average of five days of work weekly with various motion picture companies. Since the filming of further sea battles was delayed, Romaikal took me to a casting office on Spring Street and introduced me to a man who was then corralling teamsters for a Wild West production. I became a teamster. The pay was five dollars. The job consisted of driving a covered wagon, one among hundreds in action, at top speed down a long grassy slope of a location farm about twenty miles out of Hollywood. At first I had difficulties; I had never touched or handled a horse before. But the natural liking I had for dogs and horses enabled me rapidly to manage the team as well as the next man. Finally a wheel came off, and my wagon capsized. One of the megaphone men yelled enthusiastically, "Fine! Fine!"

One evening in the large dormitory of the York Hotel, where I lived, I met Virchow, one of my comrades from Hamburg. He had deserted from the *Westphalia* in New York and had come to the West Coast on one of the Luckenbach ships. He showed me letters received from Party members in Germany. The German courts were grinding out wholesale sentences against communists for treason, insurrection, rioting, conspiracy and murder. Many had been sentenced to death, but all such sentences had been commuted to life imprisonment. Among those who were condemned for life was one of my friends who had helped to storm the Eimsbuettel police station, Wilhelm Willendorf, a big-boned, sad-looking, fearless militant.

The effect which this news had on me was overwhelming. The hatred I felt for a system which destroys in cold blood the best sons of the working class was so great that I was speechless for several minutes. Inside I boiled with helpless rage, and with shame! Over there in Germany comrades went into dungeons for life, and here was I—well on my way to enjoy the Hollywood humbug. Virchow pulled a soiled sheet of printed paper from his kit-bag and handed it to me. I stared at it. It bore the title, "Sturm"— Tempest—and a subtitle, "By Seamen—For Seamen." It was an underground newspaper printed by the marine section of the Communist Party of Germany. Its contents were inflammatory. They gripped me and shook me through and through.

"I'm going back to fight," I said.

Virchow drew back. "Germany is the lousiest, toughest country in the world," he mumbled. "I'll never go back."

"Then you're a deserter."

"And what are you?"

"I'm going back."

I threw away a fair chance for a peaceful life. I journeyed to San Pedro and pestered the skippers and mates of every ship bound for Europe. The captain of the United American Lines freighter *Montpelier* signed me on as an able-bodied seaman. Thirty days later, under a gloomy North Sea sky, the *Montpelier* maneuvered through the locks and moored in Antwerp's Siberia Dock.

I went looking for Mariette. She was gone from her old place, and I concluded that she had moved to another street. So I made the rounds of the haunts of Bandura's band—*Rose of England, Monico Sam, Café Belgenland, Helgoland Bar, Susie's Paradise.* I found him in a Chinese drinking place on Brouversvliet. He looked as gaunt and hungry and dauntless as ever.

"The girl Mariette has died," Bandura said mournfully. "She was more lovable than all the debutantes west of the Rhine thrown together. We gave her a fine funeral."

I sipped my tea silently. Bandura growled:

"Take off your cap in honor of Mariette."

I took off my cap. Bandura told me about her funeral. He and his helpers had devoted two full days to collect money aboard the ships to bury Mariette with revolutionary honors. At night they had raided the parks and a number of private gardens, and had collected a mountain of fresh greens and spring flowers. They had carried her coffin on their own shoulders, and a train of waterfront agitators of many nationalities had followed them with red and black flags. Bandura had made a speech over the open grave. The inscription on the tombstone, Bandura told me, read: "Mariette, who loved and aided the toilers of the sea."

"I'm glad you did it that way," I said.

"Rest assured," Bandura said with a melancholy grin: "No decent whore has ever had more sincere mourners, nor was one ever buried with greater dignity."

I made a violent attempt to break the spell of sadness, and shouted for beer. A plump young waitress with a bloated face brought beer. She put it on the table, then she suddenly ran her arm down Bandura's neck through the opening of his shirt.

"Beer for me too?" she cried.

Bandura pushed her away. "Off with you," he snarled. "You stink."

"How goes your waterfront campaign?" I inquired. Bandura leaned forward and, with a coughing laugh, replied:

"Well, very well. Right after we had closed Mariette's grave, with all my boys assembled, the gendarmerie swooped down on us. We all went to jail for one night. A day later we were deported, some to France, others to Holland. The following night, we all turned around, and back to Antwerp we came."

Chapter Eight

PASSAGE TO CONSPIRACY

During the three days my ship remained at Antwerp I spent I every free hour with Bandura and his followers, who had greatly increased in numbers in the months of my absence. Each week ships from Helsingfors, Reval and Riga had carried to Antwerp a batch of stowaways—mostly political fugitives, all embittered, all accustomed to a hard and frugal way of existence. Among them Bandura moved like an uncrowned king; he was their leader because he lived as they lived, worked as they worked, and still proved himself the most able in this crew. He now had established contacts with bands of political harbor marauders in Marseilles, Bordeaux, London, Cardiff, Rotterdam and even in Oran of the North African coast, and in Strasbourg, the shipping center on the upper Rhine. He corresponded and co-operated with I.W.W. units on the American West Coast, and with anarchist groups in Spanish and Latin American ports.

One of Bandura's new followers was Ilja Weiss, an "activist" in my early Hamburg days. Weiss was the Hungarian who had slapped a pot of paint in the face of an officer of the Hamburg harbor police. The German police had pushed him clandestinely into Holland. Arrested again in Rotterdam, the Dutch police had pushed him into Belgium. I met Weiss in a half-dark backroom of a saloon.

"You are still a communist?" he demanded.

"Certainly."

"Well, then you must know what we have set out to do in Bandura's outfit."

I listened. Weiss worked in close co-operation with my former chief, Albert Walter, in Hamburg. The German Communist Party had emerged out of the short period of illegality which had followed the bloody October, and Walter had re-established headquarters in the Rothesoodstrasse, near the Hamburg waterfront, directing from there communist maritime activities in all parts of the world for the Profintern—the Red International of Labor Unions. The task of this organization, founded in 1920 as an auxiliary to the Comintern, was to conquer all existing trade unions or, where domination proved impossible, to wreck these unions and to set up communist bodies in their place.

The Comintern had delegated Ilja "Weiss and others to steal Bandura's organization away from its creator and leader, for whom the Comintern had no use because he stubbornly refused to take orders. Twice attempts had been made to bribe Bandura by offering him a lucrative position in the All-

Russian Transport Union in Leningrad, but the Ukrainian had derisively refused.

I admired Bandura and I felt an honest contempt for Ilja Weiss. He insinuated that a campaign had been launched by the communist faction to spread the rumor that Bandura was a narcotics addict, and that he used most of the money donated by seamen to keep several mistresses in idle luxury. The circumstances of Mariette's burial were to serve as a salient point in this intrigue. Ilja Weiss suggested that I should spread among the "activists" in every port of call the word that Bandura was a crook, that he led a double life, pretending to be a pioneer of workers' welfare, but that his private life was that of a bourgeois libertine.

"Bandura is nothing of the sort," I said.

"Maybe not," Weiss countered. "But politically, he is an irresponsible blackguard."

"Why can't we acknowledge Bandura's leadership?"

"We'd never be sure in a revolutionary crisis that he wouldn't break away with slogans of his own. He's too damned independent. How do we know he doesn't get paid by the shipowners?"

"That's ridiculous."

Weiss' greenish eyes were small and bright. "Bandura makes no difference between a fascist dictatorship and the dictatorship of the proletariat," he went on. "Every government is tyranny in his eyes. In a war against the Soviet Union, he would refuse to campaign for Russia. We must get rid of him. He is a counter-revolutionary in disguise."

"Prove it!" I cried out in a fury.

"Bandura carries on his agitation aboard Soviet ships," Weiss said with subdued ferocity. "He tells the Russian seamen that they have a right to go on strike for better food and higher pay. What is that?"

I was silent. Weiss added:

"It is one thing to strike against the capitalists; it is an entirely different thing to go on strike against a socialist state."

I was deeply disturbed. What Ilja Weiss had told me of the communist offensive to control the waterfronts made my heart beat faster. In the end we would win; the red flags of freedom and equality would fly over the most distant ocean; sailors would be masters of their ships; precious cargoes would be carried to fill the needs of peoples and not the shipowners' pockets. I was resolved to do my share to carry communism to victory on the seas. So would Bandura, I had felt sure, whose readiness to lay down his life for the workers' cause was beyond all doubt. And now came Weiss who said that Bandura was a foe of social revolution, and an enemy of the Soviet Union! This was my first encounter with the ruthless intolerance of a monolithic creed toward all individual independence of attitude and thinking. It was not Weiss who had originated the plan to defame and to break Bandura; he was simply carrying out a command. He was a Bolshevik of the East European school who would not shrink from murdering his own brother if his chiefs told him that such an act would bring victory a tiny step closer. Without such men, and such blind loyalty, the Comintern could not survive. Disloyalty I detested. A traitor was not worth a bullet. Yet, I recognized the hideous alternative: if Ilja Weiss spoke the truth, a refusal to betray Bandura would make me appear as a traitor to the communist cause.

Before the *Montpelier* left Antwerp, I asked Bandura point-blank: "Are you for workers' power in Russia?"

His gaunt face contracted as if under a spasm of pain. He fished some Dobbelman tobacco out of his hip pocket, rolled a cigarette, and lit it. Then he said calmly:

"I know why you ask this. Yes, I am for a free society of workers, but in Russia the workers have no power and no real freedom. No Party can give the workers freedom. For freedom they must fight themselves."

"The communists lead them in this fight," I protested.

"Most communists I know are fine, brave men," Bandura said. "Only their leaders—bah!" His arms flew out in a gesture of despair. "They are mutton thieves," he added fiercely.

My attempt to change Bandura's views was futile. Ilja Weiss had his way.

The *Montpelier* steamed to Hamburg. I had apprehensions that the police would arrest me for my part in the October insurrection. But my steamer flew the Stars and Stripes of America, a welcome flag in any German port, and the police did not bother the crew. I hired an unemployed German to work in my place as long as the ship was in Hamburg, and went ashore to report to Albert Walter.

The aspect of Walter's office had changed. There were new desks, new filing cabinets, and large new maps on the walls. There was a large reading-room, well equipped with communist newspapers in many languages, and a "Lenin library." The ground floor of the building was occupied by a hall for meetings and a restaurant in which drinks were served. The place was crowded with seamen and their girls, and a sprinkling of "activists" was at work to shape the opinions of the visitors. Officially the building was known as the International Port Bureau, the first in a chain of seamen's clubs which was to encircle the earth in years to come—centers of propaganda and a growing communist power on the waterfront.

Albert Walter, brown-skinned and massive, was enthusiastic over his work and hungry for the smallest details related to shipping.

"Write down all names and addresses, conditions you've found in sailors' boarding houses, seamen's missions, shipping offices, jails, and describe the methods of customs examinations in different ports, places where you crossed the border, and how you got into England. Forget nothing. Small items can be of great value to us. We're reaching out with all sails set."

I wrote the report. The same night I was called to Walter's private quarters. He lived in a modest third-floor apartment, together with his mother, a small, agile woman whose life revolved around her energetic son. Also present was Walter's trusted secretary, a fanatic young blonde named Gertrude G., and two men I had not seen before.

The two men were Atchkanov, a Russian, and Ryatt, a Lett. Both had a mandate from Moscow to act as advisers to Albert Walter in the international drive for communist domination of shipping. Atchkanov was a lively little man with a mop of unruly gray hair and restless button-eyes. He was Zinoviev's right-hand man in marine problems. Ryatt was tall and lean, with a bony, noncommittal face. He was a specialist in communist war fleet organization. Later in 1931, he became the director of the Comintern passport forging bureau, with offices on the Ogorodnikova in Leningrad.

"Ah, a real sailor," Atchkanov muttered when I entered.

Old Mrs. Walter poured Caucasian wine into glasses, and Walter distributed excellent cigars. Atchkanov read a report from Ilja Weiss on the progress of efforts to take over Bandura's organization. Turning to me, he said, "It was smart of you to establish a good personal relationship with Bandura." I replied that I had a hearty dislike for dishonest underground maneuvering.

Atchkanov smiled faintly. "Practical Bolshevism means the correct combination of legal with illegal methods of work," he said. "Understand, dear comrade, that strategical maneuvers have an important place in our operations. And what is a strategical maneuver? We launch a ruthless offensive, while declaring openly that we are waging a purely defensive campaign. We feign friendliness toward an implacable enemy so as to have a better chance to annihilate him in good time. These are strategical maneuvers."

"I like clear fronts," I said stubbornly. "If we fight someone, then why not make an open declaration of war? Trickery the workers will never understand. Why must we maneuver to bring one man to grief? The Comintern Congress gave us the direction, 'To power through conquest of the masses'."

"That is correct," interrupted Ryatt, who spoke in a harsh, staccato voice. "We must stay with the masses, bind ourselves to them, never act in isolation from the masses—*except in conspirative tasks!*" All this I comprehended and accepted. But that Bandura, who had been kind to me, should be defamed, perhaps destroyed, in such a cold-blooded manner evoked my resentment. Atchkanov and Ryatt, with characteristic persistence and patience, persuaded and argued like clever older brothers. They trusted me, and apparently needed me, and it was no hard task for them to bend me to their will.

"More elasticity!" Atchkanov cried. "Bolshevist elasticity. Comrade Lenin himself taught us that Bolshevist elasticity consists of the ability to change tactics and to employ the widest range of methods without ever losing sight of the one and only final goal." To me, still a young communist, these men were heroic figures. In Atchkanov and his kind I then saw idealists who had behind them the overwhelming authority of the victorious Soviet Revolution.

Atchkanov put his arm around my shoulder. "Comrade Walter has recommended you for a try-out in international work," he said. "You are still young in the movement, but you've done good work in the harbor and you've fought on the barricades."

I was somewhat embarrassed by his friendliness. "That's nothing," I murmured.

Albert Walter guffawed: "Did you hear that? He says that's nothing."

"One day on the barricades," observed Ryatt, "is worth three years of ordinary Party membership."

The instructions I received were, in short, as follows:

I was to keep my berth aboard the *Montpelier* and return to the Pacific Coast. Before leaving Europe, Ilja Weiss would arrange to have me appointed as Bandura's delegate to the groups with which he had contacts in the harbors of California, with the aim of bringing these groups into Albert Walter's network of harbor "activists." I was to take with me large quantities of propaganda literature to be distributed in all ports of call. Forwarding addresses in San Pedro and San Francisco were agreed upon, for the shipping of further propaganda material in English, Spanish, and Japanese. The Spanish pamphlets were for distribution to Mexicans, to the dockers in Panama and the workers of the Panama Canal Zone. The Japanese material was to go to Honolulu and other places on the Hawaiian Islands. Wherever possible, I was to recruit sympathizing seamen from other ships to join in this distribution of propaganda literature. I was to attempt to find one "activist" in each port of call reliable enough to be supplied with money and instructions for the formation of "activist" brigades after the Hamburg model. I was to become a member of the International Seamen's Union of America, then under the conservative guidance of Andrew Furuseth, to form opposition cells in his organization in a drive for a militant class war policy. If possible, I was to foster contacts with men belonging to the United States Coast Guard, particularly those who had gotten themselves into some sort of trouble, and forward their names and addresses to Albert Walter and Atchkanov. I was to "test"—by bribes—a certain official of the American Shipowners' Association in Los Angeles Harbor as to his willingness to place communists aboard American ships. I was also to take close-up photographs and furnish a detailed description of a new harpoon gun used by the whaling ships of the California Sea Products Corporation, and to study and report upon the use of airplanes in the great tuna fisheries of Southern California. Finally, I was expected to send in regular reports on all I could find out about the economic conditions and political attitudes of American waterfront workers, particularly those engaged in the vast lumber industry and on the tankships of the Standard Oil Company.

This was a bulky order. Aside from the propaganda assignments, it savored of G.P.U. business.

"Don't try to do everything at one time," Ryatt advised. "You know, before the war they sent me to prison for ten years. I soon learned I couldn't do ten years all at once. I did one day at a time, and so it was easy. That is how you must do it."

Albert Walter saw me making notes. "Don't write up too much," he said.

"But I can't remember it all."

"Well, destroy your notes as soon as you do."

I was allowed forty American dollars a month with which to finance my work. Walter counted out the first three months' budget in new American bills, and entered the sum he gave me in a tiny notebook. Walter added:

"And don't fear that you'll be alone in the wilderness. We've a great many comrades like you aboard the ships and active in the same field."

Soon all details were arranged for. As usual, I was not permitted to leave Albert Walter's apartment before Ryatt and Atchkanov, who were in the country illegally, had departed. Ryatt shook hands with me gravely. Atchkanov beamed. He almost hugged me. "Do your job well," he said in his fluent Slavic German.

After they had gone, Albert Walter threw open all windows. He was in shirt sleeves. His big chest expanded. The skin of his arms and chest had the color of old teakwood. Gertrude G., his secretary, prepared to take dictation. She perked up, quiet and alert. "Life is a joyous affair," Walter rumbled. Relaxing, Gertrude smiled for the first time that evening.

Old Mrs. Walter, moving around like a faithful ghost, had cleared off the table. "Child," she suddenly told her burly son, "it's eleven. You must go to bed."

He rose and gave her a resounding kiss.

"I'll go now, Comrade Walter," I said.

"Mack's gut," he replied, "and I'll stand by you through hell."

The night was bright, and a warm wind blew. I strode toward the harbor. I felt the urge to sing. My blood, too, was singing.

The night before the *Montpelier* left Hamburg on her westward voyage was the right kind of a night for furtive doings. I volunteered for the job of gangway watchman. All the members of the crew were ashore for a few last hours of gamboling with the Reeperbahn belles. The captain had locked himself in with two girls, a lot of wine and a substantial night-lunch, and the curtains on his cabin windows were drawn. Meanwhile, Albert Walter's contact men worked with noiseless efficiency.

Large paper suitcases, heavily loaded, were smuggled aboard. The black initials on their outsides denoted the language in which the literature they contained was printed. And late at night a surreptitious visitor, a man whom I had least expected to see, arrived. He was Hugo Marx, the Hamburg Jack-of-all-trades for the G.P.U.

"I bring you a friend," he said. "He must go to Canada in safety. You must find him a place to stow away."

I already had too many duties to attend to without bothering about a stowaway.

"Comrade Walter gave me no instructions about it," I said. "Put him on another ship."

"No. He must go with you," Hugo Marx hissed.

"Who sent him?"

The G.P.U. man snapped viciously: "Why do you seek information you don't need?" I was put out over my own impulsiveness.

"Comrade Ryatt wishes this friend to go on your ship," Marx said in a more conciliatory tone.

There the matter ended. I had suspected that the newcomer was merely another illegal emigrant who paid the Party a few dollars for a passage. Now I knew he was not. He was a communist going out on Party business. It was not in my power to ask further questions.

Hugo Marx flashed a quick, cold smile, and departed. The newcomer addressed me in excellent English: "Have you anything to eat? I was in a devil of a hurry today. I'm as hungry as a wolf."

It was too dark on deck to see his features, but I saw enough to know that this stranger had a well-built body and broad shoulders. He was of medium height, and young. When I led him to the sailors' mess room, which was situated on the after-part of the boat deck, a girl slipped out of the shadows and joined us.

"Who's she?"

"My girl," the newcomer said.

"Is she going to Canada, too?" I asked in consternation.

"Oh, no," was the answer.

We had coffee, bread and cold beef in the mess room. I realized almost immediately that the newcomer was a communist of exceptional ability. His name was Michel Avatin, a Lett. He was a former waterfront organizer for the Communist Party in Riga. He had been in Russia, and he had worked for the Comintern in England. He called himself Lambert, and he had a good British passport in that name which he handed to me for safekeeping during the voyage. Obviously he was not of proletarian family; he gave me the impression of being the descendant of a family of officers, or of having been a cadet or a junior naval officer himself. He radiated quiet self-reliance. He knew ships. His movements were swift and his appearance rather smart. His face was smooth, clean-cut and tanned. His hair was light and silky. His eyes were a steady gray, but they had, like his nose, an indefinable Asiatic quality. His mouth was thin and hard. He was as different from Bandura as any revolutionary "activist" could possibly be. I liked him instantly. So, I felt, did he like me. In Michel Avatin I met one of the most extraordinary figures in the subterranean *Apparat* of the Comintern.

The girl was very young, not more than nineteen. She was small and trim, and she had a somewhat ugly but highly intelligent face. She was Jewish, and a native of Warsaw. Michel Avatin called her Malka. Her full name was Malka Stifter. They had met and fallen in love while attending a political school in Moscow a year earlier.

I found a good hiding place for Avatin. From the *Montpelier's* spar-deck a vertical wooden hatch opened into cargo hold number three. At sea or in port this hatch was never used. I supplied Avatin with a blanket and a can containing a gallon of water, and arranged to lower a package of food for him through an airshaft at a certain hour each night. This was convenient, because I was on duty during the watch from twelve to four. The cargo in hold number three consisted of English textiles, crockery and shoes in packing cases, which we arranged to form a comfortable cave below the waterline. Before he slipped into his hiding place, Avatin said to me:

"I will take Malka into my arms. Who knows, each time may be the last."

The third mate's cabin was empty. Two days before, the third mate had had a fight with the *Montpelier's* chief officer, who was a most picturesque ruffian, with the result that the third mate deserted the ship. In the deserter's cabin Michel and Malka had their farewell embrace while I stood outside on guard. Then Malka slipped out, waving her hand to say good-by, and hastened ashore. The blackness between the cranes and sheds swallowed her. A little later Avatin came on deck.

"I am ready," he said.

The *Montpelier* left Hamburg. It took twenty days to steam from the North Sea to Panama, and twelve from Panama to San Pedro in Southern California. I read much during this voyage. The librarian of the Hamburg Port Bureau had supplied me with many books and pamphlets.

While crossing the North Atlantic, during my watches below, I would crawl at night into hold number three to pay short visits to Michel Avatin. Once he told me he had found a triangular iron scraper, and with it contrived to break open three packing cases to explore their contents. One contained shoes, and Avatin had found a pair that fitted him. The second case contained rayon stockings. The third, toys. From now on he amused himself with stuffing ladies' stockings into Oxford shoes. Then he sorted out all the left-foot shoes, and packed them into the case which originally held only stockings. That accomplished, he closed both cases with minute care.

"Two unknown merchants are due for a nightmare," he observed, adding: "I did not touch the toys. Toys are for children."

Sometimes we had brief talks of a more serious nature. Michel Avatin was bound for Vancouver. He volunteered no information about his assignment there, and I asked no questions. Hugo Marx's ominous "Why do you seek information you don't need?" still rang in my brain. It was the fundamental law of all conspirative work that no man should know more about the secrets of his organization than was essential for him to carry out his own particular duty.

One morning, twelve days out of Hamburg, an engineer announced that a stowaway had been discovered aboard the *Montpelier*. I rushed on deck. There, in the brilliant sunlight, hands in pockets, stood Michel Avatin. When he saw me, he gave no sign of recognition. It appeared that before daylight two members of the engine room crew had entered number three hold on a pilfering expedition. When they came, Avatin crawled into the farthest corner of the hold. But the invaders used flashlights, and began to break open a few boxes. Either the lights were noticed on deck, or the sounds of hammering and splintering wood were heard. Officers investigated. The pilferers fled in time, but Michel Avatin was discovered.

He was quite calm about it. He was given a spare berth in the sailors' forecastle, and was put to work with the deckhands. But when the *Montpelier* entered the Panama Canal, Avatin was put in irons and locked up in a little storeroom next to the chief mate's cabin. Canal officials came aboard and questioned him. I was so nervous I could hardly keep my mind on the ship's work and the distribution of my Spanish propaganda tracts. I put aside a chisel, a hammer and a fire-ax, and thought of ways to liberate my comrade. When the steamer nosed into the Gatun locks, I found an unguarded minute in which to speak to Avatin through the tiny porthole in his prison.

"I can give you an ax to smash the door," I said. "I'll make you a raft. You can jump overboard and paddle ashore."

Michel Avatin shook his head. "I have no business in Panama," he replied. "I am going to Vancouver."

"All the same, they'll keep you locked up in every port."

"Don't worry. I'll get out when I want to."

"Do you want the ax?" I asked.

"No. You may give me some tobacco."

"All right."

"And don't forget," Avatin muttered. "I don't know you and you don't know me. Savvy?"

"Savvy."

Out at sea again, on the Pacific side, Avatin was released and put back to work. We avoided speaking to one another, except at night and in secluded spots. I cultivated an acquaintanceship with Sparks, the radio operator, to learn what would be done with the stowaway when the ship entered American ports. I feared he would be taken off to jail. But I was soon reassured. The usual procedure with stowaways was to lock them up aboard ship in every American port of call, and to chase them back ashore in the first European harbor. Ports of call were San Pedro, San Francisco, Portland, Seattle, and Vancouver. Avatin decided to remain quietly aboard in all United States ports, but to make a dash for freedom in Vancouver, after lulling the *Montpelier's* officers into believing that he was a peaceful and docile individual. He had given the captain a false name, and he was unafraid of impending questioning by United States immigration officials.

One of the ship's oilers, a Hawaiian, made a duplicate key to Avatin's prison cell from a wax impression the Lett had managed to make of the lock. In addition to the key, all Michel Avatin needed was a good file to saw through his irons when the time to escape had come. Meanwhile he made friends with almost everyone of the crew, which was not difficult since seamen have a natural respect for anyone who shows himself to be a willing and capable hand in ship's work. Besides, Avatin was adept as a barber, a craft he had learned in a Latvian jail. Among those on whom he practiced his skill was the captain of the *Montpelier* himself. When the steamer dropped anchor in the outer harbor of San Pedro, to wait for the arrival of the port doctor and the customs and immigration authorities, Avatin was locked up again, but this time no irons were clamped over his wrists.

For three days the *Montpelier* discharged cargo in San Pedro. I contacted some of the waterfront delegates of the I.W.W., and tried to convince them of the necessity to build an international revolutionary organization of seamen and dockers. I argued: "The marine industry is international, and its rulers can only be beaten by international strikes. Of what good are strikes on American ships in American ports when three-fourths of the American merchant marine is at sea or in foreign harbors? An effective strike calls for the stopping of American ships all over the world, and to do this it is imperative to have an international fighting organization of seamen. The same goes for shipping of other nations." The Wobblies admitted that my argument was sound. "Well," I continued, "the foundation of such an international organization has been created, with headquarters in Hamburg, and traveling organizers are on the job all over the world to spread the idea and to enlist the assistance of radical waterfront groups in all important harbors."

I did not disclose that this campaign had been inaugurated and was backed by the power of Moscow and the Comintern. That was not necessary. Once a wide range of auxiliary groups had been harnessed to the scheme, the communist units would see to it that all key positions came under communist control. Essential to the success of the plan was a penetration into the conservative International Seamen's Union of America by adherents of the "Hamburg Program."

At six in the morning, an hour before the regular ship's work began, I was up again distributing leaflets and pamphlets among several thousand longshoremen who had assembled in a large shed near the waterfront where the stevedore bosses recruited their men for the day. The remnants of my Spanish literature I distributed in the shack colony of "Happy Valley," where most of the Mexican harbor workers lived. So, on each of three mornings, about two thousand pieces of Atchkanov's propaganda found their way into the hands and—I hoped—brains of the marine workers in Los Angeles Harbor. It was clear that if this were done only once a week by delegates from various ships, the propaganda wave could soon be followed up by concrete organization. Regular Communist Party units among the waterfront workers of the West Coast were still practically non-existent in 1924.

The *Montpelier* left San Pedro and steamed to San Francisco. Here again Michel Avatin permitted himself to be locked up and questioned by immigration officers. I paid off in San Francisco. My leave-taking from Michel Avatin was brief. I expressed misgivings as to his predicament. He answered with hard-boiled humor: "The British Empire is my pet. When it capsizes one fine day, I'm going to get a decoration in Moscow. Until then, attack and never tremble." I returned his British passport to him, and went on my way.

"Greet my girl Malka, should you see her," were Avatin's parting words.

Since that foggy morning in San Francisco, Michel Avatin has crossed my path many times. But neither he nor I ever saw Malka Stifter again. Her story is one of the countless tragedies which mark the trails of Comintern campaigns.

For years Avatin roved through many parts of the British Empire, on more or less important secret missions, until, in 1929, he was trapped in London by Scotland Yard agents. With G.P.U. aid, he escaped and subsequently joined the Foreign Division of the G.P.U. Malka, meanwhile, was engaged on assignments in various countries of Eastern Europe. Unhesitatingly, she sacrificed her youth and her love to the cause. In the Comintern she won a reputation for having a natural talent for the dangerous "disintegration" work among soldiers and police. She worked in the Baltic countries, in Yugoslavia—the graveyard of Bolsheviki—and in Poland. The strong positions secured by the Comintern in the Polish army were largely a result of Malka's persistent efforts. The later mutinies of 1931 in Skiemivice, Lodz, and Nova-Vileiko were due in part to Malka Stifter's groundwork. Finally she was arrested by the political police of Poland. In violation of Party orders, Avatin made a hazardous dash to Poland to find a way to liberate his girl. He did not succeed. Reports of the treatment Malka suffered at the hands of Police Inspector Zaremba, in the prison of Lvov, kindled in Michel Avatin that monumental hatred of policemen and police spies which later transformed him into a merciless professional spy-hunter and executioner. Many weeks of torture failed to extract from Malka the names of communists engaged in Polish military work. But they broke her in the end. In the prison infirmary, she gave away the names of her comrades after Police Inspector Zaremba, a sadistic fiend, had on two occasions inserted hot pieces of iron into her sexual organ. This atrocity occurred late in December, 1930, and was repeated in the second week of January, 1931. Communists released from Lvov prison brought the report to Berlin. Georgi Dimitrov, then head of the Berlin bureau, considered Malka a traitress. But Avatin, nevertheless, caused her name to be placed on the honor roll of communist martyrs.

Chapter Nine

I ATTACK THE PACIFIC

With the zeal of a crusader, I struck out on my career of an underground worker on the Pacific Coast. For a week I collected information about the Coast Guard service. I haunted the Coast Guard pier at the end of the Embarcadero, and struck up acquaintances with sailors on cutters moored after a turn of patrol at sea. I studied the requirements for enrollment in the service, and followed the men on shore-leave to learn all I could about the haunts they frequented. Late at night, I would steal aboard the cutters and place communist tracts where they would be found by the crews in the morning. At the end of the week, to round out the picture, I went to the Coast Guard station and applied for an official Lifeboat Certificate. Two Coast Guard captains subjected me to a rigid examination on the spot. Together with other applicants, I manned a lifeboat and pulled out into the bay for a test of seamanship. One of the officers, Captain Anderson, a rough old sea-dog, barked commands for maneuvers he wanted us to execute. That over, the second captain, whose name was Patricius, took charge of the theoretical end of the examination. Among the eight applicants present, I was the only one who passed the test. I received a document, signed by Captain Patricius, to the effect that I was a certified lifeboat man. With this paper in my pocket, I felt safer. That night I wrote a report to Albert Walter, detailing the information I had gathered on the possibilities of communist penetration into the Coast Guard service.

The following five months I roamed the West Coast from Puget Sound to San Diego. Rarely did I stop for longer than a week in any one place. Every steamer of the Roland Line brought consignments of propaganda literature from Hamburg, and I faithfully distributed every piece of it, not even shying from such unimportant ports as Santa Barbara or Eureka or Newport, Oregon. Money I did not receive; Albert Walter's letters complained of his heavy financial obligations elsewhere. I traveled many thousands of miles in these months, but my traveling expenses were almost nil. The coastwise vessels on which I shipped to go from one harbor to another were the lumber carriers *Robert Johnsen* and *Grays Harbor,* the freighter *Admiral Sebree* and the passenger liner *Dorothy Alexander.* Often I traveled as stowaway, chiefly using the *Yale* and *Harvard,* which were the fastest ships on the Coast.

During these months I never had a drink, never a real day of rest, and never did I go out with a girl. I lived only for the cause. Yet at times I was bitterly lonely. There was a night when I sat on a pile of timbers in the harbor of Tacoma, broken-down and ready to give up and desert. "Life," I thought, "could be so pleasant, so easy, if only I would strike out for myself; I could learn a trade, start a business, have a big new car and a good home, and life would be all velvet and sweet!" A moment later I became so angry at my own bourgeois thoughts that I snatched a piece of wood from the ground and crashed it over my own head.

Albert Walter, Atchkanov and Ryatt had reason to be content with me. By the end of November, I had brought the Hamburg bureau in contact with small but fairly stable "activist" groups in Seattle, Grays Harbor, Portland, Astoria, San Francisco, and San Pedro. I now decided to invade Hawaii.

In Hamburg I had been given the name of an official of the American Shipowners' Association who had been reported as bribable by one of Albert Walter's scouts. This official, we were led to believe, would ship any man on any desired ship for a fee of ten dollars, with no questions asked. It was important to have such a man at hand, and it was equally important that he should have no suspicion that he was assisting communist agitators to entrench themselves in strategic shipping lines. Albert Walter and Atchkanov had put it up to me to follow this lead, and to put it to a practical test.

It was easy. I went to San Pedro and asked for Mr. X., a tall, handsome, smooth-faced young man, in the offices of the Shipowners' Association. I had labored two days to make a little sailship model in a bottle, and this I presented to Mr. X. He was pleased. The following morning I wrote him a note, reading: "Please get me a ship to Honolulu." I put it into an envelope, together with ten dollars, and slipped it on his desk. Before the week had passed, I was called up for a sailor's berth aboard the *Calawaii,* one of the luxury liners of the Los Angeles Steamship Company. Asked by the chief officer if I was an American citizen, I said: "Yes, sir." I was signed on without further ado.

The *Calawaii,* painted a cool tropical white from stem to stern, was a regular vessel of the Hawaiian trade. In the course of each round trip of three weeks, the steamer spent a week in island waters with Honolulu and Hilo as the chief ports of call. Before she sailed, I lived through a hectic night, smuggling aboard my accumulated stock of suitcases and packages full of propaganda literature in the Japanese language.

The passage to Honolulu was balmy. The wild, warm, rock-bound face of Molokai, and Diamond Head pushing its gleaming snout out into the sapphire sea, seemed to laugh serenely at the conception that revolution could ever come to ride these shores. The white breakers foaming over purple cliffs, the wheeling gulls and the lush green of the hills belched gay derision at the puny proselyte of Lenin; they made me think of peacefully humming fishermen, of full-throated brown maidens with enticing hips, and of Captain Cook. Dark youngsters dived for coins in the harbor, and on the wharf the fat brown musicians of the Royal Hawaiian Band hurled a musical welcome. But beyond the crowd of bright-eyed, brightly dressed people, with flame-colored *leis* around their necks, I saw what I had searched for—a fringe of Mongolian faces rising above faded dungarees and often sleeveless denim shirts. The proletariat! I was reassured.

I found that forty percent of the population was Japanese, with Filipinos, Chinese and Portuguese the next strongest groups. Most of the Chinese became tradesmen and merchants. The real working class of Honolulu is Portuguese-Hawaiian-Japanese, with an influx of negro blood on the Portuguese side, while the plantation proletariat of the island is mainly Filipino. Contrary to the Comintern's practice in other "semi-colonial" countries, no nationalist slogans could be raised in Hawaii, since each race there is confronted by a majority of all other races. Moreover, in the streets of Honolulu words like "half-caste" or "half-breed" are taboo. All I saw and heard and read then about the racial and social constellations on the Hawaiian Islands I incorporated in a rambling thirty-page report which I dispatched to Hamburg. Five years later, in 1930, I saw this report in Moscow, in the office of Losovsky, whose real name is S. A. Dridzo, the chief of the International Propaganda and

Action Committees of the Profintern. It was marked in red pencil, *"Sehr interessant."* And a sentence which stated that Spanish, Portuguese, Chinese, Japanese and English propaganda literature should be spread concurrently in Honolulu was also heavily underlined in red.

On this first voyage, all I had for distribution were tracts and leaflets in Japanese. I saw to it that the wharves of Honolulu and Hilo were littered with them for days. I deposited them in bundles of fifty and more in waterfront ice-cream parlors, in speakeasies, and in the numerous Japanese "massage-salons" which functioned as substitutes for brothels for the poor. I retained my job aboard the *Calawaii* and returned with her to San Pedro to pick up, in addition to Japanese, all the Spanish and English propaganda material I could obtain. During my second trip to the Islands, I boarded every vessel in Honolulu harbor, including the small coastal steamers, two Japanese ships, and the square-rigged sailship *Tusitala* of New York. I was put to flight by the officers of several steamers of the Matson Line and the Dollar Steamship Company, but I found promising young sympathizers aboard the liners *City of Los Angeles* and *Molokai* and aboard the *Tusitala*. Their names I sent on to Hamburg, so that "activists" in other ports could be notified to continue the work of building communist units on these ships. In Hilo, I hired a taxicab for a six-hour drive through sugar and pineapple plantations. Whenever I saw Filipino laborers at work, I would shout to attract their attention and then fling handfuls of leaflets in Spanish out of the car. A man with a martial reddish mustache took up the pursuit in a rattling Ford, and ordered me to get off the land or go to jail. The taxi-driver apologized profusely. We drove back to Hilo. This was, I believe, the first time in history that the cry "Workers of the World, Unite!" was passed on to the plantation coolies of Hawaii.

My third voyage between California and Honolulu gave me a rare opportunity for personal contacts with a large number of Filipino workers. While in the port of Los Angeles, I noticed that hundreds of rough wooden berths in three tiers were being built into the tweendecks of the *Calawaii*. When I asked for the purpose of these mass quarters, the bosun replied, "Slave transport." We were to carry to Honolulu a large consignment of plantation workers who had arrived from Luzon a few days earlier.

At sea, the Filipinos were not allowed to come on deck. The fact that the well-fed and well-groomed men and the sleek women of the first and second class could loaf and play and dance and make love in the sunshine and under the stars, while many times their number of dark-skinned toilers were forced to camp in the crowded, evil-smelling gloom of the 'tweendecks, aroused my anger and spurred me on to tireless activity. I spent more hours among the Filipinos than on deck or in the forecastle. These sons of the land of seven thousand islands may have looked like a dull and uniform mass of slaves to the complacent outsider, but the more I dug myself into this mass and endeavored to become a part of it, the more I became aware that these men, who were fed on rice and treated like cattle, had well-defined personalities, hopes, and dreams and plans. They loved their homeland, and many of them were capable of making articulate their will to national independence. A good half of them could read, and about one-fourth could speak and understand English. The communist doctrine which in the case of oppressed peoples combines the slogans of class war with the struggle for national liberation, fell here, when translated into its simplest terms, on fertile soil. My Filipino listeners were visibly intrigued when I expounded to them the doctrine that all men, no matter what the color of their skin, were entitled to equal rights, that the first step of the fight for equal rights was the fight for equal wages with white workers, and that the best method of accomplishing that was through strikes at harvest time. I saw dusky faces light up with comprehension, and then they went on jabbering excitedly among themselves.

One of them, an elderly man with an almost herculean torso, asked me: "Is that the will of God?"

"Most certainly," I said. "God did not make rich men and poor men."

More than once, during idle moments, I felt the temptation to become a lazy and contented resident of Hawaii, the true land of flowers, champagne-like surf and tolerant living. But when I returned to San Pedro from my third voyage to the Islands, I found a letter from Hamburg awaiting me at the Soldiers' and Sailors' Y.M.C.A. As usual, it was written in a simple code—the alphabet starting with M, every fourth letter being invalid, the whole arranged something like a crossword puzzle to be read from right to left and from the bottom upward. Albert Walter wrote that his organization was preparing a world-wide campaign against seamen's missions, and for this purpose he wanted material on the doings of the Seamen's Church Institutes of America which were believed to be subsidized by the shipowners to neutralize the influences of class war propaganda. He also instructed me to collect accurate information on the living conditions of seamen aboard the tankships of the Standard Oil Company. Such information was necessary to formulate communist programs of demands for tanker crews. The Standard Oil Company was representative of American tank-shipping. Oil transports would play a vital role in future wars. Communist control of this branch of merchant shipping had been raised to a major issue in the action program of the Marine Section of the Comintern.

I left my berth on the *Calawaii* in February, 1925, and started out on a four weeks' journey through the Seamen's Church Institutes of the West Coast. The Seamen's Institutes in American ports were the best in the world. They maintained reading-rooms and libraries for seafaring men, they received and forwarded mail, served wholesome meals at lower prices than most restaurants, maintained a free employment service for deck and engine-room personnel, and offered legal advice to seamen. They often gave social evenings, dances and lectures for the men from the ships. They even showed motion pictures free of charge. Some of them had dormitories and single rooms to provide cheap quarters for jobless seamen. The atmosphere in these institutions was clean and cheerful. There were no attempts at aggressive "soul-saving." Neither were there any guards or bouncers, with the exception of the Seamen's Institute in New York, a large building on South Street. No membership fees were exacted. Every mariner was welcome as long as he did not disturb the peace of the house. Though they excluded drunks and questionable women, the Institutes were places where seamen liked to gather in idle shore hours to meet friends, to get their mail and to write their letters, to check their baggage, to read, and to play chess.

But from the communist point of view, the Seamen's Institutes were agencies of the shipowners, created to preach docility and religion. They were looked upon as supply bases for strikebreakers and as espionage centers against the always numerous rebels and malcontents in the marine industry. So they had to be exposed and fought, tooth and nail. The plan for this campaign was originated in Moscow and Hamburg in 1924. It went along with the decision to establish communist International Seamen's Clubs in all important harbors. And if the International Clubs (Interclubs) were to thrive as cultural, educational and political centers of the seafaring population, the Seamen's Institutes had to be wrecked and rooted out of existence. The war against them was waged for many years, and reached its violent climax in the early thirties when sailors' homes, including the largest of them all, in New York, became the scenes of riots and raids by wrecking squads under communist command.

It was my lot to do some of the earliest reconnoitering and skirmishing in this field. In San Pedro, San Francisco and Seattle, traveling between ports along the Pacific Highway and occasionally as a stowaway on coastal ships, I won the favor of the mild-mannered directors of the respective Seamen's Institutes by offering myself as a voluntary worker. I undertook to clean reading-rooms and offices, to visit ships in search of sailors willing and able to sing at entertainment evenings. In this way I gained an insight into the organizational structure of these Institutes, and their working methods. I obtained some of their official literature. I lay in wait for unguarded minutes, to glance over the correspondence on the managers' desks. I did some ignominious sleuthing to determine the outside sources which supplied the Institutes with funds. I even compiled rough statistics about the number of seamen who enjoyed the Institute's hospitality during a normal stay. Each evening I made detailed notes of all my observations, and at the end of a month I sent the fruits of my labors, including the printed matter I had filched, to Albert Walter in Hamburg. I heartily disliked this petty spying; I was better fitted for action than for lurking and backstairs diplomacy.

I went to San Pedro and bribed Mr. X. to ship me out aboard a Standard Oil tanker.

The ship was *El Segundo* of the Standard Oil Company of California. Half of her crew consisted of college students turned sailors for pleasure and profit. I went to work upon their minds with gusto, but with almost no results. At sea, often until midnight, the mess room rang with wild political discussions. I also studied the living conditions, the attitudes and grievances of the professional Standard Oil seamen. I induced two of their number, whom I could class as communist partisans, to enter the International Seamen's Union to carry on disruptive work inside of that organization. I had joined the Union myself during my second voyage on the *Calawaii*, and had found sufficient raw material among the members of the San Pedro branch to start an opposition group whose task was to discredit the union leaders with the rank and file and to obstruct their plans at the weekly branch meetings. The rest of *El Segundo's* crew remained unresponsive to my agitation. Standard Oil sailors were well-fed and well-paid and, as a rule, indifferent to communist arguments. Of the many American tank-ships I had visited during a year of roaming on the West Coast, crew members of only one vessel, the *Empire Arrow*, succumbed to my drive for a communist ship unit.

Back in San Pedro, three weeks after I had signed on, I dashed back to the ship, but the *El Segundo* had already departed. At my request, the marine superintendent of the Standard Oil Company, a certain Mr. Pendergast, gave me a letter of recommendation.

A year of single-handed campaigning had left me with the feeling that I was like a man who shoveled water into a barrel without a bottom. I craved for a rubbing of shoulders with men who were better than I. To none of those I had met since leaving Hamburg was I willing to concede that quality. I dreamt of being able, some day, to lead vast armies of workers into the firelines of revolution. I also dreamt of being, some day, master on the bridge of one of the finest liners afloat. But a career in the American or any other merchant marine was barred to me by the law. Aliens were not wanted. And in Germany I was wanted—for taking up arms against the government. A workers' revolution seemed to be the only way out. The old laws would be swept away, and with them their makers. But revolutions were not made in America. They were in the making in Europe and Asia. I decided to return to Europe. One of my younger brothers had come to the Coast a few months before as a sailor aboard the Norwegian freighter *Hoyanger*. We swapped a few identification papers. I would be safer in Europe if I used his name.

A curious twinge of conscience made me postpone my departure. I remembered that my Hamburg chiefs had expected me to do something about a harpoon gun used on whaling ships out of San Francisco. The matter had not been mentioned again in Albert Walter's letters, and I attached no special importance to this mission. I regarded it as one of the usual minor assignments given to young communists to test their talents for industrial espionage. I knew that a special department of the German Communist Party—and probably of the Communist Parties of other countries as well—engaged in this branch of spying to aid the better reconstruction of Soviet industry. The department was known as the *"BB-Apparat?"* (BB-Betriebs Berichterstattung—Industrial Reports).

I journeyed to San Francisco and presented the letter of recommendation given me by the Standard Oil Company in the offices of the California Sea Products Company which operated three whaling ships. I applied for a job, and the official who questioned me seemed impressed by my brawn and my eagerness to go to work. Within two days, I became a deckhand aboard the whaler *Traveler*.

Our hunting grounds were the waters off the north and south of the jagged Farallon Islands, where the playful humpbacks and the giant sulphur-bottom whales were still fairly abundant. The animals, once sighted, were killed with harpoons fired from small cannon mounted in the bows of the steamers, and were then hauled alongside and pumped full of air to keep them afloat. The floating cadavers were towed to the whaling station near Monterrey to be hung up in chains, cut to pieces, and boiled to yield material for the manufacture of soaps, perfumes and margarine. Each cruise lasted from four to five days. In ten days, the *Traveler* delivered no less than seven humpbacks and one sulphur-bottom to the slaughterhouse on the beach of Monterrey

These ten days made me ill. A live whale curving his fifty-ton bulk with wondrous elegance to the surface of the sea was a beautiful thing to behold. I was captivated by this combination of power and grace which life had taken so many years to build. Then came man, greedy, ruthless, slimy, and cunningly adjusted a grenade in the tip of his harpoon to blast to shreds heart and lungs of the whale. The sight of a whale fighting in the sea ahead, hurt, spurting blood, unable to roar his anguish or to kill his murderers, was more than I could endure. His carcass chained and trailing alongside the ship toward Monterrey, spreading an intense odor of putrefaction, what a miserable end for the good-natured titan of the sea!

The latest harpoon gun was aboard the Hawk, a newer sister ship of the Traveler. I spent an hour with the Hawk's gunner at a time when he was lovingly cleaning his shiny cannon. He answered willingly and with pride my questions regarding the intricacies of the gun and its handling. I borrowed a camera from the cook, and made pictures of the gun from six different angles. I was aware that I was doing a slipshod job, but I detested whaling. I had the film developed and sent the negatives, together with a short report, to Hamburg. And then I deserted my berth without even asking for my pay.

I was hunting for a ship in San Pedro to take me to Europe when a curt note from Albert Walter bade me sign on once more aboard the Calawaii. The note, in effect, said: "We have heard that the Filipino plantation workers in Hawaii are contract laborers who will be returned to the Philippine Islands in due time. We are, therefore, greatly interested in knowing if these workers are free enough to attend political schooling circles before returning to their homes. Comrade B. is now boatswain on the *Calawaii*, and will co-operate with you. With international salute, A. W."

When the *Calawaii* came in, I went straight aboard and demanded to see the bosun. He was a German, a man of about thirty, of the blond, taciturn, hard-bitten type, and an excellent seaman. I showed him the letter from Hamburg, and he saw to it that I was signed on in the capacity of Quartermaster. Comrade B. had been a war prisoner in Siberia. Like many other German war prisoners in Russia, he had joined the Bolshevik Party after the Soviet Revolution and taken part in the subsequent civil war. He had been sent abroad in 1923 by the Maritime Section of the Comintern as propagandist and liaison man on the west coasts of North and South America.

The second night after our arrival in Honolulu harbor, Comrade B. had rounded up four or five local communist sympathizers and escorted them aboard for a conference to determine in which districts the largest number of Filipino laborers were concentrated. The conference took place in the small two-man cabin which I shared with Comrade B. in the forward part of the ship. It was a fruitless session. The pseudo-communists of Honolulu suffered from an excessive dose of what Comintern circles contemptuously call *Lokalpatriotismus*. Comrade B. pounded away at them with great patience. We wrangled for hours, and our voices often were louder than prudence permitted. What we did not know was that another *Calawaii* quartermaster, a young member of some patriotic American organization, was eavesdropping through the thin wooden partition which separated us from the adjoining cabin.

Next day, steaming toward Hilo through cobalt seas, Comrade B. and I were called out by the *Calawaii's* chief officer, Mr. Wells, a handsome and efficient mariner, and nobody's fool. Mr. Wells, leaning against the rail, looked us over with his penetrating eyes.

"This must stop, gentlemen," he said. "I've been told that you two are I.W.W. delegates. We don't want Wobblies on our ships. Moreover, I don't want any more secret soap-boxing on my ship." For several seconds we stood dumbfounded.

"Mister Mate," Comrade B. said, "I'd like to know what rat—"

"That'll do," the mate cut in, turning abruptly. "You know what I mean. That's all."

There was no doubt in our minds as to the identity of the ship's spy. That he had reported us as I.W.W.'s was proof that he had not understood too much of our talk. My dislike for informers was so intense that I wanted to go forward to subject the spy to what Ernst Thaelmann called a "proletarian rubdown." But Comrade B., more level-headed and experienced than I, stopped me.

In Hilo, we skipped an afternoon's work and hired a ramshackle car. As was customary in that port, the *Calawaii's* jazz band played on the sundeck, and the officers and passengers were dancing with a bevy of bored debutantes from ashore. We saw Mr. Wells, his face happily flushed, whirling and gliding with a young thing in his arms, and so we slipped away unnoticed. We cruised around the island of Hawaii until dark. The roads were excellent. The towering outlines of Mauna Kea and Mauna Loa against the unmarred blue of the sky were a rare sight which gave our journey the flavor of a holiday trip. But we had only casual glances for the volcanoes. Our eyes hunted for the meandering lines of Filipino workers in the vast stretches of sugar and pineapple. Wherever we saw a sizable crew at work, we investigated the location of the men's barracks and the village nearest to them. Leisurely we walked through the villages. Comrade B. and I made notes of everything we thought might be important. It was clear that communist organizers, detailed to recruit and school Filipino plantation workers, would have to establish themselves inconspicuously in these villages; if they could manage to win the goodwill of the local Chinese, they would have plenty of opportunity for association with the Filipinos. The propaganda literature would have to be printed in neutral covers, to look like catalogues or advertising matter. An organizer would not have to go into the plantations himself. Once he had interested a few of the workers, they could carry the discussion and pamphlets into the barracks. We returned to the *Calawaii*, dusty and weary, but with the feeling that we had done a good day's work. Comrade B. did not want to send the report of our scouting expedition from Hawaii. He decided to wait until we were back in San Pedro.

That same night, after a cold shower, I went back ashore in Hilo for some refreshment in one of the ice-cream stores near the docks. When I walked into the place. I saw the youngster, whom I suspected of being the ship's informer, lurching over a small round table in the background. He had had too much *okolehau*, and he was slightly drunk and very cocky. He had a knife in his hand and amused himself with cutting a number of grass skirts and other Hawaiian souvenirs from a wall where they had been hung up for display. Seeing me, he pranced and brayed: "Hallelujah, I'm a bum . . . I won't work! I.W.W. I—Won't—Work!" Now I was sure. I lunged and with both fists struck him in the face. Then I returned to the ship. At turn-to hour, next morning, I saw that two of his front teeth were knocked out. He looked at me obliquely, keeping silent.

But he had his revenge. The *Calawaii* had hardly docked in San Pedro ten days later when immigration officers boarded the ship, leaving a watchman to guard the gangway. I was ordered to bring all my papers to the captain's salon. Comrade B. had received the same order. In the salon two immigration officials in uniform relieved me of my Able Seaman's Certificate, my Lifeboat Ticket, and my discharge book of the Shipowners' Association.

"Wait in your cabin until further notice," they told me.

A minute later a shipmate informed me that he had heard the gangway watchman say that the officers had come aboard to arrest "a couple of undesirable aliens." Then Comrade B. flew into the cabin, cursing.

"We've got to vanish," he said.

We agreed on a meeting-place ashore, and separated. We heard a voice through the companionway on deck, shouting our names. I ran through the 'tweendecks toward a port amidships, used at sea for dumping kitchen garbage. I slipped through the port. The rim of the concrete quay was too far off for me to reach. But at the bottom of the four-foot-wide gully, between the ship's side and the quay, were heavy logs chained to ring-bolts in the concrete and serving as fenders. I let myself drop to one of these logs. The surface was slimy and barnacled. I crawled along the logs, dodging a column of water which poured from a scupper, until I cleared the steamer's stern. There was an iron ladder here leading to the top of the quay. I ran up this ladder, and disappeared in the murk of a great cargo shed.

I met Comrade B. in the booth of a soothsayer in the Long Beach amusement district, a few miles from the Pacific docks. There was a hunt for us going on all over San Pedro and Wilmington. Comrade B. had salvaged his bundle of notes and his money. I had salvaged nothing. Bareheaded, in khaki shirts, dungarees and canvas shoes, we deliberated in a moving roller-coaster on what we should do. We saw no chance of ever getting another ship in any West Coast port. Both of us were refugees from the Germany of 1923, and were unwilling to invite capture and deportation. Neither of us had any identification papers. Our belongings were still aboard the *Calawaii*.

I knew an elderly girl in Long Beach, whose failure to win the man she loved had driven her to toy with communism. She worked as a waitress in a seashore restaurant. When the restaurant closed at eleven, I met her and explained our predicament to her. She declared herself willing to board the *Calawaii* to see if there were still any guards on duty. While she went aboard, Comrade B. and I waited in an empty railway car a hundred yards from the ship. She returned to report that there were two watchmen at the gangway.

In the dark night, Comrade B. and I slunk through the harbor until we found a skiff. We manned the skiff and paddled through the Pacific docks to the offshore side of the *Calawaii*. Several barges were moored alongside. In the darkness, I fell through an open hatch into the hold of a barge, and remained unconscious for some time. As if by miracle, I suffered no broken bones. Comrade B. hoisted me back on deck, and revived me with harbor water. Then he clambered up the side of the *Calawaii*, and ten minutes later he lowered our belongings into the skiff which I had meanwhile paddled under the steamer's prow. We glided silently and landed in a deserted part of the docks where there were no customs guards on duty. That night we spent in the tiny apartment of our friend, the waitress from Long Beach.

Comrade B. intended to make another stowaway journey to the Hawaiian Islands. I asked him if he needed me as his assistant.

"No," he said. "You are too tall and too conspicuous. You better go on to New York." He could not forgive me my blunder of hitting the informer in Hilo. He gave me enough money to pay my railway fare to St. Louis, where I went to the German Club, whose members were just then engaged in mass-singing and indoor gymnastics, to ask for financial assistance to continue to New York. I told them I had lost my ship, and intended to catch it again in some East Coast port so as not to lose my pay. I received three dollars and an introduction to a kindly German, a salesman of sewing machines, who was driving to New York and was glad to have a companion on his trip.

New York bewildered and oppressed me. I tarried long enough to induce one of the land-sharks, who acted as shipping masters and notaries public in dismal upstairs rooms along South Street, to procure for me a sailor's berth aboard the *Carlier,* of the Royal Lloyd Beige. A fortnight later, in the early fall of 1925, I paid off in Antwerp.

Chapter Ten

THE ROAD TO LENINGRAD

The lusty waterfront districts of Antwerp had, in my absence, undergone a thorough cleansing under the influence of an aggressive Catholic campaign. Policing had become much stricter. No longer did nude harlots lean out of the windows facing the Cathedral to yell their enticements at passing sailors. The public mass brothels had disappeared. The hordes of beachcombers and outcasts from all the coasts of the world were no longer permitted to camp on the promenades along the river. The hundreds of male and female innkeepers, stretching from the Rhine Quay to Siberia Dock, were less bland and more grouchy since Antwerp was on the way to surrender its reputation as the wildest and most vicious port in the world to Hamburg, Shanghai, and Alexandria.

And Bandura was no longer in Antwerp. I was somehow disappointed to hear that the old warrior had been induced to kowtow to Communist Party discipline. After repeated arrests and deportations to Holland and France, and persistent returns to Antwerp, he had been maneuvered into moving to the Hamburg waterfront where a tighter supervision of his doings by the Party was possible. The Antwerp harbor "activist" brigades had fallen wholly under communist control, exercised by Ilja Weiss, the Hungarian, with the assistance of a Chinese student from Berlin and a horse-faced militant, "Red" McGrath, a native of New Zealand. Fortified with a monthly subsidy from the treasury of Albert Walter, they swamped an average of eight hundred ships a month with propaganda.

A letter from Albert Walter suddenly ordered me to leave Antwerp. It appeared that I had been selected for a term of special training at the Communist University in Leningrad. My instructions were to get my sailing papers from Comrade Anton, at an address in Merxem, a suburb of Antwerp. I found myself in a well-appointed drygoods store, in the back of which was an elegantly furnished office completely equipped. A demure woman led me into this inner office, where Comrade Anton received me. He was a stern-faced six-footer, of polished manner, resembling a churchman far more than an agent of the G.P.U. Yet he was in charge, as I discovered later, of all the G.P.U. operations in Flanders. He had an *Apparat* of his own, which functioned independently and the existence of which was unknown even to Ilja Weiss and the local Party leaders.

Comrade Anton spoke faultless German, English, French, and Flemish—his mother language. He received me in a businesslike fashion. He knew in advance of my coming, and prepared for me a document typed in Russian and bearing two huge blue Soviet seals. He gave me the sum of twenty Dutch guilders, detailed instructions as to how I was to get to Russia, and told me to report to Comrade Ryatt, 15 Prospekt Ogorodnikova, in Leningrad.

My ship was the *Russ,* a German vessel chartered by the Soviets and manned by a crew approved by Albert Walter's office. She was due to sail from Rotterdam with a cargo of iron for Leningrad. I went to Holland via the "underground" route. At every important frontier-crossing, the Comintern had established a courier station charged with conducting illegally traveling communists across the borders. I went to the Belgian frontier town of Esschen by train. A well-dressed young man awaited me at the station. He had two bicycles, one for himself, and one for me. We waited until it was dark. At a leisurely pace he led me over a labyrinth of obscure country-paths toward the north. No border patrol stopped us. Two hours later we arrived at the Dutch frontier town of Rozendaal. My guide saw me aboard a train to Rotterdam; he himself returned to his relay station on the Belgian side.

Although I did not pay for my passage, I did not have to hide except during our traverse of the Kiel Canal where German officials checked the steamer through the largest canal locks in the world. Most students for the Comintern schools travel in this manner, which enables them to slip in and out of Russia without the knowledge of foreign port or border authorities.

I despair at describing my emotions when the first dim landmarks of the Soviet Union rose out of the mist—Kronstadt, the outlying islands, and then the workaday contours of Leninport. No devout worshiper could have entered a holy shrine with greater reverence than I entered Russia's westernmost metropolis.

I walked through the dreary streets of Leningrad, and my steps were light and firm. Of the many strange towns I had entered in the course of my long vagabondage, Leningrad was the least strange of all. I was like a ragged wanderer coming home at last to see if things are as they should be. Gone was all the unrest, gone the accursed lust for action at any price. I was no longer a chunk of mutinous scum in enemy country. I was content to hold my head high and let my eyes drink in the expressions in the faces of simple men and women who had their place at the helm of the first Dictatorship of the Proletariat.

No one came to tell me: "Turn! Flee, you innocent, you ridiculously happy fool! Flee before it is too late!" Had someone said it, I should have struck him down.

Throngs were on the streets. The men and women I saw were better clothed and looked better fed than I. Many faces were serious, almost sad, but many were also strong with mute determination. And smiles and laughter were common among those who sauntered in groups between drab rows of houses aching for paint. I was hungry, and dog-tired from hours of walking. My shoes were worn out. The overcoat I wore was torn. I kept on asking for the way, until at last an open-faced boy understood what I wanted. He was a student of chemistry, and a Komsomol. We walked side by side and talked.

"They should have sent somebody down to meet you at the ship," the student said. And after a while, when he learned that I had been in America:

"Is it true that workers in America have automobiles?"

"Yes, a good many of them."

"They say a worker in America is as good as dead at forty," the student said, adding pensively, "We, too, shall have automobiles." We swung into the Prospekt Ogorodnikova, and entered a massive building flanked by gardens. The thickly carpeted vestibule was dominated by a bronze bust of Lenin. There was an array of palms almost touching the lofty ceiling. Large mirrors reflected the brilliant light. Heavy leather arm-chairs were arranged along the walls. Wide doors painted ivory and gold led off in all directions. Signs at the doors bore the words "French Section," "Anglo-American Section," "Colonial Section," and others. I was in the International Club of Leningrad.

"Formerly it was the private palace of a big shipowner," the student explained. "You should have been here a few days ago for the October celebration. The *Internationale* was sung in seventeen languages at the same time."

Ryatt, the Lettish Bolshevik to whom I was to report, was not in the Club. He had gone to Moscow for a couple of days. A gloomy German functionary took care of my needs. He led me to a rambling basement restaurant which resembled a modernized medieval wine cellar. Half of the fifty large round tables were occupied. Many languages could be heard. I ate a hearty, well-cooked meal, and my beer glass was filled and refilled without my asking. From the restaurant I was led to a barber shop, and from there into a steam-chamber and bathroom where I lingered all of an hour. After the bath, a husky, taciturn woman put me to bed on a ponderous leather couch in one of the upper rooms of the Club.

"*Schlaf,*" she said curtly. "Now you must sleep."

I closed my eyes and slept long, until late the next morning.

"*Vstavayte!*" Get up!" a harsh voice said.

Above me towered a hard-faced man in white. At his side hovered a pleasant young woman. The man reminded me of the gunner of the whaler *Hawk;* the woman resembled in stature and expression the girls I had seen working as stevedores in the harbors of Finland.

"I'm the doctor," the man said. "I must examine you."

I looked for my clothes. They had disappeared. The contents of my pockets lay neatly on a table.

The woman laughed. She said something in Russian.

"She says your rags are in the furnace," the doctor translated. "She burned them."

"But what am I to put on?"

"Never mind. You'll get others."

She went away to get clothes. The doctor examined me. He could find nothing wrong. The garments which the woman brought me were not new, but they were strongly made, and they were warm. A faint smell of disinfectant clung to them.

"We take care of our boys," the doctor said. "You may go down for breakfast."

In the restaurant the sad-looking German was waiting for me. "Eat quick, it's late," he said.

"Where are we going?"

"To the G.P.U."

"The G.P.U?"

"Yes, naturally."

I thought I should be questioned. I had been warned that the secret services of capitalist countries were eager to send their spies into the Comintern schools.

On foot and in battered, overcrowded street cars we traveled into a district of palaces which had once belonged to men who were now dead and gone, or in exile. We passed the hulking Admiralty and entered one of the thoroughfares which radiate from that point. We approached the silent, thick-walled building on Majorov Prospekt.

All manner of people cluttered the grimy hallways. After a period of waiting, I was conducted to a spacious office the only decorations of which were a portrait of Lenin and another of Felix Dzerjinsky, the creator of the Tcheka. Two men in uniform sat at a table. One was short and fat. The other seemed hardly more than a pair of piercing eyes in a landscape of prominent bones.

I was not questioned. They were well informed about my past. All they wanted was to verify my identity and obtain a photograph for my communist student's pass card. I was instructed to use the name of Adolf Heller during my stay in the Soviet Union. All students used assumed names to safeguard them against informers of foreign police departments. Anonymity was essential for the work we were expected to do. I was warned to be wary about communications with strangers. I was also requested not to send letters by mail to friends or relatives abroad. All letters with foreign destination were to be turned over to the secretary of the International Club. They would be brought to Berlin by the weekly courier, and posted there so as not to show their Soviet origin. The real reason for this was a strict censorship of outgoing communications by the G.P.U. Then I was photographed.

Before I left, the cadaverous-looking official made a short speech. Except for his accentuation of each sentence with a jerk of his corpse-like head, he might have been talking to himself. No doubt, he had made the same speech a thousand times or more. "Maintain unshakable proletarian discipline," he concluded. "You are a guest of the Soviet Union. You shall become its son. Prove yourself worthy of our common historical task. Be worthy of the great tradition of the Soviet Revolution."

The morning after Ryatt's return from Moscow, I attended my first lecture in the International Division of the Communist University. The central building of this academy of Bolshevist theory and practice was the former palace of the Duma, now the Urizky Palace, facing one of the largest garden-squares in the world. The lofty windows, the columns and marble stairways, the paneled wall and enormous candelabras, the whole massive splendor of a vanished regime, brought home to the newcomer a realization of the completeness of the Bolshevist triumph. From the secret schooling circles in the Czarist prisons and underground hovels to this magnificent Palace! The somber portraits of the giants of the Revolution were everywhere. Emblazoned in stone were the words, *Workers of the World, Unite!*

Over six thousand students attended the Communist University in the winter of 1925-26. The large majority were Russians, who were trained for political and administrative work in the Party machine, the economic councils, in the trade unions and co-operatives, in the Red Army, the Red Navy and the G.P.U., and for functions in the great number of communist auxiliary organizations.

The foreign students were incorporated in the International Division which occupied twenty-odd rooms on the second floor of an adjoining building which once housed the Leningrad garrison. The Chinese, Japanese, Koreans and Malays had their own "University of the Peoples of the East" in Moscow, and a smaller one, the Pan-Pacific University, in Vladivostok. American communists had their special department in the "University of the Peoples of the West," also in Moscow. Each of the foreign groups of the Communist University also included a number of Russian communists who were being prepared for revolutionary service outside the Soviet frontiers. They were a picked lot, young and alert, and all of them were fluent in at least one language besides their native Russian.

The courses of the International Division dealt almost exclusively with aspects of class war and the struggle for communism. They did not aim at educating academic scholars. Revolutionary theories were never treated apart from actual class war experiences. The battles of the past and present—armed risings, strikes, civil wars—were analyzed and dissected, the mistakes of strategy and methods were pointed out, and lessons were drawn to guide the student in the actions of the future. All courses led up and culminated in the Leninist conception of the most important step on the road to a classless society—the seizure of power through revolution, and the establishment of the dictatorship of the proletariat under the leadership of the Communist Party. Every thought, every campaign, every action whatsoever had value only if it constituted a forward step to the seizure of power. Every omission, every scruple and laxity that could tend to retard the advance was an unpardonable crime. Revolution was not *one* way out—it was the *only* way out.

There was a special Military Department where Red Army officers lectured on the strategy of street fighting and the science of civil war. There was a special section for the study of African problems and languages, and another one—reserved for a strictly segregated and tight-lipped élite—where G.P.U. officers were the instructors. Photography, fingerprinting and police work were taught here. And known to all were the classes in which large numbers of Russian girls worked tirelessly to acquire fluency in the languages of the West. These girls were political workers. They were the "Aktivistki"—a title of which they were very proud.

The international universities of the Comintern are in reality schools established and maintained by the Russian Communist Party which is identical with the Soviet government. The Comintern being in effect no more than the foreign division of the Russian Party, we students often jokingly referred to the Comintern as the *Moskauer Fremdenlegion*—Moscow's Foreign Legion. Yet very few of our instructors were Russian. The majority of the members of our faculty were Germans, Letts, Poles, Finns and Hungarians. Most prominent among them was Otto Wilhelm Kuusinen, a leader of the Finnish Soviet revolution of 1918, one of the founders of the Comintern, who had been a trusted collaborator of Lenin. Today Kuusinen still remains a loyal servant of the Kremlin, and recently figured in the world news as the head of the Finnish puppet government set up by Stalin during the Russian invasion of Finland.

Of my other instructors, the two Hungarians, the sedate and scholarly Pap and the good-natured though volcanic Goegoes, came to grief some years later in Budapest, where they had been sent to stage a communist coup. Both were betrayed to the authorities by their own Party chief, Rakoshi. Driven to insanity by the police, Pap hanged himself in the prison of Zegedin in 1930. Goegoes died in the grip of his torturers. Another lecturer, the talented German, Arthur Ewert, who was popular because of his robust warmth and rollicking humor, rots to this day in a Brazilian prison. Most horrible was the end of Rosa Speculant, a puritanical Jewess, who lectured on propaganda. She was subsequently sent by the Comintern to Poland, and was seized there by the political police. Nothing was heard of her until an escaped fellow-prisoner arrived in Berlin with this report:

> "Police Inspector Tkaczuk came to Luck prison to question Comrade Speculant. To make her confess, he had the soles of her feet beaten with canes. Water, petroleum and urine were poured into her nostrils. Because she still refused to confess, she was raped by prison guards. They transferred her to the venereal ward of the prison hospital."

Since then a children's home on the Black Sea near Novorossisk had been named after Rosa Speculant.

High functionaries of the Comintern occasionally lectured at the University. These lectures were gala events. They had the character of Bolshevik mass meetings, and were held in the venerable main hall where formerly the ill-fated Duma convened. Outstanding among our guest lecturers was Ossip Piatnitzky, the hard-boiled chief of the organization department—the Orgbureau—of the Comintern. Piatnitzky was the man feared most by sluggish Party bureaucrats the world over. He was the man who paid or stopped, decreased or increased the subsidies of the Comintern for Parties abroad. He was the man who swung the lash of open criticism without fear or favor; where he saw a festering wound—he jabbed his fingers into it with gusto. The short, stubby, graying, blunt-faced and keen-eyed Piatnitzky waved applause aside as a waste of time. He was immensely popular among the students. Among the experts of conspirative organization he was the undisputed master. His voice rang hard, and it had a humorous tinge. He ended a three-hour speech on the "organization of victory" with the cry: "Our revolutionary fatherland, the Soviet Union, is at war with the whole of the capitalist world. Only the triumph of the world revolution can end this war."

The foreign students lived in segregated quarters, grouped according to their nationalities. Aside from official fraternity nights, close private relationships between students of different nationalities were not encouraged, because of fear that spies might have wormed their way into the student corps. I lived with a group of German and German-speaking comrades from the Baltic countries in an old tenement house in the Viborg district. On one side was the Nevka, the northern arm of the Neva estuary; on the other a vast lunatic asylum, one section of which was run by the G.P.U. We rose at half past six, awakened by a swarthy house superintendent's helper, a Georgian, who ran from room to room, shouting hoarsely, "Arise, ye prisoners of starvation ... After a breakfast of bread and tea, we were on our way. A street car bore us south across the Neva at a snail's pace, stopping at every block while hordes of passengers piled in and out. In high spirits, we often indulged in coarse flirtations in the darkness and the slashing cold of a Leningrad winter morning.

The first lecture started at nine. The subjects ranged from Marx's "theory of surplus value" to the "application of Clausewitz' Rules of Warfare in the conduct of strikes," from "revolutionary defeatism and the transformation of an imperialist war into a civil war" to "mass psychology and propaganda." Then followed an hour of discussion. Every problem from war to marriage was analyzed from a strict class viewpoint. Another lecture followed, and another hour of discussion. By that time it was one o'clock.

The hour from one to two was devoted to gymnastics, target practice with small-caliber revolvers and rifles, and other forms of physical exercise. The instructors were officers' apprentices of the Red Army, and superb examples of physical perfection they were! Individual athletic stunts were taboo. If anyone possessed exceptional prowess, he was not permitted to boast about it as young people like to do. Everything was done collectively, and the pace of motion was that of the slowest. At times three Komsomols supplied a musical rhythm with trumpets. One of the exercises consisted of doing gymnastics while standing under icy showers, a test of self-control in which the girls invariably outdid the hardiest of the male students. *Sevemoye Siyanye*—"aurora borealis '—this torture was called.

In the afternoons, we usually wrote essays or leaflets on subjects assigned by our instructors. The students had a choice between two themes, such as "Why do the Communist Parties fight the Versailles Treaty?" or "What must be the policy of the Communist Parties in the event of war between Germany and France?" I recall an assignment on the question, "Is America an imperialist state?" It followed our study of Scott Nearing's book, *The American Empire,* given us in mimeographed copies translated in various languages.

Each minute of our time was supervised by a Comintern control bureau of which Kuusinen was the invisible, and the German communists Kuehne and Schneller, the visible heads. Schneller had been a world war officer in the German army. Kuehne was a combination of a fox and a scientist, and later became the secretary of the communist bloc in the German Reichstag. At times Heinz Neumann, whose regular abode was in the Comintern building in Moscow, took a hand in the planning of our time down to the smallest detail. Many of us developed a secret animosity for this scion of a Berlin grain millionaire because of his brusque, dictatorial manner, and because of the undisguised cynicism with which he summoned likable girl students to his hotel. It was known that he had a beautiful young girl from the Caucasus region as his mistress in Moscow. Nevertheless, each time he was in Leningrad some Scandinavian or German girl was invited to gratify Heinz Neumann's appetite. The girls went to him willingly. Neumann had the reputation of being one of the few foreign communists who belonged to the inner circle around Stalin, whose name already then spelled magic to us. But the whole foreign division of the Communist University chuckled when Heinz Neumann was set upon and beaten by unnamed men in the shadow of Peter the Great's monument on Dekabrist Square. As usual, Neumann was in the company of a young woman, and both were tipsy with vodka. The following day—the Lenin-Liebknecht-Luxemburg memorial day—Neumann nursed his bruises in solitude. But the next morning he appeared in the control bureau to issue orders to student delegates about a fraternity evening with Putilov workers in the Palace of Labor. This cold-blooded libertine was an efficient Party worker.

Official supervision did not stop with the detailed disposition of our time. All our reading, our conversations, our personal associations were supervised by undercover agents of the G.P.U., which also had an informer assigned to every group of students. Only communist newspapers—a huge selection of them—were allowed to be in our hands. We were not permitted to have books other than those issued by the libraries of the University and the International Club. We were carefully steered away from all private contacts with Russian workers and students. At regular intervals, all rooms in the students' homes showed traces of a thorough search, conducted while their occupants were in school or on an excursion. G.P.U. men listened in on all group conversations. We were sincere revolutionists, and regarded the G.P.U. as our protectors. We were devoted to the Soviet Union. We had nothing to hide. We were far too busy from morning till night to stray off the ironbound communist path. Nothing ever came to my attention in all those months to indicate that a foreign communist student had gotten himself into difficulties with the G.P.U.

The student group to which I belonged counted fifty-three members, sometimes more, sometimes a few less. We lived well. We received our meals free of charge; we were given clothing when we needed and applied for it; entertainment and excursions did not cost us one kopeck. The fifty rubles each of us received fortnightly from the *Kassa* of the control bureau we could spend as we liked on drinks, cigarettes and other incidentals. But fifty-three of us were assigned to sleep in eight small rooms, the three largest of which provided quarters and sleeping space for the fifteen girls in our group. The boys were crammed, seven and eight strong, into each of the remaining chambers. We slept on collapsible army cots. When all the cots were mounted, the rooms were filled with sleeping gear from wall to wall. Usually the lights were kept burning all night, for there was always one who thought it more important to do required reading than to snatch a full measure of sleep. Iron stoves glowed red, but there were not enough to go around. Small oil lamps, battered percolators, samovars and even candles were used to battle the grim cold of winter. There were broken window-panes patched up with paper or pieces of old cloth. Yet, all the discomfort and lack of privacy never led to quarrels or peevishness among us. We took pride in showing that no hardship could daunt us.

We despised the bourgeois ideals of a settled existence, of marriage and love, of ownership and law and order. None of us looked forward to having children or a garden or only a roomful of furniture and books of his own. We thought we knew what awaited us in the years to come. We were the youth of international conspiracy. The capitalists and their hireling governments would fight us tooth and claw because they knew that our triumph would spell their death. We expected no quarter and we intended to give none. Our job was destruction—utter, uncompromising destruction—of capitalist society and the capitalist state, an uprooting and overturning of all standards and values grown out of the basic conceptions of *my* land, *my* house, *my* country, *my* wife, *my* factory or ship or mine or railroad!

Marriage among the young professionals of world revolution was discouraged. Men with families and women with children were too likely to become lovers of peace. In the always stormy and frequently short career of the professional communist normal marriage relations were blasted in the bud. In the face of the tremendous revolutionary goal set before us, cultivation of a permanent emotional alliance between one man and one woman seemed trivial and futile. But we were no celibates. We were healthy young animals as capable of erotic passion, of falling in love, and of yearning for the caresses of a beloved as any virile youths and life-hungry girls.

Debates on the merits and demerits of "free love" we left to the intellectuals of an already rotting liberalism. We were too direct in our mutual relationships to fall victim to the customs of courtship and flirtations prevalent on "the other side." Outlawed were sultry whisperings and lascivious insinuations. Outlawed was erotic jealousy. Outlawed was the pursuit and the pestering of girls who were in no mood to respond. Outlawed were false shame and morbid curiosity. It was a rule that the student who felt himself drawn to a certain girl would tell her frankly: "I desire you. Be my companion as long as the Party permits us to be together." When the feeling was reciprocal, the girl would smile and nod, and the matter was settled. And so it was also the other way around. Often two or more young men sometimes shared the intimate friendship of one girl. No secret was made of such an agreement. The recreation rooms on the ground floor of our house, where we danced and drank vodka and played chess in the evenings, became toward midnight the inalienable reservation of the lovers. The Russian Komsomol girls haunted the international students' homes in flocks, surrounding as they did the young revolutionists from foreign lands with an aura of romantic heroism. But the hordes of luckless prostitutes who shivered in the squares and doorways never entered our life. Cases of venereal disease among the students were extremely rare.

The master craftsmen in the Kremlin could not have wished for better tools. We were the unflinching prisoners of a grandiose make-believe, we who looked upon ourselves as hard-headed materialists. We dismissed the distress of today, the human wreckage littered all about us, the terror and the militarism prevailing in the country, with the stereotyped belief that we were marching forward with giant strides: "The power is ours—and the future, too!"

Of the six comrades who were my roommates during that Leningrad winter, two are dead, one is in prison. I lost all trace of the others.

In prison is Hans Sorgers. He was a cheerful, tenacious youth who danced the *Schuhplattler* at the International Club and liked to sing Bavarian mountaineer songs. He became an editor for the German Party press, stuck to his post after the Reichstag went up in flames, until an infatuation with a young Jewish girl brought him into the toils of the Gestapo. They questioned the girl after a routine roundup. Half-crazy with fear, she betrayed her lover. Fifteen years of solitary confinement in Ploetzensee prison near Berlin are his lot.

Another, Nicola Koffardschieff, a bold and earnest Bulgarian, with a head like carved oak, was an excellent chess player. He was the only one in our group who never put his arm around a girl. But he liked children. He gave them bonbons and told them stories. That was his relaxation—that, and a liter of vodka once a month. When Nicola was drunk, he became gloomy and went out to walk in the streets all night. He was a hard worker whom only children could make smile. In September, 1931, Georgi Dimitrov sent Nicola to Bulgaria on a Comintern mission. On October 30, risking his own life to liberate an arrested comrade, he was shot to death by police agents in the streets of Sofia.

And there was Kazys Kentautas, the Lithuanian, whom I will never forget. He was the best student in our group, the son of a blacksmith in Memel. He read Hegel and Feuerbach in the original, and surreptitiously he read Nietzsche's *Zarathustra*. Kazys was no fighter, but he was one of those who would walk naked into a fire to prove to himself that mind could sometimes triumph over matter. One evening in the Leningrad Palace of Labor he saw me dancing with Kristinaite, a fiery-eyed slip of a girl, who studied economics and conspiratorial organization at the Foreign Division. He fell in love with her at once. He could work himself into a state of near-intoxication simply by staring at Kristinaite's hair, which was a smooth glistening black. From that day on, he showed less interest in school, but somehow he was too shy to speak to her. I told Kristinaite about Kazys. He was training himself for work in Fascist countries—the most dangerous of all activities. Kristinaite gave me a flashing laugh and went to Kazys Kentautas. After that they were together almost every night. He was courageous enough to marry her. Kristinaite used to say, "After the revolution we shall have babies." Shortly afterwards, he was sent to work underground in Finland, she to Roumania or Greece. Later they worked together in Latvia, and in 1930 Kristinaite had a baby which she kept in a children's home in Ostrov, just across the border.

I heard nothing more from them until the end of 1933. In the Comintern service we hardly ever wrote each other private letters. One was not supposed to know where the other was, unless both had the same assignment. But in October, 1933, I discovered their names in the files of the western Secretariat of the Comintern in Copenhagen. From Latvia both had been sent to reorganize the Party in Lithuania. They were captured and thrown into the dungeons of Kovne. Kazys Kentautas was condemned to death for high treason. Kristinaite refused to make a confession. Inhuman jailers tortured her with heavy prison keys. Kristinaite went mad. To hide the consequences of their brutality the jailers murdered her a night later.

I often think of Kristinaite's flashing laughter. Had I told Kazys, when he declared his love for her: "Go away, Comrade Kentautas, she is not for you, you cannot even dance," Kristinaite might have lived a little longer.

Chapter Eleven

COURIER TO THE ORIENT

The old wanderlust stirred my blood with the coming of spring. I had had enough of lectures in the Communist University, and hungered for the winds and the freedom of the sea. Besides, the year of 1926 promised thunder. A general strike was in the offing in England, and we expected it to shake the British Empire to its foundations. In China, the revolution was clearly on its way. In the Dutch East Indies, plans hatched in the Comintern for an insurrection were afoot. I asked to be sent into the field. My request was granted. Ryatt informed me that I would serve as a courier to the Orient as soon as arrangements had been completed. In the meantime I was delegated to attend the inauguration of a Seamen's International Club in Murmansk.

Accompanied by a girl interpreter, I started out for the Arctic port. Two days and nights our train crawled northward over a desert of snow. Situated on a dismal fjord, Murmansk was at that time still a sleepy and overgrown village spread chaotically on the slopes of low, barren hills. Its lower portion was half submerged in frozen mud and slush. The spent warmth of the Gulf Stream, pawing feebly around the North Cape, made Murmansk the only ice-free Soviet harbor north of the Black Sea. It was a bleak harbor, with unkempt sheds and piers. An ancient little trawler and two small trampships hovered in the fog offshore. An indescribable gloominess lay over the place. From a smeary sky fell a drizzle that could be called neither rain nor sleet nor snow. But the houses near the station, built of rough-hewn logs, were stanch and warm.

A delegate from the Soviet Seamen's Union awaited me at the station, where the people were dirty and ragged and sulky. He had a face from which life seemed to have drained all desire. He nodded a surly welcome and motioned me to follow him, without pulling his hands out of the holes of his tattered overcoat. We made our way to the International Club, a long and low log building, decorated with a bronze bust of Lenin, pictures of Marx and other revolutionary leaders, Red banners, a large rack full of brand-new books and pamphlets, and a phonograph with a big pink-colored loudspeaker. Rain dripped through the sacking which covered the windows in lieu of glass. There was not a lavatory in the building.

The active membership of the Murmansk Interclub was made up of five Russians, two of them girls from Leningrad who knew German and English, and four foreign seamen, a German, two Scandinavians and a Scot. They were an eager lot, quite content with their task of upholding the cause of internationalism in this wettest corner of the Soviet fatherland. I delivered the main address during the inauguration ceremony, after the chairman had introduced me as a "delegate from the workers of capitalist Europe."

Upon my return to Leningrad a week later, I found instructions awaiting me to go via Berlin to Rotterdam to sign up there on a steamer bound for the Far East. Ryatt procured for me the necessary credentials, and a Swiss passport the original photograph of which had been replaced by one of myself.

"Whenever you are using a phony passport," Ryatt explained in his dry, disillusioned manner, "see that you cross the frontier at night. At night the border policemen are less attentive and flaws in the passports don't show so much under electric lights."

To avoid traveling through Poland, where the political police was the most efficient agency in a generally inefficient country, I used the slightly roundabout route through Riga, entering Germany over the East Prussian border town of Eydtkuhnen.

The express which I took from Riga had been a few short weeks before the scene of a bloody occurrence which reminded me that the profession of a Comintern courier, upon which I was embarking, is one of the most hazardous on earth. The international couriers Nette and Machmannsthal had been *en route* from Berlin to Moscow, carrying a batch of confidential documents forwarded by Soviet agents in London. The documents were carried in diplomatic pouches. Outside of Riga, shortly after the two couriers had crossed from Lithuania into Latvia, two strangers wearing black suits and black masks forced their way into the sleeping compartments occupied by the Comintern men. The invaders drew pistols and demanded the surrender of the pouches.

It was night, and the train was speeding north at close to sixty miles an hour. Nette, who had been sleeping in the top berth, reached for the pistol under his pillow. In the lower berth Machmannsthal also snatched his gun, which he had strapped to his pajamas. Instantly the masked strangers opened fire. The couriers, still entangled in their blankets, also began to shoot. Four guns blazed away at a range of less than six feet. Nette was hit through his lungs and stomach. He pitched out of his berth, but continued to fire from the floor of the rocking train. The compartment was spattered with blood from top to bottom. When the smoke cleared away, the two assassins lay dead. Nette was dying. Machmannsthal, seriously wounded, survived. The mail-by-courier was saved. Later investigations by the Riga police and the G.P.U. in Leningrad established that the dead assailants had been former White Guards in the employ of the British secret service.

In Berlin, I received my orders from Fritz Heckert, one of Moscow's chief agents abroad, and a Chinese communist whose name was, I believe, Wan-Min. Bela Kun was then also in Berlin, which was at that time the seat of the Comintern's chief agency outside of the Soviet Union. The German Republic was the most liberal and the most lax in hunting down foreign agitators. My tasks for the next few months were outlined to me over coffee and cake in the Café Bauer.

A coup was being planned for the Dutch East Indies. A victorious insurrection of the natives of Java and Sumatra, it was hoped in Moscow, would whet Japan's appetite for these rich Indonesian islands. Any Japanese move in the direction of Java would, in turn, cause Great Britain to intervene. And that, in turn, would divert British attention from what was going on in China. The strategy was to "play one capitalist country against another" for the benefit of the Soviet Union. My duty was to convey a consignment of confidential material to M. Lan, a female Chinese Comintern agent in Indonesia. The consignment consisted of a number of packages, the contents of which were too incriminating to be sent through the mails, and too bulky to be smuggled successfully along any regular passenger route. They probably also contained money. For identification purposes, I was given the snapshot of a dog. Anyone who presented to me another copy of this photograph either in Singapore or Sabang or Belawan, would be the authorized recipient of the consignment. I was to sail as a bona fide seaman from Rotterdam, where my courier mail was awaiting me. Heckert showed me a picture of M. Lan, and told me that she would probably come aboard my ship in person.

"Your salary from now on," Heckert said, "is eighty dollars a month. After your stuff is delivered in good order, send me a telegram and go on to Shanghai for further instructions."

From the "Technical Bureau"—the passport forging center which the Comintern maintained in Berlin—I received a good German seamen's book and credentials of a missionary in the employ of the Mission for Seamen in London. Before I boarded the Berlin-Amsterdam express, I was insistently warned to tell no one, "not even your mother or sweetheart," where I was going, to avoid all private communications, and to be deaf and dumb to inquiries from outsiders. *"Schweigen ist Gold,"* Wan-Min explained. "If you cannot be silent, we can't use you."

My steamer was the *Franken*, Captain Kuehnemann, of the North German Lloyd, a fine new ship then on her maiden voyage.

I shipped on her by a simple ruse. When the vessel put into Rotterdam, a communist in the crew feigned serious illness and was transferred to the marine hospital. I had no difficulty in obtaining the "sick" man's berth. But before the *Franken* sailed, I was brusquely burdened with additional responsibilities. A young local communist roused me from my bunk in the middle of the night.

"Come ashore," he panted, "there's a messenger from Hamburg."

Albert Walter in Hamburg had gotten wind of my journey to the Far East and had quickly decided to have me transact some of his business at the expense of the Berlin office which financed my trip. I dressed and scrambled ashore. In a tavern I met Hugo Marx. His pale, thin face showed the usual foxy smirk, and his eyes were half closed. He gave me a letter of instructions marked "MEMORIZE—DESTROY," and several thick envelopes containing money for the communist harbor units in Genoa, Alexandria, and Colombo.

The *Franken* steamed seaward, with my "mail" stowed away safely. The first port of call was Genoa. It rose out of the sea in the early morning, an amphitheater of pearl-gray, yellow and rose against a background of treeless green hills with crumbling forts on their crests.

A communist had to be careful in Italy. Mussolini's likeness seemed to stare through every shop window in Genoa. Hawkeyed young Blackshirts were in every street. One wrong word, one careless move, one harmless little crime of omission could consign scores of honest revolutionists to destruction in the inquisition chambers of the *Ovra*. The messenger of the Italian "underground" organization came aboard in the guise of a stevedore. He recognized me by a prearranged sign: a blue bandanna with a double knot around the neck. His open, energetic face belied all popular conceptions of the aspect of a conspirator.

"Give me a cigarette," he said genially.

I struck a match for him and waited for the password. The Genoese gave it with almost playful nonchalance. "Let's go once more to Tripolis . . ." he hummed in Italian.

That was the first line from a soldiers' song of the Turkish War.

". . . Oh, let's cut off the heads of *Arabis*," I continued.

I sauntered forward. He followed leisurely. In the bosun's locker, I handed him the envelope I had received from Hugo Marx. It had been hidden in a new coil of rope. The Italian tore the envelope open and went over its contents. It contained some typewritten sheets and a sum of money in American dollars. I arranged with him to come aboard that night to take me to a conference of waterfront functionaries. The Italian tore the envelope into tiny shreds. The money he pocketed. The letters he fastened to his thigh with a rubber band. He was ready to depart.

"Good luck," I said. "Don't forget—tonight."

"*Viva Lenin,*" he replied with quiet fervor. *"Ora e sempre!"*

"Let go, forward and aft!"

The *Franken* steamed down the coast of Italy, and several days later she bunkered at Port Said. Coal barges drew alongside, and a band of howling Arab coalheavers overran the ship. I had a letter for the communist harbor organization of Alexandria, the chief port of Egypt. I knew that my Hamburg headquarters had sent word to inform the comrades there of my coming. No doubt they would send a messenger to meet me at Port Said. I waited. For a while I expected the Alexandria courier to be among the hawkers of coral knick-knacks and Turkish delight. But he did not turn up.

The winding banks of the Suez Canal glided by, hot and yellow, deserted except for batteries of mooring poles, a few huts and donkeys, and at times a camel bearing an atrocious load. The *Franken* traversed the length of the Red Sea. Forbidding Bab-el-Mandeb appeared and vanished in a starry night. And after six days' steaming through the leaden Indian Ocean, the anchor went down in Colombo roads.

In the north, crowded and mysterious, lay India. At school in Leningrad I had heard N. M. Roy, the leading East Indian Bolshevik, lecture on the problems of the communist offensive in India. The Party was strong in the industries of Bombay, Madras, Calcutta. Participants in strikes and demonstrations were counted by the hundred thousand. Child labor, the longest hours, the lowest pay, and the highest death rate furnished superb material for agitation. But in India, the obstacles in the way of communist advance were stronger than among more primitive colonials. Primitive people are impatient and virile. The Hindu's chief vice was his senile tradition, his enervation, his passivity. The Communist Party of British India was forced to fight on many different fronts. It fought British imperialism. It fought Gandhi as a traitor to the Indian peoples. It fought the reactionary portion of the native bourgeoisie. It allied itself with the liberal faction and the intelligentsia, with the intention of cutting their throats later. It took pains not to step on the religious toes of the Moslems of the Malabar Coast. And wave after wave of propaganda literature, printed in Moscow and Leningrad, in a dozen of the hundreds of Indian languages, strove to break down the most stubborn obstacle of all — the caste system of the Hindus.

The courier of the Colombo organization, a middle-aged Lascar, was punctual. At sunset he paddled out from shore in a comfortable skiff. He clambered aboard, carrying ebony toy elephants and a bundle of gaudy shawls which he at once began to peddle among the mates and engineers. He wore mended khaki pants and a sleeveless blue shirt, dangling outside his belt. The password that had come to him from Hamburg he shouted loudly all over the ship:

"Who's got for me the London *Times*? I like to read. No matter how old."

I took him forward under the pretense that I wanted to buy a shawl, and handed him his letter. He promised to forward it to Pondicherry, the French colony, where the headquarters of the Maritime Section was established. I found no time to go ashore with him. The *Franken* was at anchor only a few short hours. We parted. As I leaned at the bulwarks, watching the Lascar paddle away in the velvety darkness, I suddenly saw him as a maniac who was trying to cross a stormy ocean in a coffin. For a moment the aim I and he and all of us struggled for seemed endlessly far away. "We are all maniacs, paddling through the night in coffins," I thought. "Dead men on furlough!" I heard the lapping of the harbor water and the thump of the chain cable in the starboard hawse-pipe. On the low shore lights burned dimly. I went below for coffee and a smoke.

The *Franken* steamed eastward, skirting the Bay of Bengal, shunning the dangerous Nicobar Islands. The approaches to Malacca Straits were dotted with shipping with liners and tramps from overseas, with filthy little coastwise steamers, with high-stemmed junks that looked like dozing bats, with native craft of outlandish shape and cut of sail. Around this passage between the Indian Ocean and the China Seas the ports of call lay within a scant day's run from each other. The first was Sabang, rich, green and bluff, a coaling station on the northern tip of Sumatra. Belawan, Pulo Penang, Singapore followed. Here, I had been told, the revolution would strike next. Here the chief consignment of the contraband I carried was to be taken ashore. My tenseness grew from day to day. I slept little. I must not miss the messenger from the Indonesian Party. Whatever the many book-sized packages contained, I had carried them halfway around the world. They were important. I scrutinized each tawny Malay stevedore as he came aboard. I watched the boatmen, the hawkers, the ships-chandlers' runners for a sign of recognition. I even wondered whether the courier I awaited might be among the little ten- and twelve-year-old girls who came aboard to wash the sailors' laundry and to peddle their hips.

Nothing happened in Sabang. No likely stranger approached me while we lay in the glaring roadstead of Penang. Then came Singapore. The lines were hardly fastened around the bitts and the metal rat-guard brought out, when a shipmate hailed me.

"Ho—come here! There's woman asking for you."

Out of a cluster of Chinese dockers stepped a small Chinese woman. She was dressed smoothly in black. Her motions were graceful, her features lean and energetic. She knew my name. In the shelter of the rudder house astern she drew what looked at first glance like a piece of cardboard from her miniature black-and-gold handbag. It was the photograph of a dog.

"Do you like this type of dog?" she inquired pleasantly.

"I have one just like this," I laughed.

So I met M. Lan, the female liaison officer of the Communist Party of Indonesia. She gave me the address of a Babu money changer's booth on a square just outside the limits of the harbor. At night, with the aid of a young Chinese, I smuggled my contraband ashore past a cordon of drowsy Sikhs. Nearby M. Lan sat smoking in a rickshaw.

To this day I do not know the exact nature of the illicit consignment I transported from Rotterdam to Singapore. Taken together, the packages weighed perhaps three hundred pounds. They may have contained Belgian automatics, or ammunition or explosives. In any case, it was dynamite, printed or real, and I was thoroughly glad to see it leave my jurisdiction without a mishap. "Transaction completed," I cabled to Fritz Heckert in Berlin.

The expected revolutionary coup came to pass less than half a year later. In November, 1926, large sections of the toilers of Java rose with guns in their hands. An insurrection in Sumatra followed. Buildings were burned to the ground, railways were blasted, much blood was spilled in battles between the insurgents and government troops. The tactics used by the rebels of Java and Sumatra were much the same as I had witnessed during the barricade fighting in Hamburg. The same, also, was the directing hand behind the scenes. The risings failed. Hundreds fell in battle. Hundreds were wounded. Thousands were captured and sent to the prison camps of New Guinea. Hundreds were summarily condemned to death by military courts.

I deserted the *Franken* in the harbor of Hongkong. The Chinese seamen and dockers were out on strike. British marines patrolled the wharves of this British Crown Colony perched on the edge of a China seething with the promise of revolt. I still had in my possession some four hundred dollars of the Comintern money originally destined for Egypt. I decided to use it for agitation among the British, American and German seamen in Hongkong harbor. But I quickly learned that such a plan was not feasible in a place where the British navy and the British secret service poked flashlights into the obscurest corners. They were hunting high and low for one Kuchiomov, a Comintern agent who had come to Hongkong to organize a continuance of the general strike. Then I learned of the case of Comrade Dosser, another agent of the Comintern who had tried to settle in Hongkong in the guise of a commercial representative. His Eurasian mistress had made an attempt to poison him in his hotel. Dosser tied her hand and foot, and changed his quarters, but was soon arrested and deported. With true Bolshevik pertinacity he returned secretly, was arrested and deported again, but escaped to Shanghai. British agents seized him there, and since then nothing more was heard of Comrade Dosser. This information caused me to decamp. I embarked for Shanghai as a deck passenger on a coastal steamer.

In Shanghai, I reported to a contact address of the Comintern in the lower part of Nanking Road. It turned out to be a barber shop. A Chinese student took my credentials, and told me to wait. The following day we boarded rickshaws and rode out into the beautiful gardens on Bubbling Well Road. To be drawn through the streets by a half-naked and sweating human draft animal made me uncomfortable. The glistening yellow back in front, the patter of bare feet on the burning asphalt, the strident gasps of a voice shouting for the right of way aroused in me an urge to leap off, to pat the perspiring shoulders, to say, "Listen, take it easy, let's have a lemonade together." But the streets of Shanghai were as unsentimental as they were full of motion. Passing me were red-faced mountains of flesh in immaculate white, bearded Sikhs stalking under their turbans with a mixture of meekness and complacent arrogance, dirty children rolling in the gutters, women grunting under fearful loads, chanting traders. And everywhere I saw unsmiling workmen, swinging along the sidewalks, bitterly poor, but able and hardy, prime material for any revolution. "China is Asia!" was a phrase I recalled hearing from the lips of a leader in Leningrad: "If we have China, we also have India and all that lies between."

We stopped at the gardens in the vicinity of the Majestic Hotel. A man with pronounced Slavic features and the manners of a courteous Parisian was waiting there. He was of a type that would fit into the role of a school teacher or of a locomotive engineer. His name was Mandalian. He was the Comintern agent in charge of operations in the district of Shanghai.

No orders regarding my next assignment had come through from Berlin. "We can use you here just as well," Mandalian observed after a few perfunctory questions. His first act was to make me surrender to him the four hundred dollars in my possession. After that we promenaded through the gardens, Mandalian talking in a rapid but disciplined voice, and I straining to catch the significance of every word.

"Don't cock your head to one side like a conspirator," he admonished me before we had sauntered a hundred yards. "There may be watchers. Be *legère*; act like an idle man chatting about the horse races."

Mandalian spoke mainly about the foreign warships and foreign soldiers in China, an armed force which constituted the greatest danger for communist revolution in China. The guns of the gray ships could not be put out of action by a frontal attack of even a million badly armed coolies. Another way had to be taken; the disintegration of the morale of foreign sailors and soldiers by means of persistent propaganda. The Comintern had created a special anti-military department to engage in this work in Shanghai, under the direction of a capable Chinese communist named Siu. The men from the foreign warships simply refused to let themselves be drawn into political discussions by Orientals whom they had been taught to despise. Comrade Siu needed a man who could meet the British and American sailors and marines on their own ground, who could talk their language and be looked upon as an equal. To Mandalian I was that man. Until I got further orders from Berlin, I was to assist Siu in the anti-military department. I met him the same day in the house of the Chinese Seamen's Union.

Comrade Siu had studied in Europe and knew German well. He was a stocky, mobile man in his thirties, married to a Russian girl who acted as his secretary. The number of functions he held was astounding. He was the Party commissar for the Shanghai Seamen's Union. He directed the work of communist spies in the well-organized remnants of the former Kolchak army, whose surviving members were stranded in Shanghai by the thousands. Siu also managed the affairs of the revolutionary student groups in Shanghai. He put a fairly new mimeograph machine at my disposal and introduced me to a group of Japanese and Chinese comrades with whom I was to work. *"Den Panzer kreuzern muessen wir die Zaehne ausziehen,"* he remarked. "Let's pull out the warships' teeth!"

We were blissfully unaware of our own grotesque audacity. Our combined force consisted of a score of assorted communists, including a handful of Japanese and two Scandinavians lusting for adventure. Equipped with a portable printing machine and a weekly allowance totaling a hundred Shanghai dollars, we set out to "pull the teeth" of the combined navies of Britain, France, Japan and America on the lower Yangtze-kiang. The sum we received to finance our fight amounted perhaps to one-fifth of the salary which the Comintern paid to Comrade Mandalian and Comrade Siu. It was they who later spoke learnedly in Moscow conventions about the reasons for the Chinese defeat; we of the rank and file had no word in the matter.

About one-third of the warship crews spent their nights ashore in relays. They frequented the music halls and tingle-tangles of the International Concessions and the brothels and sing-song dives in the Tchapai district. The girls in the brothels were Chinese, hardly more than browbeaten children under a veneer of viciousness, and without a will of their own. Most of them had been sold into slavery by their parents at the time of their first menstruation, and the owners of the brothels discarded them when they reached maturity. These houses of misery were patronized exclusively by Europeans and

Americans, and the majority of the customers were men from the foreign warships and the marine detachments. To the Chinese communists in our unit fell the task of besieging the popular brothels. They joined the waiting rickshaw coolies at the entrance, and plied every arriving bluejacket or marine with tracts containing incitements to disobedience and mutiny. One of the Chinese comrades employed his wife and sister to befriend the girls in the houses for the purpose of smuggling our leaflets into the rooms of the child prostitutes. The latter seemed intrigued by the promise that their greedy and unmerciful masters, the brothel bosses, would be dumped wholesale into the Whangpoo River after the revolution.

The foreigners in our anti-military department, the two Scandinavians, six or seven Japanese and I, concentrated on the music halls of the Nanking Road area. There was always a sprinkling of navy men and marines in the crowds that filled these places night after night. The girls here were Eurasians or the daughters of Russian refugees, rather prettily dressed, lewd, and wholly mercenary. We found some sympathizers among the Eurasians who were willing to accept sheafs of propaganda material for distribution to the bevy of bluejackets each of them had on hand, but this scheme was effectively sabotaged by some of the Russian women who seemed to be acting as undercover agents for local White Guard organizations. Besides, the rivalry between the moody, drink-hungry Russians and their flashier, younger Eurasian sisters was virulent. In the end, there was nothing for us to do but to engage the warship sailors in direct political discussions. Regularly the debates threatened to end in a fight. The bluejackets had come ashore to amuse themselves, and they resented our instructions unless we first invited them to a drink. For that, however, we lacked the money.

In the mass slaughter of communists which followed Chiang Kai-shek's break with Moscow in 1927, nearly all the Chinese comrades I had worked with in Shanghai perished. Years later, after the death penalty for communists had been decreed in Japan, I learned the fate of my Japanese companions. "Comrade Sano and his aides—Fukumoto, Nabejana Mitamura and Takara—were abducted by Japanese secret police in Shanghai and spirited aboard a ship to Kobe." The report which the Comintern received about them bore the comment: *"Vermisst; keine Org-Folgen,"* meaning: "They disappeared. Their disappearance had no damaging consequences to the organization—they kept their secrets like good Bolsheviks."

After three weeks of anti-military work, my sojourn in Shanghai ended abruptly. On a stifling day at the end of July, 1926, Siu, through his Korean courier, asked me to meet him at a corner of the Rue Moliere.

"I have news for you," Siu said.

"Instructions?"

"Right."

He told me that I was needed in San Francisco. He had an address neatly printed on a leaf of yellow cigarette paper.

"Report to this address," he said.

"How the devil am I to get to San Francisco?" I demanded. "I haven't even five dollars."

Siu shrugged his thick shoulders. "You may wait for the money, or you may travel without money. There is nothing a Bolshevik cannot do. In any case, turn over your contacts to Comrade Sano."

Chapter Twelve

FROM SHANGHAI TO SAN QUENTIN

Opposite the Customs Jetty, on the other side of the river, lay the American liner President Wilson. Her home port, San Francisco, was painted across her stern. She was due to sail at dawn. I boarded her during the night, and crawled into a lifeboat on the after deck. Early in the morning, peering through a hole I had cut into the tarpaulin, I saw that the liner was already plowing seaward. I lay face down beneath the thwarts and listened to the far-off hammering of the engines. So a peaceful day passed. I thought I was well on the way to California. But the night brought a surprise.

Unearthly howls came from somewhere quite near the lifeboat. As the howling continued, with brief intervals of quiet, I remembered that wild beasts were often transported in cages to some zoological garden, and thought such a cage had been placed on the after deck. The howling was full-voiced, long-drawn, ending on a note of utter desolation.

I finally squirmed out of the boat to investigate. The stars shone bright in a violet night. Alongside the lifeboat stood a tent. From the inky interior of the tent came the smell of flowers, and the howls.

I entered the tent and struck a match. In the tent was a coffin. The coffin was covered with flowers. At the head of the coffin, fastened to the tent pole, stood the portrait of a Chinaman. Crouched against the side of the coffin was a fat little dog. I sat down on the coffin and caressed the dog. We became friends, and the dog stopped howling.

Suddenly I was startled by the thought that the man in the coffin must be a Chinaman, the one whose portrait was fastened to the tent pole. Chinamen are never carried from China for burial in America; but wealthy Chinese who died in America were often carried to China to be buried in their homeland. I came to the conclusion that the *President Wilson* was not heading for America.

I rushed out of the tent and scanned the horizon. On the starboard side, barely visible, was a low-crouched shoreline. It told me that the *President Wilson* was steaming south, not toward California, but away from it, to Hongkong, perhaps, or Manila, or Singapore!

It was Hongkong. I changed my hiding place to a lifeboat as far away as possible from the corpse and the mourning dog, and two days later I abandoned the *President Wilson* among the piers of Kowloon.

Across the wharf lay another liner, the *Empress of Canada*. Smoke poured from her yellow funnels.

"Where's she going to?" I asked a ships chandler's runner.

"To Vancouver—she's the fastest ship on the Pacific."

Lights blazed from the run-planks and the godowns. The clatter of winches merged with the chatter of tourists and the yells of many Chinamen in the magic singsong of the waterside. Darting through the crowd, I mounted the gangway.

"Ticket, please," chanted a uniformed watchman.

I waved a piece of paper under his nose. "A telegram for Mr. Collins," I bawled, leaping past the guard into the stream of passengers.

Ships did not puzzle me. I veered into a passageway, climbed a companion, ran along the promenade deck, climbed a ladder, and rushed for the *Empress'* third funnel. No smoke came from it. It was a dummy, put there for esthetic reasons. On a long voyage the inside of a funnel was a better hiding place than a lifeboat. I climbed the narrow iron ladder to the platform near the upper rim of the stack.

The siren roared. Whistles shrilled. Soon the ship was moving. The sweetish smell of the shore dropped out of the wind and the *Empress of Canada* forged out to sea. I curled up on a soot-covered grating and slept. The smoke from the forward stacks blotted out the stars.

Before sunrise next morning I climbed down to the deck. I slipped into a luxuriously appointed bathroom. The night aloft had turned me as black as a chimney sweep. I bathed and shaved and cleaned my clothes. I washed my only shirt and dried it over the hot-water pipe. Then I went out on the promenade deck.

Immediately a short, tough-looking man in white and gold accosted me. From the marking on his sleeves I knew him to be the master-at-arms, a sort of seagoing police chief. Without ceremony he asked:

"Do you travel first class?"

"No," I told him, "third."

"I'm sorry," he said, "but this is the first class deck. The third class is forward, two decks below this."

I decamped. The 'tweendecks teemed with a conglomeration of Chinese, Eurasians and a few nondescript whites. Hawkers of soups, biscuits and colored drinks blocked the passageway.

Hungry, I asked one of the flying cooks to let me taste his soup. The soup was hot and good. Just then a deep voice boomed behind me and an enormous paw gripped my shoulders. I whirled. Before me stood a giant in a shoddy brown suit, with fierce eyes and shaggy brown hair turning gray. His breath smelled of the bottle.

I said, "I'm just taking in breakfast."

"Breakfast you call that, what?" the giant bellowed. "Up the Andes and down the Amazon River! How about it? I've been looking for a fellow like you all along. From Iquitos to Pará, astride a mahogany log! Name's Ferguson—what's yours?"

I gave him a name.

"Hell of a name," he boomed. "Come over here, an' meet my friend Killman, Augustus Killman, the best man that ever skinned a Mandarin."

Killman was tall and stringy, with a weather-burned face and deep-set gray eyes. He gripped my hand with a painful grip, and by way of reply I stepped on his toes.

"You're all right," he observed gravely.

Ferguson threw his arms around Killman's neck and mine, and roared: "Up the Andes and down the Amazon, astride a mahogany log".

It was the beginning of the most hilarious illegal voyage I had ever made. The two asked me to join a fan-tan tournament conducted by a potbellied Chinaman and a few half-caste bodyguards on the after hatch. Ferguson gave me ten dollars after I had admitted that I was penniless. I gambled, won at first, and then lost all. Ferguson lost. Killman won steadily, and by sunset his pockets bulged with accumulated rolls of silver.

"Let's go an' have supper," Ferguson said.

I told him I could not go to the dining room because I was a stowaway. Ferguson was not surprised.

"Wait here,' he said.

After dinner Ferguson and Killman invited me to their cabin. From his coat, Ferguson drew a steak, bread, butter and cheese, all wrapped up in a napkin.

"Eat," he boomed. "Up the Andes..."

For eight days I moved freely about the ship, undiscovered. Ferguson supplied me with food which he smuggled from the dining room. He also lent me a set of clean clothes. Each day ended in a wild drinking bout. The nights I spent in deck-chairs and bathrooms. Shanghai, Yokohama and the Inland Sea lay well astern. The *Empress of Canada* cleaved eastward through the open Pacific. America lay only nine days ahead.

It was then that Ferguson, whose liquor supply had given out, said he was tired of "carrying steaks in his pockets." He proposed that I should go into the dining room and take my meals with the other passengers.

I did. It was on the ninth day out of Hongkong. At Ferguson's side I had breakfast and lunch without mishap. During dinner, however, I saw the Eurasian steward count the heads at his tables. I saw him shake his head and count again. Then he disappeared.

"We'll tell him you're our son," chuckled Killman.

The steward bobbed up in the doorway. With him was a man from the purser's office. Both counted. They counted one more than they had on their list. They whispered, and the man from the purser's office narrowed his eyes and nodded. The next minute the steward handed me a sheet of note paper and pencil. Suavely he requested me to write down my name and the number of my cabin.

"G. F. Collins," I wrote. "Stateroom 36."

"Please call at once at the purser's office, sir," the steward purred.

I went topside and climbed to the lofty, soot-encrusted platform inside the upper rim of the *Empress'* third funnel. They found me after a two-hour search. A grinning sailor told me to come down. Three uniformed men received me.

"Beg pardon, sir, may we see your ticket?"
"Sorry, I have none."
"No ticket? Why?"
"No money."
They brought me to the captain.
"Who're you?" the captain demanded.
"Stowaway, sir."
"Nationality?"
"American, sir."
"That's what they all say. Name?"
"Collins."
"Humph! Why not Smith? Got any papers?"
"No, sir."
"Sell 'em?"
"Lost 'em."
The captain smiled broadly. "Got any baggage?"
"No, sir."
"See what he has in his pockets."
The master-at-arms searched me. The search produced a watch, a knife, a razor, a toothbrush and three handkerchiefs.

Then I was assigned to the bosun, a blustering Irishman, and put to work, scraping teak skylights, doors and railings from morning to night with steel scrapers and pieces of glass. I was not alone. I shared the ship's prison—an emergency lazarette on the forward part of the boat deck—with five unkempt Russians, flotsam of the Shanghai waterfront, all of them stowaways caught the first day out.

Time and space spun by. Each day five hundred miles of the Pacific Ocean rushed past the liner's flanks. I plotted and planned means of escape. Killman had procured tor me several pounds of butter. This I augmented with bosun's grease, which is used to grease the blocks and shackles. I found that if I stripped and coated my body with grease and butter, I would be able to wriggle through a porthole. I practiced at night while the Russians were asleep.

Near land the weather changed. The sky was covered with flying scud. There loomed the coast, the hills, the jutting headlands of America. The master-at-arms herded me together with the Russians into the lazarette. He counted: "One, two, three, four, five, six. All right, boys. We'll keep you here till the police come aboard." The heavy teak door slammed shut. The key turned in the lock. The ship cut shoreward, and a little later her anchor rumbled to the bottom. Quarantine. Two hours later the *Empress* nosed her way into Victoria harbor.

The Russians jabbered like excited baboons. They planned to escape after overpowering the Chinaman who would bring us food. The Chinaman came, cautiously, and shoved our breakfast through a porthole which opened on the boat deck. As soon as he had gone, I took off my clothes. I greased my body from shoulder to hip. I threw my clothes out on the boat deck. Then I followed —head out, arms out, shoulders ... I jammed on with clenched teeth. The hard brass ring took off strips of my skin.

Outside I dressed. I put on a pair of sun-glasses I had picked up during the voyage, and mingled with the crowd. People thronged over the gangway. The master-at-arms stood chatting at the rail. He did not recognize me. Two immigration officials at the gangway stopped me.

"Passport?"

I had expected that question.

"Oh, I just came aboard here to ask the mate for a job," I explained.

"How did you get aboard?" one of them snapped.

"With the ships chandler—he's my uncle."

I walked ashore, rounded the corner of a shed, and continued hastily toward the town. Soon a car stopped beside me. My heart missed a beat. A man leaned out of the car.

"Hey," he called out, "do you want a lift?"

Ten minutes later I pondered my situation in a little park on the other side of Victoria. During the day I hid in an empty barge. At night I roamed the waterfront. Far off, barely visible across the Straits of Juan de Fuca, which separates Vancouver Island from the mainland in the south, lay the United States.

I found a rowboat which was tied to a pole, slipped off the painter, and shoved out into the current-infested waters. A wind was blowing. Visibility was low. I rowed madly, heading south. The boat pitched in the sea, standing all but upright at times, and often I had to stop and bail with my cap. I sang in the night, "Death to hangmen, kings and traitors..." I fought the urge to turn around and give up. I cursed myself as a ludicrous lunatic. But I rowed. I rowed all that night. I rowed all of the following day. I rowed all through the following night. I was wolfishly hungry. I soaked my handkerchief in the rain and sucked it dry. My hands were covered with open blisters. I felt that any moment I might crumple in the bottom of the boat and wail.

About eleven in the morning of the third day I landed on a wooded shore. I pushed my boat back into the current, empty, and then collapsed and slept. It was night when I awoke. I found a road and followed it. It led to a small town—Port Angeles. I crossed through Port Angeles and struck a highway which led south.

After considerable hitch-hiking, I arrived in San Francisco, broke but triumphant. I went to report to the address Siu had given me in Shanghai, a rooming house on Clay Street, and asked for Miss Green. I was directed to a comfortable room three flights up. There I confronted a severe-looking girl who wore spectacles. But when she stepped forward, I saw at once that her austerity and her spectacles were camouflage. She had a firm-fleshed body and mischievous eyes. She was not American. Her name, I felt, was not Miss Green.

"I am the comrade from Shanghai," I said.

"You came like this?"

"I came as a stowaway."

She was not suspicious. Mandalian had sent a cable after my departure from China. She made tea and sandwiches.

"What'll be my job here?" I asked.

"You'll see," she said, obliquely.

"American Party work?"

"No. We've no contacts with the Party in the United States. It has gone down to two thousand members this year."

"Well, what am I to do?"

"You'll know soon," she smiled.

The girl went out to telephone and to get me some clothes. I bathed and slept until she returned. "The chief will see you at nine," she said.

In a cozy restaurant, near the Golden Gate Park, the chief was waiting. He was a Russian who posed as an engineer, and went under the name of Getsy. He was a slender man in his forties, with a quiet, intellectual face. His hair and eyes were gray and the suit he wore also was gray. He had the guarded, monotonous voice of a man who had acquired the trick of talking while appearing to be asleep.

Getsy was well informed about my Party record. "Avoid seeing any of your friends here on the Coast," he warned me. "No one except the people I designate must know that you are in California." Turning to the girl, he added, "Give him some money, Gushi."

The girl took a few bills from her purse and pushed them toward me over the table.

"Is there anything else you need just now?"

I looked at the girl. The name Gushi fitted her much better than the distant "Miss Green." She showed her throat and laughed. With half-closed eyes, the Russian gazed at me through the smoke of his cigarette.

Three days I loafed, with nothing to do but to follow my whims. Gushi had arranged for a room for me in the same house in which she lived. Whenever she was not busy with liaison duties for Getsy, we were together. It was obvious from her attitude that she disliked and feared her superior. She never spoke to me about the nature of his activities. She was, I gathered, the only person who knew where Getsy had his secret quarters.

"He is a comrade," she said on one occasion, "but ... he is not human. Nothing exists for him outside his work."

Even more than the run of Comintern workers on foreign missions, Gushi lived on an island of her own, which had almost nothing in common with the habits and customs of the surrounding enemy world. She was forbidden to have friends outside the staff of Getsy's *Apparat*. Every new acquaintance, no matter how harmless, was regarded with suspicion. To her and her kind—and there were thousands like her in the Soviet secret services—all the normal recreations of healthy young people were closed. She would never be able to go her own way, never have a husband and children, never have a real home. The psychological result was a cool and brazen make-believe defiance which had its roots in hidden loneliness and discontent. Gushi was glad to have me as her companion. And I was glad to have her.

"Let's forget everything," Gushi said. "Let's have an orgy."

She sent the house porter for Italian food and liquor, and then we locked the door and drew the shades. Somehow, death-like exhaustion brought on a feeling of freedom. During the day, when Gushi was away on Getsy's business, I rode to the beach and swam through the breakers. At times I thought of swimming out farther and farther, until my strength would leave me and make it impossible for me to return. But I always returned. Gushi would fold up her work when I arrived. "Any news for me?" I would ask.

Then Gushi would thrust her body forward, and say brusquely: "Not yet. Let's drink moonshine. Let's light a candle. Let's have an orgy."

On the fourth day Getsy called me to a conference. Again I met him near Golden Gate Park. He was immaculately colorless, and he gave his instructions in a cold voice. It was a matter of launching a transport of illegal communist literature to Japan. The *President Jefferson,* of the Admiral Line, was due to sail from Seattle to the Orient. Aboard the liner four communists served as members of the crew. They were to smuggle a large consignment of Japanese pamphlets to Yokohama. The position of Japan in the Orient was of the greatest significance for the revolution in China. Next to Britain, Japan was the strongest imperialist factor in the East. The success of a revolution in China depended in part upon effective obstruction—by strikes and sabotage—of Japanese intervention. Since the lines of communication between Vladivostok and Nippon were too closely guarded by the Japanese secret service, all transmissions of money and propaganda material from Moscow to Japan were diverted over the West Coast ports of the United States.

Together with Gushi, I went to Seattle to attend to the shipment which had come by way of New York, packed securely into barrels. I mobilized our assistants aboard the *President Jefferson,* saw to the re-packing of the pamphlets into many smaller units, their transportation and safe concealment aboard the ship, and fixed the passwords to be given to the recipients of the shipment. In less than a week Gushi cabled the Comintern cover address in Yokohama that the 'toys" were on their way.

Gushi was a tireless worker. All her emotional savagery evaporated when she switched her mind to organizational duties. Exalted over the smooth consummation of our assignment, I bought some pretty presents for her and two tickets for a play. She was so pleased that she squeezed my arm and began to dance.

"After the play, let's go and dance," she said. "I haven't been to a dance in eternities."

"You look different," I said, as she brushed her thick blonde hair before the mirror in our hotel room.

"I *am* different."

There was a knock on the door. It was a telegram from Getsy. He ordered me to proceed at once to Los Angeles. He was waiting for me in a hotel.

Gushi's face tightened as I read the message. Her shoulders sagged. "We'll dance another time," she said, adding, with shrill sarcasm: "We've no time to be silly, my friend. It's *marschier oder krepier!*"

"What is this about?" I asked, pointing to the telegram.

"I cannot tell you," she answered slowly.

We parted at the station. I never saw Gushi again.

Late the following night I arrived in Los Angeles. I rode straight to Getsy's hotel. He was in pajamas, a gray-faced somber figure working over papers that were spread out on the desk and on chairs. A fog of cigarette smoke hung in the room. He gathered his papers and locked them into his briefcase before he uttered a word.

"What happened in Seattle?"

"No mishap. Gushi notified Yokohama."

"Very well."

Getsy paced the room, his eyes on the carpet. "There is a serious job you must do," he said.

"All right. What is it?"

"An execution," Getsy said mildly.

I was suddenly on guard. I became tense and inexplicably nervous. This was not what I had expected. Getsy kept pacing the room. His slippers made no sound on the carpet. I noticed that his eyes avoided me. I waited. In a barely audible monotone Getsy went on:

"In the ranks of the revolution we must distinguish three types of hidden enemies. To begin with, there are the trained spies and *agents provocateurs* without whom no police department could score even a temporary victory over our units. The best of these men are smuggled into the movement from the outside; the rest are recruited from among the weaklings and unstable partisans who have stumbled into the Party by mistake. The second category are the saboteurs and disrupters of Party campaigns and Party unity. And then there are those whom we accepted as sincere revolutionists, whom we trusted and honored with important responsibilities, and who saw fit to betray our trust for their own personal gain. The individuals of this last group are by far the most dangerous and despicable. They are the slimy buccaneers who sell the lives of our comrades for money, who steal and plunder and use blackmail, who ferret out our secrets to auction them away to the highest bidder. Such creatures must be hunted down and destroyed like the vipers they are. To leave them alive would be a crime to our movement. This you surely understand. We have no means to bring traitors to an open trial. But we have the means to punish them. Sometimes the traitor flees and goes into hiding, and retribution is delayed. We search for him, and when we find him, we must punish him regardless of how much time and space he has put between himself and his treachery. It is of such a man that I speak."

It seemed as if Gushi's lips were whispering into my ear: "Dear comrade, do you see now why we needed you in America? Somewhere, far away, a tribunal of comrades has condemned a traitor to death, and you were chosen to do the hangman's work. *Marschier oder krepier*—march or croak—and close your eyes if that will make you feel better."

The cigarette I smoked burned my lips, and I snatched it from my mouth. In front of me stood Getsy in wine-colored pajamas, holding an ashtray in his thin gray hands.

"I doubt if I'll make a good terrorist," I said.

"This is not a matter of terrorism. Acts of terrorism are components of a definite revolutionary offensive. Consider this execution as an entirely internal affair."

"It's murder, Comrade Getsy."

"Nonsense. Suppose you have a family. Suppose you have children you dearly love. Suppose you invite a man whom you consider a good friend to stay in your home. Suppose this man who enjoys your hospitality takes a butcher knife and cuts the throats of your children, steals your possessions, and escapes. Is it murder to kill such a man?"

"No."

"Very well."

"Where is the fellow?"

"Here in Los Angeles," Getsy said.

He walked to a closet and rummaged in a pocket of his coat. He took out an envelope, and from it he drew a photograph the size of half a postcard.

"Look at it."

I scrutinized the photograph. It showed the head and the chest of a middle-aged man of heavy Jewish features.

"This man," Getsy said coldly.

"Executions are G.P.U. business," I said.

"Just so!"

"I think a comrade better trained than I should do it."

"I have no other man at hand. It is a pressing matter. All the preliminary work has been done. We have the address." Muttering, he said: "Don't think this is a personal affair. The decision to wipe out this snake does not come from me."

"What did he do?" I demanded.

"What affair is it of yours?" Getsy snapped.

Fear, anger and a stubborn sense of duty battled inside of me. "Suppose I resign?" I said irately. "And go back to Germany." Getsy stiffened. "Resign? I trust you said that rashly. Once in a while we dismiss a man—for cowardice, for disloyalty, maybe for unproletarian conduct. But resign?"

"I did not mean it."

"I know you did not."

"It is one thing to shoot an enemy in barricade fighting. Shoot him in self-defense. Or in a red rage. An altogether different thing is a deliberate killing," I tried to argue.

"A difference of degree, no more," said Getsy.

"If I am to take a man's life, I want to know why."

Getsy came up to me and put his hands on my shoulders. "My dear comrade," he said. 'This man is a traitor—and that's enough. Traitors must die.

That's a universal law, as old as the first tribe."

"Well, I'll have to find out."

"In our organization independent investigations are not permissible. You know that."

"Give me time to think."

Getsy resumed his pacing. I sat in a deep chair, my hands cupped over my head, trying to straighten out a disturbing turmoil in my brain: I had accepted the principle of Red Terror as a necessity. Counter-revolutionists, speculators, spies, traitors, usurers had no right to live. What then was my objection to sending a traitor to the devil with my own hands? A just man sitting by the fireside and reading that a dangerous criminal had been hanged until dead might grunt with warm satisfaction. A judge who had sentenced some luckless scarecrow to the gallows might go home afterward to enjoy a good steak and relax with his wife. But would the just man grunt with satisfaction and the judge find pleasure in his steak and the embrace of his wife if they had to do the hanging with their own hands?

Getsy was pacing to and fro, his hands clasped behind his back, talking, talking. His monotonous voice seemed to cast a spell over the whole room, until it was as gray and pitiless and impersonal as the owner of that voice himself, which was saying: "Bourgeois ethics are not our ethics. Humanitarian considerations, where enemies of the revolution or the Soviet State are concerned, savor of petty bourgeois sentimentality which is incompatible with the demands of class war and the expansion of Soviet power."

Was I a blubbering weakling? Was I seeking refuge in the moral and esthetic ramifications of a world to which I had never belonged? Getsy spoke of his life in the outlawed organizations of the Bolsheviki in Czarist times, told how the hunted revolutionary workers of St. Petersburg and Kiev had captured and executed Ochrana spies in cellars and in the woods. He spoke of Tcheka work during the years of civil war. He spoke of the legions of workers who had become the victims of treachery and were now rotting in countless prisons and graves. Must it be reported to Moscow that I refused to carry out a revolutionary task? That I indirectly strove to shield a traitor to the cause from his inevitable end? Or that I accepted the law that traitors must die, but was too weak and hesitant to uphold it in action? That a better, more devoted comrade than I must be employed for the task? Did not the Comintern possess the status of an army at war? Was it not everywhere understood that a soldier in the front line trenches who refused to level his gun at the foe had forfeited his own life?

There was no way out. Getsy stopped near enough to touch me. His voice was so low that it could not be heard more than a few feet away. Was I afraid of having my neck broken under the gallows for murder? "To prevent that is merely a question of organization," Getsy said. Thousandfold worse than hanging was ostracism from the Party. Here was a traitor who thought he had at last found a safe refuge. He would use the knowledge he had, to destroy those whose trust he had betrayed. Therefore he himself must be destroyed.

"Comrade Getsy," I wanted to say, "why not do the assassinating yourself?"

"All right," I said. "I shall do it."

Getsy let himself drop into a chair.

"When?" I asked.

"Without delay," Getsy said. "Is your head clear? Very well! Let's consider the details." The Russian's voice was dry and cold.

The following days were filled with a mad exasperation, a wild craving for sleep and escape, and futile efforts at self-hypnosis to shut out and down the agony brought on by doubts and hesitations. The specters of that bloody Hamburg October of 1923 now came back to plague me. It was not fear that troubled me. It was a battle between my blind sense of duty and the spontaneous rebellion of my nature against the alien savor of the projected enterprise. The struggle left me mutinous and in a daze. In a daze, clumsily, I tackled the assignment, in a manner that would have drawn contemptuous jeers from Hugo Marx and the fatuous Felix Neumann. I found the man whom Getsy's spies had tracked down, and assaulted him in broad daylight off a crowded street, knowing beforehand that the assault would end in failure. I struck him once with the butt of a revolver, in a gesture of violence that was more a blundering appeasement of a perverse sense of duty than the expression of an intent to destroy. My astonished quarry roared for help, and I ran like a man in a trance, vaguely aware of the fact that I had not even made the least preparation for a successful getaway.

A truck driver was running in my direction. Barbers emerged from a nearby barber shop. They rushed in pursuit of me, swinging their scissors. I ran two blocks and then darted into a small hotel, and up the stairs to reach the roof of the building. I fell on the stairs, and when I rose I saw the truck driver and three barbers storm up the staircase.

"Stand back,' I said.

The foremost barber, a lanky, fearless individual, brandished his scissors.

"Stand still, or we'll rip you to pieces."

I made no attempt to resist them. Complete indifference and a great weariness engulfed me. The barbers led me to the barber shop. A hooting crowd followed.

"Hit him on the jaw! String him up!" There were yells and laughter.

"First man who hits him gets ripped up," a barber warned.

Then police arrived. Handcuffs were snapped around my wrists. "All right, boy, come along now," a policeman said comfortably.

I was questioned by two detectives in a large room on the ground floor of the Los Angeles city jail. Both were powerful men in their thirties. Occasionally they made notes on large yellow pads. They seemed satisfied with the information I gave about myself until they touched the cause of my arrest.

"What'd you hit this man for? What was the big idea?"

I was silent.

"Why'd you do it?"

"He sneered at me and I got mad at him."

"Aw, go on. You want us to get rough with you?"

Silence.

"We're going to knock the living Jesus out of you. How'd you like that?"

I looked toward the door. Outside the sun shone brightly. A detective saw the direction of my glance. He picked up his revolver from the table.

"Don't try to run," he growled. "I'll brain you with this."

"I'm not going to run," I said.

"Who were your partners?"

"I had no partners."

"The lone wolf, what? You better tell us who your partners were."

Silence.

One of the two got up and stepped behind me. He grasped my hair and jerked my head backward. His free fist tapped the ridge of my nose.

"Come on, now—who were your partners?"

"I tell you I did it alone," I cried.

"Where do you live?"

"I had no room. I came into town this morning."

"Where'd you come from?"

"British Columbia."

"You look like a guy who's responsible for a lot of holdups around here."

"I did nothing of the sort."

"No? How long you been a gunman? Who're you working for anyhow?"

"I'm working for nobody. I came here to find a job."

By this time four or five other detectives had assembled and were standing around me in a close circle. Using their fists they began to push me back and forth in the circle. All of them muttered threats. When they stopped, one of them said: "You better come clean. Tell us all about it."

The questioning continued for another half hour, without further results. I felt depressed. Inwardly I cursed Getsy. The detectives, skeptical as they were, failed to penetrate my defense. My lips were swollen and the left side of my face was bruised before the rough-and-tumble interview ended.

I was thrown into a large, cage-like space in what seemed to be the basement of the building. The floor was of iron. The sides consisted of steel bars covered with strong wire meshing which reached from floor to ceiling. The ceiling also was of iron. Around the outside of the cage was a narrow runway for the guards and beyond that the grimy outer walls of the building. There was no window in sight. Electric lights glared day and night. Dirty canvas hammocks were suspended from steel racks in two tiers. In a corner was a faucet and a broken down toilet.

It was the filthiest jail of the many I have known. It was crammed with prisoners. The strongest, using their superior brawn, took possession of the hammocks. The weakest were forced to curl up on the iron floor. There were no blankets, no soap, and no toilet paper. Old past masters of bestiality and frightened first offenders, burglars, auto thieves, pimps and boys caught drinking from a hip flask rubbed shoulders freely. Men picking vermin out of their shirts during the day, and sexual perverts struggling with newly acquired punks during the night, were a common sight. The sounds of banging doors and names shouted by policemen and trusties made a continuous noise. Recalcitrant prisoners were manhandled by the trusties under the eyes of police officials. An exasperated negro who kept yelling for morphine was beaten perhaps ten times during a single day.

"What now?" I asked myself. "Will the Comintern make a campaign in my behalf?" Never. That was clear. The solicitude which Moscow showed for men of the caliber of Gorev-Skoblevski was not for the much more numerous lesser legionnaires in the service. No one would bicker for an exchange of prisoners in my case, even if such a thing would be feasible in America. My chiefs would expect me to "march or croak"—or both, as all the generals expect their cannon fodder to do. I listened to a fellow prisoner explain luxuriously the details of a hanging. A policeman and two trusties were beating the sick negro because he kept on howling for morphine. The negro writhed on the dirty steel, whining a prayer. His torturers had flushed faces, as if each had come straight from a successful seduction. A rough voice barked at the negro: "Pipe down, you black bastard!"

Toward the end of the second day I was called out of the cage and ushered into a small windowless room. Here I waited, surrounded by absolute silence, wondering what was to come.

Finally a detective entered. I had not seen him before. He greeted me jovially and offered me a cigarette.

I sat down, looking into his bland smile.

"Now, my boy," he began, "you know why you're here and you know that this situation can bring you in a tight spot if you don't act just right. You're a bright young fellow, and I'm not going to try to fool you because I know that won't work. I've got a son about your age; so I'm sorry to see a youngster like you in this place. I thought I'd come in and find out from you what was the trouble. Don't tell me anything if you don't want to. Those other guys who hit you don't know their face from a hole in the ground. Just too dumb, you see? I believe in giving a man a decent break. I thought I'd come to see you and let you tell me your story just as it happened. I'd be glad to help you. Now just take it easy. Don't tell me a whit if you think that's the smart thing to do."

This was dangerous. I gripped my hands tightly under the table and told the same story I had told the detectives who had first examined me.

"That's all right," my questioner continued after I had ended. "But why should a nice kid like you try to protect anybody who doesn't deserve it? You ain't the kind to beat daylights out of a fellow because he wouldn't give you a drink of water. Did that man hurt you sometime before? Or play you some dirty trick? Or was just somebody else trying to make a sucker out of you, making you bash in another guy's brains? What'd you get out of it? Nothing! And the guy who hired you, why, maybe he's wrapping himself around a good juicy steak with fried potatoes right now. Ain't I right?"

I struggled against the hypnotic effect of the man's persuasive voice. The method he used was one no prisoner expects to encounter. His eyes were kind; his face remained pleasantly relaxed. With a clumsy show of dogged-ness I held on to the original version of my motive.

The other purred on, "Why, I could get you a suspended sentence easy. A boy like you don't belong in jail. Think of all the nice girls walking around outside. Or all the boys of your age taking out the girls in their cars. Take 'em to a good dinner, take 'em to the beaches. That's fun, kid! You could stay at my house when you get out till you've found yourself a good job. I wouldn't mind that. Only I sure hate to see you in jail."

The man was an expert. He did not know how near he was to winning his clever battle when he looked at his watch and pretended to be astonished how quick the time had passed. He patted me on the shoulder and shook hands.

"Well, so long. Think it over. I'll see you again."

I did not see him again. But I was visited later by the same detectives who had questioned me immediately after the arrest. They were in shirt sleeves, and one of them had a two-foot piece of garden hose in his hand. The other put a piece of paper and a pencil on the table.

"Better write down the names of your confederates," he commanded. "Write down what you tried to do. Write 'robbery' or 'attempted murder' or whatever it was."

I bent down over the table and took the pencil into my hand. I wrote nothing.

One detective clamped my head under his crooked arm and his colleague flogged me with the piece of rubber hose. When he had finished, his face was red and he was breathing hard. The other twisted my arm. But I did not write. The detectives left me. They promised to return in five minutes to continue the procedure. That was all I saw of them.

My next abode was the county jail atop the skyscraper City Hall. This was a highly modern place of confinement, clean, and operated in an efficient manner. The prisoners were kept in batches of thirty in long, narrow cages. At night we were locked into two-man cells the doors of which were opened and closed by electricity. At no time were we let out for exercise in fresh air, as is the custom throughout Europe. But through partly opened windows we could see the street traffic far below, and the less restrained among us amused themselves by directing piercing yells at girls passing on the distant sidewalks. I studied the various types of outlaws, sneaks and simple unfortunates, and endeavored to understand their attitudes toward life. Weeks passed. I shunned all contacts with the outside world, so as not to endanger Getsy's organization.

One morning I was called to one of the small visitors' rooms. A dapper young man with long eyelashes and a flashy tie told me he was a lawyer, come to prepare my defense. I took him for a special sort of spy for the police.

"I need no lawyer," I said. "Please go away and leave me alone."

"I am satisfied," he smiled. "I see you have not weakened. Getsy sent me."

Startled, I was still distrustful. "Getsy?" I answered. "Oh, I remember. He likes to wear loud neckties."

"No," the lawyer said promptly. "His ties are gray, always gray."

That convinced me. I asked him what I should do.

"At any price, avoid questioning. We want no more inquiries. Don't wait for a trial. Plead guilty, and get it over with."

"Plead guilty to what?"

"Anything. Make them stop probing. Don't allow them to call up witnesses."

"All right."

"Ask for a public defender, and tell him you want to plead guilty."

That was all. He gave me a firm handshake, a keen glance, and then he departed as smoothly as he had come. A few days later I pleaded guilty in Superior Court to the charge of "assault with a deadly weapon." No witnesses were called; no further questions were asked. Two minutes after I had entered the court room, the judge sentenced me to from one to ten years in San Quentin prison.

BOOK TWO

THE DANCE OF DARKNESS

Chapter Thirteen

NEW WEAPONS

A thousand days I lived behind the gray walls of San Quentin, wearing the gray felon's garb, rubbing shoulders with thousands of fellow convicts under the eyes and the clubs and the guns of the guards. I entered the prison in a mutinous mood, breathing and talking rebellion, and thinking of ways of escape. A man in prison is supposed to rot. Prisons are built to break men, and when a man is broken, society has consummated its revenge. But I was determined not to be broken. I recognized quickly how impotent even the toughest criminal was against the massive authority of the prison administration. As time went by I discarded all plans of escape, crushed the inner urge to play the futile role of a mutineer, and settled down in earnest to defeat the purpose of imprisonment by making myself stronger and more capable to fill my place in the revolutionary struggles of the future. Through the first year I toiled in the roar and clatter of the prison jute mill. In the second year I advanced to the job of a prison librarian. And the third year saw me as a teacher of languages and mathematics in San Quentin's educational department. They were not peaceful years; prison life is not monotonous, but brimful of struggle and strife, victory and defeat in manifold forms.

Neither were they empty years, despite the utter absence of privacy and women. I was too occupied to suffer under such mild hardship. Far more important to me than yearning for pleasures beyond my reach was the forward plunge into a new world of zestful discoveries and intensive self-education. San Quentin gave me far more than it could take away. It had developed in me a passionate reverence for the universe of letters. I read and studied almost everything I could lay my hands on, from *Lord Jim* and *Jean Christophe* to Darwin's *Origin of Species* and Bowditch's *Epitome of Navigation*. I mastered English, learned French and Spanish, studied Astronomy, Journalism and Map-Making—courses made available to the inmates of San Quentin by the University of California. I became a contributor to the prison magazine, the *Bulletin,* and in its printing plant became proficient in the craft of typesetting. Throughout this period I remained the loyal legionnaire of the Comintern. I had established a secret prison library of revolutionary literature, and had organized Marxist schooling circles and an atheist league among the convicts. Despite the prison censorship, I had maintained contact with the Comintern network outside. So immersed was I in my self-imposed tasks that I at first regarded my parole and subsequent release as an unwelcome disturbance of an engrossing life. However, the Comintern expected my return to

Berlin. I left San Quentin in the first days of December, 1929.

"Luck to you," grinned the guard at the front gate.

Three days later I boarded a steamer bound for Europe. Le Havre was the first port of call. During the routine customs and police examination of passengers and crew a French official with wine-happy eyes singled me out for special attention. I had no French visa; neither had I any baggage or money. *"Monsieur,"* he said, "you cannot travel in France. We must detain you." He escorted me to the Immigrant Home near the waterfront. There I was led to a room which contained a bed, a table, a washstand and a chair.

Departing, the officer said, "In the morning the authorities will decide what to do with you."

I did not wait for morning. My room had a tiny window, and twelve feet beneath the window ledge was the sidewalk of a quiet street. Throughout the night a middle-aged sentry patrolled around the building, passing every two or three minutes under my window. The night was raw and squally. I watched until the sentry had rounded a corner; then I wriggled out, feet first until I hung from the ledge. I let go, and dropped to the pavement. The wind whistled between the houses. At the end of the street, lights shone on a wharf. I ran. I was free!

I tramped the streets of Le Havre all night, intoxicated with deep draughts of freedom. A man lives his life only when he is marching, I thought, when he keeps marching onward at any price. When he stops marching, he decays. The joy of life is the joy of the experience that comes from feeling one's own strength. In the thousand days spent in San Quentin I had never stopped marching. That is why I strode the streets of Le Havre, through driving rain and darkness, with eager delight, drinking the raw December air like a honeymoon wine. I climbed high to the top of the steep promontory, where the lighthouse looms, for no other purpose than to shout my gladness and my challenge into the wind-filled night.

I came to my senses toward dawn. My shabby suit had wilted like burlap in the rain. The wind had carried away my cap, and my shoes were oozing water and mud. For two hours I wandered about in search of the offices of the Communist Party of Le Havre, but in vain. I did not ask for directions. People might become suspicious at the sight of a disheveled foreigner inquiring for the communist headquarters.

I made my way to the harbor. Beyond a breakfast and a chance to dry my clothes there were three things I wanted most. I wanted to hear the word "Comrade." I wanted a woman. I wanted to feast my eyes and brain on something that was impersonal and beautiful at once. The first ship I boarded in my quest for breakfast was a British weekly boat from Cardiff. A Cockney officer, belching vituperation with enormous lung power, drove me off. It was good to hear the old Limey salt water curses. Next I boarded a Norwegian Far Eastern freighter. The Norseman was as clean as the English ship was dirty, and the Norwegian sailors met me with the traditional hospitality of their country. They gave me a powerful breakfast of coffee, oatmeal, French bread, salt fish and chewing tobacco, and while I ate they unstintingly praised the temperament of the Le Havre wenches and the natural beauties of Norway. I stripped and hung my clothes over a radiator to dry.

At noon, while the crew was in the mess room for lunch, a young Scandinavian from ashore entered, and started out on a political harangue. He then pulled wads of leaflets from under his belt and distributed them to the sailors, who addressed the newcomer as Comrade Soeder. The headline on the leaflets ran: *"Who are the enemies of the seamen?"* The emblem they displayed—a globe crossed by an anchor and a flag—was the insignia of the Maritime Section of the Comintern. Soeder was a member of the Havre "activist" brigades. I almost hugged him for joy, and told him who I was. "Welcome, comrade," he said.

"Comrade" was still a magic word to me. Toward evening we walked ashore together. Soeder warned me:

"Be careful about what you say when you meet the comrades higher up. You've been away a long time."

"Why careful?"

"Well, just be careful. There've been big clean-ups in the Comintern. The Comintern has changed its face. It has been unified. It is now going like a torpedo. One direction only. No more vagaries. No internal discussions. No compromises."

I was to learn much more about this change of face during the coming weeks. Zinoviev and Trotsky had been purged. Bukharin was pushed away from the helm of the Comintern. Stalin now dominated Russia and, therefore, the Comintern as well. He had launched the gigantic industrialization program of the Five-Year-Plan, and those who opposed him were trampled into the gutter. Purges in Moscow were followed by purges in the Comintern, whose organizations changed their role of assault troops of the world revolution for the role of defense guards of the Soviet Union. And the most militant formations of the Comintern fell into line with fervor; the Five-Year-Plan would make the Soviet Union the strongest industrial and military power on earth. That was decisive. The immense strength of the new Soviet Union would guarantee the victory of the great revolutionary offensive of the future.

No army could boast of a more rigid organization or of a more uncompromising discipline than the Comintern under Stalin. In the consciousness of every communist the word *Parteibefehl*—Party Order—towered paramount and inexorable. Any display of independence and originality of spirit was regarded as caprice and manifestation of a bourgeois heritage. Courage, devotion, tenacity were demanded, and, above all, a blind trust in the idealism and the infallibility of the Politbureau in Moscow. With this policy, the backbone of the Comintern—the strata of "activists" between the top-flight leaders and the rank and file—was well content. An army whose generals were pulling in different directions was doomed to defeat.

Soeder led me to the resident liaison agent of the Comintern and G.P.U. in Le Havre. Such agents are stationed in all important harbor and inland cities. Their official duty was to provide contacts and safe conduct for international functionaries assigned to, or passing through, their districts. They provided cover addresses for all conspirative mail and literature consignments. They received and distributed the Comintern subsidies for the local organizations.

Aside from this, they had the function of keeping a close check on the "activities" and the private lives of Party members in the area under their supervision. All official reports of the Party leaders were tested for accuracy in Berlin and Moscow by comparing them with the concurrent secret reports of the liaison agent on the spot. Invariably these agents were natives of the country in which they worked; invariably they were on the payroll of the G.P.U.

The man at the head of the *Apparat* in Le Havre was a French schoolteacher named Cance, a dark, hard-boiled little man with a clipped mustache, who thoroughly enjoyed his job. He was a captain-of-the-reserve in the army of the French Republic. He was still at his secret post as late as 1937, at the time of the abduction in Paris of the White Russian leader, General de Miller, all traces of whom were lost at Le Havre, where a Soviet steamer left on the morning after the abduction. Second in command of the Le Havre *Apparat* was his wife, a beautiful, gray-eyed, flaxen-haired young woman. They lived in a spacious, well-proportioned house of their own (58, Rue Montmirail), atop a hill overlooking the town, the mouth of the Seine, and the wide sweep of the harbor with its cleverly camouflaged shore batteries and fortifications.

M. Cance was a perfect host, and a marvel of efficiency. He jotted down the information I gave him about myself, put it instantly into code, and dispatched his young son to telegraph it to Berlin for verification. A few minutes later a succulent meal was on the table, together with wines and assorted liqueurs. Madame Cance was bewitching. Her cherry-red lips talked in a language that sounded like music. Before she married, she had been a dancer. Later in the evening she donned a flowing garment of raw silk, held together by a golden chain around her waist, and she danced while Cance played the fiddle. A pantomime which they called the "Death March of the Paris Commune" followed. It opened with a wild rhythm of advancing Communardes and ended in a frantic *"Vive la Commune!"* and a piteous whimper before the exploding rifles of the firing-squad. Soon I was reeling through a voluptuous fog, not knowing whether it was due to the uncanny performance of Madame Cance, or the quantity of liquor I had poured down my throat. A score of times I saw the sanguine face of Cance bob through the mist and I heard his soldier voice yell:

"Buvez, mon ami, et vivez joyeux!"

I had been a hard drinker in my earlier years at sea, but I was no match for Comrade Cance. He kept my glass filled and urged me to drink and to keep on drinking. He exhorted me to recount "the best adventures" of my youth. He did it to sound me out to rock-bottom.

"Certainement," Madame Cance laughed.

"It is to your own advantage, *camarade,"* her husband added.

I talked like a waterfall, as men will talk when the pressure of prison has been lifted from their brains. It was Cance's business to probe and to spy. I did not mind. I had nothing to fear. Their guest room, which was mine for the night, had sheltered, I was told, distinguished visitors: Romain Rolland,

Bela Kun, Kuusinen, Albert Walter, Andre Marty, Tom Mann and a host of other Comintern agents, like the Finn Sirola, alias Miller, the Red Army General Gussev, alias P. Green, the Briton Harry Pollitt, who had stopped off here on their way from Moscow to New York. About each of them Comrade Cance had an amusing story to tell. Bela Kun had insisted that his interpreter must be a vivacious brunette, and willing to go to bed with him. Kuusinen had had a tom-cat's aversion to cold water. General Gussev had brought his own vodka, and had demanded two girls at once. Harry Pollitt had blushed like a clergyman from Kensington. Albert Walter had been a perfect gentleman, but he detested women. Romain Rolland had droopingly regretted that he had taken his secretary along to Le Havre. And so on. With devilish versatility Comrade Cance impersonated them all. Madame Cance sipped liqueurs, and regarded her husband with steady eyes and a half-mocking smile. And then he unexpectedly produced the pictures of three girls. One by one he handed them to me, speaking the while as if explaining the layout of his garden to a friend:

"*Voici,* Suzanne—bitter-sweet and demure. *Voilà la petite* Babette, of large experience, but exquisite. *Et c'est* Marcelle—who is a real filly. They are the brides of the Comintern *au* Havre. Choose. Which one shall it be?"

I was too surprised to answer at once. Madame Cance leaned forward, and said earnestly: *"Allez, camarade, pourqois pas?* To each according to his needs." Cance gave a barking laugh.

"We are no ascetics," he announced. "The Bolsheviki and the Parisians—there are no truer hedonists in our century."

"A comrade who comes from prison deserves the best," chimed in Madame Cance.

Cance telephoned. Marcelle was away; she had gone to visit her mother in Rouen. Suzanne was at home. Cance grinned into the telephone. A comrade *de l'Amerique?* Just returned from prison? Young? Of course, she would come!

Madame Cance retired. My host experimented with the radio. Dreamy waltz music streamed into the room. "We shall retain the best of bourgeois culture after we have destroyed the bourgeoisie," he observed. "You long for beauty! Don't miss the Louvre when you pass through Paris."

"The girl—is she a prostitute?" I asked.

"Mais non," he replied quickly, *"elle est une activiste!"*

A message from Berlin, relayed over Basle to make it appear that it originated there, arrived in the middle of the night. It confirmed my identity. I was awakened by singing at seven in the morning. In the vestibule of the house, Comrade Cance snapped commands as he, his wife and son were doing their morning gymnastics. After breakfast of café-*au-lait* and dry French bread, my host supplied me with a hundred francs and an address in Paris, and drove me to the station. Suzanne was with us. She accompanied me to the train until a few seconds before its departure. Police agents looking for a supposedly homeless fugitive would never suspect him in a man escorted to a train by a chattering young lady. Soon I was speeding toward Rouen, and on, along the winding valley of the Seine, plunging through tunnels and many times crossing the meandering river. The sun shone on the boulevards when I arrived in Paris. The streets were strangely quiet. People were still resting from their Christmas celebrations.

At a Métro station I studied a plan of the city. I sauntered away at random, choosing the boulevards the names of which best appealed to my imagination, and late in the afternoon I came upon the Seine in the vicinity of the Bastille. I followed the Seine until I came to the Louvre. There I crossed a little bridge to the left bank, traversed a gloomy dungeon-like passage, and found myself in a narrow old street lined with shops of book merchants and dealers in pictures and antiquities. It was Rue de Seine. I looked for number 63, the address of the liaison agent of the G.P.U. A sulky concierge answered the bell. Following the directions I had been given by Cance, I asked to see Monsieur Ginsburg, the architect. The concierge snapped to alertness. She gave me a piercing look. *"Entrez, monsieur!"* She led me through a silent courtyard and into a building in the rear. She opened a door, using a latch key.

"Entrez, monsieur!"

I entered a small, completely empty room. Its only window opened into what seemed to be a narrow air shaft. I turned to tell the concierge that she had probably made a mistake. But the door had clicked shut. It had no knob on the inside. I was locked in. On the other side, the concierge mumbled, *"Attendez, monsieur."*

After a while I heard a man's voice, subdued, but angry. The door was opened. A slender young man of less than medium height greeted me. He had a pale, sharply cut and intelligent face, sharp greenish eyes, and a high forehead. He wore glasses. *"Bitte tausendmal um Verzeihung,"* he said in cultured German, "Our friend Cance has telephoned me about you. The concierge is a fool. Please step into the *atelier*. My name is Ginsburg."

The *atelier* was spacious and light. New steel furniture upholstered in bright colors, stacks of blueprints, bookshelves, office machines, maps, a vase full of yellow flowers, reproductions of famous paintings on the walls and a bronze miniature of the Laocoon Group on a pedestal in a corner, gave the place a mixed flavor of cold efficiency and cheerful warmth. R. W. (Roger Walter) Ginsburg was an architect, a thoroughgoing European of undefinable nationality. He had a charming young companion, a native of Alsace and a linguist of mark, whom he introduced to me as his wife. Her name was Doris. At a table, going through a stack of mail, sat two dusky, black-haired and black-eyed men. Hearing that I had come from the United States, they immediately engaged me in an excited conversation in which Doris Ginsburg acted as interpreter.

This architect's office in the Rue de Seine was probably the most cosmopolitan rendezvous of the Soviet secret services in Western Europe. Traveling instructors of the Comintern and agents of the G.P.U., coming and going on the broad road that led from Moscow to Berlin and Paris, never neglected to call on Roger Ginsburg for their mail, for an exchange of passports, for money, for safe accommodation in the homes of Party members, or to contact collaborators, to collect material for internal intrigues, and to deposit their reports for delivery to the next courier to Berlin and Moscow. No incriminating written material, other than that which callers could carry in their pockets, was ever allowed to litter the *atelier*. For each branch of his department Ginsburg maintained a separate apartment in adjoining houses, the tenants of which were Party members assigned to serve the *Apparat*. The Parisian *Sûreté,* supposedly so crafty, was a laughing stock in Ginsburg's *atelier*.

I was quartered in the Hotel d'Alsace, in a quiet street branching off from the Rue de Seine. It was a Comintern hotel, staffed by communists, and managed by a husky blonde woman who ransacked the rooms of her guests whenever it pleased her, tolerating no scrap of evidence of revolutionary schemes in her domain. She spoke English in the American way. Her "Okays" rang through ceilings and walls. When someone telephoned, she insisted on listening to what was said, though she offered no objections when her guests brought girls into their rooms, provided that the purpose was not dictation, but *l'amour!*

The two dark-haired individuals I met during my first call at the *atelier* turned out to be communist chieftains from South America. One was Urso, from Paraguay, the other was Perez, the head of the Uruguayan Communist Party. Both had come from Moscow, and they were stopping off in Paris to await the arrival of an important comrade from Berlin, one Harry Berger, to confer on the details of a certain campaign in the Latin-American countries. I almost emitted a guffaw when I saw the powerful head and the square shoulders of 'Harry Berger" appearing in the room. I recognized him in a flash. He was Arthur Ewert, who had been my political instructor at the Communist University in Leningrad. I gave no sign of recognition. Neither did he. To the South Americans, he was *Camarado* Berger. After a few jovial preliminaries, he tore into them with sledge-hammer blows of broken Spanish, berating them, I gathered, for "syndicalistic tendencies" and "opportunist deviations." Other callers interrupted, and the three departed to continue their conference in the *Jardins Tuileries*.

On two afternoons I helped Doris Ginsburg to translate reports and resolutions from German into English. One of the documents was a manifesto of the Western Secretariat of the Comintern, calling for the organization of hunger marches in every country on February 1, 1930. Another was a report on the decisions made by an international conference of negro delegates in Vladivostok. A third contained a long list of factories and mines in Algeria and Tunisia, in which communist cells had been established. This was mere routine to Doris. To me it was fascinating work. It gave me a conception of the vastness of the organization of which I was a part.

The following morning Doris asked me to act as interpreter at a conference of a group of foreign communists, with Racamond and Frachon, the leaders of the Red Trade Union bloc in France, the CGTU, which counted several hundred thousand members and was the strongest section of the Profintern. Doris herself had other pressing work. I accepted her proposal with alacrity.

The conference took place in a worker's dwelling in the suburb of St. Denis.

I met the two Frenchmen at the headquarters of the Red Trade Unions, a rambling agglomeration of buildings on Rue des Granges aux Belles, and together with a quiet girl secretary we made the tedious journey to St. Denis. Julien Racamond was a scarred old oak among men, slow-moving, quick-thinking, one of the rare communist leaders who really had influence among the masses. His colleague, Benoit Frachon, a thick-set but mobile man, enjoyed the reputation of being the foremost expert on revolutionary strategy and organization in France. Sitting between them in the Métro, I felt much like a junior lieutenant jammed in between two grizzled generals.

A strange group was waiting for us at the meeting place in St. Denis. There were four men and a woman. One was an emaciated and sad-looking East Indian. Beside him sat a pudgy, lively man whom the others addressed as Mustafa Sadi. He was a Syrian. The other two were Ratti, an Italian organizer from Marseilles, and Allan, a big, blond Scot, who looked like a prosperous merchant. The woman was quiet-eyed and reserved. She had rings on her fingers, and she crouched on the sofa with a fur coat wrapped around her. I later met her in England. She was the wife of a British Comintern agent with a long record of intrigues in Germany, the United States, and China. All of them spoke English. But Racamond and Frachon knew only French. Sentence by sentence I translated English into German, and the girl interpreter then put my German into French.

So, for the first time in my life, I had an opportunity to watch at first hand one of those informal conferences of conspirators of international caliber, which inevitably resulted in strikes, raids, shootings, headlines, and wholesale jailings in places hundreds and often thousands of miles away. This particular conference dealt with impending campaigns in Syria, Palestine, Transjordania, and Egypt. Mrs. Hardy made a report on the political situation in the Near East. Julien Racamond, heavy-handed and gruff, laid down the policy and the general line of action for the future. Benoit Frachon cleared up fine points of tactics. The subject of the conference was to decide on ways of harnessing the militant nationalist element among the Arabs to the Comintern wagon. Propaganda literature was to be shipped. Arms were to be smuggled. Agitators and organizers had to be placed in every coastal town between Alexandrette and Alexandria. Then there was talk of chartering a Greek or Turkish steamer; of a Jewish superintendent in Tel Aviv whom no one suspected of being a communist; of slogans which would not meet with the antagonism of the Moslems on religious grounds; of the organization of terror groups to harass the soldiery of Britain and France; of campaigns to fight the surrender to France of Syrian rebels who had been caught by British troops in Transjordania; of Arabs who were to be sent to a university in Moscow; of strikes and passive resistance; and of the advisability of launching a wave of sabotage acts against the railroads. The headquarters for the communist efforts in the Near East was located in Marseilles. Its traffic manager was Ratti, the Italian. Everybody present made notes, and everybody smoked and drank *vin rouge*.

This meeting had no secretary and no chairman. Racamond ruled it, and,

I gathered, that he controlled the subsidies of the Comintern for the whole Near East. Sums were mentioned: five hundred francs, seven thousand francs, twelve million francs. The East Indian bargained in a hollow voice. Mustafa Sadi got up and shrieked like a hysterical woman, tears rolling down his ample cheeks, pleading with Racamond for a thousand francs more. Allan, the burly Scot, waxed sardonic. But Racamond, ably seconded by the cold-blooded Frachon, ruled the meeting. Racamond would jump to his feet and shake his enormous fists over the head of Mustafa Sadi, as if he were about to murder him. In no time at all, five hours flew by. The meeting broke up. Racamond, cracking jokes, departed. Frachon followed him like a shadow. The East Indian looked as if he was about to fall asleep. Mustafa Sadi mopped perspiration from his forehead. Allan scanned a London *Times*. The Englishwoman yawned and wrapped her fur coat tighter about her angular figure. Things were settled. Soon the money would change hands, printing presses would thunder, couriers would start out with false passports and suitcases with double covers, and somewhere in the Near East gendarmerie and troops were scheduled to work overtime.

Back in the Rue de Seine, where I went to receive final directions for my departure to Berlin next day, Roger Ginsburg told me that Arthur Ewert wished to talk to me. Ginsburg said confidentially: "I think you should know that Comrade Ewert's position in the Comintern is not very firm. He is a capable Bolshevik, but unfortunately he has a head of his own."

The Ewert I met was very gentle and very human, almost soft, which was a strange thing in a fighter of his experience and ability. He spoke of his past. From his job in Leningrad, he had been sent to America, and for some time he had been the virtual dictator of the Communist Party of the United States. An intrigue spun by Thaelmann in Berlin had brought him back to Moscow in 1929. In such cases, it was difficult to discern where the political motives ended and the personal motives began. The two leaders then aired their differences in Moscow in the presence of Molotov and Manuilsky. Arthur Ewert was the loser. Yet Ewert was convinced that he was right. He favored an alliance with the German Social Democrats and a united front against the rapidly rising National Socialist Party of Hitler. On the other hand, Thaelmann, backed by Moscow, maintained that the Socialists, the rivals in the camp of labor, were the chief enemies of the communist movement. *"Der Hauptfeind ist die Sozialdemokratie!"* Molotov demanded that Ewert write a confession, admitting his bankruptcy, and that this document of humiliation be published in *Imprecorr,* the widely read foreign bulletin of the Comintern. Ewert was a true communist. A true communist cannot conceive of a life outside the Party. He humiliated himself. His confession was published on February 23, 1930. Ewert, as he spoke, accentuated each sentence with an almost apologetic smile.

"Why do you tell me all this?" I asked. "You are so much older in the movement than I."

"Because you are returning to Germany, my boy," he answered. "You are young. Your name still has a good sound in the movement. And it is youth that finally will decide the great issues. The young comrades in Germany should know that not Social Democracy, but Fascism, is the chief foe of the workers. I tell you we are making a horrible mistake!" Mournfully he added: "They are sending me to South America. Nothing will be decided there. The decisive battles will be fought in Germany."

This sounded convincing. But I remembered Soeder's admonition, "Be careful. We are going like a torpedo. One direction only." And Ginsburg's warning: "Unfortunately he has a head of his own."

"How can I know you are not pulling a personal oar?" I brazenly demanded.

Ewert emitted one of his broad, good-natured laughs. "Of course, I am," he said. "Tell me, who is not?"

"I don't understand you."

"You will! The advent of Stalin has changed the Comintern. Obedience counts for more now than initiative, just like it was in the old Prussian army. Look around you with critical eyes. No Communist Party has a real, home-rooted leadership. And why? Because Moscow won't permit it! The result is that a wooden-brained zealot like Ernst Thaelmann leads the strongest Communist Party outside of Russia. A top-sergeant leading a Party on which hangs the fate of the world revolution!"

I grew rebellious. "Comrade Thaelmann has been elected by the Party Congress," I said. "We owe loyalty to the leaders we elect because the principle of democratic centralism is fundamental in the Party."

"Rubbish," countered Ewert. "Stalin wiped out democracy and kept to centralism. Leaders are appointed, not elected. Every leader pulls his personal oar. Every leader strives to form his private net of spies and his secret private army to bolster him from the bottom. And the congress? I'll tell you. Congresses are called when it is too late to check tyranny from the top. Congresses are convoked only to say 'Aye' to cut-and-dried decisions. That may sound to your chaste ears like counter-revolutionary talk."

I was by now completely bewildered. This man had been my teacher. He was an authority on the credo which I had accepted body and soul. For a cornered mind, salvation lies in action. I did not ask myself who was right and who was wrong. I broke into the open with a challenge.

"Yes, Comrade Ewert, it does sound like counter-revolutionary talk!"

"And it isn't," Ewert growled.

"You pursue factional interests. Even if your life is correct, it tends to disrupt Party unity."

"I don't want to disrupt. I want you to see the truth and to let others know it."

"And then?"

"I don't want to be melodramatic. But an alliance between us and the Social Democrats might shift the course of history for many years. It must be an honest alliance."

"We cannot make an alliance with traitors," I said.

"By saying that, we are driving the strongest trade unions in the world into the bourgeois camp. We are making an error that may cost us all our lives. I don't want to bulldoze you to accept my opinion. But I want you to think it over. I want you to raise this question with the rank and file of the German Party. The whole future of the revolutionary movement hinges on what is happening in Germany this year and the next."

I bade good-by to Arthur Ewert. His eyes, deep under a bulging forehead, followed me to the door. The cold night air, lapping against my throat and crawling up my sleeves, made me aware that I was mumbling to myself. "No matter what our course," I told myself, "the Comintern is the only true revolutionary force in the world, and if men want social revolution they must follow the Comintern through fire and water, and not weaken it by bitter factional strife."

At the Hotel d'Alsace I found a typewritten note.

"See me immediately. R. G."

I walked around the corner and a block along the Rue de Seine to Ginsburg's *atelier*. Ginsburg was working over a blueprint.

"You were with Comrade Ewert all this time?" he inquired pleasantly.

"Yes ... I am tired."

"He gave you instructions?"

"No. We talked unofficially."

Roger Ginsburg put a portable *Continental* on a low steel table. He opened a drawer, and took out paper. "I will make a strong coffee with cognac," he said. "Sit down here. Write a report about everything Comrade Ewert said to you. Write it in detail, please."

"But why?"

"Parteibefehl!"

Break the character and independence of your man, and you will have an obedient trooper. That was the new weapon of the Comintern. My duty as a communist was to betray Arthur Ewert, my respected teacher. Was treachery among comrades to become henceforth the price of loyalty?

I wrote the report. Ginsburg kept toiling over his blueprints, never raising his head or looking around until I had typed the last letter of the last word and made ready to leave.

"Better sleep at my place tonight," he said. "You'll leave for Germany in a few hours."

Ginsburg's pale face was like a mask. I saw through it. He was determined to give me no chance to warn Ewert before I left Paris.

Chapter Fourteen

THE INFALLIBLES

A motherly Frenchwoman of considerable girth, one of the couriers of the Paris Apparat, escorted me to the Gare de l'Est, purchased my ticket, and put me aboard a train to Strasbourg. At the Strasbourg station, another courier recognized me by a Red Cross insignia in my coat lapel, and led me to the offices of the Strasbourg liaison agent, in a modern apartment house on Avenue Jean Jaures. The agent's name was Sorgus. He was a dark-skinned Alsatian in his thirties, a conscientious worker, whose hobby was the collecting of butterflies.

On orders from Sorgus, a tall, thin, taciturn young girl from the Strasbourg Party office accompanied me at night to the village of Lauterburg, which lies at the point where the Rhine passes into German territory. Here the Comintern maintained a border post. In a little house, which seemed to be an overturned barge with windows cut into its sides, the girl introduced me to a brawny youth. He grabbed a fishing tackle and motioned me to follow him. We went to a point where several boats lay moored to a pole. The black water gurgled. The Rhine flowed swiftly between low grassy banks. We entered a boat and pushed off, drifting downstream with the current, and pretending to fish. There were lights ahead of us. We passed them without being challenged.

"We are now in Germany," the youth said.

He brought out a pair of clumsy oars and pulled over to the right bank of the river. The oarlocks were wrapped in cloth, so that the rowing made no noise. I jumped ashore. My guide pulled away in the night. I stood on a wide meadow. The wind blew in cold gusts. I trudged away from the river toward a house without lights. There was a road. The road led into a highway. A sign at the junction read, *"Karlsruhe—4 Kilometer."*

I did not go to Berlin by the shortest route. In San Quentin I had dreamt of freedom. In Paris, I had had experiences which still lay heavily on my mind. I had spent almost nothing of the money I had received from Cance, Ginsburg, and Sorgus. So I decided to have a week for myself. I boarded the train from Karlsruhe to Heidelberg. I was back in my own country, but how little did I know it! The Rhine folk loved their land. They would live nowhere else, and they were proud that their cradles had been rocked along the Rhine. *"Nur am Rhein da moecht ich leben, nur am Rhein geboren sein . . ."* It was here, in the country between the Neckar and the Main, that I had been born, only to be taken away before my mind was ripe enough to imbibe its enchanting contours. And now, after twenty-five years of vagabondage, I beheld for the first time this land of my birth.

I took a room in a hotel overlooking the Neckar. Later in the day I mounted the ruins of the Heidelberg castle, and after that I tramped through the solitude of naked woods. The country, even in winter, was the most beautiful I had seen. The next day I again wandered alone through the woods.

In the evening I went to a bar. It was Saturday night. There was music, and a crowd of young people were eating, drinking, dancing, seemingly without a care in their lives. I sat alone at a table, drinking Niersteiner, watching enviously, but I was too bashful to ask any of the girls to dance with me. They were all so carefree and innocently frivolous. They wanted to play, and I had already forgotten how to play. Then I saw a girl at another table who also was alone and looked melancholy. She was about twenty-six, blonde, with a round face and a good figure, and she was very drunk. To drown my dejected mood and to attract her attention, I looked at her and began to sing raucously, "Hiking is the miller's joy."

"Vom Wasser haben wir's gelernt,
"Vom Wasser ...
"Das hat nicht Ruh bei Tag und Nacht,
"Is stets auf Wanderschaft bedacht,
"Das Wasser, das Wasser, das Wa-a-a-a-asser"

That girl and I, the two outcasts in the happy-go-lucky Heidelberg crowd, came together. Her name was Liese. I never asked for her second name, and she did not ask for mine. Two days we were together in Heidelberg. We bought rucksacks and provisions, and spent six glorious days hiking across the Odenwald mountains from Heidelberg to Darmstadt. Almost every mountain crest along the famous Bergstrasse bore an old, deserted castle with a moat, a drawbridge, dungeons, wells dug down into the base of the mountain, and walls often six to ten feet thick. The Comintern seemed as far away as Saturn. We were hardy and happy. Each day we grew younger.

We parted in Darmstadt. Liese returned to Heidelberg. I traveled north.

In Berlin, I reported at once to Communist Headquarters, the Karl Liebknecht House, a huge building commanding a wide square, the Buelowplatz. But for the block-long red banners in front, the Karl Liebknecht House appeared like any other business palace; but inside it was fortified and guarded like an arsenal. I gave one of the guards a written note, and asked him to report me to the organization department of the Central Committee. I waited. From somewhere came the dull hammering of presses. Doors banged and people rushed by. The hallways were plastered with blazing posters, diagrams, bulletins. In the courtyard, the bicycles and motorcycles of the Party couriers were parked by the dozen. At last the guard returned.

"Comrade Ernst will see you," he announced. "Fourth floor, room thirty-nine."

Room thirty-nine was small and bare. The windows had no curtains. There was a large desk, two hard chairs, and a picture of Stalin on the wall. The walls were painted a uniform battleship gray. Behind the desk sat a man. Two small, black, piercing eyes glowered at me.

The man was short and burly. His thin hair was combed to cover a bald spot on his head. He had chunky hands, a hard round forehead, and a thick, straight mouth. His chunky face was of an unhealthy color, and the expression on it was the most saturnine I had ever seen. It denoted power, patience, ruthlessness, distrust. But the really outstanding feature in this man were his eyes— unblinking, glistening slits without a trace of white. Before a word was said, I knew who this man was. I had seen him before. He was the stoker from the battleship *Helgoland*, who in 1918 had hoisted the first red flag of revolution over the Imperial Fleet.

Ernst Wollweber had traveled far since the day he had risen from the depths to kick one of the main props from under the Kaiser's war machine. He had become a member of the inner bureau of communist strategists in Central Europe, a member of that anonymous aristocracy of professional revolutionists without whose expert and formidable assistance the constantly publicized top-rank Party officials would be naught but garrulous generals without an officer corps to lead their army. To obtain for him constitutional immunity from arrest by police, Ernst Wollweber had been elected to the Prussian Diet. As a member of that legislative body, Wollweber had also acquired the right to free travel on German railroads between the Rhine and East Prussia. Moreover, the government paid him the substantial allowance granted to all members of German parliaments. Thus the Weimar Republic financed the journeys and maintenance of a host of agitators and organizers, elected as deputies, whose policies and actions aimed at nothing less than the complete destruction of that Republic.

"You are Comrade Ernst Wollweber," I said huskily.

The man nodded. He gave the Party salute: *"Rot Front!"* Then he growled, "Sit down." We shook hands over the desk. Wollweber's grip was hard. His face screwed itself into a mirthless grin, which revealed a row of irregular tobacco-stained teeth.

"How long have you been away from German Party work?"

"About seven years," I said.

"How are the American prisons?"

"Not bad."

"You did good work there. But the political storm center is now Germany. We need you right here." He lit a fresh cigarette with the butt of the last. "By the way," he added, "have you already communicated with Comrade Albert Walter in Hamburg?"

"Not yet. I shall write a report to him."

"That is not necessary," Wollweber said. "The Party leadership is *here*. Give your report to me."

"All right."

As he continued to question me, I had the feeling that Wollweber was circling around me with infinite caution, tightening his circle and coming a little closer after each of my answers. Suddenly he said:

"I have read your report on your conversation with Comrade Ewert."

I was startled. The Comintern's previous usage had been to forward letters of denunciations to those who had been so denounced. This had been done in a spirit of frankness and comradeship. But now it was brought home to me once more how much conditions in the Comintern had changed. Denunciations and confidential reports of comrade against comrade were welcomed now in high places. The system of secret dossiers—to be produced "when needed"—was on the way to become a component part of almost every communist leader's private arsenal.

"Oh, did Ginsburg? ..." I began.

"Say, *Comrade* Ginsburg," Wollweber interrupted. "The Party does not like the omission of certain accepted forms."

"Comrade Ginsburg requested me to write it," I explained.

I did not know where I stood. Ewert—Wollweber.... Were they friends or foes? As organization chief, Ernst Wollweber held the same position in the German Party which Ossip Piatnitzky held in the Comintern. The *Org-Leiter* could make and break men in his machine almost at will.

"It was a very interesting report," Wollweber said. "Did you and Comrade Ewert agree to communicate privately in the future?"

"No."

"Private communications between comrades sometimes have their value. More often, they are dangerous—to the younger correspondent. Your report on Comrade Ewert is in my possession. Consider that it was written for me—privately!"

"All right."

"What sort of work do you like best?"

"Maritime organization."

"Good. I'll make certain proposals concerning you at the next session of the Central Committee. Maybe you'll be put in charge of the Rhine, or the Danube, or the Berlin-Brandenburg canals. I'll let you know in a few days. In the meantime, you can acclimatize yourself to Germany."

When Wollweber spoke, each word seemed to come out in a slow sullen growl. He gave the impression of being a man who was never in a hurry, who was utterly without fear, whom nothing could surprise, and who had stripped himself deliberately of all illusions.

Ernst Wollweber arranged for my board and lodging, pending my next assignment, and introduced me to the man who was in charge of the Party archive in the rambling cellars of the Karl Liebknecht House. For over a week I had the run of Party headquarters. I read much to catch up on developments, talked with many members of the Karl Liebknecht House staff, and studied the official Party reports of the past two years. So I found my bearings in the most colossal communist machine as yet built up outside the Soviet frontiers—a machine which served in later years as a model for Communist Parties in all other countries.

The Communist Party of Germany had at that time a quarter of a million members. It published twenty-seven daily papers, with a total circulation of about five million. A dozen weekly and monthly publications and hundreds of factory sheets augmented the regular Party press. Nearly four thousand communist cells functioned in Germany, with over six hundred of them in the city of Berlin alone. Surrounding the Party, was a belt of eighty-seven auxiliary organizations which received their orders from Moscow by way of the Karl Liebknecht House.

Working silently and efficiently in the shadows of the ponderous communist edifice, was the underground G.P.U. network of the German Party. Its divisions included the *"S-Apparat"* for espionage, the *"M-Apparat"* for communist penetration into the army and navy, the *"P-Apparat"* for disintegration of police morale, the *"BB-Apparat"* for industrial espionage in favor of the Soviet Union, the Parteischutzgruppen—the armed bodyguards of Party leaders, the *"N-Apparat"* for passports, Party censorship, courier service and communications, and the various *Zersetzungs Apparate* for counter-espionage and disintegration work in the Social Democratic Party, the Catholic Center, the Monarchists, and among the military formations of the Hitler movement. Every department of the Party and every auxiliary organization was directed by a special emissary from Moscow, invested with extraordinary dictatorial powers.

The expressive word "agent" is never used in Comintern circles; the official title of the foreign commissars of the Kremlin is the awkward "International Political Instructor." Each of these international agents was a specialist in a given field. There were specialists in propaganda technique, in strike strategy, in industrial organization, women's specialists, espionage specialists, advertising experts, Red Army experts, business managers, police specialists, and specialists for each of the basic industries—steel, shipping, railroads, mining, textile, public utilities, agriculture and the chemical industry—and expert accountants sent to clear up financial tangles. Rarely were they known by their true names. They hardly ever lived in hotels. They had secret offices and secret quarters, usually in the homes of trusted Party members. All these instructors were well dressed and well paid, and seldom did any of them appear in a meeting without the protective escort of a personal courier or an alert-eyed girl who served both as secretary and mistress. It was this elusive corps of Comintern agents that formed the real leadership of the Communist Party.

But Berlin was more than the center of German communism; since 1929, it had become the field headquarters for the whole of the Communist International. Moscow was too remote from Western Europe and the Americas to carry on a close and constant supervision of the activities of its Foreign Legion. Besides, the laws of conspirative work demanded that the broad stream of international agitators in and out of Russia should be reduced to only the most necessary trickle. It was decided to let all threads end in Berlin, and to retain only a single line of communication between Berlin and Moscow. A Western Secretariat of the Comintern was therefore established in Berlin, whose jurisdiction reached from Iceland to Capetown. Appointed to act as its political chief was Georgi Dimitrov, who was responsible only to Molotov, the real ruler of the Comintern.

I met Dimitrov through Willy Muenzenberg, who had invited me, in his capacity as president of the World League against Imperialism, to speak about America at a meeting of Chinese communist students attending the Berlin University. The meeting was a success. Late that evening, Muenzenberg, who had taken a liking to me, remarked:

"Something approaching a revolutionary situation is ripening in India. How would you like to go to Calcutta?"

I answered that I was awaiting an assignment in Germany. I mentioned Wollweber's name. Muenzenberg flared up. "You have been doing international work. You should have reported to the Western Secretariat," he rattled out. "Not to Wollweber. Wollweber is Germany."

"Well, I'm a member of the German Communist Party."

"That is correct. But as an international worker, you are not under the jurisdiction of the German Central Committee. Who is Wollweber? Wollweber is a *Lokalpatriot*. He thinks Germany is the whole world. A capable comrade, but no internationalist."

I now discovered a new form of rivalry—the rivalry for power between the vertical national sections of the Comintern and the large number of horizontal international leagues. Despite all my loyalty to the Comintern, I found myself asking: "Who is stronger—Wollweber or Muenzenberg?"

Two days later, in the early morning, there was a knock at my door. A determined-looking girl courier entered.

"I come from the Westbureau," she announced. "Comrade Dimitrov wants to see you."

Dimitrov was at that time almost unknown outside of the ranks of the Comintern aristocracy. Men of his type prized anonymity. For ten years, until 1923, he had been a member of the Bulgarian parliament. He then led an armed communist rising, which ended in failure, and escaped into exile. In his absence, a court in Sofia sentenced him to death. In Moscow, after being held responsible for the catastrophic defeat of communism in Bulgaria, Dimitrov wrote a document of self-humiliation, and won the friendship of Stalin. He became the head of the Communist Balkan Federation, and was later promoted to the leadership of the Western Secretariat of the Comintern. Among the large assortment of aliases he used in Berlin, the choicest were Dr. Steiner, Alfons Kuh, Professor Jahn, and Dr. Schaafsma-Schmidt.

Dimitrov's girl courier, wary of followers, piloted me to a house on the Wilhelmstrasse, number 131-132. Here, behind the camouflage of a modern bookstore and a publishing firm called *Fuehrer Verlag*, the Comintern maintained a dozen departments, a host of typists, couriers, translators and guards. I was ushered into an elegantly furnished office. On the wall, in a massive black frame, was a portrait of—Bismarck.

My first impression of Dimitrov was disappointing. I had expected to meet a steely man, a hardened veteran of many campaigns. Instead there came out of an inner office a large, soft, flabby-faced individual, stout and dark, dressed like a dandy and smelling of heavy perfume. He wore a thick ring on his left hand. His well-manicured fingers held a black cigar. His eyes were large and bold. I soon found that he was a driving, domineering personality. He spoke German with remarkable fluency. His words came loud and hard.

"We've written *finis* to a ten-year period of revolutionary adventurism," he said. "Putschism is definitely discarded. Our program is now one of planned action; a plan extending over a number of years. We cannot achieve the revolution by fly-by-night coups, we can achieve it only with Bolshevist methods. We must organize and lead every possible strike, even the smallest—and do it *against* the will of the socialist trade union bureaucracy. A continuous barrage of independent strikes will break the mass influence of the Social Democracy, disrupt the whole system of industrial production, and deepen the capitalist crisis until it reaches a point of collapse."

Dimitrov grew more violent as he spoke:

"The Social Democrats tell the workers that it is impossible to win strikes when there's a crisis with millions of unemployed. They advise the workers to accept wage reductions without offering resistance. Here is the opportunity we communists must seize! We must cultivate a hatred in the heads of the workers against their false leaders. Each and every day we must pound it into them ten thousand times: 'The Socialist and trade union leaders are traitors! They are the most dangerous enemies of the workers! They have sold out the workers to the bourgeoisie.'"

"And the Nazi movement?" I asked, thinking of Arthur Ewert and his warning.

"The Hitler movement has no followers among the workers," he countered. "Hitler promises everything to everybody. He steals his ideas from all sides. Nobody takes him seriously anyway. He has no tradition and no background. Not even a program. Don't let yourself be distracted. The biggest obstacle on the road to proletarian revolution is the Social Democratic Party. Our foremost task is to liquidate its influence. Afterwards, we'll sweep Hitler and his *Lumpengesindel* into the garbage-can of history." Suddenly Dimitrov asked me: "What do you think of the German Party?"

"Compared with other Communist Parties, it is like an express train among pushcarts," I replied.

Dimitrov smiled long at me. His eyes, his wide mouth, his whole mobile face were smiling.

"Maybe so," he finally said. "But the locomotive might be rusty and burn a tremendous over-load of coal. Maybe ten stokers are necessary to make it move ten yards."

I was dumbfounded to hear it from the mouth of the infallible leader.

"We must never shy away from Bolshevist self-criticism," he continued. "*Selbstkritik* is a sharp weapon. The locomotive is not beyond repair. The rusty parts can be taken out; shiny, new, young parts can be put in. Maybe some of the stokers are saboteurs. Maybe the coal is not very good. Well?"

"Let's put on some good stokers and good coal," I said.

Dimitrov laughed like a gleeful boy.

"Why not?" he said. "It will run like the devil."

Then he switched to my future work. "We are sending you to Moscow," he announced. I nodded, intent on hearing more.

"Sailors belong to ships. You'll continue with the Maritime Section. We must push ahead with full strength in the shipping industry. When war comes ... you know what it means. We must have capitalist shipping in our hands. The Soviet Union needs peace. Nothing is better for taming a capitalist shark than to cut off his exports and imports. You'll meet Albert Walter in Moscow. A lot of other sailors will be there. You'll all thrash things out with Comrade Losovsky."

I was photographed on the top floor of the Karl Liebknecht House. Within a day, I received a Danish passport in the name of Rolf Gutmund, a commercial traveler and resident of Aalborg. It was a good passport. Except for a change of photograph, it had been left intact. A Soviet visa and a Polish transit visa were already entered in it. In addition, I received a special document of identification, typed in Russian, with instructions to show it only to the Soviet frontier police. I traveled with three other comrades, a Hungarian named Emmerich Sallai, a girl from Cologne sent to study at the Lenin University, and an apple-cheeked leader of the Communist Party of Switzerland. Sallai, seeing that my overcoat was shabby and light, supplied me with a heavy coat he had in reserve.

An hour before my departure, I had unexpectedly chanced upon Wollweber in the restaurant of the Karl Liebknecht House. He sat alone at a table, hunched over a glass of beer, the personification of a creature continuously brooding over conspiracies and alliances. He looked askance at me when I told him that I was going to Moscow.

"Who is sending you?'"

"Comrade Dimitrov."

He gave a faintly sardonic smile. Then he shook my hand. "Gute Reise," he growled. "Don't forget to come back."

He exchanged a few curt remarks with my travel companions before he walked away, holding his hands clasped behind him. Lights danced in the eyes of the girl from Cologne. "Do you know Comrade Ernst's nickname?" she purred intimately. "In meetings he imitates the gestures of Vladimir Ilyitch. We get him mad by calling him 'Little Lenin.' They say he practices Lenin poses in front of a mirror when he's alone."

With uncanny precision, a messenger from the Profintern singled us out in the bedlam of the station in Moscow, upon our arrival there two days later. We were driven to the Bristol Hotel, a Comintern caravansary for communist transients from abroad. I was lodged in a room together with a Finn and a Lett. Three cots, three chairs, a table, a washstand, a samovar and a picture of Stalin made up the furniture. There was an outfit for cooking, but it had broken down and was long out of use. I had hardly spent two hours in the hotel—which was more like a cosmopolitan tenement than a hotel in the European sense—when a sly-faced German engaged me in a conversation about Russia. He was too friendly. And after a while, he began to criticize openly the Five-Year-Plan and Stalin's qualities of leadership. I knew what he meant. The man was the inevitable house spy of the G.P.U. I told him to stop his counter-revolutionary nonsense or be kicked out of the room. Thereafter, whenever he saw me, he raised his right fist with a grin and shouted: *"Heil Moskau!"*

The morning after our arrival our group scattered. The girl from Cologne moved to one of the students' houses. The Swiss departed for a conference with Piatnitzky. I did not see him again. Sallai moved to the Hotel Savoy where his compatriot, Bela Kun, who had received the Order of the Red Banner, was the center of the Hungarian colony. I asked Sallai if he wanted back the overcoat he had given me. He seemed to be hurt.

"I have one just as good. Keep it, because I don't need it."

I wore the overcoat for three years. It lived longer than its original owner. For Emmerich Sallai, together with another Comintern man, was condemned to death for high treason in Budapest on July 28, 1932, and was hung the same night. Both were reported to have died with the cry, "Long live the proletarian dictatorship. We shall be avenged."

The marine conference in the Profintern was already under way. Risking a rebuke from my superiors, I stole one short day to roam through Moscow. The Five-Year-Plan propaganda dominated public life as a high mountain dominates the surrounding sea—it was visible wherever one went and, to me, it was stirring. The Kremlin had decided to sacrifice for years the normal well-being of one hundred and sixty million people to win a titanic race against a century of backwardness. "Socialism or die!" To the young communist from abroad, this "all or nothing" cry was familiar and reassuring music. "Once the Five-Year-Plan is completed, the Soviet Union will be so invincibly strong that it will insure the triumph of revolution outside of Russia." What was this not worth to a young fanatic, who was prepared to suffer every privation himself, even to give his own life for the revolution? Such reasoning made the Bolshevist indifference to the ocean of human suffering stretching before our eyes appear in a noble light.

The élite of the Maritime Section of the Comintern attended the conference in the Red Room of the Profintern building. A tall, lean Russian presided, a blond young man of reserved manners. It was Kommissarenko, the chief of the shipping and waterfront unions of Russia and Siberia. But the man who dominated the meeting was Losovsky, the head of the Profintern. He had a thin, almost hollow face, an ill-tended reddish beard, and quick, fanatical eyes. He was a clever speaker, fond of sarcasm and possessed of a lashing vitality which I thought highly unusual in a man of his decrepit appearance. The third important figure in the assembly was Albert Walter; his energetic bluffness and virility had not changed since I had seen him last.

The rest were delegates from the maritime sections of the Communist Parties of nearly a dozen countries. The conference had been called to formulate plans for the organization of an International of Seamen and Harbor Workers, and of Red waterfront unions on all continents. The new International was to be created within a year, after a worldwide preparatory campaign. Its chief task was the mobilization of seamen for the protection of the Soviet Union in case of war, by tying up the shipping of nations antagonistic to Russia. Concurrently, the new International was to serve as a battering ram for the destruction of all maritime unions which could not possibly be brought under communist control. On the fourth day of the conference, Ossip Piatnitzky, the organization chief of the Comintern, addressed us on the technique of translating propaganda into organization, and organization into action. This lynx-eyed, aggressive, yet unassuming Old Bolshevik spoke of "our tasks in Malaya, Greece or America" as if these countries were garden patches in Moscow.

Of special interest to me were the reports on the steady progress of communism along the American seaboard ever since the early haphazard days when I had been one of the legion of traveling delegates from Hamburg to carry propaganda literature across the Atlantic. International Seamen's Clubs had been established, with Profintern funds, in the nine most important ports of the United States. Using the working methods developed in Hamburg, these clubs had consolidated their growing influence, and gave rise to a national organization which was called the Marine Workers' League. Losovsky had granted a special monthly subsidy for the publication of a communist newspaper for American seamen, the *Marine Workers' Voice*. The Moscow conference, accepting a plan drawn up by Kommissarenko, decided that the time had come to engineer into existence a Red trade union of American waterfront workers. Two young American communists, possessing leadership qualities and the necessary ruthlessness, had risen from obscurity to a place high in Losovsky's favor. Losovsky spoke of them with almost fatherly affection. One was George Mink. The other was Tom Ray. Losovsky and Walter agreed to give Mink the leadership of the Atlantic coast, and Ray that of the Pacific, with respective headquarters in New York and San Francisco. Mink and Ray were placed on the payroll of the Profintern; Losovsky decreed that they should receive additional monthly allowances to cover the costs of the *Marine Workers' Voice,* of the maintenance of the International Clubs, and of sending a crew of organizers into all harbors between Norfolk and Seattle. Like all Soviet funds for maritime work abroad, this money was to be conveyed to its destination through Albert Walter's office in Hamburg. Finances were also provided for a convention of American waterfront communists, held in April, 1930, three months after the Moscow conference, in New York, to organize the Marine Workers Industrial Union. It was attended by 118 delegates from Atlantic, Pacific, Gulf and Great Lake ports. George Mink, Tom Ray and a certain La Rocca were then summoned to Moscow to submit reports and receive further instructions.

Each evening, after a day of drawing the blueprints for future campaigns, ended with an outright saturnalia. The only groups that kept aloof from these orgies were the Russians, the grave-faced Chinese, and the older communists, who withdrew to prepare their notes for the next day's speeches and arguments. The rest of the delegates repaired to their hotels, the Bristol and the famous Lux, where most of the foreign Comintern workers had their crowded quarters. Vodka, wine and a variety of cheap candies and cakes were always on hand. Often there were as many as twenty-five of us in a room six or eight yards square. The sudden stripping of an unsuspecting newcomer, mutual dousing with cold water, vodka-drinking tournaments, and "nationalization of women"—a juicy satire on bourgeois propaganda—were popular games. Men appeared in women's clothes, girls dressed as peasants or stevedores, and—with lights turned out—each participant was obliged to regain his original outer garments before the master of ceremonies decided to switch on the lights. Mock "proletarian courts" then meted out punishment to those caught in diverse stages of dishabillement. Our frolics usually terminated at midnight; no communist wished to risk being caught catching up on his sleep during the next day's duties. The older Bolsheviks knew no pity in this respect.

On the last day of the conference Albert Walter showed me a letter from Wollweber, written in Berlin. The "Little Lenin" was jealous of the attention Walter was receiving in Moscow. He complained to the Comintern that the most promising young elements were being stolen from the German Party for international assignments. "He is a peasant," Walter burst out. "Don't let him dupe you."

"But why all this confounded sneaking?" I cried.

"Human nature is the most stubborn concoction imaginable," Walter replied grimly.

The next day I was commissioned to go to Antwerp to take charge of the activities of the communist waterfront units and the International Clubs in Rotterdam, Antwerp, Ghent and Dunkerque. My monthly salary was $100; my monthly organizational budget $750. I was glad to return to the firing lines. I detested the life of a politician.

News of the rising strife in Germany burst like a warning squall into the sleepy atmosphere of my compartment as I passed through Berlin. The news hawkers howled on the platforms, *"Bloody Riots in Berlin and Hamburg! Nazi Sturmfuehrer Murdered!"* The Party had led the unemployed masses into battle against the police. There had been barricade fighting in industrial districts. Hamburg reported dead and wounded. On February 23, in Berlin, the Storm Troop leader Horst Wessel had died from bullets fired by communist assassins. Dr. Goebbels' newspaper, the *Angriff,* clamored for revenge. The struggle for the conquest of Berlin, of Germany, of the world, was thrown into a swifter pace. From an adjoining railway car, packed with Brownshirts, singing came.

It was the Horst Wessel Song, written by the murdered Nazi student, the battle-song which was destined to rank equal with *Deutschland ueber Alles* in later years.

My train pulled out of Berlin. Westward it rolled, toward the Rhine. The first smell of spring was in the air.

Chapter Fifteen

FIRELEI

In Antwerp I met Firelei.

I saw her for the first time in the Museum of Art, where I occasionally went to enjoy a quiet hour away from strident reality. Among the full-bodied austerity of the Dutch masters she sat, a splash of living beauty and color, the daughter of an impudent and fearless age. She had an open sketchbook on her knees, and the crayon in her right hand flew over the paper. She had small, but able hands. She peered intently at the somber portrait of a woman on the wall in front of her. Her glance leaped to the paper on her knees and her right hand drew swift contours. And then her eyes swung back again to the likeness of the older, sturdier woman on the wall.

I halted and looked over her shoulder. She was so absorbed in her work that she was unaware of my intrusion. Some powerful and intangible influence took hold of me. It was beyond explanation, and utterly new. There was an inimitable harmony between her attitude of concentration and the easy grace of her posture and motions. I came as close to her as I dared. A blue Basque cap clung smoothly to her dark blonde hair. Her hair had a satiny hue; it glistened faintly under the lights. She was slender, and firmly made. Her knees and legs were of the kind that convinced one that there could be no trace of lassitude or laziness in her make-up. The skin of her arms and the nape of her neck had all the freshness of a Nordic woman addicted to sunlight and wind. It was a clear ivory, with the blood pulsing close to the surface. I watched with the breathless excitement of a half-starved wanderer who sees lighted trees through windows on a raw Christmas night, feeling empty-handed and poor.

I was so close now that I touched her. She looked up in a flash. She had full, mobile lips. Her eyes were gray and searching. "What are you doing here? What do you want of me?" they seemed to ask. I dropped my glance. I murmured a silly excuse. Then I fled, hot with shame and anger at myself.

I had much to do that day. A large consignment of literature had to be smuggled aboard a French vessel bound for Saigon. It had to be done with utmost circumspection, for not a month passed in Cochin-China without some heads of communist militants falling under the guillotine. Willy Muenzenberg had sent an Annamite "activist," Le Huan, to Antwerp with orders to proceed to Saigon. I had to take care of him. But all these duties failed to draw my mind away from the girl I had seen in the Museum of Art.

I cursed at myself: "You fool, know your limits. Such a fine girl is not for you! Call her a bourgeois bitch, and be done with it. Stick to the Komsomol girls and the sluts from Skipper Street. To them you are like a king. To her, you are a nuisance, a scavenger, a rootless ragamuffin ... Call her a bourgeois bitch, and be done with it!"

Yet the next day and the days following I hastened to the Art Museum and skulked for hours through the high-ceilinged halls, suffering pain from the knowledge that I was neglecting my duties as a revolutionist. I could not find her in the Museum.

The sun shone warm, and the people of Antwerp began to come out to sit gossiping on their stoops. It was March. Le Huan was on the way to Cochin-China, not knowing that he was going straight to his death in the Prison of Annam. A melancholy young Polish Jew, named Hirsch, arrived from Paris with a mandate to go to Galicia. I put him aboard a ship bound for Gdynia. I received three postcards from him, in which he wrote that all was going well in Poland. Then came a curt note from Berlin, instructing me to strike Comrade Hirsch off my list. Hirsch had been caught by police. Some months later, on June 12, he was hung for high treason in Lemberg. Our campaign of agitation went on with meetings in the International Clubs, propaganda among the dockers and rivermen, and furious paper attacks against the socialists and their unconquerable trade unions. There were huge consignments of printed matter, arriving from Berlin and Moscow, for shipment to Jamaica, to Siam, to India. The sun shone warmer, and the boldest of the café owners on the Meir put out their first tables on the sidewalk.

And then I suddenly met her again. I was sauntering along the waterfront. The harbor was full of ships and noise. The air was redolent of tar and brine, and the Antwerp cathedral stood massively against the blue sky. On a rusty bitt, at the edge of a wharf, sat the girl. Her legs dangled over the green water of the docks. Again she was drawing, her eyes leaping diligently from the paper to a conglomeration of river craft moored nearby, and back. Behind the river ships reared an assembly of cranes and sheds, and beyond them the roofs of Antwerp and the tower of the cathedral glistened in the sunlight.

I came nearer. This time I would speak to her. In the workaday patchwork of sunlight and shadow she seemed far less distant than in the church-like sanctity of the Museum. The harbor was my domain.

The river barges had romantic names. They hailed from Amsterdam and Strasbourg, and some had come all the way from Rouen and Paris. On their decks, men squatted in the sunshine. Some smoked their pipes, resting. Big-hipped women called to each other from ship to ship. A fat little dog was barking at a line of fluttering laundry. The girl had drawn the stern of a French Rhine barge. There were mooring lines and the large horizontal steering wheel, and a contented woman nursing a baby in the shadow of a companionway. The girl saw me. She gave me a smile of recognition. I looked at her drawing.

"It looks real," I said. She flushed.

"It is so difficult to capture the moods of the docks," she observed.

"Have docks moods?"

She laughed and closed her sketchbook. She was a girl who liked to laugh. She was not "bourgeois." Hers was a captivating simplicity that made the application of a label seem idiotic.

"You've forgotten the name of the ship," I said. "A ship must have a name. It's *Oran*."

"Yes, yes. I must put in the name." She hesitated for a moment. Then she opened the book defiantly. "So—O-R-A-N."

She spoke in English, as I had before her. She formulated each word with utmost care. With a light toss of her head, she said: "English is the language of sailors, no?"

"That's right."

"Are you a sailor?"

"Sure."

"Where is your ship?"

"I'm ashore. I'm looking for another ship."

"I have an uncle who was a captain. He always said a sailor without a ship is like a pastor without a church. Where did your last ship come from?"

"From Galveston."

"Where is Galveston?"

"In America. In Texas."

"Oh—I have heard of Texas. What did you bring to Ant-werp-en?"

"Grain," I said.

"Sailors are lucky, I think."

"Ha, why?"

The girl did not answer at once. Then she leaned back and said: "Panama, Sumatra, Honolulu, Madagascar, Oran. ... I like the names so much."

She drew up her knees and clasped her arms around them. She looked toward the river, where a large Japanese ship was outbound in the wake of smoking tugs. "Do you like Antwerp-en?" she

"Yes. Is it your home?"

She shook her head. "I am here to study," she said seriously. "Are you an artist?"

"Oh, no." She smiled quickly. "I still must learn how to use my eyes and hands. I love lines and colors when they have a meaning, like sounds and moods. I wanted to study in Paris, but my parents would not permit it. So I came to Flanders."

"You look like a Flemish girl."

"My mother was Flemish. Flanders is rich! The town of Ghent was once the Venice of the North. It once had more ships and merchant princes than all of England."

"Do you admire merchant princes?"

The girl laughed merrily. A ship nosed into the dock. The Danish flag flew from its stern. Hoarse yells from rough throats hung in the wind.

"Where is your home?" asked the girl.

"Wherever ships are," I said.

"Look!" she cried out.

A group of men clambered ashore from a British steamer tied to the wharf a little way off. They were Lascars, cadaverous fellows, with turbans on their heads and bright cotton shirts protruding from under sweaters fluttering about their thin thighs. As they passed us, a tall man with velvety deer eyes and a drooping mustache bared all his yellow teeth in a grin.

"Stokers," I said.

"Where are they going?"

"To Skipper Street."

The girl made a grimace of distaste, and said resolutely: "Sit quietly on this bitt. I shall try to make a sketch of you."

"What will you call it?"

" 'A sailor looking for a ship,' " she replied. "Hook your thumbs in your belt, and sit still."

We spoke little. Winches rumbled near and far. From the river drifted a ragged concert of siren blasts. The eyes of the girl were now intent and strangely impersonal. They shuttled between the sketchbook and me. I became as self-conscious as a schoolboy whose secrets were being dragged into the light. A small cluster of stevedores drew up, and glued their eyes to the girl. One of them shouted admiringly: *"Ah, la garconne!"* He brought the tips of his toil-hardened fingers to his mouth, in the French manner, releasing them with the sound of a vigorous kiss. The girl answered with a mischievous glance in their direction. "Please, my friends," she said in Flemish, "try not to disturb me." After that, she was able to finish her sketch, while we talked of many things.

I called her Firelei. The name fitted her well, I thought. We met as often during the following weeks as I could contrive to snatch a few hours' leave from the constant rush of my duties. I was hopelessly, vehemently in love. I had considered love a hypocritical habit of the despised bourgeoisie. But now I wanted Firelei to be my mate and comrade at any price. She liked me. I was of a different tribe than the young men a girl of her type was wont to meet. She was at a loss to place me in any of the traditional categories of the social order she knew. In her eyes, I was neither bourgeois nor a worker, nor did I belong to the conventional boheme. She saw me as an individualist and a rebel. And Firelei, like most of post-war Europe's best youth, was a rebel, too, a rebel against the conventions of a generation that had forfeited the privilege to show youth the way into the future. Youth had learned to cleave a path of its own. This we both understood and accepted. But Firelei knew nothing of the real nature of my work. "Communist" was a very fashionable word in the Europe of 1930. It suggested unwashed individuals reeking of sweat and cheap coffee, gathering into hordes and yelling "Down!" in the streets. I feared that she would sever relations with me and flee if I told her who I was.

Firelei was half German, half Flemish. Her father was a businessman in Mainz on the Rhine. The German revolution of 1918 had come two months after her eleventh birthday. After her graduation from a Lyceum, she had attended art school in Frankfort, and then in Munich, where she met an engineering student with whom she ran away on a hiking tour across the Alps. Her father, who had gone in pursuit, brought Firelei back to Mainz and maneuvered her into accepting a job in the advertising department of a fashion house. She worked for nearly three years in Mainz, uninterruptedly at war with her parents. The family was *Deutsch-National;* it moved in pro-monarchist circles. But Firelei detested soldiers and all authority that lives on a dogma and a uniform. She was sensitive and stubborn. Prolonged discontent and an inborn love of freedom made her reckless. She threw up her job, and went to Paris to develop further her clear artistic talent. The family implored, raged, begged her to return. In a German provincial town it was a disgrace to have a daughter run wild in Paris. Firelei, living ten days on bread and cheese, replied with a demand for a monthly allowance. They compromised by permitting her to go for a year to Antwerp, where she had an uncle, a retired sea captain who had lost his left leg on the Congo River. It was in his house that Firelei lived.

Sometimes my work took me to Rotterdam, Ghent and Dunkerque. I was away from Antwerp two and three days at a time. When Firelei came, eager to have my companionship, she often could not find me. Unavoidably she came to the conclusion that, for a sailor, I was leading a very strange life. Her uncle, a shrewd and physically powerful man, became suspicious of my activities. I did not want to lie to Firelei. I did not want to give her up. I decided to tell her the truth. Tossing and muttering in sleepless nights I came to the point where I decided to discard the Comintern, if need be, to win the girl I loved.

But the hold the Comintern has on the minds of its indentured servants can be compared only with the grip the Jesuit Order has on its members. Events of great magnitude ripening in India and Cochin-China swept me back to my post. Some four thousand

Lascars served in the crews of British and German ships for which Antwerp was a regular port of call. These Lascars formed the pipeline through which the Comintern pumped an incessant stream of propaganda, instructions, and rank-and-file agents into all East Indian harbors.

In Comintern circles there was already talk of "The Indian Revolution." Throughout the spring of 1930, many communists allowed themselves to become intoxicated with the prospects of "capsizing" the British Empire by bringing the Soviets to power in India. There was street fighting in Calcutta and other towns. The newly-founded Red Trade Union in India was under the direction of the Pan-Pacific Secretariat of the Profintern, which the American Earl Browder had established in 1927 in Shanghai with funds allotted him by Losovsky.

My sense of duty toward the revolution plunged me into painful inner struggles. Had I the right to draw Firelei into such a life of conspiracy and violence? She meant infinitely more to me than the luckless Hindus. But I clung to the Comintern as a peasant clings to the land of his forbears. The Comintern was the earth which gave me life and purpose. And there was

Firelei—rooted in a different soil. I wrestled with the thought that she was far too good, too fine, to be destroyed in the Comintern service. I wrestled with the idea that I must discard one to win, and to keep, the other.

I was afraid of the hidden weakness and potential treachery which is the heritage of every human being. It seemed much simpler to persist in the unthinking "Either—Or! " But where, I asked myself, lay triumph, and where defeat?

One night Firelei became mine. I told her that I had been in prison. I told her that I was in the employ of the Communist International. I told her that I was proud to be a revolutionist, and that I never would be anything else. Firelei's point of view was one of chaste and youthful idealism. Had not all the great thinkers and poets and artists been revolutionists at heart? She knew nothing of the ugly realism of the communist movement.

"When we gain power," I said to her, "all human suffering will end. Life will be joyous. Oppression, marching armies, unjust laws, hunger and wretchedness will be remembered only as specters of a vanquished past."

Firelei had a woman's inborn compassion for noble souls. I showed her a report from the Belgian Congo, describing the fearful conditions under which the wretched natives were forced to work in the copper mines and cotton districts around Barna and Leopoldsville.

"It is against this inhumanity that we are fighting," I said.

I showed Firelei another report, dealing with the lives of communists condemned by Fascist courts to the prison of Santo Stefano, an island five miles from Naples. I told of prisoners chained in the hold of a ship, of men who were not permitted to see the sun or to hear a human voice year after year, of sickness and death in the dungeons, of a cemetery without names and crosses on the farthest end of the island, of bad food and gendarmes grown vicious out of boredom. Firelei had tears in her eyes.

"We must rescue them," I said. "For that we fight.'

I showed her a third report, which had come through from Saigon. It told of the struggle of the coolies for the right to organize in Red unions, of strikes against the most pitiful wages on earth, of the ferocity of the Resident Governor of Annam and the French gendarmerie, of the killing of workers, and of the slaughter of peasants who had refused to pay exorbitant government taxes.

"The coolies in Cochin-China feel and love like you and I do," I said. "They have a right to shape their own destiny. Their struggle is just, and we must fight to help them."

I unfolded to Firelei a world that was like a gruesome picture-book of injustice and misery brought about by a handful of rich men in London, Paris, Brussels, and New York. She was not equipped to challenge this Marxist interpretation of poverty, mass joblessness, and war. She idealized me and I idealized her. We were together now night after night, engulfed in a wave of delirious happiness that surpassed in intensity all conceptions we had had of the human capacity for unrestrained self-surrender. Not many days passed before she said: "Let me help you in your work."

Firelei was not a communist. Her free-and-easy nature rebelled against being made a cog in an organization where blind obedience and totality of leadership were paramount. She volunteered her help out of a new feeling of comradeship, and out of an altruistic desire to alleviate the suffering of helpless people. I strove to keep her away from the ugly phases of communist practice. She painted posters, drew caricatures, and designed decoration schemes for the International Clubs. She became fascinated by *motifs* that had hitherto lain completely beyond her horizon. Her work had originality because she knew nothing of the Russian pattern, and it soon attracted the attention of the propaganda department of the Western Secretariat. "Who is the comrade who can draw so well?" asked a letter from Berlin. I ignored the inquiry. Firelei was more interested in the constellations of lines and colors, and the effects they could exercise on the emotions—including her own, than in the strategy and tactics of political conspiracy.

We discovered that we had in common a love of the sea, of growing things, and of a life of motion. Each week I deserted my Comintern duties for one day to hire a boat and go sailing with Firelei on the lower reaches of the Schelde. At times we sailed to Vlissingen for a walk over the dunes and to spend a night around a fire on the beach. We swam, won friends among fisherfolk, made love, dug for clams, and I taught Firelei what I knew of the stars and planets overhead. For the moment we asked no more. We belonged to each other.

Firelei's uncle grew more belligerent each time his niece returned home defiantly at dawn. I came to regard him as my personal enemy. Most Flemings are easy-going, but they can be brusque and harsh when their own interest or the honor of their clan is involved. The retired sea captain at first only threatened to send Firelei back to her parents in Mainz. As the girl continued to defy his ideas of propriety, he resorted to violence. One day Firelei came to me pale and disturbed.

"Uncle Bert has tried to lock me up." Her laughter had a faintly hysterical note. "I did not permit it and he beat me. What shall I do now?"

"Move out," I said. "Make no concessions. Bring him to his knees."

"Where should I go?"

"To me."

"Naturally. But they'll stop my allowance."

"Freedom is worth more than money."

"But you've barely enough to live on yourself."

It was true. The larger part of my monthly salary dribbled away to meet unexpected organizational expenses, and there were months in which I received no pay at all. The Comintern had a way of demonstrating to its employees their dependence on the treasuries in Moscow and Berlin by sudden stoppages of subsidies. Such sporadic periods of penury were a loyalty test devised by the thrifty Piatnitzky. However, they never lasted longer than a month.

"When you and I are together, there's no obstacle we cannot overcome," I said to Firelei.

From then on we lived together. Firelei's uncle refused to allow her to take her belongings from the house. "Beware of the sailor," he warned her. "Only a renegade discards his home." I mobilized a squad of communist longshoremen for a night raid on the old sea captain's house. Firelei's belongings, which included several trunks full of books, were transferred without a serious mishap to my quarters under the roof of a six-story tenement facing Antwerp's marketplace. Our abode was rather unkempt and gloomy when Firelei moved in, but after a few busy days her sense of beauty and harmony transformed it into a cheerful anchorage for both of us. The walls were painted with good ship's paint filched from boat lockers by some of my seafaring aides; the furniture was restored and rearranged; pictures found their places on the walls, bookshelves were installed, and Firelei saw to it that there were always flowers about the room. It was the nearest thing to a home I had had in the twelve years since the Great War.

Up to this time Firelei had rarely met any of my communist associates. Now it became unavoidable that she would meet them more frequently and observe them at close range. These communists were not of the local Party organization, with which I had little to do, but men and women engaged in the international *Apparat* of the Comintern, passing through Antwerp on their various missions. At times they stayed overnight at my den, and, accepting as a matter of course that Firelei was a member of the service, they often spoke without reservation, as men will in a place they consider safe after a long and hazardous journey. It became apparent to Firelei that communist activities were closely linked with the Soviet secret police.

One of my visitors—*en route* from England to Berlin—was a Macedonian whose name was on the "wanted" list of every political police in Europe in connection with the assassination in Sofia of Nikolaus Mileff shortly after the latter's appointment as Bulgarian envoy to Washington. Another, a Eurasian Bolshevik, told of his escape from Pamekasan Prison on Madura Island in the Dutch East Indies, where some six hundred leaders of the armed insurrection of 1926-1927 in Java and Sumatra were confined. This emaciated Eurasian, who called himself "Waldemar," was a cut-throat who might have fitted into any pirate tale. Before his transfer to Madura Island, he had spent two years in the Digul River prison camps in the jungles of Dutch New Guinea under harrowing conditions. He prided himself on having organized prison mutinies and engineered the murder of several guards. "With this," he said, abruptly pulling a long thin dagger from under his belt and caressing it in Firelei's presence. He had come to Antwerp as a stowaway from Singapore. I escorted him to Verviers, where the communist in charge of the border station smuggled him through the frontier woods to Aachen and put him aboard a train bound for Berlin. Still another, a Russian waiting in Antwerp for a Soviet steamer to take him to Leningrad, tried to create a favorable impression on the silently listening Firelei by telling her of his exploits as a G.P.U. agent in Bangkok, where he claimed to have pressed a number of maids of the Rajhani Hotel into a Soviet commercial espionage organization which called itself "Association of Employees of Europeans."

The more Firelei learned of the underground machine of the Comintern, the more pronounced became her distaste for the communist movement as a whole. The single-track fanaticism, the matter-of-fact callousness, and the intolerance of many of the communists she met, appalled her.

"How can people who talk of nothing but destruction and bloodshed lead humanity to freedom and happiness?" she asked.

"You must understand that we are at war," I answered. "The purpose of war is to annihilate the enemy. We must destroy before we can build anew."

"But why must we borrow the methods from Russia? Everything you do is aimed at violence. I don't like violence."

"Every birth is like a revolution—violent! Even the most gentle child enters life amid screams and blood."

"I have so much to learn," Firelei said.

"You must learn how to hate," I told her.

"I wish we could go away and live our own lives," Firelei concluded.

One night I returned very late from a dash to Rotterdam. I was surprised to see that the light was still burning in our room. Firelei was not asleep. I found her poring over a sheaf of manuscripts I had written, partly in San Quentin and partly during odd hours, to take my mind off the often sickening pressure of Comintern business. The stack included the manuscript of a book, and a number of short sketches and articles dealing with the experiences and observations of my early years aboard sailing ships. Firelei's voice was tinged with jubilation.

"This is a discovery!" she exclaimed. "Why have you never told me that you write? Why don't you send these pieces out to be published? Let's do it! I think they are vivid, really good."

I saw at once that Firelei hoped that my writing could open for her and me a life away from the Comintern.

"They are not Marxist," I said. "I just wrote them because I dream sometimes of going back to a sailor's life."

"Just because of that! Let me send them out."

She begged irresistibly. Next morning she went to the city library to explore publications likely to accept material portraying the ways of ships and sailors. The following days she toiled at my typewriter, putting a number of manuscripts she had selected into shape. She worked devotedly, and with an enthusiasm that astonished me. The book manuscript which I had named "Scum's Wake" she promptly dispatched to a publishing house in New York. A description of a sailing vessel maneuvering through a foggy English Channel night went to the *Blue Peter*, a nautical magazine appearing in London. A story of Heligoland, to which Firelei affixed the title "Silver Bridges," was sent to a tourist periodical in Hamburg, and an account of my stowaway voyage from Shanghai to Vancouver was put on its way to a New York travel magazine. Firelei continued to re-type more of my manuscripts during spare hours.

Weeks flew by fast. And then came one triumph after another to the girl I loved. *Blue Peter* accepted my article, "Fog." From New York came a fairly handsome check for my stowaway yarn, and the German tourist journal was equally fast in paying for "Silver Bridges." The American publishing house reported that "Scum's Wake" was under consideration. The magazine editors asked me to send them more stories. I stared at the checks, not knowing what to do. I was half bewildered by such unlooked-for success, and apprehensive of a publicity I did not want. For me to write for bourgeois publications was like trading with the enemy. But not so to Firelei.

"Follow it up," she pushed me with bright eagerness. "Write some more." Firelei did all she could to overcome my foolish resistance.

"Go on writing," she urged. "In this way we will win freedom."

"Freedom from what?"

"From people who hold you in their hands like a pawn."

"Listen," I objected. "I belong to the Comintern."

"You belong to yourself—and to me!"

"I cannot do it. I believe that loyalty to a chosen cause is the greatest thing in a man's life."

Firelei came close to me. She murmured endearments. "Let us be ourselves," she said. "We need not be dependent. We are fit enough to shape our own destiny. We need not rummage in secrecy and ugliness."

Firelei was afraid of the future. She knew enough now of the Comintern service to realize that, sooner or later, it would disrupt and smash any harmonious relationship between any man and woman in its ranks.

"What is on your mind?" I asked her brusquely.

"Shall I tell you?"

"Do."

"I want a baby."

I could not find the answer to give her. We had never spoken of marriage. We both believed that a union between a man and a woman cannot be made holier or more enduring by the official blessings of a functionary or a clergyman. But we both believed that it was a crime to have a child when the possibility of bringing it up in security and happy surroundings was lacking, and when the parents lived in constant fear of sudden flight or of a prolonged plunge into prison.

"I am bound to serve the cause as long as I live," I said, well aware of waverings inside.

"Write, all the same. You may change your mind some day," Firelei said quietly.

I found time to write. I played with the idea of breaking away and striking out on my own the way a soldier toys with the thought of deserting his muddy trench to return to a distant homestead, never earnestly believing that it can be realized. The ties which held me shackled to the communist machine were stronger than I cared to admit to myself. Nevertheless, I wrote, with Firelei at my side. Whenever I began a piece, I finished it in a single sitting which usually ended at dawn. Five or six articles and stories, all of which had the sea as their background, went out to various magazines. The editors sent me checks in return, and printed what I had written. Strangely enough, all this did not excite me at all. I took it as a matter of course, in the belief that "there is nothing a Bolshevik cannot do." Had I not won Firelei? My self-confidence still bordered on the monstrous. I would not have shied away from an assignment to sail a canoe around Cape Horn or to take charge of the government of Afghanistan. Meanwhile Firelei was making plans for my literary career, and talked of renting a fisherman's cottage on a desolate spot of the Flanders coast.

The end of this period of wavering came like a sudden awakening from a long and erratic dream. It came in the form of a messenger from Ernst Wollweber in Berlin. The messenger was Michel Avatin, the Lett, whom I had helped to conduct across the ocean aboard the *Montpelier* six years earlier. The years, it seemed, had not made him older. Compact, firm-faced, swift-moving and ever at ease, he appeared one evening at the International Club in Antwerp and embarked immediately on a thorough overhauling of the organization which I had a mandate to direct. I liked to work with Avatin. He was efficient and incorruptible. His reputation in the Comintern was that of a man who never crawled, never begged favor, never accorded mercy to shirkers. He was known to have friends and backers high in the councils of the G.P.U. and the Russian Party. But he was the kind of man who never demanded anything of anyone that he would not be able and willing to do himself.

Avatin exercised many functions as a representative of the Foreign Division of the G.P.U. His routine check-up on the soundness of the Comintern's international *Apparat* in the Lowlands was only part of his mission. His main job was that of director of the Party's *"S-Apparat,"* the espionage department, in Germany and the smaller adjoining countries. In Antwerp, he requested my assistance in compiling a select list of little-known but reliable young communists to be planted within the Russian White Guard organizations in Belgium and Holland. Avatin also went into conference with one of his aides, who was an employee of the Italian consulate in Antwerp. Mussolini's *Ovra* was very active in luring exiled Italian revolutionists to Southern France, particularly to Marseilles, where they were occasionally abducted to Italy. The conference between the Lettish spy hunter and the Italian took place in the suburban office of Comrade Anton, the resident agent of the G.P.U. in Antwerp.

"When you catch an *Ovra* spy, what do you do with him?" I asked Michel Avatin.

"We cross-examine the unimportant ones, then give them a hard beating, and let them flee. The dangerous spies we execute, to strike fear into their colleagues."

Abruptly, while we were striding along a street, Avatin said: "Take me to your quarters. I have instructions for you from Comrade Wollweber."

"But I am not under Wollweber's jurisdiction."

"Perhaps you are. He has taken over our military work in Central Europe."

The tone in which Avatin said this was casual, but I thought it had a mildly ominous undertone. "Central Europe" embraced Switzerland, Czechoslovakia, the Netherlands and Belgium. We mounted the six flights of stairs to my garret quarters. In a flash Avatin's eyes had taken in every detail of the place. Firelei was there. There was a startled look in her eyes. Her lips parted, she moved forward to greet the Lett, a stranger to her. It was obvious that Avatin's appearance—a strongly masculine mixture of Viking and Mongol—had instantly caught her artistic interest.

Michel Avatin shot a questioning glance in my direction.

"She is my comrade," I said.

"Party member?"

"No."

"I regret," Avatin muttered. "Please ask her to leave us alone for one hour."

Firelei picked up a book, and left the apartment without uttering a word.

Chapter Sixteen

FIRELEI MAKES HER DECISION

As Michel Avatin faced me squarely, he was the image of all the power of the Comintern and the G.P.U. He possessed the uncompromising poise of a fanatic who regarded himself as a member of the ruling caste of one-sixth of the surface of the earth.

"How can you, an international representative engaged in illegal work," he demanded, "allow someone who is not a Party member to know an address on the secrecy of which depends the safety of our conspirative *Apparat*?"

"Which address?"

"*This* address. *Your* address."

"The girl is trustworthy," I said.

"Trustworthiness is a mere assumption until it has been tested in the fire," countered Avatin. "She is not a Party member."

Our conversation became increasingly bitter. A Party spy in the Antwerp *Apparat* had collected a lot of details about my personal life, and reported them to Comrade Anton who, doing his duty as a G.P.U. representative, had included them in his regular reports to Berlin. Avatin spoke quite frankly about this system of "mutual Bolshevist control." The reports had reached Ernst Wollweber who, with the assent of Dimitrov, had just then decided to place me in charge of the illicit traffic in firearms from Belgium to Germany. It was shortly after Chancellor Bruening, the Catholic leader, had dissolved the Reichstag and fixed September 14 as the date for a general election. The election struggle was being carried on in a spirit of civil war. To the surprise of all, the Nazi Party, under Hitler and Goering, struck out for power with unexpected ferocity. Communists fought Socialists. Socialists fought the Hitler troops. Hitler guards fought Communists. Ernst Thaelmann, the Communist Party figurehead, had announced: "After the destruction of the Socialists, the final struggle for power in Germany will be between Bolshevism and Fascism." The military section of the German Communist Party needed arms which were hard to get in Germany. They had to be smuggled in from the border countries. Wollweber had selected me to take charge of this enterprise on the Belgian side. The fact that Firelei was not a trained and tested Party member, endangered—in communist eyes—not only this project, but also all other illegal enterprises with which I was connected.

"You are long enough in the movement to understand this," said Avatin. "You must either drop your girl or make a communist of her. Let danger test her loyalty. Then we will welcome her warmly."

"I suppose the alternative is that I'll be kicked out of the Party?"

"There is no such alternative."

"I know it."

"We cannot release anyone who has worked in the *Apparat*. What is a girl? The world is full of girls. To us, the Party is everything, the beginning and end of all things."

"Perhaps Firelei does not want to enter the Party."

"If she loves you—and does not want to lose you—she will become a member of our Party," Avatin said.

"And otherwise both she and I would have to go to the Soviet Union?"

"That is the only way, comrade."

Avatin had a way of suddenly changing his tune. Now he used persuasion, and spoke like an anxious friend. "Comrade, the path you are taking is the wrong path." Now he spoke with the double-edged pride of a zealous officer about to lead his troops to glory and death. "We live for the revolution—it is impossible for us to live any other life."

Totalitarian faith and reckless obedience won. Avatin and I and countless others knew only one master—the Party and the Comintern, and had but one obsession, that the battle for revolution was the only worthwhile aim in our age. It was *Parteibefehl* that I should discard Firelei or win her unconditionally to the cause. It was *Parteibefehl* that I should cease writing for publications which Leninist theory identified with the enemy camp. I stopped writing. I scrapped my dreams of independence which now looked insipid and false. I became rude when Firelei hesitated to let me bend her to my will. I purchased guns in Brussels and Antwerp and had them smuggled into Germany by maritime couriers. I worked to exhaustion so as not to have time to think. I was violently at war with the avid individualist who was my other self. A strange harshness took hold of me, and I trampled on the beauty and tenderness I had barely learned to cherish. Firelei left me, horrified, not comprehending the sudden change. I traced her, and all night I stood on the street in front of her refuge and roared her name like a wild beast. Two policemen brought me to my senses. They released me after I explained that I was not a madman.

After four days' absence, Firelei returned to me. Her infatuation was stronger by far than her instinctive insistence on a normal way of life. Her capacity for self-abasement was as great as mine.

During the following two weeks, rush work kept me busy for sixteen hours a day and more. Two middle-aged men, who looked like prosperous merchants, came to Antwerp by airplane from Paris with credentials from Dimitrov. I had been advised by the Western Secretariat in Berlin, in a coded message, to assist the two arrivals in every possible way. The two were the chiefs of the South American bureau of the Communist International with headquarters in Paris. One was Gustav Sabottka, a Czech, who also headed Moscow's international campaigns among the miners. The other was a quiet-spoken Russian or Pole, who used an American passport and was known to communists in Belgium and France as "Comrade René." Both had a formidable reputation in the confidential circles of the Soviet secret service abroad. They were accompanied by two smart-looking female secretaries and a bodyguard of three Frenchmen of the Paris Red Front League. The girls smelled of *eau-de-cologne* and the men of atrocious French cigars. Comrade Anton and I had a communist family move from its home in the Merxem suburb, to provide a temporary abode for the South American bureau. In such cases, secret private quarters were essential, because hotels were obliged to report their guest lists daily to the police.

The newcomers' sudden descent on Antwerp had to do with the Comintern's preparations for major coups in a number of South American countries. In most of these countries the Communist Parties operated illegally, necessitating the maintenance of a system of communications which was independent of the mails and cables. For this purpose, we had a net of maritime couriers on ships sailing out of Marseilles, but a sudden raid by the French Sfirete, in connection with communist schemes in Syria and the Near East, had disrupted the Marseilles organization. So it had been decided to move the communications center for South America to Antwerp, until the damage suffered in Marseilles could be repaired.

The organizations at my command in Rotterdam and Antwerp now concentrated for a number of days exclusively on pressing communists, sailing on ships in the South American run, into the Comintern courier service. As a safeguard, they were freed from all regular Party duties. Huge batches of printed matter and much money went to Buenos Aires and Montevideo. These emergency couriers were virtual prisoners of the international *Apparat*, under the surveillance of our lynx-eyed watchers and G.P.U. operatives on the docks of the terminal ports on both sides of the Atlantic. We took these precautions to prevent consignments from becoming "lost." Even out at sea a courier was under the secret surveillance of a fellow-communist in the vessel's crew.

Most of the propaganda literature shipped from Antwerp was destined for distribution among Latin American armies and navies, exhorting the men to mutiny in case of an acute crisis. I learned that astonishing numbers of undercover agents were on their way to South American states. The Communist Parties there were known to have strong anarchist tendencies. Moscow did not trust the Latin American leaders out of sight, and therefore had them amply covered with Comintern supervisors.

Sabottka and René were well satisfied with the prompt way in which I adapted my organization to serve their emergency needs. René became particularly friendly with me. He intimated that he could use me as an organizer on South American rivers. Both of them, beyond a tentative effort at flirtation, ignored Firelei. Sabottka referred to her, in speaking to me, as "your enticing bourgeois wife." I resented it bitterly. But I did my duty as a communist. Private likes and dislikes had no right to survive. René pulled my hair in a fatherly manner. "I shall mention your excellent co-operation in my next report to Moscow," he promised.

Firelei's father appeared unexpectedly in Antwerp. He came to take his daughter back to Germany. Since Firelei wished that I should speak to him, I met him in a hotel room I had rented for the interview. He was a well-preserved and slightly paunchy man, with red cheeks and the outward signs of opulence. He had come, expecting to see his daughter. Instead, he found me. From the first instant I met him as an enemy, determined to repulse him swiftly, ruthlessly, and finally. Inside, I felt I was soft. Brutal aggression was the best defense against this softness.

"Was wuenschen Sie?" I asked, with forced bluntness.

"Where is my daughter?" the man asked huskily.

"Your daughter belongs to me!"

The man pleaded and blustered like a desperate beggar under a rich man's portal. He squirmed and implored. He made threats. He asked for consideration and pity I was sorry for him. I became unnecessarily cruel. "Leave now or I'll throw you down the stairs," I threatened. Firelei's father departed, shaking his fist at me. "I'm going to have your past investigated," he half shouted, half muttered. "I'll make it as hot as hell for you—you communist!"

To him, I knew, I was a vicious hoodlum. I told Firelei what had happened. She suddenly recalled that it was her father's birthday. That made her restive. For a long time she moved aimlessly about the room. She mentioned the rollicking festivals with which her family traditionally celebrated the birthdays of any of their clan. There would be a festival that night at Uncle Bert's. There would be wine and champagne and tables laden with food. On past occasions, Firelei had spoken of these jamborees with disgust, and had said: "They are gobbling and guzzling away a thousand marks in one night while people outside must gnaw dry bread." Now Firelei decided to go to the home of her sea-captain uncle to placate her father, and to try for some sort of truce with the family.

"I will make it clear to him that there is no reason why they should worry and suffer because of me," Firelei said.

"Do you intend to go alone?"

"No. We'll go together. We have nothing to be ashamed of, and nothing to fear."

We went late. A meeting had detained me. Approaching the house, a well-constructed three-story building of gray stone and brick, with a carefully tended little garden on one side, we heard the muffled sounds of feasting. A group was singing—

"Trink, trink Bruederlein trink,
"Lasset die Sorgen zu Hause ..."

I rang the bell. A Flemish maid opened the front door. Firelei walked through the vestibule to a large living room. Many people were there. I heard the clinking of glasses. The furniture had been moved aside to make room for dancing. The singing continued. A jovial roar arose as Firelei entered the living room, but when I followed her all the people suddenly became silent.

I felt the hostility in their heavy stares. Then one of the men rose, and stumped toward me. He was a broad-shouldered Fleming with a full, once weather-beaten face and iron-gray hair. He was Firelei's uncle. It was not easy to discern that one of his legs was artificial. His outstretched arm pointed toward the door.

"Leave my house," he said.

"If you make him leave, I shall leave with him," Firelei said.

Seconds loaded with painful consternation followed. Firelei's father pushed forward, muttering. Other men began to grumble. A woman gasped:

"Jesus-Maria, what a girl!"

"Leave my house!" the one-legged sea-captain repeated imperiously.

"What is the matter with you all?" asked Firelei. I now faced her father.

"I'm sorry about this morning," I mumbled. "Let's try to talk sense."

Five or six people rose, and tramped past us to get their hats. Others walked about the room, not knowing what to do. There was general confusion. Someone crashed his fist on a table. A carafe was pushed over and splintered. A woman rocked to and fro, her hands clasped to her face. Firelei stood immobile. Her left hand touched her throat. Her slender form was upright in the commotion. Her face was pallid. Her eyes showed amazement, her lips bewilderment and scorn. The one-legged man stood in front of me, both hairy fists raised high. He roared into my face:

"How can you do such a thing to me? How can you do such a thing to me?"

Other men gathered around us. The thought of being pounced upon by a number of enraged and half-drunk citizens seemed ridiculous. The men were advancing, and I backed against a wall, looking for Firelei. An elderly woman with black curls grasped Firelei's wrists, and was trying to drag her into an adjoining room. She struggled to free herself. Another woman and a man seized her arms and jerked her about. Meanwhile, the advancing men, led by the sea-captain, were pushing me toward the street door.

"How can you do such a thing to me?" he raged.

"Shut up," I yelled. "You're crazy!"

"Go," he shouted with all the force of his lungs. "Go, I tell you, go!"

It was a bitter burlesque. I suddenly lunged forward, and the men gave way. I leaped across the room where Firelei was still struggling, her dress torn. Her assailants were terrified. They let her go. The one-legged man, his eyes blazing under thick brows, interfered. Firelei cried:

"Uncle Bert, you drank too much, you don't know what you're doing."

The front door slammed with such force that the house vibrated. A man had fallen over the table. He wept. The sea-captain seized Firelei's shoulders. He almost lifted her off the floor.

"A disgrace! A damned disgrace!" he shouted madly. Firelei's father joined him.

"You won't inherit a penny," he threatened. "I won't give you the dirt under a fingernail." He seemed to have gone berserk. Sounds like those of fog-horns came from the throat of the one-legged man:

"A disgrace! Freethinkers and whores!"

Firelei struck him across the mouth. He was silenced.

The black-haired woman wailed, "Our girl, our baby ..."

Firelei was disheveled and frantic. Never had she expected a welcome like this. I led her out of the house. We hurried down the street. For a dozen paces the one-legged man stumped behind us. Then he stopped.

We went in the direction of the harbor. Brassy music brayed from behind the windows of the dives. Sailors rolled toward pleasure. At the corners, prostitutes smoked cigarettes and coaxed passing mariners.

"This was beastly," I panted.

"It was pitiful," Firelei said.

We walked on in silence, skirting the bank of the Schelde until we came to the gloomy battlements of the *Steen,* an ancient fortress of the Jesuits.

"And now—what?" I asked Firelei.

"Where you go—I go," she answered.

Another week passed. Firelei had stubbornly refused to register as a member of the Party, which to her was an alien, impersonal monster.

"Men were not made for uniforms," she said emphatically. "Neither real ones, nor spiritual ones. I can help you in all sincerity without yelling 'Hurrah!' or 'Down at things I know so little about."

My nerves were frayed, my attitude toward Firelei became unfair. I was worn out from overwork and lack of sleep. I was no longer sure of my footing. Life seemed an idiotic carnival, a senseless clamor without respite and joy. One day, Firelei asked me: "Why must you hurt me when you are dissatisfied with yourself?"

"Am I hurting you?"

And then I rushed off to meet René. He was in the company of the eternally calm and mournful Comrade Anton. Also present was an intelligent-looking young man I had not seen before. He was a German, Karl S., a graduate of the Western University in Moscow. He had been sent to Antwerp to relieve me of my duties. I was given another assignment.

"You will acquaint Comrade Karl with the details of your *Apparat*" René said, adding with a fine smile, "I have made arrangements with Comrade Walter. You are going on a trip to Buenos Aires. Your steamer is leaving Southampton in two days. Tell no one where you are going. We shall spread the intelligence that you have returned to Germany."

Little time remained to prepare for my departure. I surrendered to Karl S. all the material, contacts and information he needed to carry on. Then I hastened to the garret that had been home to Firelei and myself through four crowded months. I was standing in front of the bed, packing a suitcase, when Firelei came in. Without saying a word she stepped close to me and put her arms around my neck. But my thoughts were already at the La Plata.

"Please leave me alone," I said.

"Why should I leave you alone?"

"I don't know. I have no time. You disturb me."

Firelei laughed.

"Grumpy-one," she said. "A pleasant welcome you give me.... Or is it farewell? Are you going away?"

"Yes, tonight."

"Where? I am going with you."

"I'm going for the Comintern. I must go alone. I cannot tell you where I am going, but I shall be back before long."

I pretended that I did not hear her sigh. She disengaged her arms, and slumped into a chair.

"Jan," she said, using the name I had adopted for the Lowlands waterfront, "Jan, listen to me, I want to talk to you."

"Go ahead."

"Tell me, am I no more to you than a handy object in bed?" I stopped packing. "No," I said, "you are my comrade."

"Comrade!" she cried, "I hate the word. I hate the bed. I hate the dreary life we are leading. You are always away. You never come to me before midnight. You do not even ask me for food or money. Must it be like that? Must we be so miserably empty when we are together? Why don't we take a holiday and walk through the fields? Why can't we get some flowers and some wine, and have an evening to ourselves?"

I saw her fight back the tears. Firelei was ashamed of tears. "I'm sorry I have made you suffer," I said. "But can't you understand that we are in the midst of the biggest social upheaval of all times, that I follow the most sublime aim any man can follow? I belong to the Cause; I belong to it brain and hide. You've said to me once 'Where you go—I go.' I wish you would follow me. No word has a deeper meaning than the word Comrade."

"I cannot, Jan."

Firelei's face was ghastly pale. Her lips twitched. The tip of her left foot tapped the floor in a nervous tattoo.

"Why can't you?" I demanded harshly.

"Because I can see how these last months have changed you. You have become a serf. A fanatical serf. Whenever you speak of the Party, the muscles in your face seem frozen hard and your eyes are cruel and wild. The Cause, always the Cause."

"It's splendid," I said, "and true!"

"It's ugly," she answered. "It takes everything and gives nothing."

"That's not ugly."

"Yes, it's ugly—a mass of sweating, shouting scarecrows is ugly! "

Firelei crossed the room to where a water color portrait, which she had made of herself in front of a mirror, was fastened on the wall. It had been remarkably well done. She paused in front of it, her eyes scanning every line of the picture.

"Look," she said, "this is I. My breasts are small and firm, my legs are slender and strong, the lines of my hips are enticing and my voice is melodious. I know it, because you have told me so. My eyes are gray, and they like to laugh. When they laugh, they sparkle. They tell me that I belong to you with body and soul. You are much stronger than I. What you make of me, I am."

"You are my comrade," I said.

"Am I?" Firelei smiled. "I dreamt that you had a powerful dog. The dog had the face of Avatin. It forced me to eat in one room while you ate in another. Then you saw me give poison to your dog, and you came and broke my wrists and struck me in the face with the plate from which the dog was eating. When I fell, you told the dog to kill me."

"Firelei! Firelei!" I shouted.

She was still gazing at her likeness. She turned.

"Don't shout," she said softly.

I implored her to be sensible.

"How can I be sensible when you are out of your mind?" she answered serenely.

I hesitated, and said: "I shall take a later train to Vlissingen."

"No," Firelei replied. "You still have an hour before the last train. You are going to England? I have bought candles and a bottle of Madeira. Let us put on our best clothes. Then we will darken the room and light the candles. Let's pretend you've just come back from your voyage."

I boarded the liner *Monte Pascoal* at Southampton Roads, traveling second class, and armed with credentials purporting me to be a representative of the Universum Publishing House in Berlin. The contraband I carried included six reels of film in flat steel cases. I did not know the contents of the films. All I knew was that Sabottka and René attached great importance to having them safely delivered to the central Profintern office in Montevideo (Confederacion Sindical Latino Americana). I also carried several large money envelopes, which were to be called for by one of Arthur Ewert's South American couriers. Money for Latin America was usually transmitted through the Soviet Trade Delegation *(Yujamtorg)* in Buenos Aires. In Comintern circles it was understood—though never mentioned or discussed—that funds not sent by cable, but by secret courier, consisted of currency forged for the Comintern by German craftsmen in Berlin. This was especially true of German, Belgian, French and American currency in denominations of 100. I did not know whether the money I carried to Buenos Aires was counterfeit or not. Its transmission, however, was organized with extraordinary circumspection. It was a very large sum. How large, I had no way of knowing. The three envelopes were marked A, U, and C—Argentine, Uruguay, Chile. Before my departure, there had arrived a beautiful cowhide suitcase built by an expert in Berlin. The money envelopes were placed into its hollow cover in the presence of René, Comrade Anton, and myself. Anton then glued the lining into place. To gain access to the consignment, it would now be necessary to cut open the cover of the suitcase. I then filled the suitcase with harmless papers of the Universum Publishers and with soiled laundry. "It is almost fool-proof," René smiled. "It makes you feel secure. When one feels secure, one acts inconspicuously."

I had paid the rent for my garret quarters for three months in advance. I would be back, I hoped, within sixty days. Firelei promised to face this period of loneliness bravely.

During the voyage to Montevideo I brushed up on my Spanish, became the most persistent visitor of the ship's library, and slept much, and conscientiously avoided all personal contacts with my fellow passengers. Vigo, Lisbon, Rio de Janeiro and Santos were ports of call. I resisted the powerful lure of these ports with success. I did not go ashore with the gay caravans of sightseers, because I was afraid to leave my contraband at the mercy of any possibly inquisitive steward or ship detective. The night before the *Monte Pascoal* entered the yellow mouth of the La Plata, heading for the anchorage off Montevideo, I hid the metal cases containing the films in the biscuit-tank of one of the steamer's lifeboats. The passport and customs inspection by the Uruguayan authorities were perfunctory for the passengers of the first and second class. With a firm grip on my new cowhide suitcase, I journeyed ashore by the first launch.

As I walked from the landing, through the knots of shouting cab-drivers, I noticed that I was shadowed by two well-dressed individuals. One of them kept some twenty yards behind me, the other followed on the opposite side of the street. My first thought was, "Police!" I quickened my stride, turning corner after corner. The two followed. I was debating with myself whether to hail a taxi or to break into a run. The bright yellow suitcase I carried was an object too easily identified. "If I ran, I'd be arrested at once," I calculated. "If I jumped into a taxi my pursuer would take the number of the car or even follow me in another." In desperation, I tried another trick. I pulled a travel booklet out of my pocket, simultaneously throwing a furtive look over my shoulder. I tore the paper into small pieces, so that my shadowers could see what I was doing, and then scattered the shreds into the street. The two sleuths, I felt sure, would stop to pick up the scattered bits of paper. I halted, pretending to look into a shop window, and watched them from the corner of my eyes. They did not stoop to gather the papers. The one behind me grinned brightly, waving both hands in a gesture which among seamen signifies "All clear." I waited, every nerve tense. The man came straight up to me. His companion crossed the street.

"*Zum Teufel,*" the first one laughed, "you run off like a cockroach, you with your long legs."

He had spoken in German. His companion nodded a welcome.

"We come from Harry Berger," the German said.

Harry Berger was the cover name for Arthur Ewert. The two were guards sent to meet me to insure the safety of my consignment. We all boarded a cab, and drove to a small restaurant on the Calle Viejo, the back room of which was the office of the Montevideo liaison agent. There I produced my credentials, which had been typed on linen and sewed into the shoulder-lining of my coat. The liaison agent, a burly, fluff-faced German, at once dispatched a courier to the *Monte Pascoal* to smuggle the heavy metal film containers ashore.

Montevideo and Buenos Aires served as Comintern headquarters for all countries south of the Panama Canal. Communism in South America was entirely under the direction of foreign agents. Russians, Germans, Poles, Letts and Finns were in responsible positions, and there were a number of New Yorkers in the corps of traveling agitators.

My stopover in Montevideo lasted several weeks. A female representative of the Yujemtorg office in Buenos Aires came to Montevideo on one of the week-end excursion steamers. She was a thin, bloodless person of about thirty-five, smartly dressed and harshly matter-of-fact. She was the secretary of the Bolshevik Party cell among the *Yujamtorg* personnel, and probably a stationary agent of the G.P.U. To her I surrendered the cowhide suitcase. She scrutinized the lining of its cover with a magnifying glass, and, finding the identification marks and the lining intact, she handed me a receipt for "one case of electric bulbs." Incidentally, less than a year later, on July 31, 1931, the *Yujamtorg* was raided and closed by the Buenos Aires police. It then moved across the La Plata, and was re-established in Montevideo. Proof of the close connection between the *Yujamtorg* and the bloody communist insurrections in Brazil caused the Uruguayan government to close its offices and expel the Soviet trade envoy, Minkin, in December, 1935. It was then that Arthur Ewert was arrested as the leader of the revolutionary outbreaks in Brazil, where he is still imprisoned, although renounced and abandoned by the Comintern.

The hospitality of the communists of Montevideo exceeded anything I had so far encountered in Europe or in the United States. I was given a luxurious room in a private house on the outskirts of the city. I was lavishly fed. Each day brought invitations to dinner in the homes of local communists—which included doctors, tallymen and tugboat captains now on the payroll of the Profintern. There were many pretty girls showing their eagerness to throw themselves into the arms of the foreign *camarado*. Germans in general were at that period most popular in South America. Even the tough-looking *hombres* in the communist rank and file tried to outdo each other to win the patronage of a Bolshevik from overseas. Often enough a meeting ended with a dusky comrade sidling up to me and, with flashing of eyes and teeth, suggesting in an intimate whisper: *"Oiga—senorita pequenc y hermosa? Vamanos! Pagaro!"* I declined. I was hungrily waiting for a letter from Firelei. I had told her to turn over mail for me to Comrade Anton, who would forward it. But none arrived.

My sojourn ended after I had spoken as a delegate of the Maritime Section of the Comintern at a conference of waterfront functionaries from Peru, Chile, Uruguay and the Argentine. Action programs were drafted for the seamen, the dockers, the rivermen and the personnel of the South American navies. I cited the details of the mutiny of the German fleet in 1918 to impress the Latin

Americans with the importance of building up communist units in every navy. I spoke enthusiastically, and even the cheeks of my interpreter were hot with enthusiasm.

Little did I dream then that in September, 1931, during the presidential election campaign, the Comintern would make a serious bid for power in Chile. The country became paralyzed by strikes and riots. The slogan "All power to the Soviets!" was raised. The Chilean fleet mutinied and the mutineers seized naval bases. Martial law was declared and eighty government airplanes bombed and machine-gunned the mutineers. The revolt was crushed. Three hundred and twenty mutineers died in the battle. A score of ringleaders were sentenced to death, and many more sent to prison.

My job was done. I crossed to Buenos Aires and there embarked on the *Cap Arcona* for Europe. No letter from Firelei had reached me. This deeply worried me. The fast liner hammered northward, no man aboard her more impatient to get home than I. Aboard the *Cap Arcona,* I made a disquieting discovery. The German Reichstag elections had taken place during my absence from Europe. The Communist Party had gained a million votes, and had become the third strongest party in the land. The Socialists had lost many hundred thousands of their followers. The Comintern policy of wrecking them had not been in vain! But the surprise that came like a thunderclap from the clear skies was the tremendous advance of the Hitler movement, which up to this time had been regarded worthy only of disdain. In one gigantic leap the National Socialists had increased their mandates in the Reichstag from 12 to 107; they who only two years earlier had but one-fifth of the communist strength now ranked as the second strongest political party in the country. Some new, hitherto unknown force was rising with the ominous roar of a yet distant tide-rip. And I first saw its signs aboard the *Cap Arcona.*

The crew of the ship, one of the largest in the German merchant fleet, contained a strong, disciplined, well-organized cell of Nazi storm troopers, who flooded the vessel with their propaganda. I observed them doing drills and gymnastics during their watch below. They were a band whose elan and defiance of all outsiders compared with nothing I had as yet perceived under the German flag. They exercised their rule through a combination of propaganda and terror. All of them were young, representing a high type of German youth. I came to the conclusion that is was time to do something, to do it soon, to do it with all the energy and persistence at our command. I remembered the warning voice of Arthur Ewert: "We shall be destroyed!"

Upon my arrival in Hamburg I submitted my report and I was immediately given a new assignment which called for my presence for some months in Bremen and the Weser country. Ernst Wollweber in addition to his many other controlling functions, had acquired the chieftainship of all communist forces in German shipping, railroads and communications. Ernst Thaelmann and his satellites were more often in Moscow than in Berlin. Maneuvering in the dark with much patience and genuine ability, Ernst Wollweber, the saturnine ex-mutineer whose cradle had been rocked among the coal mines of Silesia, became more and more the dominating force behind the scenes of the strongest and best-organized communist movement outside of Russia. I was now directly responsible to Wollweber, and subject to his orders.

I telegraphed to Firelei, but received no reply. I notified Wollweber that I intended to make a dash to Antwerp for a day or two. He replied that the Party could not recognize the validity of private enterprises on the part of its employees. I wrote back to Berlin by airmail that I had no "private enterprises," but requested a short leave of absence to find Firelei and to arrange for her coming to Bremen. I stressed the fact that Firelei's artistic talents would be of value to the propaganda department of the Party. Wollweber answered in what approached an ultimatum. "Intimate contacts between responsible comrades and un-proletarian outsiders are out of the question," he wrote. "I have made that clear to you before. Please accept my standpoint. Unless the person (Firelei) becomes a member of our organization and submits to its discipline, we must reject her as a possible danger to our *Apparat*. If you cannot understand that, you have not grasped the Leninist definition of what a Bolshevist Party should be."

I went to Antwerp. It was the beginning of November. A wet wind howled in from the North Sea, and rain-water gurgled in the gutters. I stormed up the stairways to the garret where Firelei and I had had so many happy hours together. At the top landing I stopped for breath. My heart pounded. I drew the key, unlocked the door, and entered. The place was empty. A thin layer of dust was on the floor. There were no books, no clothes, no curtained windows that faced the tower of the Cathedral. Only gaping, depressing emptiness. Firelei had left no message. Then my eyes struck something horrible. There was the picture Firelei had painted of herself, tall, silent, and tender in its colors. Dismally it stared at the stripped room. It was the portrait of a murdered girl. The plaster on the walls showed through where the eyes had been. The eyes had been cut out.

I began a frantic search. The landlord knew nothing. He only grumbled about the nuisance of having lone women go and make a mess of things. I raced to the house of Firelei's uncle, but the door there was slammed into my face. I questioned the neighbors. No, they said, the German painter-girl had not come back to the sea-captain's home. I phoned the police. I questioned Comrade Anton and all other Antwerp communists who might have known her. None of them knew where Firelei had gone, except, perhaps, Anton—and he refused to tell because I had not come to Belgium in an official capacity. "Maybe she has returned to her parents in Germany," he suggested. "Daughters of the *petit bourgeoisie* capitulate at the first serious obstacle."

It was not true. The large-bosomed and large-hearted *madame* of the Café Banana, where Firelei went at times to sketch waterfront types, knew what had happened to my girl.

"She is in the hospital, the poor *meisje*," she said in her masculine voice. "She was very ill. But she is better now, nearly well. Why in the name of the Saviour did you not take better care of her?"

"What happened? Tell me quick!"

"An abortion," the woman said. *"Godsverdumme,* she was brave enough to do it herself. She nearly bled to death when they came for her."

Intense remorse, self-accusation, pangs of conscience racked my whole being. I fought them with gnashing teeth. Through the eyes of the twisted rationalism of a communist such mental agony was the attribute of weaklings. I tried to think: "Daily throughout the world, men and women stumble and fall. Shall we stop our advance because of personal calamities inevitable as sunrise?"

"Firelei loves flowers," I thought. "They would be a sign that I stood with her." I bought flowers, and with them I tiptoed to her bedside. How could I ever forget the expression of joyful relief on her face when she saw me? A long time we looked at each other, holding hands, not saying a word.

Firelei spoke first, after a long, radiant smile.

"You have come back," she said.

I talked of many things that I knew would please her. And then I asked: "Why did you do it?"

"I thought you'd never come back," she answered softly. "I have learned how it feels to die."

Day after day I lingered in Antwerp. Firelei's recovery was like the coming of spring. A wire from Wollweber reminded me that it was November, the stormiest month of the year.

"Return without delay," the wire said.

"I must go," I told Firelei.

"Soon I shall be well enough to follow you," she said happily. "It will be good to share life with you."

"All our life we will be comrades," I said.

The color in her cheeks had disappeared. Her face looked thinner, harder, more determined.

"I have changed my mind," she said. "I had much time to think. The day I come to Bremen you must make me a member of the Communist Party."

Inadvertently I recoiled. I knew that it was not her acceptance of Bolshevism, but her love for me, which brought her to this decision.

"In Bremen you will meet my mother," I said.

"I am glad," Firelei smiled. "She and I will be friends, I feel sure."

Chapter Seventeen

BETWEEN THE HAMMER AND THE ANVIL

Captain Goering, Hitler's right-hand man, was scheduled to appear as the main speaker at a mass meeting of the National Socialists in Bremen. The chief of the anti-Nazi division of the Communist Party, the ruthless Heinz Neumann, gave the command to break up the meeting. Our local leaders shunned this duty, perhaps because they learned to respect Goering's storm troopers. As a newcomer, I was delegated to do the job. This was part of my new assignment.

A hundred picked men from the Red Front League were placed at my disposal for the Goering affair. They were fearless young roughnecks, one and all. We had a special leaflet printed for distribution at the meeting, under the headline: *"Ten questions Nazi Goering fears to answer."* I detailed my men into groups of five and instructed them to mingle with the crowd in the hall and to go into action at the shout, "The National Socialists are neither national nor socialist." Each man was armed with a blackjack and brass knuckles, and a batch of fifty leaflets.

The meeting was to begin at eight in the Kasino, the largest hall in town. A steady stream of men and women flowed through all the streets leading to the Kasino. A platoon of policemen occupied all surrounding corners. Girls and young men roamed the sidewalks. Some wore red bands around their sleeves—they sold communist publications. Others wore the swastika insignia—they shouted Hitler slogans in raucous chorus. Here and there a minor affray broke out, but was quickly squelched by the police. Brownshirted troopers marched by in closed formations. A howl went up: "Down with the Brown murderers!"

"Down with the Muscovite pest!" came in prompt reply. Thousands jammed the hall. Ranged along the walls and in front of the speaker's stage, storm troopers stood shoulder to shoulder. A brass band played a war march. Crimson banners of gigantic dimensions covered the walls. A hundred bearers of swastika flags formed the background of the stage. In the huge crowd, my crew of communists were like a drop in a river.

All of a sudden the array of Brownshirts lining the walls stood at attention. Right arms flew upward. The band blared fanfares. The massive walls of the building seemed to shake as the human mass broke out in one tremendous roar:

"Heil! Heil!"

A score of stalwarts goose-stepped down the aisle toward the stage. They were followed by uniformed men bearing storm banners. The golden swastika which topped the banners glittered under the lights. And then a grim-faced, burly man in civilian clothes strode down the aisle. His chunky right arm was raised in the Hitler salute. Another column of stalwarts followed directly behind him. A bell rang. The roar ceased. A whip-like man, with a military voice, announced that Captain Goering would speak on "Versailles must die so Germany may live."

The chunky man stepped forward, glowering at the audience, his broad muscular face brilliant under the spotlight. A beautiful blonde girl presented to the Nazi chieftain a bouquet of roses as large as a wheel. Captain Goering sniffed the roses, and grinned. Then he took off his coat and threw it carelessly behind him under the table. He rolled up his shirt sleeves and loosened his belt. Laughter of approval mixed with applause. Goering swung his arms, as if to limber up, and the applause rose to a booming roar.

Captain Goering spoke. His speech was rude and vigorous, scornful of politeness, and so simple that a child often could have understood him. What convinced his hearers, however, were less his words than the impression of truculent and brutal personal honesty which he created. His voice and his fists pounded the Treaty of Versailles. He paced up and down on the stage, fists clenched, hairy arms flying, his face streaming with sweat. His voice became a gale of menacing sounds. He worked himself into a blazing fury. He yelled and growled and hammered. He grumbled and pranced in mad outbursts of wrath. He attacked everything in the world from God down to pawnbrokers and nudists, excepting only the Army. He unleashed a wild surf of hatred, and sent it thundering into his audience. I was amazed to find the mass of stolid Germans more excited than a crowd of Spaniards in a bull ring. I tried to be cool, tried to take notes on what I intended to say after Captain Goering had finished, but soon gave it up. The man fascinated me.

At last Goering ended amid an earthquake of applause. He sat down and mopped his face. He fished his coat from under the table and wrapped it carelessly around his shoulders. The whip-like man with the military voice rose and asked if any representatives of enemy parties wished to speak ten minutes each to refute Captain Goering, who would be glad to answer all questions raised. I rose and stepped forward, automatically obeying my *"Parteibefehl!"* I felt my scalp shrivel and grow cold. I handed the whip-like man a slip of paper, bearing my name and Party affiliation.

The whip-like man announced: "A representative of the Communist Party now has the word. I beg the meeting to maintain discipline."

I mounted the stage. A deathly silence descended upon the great hall. Troopers of Goering's bodyguard eyed me curiously.

After the first sentence, my self-confidence returned. There were snickers and catcalls, but there was also the frenetic applause of my hundred aides in the crowd. I pointed out that the Treaty of Versailles was the consequence of a lost war, and that the war had been provoked by capitalists for imperialist purposes. "All Germany knows," I went on to say, "that the Nazi Party is financed by capitalists exploiting the German nation. The National Socialist Party is neither national nor socialist—yet it calls itself a workers' party!" At this point I turned and pointed toward Captain Goering: "Does this man look like a worker?"

Goering thrust his bull-head forward. Half a dozen troopers jumped on the stage and rushed me. *"Raus mit dem Halunken!"* Goering ordered, "Out with this scoundrel!" That same instant my aides, in groups of five, rose in the crowd and hurled fistfuls of the small red leaflets though the densely packed auditorium. There was general tumult. I leaped off the stage over the heads of the troopers below, and plunged headlong into the crowd. A blackjack came down on my head. In the excitement I barely noticed the impact. The Brownshirts had left their points of vantage along the walls, and were lunging toward the center of the hall, to fall upon the intruders. A terrifying melee followed. Blackjacks, brass knuckles, clubs, heavy buckled belts, glasses and bottles were the weapons used. Pieces of glass and chairs hurtled over the heads of the audience. Men from both sides broke off chair legs, and used them as bludgeons. Women fainted in the crash and scream of battle. Already dozens of heads and faces were bleeding, clothes were torn as the fighters dodged about amid masses of terrified but helpless spectators. The troopers fought like lions. Systematically they pressed us toward the main exit. The band struck up a martial tune. Hermann Goering stood calmly on the stage, his fists on his hips. My plan had been to create such a pandemonium in the packed hall that the police forces waiting outside would barge in and close the meeting. But the police did not intervene; it was controlled by Social Democrats, who were satisfied to let the antidemocratic forces break each others' heads undisturbed.

All about me communists were fighting now to gain the street. They ran off like hares. I also ran. Rounding a corner, I passed a big open motor lorry. In it sat thirty policemen, motionless, holding their rifles like silent specters.

My mother, who lived a quiet life in her tiny Bremen apartment, received Firelei well. She abhorred communism, because it preached violence and denied God, but her urge to aid those in need knew no discrimination. Had a drunken murderer come to her for help, she would have given it to him. Her three small rooms were full of memories of the past. My mother loved to regard her home as an open haven for her five wandering children and their friends. Both of my brothers, sturdy six-footers obsessed by an invincible wanderlust, had gone to sea. My two sisters also were away, the older one as a nurse in a Berlin hospital, the younger as a photographic expert with the scientific expeditions of Dr. Leo Frobenius, the African explorer in the wilds of Sudan. "Oh, but they always come back to me," my mother smiled, content to wait.

One day Firelei said to me: "Mother is worried about you. When you became a communist, she tried hard to understand communism, but she could not. It breaks her heart to see you work only for destruction and strife. She prays that you should turn away from it."

"It is too late," I said.

"Another thinks it is never too late. She has begged me to influence you to go to navigation school to study for the next officers' examinations. She says it has always been your dream to stand as a captain on the bridge of a liner."

"It is still my dream," I said, struggling to hide a treacherous upsurge of emotion. "Only tell me—who would entrust a known communist and an ex-convict with a valuable ship? No, no, it is far too late!"

"Why not do it, and see what comes of it?" Firelei implored. "There is nothing you cannot do. With a navigator's license in your pocket, you will surely find a berth. Remember, it is never, never too late!"

I did not neglect my various Party duties. But I found time to enroll as a student at the Nautical School in Bremen. Its director, Captain Preuss, had known my father well. He received me warmly.

"Sieh, wer kommt denn da!" he boomed. "Well, well, my boy, have you become tired of the Bolshevist nonsense?"

"How do you know I'm a Bolshevik?" I asked, somewhat embarrassed.

"Allah told me," laughed Preuss, adding seriously: "Don't be a fool. Shipowners have their information service. You've been giving them a lot of trouble lately. They've got your name on the blacklist—in red ink, I assure you. However—repent, and we shall see what we can do."

Attending school consumed but little of my time. I had mastered the essential mathematics and nautical astronomy in San Quentin, and had to put in but a few hours at school each week to conform with the government regulations for prospective ships' officers. I had no reason at this time for shouldering the additional burden of studies other than that of trying to please my mother. I was overworked, ate insufficiently, and slept too little. But my mother was overjoyed; in her innocent heart she believed that she had won a victory over the Comintern.

I found the Nautical School a citadel of Hitler. The staff of thirty teachers was composed of Nazis. The roughly three hundred students were Nazis. The officers' club—the Tritonia—was dominated by Nazis. The school was swamped with Nazi literature. During recesses, the school roared with Nazi meetings. Many of the students came to the lectures in storm troopers' uniforms. Every coat lapel around me boasted the flashy swastika insignia. I was the only communist there.

"Why are you a Nazi?" I asked one of them. It was toward the end of 1930.

"Look what this so-called democracy has done for us," he answered with complete self-assurance. "Half of our ships are rotting in graveyards. Adolf Hitler will lead Germany to its rightful place among the nations. We shall have colonies. We are going to expand in all directions. We are going to have the finest merchant marine in the world. Under Hitler, our ships will sail—and not rot."

"A program of imperialist expansion," I commented.

"Most certainly!"

"That'll mean war."

"What of it? Men were born to wage—and win—wars."

"The German people want no war."

"*We* are the German people."

"Look at Russia," I said. "It is the only country in the world whose merchant marine is growing."

"Don't tell me about Russia," replied the Nazi. "I've been to Vladivostok with my last ship. The girls there come aboard to let themselves be raped five times for a tin of sardines. That's Bolshevism for you!"

"The Russians exported more grain than Canada did last year," I countered.

"I advise you to stop your communist propaganda in this school," the Nazi said coldly. "Some of our boys might bring their riding whips and flog you out of the building. So hold your tongue."

Firelei, whose deep love for me had driven her into the movement, soon won considerable popularity in the German Communist Party. She painted posters which the Party used in nationwide drives. Her caricatures of Hindenburg and Hitler and other enemy leaders were reproduced in the Party press. She organized theatrical groups which toured the German Northwest; the most famous and talented of these groups was called the "Red Reporters." Without receiving a penny of remuneration, she worked from morning till night. She was kept too busy to realize that her plunge into Party work doomed her hopes for a legitimate career as an artist. At times, when she was tired, she would ponder and ask, "Where does all this lead to?"

"Forward and upward!" I would answer. "We have no time to be tired."

I had stopped my sallies into the field of literature. When I wrote, I wrote for the Party press. My articles and sketches appeared in a number of communist dailies and weeklies. On orders from Wollweber, I had cut short all efforts to publish my book, "Scum's Wake," in the United States. Instead it was censored by the literary department of the Comintern, to eliminate deviations from official Stalinist policy, and in mutilated form it appeared in the camouflaged German communist press controlled by Willy Muenzenberg and several trade union publications in Soviet Russia. Since I was a salaried employee of the Comintern, I was formally requested to contribute the payments due to me toward "the successful completion of the Five-Year-Plan." I did so cheerfully. As a reward, I was nominated to the post of honorary president of the League of Proletarian Writers in the Northwest District.

I had also written two one-act plays which were entitled "Signal of Mutiny" and "The Sailor's Enemies." They were both accepted by the Party and subsequently performed by the communist theatrical groups aboard the largest liners of the North German Lloyd in Bremerhaven, including the crack ships *Columbus* and *Bremen,* causing a greater disturbance in shipowners' circles than a month of intensive strike agitation. The plays were open incitements to mutiny, veritable commands to the crews to seize the ships and to hoist the red flags when the time was ripe. Simultaneously with these performances went a dogged propaganda aboard the vessels of the North German Lloyd, the company that practically dominated the old Hanseatic metropolis of Bremen. Great, therefore, was my astonishment, when I was approached one day by a representative of the *Lloyd Verlag,* the publishing house of the North German Lloyd. The representative invited me to call at the editorial headquarters of the company for a confidential conversation with the editor-in-chief of the *Lloyd Journal.* Loyally I wired Wollweber informing him of the fact.

"Be careful," he replied, "their object is bribery. But the contact may be of value."

The editor-in-chief received me graciously. She was a cultured woman, a certain Miss von Thuelen, the sister of one of the most powerful personages in the North German Lloyd. Serenely she informed me that the company had been informed that I experienced financial difficulties in completing my term at the Nautical School. She offered me a contract to write one article a month for her magazine, a total of twelve pieces at two hundred marks each. I refused. She then asked me if I would consider translating the official tourist guide for 1931 of the North German Lloyd from German into English. This tourist guide was well known in all North Atlantic ports. It was a two-hundred-page book praising the beauties of Germany. Miss von Thuelen offered me a thousand marks to do the job. I accepted. The tacit understanding was that I should refrain from all further efforts at stirring up trouble among the crews of the Lloyd ships.

Wollweber considered planting me as an undercover agent of the Comintern inside the North German Lloyd. This plan, however, was torpedoed by Heinz Neumann, who wanted me for his anti-Nazi campaigns. I did only a small part of the translation myself. The bulk was done in record time by official translators of the Communist Party. After ten days, I was able to deliver the English version of the tourist guide. I received a check for one thousand marks. The money went into the treasury of the Communist Party, and I continued to harass the North German Lloyd at every possible turn. Again I had wantonly thrown away a chance of building up for myself an independent existence within the law. Firelei was stunned by my recklessness. My mother was deeply hurt by my treachery.

Wollweber was on one of his tours of inspection to all the communist units in the transport industry of Central Europe. The man was uncanny. No detail, no weakness escaped him. He was a beast with the brain of a malevolent scientist. There was nothing he feared, except publicity. I said to him good-naturedly, "They call you the 'Little Lenin,' but you're much more like Stalin than Lenin."

At that Wollweber stopped short. "What makes you think that?" he asked, showing his tobacco-stained teeth in a grin.

"Well," I said warily, "Comrade Lenin was always before the masses."

"What have you got against Comrade Stalin?" Wollweber scowled.

"Nothing," I said.

"Comrade Stalin is the greatest living statesman," Wollweber declared, as if he were sentencing someone to be hung. "No one who questions this assertion can ever be used in a vital function."

That evening, the day's work done, Ernst Wollweber said to me: "Now let's go and be happy."

"What is it that you need to be happy?"

"A quiet place, where a man can let go of the life-lines, and drink a case of beer in peace."

I laughed. I invited Wollweber to my quarters in the proletarian Westend of the city. I bought two cases of beer and cajoled the landlady into preparing a large amount of *Bratwurst* and potato salad. Wollweber arrived at nine. Always suspicious, he sent his secretary ahead to investigate the house before he entered it himself. The secretary was a small girl of twenty, fairly attractive but tight-lipped, and devoted to her master like a well-trained dog.

Wollweber was a heavy drinker, though he hardly ever touched a drop of alcohol unless he felt himself perfectly safe from the long arms of his many enemies. This time he drank without restraint; his small, gleaming black eyes fastened themselves like sucking animals on Firelei. His hands soon followed, but Firelei laughed them away. With a few swift strokes, she drew a caricature of the plainly amorous Wollweber and named it "Cannibal looking for a bride." Wollweber guffawed, but the epithet "Cannibal" became as popular as that of "Little Lenin."

Wollweber talked of his youth. Early in the Great War his father, a miner, had been killed on the Russian front, and Ernst had become a member of the Socialist Youth at the age of seventeen. His trade had been that of a riverman. He had plied the German waterways, smuggling defeatist propaganda from Berlin to the western front until, one day, he helped a group of "activists" sink a number of cement barges in a canal in Belgium to block the transports of war material to the front. The Socialists expelled him for his radicalism, and Wollweber joined the Spartakus Bund and, at the same time, volunteered for the Imperial Navy. He had fought in the Battle of Jutland, and had then become one of the chief organizers of the final mutiny in the German fleet. Wollweber boasted of his prowess both as a revolutionist and a man, and all the while he edged himself closer to Firelei. His little secretary-mistress watched him like a hypnotized mouse. Abruptly Wollweber turned to me.

"This chit of yours," he growled. "I must have her in bed." Pointing to his frightened secretary, he added: "You take Helen, she's a nice little hare."

The drinking bout ended suddenly. Firelei, Helen and I decamped, seeking-emergency quarters in a hotel and leaving the "Little Lenin" alone in charge of my abode. Returning next morning to see what had happened to my chief, I found him in bed with a Junoesque prostitute he had managed to pick up in the street after our departure. Wollweber had sobered up. He paid the girl, and told her to be off.

"Bah," he snarled when we were alone, "after a night like this I could puke at myself. Life is a leprous hell-hole. Unsatisfactory, altogether unsatisfactory."

A few minutes later, after a dousing with cold water, he was again the old, disillusioned warrior. "Let me see your plans for the Weser mobilization," he growled. "We must put more punch into it. By February we must come to strikes that will tear the transport industry to ribbons."

The Hitler movement was sweeping the country like a storm flood, washing away the parties in the middle. Because it was my business to fight it, at meetings, in the factories, in the streets and on ships, I studied its methods. The Nazis waged their campaigns with unlimited courage and ruthlessness, with devotion and cynicism. They promised higher wages to the workers, higher profits to industry, and well-paid jobs to the unemployed. They promised the liquidation of department stores to small traders. They promised land to the farmhands, tax-exemption and higher income to the farmers, and government subsidies and cheap labor to the large landowners. They promised to outlaw strikes and at the same time supported every strike to curry favor with the toilers. They ranted against capitalism and bargained with captains of industry behind the scenes. They held out the promise of careers and of power to students and intellectuals, who rallied to the Nazi banner by the thousands. Nazi propaganda was as quick as lightning, seizing upon every mistake made by other political groups. Hand in hand with this propaganda went a superbly organized terror. Merchants were terrorized into surrendering part of their profits to the Nazi Party. Liberals were terrorized until they dared not hold public meetings. Brown-shirted raiding detachments, schooled in the technique of terror, clubbed, stabbed and shot opponents in daily affrays.

We raised the slogan, "Strike the Nazi wherever you meet him!" But it was a secondary motto for us. The paramount aim of the Communist Party was still the destruction of Social Democracy, the "principal foe" blocking the road toward a Soviet Germany. So it was that in organizing a maritime strike campaign, I concentrated my main efforts on the destruction of the socialist-controlled trade unions. With the aid of many hundreds of thousands of leaflets, we stirred up the discontent of the workers and lashed them to wild hatred against the employers, against the police and against the Social Democratic leaders—who favored arbitration.

The tactics employed by the Comintern to wreck the socialist trade unions was that of the "united front." Every communist meeting, newspaper, leaflet raised the slogan of the "united front" on every occasion. In the beginning, because of my sincere belief in the desirability of co-operation with the socialists, I took it literally. I went to the headquarters of the socialist Transport Workers' Union in Bremen to propose to its chief a plan of united action in the strike then imminent. One of the numerous G.P.U. spies in our Party got wind of my visit, and sent a confidential report to Berlin, in which he accused me of secret counter-revolutionary negotiations with a notorious "Social-Fascist"—a term then in vogue among communists. The report was forwarded to Herrmann Remmele, communist Reichstag deputy, then touring Western Germany. He promptly collared me, and gave me a rough-and-tumble lecture on what the Comintern meant by the "united front."

Comrade Remmele made it clear that no "united front" was wanted unless it preserved communist leadership. The aim was to unite with the rank and file against the will of their socialist leaders. This was called the "united front from *below*," and was calculated to drive a wedge between the rival leaders and their masses, and to split the trade unions. All communist proposals were intentionally so worded as to be rejected by the socialist chiefs. These proposals invariably ended with the appeal, "Defend the Soviet Union, the fatherland of all workers!" The socialist leaders rejected this formula, and the communists then cried, "Traitors! Saboteurs of co-operation!" Thus the "united front" maneuver became one of the main causes of the impotence of organized German labor in the face of Hitler's march to power.

I bowed to Remmele's order. "That is the Party line," he said. "Any deviation from it is equal to treason!" Five years later this veteran of the Bolshevist movement, the author of a volume in praise of the Soviet Union, who had been condemned to prison in Germany and fled to Russia, came to the end of the "Party line." He was shot in the dungeons of the G.P.U., in Moscow as a "Gestapo spy."

The blind hatred for the Social Democrats took a decisive turn about the middle of January, 1931, when Georgi Dimitrov issued a secret memorandum of instructions to all leaders and sub-leaders of the communist columns. A special committee, headed by Thaelmann, Heinz Neumann and Wollweber, was set up to carry the instructions into effect. Summed up in one sentence the instructions were: *"United action of the Communist Party and the Hitler movement to accelerate the disintegration of the crumbling democratic bloc which governs Germany."*

My chief aide, a leather-faced engineer named Salomon, and I stared at each other in consternation.

"Who is crazy?" Salomon muttered. "We—or the Central Committee?"

"Without the help of the Social Democratic Party, the German bourgeoisie cannot survive," Wollweber growled in a meeting of Party functionaries. "With the liquidation of the Social-Fascists, we are preparing the soil for civil war. We shall then give Hitler our answer on the barricades."

Those who objected were threatened with expulsion from the Party. Discipline forbade the rank and file to discuss the issue. From then on, in spite of the steadily increasing fierceness of their guerrilla warfare, the Communist Party and the Hitler movement joined forces to slash the throat of an already tottering democracy.

It was a weird alliance, never officially proclaimed or recognized by either the Red or the Brown bureaucracy, but a grim fact all the same. Many of the simple Party members resisted stubbornly; too disciplined to denounce openly the Central Committee, they embarked on a silent campaign of passive resistance, if not sabotage. However, the most active and loyal communist elements—I among them—went ahead energetically to translate this latest *Parteibefehl* into action. A temporary truce and a combining of forces were agreed on by the followers of Stalin and Hitler whenever they saw an opportunity to raid and break up meetings and demonstrations of the democratic front. During 1931 alone, I participated in dozens of such terroristic enterprises in concert with the rowdiest Nazi elements. I and my comrades simply followed Party orders. I shall describe a few of such enterprises to characterize this Dimitrov-Hitler alliance and to illustrate what was going on all over Germany at that time.

In the spring of 1931, the socialist Transport Workers' Union had called a conference of ship and dock delegates of all the main ports of Western Germany. The conference took place in the House of Labor in Bremen. It was public and the workers were invited to listen to the proceedings. The Communist Party sent a courier to the headquarters of the Nazi Party, with a request for co-operation in the blasting of the trade union conference. The Hitlerites agreed, as they always did in such cases. When the conference opened, the galleries were packed with two to three hundred Communists and Nazis. I was in charge of operations for the Communist Party and a storm troop leader named Walter Tidow —for the Nazis. In less than two minutes, we had agreed on a plan of action. As soon as the conference of the Social Democrats was well under way, I got up and launched a harangue from the gallery. In another part of the hall Tidow did the same. The trade union delegates were at first speechless. Then the chairman gave the order to eject the two troublemakers, me and Tidow, from the building. We sat quietly, derisively watching two squads of husky trade unionists advance toward us with the intention of throwing us out. We refused to budge. As soon as the first trade union delegate touched one of us, our followers rose and bedlam started. The furniture was smashed, the participants beaten, the hall turned into a shambles. We gained the street and scattered before ambulances and the *Rollkommandos* of the police arrived. The next day, both the Nazi and our own Party press brought out front page accounts of how "socialist" workers, incensed over the "treachery" of their own corrupt leaders had given them a thorough "proletarian rub-down."

On another occasion the German liberals were the victim. The Democratic Party had called a public mass meeting in defense of the German Constitution. It had summoned its military organization, the "Young German Knights," to protect this meeting against extremist raiders. A large police force also took up positions in the great hall. The day before the meeting, the Nazi Party had approached the Communist Party with a request for aid to smash the rally of the Democrats. A truce was established between the

Red and Brown guerrillas. Both sides concentrated to wipe the Democrats off the political map. I was assigned to lead the Communist wrecking party; the Nazi faction was again under the command of Tidow, a soldier of fortune in the clique of Captain Roehm. Our hordes came early, filling the hall before the Democrats arrived in force. The main speaker of the evening was General von Lettow Vorbeck, the defender of German East Africa during the Great War. We granted Lettow Vorbeck a bare ten minutes of uninterrupted speaking. Then, at a signal, a group of Nazis and Communists in the front row of the auditorium began to shout the vilest terms of abuse at the General. Police and "Young German Knights" immediately intervened to silence the marauders. In a few seconds a grand battle was in progress. Bottles and chairs whistled through the air. Well over a thousand raiders tangled with hundreds of "Knights" and police and several thousand innocent listeners. Tidow's men and my own had brought with them itching powder, stink bombs and a large number of white mice. The itching powder and the mice were used to drive the women present from the meeting. General von Lettow Vorbeck was locked in a lavatory beneath the stage. The police did not dare to use their weapons for fear of hitting noncombatants. Eventually, the police drove us into the street, where the affray continued far into the night. The mass rally of the Democrats was shattered beyond hope, like so many others of their meetings throughout the Reich.

Communist co-operation with the Hitler movement for reasons of political expediency did not stop at wrecking the meetings and demonstrations of opponents. In the spring of 1931, the German Nationalists moved for a plebiscite to oust the Social Democratic government of Prussia. Together with the followers of Hitler, they collected the number of signatures required by law to force the Berlin government to make the plebiscite mandatory. Tensely we Communists awaited the answer to the questions. "How are we to vote? If we vote with the Nazis, the Socialist government of Prussia might fall, and a combination of Hitlerites and Monarchists will come to power in Prussia, the dominant state within the Reich. Surely we are not to give our votes to make Hitler ruler of Prussia?"

The Communist high command, under Dimitrov, gave us the answer by telegram and letter, and through circulars, pamphlets, and headlines in the Party press. *"Down with the Social Democrats, the chief enemy of the workers! Communists, your duty is to sweep the Socialist traitors out of the government offices!"* So, while Communist and Nazi terror groups blazed away at each other in nightly skirmishes, Communists went loyally to the polls to give their votes in support of a drive launched by the Monarchist Hugenberg and the Fascist Hitler.

The wave of strikes which we had engineered in the early months of 1931 was water on the Nazi mill. The miners struck in the Ruhr, in Saxony, and Silesia. In my own province, along the seaboard, the waterfront workers followed. We endeavored frantically to turn this strike into a major political battle by leading the masses into conflicts with the police. But the workers, taught by many bitter experiences, were either too tired or lacked confidence in the power of the Communist Party. Under such conditions, the encounters tended to be short and hectic.

Hamburg and Bremen were at that time the most important ports of call for the Soviet merchant marine. We received instructions from special emissaries to exempt Russian shipping from the strike. It was *Parteibefehl*. So when the dockers struck, all ships were affected except those flying the Soviet ensign. Our strike committees formed special stevedoring gangs to load and unload Russian vessels while the craft of other nations lay paralyzed. The mass of strikers protested. Nazi agitators exploited the opportunity with the cry: "The Soviet Union organizes scabbing! While the workers starve, the communists draw pay from Soviet steamers! The Communist Party places the profit interest of the Soviet Union above the bread-and-butter interest of German proletarians!"

Many of us were sick at heart at the transformation of the Soviet government into the foremost strike-breaking firm in Germany. But our Party leaders were adamant. "Those who strike against the Hammer and Sickle," they proclaimed, "are saboteurs of the Five-Year-Plan, traitors to the first Land of Socialism!" Striking workers who opposed this decree were clubbed at meetings and driven off the waterfront by Red Front squads, and often straight into the outstretched arms of the Hitlerites.

At the same time, the Nazi brigades muscled into our ranks for the purpose of infiltrating those industries which had remained immune to their propaganda. In Bremen and Minden, the Nazis perpetrated bold coups and threatened to attain a majority in the strike committees. The job of driving the Nazi squads off the docks and out of these committees was given to Edgar Andree, one of the leaders of the outlawed Red Front Fighters' League. I had met him in 1923, in the lair of Maria Schipora. This warmhearted giant and superb fighter displayed uncompromising cruelty when it came to grinding Hitler's columns into the dust.

Edgar Andree had won great popularity among us after he had successfully smashed Nazi meetings in which Dr. Joseph Goebbels had been the chief speaker. Andree organized Red terror units in all North German towns, armed them with stilettos and Belgian automatics, and gave them the order: "For every communist murdered, five storm troopers must be killed!" It was Andree who was mainly responsible for the creation of a special military organization named the "Anti-Fascist Guard." No man inspired greater fear and hatred in the hearts of the storm troopers than Edgar Andree. *Our undercover agents in the Hitler formations reported that the storm troop commanders, Karl Ernst of Berlin and Fiebelkorn of Hamburg, had decreed, "Andree muss sterben-sterben!*—Andree must die!"

By this time, two years before Hitler's ascent to power, the framework of the Gestapo was already in existence. The Nazis had adopted the pattern and technique of the Tcheka, and the élite of the storm troopers had proved itself most gifted in copying the model of mass terror originated in Soviet Russia. From now on, it was terror against terror.

The Nazi decision to "liquidate" Edgar Andree, we knew, would be carried out at any risk. Andree called a secret conference on March 4 to discuss the establishment of a special school to train the Anti-Fascist Guard in terrorist warfare. I was invited to the conference, and had been requested to bring with me a list of fearless young communists fit to lead terrorist drives against the storm troopers. We met in utmost secrecy in the backroom of a tavern in Fuenfhausen, a village a few miles from Hamburg. But Andree himself was not present, as he had received sudden orders shortly before the meeting to fly to Paris on a pressing military mission.

The conference at Fuenfhausen ended quite late. After a glass of beer at the bar, I boarded the night omnibus for Hamburg. With me were two other communists, Karl Henning, a member of the
Hamburg senate, and a comrade named Cahnbley, who was in charge of the secret printing of illegal army and navy propaganda.

Outside of Fuenfhausen the bus stopped. Three young men, one in the uniform of a Nazi storm trooper, entered and sat down near the driver. There was nothing unusual in that; the Hitlerites drummed day and night in these outlying communities. But while the bus was speeding along the open road, the three newcomers suddenly leaped up and drew guns. The uniformed trooper pressed his automatic into the driver's back.

"Just keep her going,' he said calmly.

The other two faced the rear of the car, their fingers on the triggers of their pistols. In a flash I realized that there had been a spy at the Fuenfhausen conference, and that these three were assassins. One of them, a tall, blue-eyed youngster, leveled his gun at Cahnbley.

"You're Andree," he barked. "We are looking for you."

Cahnbley shrunk back in his seat. The other passengers sat like frozen corpses. Comrade Henning intervened.

"Leave him alone," he said. "That's not Edgar Andree."

The pistols swung around. One of the Nazis snapped: "I know you. We've got you on the list, you're Henning."

"Put down your shooting irons," Henning said.

I exchanged a glance with Cahnbley. The next instant we lunged at the assassins. Their guns roared. Glass splintered. The trooper in front was firing at Cahnbley and me. A woman shrieked.

We were unarmed. Comrade Henning slumped across the lap of a woman beside him, and groaned. The tall young Nazi was still firing at Henning. Some of the bullets struck the woman's legs. She squirmed and screamed.

Comrade Cahnbley had pulled off a shoe and was attacking the Brownshirt in front of him The smell of burnt powder filled the bus. A small child crumpled. The guns roared deafeningly. Suddenly Cahnbley reached for his face, and pitched atop two women in the aisle. Both women were bleeding. A bullet grazed the top of my head: I reeled and slumped between two seats.

The bus stopped. Struggling against unconsciousness, I heard the assassins order all passengers out on the highway. I closed my eyes and lay still, pretending to be dead, and was dragged out of the bus and thrown into a ditch by the road. The Nazis commanded the chauffeur to drive on alone. They cut the telephone wires overhead, and were picked up by a car which had followed the bus.

Men were busy with flashlights. Blood ran down the back of my head. Henning was dead, hit seven times in the head and chest. Cahnbley had lost an eye and part of his nose. The wounded child whimpered. Two wounded women were unconscious, the third kept screaming at the top of her voice. Someone bathed my head in cold water. Before the police arrived, I staggered away in the dark. A milk truck brought me to Hamburg.

Two nights later I sat on the platform of a communist mass meeting in the Sagebiel Hall of Hamburg. Ernst Thaelmann, the Party leader, spoke. He called for the formation of Red Vigilante committees in town and country to meet the Nazi terror.

After Thaelmann, I stood up to address the meeting. The chairman referred to the bandage I wore around my head as a "badge of revolutionary honor." I urged the masses to drive Nazi invaders out of the working class districts, and to avenge the death of Comrade Henning. I terminated my speech with the cry, "Death to Fascism! Germany is not Italy!"

From fifteen thousand throats came the cry for vengeance:

"Rache! Rache!"

Michel Avatin, of the G.P.U., was assigned to track down the murderers of Henning. They were apprehended, but had to be surrendered to the police. The judges before whom they were tried were, like most German judges, Nazi sympathizers. The assassins received prison terms, and were freed shortly after Hitler came to power. All three subsequently became members of the Hamburg Gestapo.

Chapter Eighteen

SOVIET SKIPPER

Captain Preuss, the director of the Nautical School, called me to his private office. In his weatherbeaten face his eyes were keen and young. His large, hairy ears, which gave his countenance a faintly humorous aspect, seemed to jerk forward with an air of immense belligerency.

"Ships must sail," he said in his explosive manner, "and the smartest youngsters on God's earth are just good enough to sail them. *Accord?*"

"Aye, sir."

"Hell's bells!" Captain Preuss went on. "This is the end of February. The navigators' examinations are a week away. And what do you do? Frazzle your time away with the Red stinkers! You could make the angels sick! I could ring eight bells and kick you out. But I happen to be a soft-hearted jackass. I want you to realize that you are at a point where the channels fork. One course, the one you're on now, leads into the mudbanks; the other leads to clean deepwater. I wouldn't give a hoot if you weren't an old sailor's son."

The captain's words cleaved apart the artificial bridge I had built within me to close the gap between contradictory urges—the rebel urge and the urge to be a commander of ships. Captain Preuss' voice now came in a gentle rumble:

"We all have our follies and our dreams, my boy. Some dreams we can make come true, others—never! They are murdered by their own realization. You can go the decent way." Biting off the end of a cigar, he added: "Or you can go to hell."

I could not find the strength to fight my way to a clear-cut decision. But I decided to pass the ships' officers' examinations. "Perhaps I will strip off the chains," I thought, "and make the big jump yet!"

Keeping myself awake nights with black coffee, cognac and endless cigarettes, I snatched time from Party work to prepare for the examinations, which covered the theory of magnetism, dead reckonings, spherical trigonometry, salvage laws, cargo stowage, business English, treatment of scurvy, and Sumner lines. I struggled with azimuths and amplitudes, with longitude sights and exmeridian altitudes, chronometer errors and the receiving and sending of wireless messages in Morse. I was thankful for what I had learned in San Quentin when I emerged as the second best in a group of seventeen students, and even received honorable mention in the bourgeois press of Bremen. I was presented with a document which gave me the right to serve as navigator on ships of any tonnage on any ocean.

I looked long at my navigator's certificate. "You scrap of paper," I thought, "to me you are of no greater worth than a share in rubber plantations on the moon!" Was I not on the blacklist of every shipowner in the land?

The next three weeks I was immersed in a crusade among the waterfront workers along the Rhine. Firelei had gone through a course in a Party school, and was now attached to the publicity department of *Weltfilm* in Hamburg, a company dealing in Soviet motion pictures. On my return trip I found a letter inviting me to call at the headquarters of the North German Lloyd.

I was ushered into the office of Captain von Thuelen, chief of the nautical division. He explained to me that his company, one of the largest and oldest shipping concerns in the world, was always on the lookout for talented young men to join the officer corps of the fleet. Gruffly he deplored my alliance with Communism, advised me to break with radical politics, and offered me a job as junior officer on one of the Far East liners! Von Thuelen was joined by Captain Paul Koenig, the man who had navigated the German freight submarine *Deutschland* from Bremen to Baltimore and back during the World War. Both of these powerful old seadogs promised me a fine career on condition that I sever all connections with the Communist Party.

This was an opportunity which did not come twice in the course of a lifetime. And I knew it. A good, respectable job, security, and the prospect of an honorable career were within my grasp. I had to choose between the realization of my boyhood dream and the perilous uncertainties of the life of a professional revolutionist. For several minutes I fought a violent inner battle.

In the end, I declined. Bourgeois honor was not my honor. I was bound up with the Comintern, and live and die with the Comintern I would. I thanked the master mariners for their kindness. They could not grasp why any young seaman would reject such an offer. To them, I was an utter, unredeemable fool.

Like a blind man I stumbled down the thickly-carpeted stairways of the North German Lloyd building. Out on the street, heedless of the stares of passers-by, I wept like an unhappy child, overwhelmed by a wave of helpless, terrible anger at myself. I had burned behind me the last bridge to the world of normal duty and normal pleasure.

Firelei was pale and silent when I told her what had happened.

"Must it be so?" her sadness seemed to say. "Everything for the cause—and nothing for ourselves?"

The Party got wind of the fact that I had an officer's ticket. At the end of May I was called to Berlin, and the girl courier who met me at the station led me straight to a conference in Ernst Thaelmann's office in the Karl Liebknecht House. Fritz Heckert and Dimitrov were present.

Dimitrov, strongly perfumed as always, grinned from ear to ear. "You're the first ship's officer who is also a member of the Communist Party," he said.

Fritz Heckert, stroking his flabby abdomen, came to the point: "You must now get about among the officers and engineers of the merchant marine, to build up revolutionary cells in that group."

I did not tell the comrades that I had been offered an officer's berth. They took it as a matter of course that, as a known agitator, my name was on the blacklists in every shipowner's office between Koenigsberg and Emden. But Heckert and Dimitrov lost no time in developing their plan of campaign, which called for my joining the largest of the seven existing unions for captains, mates and engineers, and the organization of a "Unity League for Ships' Officers"—a front organization for the actual work of Communist Party units. I was allowed an initial budget of eight hundred American dollars, with later monthly budgets to fit my needs. This money was to come from the West European Bureau of the Profintern, which then received one hundred thousand dollars monthly from Moscow, and was under the control of Fritz Heckert in Berlin.

Ernst Thaelmann proposed that I should first go for a short sojourn to the Soviet Union to study methods and conditions in the nautical union there. Dimitrov and Heckert agreed at once.

"Without having had actual experience as a ship's officer," I objected, "I shall be discredited and kicked out of the first officers' meeting I enter. The Nazi organizers will stand up and say: 'Look, this man has never stood on a bridge, and now he comes to tell the mates and engineers to fight under his direction.' "

"All right," Dimitrov said. "We'll get you a ship. We'll get you a job as captain on a Soviet ship. You must arrange to have some Nazis in your crew who will see with their own eyes that you are the real commander of the ship."

That sounded fantastic. But the adventurous flavor of this proposition made my blood tingle. Dimitrov promised to inform me when he had found a suitable ship. Fritz Heckert then telephoned his secretary, Liselotte, a thin dark girl who was also his bed-mate, to bring eight hundred dollars from the Soviet Trade Mission. Twenty minutes later she arrived, carrying the money, in five- and ten-dollar bills, in a battered briefcase.

In Hamburg, I spent seven days exploring the various officers' unions and boarding dozens of ships to interview mates and engineers. Then I wrote the first issue of the new ships' officers' bulletin, which I called *The Bridge,* and had an edition of five thousand copies printed on the Party presses. I divided the lot into parcels and shipped them to the International Seamen's Clubs in Danzig, Kiel, Stettin, Luebeck, Hamburg, Bremen and a number of smaller ports. I then went off with a member of the Party motorcycle squad on a trip through all German harbors.

I was in Danzig when a message from Berlin reached me. It read:

"Report to Soviet consul in Bremen to take command of Soviet Pioner. Choose your own crew. Wollweber."

My heart pounded. The magicians of the Comintern had turned the trick. At twenty-seven, with no practical experience as a navigator, I was told to go and become a skipper! I made a mad race for Hamburg by motorcycle. At nine o'clock the next morning I was with Firelei. Breathlessly I told her of my mission.

"Take me along," she said at once.

"But the Party," I demanded. "You can't run off without a leave of absence."

"Party or no Party," she decided. "If you become a captain, I request to be signed on as cabin boy."

I called the Hamburg chieftain of the Ships' Officers' League, Comrade Karl Meininger, a former leader of the Freethinkers' Society, and put him in charge of all our units in German ports during my absence. (Incidentally, this Meininger was arrested by the Gestapo in 1934, convicted to prison for high treason, escaped from Germany in 1936, and subsequently became a master mariner of a Palestine merchant vessel.) Then Firelei and I hastily packed some belongings, and we took the train across the heath of Lueneburg to Bremen.

At the Soviet consulate in Bremen, I met an official of the *Sovtorgflot,* the Russian shipping trust, who was supervising the construction of Soviet ships in German shipyards. The consul introduced him as Captain Kostin, supposedly a former submarine commander in the Czarist navy.

"Our friends in Berlin have recommended you highly," the consul said to me. "I assume that you're thoroughly familiar with all phases related to the captaining of a valuable ship?"

"Of course," I answered brazenly.

The fact that "our friends in Berlin," who had recommended me, knew nothing more about ships than that they began at the bow and ended at the stern did not disturb the consul at all. Captain Kostin, a vivacious little man, patted my shoulder and led me to his automobile which was parked in front of the consulate. Together we journeyed out to the Vulkan Shipyards.

My ship, the *Pioner*—Russian for Pioneer—was a large and fine sea-going tub, just completed, and designed for service on the northern coast of Siberia. My duty was to take the ship around the North Cape of Norway to Murmansk, where a Russian crew would take charge of the vessel and conduct it farther to the mouth of the Yenisei River. It incorporated the highest craftsmanship with the latest in shipbuilding technique, and was equipped with two 800 h.p. Diesel engines.

Captain Kostin, I soon discovered, was a rank amateur in things nautical. He did not know what a sea-anchor was. He did not even know the workings of a compass. Had it not been for the honesty of the capitalist shipbuilders of Germany, Captain Kostin would have sent without hesitation any leaking coffin to brave the ice-infested Northern Sea Route as long as that coffin had the general contours of a ship. My first thought was to report this fraud to the G.P.U.; Kostin, in my eyes, deserved to be shot.

But Firelei saved Captain Kostin's life. She thought him a lovable chap. He entertained us royally, gave us elaborate dinners, rooms in the best hotel, and told us with great enthusiasm that soon Murmansk would be the foremost fisheries port in the world.

I had a free hand in fitting out the *Pioner*. I bought a mountain of provisions to last us not only through the voyage north, but also for the return trip by rail, for I knew that Russia was then an extremely hungry country. When I began to choose my crew, however, I ran into trouble.

Besides Firelei, whom I made the *Pioner's* cook, I needed ten men; a machinist, three oilers, a mate, four able seamen and a cook's helper. I intended to recruit at least four of my crew from the unemployed members of the officers' unions, possibly members of the Nazi Party, to have impeccable witnesses that I had really been a skipper. The other six were to be bona fide seamen from the ranks of the Communist Party. But the communist high command in Bremen, headed by Comrades Robert Stamm and Nickel, disrupted my plans.

Stamm and Nickel maintained that I was liable to their orders. They stormed against the plan of taking along a few Nazis. They asserted that Nazis would wreck the ship *en route*, commit acts of sabotage, and engage in espionage once they were in the Soviet Union. All of the *Pioner's* crew had to be Party members, and Stamm and Nickel were going to supply them.

We compromised in the end. The Party Committee was to furnish five crew members, leaving me to select the other five, provided none of them belonged to an enemy organization. After the contract was signed, the visas affixed to our papers, and the *Pioner* ready to sail, I found that among the five men the Party had supplied not one had ever worked aboard a ship. They were simply favorites of the Bremen Party chiefs, out to earn some easy money, regarding the trip as a junket to the proletarian fatherland.

With Red flags flying, sirens screaming, delegations from the Party bidding us farewell, and with Captain Kostin throwing smiles and kisses at Firelei, the *Pioner* pulled into the river and pointed its bluff nose toward the North Sea. I paced the bridge, hiding my pride, and trying to assume a most casual professional manner, but watching meanwhile like a lynx every act of the grizzled old Weser pilot as he eased the ship down the river.

I had no experienced mate. My engineer was in reality an auto mechanic. Of my sailors, only two could steer a ship. The rest made up by electing a ship's committee, a provisions commission, and a *Kultur Kommissar* to organize Marxist entertainment during the voyage. Below the town of Brake, we met the tide and ran into short, choppy seas. Before we had reached Bremerhaven, where the river meets the North Sea, the president of the provisions commission and the *Kultur Kommissar* draped greenish faces over the stern rail.

"You've a nerve," the grizzled Weser pilot turned to me. "For a million rubles, I wouldn't go to Murmansk on this ship!"

Off Bremerhaven, the customs launch came alongside to take the seals off our stores which we had bought in a free-port zone. They included several cases of cognac and some thousands of cigarettes. To my consternation, the customs inspector came raging on the bridge.

"The seals in your storeroom are broken," he yelled. "Who gave you authority to break customs seals before leaving German waters?"

I went below, the inspector fuming at my heels. I found that the comrades of the provisions commission, not knowing the freeport regulations, had broken the seals in their eagerness to plan the provisioning of our expedition. Now they stood there sheepishly. Some grumbled about "bourgeois provocation" on the part of the customs officials.

"Who broke those seals?" the inspector continued to rage. "How many cigarettes have been smuggled ashore between here and Bremen? How many bottles of cognac, how many pounds of tinned butter, have been smuggled ashore? I have to confiscate the ship! I order this vessel to put into Bremerhaven for investigation!"

All protests were futile. Three customs guards were put aboard the *Pioner,* which, at a snail's pace, crawled toward Bremerhaven where other guards tied her unceremoniously to a pier.

Ten hours of bickering and negotiations followed. At the customs house, I was interrogated as if I were a pirate. The *Pioner* was searched from stem to stern. Every bottle of cognac, every cigarette, every pound of butter and coffee and rice was accounted for. While I answered questions and signed declarations to satisfy the authorities, my comrades aboard took the opportunity to launch a series of flying meetings among longshoremen and wharf policemen.

The Weser pilot, after having sworn that nothing had been smuggled ashore, departed with the remark: "Young man, you'll never get to Murmansk."

"We fine you three hundred marks, and twenty-three marks for costs," the customs official, who had conducted the investigation, announced. "You can pay the fine and clear out. You can also contest the fine. In the latter case, this ship will be detained until the court decides the issue."

With gnashing teeth I paid the fine. It almost emptied the *Pioner's* cashbox. Then I returned to the ship, and told the *Kultur Kommissar* and the three comrades of the provisions commission that they were fired.

"You have no authority to fire us," they objected. "We shall call a meeting of the crew to pass upon the matter."

"You are fired, without pay," I snarled. "You're fired! Pack your bags and get off my ship!"

"We refuse to leave the ship."

"Get off!"

"This is unproletarian conduct," they protested. "We shall appeal to the Party."

"Get off my ship," I said, "or I'll have you arrested as mutineers." They refused to budge. Firelei and my engineer, who enjoyed a somewhat macabre sense of humor, connected the fire hose and the engineer set the pumps working.

"Get off my ship," I commanded again.

"You'll answer for this before the Party Control Commission," the *Kultur Kommissar* blustered.

"Douse them!"

Firelei and the engineer turned the spurting hose on the recalcitrant comrades, pursuing them around the deck and into their cabin with a jet of oily harbor water. Finally, all four escaped to the wharf. The engineer, Comrade Lausen, stood guard with a monkey wrench to prevent them from coming back aboard.

I sped to the communist Port Bureau in a taxi, and hired four new seamen. Then I mobilized the Party newspaper truck, and sent the four men to Bremen to get their visas from the Soviet consul. Within eight hours they were back.

In the meantime, a courier from Captain Kostin arrived in Bremerhaven with this message:

"*Dear Comrade,* you will please proceed with *SS Pioner* to Kiel to take in tow *SS Lososi. Lososi* is moored at the coal hulk in Kiel fjord, and must be towed to Murmansk by SS *Pioner*. I shall meet you at Kiel. With international greetings, Kostin."

Pioner was soon under way. Once in open water, I turned eastward between the islands of Heligoland and Scharhoem, ran into the Elbe estuary, passed Cuxhaven, and entered the locks of Brunsbuettel on the North Sea end of the Kiel Canal. When the Cuxhaven coast guard station ran up a signal: "What ship?" I replied proudly, "*Pioner*, Bremen to Murmansk."

Much dangerous water lay between Kiel and the North Cape, but I was determined to bring my ship to Murmansk or never show my face again to any living creature! Before we left the Brunsbuettel locks, with the Canal pilot aboard, I received a telegram from Bremen. I knew immediately that it was a telegram from the Communist Party, inspired by the *Kultur Kommissar* and the provisions commission I had so rudely driven off the *Pioner*.

It read:

"*You are herewith expelled from the Communist Party for gross opportunism and unproletarian conduct. Leave ship Pioner at once. Nickel.*"

I called a ship-chandler's runner and asked him to send a wire for me to the Communist Party in Bremen.

"*Go to hell,*" I wired. "*I and Pioner on way to Murmansk.*"

We passed through the Kiel Canal at night. It was like steaming along a brightly lit highway. At dawn, churning in the opposite direction, a flotilla of destroyers passed by. Politely I dipped the red Soviet flag when the low gray warships were abeam, and I had the satisfaction of seeing units of the German navy dip their ensigns in return, thus taking notice of a ship of which I was commander.

On the giant locks of Holtenau, at the Baltic end, stood dapper little Captain Kostin, grinning a welcome. He boarded the *Pioner* before we proceeded to the roadstead where, moored to an ancient coal hulk, lay the high seas trawler *Lososi*, newly built in Germania shipyards of Kiel. The *Lososi*, I saw at first glance, was one of the most modern trawlers afloat. She was more than twice the size of the *Pioner*.

The *Lososi* had no crew. Captain Kostin maintained that no crew was necessary, since the *Pioner* was going to take the trawler in tow. I said that I needed at least three men to man the *Lososi*, even if we towed her. A ship in tow had nevertheless to be steered, particularly in the rock-infested waters off the Norwegian coast. Captain Kostin explained in his effervescent manner that *Sovtorgflot* had made no arrangements for manning the *Lososi*.

"Well, in this case," I argued, "you are *Sovtorgflot*. Therefore you can give me power of attorney to hire three more men."

"That's utterly impossible," Captain Kostin protested. "I cannot take such a responsibility."

He handed me the *Lososi's* papers, and grudgingly I signed a receipt for one new trawler.

"By the way," Captain Kostin said, "have you a chart of Trondheim Fjord?"

"No."

"By all means, get a chart of Trondheim Fjord," he said. "There is a small port, called Muruviken. On your way to Murmansk, you'll put into Muruviken for two hundred tons of woodpulp. This woodpulp is for Murmansk."

"Woodpulp?" I repeated, bewildered.

"Woodpulp, of course, woodpulp. Put the woodpulp into the *Lososi* and bring it to Murmansk. Here are the papers; everything is in perfect order."

With the woodpulp papers he handed me a bottle of Kupferberg Gold champagne, and jumped into a waiting launch. He had to go back to Bremen to "supervise" the launching of another tug. As the launch drew off, I shouted after him:

"Hey, how about a line to tow the *Lososi*?"

"There's a good towline on the *Pioner*," he shouted back, cheerfully waving both arms.

I took two sailors forward to open the fore peak and break out the towline. The line turned out to be merely the cut-off end of a hawser, less than a hundred feet in length, far too short to tow a ship like the *Lososi* over a good portion of the Atlantic Ocean. With so short a line, a heavy sea running up from astern would threaten to hurl one ship on top of the other, and smash both. Besides, a short line, having no spring effect, would snap at a sudden jerk. I decided that I would have to procure another line.

The fact that the *Lososi* had no crew did not bother me. I could put three men from the *Pioner* to steer the *Lososi*, leaving the leading vessel with a crew of nine. If the Russian workers could complete the Five-Year-Plan on dry bread and cucumbers in three years, then why could not I bring to Murmansk two ships with one crew?

I went ashore and telephoned *Derutra,* the Soviet shipping company, in Hamburg. A cheerful voice with a thick Russian accent answered.

"I need a towline," I said. "I need a full-length towline, otherwise I cannot leave for Murmansk."

"A towline? Please, comrade, explain."

At length I explained the nature and the purpose of a towline, and after that I explained why I could not sail without it. "I need a good, long towline," I concluded. "I need it at once."

The voice at the other end of the wire paused. I heard sounds of an argument in Russian. Then the voice answered:

"You may need a towline, comrade. I am sure you do. It is a serious expense. I cannot—well, you better talk to the comrade in charge of foreign purchases."

The comrade in charge of foreign purchases reported his presence.

"I need a towline... Again I explained my problem from beginning to end.

"Very well," said Comrade Foreign Purchases. "But what guarantee do we have that the towline will be shipped back to us once it is in Murmansk? We shall never see it again. We—"

"But I *need a towline,*" I groaned into the telephone.

"Of course, of course, but ... I cannot make a decision on the spur of the moment, comrade. I shall connect you with Comrade Vice President. He will be pleased to arrange the matter...." Comrade Vice President was at the telephone.

"I need a towline ..." I reiterated.

"Certainly, comrade ... only permit me to have my Comrade Secretary consult the *Pioner* inventory list.... Have an instant's patience, please."

"I need a towline," I barked. "Without a towline I can t sail. A towline costs three hundred marks. It is cheaper to buy a towline now than to waste money on port taxes."

"We understand perfectly," the other replied suavely. "But ... suppose a towline is not really required. I cannot buy a towline without possessing myself of all the pertinent facts."

"Comrade Vice President—*I need a towline...*"

"Yes, yes." And then, disconsolately: "Please wait. I cannot personally take the responsibility."

I waited. I called again. I was on the telephone for an hour. Finally Hamburg answered "We have no power to buy a towline for you. Our inventory shows that there's a good towline on the *Pioner*

I wrangled some more. *Derutra* in Hamburg told me to take up the matter with the Soviet Trade Embassy in Berlin. I phoned Berlin.

"I need a towline," I said, "to bring two new Soviet vessels to Murmansk. Without a towline, both ships will be marooned in Kiel."

At the Berlin end of the wire a heavy voice said: "All right. We shall discuss the matter. Call us again in twenty-four hours." Twenty-four hours I waited. The expense for twenty-four hours in port ran close to a hundred marks. Then I called Berlin again.

"This is the master of the *Pioner* speaking. How about a towline?"

"Oh, yes, a towline. We have communicated with Hamburg. Hamburg informed us that there is a good towline aboard the *Pioner*. Please make use of it."

"There is no towline," I yelled in a rage. "There's a line—as short as a dog's tail ... no good for towing. ... I want a real towline."

"Oh, a line for towing?"

"Yes, a line for towing!"

"Please have patience. We cannot decide off-hand."

I then telephoned Captain Kostin in Bremen. His secretary said that Captain Kostin had been called to Berlin about some business concerning a towline.

Another day went by. Another hundred marks of Russian money went to the devil. Early next morning I called Berlin again.

"This is the master of the *Pioner* and *Lososi*. I need a towline to . . ."

"The comrades are not in yet," a female voice interrupted. "Call again at ten o'clock."

I called at ten.

"How about that towline?" I ranted.

"Exactly," the thick voice I had heard two days before answered. "Yes, the towline. We are sending a man tomorrow to establish the fact that there's really no towline aboard the *Pioner*."

"You crooks," I barked into the telephone. "You are sabotaging the Five-Year-Plan. If I have no towline by tonight, I'm going to take the *Pioner* to sea and leave the *Lososi* behind."

After that I called a meeting of my crew to consider what to do. Comrade Lausen, my engineer, suggested that we sneak alongside some tug after dark, and steal a line. We rejected, this proposal for fear that it might end in the confiscation of our ship. I went ashore to a ship-chandler and bought the best towline I could find. I did not pay cash, but told the manager of the firm to present the note I signed to the Soviet Trade Mission in Berlin. Returning with my towline in a water taxi to the *Pioner*, I found three stony-faced Russians on board. They said they had just arrived from 'Berlin to man the trawler *Lososi!*

I divided the Russians into three watches, one man per watch, and convinced myself that they could steer. That done, all hands turned out to secure one end of our precious towline around the *Lososi's* forecastle and foremast, and late in the afternoon we cleared the anchorage of Kiel and headed out into the Baltic.

Luckily, the weather was fine until we had negotiated the Sound between Denmark and Sweden. We did not make more than six knots an hour. In the Kattegat, between Gothenburg and the Cape of Skagen, we ran into a stiff north-wester. The *Pioner*, with a draft of less than five feet, pitched wildly in the seas.

Off Skagen I changed course to the westward, making for the southernmost tip of Norway. In the reddish rays of a setting sun I saw the three Russians leaping up and down on the dancing forecastle head of the trawler astern, and gesticulating madly. Frantically they pointed toward the towline. Through a pair of powerful glasses—the *Pioner* had the best possible equipment—I discerned that the towline was chafing through where they entered the *Lososi's* hawse pipes. At any minute the line threatened to part and set the trawler adrift.

I hove to with the *Pioner* and lowered a dinghy and sent three men into the dinghy. The towline hung slack. The *Lososi* turned slowly and wallowed in the beam sea. The three men in the dinghy rowed over to the *Lososi*, and together with the Russians they heaved in some of the towline. Since there was no steam on the trawler, this work had to be done by hand. The back-breaking job took all of four hours. The damaged spot in the line was hauled in, the line refastened and the points of friction guarded against further damage by wads of canvas and burlap. When the three men returned to the *Pioner*, the dinghy capsized. All three, however, could swim, and we hauled them aboard with heaving lines. So pronounced was our eagerness to safeguard the interests of the Soviet Union that we lowered another boat and set out to salvage the overturned dinghy! It was well after midnight when we resumed our westward course, both ships pounding and spanking in the choppy seas. We on the *Pioner* saw the *Lososi* meander back and forth like a pendulum. At first we blamed the North Sea for this crazy swinging of the trawler, but later I discovered that, after nightfall, our Russian colleagues had simply gone to sleep, leaving the ship to steer by itself. On the following day, with the coast of Norway in sight, I stopped again, had the Russians brought aboard the *Pioner*, and transferred three of the latter's crew to handle the bigger *Lososi*.

Standing well off the coast, I kept the two ships on a northerly course during the three following days. Needless to say, I rarely slept. Day and night I remained on the bridge, hollow-eyed, oblivious to hunger, and finding it a fascinating business to navigate two undermanned ships with no one to rely on except myself. The world of political strife seemed to belong to another planet. Acutely I felt that my love of the open sea stood in grim conflict with my loyalty to the Comintern. Still, were the ships to be wrecked because of my insufficient nautical experience, I was firmly resolved to kill myself rather than to face the sneers of Dimitrov and Heckert. To these comrades, I was a Bolshevik, and I believed that there was no task a real Bolshevik could not accomplish.

Firelei learned to steer the *Pioner*. She proved to be one of my best helmsmen, and she quickly developed the knack of using a sextant for latitude observations of the sun at noon and of Stella Polaris at night. When she steered the ship, she sang. Looking out over the wide expanse of the sea, she told me: "Now I know why sailors like to sing when they're at work."

I began to hug the coast around Cape Statland, for I remembered the woodpulp and I did not want to miss Trondheim Fjord. The Fjord pilot came aboard, guzzled nearly half a bottle of the *Pioner's* cognac, and brought both ships safely to the ramshackle pier of a lumber mill in the village of Muruviken.

We learned that the waterfront workers along the whole coast of Norway were on strike. Yet we had to take on a load of wood-pulp for the Soviet Union. The Five-Year-Plan recognized no strikes. It could not wait. The Soviet representative in Oslo had made arrangements, through the Norwegian Communist Party, to have the woodpulp loaded by scabs on the *Lososi*. But my men of the *Pioner* disliked the idea of working with strikebreakers. I had to talk for hours before I could convince my crew that strikes were fought against the capitalists, and not against the Homeland of Socialism. Only the three Russians did not care. Strangely enough, they were the least class conscious members of the gang under my command.

The news that two vessels flying the hammer-and-sickle were in port spread like wildfire along Trondheim Fjord. Six hours after we had tied up to the wharf, the Communist Party membership of Trondheim, a town of 60,000 inhabitants, turned out in full force. They came on trucks, on bicycles and buses to Muruviken, to greet the victorious revolutionary workers who sailed ships under Soviet banners. More than three hundred Norwegian comrades, men and women and children, swamped the *Pioner* and *Lososi*. Their astonishment was great when, instead of a full crew of doughty Russians, they found a lot of Germans at home under the magic Soviet insignia, for they had brought placards and banners bearing the inscription: "Greetings to the builders of Socialism."

All the same, we had a fine time. I organized an "international fraternity meeting," opened our cognac and cigarette stores, harangued the Norwegian comrades on the success of the *Piatiletka* (Five-Year-Plan), and toward evening I left Comrade Lausen in charge of a crowd of revelers aboard the ships and, together with Firelei and the Party Committee of Trondheim, I was driven to address a workers' meeting. It was a meeting of strikers. They cheered loudly when I was introduced to them as the Russian skipper of Russian ships.

I returned to Muruviken at two in the morning. Many of the portholes of the *Pioner* and *Lososi* still showed light, and weird noises came from the insides of the ships. The decks were littered with drunken Norwegians, sprawled among empty bottles and broken glass. Aboard the *Lososi*, a few couples were dancing to the tunes of a *balalaika* played by one of my Russian sailors. Every bunk in the crew's quarters of the *Pioner* contained a female Norwegian communist in the arms of a German comrade. At intervals, the girls and women, with bursts of shrieking laughter, were exchanged among the owners of the bunks. Firelei, tipsy herself, remembered the fire hose she had used against the *Kultur Kommissar* in Bremerhaven. She tied a pail to a lanyard, filled it with the brine of Trondheim Fjord, and kept dashing the brine into every bunk until the irate Comrade Lausen seized her and threw her overboard. I stripped and jumped overboard after her. That was a signal. Soon every man able to swim discarded his clothes and followed me into the water for a merry time in the gentle light of the northland night. At dawn I commandeered all the taxis that could be found in Muruviken, and bundled my Norwegian guests pell-mell into them. Instead of money, each taxi driver received a bottle of cognac. Quiet began to settle on the *Pioner* and *Lososi*.

Next afternoon, with the woodpulp aboard, I conducted a thorough search of both ships before we put out to sea. My suspicions were verified. Four male and two female Norwegian communists were dragged from their hiding places and hustled ashore. With the motors hammering as sound as ever, and the coast pilot aboard, *Pioner* headed seaward, dragging the *Lososi* with two hundred tons of woodpulp in her wake.

The Norwegian coast pilot was in charge of the ships, and I caught up with my sleep. We proceeded northward along the inland passage, between the coast and the maze of rock-bound islands, and the nights became so light that newspapers could be read under the eerily flaming midnight sky. We passed Boervik and Bodoe, wound our way through the sinuous channels east of the Lofot Islands, left Narvik, Tromsoe and Hammerfest—said to be the northernmost town on earth—astern. At Gjoesvaer Island, close to the North Cape, I discharged the pilot, cleared the Cape and pointed the *Pioner's* prow eastward into the Arctic Ocean. We were now in a luminous, mirror-like sea, three hundred miles north of the Arctic Circle. At midnight the sun hung, like a glowing orange, low over the northern horizon.

I navigated with the greatest caution. Nordkyn and the Vardoe promontory hove into sight and vanished. A school of whales gamboled in the velvety sea. I shaped a course for Kildin Island, which lies just east of the entrance to Kola Bay.

Seventeen days after leaving Kiel we entered Kola Bay. The low shores were shrouded in fog, and I made the Planer's siren roar every minute as the ships edged yard after yard into Russian waters. When the Murmansk pilot boat appeared like a specter out of the mist, with screaming gulls wheeling overhead, I felt like shouting with joy. Our safe arrival in Russia I regarded as the greatest triumph of my life. Lined up along the rail, the crew of the *Pioner* eyed the pot-bellied Russian pilot as though he were some fabulous god. But this Soviet citizen showed no interest in the new ships we had brought. His first thought was a cup of good coffee and a dish of ham and eggs—two items which Firelei promptly supplied.

Chapter Nineteen

IMPOTENT AND OMNIPOTENT

A squad of G.P.U. men boarded the *Pioner* in the Murmansk harbor, but no marine official came to receive the two fine and costly ships I had navigated with so much pride, and with so much zeal for the Five-Year-Plan. The leader of the G.P.U. was a wiry, swarthy fellow, with inquisitive button eyes, who spoke English fluently. Each member of my crew was examined to the marrow of his bones. Since all of us possessed the black Communist Party membership books, the G.P.U. officials willingly fraternized with us as soon as they had completed our examination. But not one of them expressed any interest whatever in the two brand-new ships.

I scrutinized the harbor with keen interest. An atmosphere of mud, toil and fish enveloped it. The sleepy village of Murmansk had become a veritable volcano of activity since my last visit there at the beginning of 1926. The town had expanded, and new settlements of large log houses stretched away in many directions. Giant fish sheds had been erected out of logs and corrugated iron. A large fleet of high seas trawlers lay moored to the wharves or were anchored in the bay. Winches rattled without cessation; loads of fish swung through the air. Men and women ran about, worked, shouted. A long, new, massively built pier jutted out far into the harbor. I gazed at it, and wondered.

"Look at the pier," I said to the G.P.U. leader. "The superstructure looks wrong. It's built so that there's no room for the stevedores to stand and work."

"Yes," the G.P.U. man answered sullenly. "Sabotage! We shot the engineer."

Next I pointed to a cluster of trawlers anchored offshore. They were new ships, but they looked broken down and rusty.

"Why are these ships laid up?" I asked. "Why are they not at work, at sea, catching fish? Why are they so rusty?"

"We have no shipyard here to repair them," my guide said, "and paint is scarce." He shrugged his shoulders. *"Nitchevo,* soon we shall build a shipyard and repair them."

No one, as yet, had come to claim the *Pioner* and *Lososi*. I demanded to know to whom I had to turn over the ships.

"The port captain," the G.P.U. official informed me. "He will see you soon."

All day passed and no port captain appeared. But the manager of the wharf, where the two ships lay moored, a clean-shaven ruffian in polished boots, came storming, telling me to move my ships to the other side of the harbor, because he had no room for them on his pier.

I brought out lines in boats to the other side of the harbor basin, and hauled the two orphaned vessels across. The watchman there protested strongly for some obscure reason of his own. I paid no attention to his protestations and he ran off, threatening to report me to the port captain for disobedience. But the port captain still remained a mythical figure.

Toward evening the *Pioner* was haunted by a great number of ragged women and children. They sneaked aboard to beg for bread or any other provisions we could spare. Firelei cooked a stew of potatoes, salt pork and peas, and our Russian visitors gobbled up enormous portions down to the last scrap. Fed, the women began to ransack every cabin which was not locked. They tried to carry off blankets and shoes and even alarm-clocks. In the end, I was forced to gather my crew and drive them off by main force. Later some of the younger women came back and offered to share the bunks with the members of the *Pioner* crew for a pair of socks, a piece of good soap, or a can of corned beef.

At eight o'clock, the local G.P.U. chief boarded the *Pioner* and invited us to spend the night with him ashore. Firelei and I accepted gladly, and asked him to show us Murmansk.

"How is it that so many women come to beg food? Why are there so many prostitutes? Is there no work for them?" inquired Firelei.

"We have plenty of work for all," the G.P.U. man said. "But many of our citizens still have more interest in useless fineries than in the big things we accomplish. Did they bother you? I shall have them arrested!"

Every street in Murmansk was crossed by red banners bearing Five-Year-Plan slogans. Every street was crowded with work-stained men and women. The streets had no pavement. The board sidewalks were broken in many places, and people had to balance themselves in single file over planks thrown across holes in the ground, or wade across patches of knee-deep morass.

"Never mind the rotten streets," the G.P.U. man told us. "In two years we shall have paved roads.'

We passed the rambling log building of the International Club, which I had helped to inaugurate more than five years before. At that time I had had a vision of this club developing into a center of culture. What I saw now was a grimy den, crammed with noisy workers of all ages and sexes, some of them reading ragged newspapers, others eating fish which they had brought wrapped up in paper, but most of them drinking vodka under the busts and portraits of Stalin and Lenin.

The smell of damp clothes, unwashed bodies, and fish was everywhere. An abandoned truck was sunk deep in the mud of the main street. Often we stepped over men and women who had gone to sleep, drunk, on a piece of wood in the mire. Utter squalor and dull indifference met my eyes everywhere. The only modern stone buildings in town were the bank and the house of the G.P.U. In most of the log houses, every room was occupied by a family, often by two. Single workers were quartered at the rate of five to eight men and women in a room. The constant arrival of new hordes of toilers resulted in the overcrowding of the newly constructed log houses before plumbing, lights or even partitions could be installed. I saw families of five housed in rooms which contained no furniture beyond a huge pile of rags, a packing case and a few nails in the wall—and the inevitable color print of Stalin. Only my fanatical belief that the industrialization of the Soviet Union, even though it entailed unprecedented mass suffering, was essential to our victory in the whole world, sustained me.

Our exploration of Murmansk, "the frontier of socialist labor," was not without a humorous side. Firelei, commenting on the many drunken people who sprawled in the streets, asked our G.P.U. mentor if the Party organization of Murmansk could not provide more wholesome entertainment for the workers.

The G.P.U. man drew himself up truculently. "Drunks?" he asked. "Have you seen a drunk? Has he offended you? Where? I shall arrest him immediately!"

We entered a long barnlike structure which served as the only cinema theater in town. It was packed with ill-smelling humanity. There were no vacant seats. The G.P.U. chief tapped three spectators on their shoulders and told them to get up and surrender their seats. They grumbled at first, but when they turned and noticed the smartly pressed uniform of the political police, they jumped up with alacrity. We said we could stand, but our guide would hear nothing of it.

We saw a Hollywood "Wild West" picture, with hard-riding cowboys in five-gallon hats doing a lot of shooting. The G.P.U. man, proud of his English, insisted on explaining every scene to us in a loud voice. Voices in the audience clamored for silence. Our host roared his defiance, and continued to expound who stole whose cattle, and who shot whom.

"Damn good picture," he proclaimed at the end.

We went back to the *Pioner* at a very late hour. We found Murmansk wide awake. The whole population worked in three shifts, and under the gloomy midnight sun work progressed as in broad daylight. Hundreds of women and a few men were building a fence around a portion of the harbor. They dug deep holes in the swampy ground and sank concrete pillars into the holes. We stopped to watch a group of elderly women doing this labor. Their coats and skirts were old and ragged, their boots were cracked open at the seams, and the mud ran out of them. Their faces looked emaciated. Each time they struck their picks into the stubborn earth, they emitted long-drawn grunts.

"Are they convicts?" Firelei asked uneasily.

"No, no," the G.P.U. man answered emphatically. "Many thousands come to work in the factories in Leningrad. There they are formed into brigades and sent to work in Murmansk. After one year in Murmansk, they are allowed to look for work in Leningrad."

"Do they always work at night?"

"Some work in the daytime, others at night. Time is precious, and the USSR needs fish." Then he went on to tell us that the G.P.U. had crushed a movement of passive resistance among these workers some three months earlier.

"They whispered from ear to ear, 'Take your time, go slow!' We arrested four hundred."

"What happened to them?" asked Firelei.

"We shot the leaders here. The others we sent away in a train."

"What became of them?"

"I don't know. We have no time to waste on saboteurs."

Back in our cabin aboard the *Pioner*, Firelei threw herself on the bed and wept. The superficial view she had had of Murmansk had revealed to her greater horrors than any she had seen in hunger-ridden Germany. This was not the Socialist Fatherland she had looked forward to with such eagerness.

"Is this what we are fighting for?" she asked.

"The masses of this country are backward," I argued. "What we have seen illustrates the superhuman efforts made by the Bolsheviki to liquidate the heritage of Czarism. No price can be too high to build a socialist society."

I knew that sounded hollow, but I was fiercely determined to defend my faith.

When no one had shown up the following morning to claim the two ships in my care, I went in search of the port captain. I found him in a dingy office behind a battery of telephones, a lean and melancholy man, with a bristly face and dirty fingernails. He wore an unkempt white linen suit. His feet were on the desk, next to a glass of tea.

"I am the captain of the *Pioner* and *Lososi*," I said. "I want to hand over the ships to your care."

The port captain, an official of the North State Fisheries, looked startled.

"Ships?" he muttered. "What ships?"

"New ships I brought over from Bremen and Kiel, two new ships."

He looked perplexed. Laboriously he hoisted himself out of his chair. He now addressed himself to a burly, red-faced, blue-uniformed assistant:

"Two ships have come in from Germany. Are they in good condition?"

"I shall inspect them," the assistant rumbled.

The port captain told me to come back in two hours. He would have to telephone headquarters in Leningrad to verify my statement.

When I returned, I found the port captain beaming. He offered me tea, cake, cigarettes.

"I have called Leningrad," he said. "We've been expecting these two ships for weeks."

It took the port captain three days to assemble a crew to take over the *Pioner* and *Lososi*. Meanwhile he invited me to be his guest. His wife, who was typist at the bank, fed me cabbage soup, fish, caviar, black bread and vodka. But most of his time the port captain spent aboard the *Pioner*, enjoying our tinned beef, butter, jam, and cognac.

Finally, the Russian crews for both vessels arrived. There were twenty-seven men for the *Pioner* and more than forty for the *Lososi*. Hailing from the Yenisei country in Siberia, from Archangelsk and from various points of the Kola peninsula, they were an adventurous-looking, boisterous, hard-bitten lot. They filled the ships with gleeful shouts, admired their cleanliness and newness, tested their outlandish fixtures, spat on the scrubbed decks, jumped on the mattresses with their mud-caked boots, banged doors, scattered the contents of tool chests, turned the shining galley into a chaotic mess, cut the leather straps from the wheel house windows, and then settled down in comfortable groups around the inevitable vodka bottles, which appeared out of the shapeless bundles they had brought with them. In an hour the two new ships were transformed into battered madhouses.

The Russian captain assigned to bring the *Pioner* to Siberian waters was a blond youngster, not more than twenty-one years old.

I surprised him in the act of dumping my belongings out of the door of the captain's stateroom.

"I now take charge of this ship," he announced. "Therefore this cabin is mine."

When I demanded that he put my things back and find other quarters for himself until I had made arrangements for my return passage to Germany, his cockiness subsided. Just then the radio operator, a fellow with Mongol features and immense shoulders, reminded him that his crew was hungry, and that he should request the surrender of the *Pioner's* storeroom keys from me.

"Give me the keys," he said. "We need meat, we need flour, we need canned goods."

I knew that if I gave him the keys, our stores would certainly evaporate, and I needed the remaining provisions to feed my men during their voyage home.

"Nothing doing," I retorted.

After a lengthy squabble, he sent some of his men to filch a sackful of codfish from the nearest shed. Soon the once sleek *Pioner* smelled of fish and grease from bridge to bilges.

"I now take charge of this ship," the Russian skipper repeated. "You and your crew, you can go."

I requested him to sign a paper stating that he had received the ship *Pioner* and all inventory aboard in good condition. He signed the receipt with a flourish, without troubling to check on the condition of ship and gear. The same performance took place aboard the *Lososi*, whose new master was a Lett with a long reddish mustache. I and my crew packed our bags, and the Russians, happy with vodka, carried our luggage to the railway station, shouting and singing all the way. As we marched through the morass, Comrade Lausen marveled:

"These Russians up here look like men, but act like overgrown children. We could have sold everything movable in Kiel and Trondheim, and delivered two empty ships here, and none of 'em would have been the wiser."

My engineer spoke the truth. Already some costly nautical instruments had disappeared, and the electric range in the galley was out of order. The two hundred tons of woodpulp we had picked up in Norway, with the aid of scabs, belonged to a consignment needed in Leningrad. But this valuable cargo now lay on the wharf in a disconsolate heap, not even covered by tarpaulins, and cloud-banks in the sky promised rain.

For two days we camped amid a reeking crowd at the Murmansk station, waiting for a train to Leningrad. Trains departed twice a day, but they were so full that we could find no room aboard. And we lacked the hardiness to join the huddled bevies of voyagers atop the roofs of the coaches.

I enlisted the energetic intervention of my friend from the G.P.U., and the fifth train took us along. It included two upholstered cars, which were almost empty; their only passengers were three or four higher Soviet officials. The rest of the train, nearly half a mile long, was made up of box cars and "hard" coaches. Our party, of the *Pioner* crew, traveled in one of these coaches. Each of us occupied a sort of wooden shelf on hinges, allowing one to stretch out. On the way, the porter brought us sheets and blankets, luxuries which our mass of Russian fellow-voyagers had to do without.

The Russians all about us regarded us as if we were wondrous animals; we carried with us meat and butter in tins. When we ate, women flopped from nearby shelves and begged. The conductor drove them off, and for a while I thought we would be mobbed.

"When you sleep," he warned us, "keep on your shoes."

During our first night on the train, many articles of clothing were stolen from us while we slept. After that, I found it necessary to divide my crew into watches, to safeguard our poor belongings from the luckless proletarians about us, who had an urge to help themselves. More than once, in our crowded coach, a young girl accosted a German sailor, offering him a trip to the lavatory in return for a bar of sunlight soap.

Three nights we spent on the train. When we reached the outskirts of Leningrad, I distributed the rest of our provisions among several Russian families who were rich in children. One mother said to me, "God bless you." They ate the food then and there, and carefully stowed the empty tins into their bundles. A north-bound train passed us—bound for Murmansk. Firelei and I counted seventy-six cars in this train. Dense clusters of faces and bodies were visible through every window. It had little in common with the deluxe express trains on the Moscow run. It resembled, like our own train, a decrepit mule forced to carry a mountain. In the rush and clangor of the Leningrad station, we stood in file for six long hours to check what little baggage we had.

My comrades passed the time in excursions to the former Czar's palaces, which were now museums and children's homes. They visited the Smolny and the Red Putilov plant. Most of the time, my men went hungry; no meals were to be had before two in the afternoon, except in restaurants where a tough steak cost eighteen rubles.

Our ship, the *Smolny*, left Leningrad almost three days behind schedule. Before the ship steamed seaward, a detachment of G.P.U. soldiers swarmed aboard and searched most passengers to the skin.

Off Kronstadt, Engineer Lausen heaved a deep sigh. "I'd hate to be buried in this land," he said bluntly. "Wait till we have a Soviet Germany—then we'll show the Muscovites what efficiency in Socialism is. Those fine ships in Murmansk—all rusty and rotten . . . *verflucht!*"

My own faith in the Bolshevist rule and in the magic achievements of the *Piatiletka* had been badly jolted, too, by my Murmansk voyage. This, my first journey in a non-political capacity to the Soviet Union, had bared to me an incongruous duality in the Socialist Fatherland. I had found, on the one hand, a studied insensibility towards human suffering, slavish fear of responsibility, vast incompetence, and a tragi-comic inefficiency. On the other hand, I well knew the deadly efficiency which prevailed in the activities of the infallible Party and G.P.U., where ruthless decisions were swift and "activism" was enthroned. It was this strange and bewildering bedfellowship of mass impotence and ruling caste omnipotence which had made Comrade Lausen burst out in despair: ". . . *verflucht!*"

It was a mood which lingered with me after we had left Leningrad. It might have eventually freed me from the Soviet obsession had not circumstances brought me back to Leningrad two months later as a commanding officer belonging to the "infallible and omnipotent" élite of Bolshevism.

After my return from Murmansk, I became a member of the inner circle guiding the Maritime Section of the Comintern. Early in September, 1931, I received an order to report to Dimitrov in Berlin. A girl courier of the Western Secretariat at once led me to an obscure coffee house in the Moabit district. After some time Dimitrov, Wollweber, several other Germans, and a Russian whom I had not met before, arrived. They came one by one, Dimitrov first sending his secretary ahead to investigate if any unwanted outsiders were around. This conference laid down a plan of action for a strike based on tactics new in the history of industrial warfare.

The Comintern planned a major blow against German shipping. On October 1, all German merchant ships were to be stopped, not only in Germany, but in all foreign ports and on the high seas as well. The pretext for this strike was a scheduled wage cut for seamen; the object was to paralyze Germany's foreign trade with one stupendous blow. Already action committees had been created in all important harbors. A force of sixteen agents was detailed to lead the planned coup. Wireless messages were to be sent to all ships at sea which had radio operators sympathizing with communism. The initial blow was to be struck against German vessels in Soviet harbors, as a signal for German crews all over the world to follow suit. Wollweber and Albert Walter were put in charge of the campaign in Germany. I was assigned to lead the action in the harbors of the Scandinavian countries and the Soviet Union. Others were dispatched to direct the assault against German shipping in Holland, Belgium, France, England and the United States. A young American, Marcel Laroque, active in the Maritime Section of the Communist Party of the United States, was made director of operations in Antwerp.

We disposed our forces according to plan. The chiefs of the communist units on all outgoing ships received their secret instructions. Two days after the Berlin conference, I was on my way to Leningrad, stopping off *en route* in

Copenhagen, Gothenburg and Stockholm. I crossed by boat from Stockholm to Turku, and reached Leningrad by train along the south coast of Finland. A special mandate from the Western Secretariat put all functionaries of the Leningrad International Club at my disposal. I dispatched the head of the German Section in Leningrad, Fritz Richter, to Odessa, to take care of German ships in the Black Sea ports. I remained in Leningrad, establishing headquarters in the vicinity of the port.

Our preparations were carried out with a minimum of publicity. Quarters for striking seamen were arranged for. A squad of young women from the foreign language schools was made responsible for the entertainment of strikers to keep them away from their ships and the waterfront. A detachment of German-speaking G.P.U. agents with marine experience was put at my disposal. They were disguised to play the role of striking sailors, and assigned to prevent any German ship from bolting in the night after it had entered the harbor. The Soviet longshoremen were to declare a sympathy strike and refuse to work tied-up German vessels. Already *Sovtorgflot* had chartered sufficient additional British and Scandinavian tonnage to avoid a stoppage of Soviet export normally carried in German bottoms.

At dawn, October 1, the call for strike and mutiny was broadcast. Three German steamers were in the port of Leningrad. Committees in European harbors reported that twenty-five other German ships were at sea on their way to Leningrad. German shipping, unaware of the international conspiracy against it, sailed serenely into the trap.

The German ships in Leningrad were the *Anita Russ, Asta* and *Bolheim*. I went aboard each of them with a bodyguard of three G.P.U. men, shouldered past the protesting officers, and called a meeting of the crew. I declared that the strike was on, that the German shipowners had to be taught a lesson they would never forget. The communists in each crew promptly voted in favor of joining the strike. The rest were told that they would be treated as strikebreakers if they did not join. A few rebelled. Aboard the *Asta,* the chief officer blocked the gangway with a gun in his hand. Gangs of Russian longshoremen, led by a G.P.U. man, now boarded the ships. The *Asta* officer was struck down. The rebels in the crews were bundled ashore by main force.

An hour later, I telegraphed to Hamburg, Bremen, Antwerp and Rotterdam: *"German crews in Leningrad strike one hundred percent. Appeal to all other crews to follow example of Leningrad mutineers."*

The news was flashed around the globe. In Hamburg, Bremen, Kiel, Stettin, in Belgium and Holland, in Bordeaux, Philadelphia and Bombay, German sailors tied up their ships. Rumors of mutinies on the high seas poured in. More than a hundred crews struck. In each case the strike decision was enforced by the Party unit aboard the respective ship. Vessels which had no communists in their crews did not join the action, except in Russian ports, where the seamen were forced to abandon their ships with the help of the Soviet police.

. By October 9, twenty-one German ships were held imprisoned in Leningrad harbor. By October 13, their number had increased to thirty-six.

The crews of five German steamers were taken ashore in Odessa. Occasionally the officers of a ship attempted to take their craft to sea at night, leaving their crews behind. I had foreseen that. We had set up Vigilante Committees to keep watch on every quay. Runaway steamers were forced to return, and their captains were fined by the Soviet authorities for "conspiring to go to sea with undermanned ships."

The German government protested vigorously against this detention of German ships in Soviet ports, and against the mass abduction of German sailors. The Soviet government replied that the German seamen were striking of their own volition, and that it had no legal power to intervene.

Meanwhile, the seven hundred "striking" seamen in Leningrad were lavishly entertained. The picketing of their ships was done by Komsomols and the G.P.U. The daily strike meeting was really a banquet, followed by floor shows and dancing. In their own words, the German sailors "lived like lords." Most of them had acquired Russian sweethearts—*"Streik-Liebchen."* Excursions were arranged for them, as well as evenings at the theaters and visits to model factories and museums. Everything possible was done to keep the German workers from mingling with their Russian fellow-toilers.

On the morning of October 19, a telegram arrived from Berlin. The strike was called off! The wage cut was accepted. The seamen were to be advised to return to their ships. I was stunned. It was defeat. But why?

I learned the answer later. The Hitlerites, who had supported the strike in its early stages, had executed one of their about-fronts, and made an offer to the shipowners to man the marooned vessels with Nazis. Soon ships began to leave Hamburg manned exclusively by storm troopers. To thwart the conquest of the merchant marine by Hitler, the Communist Party had commanded its followers to return aboard the ships. The strike was over.

Then came the aftermath. The maritime laws of the Weimar Republic had been taken over unchanged from the Kaiser's time. Under these laws, seamen who struck on the high seas or in foreign ports were guilty of mutiny. In German ports and in the pilothouse of the Kiel Canal, special courts were set up to sentence the mutineers. The courts worked in three shifts, twenty-four hours a day. Crews who had struck abroad were met by police upon arrival in German waters. Police boarded the incoming steamers. They arrested the mutineers and brought them to court. One hundred and forty-two ringleaders who had heeded the communist call to action were sent to prison. Twenty-five of the ships which had been tied up in Leningrad became overdue. Their crews, knowing what awaited them in Germany, mutinied at sea. Fires were doused, engines disabled with sand. Lifeboats loaded with mutineers left their ships to drift helplessly on the Baltic. Government airplanes were sent out to locate the distressed vessels.

Like most communist campaigns, this one, too, left a wake of shattered hopes, broken homes, and misery for its guileless participants.

I returned to Germany aboard the Soviet steamer *Kooperatzia*. As soon as I set foot on German soil, I was accosted by two burly men in civilian clothes. They flashed their badges.

"Show your papers!"
"What's the matter?"
"We'll show you. You're under arrest!"

They escorted me to the central jail in the heart of Hamburg.

I was photographed and fingerprinted and locked in a solitary cell. The charge brought against me by the German government was "sabotage and incitement to mutiny and rebellion."

I was not the only one who had been arrested for engineering the mass mutiny in German shipping. From information whispered by the prisoner who distributed our food, and from a constant surf of yells that came from hundreds of cell windows, I gathered that half of the great prison was filled with arrested communists. That was heartening. Detectives came to question me. They cajoled and threatened. I refused to answer. I refused to eat. I joined the chorus of yellers, and would hoist myself up on the bars to look out of the window. I did everything I could do to violate the official rules of conduct. I knew that my comrades did the same. In the face of such mass action, the jailers were bewildered and helpless. All day communist demonstrations surged outside the prison yards. I heard the singing crowd, the chorus of shouts, and the sounds of police attacks on the mass of demonstrators.

Among the prisoners were Albert Walter, Edgar Andree and Christian Heuck, a Reichstag deputy from Kiel. (Heuck hanged himself in 1933 shortly after his arrest by the Gestapo.) All three had been seized in violation of their constitutional immunity. The whole non-communist press, from the Nazis to the Social Democrats, demanded drastic punishment for the arrested.

Nothing happened. The investigations of the police and the courts got nowhere. The Soviet Union was at that time Germany's best customer. The Soviet flag ranked second only to the Union Jack among the foreign shipping in German harbors. The German government realized that a prosecution of the strike leaders would inevitably incriminate and compromise the Soviet Union, and feared the consequences to the trade and political relations between Moscow and Berlin.

After nine days in jail, we all were released without further ado. We stepped out into the gray November light, dirty, unshaven, weakened by our hunger strike. Girls from the Communist Sport Clubs received us in the streets with red banners. They served Wiener sausages and beer. We celebrated our triumph. It was true that the strike had ended in defeat for the German workers; nevertheless, for the Soviet Union it was a triumph.

Chapter Twenty

THE MAN HUNTERS

Toward the close of 1931, the Maritime Section of the Comintern turned a large share of its attention to the merchant fleet of Japan. Events in Manchuria had been rushing to an unmistakable crisis. The Japanese army was on the point of seizing that country. Relations between Moscow and Tokio grew more threatening daily. The Comintern had launched a worldwide anti-Japanese campaign. Our seamen's organization started a sabotage offensive against the transport of war supplies to Japan, and against Nippon's merchant marine in general.

This was, to my knowledge, the first time that communist sabotage methods were put to the test on a large scale. The Comintern network was too feeble in Japan, partly because the death penalty had been decreed there for communists, to paralyze its harbors by strikes. In accordance with the general rule of "action at any price," sabotage was employed wherever strikes could not be effective.

Sand was manipulated into the bearings of the steamers' propeller shafts. Cargo winches were disabled. Winch runners and hawsers were treated so that they would break when put under stress. Labels and inscriptions on boxes and crates were changed. At sea, in bad weather, ventilator shafts were turned into the wind to allow sea water to pour into the cargo holds. At night gallons of kerosene or benzine were poured through the airshafts, and a few fistfuls of kerosene-soaked oakum followed. As the weeks passed on, each Vigilante chief evolved his own set of tricks. Japanese ship guards were reinforced to no avail.

Soon evidence cropped up to show that Japanese secret service agents were busy in European ports to check the wave of sabotage acts. A Chinese language student at the Berlin University, a highly intelligent lad known in our Chinese section as "Comrade Yang," was sent to Rotterdam to take charge of our sabotage brigades in Dutch ports. In the guise of a laundryman's runner, he personally boarded every incoming Japanese ship to investigate sabotage possibilities and to lay plans which then were executed by members of his Port Vigilante Committee and helpers in the steamer's crew. One day Yang was overpowered by secret service agents aboard a Japanese vessel. He was kept a prisoner. The ship left Rotterdam, bound for Yokohama by way of Le Havre, Oran, Port Said. A hue and cry was raised in Comintern circles over this incident. Yang's delivery to the police of Nippon spelled certain death for him. It also tended to demoralize the spirit of our sabotage groups everywhere. Kommissarenko gave me the assignment to do everything necessary to save Yang from the hangman in Yokohama.

I wrote an appeal for action and had it translated into seven languages under the heading, "Rescue the kidnapped Chinese coolie!" I notified our units in Le Havre, Oran, and Alexandria to leave nothing undone to help Yang escape from his floating prison. The ship meanwhile called at Le Havre. An attempt by local communists to free our Chinese comrade was foiled by the French police. The steamer proceeded to the next port of call, Oran, on the North African coast, with Yang still aboard. Kommissarenko was very angry. Others who had known the cheerful little Chinaman already considered him as good as dead. After a sleepless night I came to the conclusion that there was only one man capable of liberating Yang despite hell and high water. This man was Michel Avatin, the Lett of the *S-Apparat*—Espionage Defense department—of the Comintern. Avatin was in Berlin. Since he was under G.P.U. jurisdiction, I had no power to summon him.

"Give me Avatin for three weeks," I told Kommissarenko.

For a while the Russian thought it over. His calm, blond face betrayed nothing. Then he said:

"Avatin, of course. I should have thought of him before." Avatin arrived in Hamburg late that night. He came straight to my apartment on the Schaarmarkt, and roused Firelei. I was not home. Firelei notified me of Avatin's arrival. I hastened to meet him.

I found Michel Avatin sunk in an easy chair, sipping coffee and looking over a sheaf of drawings by Kaethe Kollwitz. I was much agitated about Yang. Avatin's presence calmed me immediately. Neither earthquake nor mass murder could disturb him in the least, it seemed. He listened to the facts as I outlined them, asked a few questions pertaining to communication, then nodded, brooded for a minute—and got up.

"Very well, comrade," he said. "I'm going to Oran."

The available time was short. Yang would arrive in Oran within four or five days. But no one in all the Comintern had Avatin's reputation of being able to travel the greatest distance in the shortest possible time and with a minimum of effort and noise.

A week of acute suspense followed. I felt as if I were waiting for my own reprieve from execution. Finally a telegram arrived early one morning.

"All clear. M. Lambert."

"Lambert" was one of Avatin's cover names. I was exuberant with joy. Yang was free!

Avatin flew from Hamburg to Amsterdam, from Amsterdam to Paris, from Paris to Marseilles. In Marseilles, he conscripted the services of a tested Greek G.P.U. agent named Michael. Together with Michael he traveled as stowaway to Algiers, hiding under the boilers of a Mediterranean steamer. From Algiers, the two proceeded by rail to Oran. There was an International Club in Oran. Avatin mobilized the harbor "activists" and the communist units among the dockers of Oran. When the ship on which Yang was kept a prisoner arrived to take on bunker coal, Avatin was ready. He and a group of his aides were armed with axes and crowbars.

"It was as simple as stealing a horse," Michel Avatin told me later. "Our Africans have guts! I went aboard to find out where Yang was hidden. He was in a cabin way below decks, handcuffed. Our Africans stormed the ship and set little fires. While the Japs turned out to extinguish them, my ax-men broke the door and made off with Comrade Yang. I put him in a car and drove out with him into the desert till everything had quieted down."

In the Soviet secret service Avatin was an exceptional figure, and immensely popular. He never remained behind the lines while sending his men into fire. He advanced into danger with his aides, leading them on.

One of Avatin's superiors, a lanky, taciturn and stony-faced Lett named Schmidt, had arrived in Hamburg on a special mission for the G.P.U. His arrival was surrounded by extraordinary mystery. Instead of merely slipping into the country with false papers, he was smuggled ashore at night from a Soviet vessel. Schmidt's compatriot, Michel Avatin, came over from Berlin to meet him.

Schmidt's mission had to do with stamping out foreign espionage within Soviet ranks. His task was to deliver a blow to the *Auslandsabteilung,* the Foreign Division of the Nazi Party. Since no one in the Comintern was better informed than I on the Nazi doings in the merchant marine, I was summoned to take part in the conferences between Schmidt and Avatin.

The Nazi Foreign Division was the organization of National Socialists outside of the German frontiers. It commanded strong columns in the United States and most South American countries, in the Balkans, and to a lesser extent in Western Europe and Scandinavia. In the Far East and in France, it co-operated with elements of the former Czarist army. The *Auslandsabteilung* played a dual role. Officially it endeavored to carry Nazi propaganda into the homes and offices of the thirty million Germans living abroad. Unofficially it maintained a more effective network of international military espionage than the German secret service; the results of Nazi military espionage were transmitted to the general staff and the officer corps of the Reichsnjoehr, and was one of the chief means of widening and consolidating Nazi influence in the armed forces of the German republic. Occasional trials before German courts and convictions of many officers for Nazi agitation were never serious enough to affect this state of secret collaboration. The Nazi "points of support" (*Stuetzpunkte*) on vessels of the merchant marine formed the living and efficient link between Hitler's units abroad and the headquarters of the Foreign Division in Hamburg. Chief of the *Auslandsabteilung* in 1932 was Herr Thiele, a former executive official of the North German Lloyd. Each group of nations stood under the direction of a departmental head. The heads of the departments were responsible to Thiele, and Thiele only to Hitler. Thiele disappeared in the Blood Purge of June, 1934. Wilhelm Bohle and Rudolf Hess took over the direction of the Nazi Foreign Division.

It appeared that in December, 1931, the G.P.U. had discovered a member of the Nazi Party among the students of the Western University in Moscow.

This spy committed suicide in the Lubianka Prison not many days later. Before he died, he had revealed to his questioners that the Hitler movement had established an information service on Soviet affairs through a chain of contact men on Soviet soil. A number of German engineers and mechanical experts were suspected of being secret members of the National Socialist Party. It was also suspected that they were co-operating with anti-Stalin forces in the industrial centers of the Soviet Union. A certain Professor Ernst Schwartz, who had an apartment in Hamburg and a house in Frohnau, a suburb in Berlin, had been designated as the chief of the Nazi espionage service in the Soviet Union. The G.P.U. sought documentary proof to warrant the arrest of German nationals in Russia. Comrade Schmidt had been assigned to handle the matter in Germany. He and Avatin concocted the following plan:

Six communists from Hamburg, who must be unknown to Berlin police, were to follow all movements of Professor Schwartz for a period of two weeks. At a given hour they would detain him, while another squad of our Espionage Defense *Apparat* raided the Professor's Berlin residence and his apartment in Hamburg. All his books, files and documents were to be seized and conveyed to Hamburg to await shipment to a Soviet port by the next Russian steamer. The six shadows were supplied by Hugo Marx, the Hamburg liaison agent of the G.P.U. My job was to see to the safe transfer of Professor Schwartz' documents from Berlin to Hamburg, and aboard ship. Avatin would direct the action. Schmidt would remain the guiding spirit in the background.

All I knew of the conspiracy was what Michel Avatin and Comrade Schmidt deemed necessary for me to know, no more. Each of us proceeded separately to Berlin, where we met in a communist restaurant on Hedemannstrasse. While our operatives spread their net around Professor Schwartz, I took quarters in a hut belonging to *Laubenkolonie*—a colony of cottages and small gardens—outside of Berlin, known as Felseneck. Situated between the capital and the suburban town of Reinickendorf, it contained less than a hundred cottages, and was more a secret camp of the communist military organization than a community of gardeners. The country surrounding Felseneck was rather lonely and undeveloped, despite the nearness of newly erected apartment blocks at the edge of Berlin-Schoenau. Ill-kept hedges, fences, piles of debris and garbage heaps added to the inhospitality of the place. This was important, for the Felseneck colony contained several houses which served as guard-stations for the German G.P.U. Here I awaited the delivery of the documentary loot from Professor Schwartz' villa.

The material which Avatin's aides gathered about Professor Schwartz showed that he had headed the intelligence bureau attached to the headquarters of Captain Roehm, the supreme chief of the storm troops. When the Foreign Division of the Nazi Party was established in the spring of 1931, Schwartz, who knew Russia from World War service, had been assigned to a special section dealing with Soviet affairs. If it was true that he was in charge of numerous Russian contacts, a raid on his archives could possibly lead to the extermination of all Nazi agents in the Soviet Union. Schwartz was fifty-four years old. His official rank was that of a storm troop leader. To camouflage the real nature of his activities, he posed as a portrait painter. Where and when he had obtained the title of professor remained a mystery.

Avatin's crew struck on the evening of January 18. Professor Schwartz was lured away from his Frohnau residence by a faked call from the office of Dr. Joseph Goebbels, who was then the chieftain of the Nazi Party in the Berlin district. The caller was a G.P.U. man. While Schwartz was away, G.P.U. men raided his villa, tying up the Professor's wife and two servants, and escaping with two trunks full of material taken from his files. The trunks were first brought to 34 Choriner Strasse, a communist relay station in the north of Berlin.

But if the G.P.U. had its spies inside the Hitler movement, so did the Nazi Party's secret police chiefs—Heinrich Himmler and one Diels—have their agents in the communist organizations. A flying squad of storm troopers swooped down unexpectedly on the house at 34 Choriner Strasse. But the loot taken from Professor Schwartz' home was then already on its way to the Felseneck colony. The Brownshirts stormed the relay station on Choriner Strasse with guns in their hands. Red Front guards on duty in the house replied with fire. Four of the Nazi raiders were shot before the police arrived.

Nazi headquarters was informed through some spy in communist ranks that Professor Schwartz' archives were being rushed to a hiding place in Felseneck. Ernst Schwartz himself sped to a roadhouse named *Waidmannslust*, which was a storm trooper's stronghold an hour's marching distance from Felseneck. He put himself at the head of a force of armed Brownshirts, and moved post haste against the communist colony.

While all this was going on, I sat serenely in a cottage by a potbellied stove, discussing with comrades the general political situation, and waiting for the load of papers to take to Hamburg. The two trunks containing the filched documents never arrived, however, in Felseneck colony. They were lost without trace in the vastness of the Berlin suburbs. The two comrades who drove the hired car which carried the trunks were never heard of again. It was later learned that they had lost their nerve and deserted.

A courier burst in upon us. Breathlessly he reported that a column of two hundred armed Nazis was invading Felseneck. I rose to investigate, and to find the leaders of the colony. It was too late. From far and near came the alarm shouts of the Red Front guards. It was one o'clock, and the night was dark. Lights sprung up in the shacks. Those who had guns spread out in skirmish line through the gardens. Yells, the sound of crashing wood and splintering glass were heard. The storm troopers, advancing slowly, demolished and ransacked every hut, beginning at the periphery of the colony and working their way toward the center. Rocks flew through windows. Doors were kicked in. The night was filled with roars and the crackling of pistol fire.

I was not armed. I knew of nothing better to do than to crouch behind a fence and wait, a broken brick in each fist. From the lanes, from shattered windows, from behind the fences and the naked hedges pistols shot tongues of flame. The shooting was wild. The confusion was great. At times it was impossible to discern who was friend and who was foe, for the storm troopers wore no uniforms and carried no insignia. Storm troopers invaded a cottage twenty yards away. Its occupant, a young worker named Fritz Klemke, darted out of the door. A second later I heard him shriek through the barking guns. He died quickly.

I saw men and women running in the night. I ran with them. Searchlights blazed up on both sides of the colony. There was the shrill twittering of police trucks and the heavy cracking of service revolvers. Police were closing in, but the lorries could not get through the narrow lanes of the colony. Attackers and defenders alike scattered in the darkness. In the cold, dim light of the morning I reached the Tiergarten, miles away from the scene of the massacre. I wandered through the Tiergarten to the Brandenburg Gate. The streets were empty. I found a restaurant open, and ordered coffee. It had never tasted better to me.

Later in the day I went in search of Avatin. I was told that he had gone to Essen, in Western Germany. Schmidt also decamped. The newspapers were making a terrible noise about the Felseneck affair. Two policemen had been among the victims of the affray. The Berlin police arrested fifty-four storm troopers and twelve communists, and a big inquiry was on. I fled to Hamburg.

The police found clues linking the Felseneck massacre to communist operations in Hamburg. Police Commissioner Braschwitz of the political police in Berlin, made a special trip to Hamburg to question Edgar Andree, the chief of the Red Front Fighters, but to no avail. Incidentally, Braschwitz later joined the Nazis and became one of the chiefs of the Gestapo.

Professor Schwartz was found dead on the doorstep of a Felseneck cottage. The wall of the cottage, owned by a communist named Hohmann, showed thirty-odd bullet marks. According to the police report, Schwartz had been stabbed in the back "with an unusually long knife."

To avenge the murder of Professor Schwartz, the storm troop formations among the students of the Berlin University launched a murderous attack on the members of the communist student units. The latter called for reinforcements. The fighting became so violent that the police closed the university "until further notice."

The *S-Apparat* of the Party had discovered the identity of Himmler's spy in the Felseneck colony. He was a twenty-one-year-old youth named Bernhard Wittkowsky. Shortly afterwards his body was found on the outskirts of Berlin, his head bashed in. In the distant city of Essen another Nazi spy, Arnold Guse, was located and assassinated the following day.

Hitler offered publicly a reward of five hundred marks for the disclosure of the names of the G.P.U. killers. It brought no results.

When I saw Avatin again at the end of January, he seemed unchanged. We talked about the failure of the Berlin expedition and the death of the Nazis.

"Who did it?" I asked abruptly.

Avatin gave me a quick glance. "Does it matter?" he replied. "They were bitter enemies of the proletariat."

When the hue and cry over the Felseneck massacre had died down, Schmidt tackled his next assignment. It seemed that the British espionage forces had secured a foothold among the crews of Russian vessels. The British secret service employed for this purpose agents connected with the foreign branches of the bitterly anti-Bolshevik British National Union of Seamen. In Hamburg, the agent who cultivated contacts in the Soviet merchant marine was a certain Andersen, a Scandinavian of cunning and ability. Comrade Schmidt was sent from Moscow to carry out a major operation on Mr. Andersen. A squad of German communists was assigned to assist Schmidt in his undertaking. They dogged every step Mr. Andersen was taking. They burglarized his offices on the Schaarsteinweg (only a few houses away from the maritime headquarters of the Nazis, the *Stellahaus*) and found a way of intercepting Andersen's mail.

This brought certain results. There was a reshuffling of the crews of seven or eight Soviet steamers, and a few Russians who had been popular figures in the International Club disappeared. In February, 1932, arrangements were made to abduct Mr. Andersen and take him to the Soviet Union aboard a Russian vessel. From Schmidt, whose brooding eyes always seemed to be searching the floor in front of his feet, and Herrmann Schubert, Reichstag deputy and Hamburg Party chief, I received the order to put ten reliable men from my *Apparat* at the disposal of Karl Stevens, known as "Punch." Stevens was one of the most ruthless functionaries in the Espionage Defense department. Stevens and his crew of ten were to seize Mr. Andersen.

But Andersen had been informed by his own spies of what was afoot. When Stevens and his raiders burst into Andersen's office early one morning, they were met by a mob of British seamen armed with clubs and brass knuckles. A fierce hand-to-hand fight ensued. The office was demolished and Mr. Andersen lay under a table with a broken skull. The police arrived and the raiders were obliged to scatter and flee. Mr. Andersen, after a sojourn in the hospital, returned to England. In retaliation, a strong band of armed men raided the International Club in Hamburg. They came at night, at a time when the Club was crowded with seamen of many nations and their girls. Next morning, I counted some two hundred chairs the legs of which had been broken off by the men who had used them as weapons against the assailants. As usual, the police arrived after the fracas had ended, and their questioning was only a perfunctory gathering of material for an official report.

Shortly afterward British newspapers, reporting the assault on Andersen, characterized the International Club in Hamburg as a "den of assassins."

"Punch" Stevens vanished from the Hamburg waterfront to evade apprehension by police for another crime. Years later, while I was in a Nazi prison, I learned from fellow-prisoners that in the spring of 1934 a Gestapo agent had recognized Stevens wearing a storm trooper's uniform. He was seized and questioned. Under torture, Stevens admitted that he had joined the Nazi formations as a G.P.U. assignment. Three months later the *Sondergericht*—the Special Tribunal—condemned him to life imprisonment. For all that, he was more fortunate than his chief, Herrmann Schubert, one of the pillars of

German communism, who fled to Russia, where he became a professor at the Lenin School. Together with many other prominent communist exiles, Comrade Schubert was executed in the dungeons of the G.P.U. during Stalin's great purge.

During the first six months of 1932 four abductions over the sea route were carried out by the German *Apparat* of the G.P.U. in Hamburg. The fate of one of the four victims touched me to the quick. The long arm of Stalin reached my friend, the Ukrainian Bandura, whom I had learned to like and respect in the days when he was the chief of the waterfront agitators in Antwerp.

Bandura, who had joined the Communist Party because he loved the rebels of the waterfront as if they were his own children, cut a most pathetic figure in Hamburg where he had been transferred. Eternally cadaverous and in rags, abused and imposed on by the "100% Stalinists" in the organization, he was nevertheless loyal and dauntless in the defense of seamen's interests. For all his devotion, he was treated as an outcast, under suspicion of nursing heretical "syndicalist tendencies" in the Party.

Bandura was bitterly unhappy. Since his early youth, he had known no other life than that of a class war fighter. More and more he took to drink, which he procured from the French ships where he had successfully built up a number of units.

"I live in a reeking bilge, no one understands me," he blurted out one day, despair spread all over his wasted face. "Everyone who was good to me, I lost—my wife my friends, my children— everybody! everybody!" The intensity of his despair shock me. "What is it that you people want me to do? Please tell me that!" he roared piteously. I could not help him. Only those who know the communist method of completely isolating one suspected of heresy will understand Bandura's position. It is a deadly method. It is like depriving a fish of water, yet keeping it alive to suffer.

A strange friendship came into being between Bandura and Firelei. It began on a day early in February, when Firelei and I had married. Her parents, realizing that no force at their command could part us, had adopted a conciliatory attitude and given her sufficient money to establish a cheerful home. We had rushed through the marriage ceremony in Hamburg, and from there we had hastened into the harbor to attend a conference aboard a Soviet vessel. Bandura had been there, and so was an official representative of the Russian trade unions who, jealous of Bandura's popularity among Soviet seamen, had launched a savage campaign to discredit the Ukrainian. Firelei's inborn sense of justice had prompted her to defend Bandura, and from that day on the shaggy wanderer had shown her the attachment of a loyal dog.

One day Firelei said to him, "Comrade Bandura, come home with me, you need a bath and a good meal." The unkempt old warrior had meekly trotted away behind her. Since then I met him often in our apartment. Bandura would come to relax and gather hope. Sipping coffee, he would say to Firelei:

"Say something."

"What should I talk about?" Firelei would ask.

"It does not matter," Bandura would grumble. "Speak of the birds. Speak of the trees. Speak of the child that is to come. Just speak for me."

Firelei was with child. When I saw him together with Firelei I thought of a battered, broken old oak in the company of a graceful young birch. She admired Bandura for his knowledge of life and for the superb human qualities which lived under his derelict exterior. Firelei would speak for a while, and then Bandura would talk, talk for an hour or more. He would talk about life. About the dreams of his youth. About beauty no prison or hardship could break. About the rivers along which he had traveled. But he never talked politics when he was with Firelei. When Bandura left her, he would say:

"Your son, I shall love him! I am not poor now, I am rich!"

"Comrade Bandura should never have become a revolutionist," Firelei said to me.

"Why not?"

"As a boy he wanted to be a gardener. If the Great War had not smashed into his life, he'd be a wise old gardener by now." Off and on I had received reports from our harbor "activists" that they had encountered Bandura on Russian ships in the harbor, and ashore in the music dens of St. Pauli in the company of Soviet sailors. Bandura had no business to take him to Russian vessels. He was the head of the "activist" columns which covered steamers under the flags of France, Yugoslavia and Greece. Persons visiting Soviet ships were required to have a pass issued by the Soviet consul general. Bandura had no such permit. "What of it?" I thought. "Bandura is a Slav, he craves the company of his countrymen." There exists an agreement between the G.P.U. and the Comintern representatives in the various ports which provides that Soviet seamen in harbors outside of Russia should get little opportunity to cruise around at will amid "capitalist" surroundings. The enticement of such surroundings had often enough resulted in the desertion of Russian sailors, especially of those who were not confirmed communists. Soviet ships in foreign ports were under the constant supervision not only of their own leading committees and suspicious shoreside police, but also of the local Communist Vigilantes. The official reason given for this supervision was to prevent sabotage by anti-Stalinist elements. The real reason was to impress Soviet mariners with the fact that the G.P.U. is everywhere. The head of this protective squad in Hamburg was Hugo Marx, the pale-faced and vain G.P.U. fox, who had entered my life in the stormy months of 1923. Aside from his function as head of the Vigilantes, Hugo Marx held the job of foreman in the communist stevedoring firm known as *Stauerei Einheit,* which chiefly loaded and discharged Soviet steamers. One morning Hugo Marx appeared unannounced in my office, locked the door, glanced swiftly over his shoulder, and hissed peremptorily:

"We'll have to drop Bandura."

"Why so?"

"We've watched him closely. He's been giving us trouble for years. Who knows if he's not in the pay of Trotsky?"

I scoffed: "If Bandura is a Trotskyist, then I'm a Christian Scientist."

Hugo Marx produced a list of names of Russian ships.

"Here are the ships on which Bandura agitated against the Soviet government in the last twelve months," he buzzed. "I'm in possession of written reports from each of these ships."

"What's his line of agitation?" I demanded.

"His line is that the Bolshevist Party under Stalin has made itself independent of the Russian proletariat. Here are his exact words: 'Democratic centralism has become bureaucratic centrism. You have no socialism in Russia, but dictatorship of a counter-revolutionary gang of eunuchs. Stalin must go before the workers' power can be resurrected.' Now, what about that, I ask you?"

I was silent. These were no trumped-up charges. Bandura was well informed on what was happening in the Soviet Union. Bandura, despite his homelessness, was a peasant. He knew the significance of man-made famines. He knew what the G.P.U. troops were then doing to the peasants in the Ukraine. And so, Bandura, the rebel, struck back as best he could.

"Bandura tells the Russian seamen that the workers in other countries hate Stalin," Hugo Marx continued. "One of the sailors on the *Krasny Profintern* objected. He told Bandura he's read in *Pravda* that Comrade Stalin was beloved and trusted by the world proletariat. What do you think Bandura said to that? '*Pravda* lies, no one loves Stalin,' that was his answer."

"Well, what are you going to do? Expel him from the Party?"

"No. We're going to send him away."

"To the Soviet Union?"

"It depends on what we can arrange. It is for Berlin to decide. The comrades at the bottom must know nothing. To them it must be explained that Bandura has been sent on a mission to Poland." Hugo Marx departed. A day later I saw Bandura.

"Comrade Bandura," I told him, "I know you can keep a secret."

Bandura was half drunk. He had just returned from a tour of the French ships in the harbor. He pointed to his heart. "Many great secrets are locked here," he said. "They are safe with Bandura."

"The G.P.U. has reports on your talks with men on Russian steamers," I said. "They do not like it. You had better disappear. Go to Rotterdam or Marseilles or anywhere."

Bandura laughed. "You want to get rid of me?"

"I speak in earnest. I am giving you warning."

"The G.P.U. has the same odor as the killers of Karl Liebknecht," Bandura grumbled. "They are the traitors, not I."

"All the same, they have power."

"And I have faith, comrade. I had faith before you were born. Where is your wife?"

"Firelei?"

"I want to see her."

"You cannot."

"I understand," the Ukrainian said with cutting derision. "I am a man who spreads the pest. I believe in liberty. You believe in howling with the pack. Good-by. Tell your wife that I thank her much for her kindness."

"Take care no one sees you when you leave."

Bandura did not leave Hamburg. He was seized by G.P.U. men, and kept for nine days in a secret detention place, at 19 Kohlhofen. In the first days of June, 1932, in the middle of a mild summer night, he was escorted aboard the *Dnepr*. Bandura offered no resistance. The *Dnepr* sailed for Leningrad. Bandura was one of the first in the legion of foreign communists exiled to the Solovietzky Islands in the White Sea, the isles of "tears that turn to ice."

"What has happened to Comrade Bandura?" the "activists" of Hamburg asked more than once after his disappearance.

"He has been sent to Gdynia," was the answer.

And three weeks later another legend was let loose. It ran: "Comrade Bandura has been arrested by Polish police in Gdynia."

In the torrent of events, the fighting Ukrainian was quickly forgotten.

Three other men were abducted and put on the road to Leningrad during the first half of 1932. They were spirited out of Hamburg aboard the Soviet steamers *Alexey Rykov* and *Rosa Luxemburg*. All these kidnappings were carried out under the eyes of the German authorities, without arousing the slightest suspicion. By this time the underground G.P.U. network had grown so widespread and efficient abroad that it functioned like a veritable empire within empire on several continents.

One of the three victims had been a member of the Soviet Trade Mission in Berlin. He had stolen a substantial sum of money and decamped to Cologne, where he attempted to establish himself as an exporter of toys. He was seized in Cologne by Michel Avatin and his aides, and brought back to Berlin. There a "proletarian court," composed of two G.P.U. officials and two members of the communist unit of the Soviet Trade Mission staff, ruled that he be returned to Russia. Under G.P.U. guard, he was brought to Hamburg, a pudgy, dejected-looking man with horn-rimmed glasses. To prevent him from committing suicide, he was kept day and night in irons. One of the crew of the Soviet freighter *Rosa Luxemburg* was instructed to "disappear" in Hamburg, and the luckless embezzler from Berlin was then registered in his place as a regular member of the crew. He was never heard of again, and it was taken for granted that he was shot in Soviet Russia.

The two other involuntary passengers to Russia were Italians. Mussolini's political police, the *Ovra*, was very active in Germany and Austria. Almost every Italian consulate had a political spy attached to it. One of the two was seized by the G.P.U. in Vienna, where he had played the role of an anti-Fascist officer of the Milan garrison. He had described himself as a fugitive from the *Ovra*, and a member of the outlawed Communist Party of Italy. His real job was to spy on the transports of communist propaganda, printed in Vienna and in the Italian language, being smuggled across the Alpine frontier to

Italy. He was paid two thousand liras for each seizure of such a clandestine transport. He arrived in Hamburg, in G.P.U. custody, more dead than alive, and was shipped to Leningrad aboard the *Alexey Rykov*.

The second victim was an Italian spy attached to the consulate in Hamburg. He appeared in my office about May 20, 1932, posing as a communist who had broken out of a jail in Turin. He carried newspaper clippings to prove his story, and volunteered to work in the Italian section of the International Club in Hamburg, which was very active at the time. Supplied with a special subsidy, it published a newspaper and pamphlets which were smuggled into Italy aboard Italian ships. Among the Italian vessels trading with North European ports there was not one which did not have a communist cell among its crew. The spy's task was to ferret out the names of these contact men, so that the *Ovra* could arrest them when they arrived in Italian ports.

I did not suspect the newcomer of being a spy. He made a good impression and talked liked a trained communist. In an international shipping center like Hamburg political refugees arrived almost every day, some along the highways, others as stowaways. When I notified the Party's Espionage Defense *Apparat* to investigate the record of the new arrival, I merely adhered to our accepted routine. Every newcomer who could not produce official Party credentials was kept under surveillance until we were convinced of his trustworthiness. It was purely a measure of self-preservation.

The Italian was assigned to quarters with a family of Party members. When he went into the harbor, he was shadowed by our Vigilantes. A girl from the Young Communist League was assigned to cultivate his friendship. I took care not to assign him to Italian ships. He spoke French, and was detailed for a test period to the French section.

The Italian's name was Giacomo Bianchi. At first he displayed none of the faults and mistakes committed by the run of spies. No compromising material was hidden in his room. He abstained from asking questions not pertaining to his allotted duties. He spent no more money than his meager weekly allowance paid by the French section. He received no mail and wrote no letters. Nevertheless, he betrayed himself. I was about to call off his surveillance and accept him as a reliable member of our circle, when Hugo Marx appeared like a ghost and whispered, "Better be careful."

"Have you found anything?" I asked.

Marx nodded. The night before, a crew of Italian sailors had attended one of the political dances at the International Club. Giacomo Bianchi had also been there, talking to French seamen. The Italians had been treated with beer by a group of Russians and had enjoyed themselves hugely. But by no gesture or word had Giacomo betrayed that he was aware of the presence of his anti-Fascist compatriots.

"This is suspicious," Hugo Marx whispered. "Giacomo is a spy. Were he not a spy, he would have talked with his fellow-Italians. To hide the fact that he is a spy, he avoided talking to them in the presence of others."

Oar surveillance of Giacomo was tightened. One night, in bed with the girl from the Young Communist League, he promised to take her on a tour to Italy. She had assented, snuggled closer and prodded him to tell more. "I have influential connections," Giacomo had hinted mysteriously. Next morning we had the report. A few days later Giacomo was shadowed to a restaurant where he had supper with a stranger. The stranger was trailed to the Italian consulate quarters. A day later this stranger was photographed by one of Hugo Marx's helpers. The photograph was put into the girl's handbag. The next night, while she sat with Giacomo in the restaurant of the International Club, the girl drew out the photograph. Showing it to Giacomo, she said: "We have caught an Italian informer. He has given us a list of his assistants. Let's rejoice!"

Giacomo did not wait. He excused himself and hurried away. Two agents of the G.P.U. caught him in his room while he was hastily packing his belongings.

The spy was almost tortured to death in the beer storage cellar of the International Club. The torture was administered by the members of the Italian section. They had a ferocious hatred for *Ovra* informers, and wanted to kill him as painfully as possible. He was beaten between the legs until he gave away all he knew about the *Ovra* activities in Germany. After that, it was impossible for the G.P.U. to release him. He would have informed the police and warned his fellow-spies. But for my intervention, the Italians would have murdered him on the spot. It would not do to have a corpse on the premises. Giacomo was removed to 19 Kohlhofen, the secret prison of the G.P.U. in Hamburg. I did not see him again. After some weeks, he was transported to the Soviet Union aboard the *Alexey Rykov*. Not even the girl who had been his mistress knew what had become of him. She was told that Giacomo had escaped to Holland.

Chapter Twenty-one

STALIN OVER THE SEVEN SEAS

Stalin's power on the seven seas had developed by 1932 into a vast maze of imposing facades and underground passages. This far-flung dominion waged propaganda campaigns, maintained numerous smuggling rings, ran schools for agitators and wreckers, initiated mass strikes, organized mass sabotage, instigated naval mutinies, engaged in various forms of espionage, carried out assassinations, employed crews of expert kidnapers, and operated prison ships disguised as merchantmen.

Control of the marine industries of all capitalist countries was always regarded in Moscow as of foremost strategic importance. To be able to paralyze at will international ocean and river traffic was deemed vital to the defense of the Soviet Union. Ever since the conference of the Comintern's Maritime Section, held in Moscow in 1930, which I had attended, an ostensibly independent international body had been functioning among the waterfront workers of the world. It went under the name of the International of Seamen and Harbor Workers—ISH for short, but was in reality a masked continuation of the Comintern's Maritime Section. Like the Comintern and the Profintern, ISH was designated to appear as a sovereign, self-governing organization. To make its camouflage more effective, its headquarters was established not in Moscow, but in Hamburg, at 8 Rothesoodstrasse.

The chief of the ISH was Albert Walter. He received a monthly subsidy of $52,000 for international waterfront activities. The source of this money was *Sovtorgflot*, the Soviet Shipping Trust, which deducted it from the wages of Soviet seamen and longshoremen.

I had been nominated in August, 1931, by Georgi Dimitrov to the Political Bureau of the ISH, and was attached to its headquarters. My salary was $200 a month. From this vantage point, I became intimately conversant with every major communist activity in international shipping.

The operations of the ISH comprised three distinctive fields: (1) revolutionary action, (2) communications between the Moscow-Berlin centers and the rest of the world, (3) marine espionage.

The campaign among ships' officers was only a small fraction of the assignments put on my shoulders shortly after my arrival at the Hamburg headquarters. In the Comintern, the life-juices of men are burned out at an appalling rate. The curse of overwork and suffocation in the ocean of detail was on all of us. Functionaries staggered under a dozen, and more, tasks. Protests were of no avail. We used to joke: "A bourgeois consists of flesh and bone; a communist consists of functions."

The ISH possessed organizations in twenty-two countries and nineteen colonies. Aside from its stationary functionaries, the ISH employed a corps of fifteen "political instructors" who were constantly on the road, each of them responsible for the smooth functioning of the communist waterfront *Apparat* in his territory —the Levant, the West Indies, the U. S. A. and Canada, the Scandinavian countries, etc. The ISH operated forty-seven International Clubs in as many different ports. Its central publication, the ISH-Bulletin, was issued in thirteen languages, printed in Hamburg, and dispatched from there to Red waterfront organizers all over the world. Of the total monthly budget, only about $8,000 went to pay for the maintenance of ISH headquarters and field staff. The remaining $44,000 was sent abroad as subsidies to the organizations affiliated with the ISH.

To countries which tolerated Communist Parties within their frontiers, the subsidies were usually sent by cable to neutral cover addresses or spurious business firms; to countries where the Communist Party was forced to exist illegally, subsidies were conveyed by the Comintern's maritime courier system. Later, however, the stringent laws prohibiting the export of currency in a large number of countries forced us to abandon use of the cables for money transfers. Couriers serving in the crews of vessels and communists serving as employees on international trains became more and more the carriers of confidential Comintern mail. Banks, for obvious reasons, were almost never used for the transmission of funds. Utmost care was exercised to avoid all incriminating contacts between the communist *Apparat* and the official diplomatic agencies of the Soviet Union.

In the United States, recipients of these communist waterfront subsidies were, from 1930 to 1933, George Mink, and subsequently Roy ("Horseface") Hudson. The addresses to which this writer dispatched funds were 140 Broad Street, and Box 13, Station O, both in New York City. These subsidies included allowances for the *Marine Workers' Voice,* for the maintenance of International Clubs, for wages of organizers, for the support of a special communist group in the Panama Canal Zone, and for communist activities in the U. S. Navy and Coast Guard. George Mink later became one of the chief G.P.U. international operatives; Roy Hudson became a member of the Central Executive Committee of the American Communist Party.

During this period, while serving as a member of the executive of the ISH, I came in contact with several American communists. Some of them worked under my personal direction. Two were destined to rise high in Stalin's favor. They were George Mink, of G.P.U. fame, and James W. Ford, the negro who became the Communist Party's perennial candidate for Vice President of the United States. We regarded Ford as a careerist, of no great courage and even less industry, but possessing an uncanny knack of wheedling close to those in charge of budgets. Very dark of skin, inclining to corpulence, soft-spoken and well-dressed, Comrade Ford went about his duties in a quiet diplomatic manner, displaying considerable ability for unobtrusive political intrigue.

In 1930, James Ford was appointed to the post of secretary-general of the International Committee of Negro Workers, with headquarters in Hamburg, selected because of its excellent shipping connections with the West Indies and the shores of Africa. Ford's office was located in the building of the Hamburg International Club. He was supplied with secret quarters, a monthly subsidy from Moscow, and a young mistress who, incidentally, was also a member of the G.P.U. Negro agents from the Moscow school were dispatched to Britain, Jamaica, the United States, and to South Africa. James Ford's organization—referred to in short as the *Negerkomitee*—flourished. Countless manifestos, brochures and a monthly magazine, the "Negro Worker," came off the Communist Party presses in Hamburg, and found their way to all parts of the world inhabited by negroes. Since the contents of the "Negro Worker" were very inflammatory, the greater portion of each edition had to be smuggled to its destinations by the maritime couriers of my *Apparat*. All agitation and organization efforts of the *Negerkomitee* were directed toward inciting the colonials to strikes and rebellion, particularly in the British possessions. But the least active in these machinations was James Ford himself. He was too much of an intellectual to be a revolutionary "activist," and he detested danger. A political instructor from Moscow, a Pole named "Adolf," once said to me, "This Ford is an expensive parade-horse. He swallows too much money and he sleeps too much."

Albert Walter raged. "Let's get rid of this fraud, let's chase him back to America," he proposed to Moscow.

"Ford must stay for representative purposes. He is a good speaker," Losovsky wired back.

The end came suddenly. A large batch of copies of the "Negro Worker" had been smuggled to Durban and Capetown. There was much unrest and some violence among the dockers in South African ports. The British Secret Service traced the seditious "Negro Worker" to Hamburg. The Colonial Office in London lodged a protest with the German government, accusing it of sheltering instigators of uprisings in the British Empire. A police raid on our Hamburg headquarters was the result. Fearing arrest, James Ford rushed out of the building, jumped on a bicycle, and attempted to speed away to safety. The attempt was futile and ridiculous. In a North German town like Hamburg, no negro could make himself more conspicuous than by racing off on a bicycle with policemen in pursuit. In Comintern service, to become conspicuous means to become useless for conspirative work. Ford was summarily relieved of his international functions. But Losovsky saved Ford. Ford packed his bags and vanished. A more efficient colleague, one George Padmore, arrived from Moscow to take charge of the Negro Committee. After a short period of "exile" in Moscow, Ford returned to America where the communist press hailed him as "the great negro leader."

Of an altogether different stripe from Ford was his fellow-countryman, George Mink, also destined to become a special favorite of the Kremlin—in other and more perilous fields. He appeared in Germany in the latter part of 1931, when I met him in the ante-chamber of Dimitrov's establishment, the

Fuehrer Verlag, in Berlin. He was an unusual type of man, young, dapper, with slightly Jewish features and full of watchful, cynical arrogance. He was rather short, but strongly built. His mouth was small and cruel, his teeth irregular, and his eyes, of a greenish-brown color, had a faint wild-animal glint. Yet to an uncritical eye Mink appeared as a nondescript mediocrity. On the occasion of our meeting, he received a considerable sum of money—several thousand dollars—in American currency for waterfront activities in the United States. The money was paid to him by Fritz Heckert, Reichstag deputy and treasurer of the Western Secretariat of the Comintern.

"Who is this fellow?" I asked.

"A gangster from New York," Heckert answered jocularly. "Better go with him on the same train. He's also going to Hamburg to take a boat for the United States. Mink likes the girls, and he's got a lot of money with him."

Soon Mink and I sat snugly in a compartment of the Berlin-Hamburg express. We were alone. Mink produced a bottle of French cognac and a sheaf of lewd photographs. "The tarts like such pictures," he explained. "One look, and they fall on their backs." We drank cognac and talked. Mink knew that I was a member of the ISH executive. He wanted to make a good impression. So he boasted of his exploits.

He had joined the Communist Party in 1926 in Philadelphia, where he had worked as a taxi driver. As a sideline, he went marauding on the docks. His chest swelled with pride when he mentioned that his cronies had dubbed him "Mink, the harbor pirate." He had come to the conclusion that the life of a professional communist would appeal to him. He moved to New York in 1927 and on his own, wrote confidential reports and offered his services to Losovsky in Moscow. His energy and his lack of scruples, coupled with his experience as a "harbor pirate," qualified him for an appointment to bring American shipping under the Comintern banner. He organized the first International Clubs on the American seaboard. He was called to Moscow in 1928, agreed to spy for the G.P.U. on fellow-communists suspected of unreliability, and won the patronage of Losovsky to whom Mink claimed to be distantly related. Supplied with a false passport, funds and special powers, George Mink toured the United States, Mexico and other Latin American countries. From 1930 on, however, Mink was more often in Berlin, Hamburg and Moscow than in New York. Officially, he was engaged in revolutionary trade union work; secretly, he had become part and parcel of the Counter-Espionage *Apparat* of the G.P.U.

Early in 1932, following a secret radio message, the officers of the Hamburg-America liner *Milwaukee* raided certain cabins aboard their ship, which was at the time on the high seas, bound to Hamburg from New York. The occupants of the raided quarters were three G.P.U. couriers serving as stewards on the Milwaukee. They were Ferdinand Barth, Camillo F., and Carl R. Typed reports, photostats, code messages, blueprints and photographs—the whole haul of one month's industrial spying in America—was discovered hidden in their mattresses. The three couriers were put in irons and later surrendered to police for questioning. One of the comrades in the Hamburg *Appa-*

rat who was responsible for the safe conduct of such espionage matter resigned from the Party a few days later. But G.P.U. men in possession of organizational secrets are never permitted to resign. This comrade, a young technician named Hans Wissinger, was requested to go to the Soviet Union. Prizing his freedom, he refused. The chiefs of the *S-Apparat* then decided to do away with Wissinger. Among the men assigned to carry out this mission were Hugo Marx and George Mink. Marx and Mink were birds of a feather.

The executioners did not bother to inquire into Wissinger's guilt or innocence. On May 22, at dawn, Hans Wissinger was found shot to death in his bed in his apartment on the Muehlenstrasse. In the International Club, which was only a few doors from the scene of the murder, the killing of Wissinger created a considerable stir. He had been well known to the Hamburg "activist" corps. Albert Walter angrily demanded to know who had been indiscreet and foolhardy enough to carry out a "liquidation" within a stone's throw of the official ISH building. He summoned Hugo Marx.

"Ask George Mink," Hugo Marx answered drily.

The communist press, to avoid a scandal, attributed the killing of Wissinger to Nazi terrorists. Later that day I found George Mink at the International Seamen's Congress, which was then in session in Hamburg. He sat in the adjoining restaurant, drunk and singing, surrounded by a flock of female Party stenographers. I accosted Mink:

"Did you know Wissinger?"

"What about him?" he demanded.

"Perhaps he was innocent," I said. "Perhaps you have made a mistake."

Mink gave the standard G.P.U. answer: "We never make mistakes! We never strike at innocent men."

Among the crowd of international Bolsheviks which populated Hamburg in the early thirties, George Mink was hated and despised. Even his own compatriots openly regarded Mink as a gangster. Albert Walter referred to him as the "cut-throat from the Bowery." Later in 1932, during an outbreak of factional strife between Ernst Thaelmann and the ISH chief, Mink was charged by the Berlin G.P.U. office with collecting damaging material against Comrade Walter.

Sailors are a rough tribe. One morning men from Albert Walter's bodyguard seized George Mink and searched him. Hidden in his pocket they found a miniature camera. Since the carrying of photographic paraphernalia in communist offices of international importance is strictly forbidden, Albert Walter was informed of the find.

The old sailor raged. "Beat him up," he ordered. "Trounce him!"

That was music to the ears of the Hamburg comrades. They hauled George Mink over a table and flogged him. Then they threw him down the stairway.

In the meantime Mink had vanished from my horizon. In 1935, when I was a prisoner of the Gestapo, I was questioned about him. I learned then that he had been arrested in Copenhagen where the central offices of the Foreign

Division of the G.P.U. had been moved upon Hitler's advent to power. One night at the end of May, 1935, a chambermaid in the Hotel Nordland in Copenhagen was heard yelling for help. Other employees of the hotel rushed into the room and found one of their guests—George Mink— attempting to rape the maid. Mink was turned over to the Copenhagen police. He was charged with an offense against public decency. But when detectives searched his room they found secret codes, cyphered addresses, false passports and three thousand American dollars of doubtful origin. George Mink and several of his associates were seized and charged with espionage in behalf of the Soviet Union. On July 30, 1935, in a trial held behind closed doors, Mink was sentenced to eighteen months in prison.

After his release, George Mink went to Moscow. Only Losovsky's powerful influence saved him from being permanently shelved for his imprudent behavior in Copenhagen. The G.P.U. supplied him with a passport in the name of "Alfred Hertz," and dispatched him to Barcelona. Mink did not fight in the front lines against the advancing armies of General Franco. He operated in the safe hinterland. His apartment in the Hotel Continental became the breeding-place of many of the murderous G.P.U. night raids on the homes of anti-Stalinists in Barcelona.

Another American who played a prominent part in Stalin's crusade on the seven seas was a certain Comrade Appelman, a former Party organizer in Albany, New York, who went under the *nom de guerre* of Mike Pell. He had worked for the Comintern in Germany and Soviet Russia, and had organized the first anti-war committees among the crews of American transatlantic liners, led by the *President Roosevelt*.

Late in May, 1932, Mike appeared at the first International Seamen's Congress held in Altona, a Red suburb of Hamburg, as a member of the large delegation of the United States waterfront workers, of which George Mink was the leader. This Congress, called by the "independent" ISH, was a "united front" affair. To all appearances, the delegates were to deliberate on a basis of complete equality, "irrespective of race, color or political creed." In reality, the Congress was ordered and financed by the Kremlin from beginning to end; even the fares of the delegates from far-off corners of the earth were paid out of our funds.

The delegates began to arrive in Hamburg three weeks before the event. They came by train and airplane and passenger liner, and some arrived from across the seas as stowaways. They came from Capetown and San Francisco and Sydney, and from a hundred harbors in between, pilgrims to the grand masquerade of Stalin's power on the seven seas. They were turned over to Communist Reception Committees who supplied them with private quarters, food, money and entertainment. A member of the Espionage Defense was assigned to each delegation, ostensibly as guide and interpreter, actually as a spy to ferret out possible anti-Stalinist sentiments among the visitors from abroad. Counted together, the delegates represented approximately a million seamen, dockers and rivermen. Only a minority were communists. Yet, the majority of non-communist elements was hopelessly at the mercy of the communist "fraction" (caucus), which never acknowledging its existence to the outsiders, operated secretly as a disciplined body to dominate the seemingly democratic procedure of the convention

All resolutions, speeches and programs were written in advance in our communist headquarters. All chief speakers were communists in various disguises, and they were told exactly what to say before they were allowed to utter a word. Among the mass of foreign delegates there was only one who saw through this fraudulent system of wire-pulling, and rose to protest against it openly. He was Engler, a delegate from Rouen, France. Engler was quickly taken care of. Two assistants of Hugo Marx, posing as German policemen, visited Engler the same night. They told him that the German authorities considered him an undesirable alien. Then they escorted him to Cologne and put him on a train to Paris with the admonition, "If you return to Germany, Herr Engler, you will go to jail."

Several speakers were chosen by Kommissarenko from the strong American delegation which attended the Congress. Louis Engdahl of Chicago, who was then touring Europe with Ada Wright, the mother of one of the negroes in the famous Scottsboro case, spoke on "International Solidarity." Harry Hynes, the national organizer of the Red Marine Workers Union of America, expounded the technique of strikes on the waterfront. (Harry Hynes was later killed in Spain.) Thomas Ray, of San Francisco, spoke about the tasks of seamen in the event of war against the Soviet Union. (Thomas Ray subsequently became the directing force behind the National Maritime Union of America.) None of these speakers voiced their own original thoughts. Engdahl's speech was written by Willy Muenzenberg, Hynes's exposition had come from Kommissarenko's brain, and Tom Ray's lecture on the art of mutiny and sabotage against munitions transports had been drafted by me.

Many of the delegates were outright impostors. Chinese students from Berlin spoke as the "representatives" of the dockers in Canton and Wei-hei-wei. A negro from Trinidad, who had spent most of his life in London, was acclaimed as the delegate of the negro river workers on the lower Mississippi. Such tricks are a feature of every international communist convention.

On the second day of the proceedings it became clear that no delegation from East Indian ports could arrive in Hamburg. The British government had refused passports to the East Indians, and had imprisoned the leader of their delegation. Kommissarenko went about the congress hall, muttering to himself. Suddenly he turned to me, saying: "India is important. We need a Hindu at this Congress. Go and scare up a Hindu, bring him here, and we will make him speak."

I went out to hunt for a likely Hindu. The steamer Drachenfels of the Hansa Line was in port. Its stokers were Hindus. I hastened down to the harbor and boarded the Drachenfels. The Hindus aboard did not understand me when I talked to them about a congress. I tried another method.

"Like 'em singsong-missy? Like 'em young little singsong-baby? You boys quick come with me. No charge."

Three of the East Indians were willing to go. Two wore scraggy beards. The third was clean-shaven, but as thin as a skeleton. All three wore grimy turbans and shirts dangling out over their belts. Licking their chops in anticipation, they followed me into a taxicab. We drove straight to the Congress.

"Come inside," I said. "See 'em singsong-babies. Right here." The three were stunned when they saw themselves in a hall full of men bent over papers; bewildered they stared at the red banners all around them. I led my victims past the table, where the international praesidium sat, and on to the speaker's podium. I pushed the clean-shaven one ahead. There was the sound of drums, and then silence. Ernst Wollweber, the president of the Congress, rose and announced with a thunderous growl that in spite of the attempts of Scotland Yard to sabotage the participation of an East Indian delegation, the East Indian comrades had found a way to come to the Congress. He ended with the call:

"The representative of the Dockers' Union of Calcutta now has the word."

The three Hindus stood helpless on the stage and grinned.

The young American, Mike Appelman, now took charge of the situation. He glowered ferociously at the Hindus.

"How long you work?" asked Mike in a fierce whisper.

"Six to six," said a Hindu.

"The East Indian comrade says that the imperialist exploiters force East Indian workers to labor uninterruptedly from six in the morning to six at night, a minimum of twelve hours a day, and seven days a week," interpreted Appelman, turning to the audience.

"How much your pay?" Appelman snapped at the Hindu.

"Three pounds."

"East Indian proletarians must slave 360 hours a month for 60 shillings, or six hours for the equivalent of a quarter dollar," announced Appelman to the Congress.

"What you eat for supper?" he asked the Hindu.

"Rice!"

"They are fed like animals. Three times a day a handful of rice, that is the ration of East Indian workers!" bellowed Appelman.

"You like more money? Better supper? Beat up the boss?" he coaxed his quarry.

The Hindu stared. Then he grinned, and nodded.

"The East Indian workers declare themselves willing to join in the struggle of the classes, the struggle for higher pay and shorter hours, for freedom from exploitation, for Socialism, for the protection of the Soviet Union against attacks of the imperialist sharks!" Appelman thundered.

The Congress roared applause. The band struck up the *Internationale*, and the delegates rose to their feet and sang. Quickly the three Hindus were hustled out of the hall. At the entrance, they demanded to know when they would meet the promised "sing-song-missies."

"Beat it, you bums," they were told. "Get back to your ship!"

The virtual dictator of the Congress which drafted the program of demands for the seamen and dockers of all nations, was the Russian Kommissarenko. He was also the dictator of the Soviet Transport Workers Union and its four hundred thousand members. Comrade Kommissarenko held up before the full session of the Congress, the methods and conditions in Soviet shipping as models for all the other merchant marines in the world. "Our struggle will not cease," he scouted, "until the Red banners of proletarian freedom fly from the mastheads of the last ship afloat." But in a *Sonderkonferenz*—a caucus meeting of responsible ISH functionaries, Kommissarenko spoke in a far more cold-blooded vein. Here he discussed with us the special political tasks of the communist ship units, particularly those of Russian vessels. As one of the heads of the Maritime *Apparat*, I had come in frequent contact with Soviet ships. They were prison ships—camouflaged as ships of freedom—in more than one sense: prison ships for their crews, who were subject to special maritime laws which were unsurpassed in ferocity even by the Kaiser's ill-famed punitive *Seemannsordnung*; and prison ships for recalcitrant foreign communists whom the G.P.U. thought imprudent to leave at large. Kommissarenko took all this for granted; he was speaking as a Bolshevik to Bolsheviks.

Following the inauguration of the Five-Year-Plan and the concurrent transformation of the Comintern into an arm of the Soviet secret service, the kidnapping of possibly dangerous police spies and communist renegades abroad became a matter of routine. The victims ranged from officials in the Soviet diplomatic corps and its trade missions to police informers, agents provocateurs, spies of foreign governments, embezzlers of Soviet and Comintern funds, leaders of anti-Stalin organizations, hostages, obstructionists and saboteurs, and such renegades whose knowledge of the Kremlin's secret service *Apparat* tended to imperil the lives of important undercover agents and the existence of an organization built up painstakingly and at great expense to Moscow.

Of all this the communist rank and file knew, of course, nothing that could be termed concrete. The comrades drafted into the underground Espionage Defense corps, which co-operated with the G.P.U. in the abductions, never came from the ranks of known leaders. They were taken from the strata which lay between the top committees and the obedient communist herd. The men recruited for this so-called *S-Apparat* had to meet three fundamental requirements: an impeccable record of three years of Party activities, at least one arrest in which they had divulged nothing harmful to the police, and a fanatical belief in the historic world mission of the Soviet Union. They had to be young, resolute, and blindly devoted to the cause. Once they were taken over by the Espionage Defense, they faded completely out of the official picture of the Party.

The procedure used in the abduction of a spy or a traitor seldom varies. Abduction is given preference over assassinations on foreign territory, unless the victim is so obscure a personality that no one would take much interest in the circumstances of his death. First comes, in most instances, a friendly offer of a job in the Soviet Union. If the victim agrees to go, he may not even be shot or exiled when he gets to Russia; he may really get the job, an unimportant sinecure a thousand miles or more from the nearest frontier station, with the certainty that he will never, never be allowed to leave the Socialist Fatherland. Most of the communists who are so "invited" go voluntarily, resigned to their fate. They are apt to look upon a life outside the Soviet movement as worse than death. To them, self-surrender to the G.P.U. is a last gesture of loyalty to the cause which had already taken their best—the sky-storming enthusiasm of their youth!

But once the serene G.P.U. invitation to "go to Moscow and take a rest" is rejected, the Espionage Defense corps goes into action. The G.P.U. does not wait for the arrival of a Soviet ship in some nearby port before it seizes its quarry. The victim is seized at the first good opportunity and kept imprisoned—sometimes for months—awaiting the arrival of a Soviet vessel manned by a hand-picked crew. The G.P.U. has secret places of detention in or near key cities. In Hamburg, it was the cellar of a house which harbored a book-distribution firm, the Viva, at 19 Kohlhofen, in the heart of the city. In Berlin, it was a summer house on Schoenholzerweg, on the outskirts of Reinickendorf-Ost, a town not far from the capital. In Copenhagen, it was a summer cottage owned by Richard Jensen on the highway from Copenhagen to Kjoege. In Paris, it was a house on the Rue d'Alembert, managed by Beaugrand, a member of the French parliament living at 221 Rue Etienne Marcelle in the Montreuil district, just around the corner from the Paris outpost of the G.P.U. There were many more such Soviet secret detention places in foreign lands, the exact location of which I have no way of knowing. From these illegal jails the prisoner is spirited aboard a Soviet ship during the night before sailing.

Quite apart from the official sessions of the Congress, secret organizational conferences, to which only communists were admitted, convened in adjoining halls. The subjects which were discussed here were of an intimately conspirative nature—communication networks, personnel questions, subsidies, new wrinkles in the engineering of strikes, concrete plans of action against the shipping of various nations, and the work of communists in the navies of capitalist countries. In one such meeting, which I directed, the tactics used in naval mutinies of the past were thoroughly analyzed, mistakes made clear, and successful methods recommended for application in the naval campaigns of the future. A Russian delegate who had come with the Soviet vessel Dnepr expounded the methods employed by the Bolsheviks in the Czar's Baltic fleet. A German, the Reichstag Deputy Willy Leow, explained the numerical factors involved in the victorious mutiny in the German Imperial Navy. Comrade Languinier, a Frenchman, analyzed the risings of French warship sailors in Toulon. Delegates from the Danish navy and the Polish naval base of Gdynia followed. But the greatest interest was reserved for the lessons of the naval revolt of Chile and the mutiny of the British Home

Fleet at Invergordon, both of which had taken place during September, 1931. George Mink reported on the events in Chile, while Cole, a delegate from Liverpool, spoke on "The Spirit of Invergordon."

The mutiny of the British fleet at Invergordon was a political event of the first magnitude. It had rocked not only the British Empire, but also the faith of millions of non-Britishers in the immunity of Albion's battleships to the bacillus of rebellion. The mutiny began on the night of September 12, after Sir Austen Chamberlain had announced in the House of Commons that a reduction in pay had been decided upon for all lower ratings in the navy. That night the sailors gathered thickly in the shoreside canteens—and the agitators went to work. Able Seaman Bond, of H.M.S. *Rodney*—which ranked among the most powerful units of the Home Fleet—jumped atop a table and called on the sailors to answer the government's decision with a strike. The next speaker was Len Wincott, the organizer among the ringleaders. Ship delegates were elected to carry the strike call to all the vessels of the fleet. A day later ship committees were elected. On Monday, September 14, a meeting of crews' delegates fixed the beginning of the strike for 6 A. M., Tuesday morning. A glass was thrown at a naval officer who attempted to dissolve the meeting. The sailors returned to their ships, some singing the "Red Flag," a communist battlesong. Through the night shouts leaped from ship to ship: "Don't forget tomorrow morning!"

"Tomorrow morning" came. First to strike were the sailors aboard the *Rodney*. Their cheers rolled over the roadstead. Two hours later all crews of the Home Fleet were on strike. The sword and shield of the British Empire was paralyzed. After thirty-six hours the Admiralty capitulated before the mutineers. The affair was hushed up. Neither trials nor convictions followed. Twenty-four ringleaders were merely discharged from naval service—"for subversive conduct"—and given free railway tickets home. In the subsequent discussions of the lessons of the Invergordon mutiny at the Hamburg Congress, one of the Russian emissaries observed that such a naval strike "transformed the British Lion into a harmless pussy-cat." The latter phrase was snapped up and internationally popularized by the American delegate, Mike Appelman, in a book, "S.S. Utah," which in thinly disguised fiction form outlined the technique of organizing strikes and mutiny on the high seas, and which was published by the subsidiaries of the Comintern in Russia, Germany, the Scandinavian countries and in America. The Invergordon mutiny created in the minds of many uninitiated Bolsheviks an unwarranted optimism regarding the possibility of "capsizing" the British Empire. However, my misadventures in England in the course of my next assignment, confirmed the opinion of our leaders that, in spite of the "spirit of Invergordon," our forces were far from whittling down the claws of the British Lion.

Chapter Twenty-two

INSPECTOR-GENERAL FOR ENGLAND

I was summoned to Berlin after the International Seamen's Congress had closed and the last of the delegates had received the funds for their homeward passage. Georgi Dimitrov's welcome was exceptionally friendly.

"Dear comrade," he told me, "we are sending you to England. You will find a delicate situation there. Our British movement is a pain. It will not grow, neither will it die. Harry Pollitt and his crowd are as snobbish and as incapable of revolutionary mass work as they are English."

For five long hours I received detailed instructions pertaining to my mission. They included an overhauling of the financial management of the London *Daily Worker* and the communist shipping paper, the *Seafarer*, as well as a tour of British ports, a reorganization of the communist trade union opposition, known as the "Minority Movement," of the East Indian Seamen's Union, the headquarters of which was in London, and the West Indian Society—an international negro organization centered in Cardiff, Wales.

It was by far the most important job I had ever been assigned to tackle. I spent two more days in going over the British correspondence in the files of the Western Secretariat of the Comintern. I found that the reports sent in by the British Central Committee were a mixture of diplomacy, self-righteousness and claims to successes which had not been attained. Every letter ended with a shrill request for money. The British Party had almost no income of its own. Perhaps five percent of its recorded members paid dues. Every phase of Party activity was dependent on subsidies from Moscow.

Incidentally, it may be noted that the British files of the Western Secretariat were not kept at the main offices which were housed at the *Fuehrer Verlag*. The records pertaining to each individual nation were kept in different private apartments of trusted Party members. This decentralization of documentary material made it impossible for the police to seize in one raid the bulk of confidential Comintern records in Berlin. Even the efficient Gestapo failed to get them. In the spring of 1933, they were transferred in small batches to Copenhagen.

Painstaking preparations were made to ensure my safe entry into the United Kingdom and the efficacy of my lines of communication. Britain was one of the freest countries on earth. But it had in Scotland Yard a police machine that worked with almost omniscient precision. Scotland Yard spies were everywhere. The British passport authorities had a reputation for discovering at a glance the most subtle forgeries in traveling documents. In the

Comintern we knew that no well-known agent could ever hope to pass a British port of entry without official molestation. Numerous Comintern men had in previous years been seized and deported by Scotland Yard.

I received three false passports to cover my sojourn in England. There was a Dutch passport in the name of Gerhart Smett, which I was to use for entry and for registration with the London police. A Norwegian passport in the name of Alfson Petersen was to serve as my identification for the British Communist Party. I kept in reserve an American passport, originally issued to one Kurt Peter, to be used only in an emergency or for sudden flight from arrest. The description in all of these passports fitted me perfectly. The only items which had been changed were the photographs and the bearer's signature. In addition, I carried business credentials introducing me as the representative of a wholesale fish merchant in Rotterdam. The fish merchant actually existed; he was paid to acknowledge this letter of recommendation in case of an inquiry. All these documents were issued by the Comintern counterfeiting center, which had its offices in Berlin SW68-72 Lindenstrasse.

Taking the plane for Croydon from Hamburg-Fuhlsbuettel, I carried only the Dutch passport and the fish merchant's letter. The other passports, addresses and the Comintern credentials were then brought to me by two maritime couriers who handled our secret communications to and from England. Both were engineers serving on the British weekly boats *Teal* and *Lapwing*.

I bade Firelei farewell and flew to London on a crystal-clear day. The examination at Croydon caused me some uneasy moments. Passport officers on duty perused every page of my Dutch passport. Then they began to thumb leisurely through their suspect list. A few questions followed. I passed. A bus brought me into London.

I met Harry Pollitt, communist leader of Great Britain, at the *Brasserie Universelle* in the Piccadilly district. He was a handsome, well-built and elegantly-attired man in his late thirties, an excellent and tireless talker, with a very high opinion of his own abilities. He received me with a forced joviality which gave me the impression that he looked with hidden disfavor on my presence in London. "Something is rotten in Denmark," I thought. "Comrade Pollitt must not be permitted to obscure the facts." From the first we were enemies. Pollitt's resentment was sugar-coated. To him I was an ignorant interloper in British affairs. But no one in any Communist Party dares openly to question the authority of "the man from Moscow." When Pollitt offered me quarters with a communist family, I declined. The nature of the business I had come to do was unpleasant. The hazard of residing at an address known to functionaries suspected of corruption was obvious. I also declined to make use of a girl secretary Pollitt offered to assign to me. I was quite certain that she would be a spy of the Central Committee.

"She's a good-looking chit," Pollitt tempted.

"Don't bother," I said. "I'll have my own *Apparat.*'

The British Party chief seemed to sniff the air cautiously. He thought I was a Russian.

I took lodgings in one of the innumerable boarding-houses around Euston Station. Then I proceeded to gather a nucleus of reliable assistants whose names and addresses had been transmitted, with other material, by the courier aboard the *Teal*. My aides were Joe Keenan, a hard-boiled little Australian and a veteran of many Comintern enterprises, "Red" McGrath, the lanky New Zealander with whom I had co-operated in Antwerp in the years following the Hamburg insurrection of 1923, Patrick Murphy, one of the few hard-drinking, hard-fighting Irishmen in the G.P.U. service, and a girl named Cilly. Cilly was young and tall and dark, coolly independent and chic; she was a German girl who had worked for the Soviet Trade Mission in London, the *Arcos*, until that institution had been raided by Scotland Yard. We met in a tea-room to exchange observations and to get our bearings.

In the Comintern, the British Party occupied a singular position. It had never had a shake-up. It had never been torn asunder by factional struggles. Yet, since the general strike of 1926, it had become the most useless and expensive toy of the Communist International. It had swallowed money to the tune of a quarter of a million dollars yearly. After ten years of existence, it counted less than one-tenth of the number of units commanded by the Party in the city of Hamburg alone. "What is the reason for this stagnation?" I asked myself.

The chief reason was perhaps the mental attitude of the British worker. Another reason was to be found in the ineptitude and arrogance of the Party leadership, and its corrupt point of view that revolution was a good business, provided revolution did not come. And the third factor was the proficiency of British trade union leaders and of Scotland Yard in the art of sterilizing in the gentlest manner any communist attempt at an offensive.

I decided to attend to the London *Daily Worker* first. The editorial and business offices of this central Party organ were under Scotland Yard supervision from nine o'clock each morning to punctually six at night. Two detectives were always on duty. I saw them standing on the other side of the street, lounging in doorways, pretending to be engrossed in newspapers, actually sizing up every person that entered or left the building. Our check-up had to be done at night, without a forewarning to those concerned.

Joe Keenan and Pat Murphy rounded up the staff in their homes. Our session lasted until seven next morning. This was repeated twice more in the course of a week. The bevy of well-groomed Britishers—not a worker among them—was furious about my "G.P.U. methods" of investigation and cross-examination. But they exercised prudent restraint, fearful for their jobs. Our conferences were stormy, nerve-racking affairs. But that is the joy of overhauling an organization financed fully by Moscow; "the man from Moscow" can slash away at will, become sarcastic, go berserk, and insult the Moscow-paid pawns to his heart's content—and not one of them will stand up for fear of being mentioned in a "confidential report."

The *Daily Worker* had been launched in 1930 with an initial subsidy of $45,000, supplied by the Soviet Government *via* the Comintern with the understanding that each issue should comprise a minimum of one hundred thousand copies. In addition to the initial subsidy, $2,600 had been sent each month by the Western Secretariat to pay for the wages of the *Daily Worker* staff. In April, 1931, the British Central Committee had reported to Berlin and Moscow that the circulation of the *Daily Worker* had been raised to over two hundred thousand, and had requested a monthly budget of $4,000 to pay for the greatly increased number of comrades employed by the Party press department. The discrepancy between the allegedly rising circulation of the paper and the dismal stagnation of other Party activities had given rise to suspicion in the heads of responsible Comintern functionaries. After a most bitter investigation, this is what I found:

The circulation of the *Daily Worker* was not two hundred thousand, but a bare thirty thousand. The editorial business personnel had not been increased. Where did the Comintern money go? A small part of it had been used to buy advertisements! Businessmen were paid by the *Daily Worker* to use its space with the design of demonstrating the paper's growing influence to Moscow. The rest of the money went in the form of salaries and "expenses" to a small clique of Central Committee members. "Expenses" included fairly luxurious apartments, maintenance of mistresses, vacation trips to the South Shore, and fur coats and automobiles for the wives of prominent British Stalinists.

The British comrades tried hard to explain the facts away by talking for hours about the vicissitudes to which the *Daily Worker* had been subjected by the British authorities. The *Daily Worker* had been banned from the official newspaper trains. In 1931, the chief printer had been sent to jail for nine months. Frank Paterson, one of the ostensible owners of the paper, had been condemned to two years of hard labor. One of the editors, Comrade Allison, had gone to prison for three years. Another, Comrade Shepherd, had been sentenced to twenty months of hard labor in connection with the Invergordon mutiny of the British fleet. And so on. I laughed off these explanations. Anti-communist terror in Britain was a kindergarten affair when compared to the hardships encountered by our comrades in most European and Asiatic countries. Ruthlessly I cut down wages to four pounds sterling a week and "expenses" to nothing. I had brought with me from Berlin the subsidies for June and July, and I hung on to them like a hardheaded miser. After all wages were paid, there was a surplus of nearly $ 1,600, which I used to improve the circulation machinery. I sent off a long report on my findings to Hamburg, by my courier aboard the *Lapwing*. From Hamburg it was forwarded to Berlin, from Berlin to Moscow. One by one, with the exception of Gallacher, the Lenins of the British Empire were called to Moscow.

The conditions that existed in the offices of the *Daily Worker*, I found, were duplicated in most of the other departments of the communist movement in Britain. It was led by a corrupt clique of bureaucrats looting not only the Comintern treasury, but also the pockets of their own rank and file. In the blazing summer heat of London, I investigated almost a score of communist offices bearing the name-plates of the many auxiliary organizations, and everywhere the picture was the same: well-groomed and voluble officials loafing behind a shiny desk, trim-looking secretaries, office hours from nine to four, heaps of paper plans and resolutions, portraits of Lenin and Stalin on the wall, and no contact worth mentioning with the laboring masses of Great Britain.

One of my tasks was the inspection of the London bureau of the Friends of the Soviet Union, outwardly an "independent" body. Since the end of 1930 this organization had received a special monthly allowance with which to combat the intensive British anti-Soviet campaign that centered around the employment of slave labor in the vast lumber camps of the G.P.U. in the country around Archangelsk. The Friends of the Soviet Union in London had received huge consignments of the handsome and expensive pictorial review, *U.S.S.R. in Construction,* and money with which to finance a large-scale distribution of this publication among British teachers, college professors, and professional groups. Probing through the records and the premises of the "Friends" in London, I found that the money had been spent to no good purpose while big stacks of *U.S.S.R. in Construction* reposed in the cellars, thickly covered with dust.

The British Party had in its ranks no groups of militant character. When one of the officials wanted a batch of leaflets distributed, he was obliged to hire some down-and-outer for a union wage of five shillings a day to do the job. A good proportion of these Party "volunteers" earned their meager bread and butter by acting as small-time informers for Scotland Yard. (Later that year, when Scotland Yard agents had arrested me, a London police inspector told me gravely: "We've got you communists hamstrung. Why, if we want to know something, we walk right into any of your offices and buy the information we are looking for.")

One of the coups which won me credit in Moscow was the liquidation of the cozy nest which two top-flight British communists, Comrades Thompson and George Hardy, had feathered for themselves at Comintern expense. Thompson and Hardy were the team at the head of the most important department in the Communist Party of Great Britain—in charge of the harbors, the docks, the fisheries and the vast British merchant marine. Thompson was a hard-voiced giant, formerly an official of the British Trade Union Congress. George Hardy was a soft-footed, foxy schemer, who had transacted Comintern business in many far places, in India, Moscow and Vladivostok, in South Africa, Shanghai and the United States. I had met both Hardy and Thompson briefly in Berlin and Hamburg during the previous year. Both looked like prosperous merchants, and their women were sufficiently groomed to have stepped fresh out of some fashionable country club.

"When you deal with these two, be rough, be aggressive," Dimitrov had advised me. "They're liable to sell you the Nelson Statue on Trafalgar Square, if you don't look out."

I found what I had expected to find. The communist waterfront organizations in Great Britain registered some fourteen hundred members, but not one of them had paid dues beyond an initiation fee. The International Seamen's Clubs in British ports were not political centers, but unsavory cafés run for the personal profit of Hardy and Thompson. The International Club in Freetown, Sierra Leone, on the West Coast of Africa, which was budgeted and directed from London, had been transformed from a communist rallying point to something that closely resembled a slave-trading center. Returning negro comrades told the tale. Hardy had sold the Freetown unit to a clique of "Krubosses," men who supplied coastal vessels with longshoremen for a fee amounting to one-third of the negroes' wages. Thompson did a flourishing business by importing Arab and Chinese seamen for placement on British ships far below the regular wage standards. The monthly ISH subsidy of $2,500, which Hardy and Thompson received through Albert Walter to make British shipping Red, was distributed in the following manner: Hardy paid himself a salary of $1,000, Thompson paid himself a salary of $1,000, and the remaining $500 they used for printing a newspaper, the *Seafarer,* not for distribution among dockers and seamen, but solely for dispatch to German and Soviet ports as "proof" of their activities in England. Patiently I collected voluminous details for a report to Georgi Dimitrov. My courier on the *Teal* relayed the report to Hamburg. Meanwhile George Hardy, aware that something threatening was afoot, collected counter-material against the Maritime Center in Hamburg and myself. He accused me of having organized a burglary on his office on Commercial Road, and of the theft of his personal files. He entrusted this counter-report to his wife and sent her to deliver it in Moscow. It would have been easy to stop Mrs. Hardy in Berlin. However, she was allowed to proceed.

From Berlin I soon received instructions to break Hardy and Thompson with every means at my command, and to install a new leadership in their *Apparat*. The methods of "breaking" men were as familiar to me as they were to anyone who had grown up in the communist movement. First I stopped all payment of subsidies. The *Seafarer* ceased to appear. One after one, the seven existing International Clubs in British ports were forced to shut down. Through unsigned leaflets spread among their own followers, I accused Hardy and Thompson of stealing workers' money and of complicity with Scotland Yard. I had caused damaging personal data on Hardy to reach the hands of the bitterest foes of communism, Bevin and Spence, the leaders of the British maritime unions. Soon this material began to appear on the front page of Mr. Spence's journal, the *Seaman,* and found its way into every foc's'le under the British flag. As a result, Hardy accused Thompson of treachery, and Thompson gave Hardy a tremendous thrashing in front of Charley Brown's famous tavern on West India Dock Road. By way of revenge, Hardy denounced me to Scotland Yard, and detectives began to comb the East End, asking for a "Russian with an American accent." Several times I had the distinct *feeling* of being trailed. But, fortunately, the average detective can be recognized a hundred yards off.

The campaign to break Hardy and Thompson was a complete success. The blustering Thompson was not dangerous; he was permitted to resign. George Hardy was ordered to go to Moscow. For two weeks he hesitated. "Goddamn you sons-of-bitches," he told me, "you've got my wife there."

"You sent her there, didn't you?" I answered.

George Hardy was, after all, an Englishman. He went to Moscow. He was permitted to remain alive. But he has, to the best of my knowledge, never emerged from his oblivion.

The new leadership for the Comintern work in the field of British Empire shipping was selected at the World Congress against Imperialist War in Amsterdam, financed and engineered by the Kremlin in August, 1932. It was sponsored by a fine array of liberal "innocents," ranging from Romain Rolland to Patel—the Chairman of the East Indian National Congress. It also brought together the international Comintern élite. In one of the secret conferences which accompanied the open "show" session, the successors to Thompson and Hardy were appointed.

After Hardy and Thompson were pushed out of the way, I concentrated on the West Indian Association. This was a league of negroes, built up in the course of years by a negro named O'Connell, controlling numerous local units in Jamaica, Haiti, the Dominican Republic and on the lesser islands. It stood for the defense of negro rights and the promotion of cultural relations among the various negro centers. O'Connell, who had his head office in Cardiff, was an energetic individual, very dark of skin, but with the nose of an Arab horseman and the chin of a pugilist. He was not a member of the Communist Party, but held the card of one of the more important auxiliaries—the Friends of the Soviet Union. My instructions were to plant a communist adviser in O'Connell's office, and to enchain O'Connell by inducing him to accept a regular subsidy of a few hundred dollars from the International Secretariat for the Friends of the Soviet Union. Actually such a Secretariat did not exist; the "Secretariat" was Willy Muenzenberg. The aim was, of course, to use O'Connell's Association as a communist transmission-belt among the negro populace of the West Indies. The assistant I had intended to put into O'Connell's office was a London negro named Jones, a graduate of the Lenin School in Moscow. What I did not suspect, however, was that Comrade Jones had been for years, and still was, on the payroll of Scotland Yard.

My mission ended in bleak defeat. I journeyed to Cardiff. O'Connell was willing to accept the money I offered to support his organization, but he stubbornly insisted that the West Indies were one thing, and Moscow another. Bluntly he told me: "I represent my negro brothers; you want me to represent Russia among the West Indians. I cannot be a servant to two masters. My conscience rules that out."

"But we are deeply interested in helping the colored people in their just fight," I explained.

"Who are 'we'?" O'Connell barked. " 'We' is Moscow. Moscow is deeply interested in helping Moscow."

I then tried another method. There were several negroes in Cardiff who were both members of the Communist Party and of the West Indian Association. They did not amount to much, but they were there. I printed a leaflet denouncing O'Connell as a "traitor" to the negro cause, pointing out that the final liberation of the negroes could only be accomplished by revolutionary means, and urged the members of the Association to depose O'Connell. The leaflet was distributed in Cardiff and on ships manned by West Indian negroes. O'Connell reacted promptly. He called an open meeting of his followers to make short shrift of the Stalinist opposition.

I summoned Jones from London and a handful of other negro communists from Liverpool and Birkenhead to strengthen our group in the forthcoming meeting. Roles were assigned in advance to all participants. I established a temporary headquarters in a fish-and-chips shop a few doors away from the meeting hall, maintaining contact with the communist caucus by two negro couriers. Besides O'Connell, the Association had no formidable speakers. On the other hand, each member of our unit was able to deliver a harangue. I felt confident that we would carry the day. Once a communist bloc was established inside the Association, O'Connell could either be forced to abdicate or come to terms.

O'Connell won the battle. He had been informed about every detail of my plan. Plainclothesmen hovered about the meeting. O'Connell opened the meeting by calling every member of the communist group by name, including Jones, and demanded that they should leave the building. A scuffle ensued, a few heads were broken, and then the policemen closed in and arrested every communist in the meeting on a charge of "disturbing the peace." I cursed myself for a crude blunderer. The Cardiff police, too, were now scouting for "the Russian with an American accent." I fled out of Wales in disgrace. Arriving in London, I reported my failure to Berlin. Orders arrived from Berlin to break O'Connell or to wreck his Association. Pat Murphy was sent to Cardiff to continue the campaign. It ended, months after I had left England, with the liquidation of the West Indian Association. The Cardiff offices moved several times before they finally closed down. O'Connell sank into obscurity.

In the middle of July, I was suddenly recalled to Germany. The atmosphere I found upon landing in Hamburg convinced me that great and implacable forces were moving against each other for a final cataclysmic clash. But the crashing events in my homeland belong to another chapter. I returned to London in August, this time by boat via Grimsby. There were still the affairs of the East Indian Seamen's Union to be straightened out.

Moscow had demanded that the headquarters of the Union be transferred from London to Calcutta. A closer contact with the home bases of the East Indian waterfront workers was desired. But for some mysterious reason the Central Committee of the British Party and the leader of the East Indian Seamen's Union had consistently sabotaged every attempt to transfer the head office to Calcutta.

"We know little about this outfit," Albert Walter had told me. "The head of the Union is a Hindu. He's a fat, good-for-nothing loafer, but he has more shipping contacts to India than anyone else. Find him, and put some TNT under his hindquarters. He calls himself Vakil."

As is done in all such cases, I began by stopping the Hindu's budget. Three of my aides, working in eight-hour shifts, kept his place under observation from the window of a room I had rented in a house on the opposite side of the street. Vakil's headquarters occupied an old two-story house, with six rooms distributed above a large ground-floor store which now served as a meeting-hall and club-room. I reasoned in the following manner: "The Hindu refuses to move his firm to Calcutta. For this he must have a reason. I must find out whom he meets, what he does, and what influence keeps him stubbornly in London." A week of surveillance revealed nothing, except the picturesque figures of the Lascars from the ships in port who visited him. Vakil himself went into the harbor each morning to board vessels with East Indian crews; on these journeys he carried a sample case filled with cheap watches and other trinkets. That was his camouflage to avoid being challenged by the policemen who guard the gates to all London docks.

In order not to lose more time in fruitless surveillance, I decided to interview the Babu without further reconnaissances. I entered his place unannounced, on a Sunday evening. Vakil's office on the first floor was a greasy little room, with posters on the walls, piles of East Indian literature on shelves, and a primitive printing press in a corner. A train of curious Lascars had followed me from the club-room up the stairway to see what the Occidental wanted in their building. I ordered them to go back to the ground floor. They complied, plainly frightened, taking me for a policeman.

The Babu was a large, brown, fat man, approaching fifty. He was dressed like any East End innkeeper, and his small, sly eyes squinted at the world between barricades of fat. He was not alone. Two turbaned individuals squatted near him on low chairs. They all jumped up when I walked into the office.

"What may be your wish, sir?" said Vakil with dignity.

"I come from the International of Seamen and Harbor Workers."

"Ah!"

We sat down. Vakil's two companions wanted to leave. But I prevented that. "I am the first to leave," I decreed. "You can go after I have gone." We talked. All my probing as to why the chief of the East Indian Seamen's Union refused to transfer his headquarters to Calcutta led to no results. Vakil talked volubly. He boasted of his contacts with India, pointed out the trust placed in him by the Lascar sailors, and then embarked on long lamentations about the lack of co-operation from our international organization. All this, I soon realized, was only designed to keep me from prying into his affairs.

"Give me a list of all your contact men on ships to East India," I demanded. "Show me your correspondence with the East Indian units. Show me your financial records."

"Oh, but they're written in a language you could not read," the Babu countered.

I settled down to a night of gathering fragmentary notes about his organization. Vakil's answers to my questions came reluctantly. Many were evasive, more were obviously false. I tried then what is known in the Comintern as the "Thaelmann method." I brought my fist down on the table and rose, overturning the chair. Leaning forward with all the truculence I could mobilize, I roared: "Comrade Vakil, your actions are not those of a revolutionist. I thought I had to deal with a Bolshevik. Where is your Bolshevist frankness? I see now that I have to deal with a shyster. I want no subterfuges. I cannot permit you to play in the dark with the vital interests of our East Indian class brothers! We put you in charge of this organization. We have a right to know what you have done with it!"

Vakil slumped in his chair,, his arms dangling limply.

"My word!" he said finally. "Your impudence is remarkable!"

"Let's come to terms," I said.

"Ah!"

"Remember we are stronger than you. Do you imagine we can permit anyone to steal one of our organizations, and let him get away with it?"

"Do not forget," the Babu murmured, "we are in London."

I pretended not to understand the threat, and requested him to prepare a report on his organization. I promised to return for it in the morning. Vakil agreed.

I called Joe Keenan from the nearest telephone, instructing him to rouse our three assistants. At two o'clock in the morning we met at the entrance of Blackwall Tunnel, at the end of East India Dock Road. From there we proceeded to the Babu's headquarters.

Vakil was already in bed. He appeared at the door in grimy green pajamas. We pushed him back into the house and entered. Then we searched the building. Outside of our group, only Vakil and his two turbaned aides were present. The latter two were locked in a back room and placed under guard. Vakil we herded into his cluttered office.

A strange inquisition followed. The Babu was a weakling. Under threats, he divulged everything we wanted to know, including the secret of his refusal to transfer his *Apparat* to Calcutta. At times his blubbering fear was so grotesque that we could hardly keep from breaking into laughter. Vakil had transformed the East Indian Seamen's Union into an opium smuggling ring which had its customers in London. His ships' delegates in the East India trade bought the drug in small quantities in various ports of India. The necessary capital was supplied by Vakil. They purchased the opium for an equivalent of $2.30 per kilogram, and smuggled it into London, where Vakil paid them a commission of twenty percent. The Babu then sold the opium to the local traders for whatever he could get.

"What did you do with the money?"

"The profits were very small. I am a man with a large family," Vakil said mildly.

The truth was that Vakil had no family at all, but he had become the owner of several houses in Whitechapel. I told Vakil that he had to relinquish all control of the Indian Seamen's Union effective at once. I threatened to denounce him to the British authorities if he persisted in using union members for the opium traffic. In reality, I had no such intention; men of Vakil's type would not hesitate to denounce our East Indian adherents on the ships should he get into trouble himself. I seized all papers, documents and files I could find in the building. My companions packed them into sacks, and one at a time the sacks were carried away to an apartment on High Street, in the deepest slums of Poplar, which I had rented after my first arrival in England to serve as a secret depot for colonial propaganda material. I wrote immediately a detailed report on the case to Berlin. The Babu's records followed a week later, in charge of our courier aboard the *Lapwing*.

The "breaking" of Vakil had a sequel. Again my presence in London was denounced to Scotland Yard, either by Vakil himself, or by the Central Committee of the British Communist Party, which fiercely resented my highhanded intrusion in British affairs.

Another East Indian, a student named Gani, had been sent from Berlin to direct the alienation of East Indian seamen from Vakil and to organize the transfer of the Union to Calcutta. One afternoon, when I left Gani after a conference we had had in the Poplar town hall, the safest of places for communist conspiracy, I hastened toward the other side of London to meet Cilly, my secretary, at the King's Cross Station. I took the Commercial Road bus to Aldgate. A soon as I had stepped off the bus, to cross over to Aldgate Station, the subway terminal, two burly individuals stepped from behind a corner and grasped my arm.

"Hello," I said, "what are you chaps up to?"

"You bloody well answer the description of a foreigner we are looking for," one of the men replied.

Both flashed badges.

"We are from Scotland Yard," they murmured in unison.

I had in my pocket some notes on my conversation with Gani, and other notes pertaining to a letter I had intended to dictate to Cilly. The letter had been intended for our unit chiefs in Cardiff, Liverpool, Glasgow, and the Tyne ports. I crushed the notes into one lump in my pocket, jerked them out with lightning speed, stuffed them into my mouth and began to chew frantically. I was choking.

One of the detectives was patting my back with vigor.

"Spit out the documents, brother," he counseled.

A few of the notes I had succeeded in swallowing, one or two I spat out, rubbing them to shreds with my feet as soon as they fell to the pavement. The detectives dragged the others out of my mouth with strong stubby fingers. I had felt too secure. I had neglected one of the most important rules of conspirative technique, the rule which said: "Never carry written material in your pockets; let it be carried by an unknown assistant, or hide it in the lining of your clothes or the cavities of your body."

Scotland Yard agents prove their efficiency by never making an unnecessary show of force, a show so dear to the policemen of most other nations. There were neither manacles, nor jiu-jitsu grips, nor a police-wagon clanging through crowded streets. Simply a little push into the ribs, and a drawled, "Aw, come along now; you wouldn't resist, would you?"

"No," I said.

"Where were you going?" they asked.

"I was going to my apartment to pack up and leave the country," I told them.

"All right. Then let's all go to your apartment."

We entered Aldgate Station and boarded a westbound train. I sat in a corner by a window, a detective at my right, the other on the opposite seat. It was all quite pleasant. The Yard men joked, asked me how I liked Piccadilly and how the English girls compared with the girls of my own country.

"The Russian girls are supposed to make great paramours," one detective said.

I was on guard.

"I don't know. I've heard that too."

"Aren't you a Russki?"

"No."

"Well, well, fancy that! How do you like England?"

"I don't like it."

"Well, if you'd come to us right away, we'd have showed you around a bit. I'm sure you would have liked England."

"Maybe."

"What do you think is the best country in the world?"

"The United States."

"Not Russia?"

"No."

"We sure appreciate your frankness," one of the men said with irony. "But you fellows will never get anywhere in Britain. Who in hell wants to sleep seven in a bed as they do in Russia? Or don't they?"

"Don't know. I've never been in Russia."

We left the subway in the West Center of London and sauntered to my quarters which contained nothing that could compromise me. By leading them there I hoped to keep the sleuths away from the East End, where most communist centers of operation were located. On the way, we stopped at a public house. I bought the detectives a drink, and then they bought drinks in their turn, and the game of cat-and-mouse went on. After we reached my rooming house quarters, the two detectives stripped me naked and searched every inch of my clothing and the room. The questioning that followed lasted many hours. I first led them far afield, but was later tricked into contradictions, and when I admitted that I had told them a cock-and-bull story, we all laughed as if we greatly enjoyed each other's company, and the detectives ordered tea and sandwiches. Even after they had become convinced that I would reveal nothing and admit nothing, not even the obvious fact that my passport was a fine piece of forgery, did they become rough or menacing in their methods.

"Listen here," one of them suggested suddenly, "if you'd work for us, you could make a little money on the side. The job you've got now is not very lucrative, is it? Anybody can use a few extra

"I told you already I don't like England."

"Where did you intend to go from here?"

"To Germany. I got a nice girl there."

"Well, mayhap you will not see your girl so soon. We might charge you with entering the country under false pretenses."

"Suit yourselves," I said.

There is a Comintern saying pertaining to deportation methods which runs like this: "In Russia you are shoved *under* the country, elsewhere you are *kicked* out of the country, but in England you are *bowed* out of the country." I can certify to its correctness. For one of the detectives announced, after they had given up further questioning as useless:

"We want no unpleasantness, you know. The Home Office is content to send you fellows where you came from, and just put you on the suspect list. We're going to put you on a boat in the morning. Just let us keep that passport of yours."

"What! No photographing? No fingerprinting?"

The detectives grinned. "We have your picture in the passport, and your fingerprints we've got on the glasses you handled in the public house a little while ago."

I became suspicious that these men might not be agents of the British Government at all, but impostors. Why were they so casual? Why did they not take me to headquarters? I demanded to see their credentials.

"Anybody can show a badge," I said.

"Oh, certainly."

Both produced their Scotland Yard identification cards. My respect for that police force grew enormously.

"You're a nice chap, and so are we. We won't make a scandal about it. But any time you fancy earning a few extra pounds—why, drop us a postal card."

One of the two kept me a prisoner in my own room for the rest of the night. The other departed to attend to the formalities of "bowing" me out of England. A police inspector and another agent arrived in the morning.

"We sure give you credit for carrying no correspondence in your luggage," the inspector commented while he watched me packing my belongings. "Do me a favor and don't come back to England. It's absolutely unprofitable for you, and a nuisance for us."

I was escorted by train to Grimsby. There I was put aboard one of the liners of the London and North Eastern Railroad. A detective accompanied me until we were outside of British territorial waters. He departed with the pilot.

•••

The second part of the sequence to the "breaking" of the fat Babu in London was tragi-comic. He wrote to Albert Walter, the chief of the ISH, that he would denounce all East Indian communists he knew to the British Secret Service, if the records taken from his office were not returned within a month. The matter was referred to the G.P.U. office in the Hedemannstrasse in Berlin. At first Michel Avatin was assigned to go to London to "silence" Vakil. But Avatin was known to Scotland Yard and too valuable a man to lose in such a minor action. Another man, one Patra, was dispatched in his stead. Patra, a tall, thin, keen-eyed fellow from the Balkans, had worked since January, 1932, in the special *Apparat* directed by the taciturn Lett Schmidt, whom I had met before in Hamburg, where he was wont to arrive in the guise of a sailor aboard various Soviet ships. Patra went to London.

Years later, through a fellow-prisoner in the Gestapo cellars of the Polizeipraesidium on the Alexanderplatz in Berlin, I heard what had happened to the Babu. He had been chloroformed in his den near the London East India Docks, put into a trunk, and was thus smuggled past the English dock policemen aboard a Russian ship in Tilbury. Vakil was brought to Leningrad in good health.

"What happened to the Hindu in Russia?" I inquired.

"I don't know," the other said. "They say he became an attendant in a hospital."

Chapter Twenty-three

HOW WE ENGINEERED MUTINIES

Several days after my expulsion from Britain I received orders through Albert Walter to go back into the Lion's mouth.

"But I've just been 'bowed' out of there," I objected.

"That's just it," the bronzed old sailor rumbled. "They don't expect you back right away, and that's why you have an excellent chance to slip in again."

I was given another passport and credentials, together with five hundred dollars. I was not to go to London, but to Glasgow. The Scottish section of the British waterfront union, controlled by the powerful labor leader Ernest Bevin, had broken away from its mother organization and was conducting independent strikes in Grangemouth and Glasgow. A report from the resident G.P.U. agent in Glasgow had revealed that three men in the leading committee of the splinter union were communist sympathizers. Moscow's plan was to bring about its affiliation with the Profintern. To this end, financial support for the harbor strikes in Scotland had been sent by the Comintern. So I was assigned to interview the communist sympathizers in the Glasgow leadership, and to pave the way for a communist invasion to conquer their union. This was to be done in co-operation with Gallacher, the only communist member of the House of Commons. I had met Gallacher, a rough and aggressive type, in London, and knew that he was at loggerheads with Harry Pollitt, his Party chief.

Without delay I embarked on a small British trampship for Newcastle. The only other passenger was a Newcastle merchant named Bates. During the passage, I cultivated the friendship of this man to such an extent that he invited me for a week-end at his home just as our steamer was nosing its way between the grimy banks of the Tyne. As a guest of a prominent citizen of Newcastle, I felt sure that I would not be bothered overmuch by the Newcastle passport inspectors. However, the uncanny efficiency of the British police thwarted my plans.

No sooner had the ship been moored to her Newcastle wharf when two burly plainclothes officers boarded it and accosted me.

"Your passport, please! We've been advised of your coming!"

Forlornly I sat in the cabin, watching the two detectives scrutinize my passport through large magnifying glasses, while Mr. Bates, waiting for me on the quay, honked the horn of his car. One detective looked hard at me.

"This passport has been tampered with," he said slowly.

The other detective rapped his knuckles on the table.

"This passport has been tampered with," he echoed.

My person and my belongings were searched with minute care. They did not find what they were looking for. The addresses and memoranda I needed for my work had been entrusted for transmission to a maritime courier aboard another ship. I bluntly refused to answer any questions.

"Come along!"

I was brought to the jail of the harbor police. It was run by men who wore the uniforms of the British Navy. It was a brick building, kept scrupulously clean. Each individual cell had its own fireplace. Before I was locked into a cell, I was given tea and a plate of ham-and-eggs, and a warder lighted a wood fire. Late at night I was called out into the guard-room for questioning. Strangely, no detectives were present. My interviewer was an elderly officer in a naval uniform. His face was drawn and deeply lined, suggesting the hidden anger of a man half-crazed from insomnia.

"Why did you come to the United Kingdom on a false passport?"

"I refuse to answer."

"You refuse to answer?"

"Yes."

The officer snapped into a weird fury. I had the impression that I was dealing with a lunatic. I stepped back against the wall, the officer following me, crouched as if ready to spring.

"Sir!" he shrieked. "I am 'sir' to you, do you comprehend that? I am 'sir,' you unspeakable hoodlum!"

"Sir," I muttered, taken aback by the unexpected onslaught.

"You damned communists," he yelled. "You want to set the world afire. Not while I live! You are as bad as the Germans who sank our ships from ambush in the war. You are worse. You are ..."

At first I thought that this was an attempt at intimidation, an effort to frighten me and to make me yield information. But it was not that. I realized that my examiner was out of his mind. Not until he had exhausted himself was I locked again into my cell.

The sheets of my bed were white and crisp, the blankets were clean, the fire crackled and then it died down. I slept soundly. Next morning, when the detectives came to settle down to an ordeal of questioning, I told them about my night experience with the commander of the jail. The detectives apologized for the official's rudeness. They explained that the top of his skull had been blown off when his ship was torpedoed by a submarine in 1916, and that he now wore a silver skull.

Two days and nights I lingered in the Newcastle jail. The detectives, after convincing themselves that I would not give them any information about myself and my employers, talked chiefly about England and occasionally indulged in amiable mockery at my futile attempt to enter it for a second time. I tried to gain some indication as to the identity of the Scotland Yard informer in Hamburg who had advised them of my coming. They merely laughed. "We don't need informers. We sniff in the air and we know. Aha! Someone's coming."

Again I was expelled from Britain. I was returned to Hamburg on the same ship on which I had come to Newcastle. After that, my name was definitely stricken from the list of Comintern men eligible for assignments in England. Once a man had become known to Scotland Yard, the best disguise, it seemed, would avail him nothing. To the Comintern, Great Britain has always been one of the least dangerous yet one of the most difficult terrains.

"Get ready to go to Holland at once," Albert Walter said to me in his blunt, though ever-enthusiastic way. "I have communicated with the Western Secretariat. A Dutch shipping strike is looming. Get it started. Pick out the biggest ship on which we have a strong unit. What we want is a sensational action, *ein Fanal*—a beacon—a striking example for other crews to follow. And don't forget to whack away at the Social Democrats in your strike manifestos"

I arrived in Rotterdam early the following morning. The Dutch shipping strike was mildly supported by the Social Democrats. What the Comintern wanted was an action of violent lawlessness which would be condemned by the Socialist leaders, and would thus afford us an opportunity to designate them as traitors to the seamen's cause.

Liaison agent and political instructor for our maritime units in the Dutch merchant marine was Willem Schaap, whose quiet manners and gentle blue eyes were belied by his silently driving energy. The Central Committee of the Dutch Party had been advised from Berlin to assign all its forces to aid in a spectacular waterfront coup—forces made up of 5,700 communists organized in 142 cells. Moscow's purpose in ordering this action went far beyond the confines of Dutch shipping proper. In the Far East, the Communist Party of Indonesia was preparing for a blow against Dutch colonial rule. The Indonesian communists, still remembering their bloody defeats in the insurrections of 1926 and 1927, were to be encouraged by a demonstration of communist power in the mother country. If they saw that the Communist Party was strong enough to disrupt shipping between Holland and the Colonies, they would take heart and launch a new offensive for "national liberation." As usual, the pretext seized upon to launch these actions was threatening wage cuts. As usual, the underlying reason for the planned *coup de main* was the Soviet Government's frantic fear of an imperialist invasion of Russia, and its resultant aim to divert the eyes of Britain, France and Japan to imbroglios far from the Soviet frontiers.

In Willem Schaap's office, I and Comrade de Groot—a member of the Dutch Central Committee—looked over the lists of communist units on Dutch vessels. We chose the liner *Rotterdam* for our initial action. The *Rotterdam* was the pride of the Dutch merchant marine, a large luxury liner then on the way to *Rotterdam* from New York with the Dutch Olympic team among her several hundred passengers. The communist cell aboard this vessel counted twenty-seven members, including seven Germans who had gone through the experience of the German shipping strike during the previous year. Among the communist sympathizers was the ship's junior radio officer.

The liner was scheduled to call at British and French channel ports *en route*. I had no doubt that the Holland America Line, owner of the ship, was informed of the imminent strike, and would therefore order the *Rotterdam's* captain not to enter any Dutch port until the dispute was settled. Those were the usual tactics of shipowners. By keeping their ships away from home ports, they hoped to keep their crews uninformed about impending conflicts. This gave us the opening for which we searched. Early in September, I sent Willem Schaap to the English South Coast to intercept the *Rotterdam*, and to organize mutiny in case the owners should attempt to prevent the ship from proceeding to its regular terminal harbor in Holland. I was confident that our force of twenty-seven communists would be strong enough to swing the crew of two hundred into action.

While the *Rotterdam* approached Cape Landsend, our columns in the harbor of Rotterdam worked day and night. We called dozens of meetings and distributed many thousands of strike manifestos. We sent agitation squads aboard every ship in port. At night, our detachments went into the harbors in boats, and armed with paint and brushes, they smeared the strike slogans on ships' sides, quays and cargo sheds. Action Committees were formed. Communist employees in the offices of the Holland America Line were instructed to keep us informed on the shipowners' plans. Our agents in the Rotterdam police department were put on the alert to warn us in advance of intended raids.

As I had expected, the liner *Rotterdam* received a wireless message from her owners, ordering her to discharge passengers in Plymouth and Boulogne, and to return to New York without touching any Netherlands port. Willem Schaap hastened to Plymouth, slipped aboard the Rotterdam, and remained there during the steamer's crossing to the French coast. This gave him time to map out the plan of battle with the members of the ship's communist unit.

At a fixed hour, our column aboard the *Rotterdam*—then at sea, steaming toward New York—went into action. Through the assistant radio officer and the head of the communist unit, the crew was told that a wireless message had been received to the effect that Dutch seamen were solidly on strike in all Netherlands ports and that the strikers had appealed to the *Rotterdam* crew to force their captain to return to home waters. In reality, no such message had been received. In reality, Dutch shipping had not as yet been tied up solidly. Our plan was to bring about such a tie-up through an electrifying mutiny aboard the *Rotterdam*.

The mutiny proceeded according to plan. A delegation of communists presented an ultimatum to the liner's master, Captain van Dulken. They demanded that the ship should not proceed to New York, but return to home waters to join the strike.

Captain van Dulken refused. He informed the crew that there was no general strike in Dutch shipping. The German communists in the delegation called him a liar, insisted on the correctness of the counterfeit wireless message, and repeated their demands in the name of the liner's crew. Again Captain van Dulken refused.

The communists acted boldly. At the head of a horde of volunteers from among the rest of the crew, they invaded the engine room, extinguished the fires, and stopped the engines. Helpless as a giant coffin, the liner drifted about the western reaches of the English channel. The news of a mutiny on the high seas aboard one of the largest ships in the Dutch fleet swept away the remnants of strike-resistance in Rotterdam. Overnight all shipping was stopped. Except for the mass pickets and regiments of police, the harbor lay dead.

The radical turn of the movement was more than the leaders of the moderate Dutch Federation of Seamen had bargained for. They objected against tactics which violated the laws of the land. I leaped at the chance. All along the waterfront, crimson leaflets were distributed, denouncing the Socialist chiefs as "traitors who sell the sailors' hides to the shipowners by refusing to carry on the struggle with all means, inside and *outside* the law!" As a result, Dutch seamen flocked in droves into the communist camp.

The Dutch shipowners made attempts to man their marooned vessels with Chinese seamen, some three hundred of whom were scattered in Oriental boarding houses along the harbor front of Rotterdam. At the suggestion of Willem Schaap and his Chinese assistant we decided to scare off the Chinese sailors by what Comrade Schaap chose to refer to as "psychological terror." The head of the Red Front Fighters' League in Rotterdam was appointed to the job of "chief psychologist." He armed himself with a band of Party guerrillas and a list of Chinese boarding houses. Some members of this host posed as officials of the Dutch Federation of Seamen, others as members of the Rotterdam alien police. They made the rounds of the boarding houses and threatened the jobless Oriental mariners with "immediate deportation to China" if they should dare to occupy the berths of striking Netherlands seamen. A few Chinese who disregarded this order were slugged with sandbags. The great majority, however, stoically succumbed to Comrade Schaap's "psychological" treatment.

Meanwhile play and counterplay aboard the *Rotterdam* continued. Captain van Dulken pretended to capitulate to the crew's demands to tie up his ship in Rotterdam. But in the middle of the night, he secretly changed course, again heading for New York. At sunrise the communist stokers discovered the skipper's trick. The sun should have risen over the bows. Instead it rose over the stern. The ship was steaming west. Again the fires were killed, again the big ship drifted helplessly between Cape Lizard and Ushant.

"Back to Rotterdam," the action committee threatened, "or we will put the scow on the Cornwall rocks."

Captain van Dulken had no choice. Aboard the *Rotterdam* the communists were masters. The helm was put hard over once more. In the night of Monday, September 5, the big ship dropped anchor off North Hinder Lightship, and her captain wirelessed the Dutch Admiralty: *"Mutiny—request aid."*

In Rotterdam harbor marines were loaded aboard a pilot ship to go out and down the mutineers. The gunboat *Meerlant* was dispatched by the Admiralty to escort the Rotterdam into port. I had foreseen this emergency, and prepared for it. An "activist" squad distributed leaflets among the embarking marines. "Proletarians in uniform," the leaflets said, "refuse to arrest your brothers aboard the *Rotterdam!* Their fight is your fight. Remember the glorious tradition of the *Potemkin* mutineers!" There was a minor disturbance when a small group of marines refused to participate in the expedition against the *Rotterdam* rebels. However, they were quickly disarmed and arrested.

Between two and three in the morning of September 6, the embattled liner was brought into Rotterdam. The decks were occupied by a company of marines; the gunboat *Meerlant* followed close astern. Ten ringleaders were arrested and flung into prison, charged with mutiny and sedition. Among them were our seven German comrades.

Far grimmer was the outcome of another mutiny which took place, under the Dutch flag, on the other side of the world a few short months later. Its preparation and its technique were closely linked with the lessons gained in the rebellion aboard the *Rotterdam*, and were the results of the silent efforts of the M-Department—the Military Section—of the Comintern.

There are branches of the M-Department in all major Communist Parties. They are the active organs of "Revolutionary Defeatism," the arms of the Kremlin in the armies and navies of other countries. The units of the M-Department were trained to carry on untiring, obstinate and systematic revolutionary propaganda within the armed forces of capitalist nations. The aim of this campaign, as we well knew, was the complete disintegration of discipline and morale in "imperialist" armies and navies. The recruiting for the Communist Party of former members of armies and navies was also considered of great value. Ex-soldiers and sailors were used to establish and build up contacts with men still under the colors. In the event of war, this whole *Apparat* was expected to organize military sabotage, mutinies and soldiers' strikes whenever the interest of the Soviet Union dictated such action. The analytical reviews of the well-known naval mutinies in the Black Sea, in Toulon, in the German Imperial Fleet, of the British Fleet at Invergordon, and of the Chilean warships were required reading for all responsible functionaries in the Maritime Section of the Comintern and the M-Department.

Particularly strong were the communist positions inside the navies of Germany, Denmark, France, and Holland. There existed since 1931 special schools in Rouen, Hamburg and Rotterdam for the training of communists for naval work. In the middle of September, 1932, after the strike of Dutch seamen had ended, I was ordered to put eight members of the Dutch Young Communist League through a ten-day course of training in naval work. The eight young communists were scheduled for military service in the armed forces of their country. Being seamen by profession, they would enter the navy and were expected to apply for service in the East Indian squadron of the Dutch fleet.

I regarded this as a minor assignment. The ten days went by like a holiday.

The schooling of the eager youngsters took place in the building of the International Club, 7 Willemskade, a house overlooking the wide inner harbor of Rotterdam, with liners and warships in plain sight of the apprentices in naval conspiracy.

The last of my lectures was also attended by a young Chinese Comintern agent, who had arrived from Moscow on his way to Indonesia. This comrade, a quiet, attentive man, sat silently in a corner, listening and occasionally taking notes. Willem Schaap introduced him to me as "Leo Chang."

"What has he got to do with the Dutch navy?" I inquired.

"He's going to take care of the Colonial Squadron," Schaap replied.

"Leo Chang," after a string of conferences with the M-Department in Rotterdam, departed for Batavia. I returned to Hamburg, and was soon too immersed in other duties to pay much attention to what the Comintern units in the Dutch navy and "Leo Chang" were cooking up in Indonesia. What happened four months later in Far Eastern waters was so startling that it overshadowed for a brief spell in our minds even the gathering Nazi holocaust. However, because the events occurred a few days after Hitler became Chancellor and at a time when the United States was in the midst of a grave financial crisis, they remain to this day a little-known chapter of our times.

The naval garrison at Soerabaja, Java, rose in revolt. The Dutch Government, seeing the very existence of its vast East Indian empire imperiled, acted swiftly. Four hundred and twenty-five of the Soerabaja mutineers were put in irons and thrown into prison.

The Comintern shouted: "Down with the imperialists! Liberate the prisoners of Soerabaja!" It was too fine an opportunity to miss.

In Kotoraj, a small port of northern Sumatra, lay the Dutch battleship *De Zeven Provincien*. Aboard this warship, the M-Department of the Comintern had a strong unit, and also an action committee composed of Dutch and Javanese marines. "Chang," the Comintern emissary, had studied in Moscow, among other things, the feat of the *Potemkin* mutineers in the Czar's Navy. A courier arrived from Singapore, the Comintern headquarters for the Dutch East Indies, with instructions. The sailors of *De Zeven Provincien* were to seize the warship, steam for Java coast, and bombard the naval station of Soerabaja. Such an action could well serve as a signal for the hoisting of red flags on all other naval units, and a general rising in the Dutch East Indies.

The commander and officers, except nine, of *De Zeven Provincien* were ashore in Kotaraj. Shortly before dawn on February 5, the mutineers struck. At bayonet point, eight of the nine remaining officers were handcuffed. One escaped by jumping overboard; he swam ashore. Then, just before daylight, the mutineers steamed out to sea with the captured battleship. They set course for Java.

Immediately Moscow hailed this abduction of a warship as a significant and tremendous success. Comrade Dimitrov, in Berlin, ordered me to issue a manifesto in support of the mutiny. "Navy men of all countries," I wrote, "prepare to follow the glorious example of the *De Zeven Provincien* mutineers!" This proclamation was printed in German, Dutch, English, Scandinavian and French editions, and distributed clandestinely aboard the warships of the respective nations.

Simultaneously, the Comintern machine in Holland as well as in the Netherlands Indies went into action. Meetings were called. Proclamations, printed on miniature presses, previously smuggled to Singapore and Batavia, were distributed by the hundreds of thousands. They called the workers to solidarity actions, to demonstrations and strikes as a necessary prelude to armed insurrection.

Already the Dutch crews of other warships had rebelled. Forty-five of the ringleaders were arrested. Flying squadrons ordered to pursue *De Zeven Provincien* were delayed because the workers of the airplane base had gone on strike. Whipped on by action committees, part of the native laboring population of Soerabaja went on strike. Many were arrested.

In the capital of the Netherlands, the government met hastily. Decrees were issued to counteract subversive schemes in the Colonies. Members of the army and navy were subjected to punishment for having communist literature in their possession.

Meanwhile, Comrade "Chang" issued orders to seize the navy arsenal in Soerabaja to arm the revolutionary proletariat.

The mutineers of *De Zeven Provincien* were steaming down the coast of Sumatra. From Celebes a loyal squadron of cruisers and destroyers steamed full speed through Java Sea to intercept the mutineers.

It is an ironical fact that a government spy among the crew of *De Zeven Provincien* had warned her skipper of the impending mutiny. But the skipper, comfortably ashore for the night, had laughed. Two hours later the abduction of the battleship had taken place. Now, with seven officers and twenty marines, he was speeding aboard the government vessel *Aldebaran* in pursuit of his runaway command. But *De Zeven Provincien* was faster. It was not easy to catch her. Besides, her armament included 11-inch guns. In the Comintern, we fervently—and foolishly—hoped that the roar of these 11-inch guns would set an end to 300 years of Dutch rule over the islands of spices!

In Batavia, a squadron of flying boats, armed with machine guns and bombs, was taking off to sea under sealed orders. Two submarines, two destroyers and a mine-layer joined in the hunt for *De Zeven Provincien*. Reinforcements were sent to protect the arsenals of Soerabaja. There, the loyal cruiser *Java* and the destroyers *Evertsen* and *Piet Hein* lay in wait to meet the approaching mutineers. The commander of the kidnapped battleship had shifted to the faster vessel *Eridanus*, which glued itself to the wake of *De Zeven Provincien*, constantly signaling the latter's position.

Then came defeat. The solidarity actions ashore petered out. The mutineers were now alone. Trouble broke out in their own ranks; they sent contradictory radio messages into the world and *De Zeven Provincien*, heading down the western coast of Sumatra, made no more than seven knots. M. Wibaut, a leading Socialist, publicly condemned the attitude of the mutineers. Mass meetings pledged themselves to support the government. The Comintern, recognizing defeat, coldly abandoned the mutineers to their fate.

The mutineers, seeing themselves deserted, offered to surrender, provided their liberty would be guaranteed.

The government replied: "No negotiations! Unconditional surrender!" Army units were concentrated in western Java to prevent a landing of the mutineers. In addition to the assembled East Indian squadron, six seaplanes, a cable ship and a navy tug joined the hunt.

After five days the combined government forces cornered De Z-even Provincien off southern Sumatra. The mutineers had no anti-aircraft guns. A sea plane dropped a message.

"Surrender or we open fire," the message said.

The mutineers refused to hoist the white flag. Stubbornly *De Zeven Provincien* continued on her course.

"Surrender!" another signal repeated.

"Stand off!" was the curt retort of the mutineers.

Planes roared overhead. They dropped bombs. A direct hit abaft the bridge set *De Zeven Provincien* afire, killing 2 2 mutineers and wounding 25 others. In a panic the mutineers rushed for the boats. The government forces were prepared to annihilate the captured and imprisoned officers together with the insurgents. To the last minute the members of the action committee sent radio messages condemning wage cuts and demanding justice.

The bitter end had come. The survivors were clapped into prison. Later a court martial in Soerabaja condemned 19 Javanese and 5 Dutch ringleaders to penal servitude ranging from 1 to 18 years.

Firelei was too happy for words to see me back home. I thought her more beautiful, more lovable than ever. It was September 25, 1932. Two days later our son was born. I stood at the head of Firelei's bed, holding her hands, oblivious of the hours. On the wall above the bed was a picture showing Lenin in a pensive pose. A Party physician and a nurse from the corps of communist Samaritans attended. Firelei fought bravely, as any woman does who is not afraid of life. To me it seemed that the birth of a child was a greater event in the existence of the individual than a revolution. They had much in common, birth and revolution. Both were violent. Both were paid for with struggle, pain, blood. Both marked the beginning of new life, and no one could tell beforehand what course it would finally take. Something red and ugly and slimy was belched into the world.

"A boy," the doctor grunted.

"A boy," Firelei cried in wondrous exhilaration. "Do you hear? A boy! Oh, how beautiful!" And then, whispering fearfully: "He doesn't cry! Why doesn't he cry?" And a moment later: "Oh, did you hear? He cried! He got spanked and he cried! Oh, how beautiful, how beautiful!" Firelei's gentle, happy voice filled our Spartan apartment and all the universe with the cry: "How beautiful!" Then she relaxed, contented.

We called the child Jan.

Chapter Twenty-four

THE SWASTIKA CASTS ITS SHADOW

One day I asked Ernst Thaelmann:

"What will happen when Adolf Hitler seizes power?"

"Let him," he answered, "he won't last long. The workers will rise. There will be civil war."

In the spring of 1932 a working alliance between the powerful Socialist and Communist Parties of Germany would have dammed the tide and thereby changed the course of world history. This conviction grows out of my experience as an active participant in one of the embattled armies, for it is as such that I am writing of the events preceding the rise of Hitler to power, and not as a would-be objective historian or eyewitness.

Early in 1932 the Hitlerites already had control of the governments of Thuringia and Brunswick, but Prussia—which is two-thirds of Germany—was still firmly in socialist hands. On March 17, the socialist-controlled police of Prussia, to thwart a planned storm trooper march on Berlin, raided Nazi headquarters in Berlin and in hundreds of lesser towns. On April 17, a government decree outlawed the military organization of the Nazi Party. Police raided and closed the strongholds of the Brown Guards.

The prohibition of the storm troop organizations became a farce, though it had been based on serious intentions. The military formations of the Nazis continued to exist, and to grow. The only visible effect of the new law was that the Hitler guards wore white shirts instead of brown ones.

Thirteen million Nazis were confronted by eight million Social Democrats and half that number of militant Catholics. The balance of power lay in the hands of the Communist Party and its five million followers. For a time it seemed as if the March and April raids on the Nazi fortresses signaled the beginning of a general offensive to drive Hitlerism into impotent obscurity. The communist rank and file was eager to pitch in and help. But in Moscow, at the Eleventh Session of the Executive Committee of the Comintern, D. Z. Manuilsky, the mouthpiece of Stalin in the Communist International, rose and said:

"In order to deceive the masses, the Social Democrats deliberately proclaim that the chief enemy of the working class is Fascism. It is not true that Fascism of the Hitler type represents the chief enemy . . ."

Manuilsky's voice was the voice of the Kremlin. To communists the world over it was law. It created a hideous confusion among the leaders of the German Party. Sickly half-measures were the result, a swinging between extremes which ranged all the way from outright co-operation with the Hitler movement to murderous ambushes against isolated storm trooper detachments.

Election battles followed each other like waves before a storm. Each time I returned to Germany during 1932, I found myself in the middle of a wild election fight. The armies which were pitted against each other in those months were more numerous than the armies which fought the World War.

The rough figures of two elections, the first and the last of democratic Germany, tell eloquently how much democracy was worth in Germany in 1932:

In the National Assembly elections of 1919 the parties which supported the democratic Weimar Constitution commanded 25,723,000 votes. The parties which condemned the Weimar Constitution received only 4,667,000.

In the last free Reichstag elections in November, 1932, the Democratic Front mustered 13,314,000 adherents, while the legions of absolutism and dictatorship had surged up to 21,337,000.

In the fourteen years of its existence, German democracy thus lost 12,670,000 of its one-time supporters, while the parties pledged to put democracy to death had won 16,670,000 new fighters.

Adolf Hitler had sent a special emissary to Hamburg to direct a drive to smash the organizational monopoly which the Communist Party had attained in a large part of the German merchant marine. Hitler's agent was one Heines, one of the crowd of former officers with which the Nazi Party fairly swarmed, a blood-thirsty ruffian of Captain Roehm's crew of *pederasts*. This Heines had been condemned to death for murder in the 1920's, but was freed by the Hindenburg Amnesty. In 1933 Hitler made Heines police president of Breslau. Heines was executed by the Gestapo in the Nazi "Blood Purge" of June, 1934.

A day after Heines arrived in Hamburg, the Communist Reichstag deputy Heinz Neumann made his appearance. Long a specialist in the art of terror, he proceeded to dictate to the Hamburg Party chiefs the details of an offensive of bloodshed. "*Blut muss fliessen*—blood must flow," was the young Berliner's favorite phrase. Neumann was feared in the Party. He was known as a favorite of Stalin.

"Give me a man I can use to make hell hot for Nazi Heines in Hamburg," he demanded. The Hamburg Party head, Herrmann Schubert, assigned me to do Neumann's bidding in the anti-Heines campaign.

"Our most vicious fault is our womanish humaneness," were the Berliner's first words to me in an interview which took place in my Hamburg apartment. "Why not rid ourselves of this indecent squeamishness? The Hitler bandits! The rock-headed Social Democratic saboteurs! With such people words are useless!"

Heinz Neumann was not representative of the general type of Party leader. To a certain degree he had preserved his independence of thought; he demanded discipline, but hated it himself, and the keynote of his character was a reckless and brilliant irresponsibility. He had a fine, intelligent face, and a ready smile. His eyes were large and cruel. He acted as if the world had been created for him, Heinz Neumann, to move in. His contempt for the simple, plodding worker bespoke his bourgeois ancestry. To many young female communists he was still the romantic knight of revolutionary adventure. He could take them and throw them away whenever he liked. Among Party belles the phrase, "I have slept with Heinz Neumann," sounded like the proud equivalent of "I have received the Order of the Red Banner." Comrade Neumann was obsessed with a craving for ruthless action. To him, every socialist worker who rejected Soviet leadership was equal to the most rabid Brownshirt, and therefore ripe for the knife or the bullet. "The socialists are social-fascists," he liked to snarl in the middle of a conference. "They are the left-wing of the Hitler movement." But, like most killers who have their subordinates do the killing, Heinz Neumann was a physical coward.

His instructions as to the methods of frustrating the Heines campaign on the Hamburg waterfront can be summed up in a single sentence: "Break up the first seamen's meeting called by Heines, and shoot down every Brownshirt on sight."

The first part of this order I carried out. I entered the meetings with a force of several hundred communist sailors and dockers, and burst them asunder. I rejected Heinz Neumann's proposal of mass murder after the Nazis had fled out of the hall into the streets, because I knew that the storm troops would inevitably retaliate. The loathsome aspect of the frequent shooting affairs was that as often as not innocent passers-by, including women, had been the victims. Neumann was furious about my "squeamishness." His fury seemed justified after a picked force of two hundred Nazi Elite Guards in their turn blasted a communist meeting which eight hundred men and women attended. At about this time—the beginning of May—the Marine Storm of the Nazi Party had established a stronghold on the Schaarmarkt, in the heart of the Hamburg waterfront district.

Neumann, his thin face invaded by a nervous pallor and his eyes spurting cold rage, insisted, "We must show the Hitler bandits that they cannot settle down with impunity on the Red waterfront. I give you ten days' time. *Ich will Leichen sehen*—I want to see corpses."

Of the seven Party leaders present not one dared to object. Trembling from head to foot, I said:

"Comrade Neumann, I am a bad hand at butchery. My field is organization and communication." With that, I left the conference, and have been thankful for it ever since. Had I followed Neumann's orders, I should not be alive today. The men who took my place in the Berliner's cortege of terrorists all died horribly.

Heinz Neumann entrusted the job of producing Nazi corpses along the harbor of Hamburg to Johnny Dettmer, a reckless blond giant I had known already in 1923, when he had engaged in smuggling Russian rifles into Germany to arm the Red Hundreds. Comrade Dettmer was not "squeamish." At the head of the "Red Marines," a section of the Party's outlawed military organization, he produced corpses in sufficient numbers to gladden even the heart of Heinz Neumann.

Early one morning a squad of seven young Nazis were on their way to distribute propaganda to the dockers at the harbor gates.

Johnny Dettmer's crew sauntered up behind them on Admiralty Street, and shot all seven in the back. In the dawn of another morning, members of the Hitler Youth, boys and girls, were marching toward an excursion steamer they had chartered for a holiday trip. The approaches to the excursion piers led through park-like surroundings. Behind trees and bushes Johnny Dettmer's crew lay in ambush. Boys and girls, none of them over sixteen, were hit indiscriminately by dumdum bullets from the guns of the Red Marines. On another occasion, on the night of May 19, 1932, a group of young Nazis on their way home from a meeting were pounced on by Red Marines in a dark street (Herrengraben), and dragged into the doorways of near-by houses. Here eight or nine of them were lacerated with knives. One Nazi had his eyes stabbed out with a screw driver. Another, the storm trooper Heinzelmann, was stabbed eleven times. Members of the Red Marines then sat on their victim, slashed off his genitals, and severed his vertebrae. I and other comrades with me were stiff with horror on hearing the details of these exploits. But we had learned how to hold our tongues. In the Party, heresies were discovered with a facility and ingenuity that outrivaled the Spanish Inquisition. The purpose of these instances of screaming terrorism—to frighten the Brownshirts away from the waterfront—was not achieved. The Hitler bands continued to push their spearheads into the working class domain with unshakable courage and tenacity.

After this series of wholesale murders, Heinz Neumann suddenly vanished from the stage of German and International Bolshevism. Intrigues spun against him by the Thaelmann-Pieck leadership became his undoing. Ernst Thaelmann seized upon Neumann's heretical interpretation of the bastard conception of "Social-Fascist" to break one of his most talented rivals. The later misadventures of the Berlin millionaire's son are not without a searing irony. Neumann was exiled to Moscow, where he sulked for nearly two years. When the aging Wilhelm Pieck, Thaelmann's nominal successor and the young Berliner's bitter enemy, arrived in Moscow after the German debacle, Neumann was commissioned to go to Germany to lead the "underground" movement against Hitler. Such an assignment was tantamount to a death sentence. Instead, Neumann went to Switzerland and launched a campaign to send Comrade Pieck to Germany in his place. Neumann was ordered to return to Russia—and refused. The G.P.U. then denounced him to the Swiss police, who arrested Neumann on a charge of having entered Switzerland on false passports. The Nazi government demanded that the Swiss authorities surrender Neumann to the Gestapo to face charges of murder and treason. Neumann's choice was: Germany—or Russia. He chose Russia, recanted, humiliated himself before the Central Control Commission in Moscow, and won Stalin's forgiveness. In 1936, just before the outbreak of the Spanish civil war, Neumann appeared in Spain with a mandate from the Comintern, and using the name of Enrique Fisher. He plunged straight into a jurisdictional quarrel with the G.P.U. machine in Madrid. He was seized by the G.P.U. in Spain and brought back to the Soviet Union at the height of Stalin's great purge. Heinz Neumann, the chief terrorist of the Comintern and the author of the slogan, ' Strike the Nazi wherever you meet him!" died from a bullet fired by Stalin's executioner.

In 1937, in Copenhagen, I had occasion to ask Ernst Wollweber:

"Why was Comrade Neumann executed?"

"Don't call him 'comrade!'" the Silesian had growled, "he was a spy of the Gestapo."

Hitler's finest involuntary allies were we, the communists. Our rank and file, in its largely instinctive struggle against the Nazi advance, was checked almost weekly by the infallibles in our high councils in Moscow and Berlin. How often was I admonished by my superiors, and admonished in turn the comrades working under my direction: "Don't concentrate your efforts on Hitler; hew to the Line; we must deliver our hardest blows against the 'Social-Fascists'—the Social Democratic Party! They and their trade unions must be smashed if we are to win the majority of the workers for the Dictatorship of the Proletariat!" We followed instructions with vigor, for we had been trained to subject ourselves to an exact control and to a personal discipline that savored more of Bismarck than of the Karl Marx we worshiped.

Firelei saw through it all.

"We are as loyal as phonograph records," she once remarked to me.

"That is our strength," I had answered. "To conquer the earth we must have a World Party without a division of opinion in its ranks."

"An Eiffel tower of phonograph plates, all playing the *Internationale*," Firelei smiled back at me.

I had become angry. Intolerance was the air we breathed. Firelei was too good a soldier to break from the ranks.

In the spring of 1932, the democratic parties in Germany joined forces for their one and only major attempt to stem the Nazi stormflood by a concerted counter-drive "within the boundaries of Constitution and law." They formed a cartel of organizations which, numerically and financially, was far stronger than the Hitler movement. They named the cartel the Iron Front, and established the *Aktivisierung*—activization—of all republican resources against Hitler as its aim. The daily Nazi average of two thousand mass meetings was to be countered by an equal number of "Stop Hitler" rallies. The leaders of the Iron Front proclaimed their intention to re-conquer Germany by a continuous barrage of mass meetings. They copied the Nazi and communist propaganda technique, but emasculated their campaign from the start by rejecting the use of strong-arm methods alongside their propaganda. Shock-brigades of trade-unionists—*Hammerschaften*—were formed to protect the meetings and propaganda squads of the Iron Front against storm troop raids.

No sooner had the Iron Front launched its counter-offensive than all the units of the Communist Party received instructions to sabotage the enterprises of the Iron Front at every turn. This we did. Propaganda detachments of the Iron Front were forcibly relieved of their arms and of the leaflets and papers they had set out to distribute. Iron Front meetings were disrupted by packing the halls in advance with storm troopers and communists. Communists professing to be democrats entered the Iron Front organizations by the hundreds for the sole purpose of creating confusion. And accompanying these underhanded jabs was a tremendous campaign in the Nazi and the communist press. The leaders of the Iron Front, backed by the government of Chancellor Bruening, made only feeble efforts to strike back. A dozen communist newspapers were suppressed, and a score of communist editors sent to prison for "literary high treason." When the Nazi storm trooper organizations were outlawed by decree, in April, the directors of the Iron Front had the power to follow up this measure with a general offensive, but they lacked the pluck. They were afraid of revolution. They were afraid, it seemed, even of their own power.

The government of Chancellor Bruening, which had been supported by the democratic bloc, was dismissed on May 30, 1932. Democracy's attempt to rule by decree had ended in failure. Franz von Papen, ex-spy and lion of the Gentlemen's Club of intriguing noblemen, became Chancellor, and General Schleicher, the head of the *Reichswehr*, his Minister of War. Hitler had given his word of honor to support the Papen Cabinet—on two conditions: immediate dissolution of the Reichstag and new elections, and repeal of the government ban against the storm troops. The conditions were granted. Rearming of the nation became the chief topic among the adherents of the new regime. "Death to Bolshevism" was the war-cry under which rearming was to be accomplished without stirring up noisome attention abroad, particularly in France. The storm troops unleashed a new wave of terror. The number of political killings reached a new high during the first week of June. Hitler presented the Papen Government with a sudden ultimatum. The ultimatum demanded the proclamation of martial law, suppression of the Communist Party, and control of the Prussian police by National Socialists. Von Papen refused; Hitler threatened to let "events take their course"; von Papen, fearing that the Hitler movement would surge upward beyond the government's control, prepared for a *coup de main* himself.

The Nazi storm brigades were reported to be concentrating in huge camps around Berlin. The *Reichswehr* had been put in a state of highest alarm. The storm troopers spoke openly of the coming "night of long knives." Chancellor von Papen prepared to strike in Prussia; a reactionary Nationalist government in the Reich and a socialist-controlled government in the largest German state were incompatible bed-fellows. The cry, "Drive the Marxists out of the Prussian ministries!" swelled to a thunderous surf. Prussia was democracy's last fortress. Upon my return from England, I repaired posthaste to a meeting in the Karl Liebknecht House.

It was an extraordinary meeting. The whole Central Committee of the Party was assembled there, together with the leaders of all auxiliary organizations and the members of the traveling corps. It was a stormy meeting which lasted from eight in the evening to five in the morning. A dozen factions were at loggerheads; roars and screams punctuated the debates, and at times I thought that the élite of German Bolshevism would come to blows. Some advocated that the full fury of the Party should be turned against Hitler.' Some spoke for a last-minute alliance with the Social Democrats. Others held that a violent Nazi coup would drive the socialist workers into the communist camp. However, the tenet that the socialists were the main foe of Soviet power prevailed. Ernst Thaelmann raged like a maddened bull, formidably seconded by Hugo Eberlein, the Party treasurer, Herrmann Schubert, the Vice President and by Willy Leow, Leo Flieg, Fritz Schulte and other members of the Reichstag and the Central Committee. Ernst Wollweber and Hans Kippenberger sat silently, and so did Hotopp, a leader of the League of Proletarian Writers. In the end, all proposals to form an honest alliance with the Social Democrats were defeated. The old line prevailed.

"You communists, by your policy of disrupting the front of labor, are chiefly responsible for the counter-revolutionary upsurge in Germany," challenged the socialist press.

"Traitors!" screamed the communist press in answer. "Bridge builders of Fascism!"

Today, looking back on that assembly of confusion in the Karl Liebknecht House is looking upon an assembly of corpses. After the Reichstag Fire, most of the participants in that savage, but fruitless, meeting succeeded in escaping the Gestapo. Stripped of their power, they met again in Moscow, of no further use to their masters in the Kremlin. The G.P.U. proceeded to complete the job which the Gestapo had wished, but failed, to do. Kippenberger and Schubert, Leo Flieg, Birkenhauer and Hugo Eberlein; the *Rote Fahne* editors, Suesskind and Knoth and Nofke; Thaelmann's secretaries, Werner Hirsch and Meyer; the leading Prussian communists, Dr. Lothar Wolf and Dr. Fritz Halle; the writers Hotopp, C. Haus, Kurt Sauerland and Emel; Fritz Schulte and Heinrich Kurella—the editors of *Imprecorr*; Bertha Gropper, the garçonne of the communist Reichstag delegation; and others whose names could fill page after page—they all were destined to join Heinz Neumann in the graveyards of the G.P.U.

Hitler, Goering, Goebbels and their host of four thousand speakers roared over the land in airplanes and high-powered cars. Night after night they descended in German towns to speak to the masses. No community was too remote or too obscure for their invasion: Koenigsberg on Thursday, Cassel on Friday, Hamburg on Saturday. Hitler tore through the air in the day, and at night he hypnotized the multitudes into a chauvinistic frenzy.

Our leader, Ernst Thaelmann, proclaimed that the sharpening of the conflict now gave our policy "the strategic slogan of the People's Revolution." Words! We all knew that we were not strong enough to make a revolution. The *Reichswehr* was full of hidden Nazis. The German police outside of Prussia was infested with Nazis. There was only one force in the land strong enough to crush the Brownshirts and Steel Helmets in open civil war. The trade unions, controlled by the Social Democratic Party, were that force. But its leaders flinched at the prospect of civil war.

The Communist Party set out to play a most desperate game. Secret instructions were dispatched to all unit leaders, ordering the seizure of the next opportunity to provoke a mass slaughter between the storm troops and the workers. A great number of killed working people, it was hoped, would incite the masses of trade unionists to counter-action over the heads of their own leaders. The Communist Party would then put itself at the head of the angry masses with the demand for a general strike and the arming of organized labor. The aim was to bring about civil war and complete alienation of the socialist masses from their traditional leadership. The scheme was as criminal as it was absurd. But we communists, living in a make-believe world of our own, went forward with the optimism of megalomaniacs from Mars.

The awakening was rude. It began on a Sunday in July. The high command of the storm troops had ordered all Brownshirt formations of the North Sea districts to assemble for a march through the communist quarters of Hambug-Altona. Immediately the Communist Party concentrated its military formations in Hamburg for a counter-demonstration. The intention was to have the two armed parades, each counting tens of thousands of marchers, to clash head-on in narrow streets. In addition, every able-bodied communist not participating in the demonstration was assigned to one of the many points of assembly in the suburbs. Each brigade thus assembled was supplied with a list of names and addresses of Nazi and Steel Helmet functionaries in the district.

In the event the meeting of the two demonstrations in Altona did result in a massacre, our orders were to invade the homes of known Hitler followers and to make short shrift of all who fell into our hands. An elaborate courier service connected the scores of shock-brigades with the communist supreme command of three—Herrmann Schubert, the Hamburg Party chief, Ernst Wollweber, representing the Central Committee, and Edgar Andree, the chief of the military *Apparat*. A greater number of armed communists lay in wait in the tenements that Sunday morning than on the eve of, the ill-fated armed insurrection of October, 1923. Squads of girls and women were in readiness to take care of the wounded and those eventually hunted by police. *"Der Tag der langen Messer"*—"the day of long knives"—was in the offing.

The socialist police chief of Altona, Eggerstedt, outlawed the planned communist counter-demonstration at the last moment. At the same time, he reaffirmed the permission given to the Nazis to march, and furnished them with police protection. (The same Eggerstedt was later murdered in cold blood in a Gestapo concentration camp near Papenburg two days after his arrival there.) Communist spies in the storm troops ferreted out the route the Nazi parade was to take. Armed units of Red Front Fighters were stationed in advance on the roofs of houses along the route of the storm troop invasion. Charged with leading the sailors' and dockers' units of the Party, I had these forces, some eight hundred strong, assembled in a large number of waterfront taverns all along the wide river front of Hamburg and Altona. Our *ordre de jour* was to rout all Hitlerites from the ships and out of the harbor after the massacre of the Nazi demonstration in Altona had become a success.

The storm troops marched. They marched with bands crashing and swastikas flying. Their demonstration was flanked by police. Police lorries with machine guns preceded and followed the marchers. The parade entered the sinuous old districts of the city, winding forward like an immense brown snake. The blare of trumpets and the rolling of the drums reverberated from the walls of dingy houses. The side streets along the route seethed with many thousands of workers and their womenfolk, shaking fists, hurling rocks and garbage at the Brownshirts, and shouting abuse.

The storm troops marched like one machine. The faces of the youngsters were set and pale. At minute intervals, at a signal of detachment leaders, they broke into a hollow roar:

"Death to the Red Pest! Germany—arise!"

Then the first shots cracked from the roofs. The roofs were too slanting and the streets too narrow to take a direct aim at the marching troopers. The shooting was directed at the bases of houses facing the snipers. The ricocheting bullets flew then into the Brownshirt columns. Some women who had been watching the parade from the windows of their apartments were hit and fell screaming. The storm troopers crowded into the houses to trap the attackers on the roofs. Garbage cans hurtled out of windows.

Police trucks pounded into battle. Machine guns raked the roofs and the windows. Policemen hurled gas grenades and people ran like cockroaches. The storm troops were broken up in irregular, badly shaken groups. Some continued their march; most of them fled. The communist *Feuergruppen*, who had set out to annihilate the Brownshirts, now found themselves locked in a hopeless combat with the police. The "day of long knives" ended in failure and bewilderment. Our waiting units around the field of battle waited vainly for the order to strike. Eighteen dead and two hundred wounded littered the cobbled streets. Many more wounded and a few dying men were hidden in the homes of communists, where they were attended by communist Samaritans. When I returned home, still dazed by the disaster, Firelei met me at the door. "Be quiet," she said, "we have three wounded comrades here."

"Will they pull through?"

She nodded. "Such a day poisons the heart," she added in a low voice.

This was the "Bloody Sunday of Altona," which precipitated the ill-famed but historical "Rape of Prussia." The Western Secretariat of the Comintern could have done Hitler no greater favor than to provoke the Altona massacre. Chancellor von Papen seized upon the pretext that the Social Democratic Government of Prussia had proved itself unable to preserve law and order in that state, and demanded evacuation of the Berlin government buildings by Ministers Severing and Braun. These two Social Democratic heads of the Prussian Government in turn branded the ultimatum of von Papen as unconstitutional, and announced that they would yield only to brute violence. Von Papen's *coup d'état* became an accomplished fact on July 20, a few days after the butchery in Altona. A newly-appointed police president of Berlin, accompanied by fifteen soldiers, invaded the Prussian Government palace and arrested the ministers. The socialist chieftains followed the soldiers to the *Reichswehr* barracks, where they were released a few hours later against their pledge to do nothing. Thus, a handful of men had put out of office, in violation of the Weimar Constitution, a body of Prussian Government officials who had at least thirty thousand armed and trained policemen under their rightful command.

The communist masses were on the streets. Millions of manifestos calling for a general strike were distributed by our "activist" brigades. Mass arrests of communists followed. The Social Democratic forces did not stir. Too thoroughly already had the hearts of the workers been poisoned by brother-strife and mutual distrust. A clever and ruthless young man, Dr. Herrmann Diels, who had been von Papen's spy in the Prussian Cabinet, and who also was Hitler's spy in the Papen machine, was made head of the Political Police of Prussia. The formal organization of what was to become the Gestapo (*Geheime Staatspolizei*)—already existing in embryo within the Nazi Party—was begun by Diels on July 20.

Fourteen Nazis and communists were killed on July 31, the day of the new Reichstag election. Nazis emerged as the strongest political movement in the country. The Socialists still maintained the second place. The Communist Party came third. On August 13, Adolf Hitler, in reply to his clamorous insistence, was offered a share in the government. He rejected the offer. He wanted all— or nothing. On August 30, Captain Goering became the President of the Reichstag. But that body proved itself again unable to function; there was no majority capable of forming a government. The deputies rejected the Papen Government by a vote of 513 against 32. Whereupon Chancellor von Papen dissolved the Reichstag. That happened on September 12. New elections were scheduled to take place on November 6. I returned from my assignment in Holland in time to plunge into the caldron.

In the savagery of the election war which filled all of October to the brim neither I nor my comrades found time for an hour's reflection or a single night's normal sleep. For the moment we shelved all international duties to bring every ounce of our strength to bear on the German field.

Every few days there was a general alarm of all Party members, alarms caused by rumors that Hitler had set the date for his march on Berlin. Thrice within a month I was arrested by Hamburg police; each time I spent the night in the cellars of the grim city prison; each time the cellars were crammed with communists, Steel Helmets, storm troopers and members of lesser belligerent organizations. The political struggle did not cease even in the jails. It was the most active and most dreary month of my existence. The Party commanded, and I rushed like a robot, one among uncounted other robots, a cog in a hideous welter of senseless machinery. To Firelei and to me, the only non-combatant in our sphere seemed to be our son, little Jan. His robust smallness, when he drowsed in his basket or squirmed in his bath, was a delight to the many overworked and frantic or grimly-determined male and female revolutionists who stamped in and out of our rooms at all hours of the day and night. The astonished stares, the pensive smiles and the gruff chuckles of the comrades—in the presence of Jan—contained something of the expression on the face of a convict who hears a child's guileless laughter penetrate his world of stone.

October also was a month of strikes. It was a standing order of the Comintern to organize strikes whenever and wherever possible, to disorganize production and transport, and thus to sharpen the conflicts and the distress caused by the economic and political crisis. Chancellor von Papen's measures to fight unemployment provided an excellent soil for the growth of a wild strike wave. One-third of the German working population was jobless; it was this army of the workless which furnished the most devoted and reckless militants for the communist and storm troop ranks. Von Papen's plan was to increase the number of the employed without a corresponding increase in the national wage total. The Communist Party roused the masses to lay down their tools, and every strike was linked with the cry, "Away with the Papen regime!" Meanwhile the Hitler movement had also declared an open war against the government. Five storm troopers who, in Silesia, had tortured to death a communist by shooting him thirty-five times while his mother was forced to look on, had been condemned to death by a Special Tribunal. Hitler, in answer, had publicly adopted the convicted murderers as his "blood brothers," and launched a frontal attack against von Papen. "Down with the Papen regime!" became also the war-cry of the Nazis. Communists and Brownshirts combined forces in a common effort to wreck the Papen plan by an avalanche of strikes.

November 3, at 4 A. M. on the eve of the elections, the strike wave culminated in the great Berlin transportation strike. Communists and Nazis stood shoulder to shoulder in the picket lines, in the raiding squads and in the action committees. Chancellor von Papen threatened martial law and the calling out of the *Reichswehr*. The National Socialists and the Communist Party countered with an armed concentration of their brigades in the environs and the suburbs of Berlin. The strike continued, dominating the elections of November. Hitler lost nearly two million votes and 33 mandates in the Reichstag.

We all breathed freer. The Party press burst out in jubilation. "Hitler's Ship is Sinking!" the headlines announced. The socialists lost seven hundred thousand followers who had joined the communist camp. With almost six million votes, the Communist Party now commanded an even 100 mandates in the Reichstag. But in truth the battle had again ended in a stalemate. The Hitler movement, though on the decline, was still the strongest party in the land. No parliamentary majority was possible; again the Reichstag was a machine that could not run. The strikes went on. Twelve days later von Papen tendered his resignation.

General von Schleicher became Chancellor of the Reich on December 2. They called him the "Social General." Secret rearming of the nation with the aid of the trade union millions was the gist of his program. He sought to alleviate the acute factional bitterness in the country by a sweeping amnesty of political prisoners. Thousands of incarcerated communists and storm troopers left the German jails; they were soldiers immediately returning to battle.

"Away with Schleicher!" raged the Nazi press.

"Down with the Schleicher Government!" the communists echoed.

Chapter Twenty-five

SCANDINAVIAN INTERLUDE

I was called to Berlin on December 6, 1932, to report to Georgi Dimitrov. He looked fat and happy. Under the thunderclouds of July he had feared that the Western Secretariat of the Comintern, which he headed, would be forced to evacuate from Berlin. No such precaution, he thought, was necessary now. The nervousness which had invaded Comintern circles had subsided somewhat after Hitler's election setback in November. Once more attention was turned away from the Brown Menace and directed toward the "chief enemy," the Social Democratic forces. Hitler was on the way out, Dimitrov assured me. "Hitler will never come to power," he insisted.

I met in Dimitrov's office on the Wilhelmstrasse a secretary I had not seen there before, a girl of athletic build and mannish gait, who followed her master around like a faithful dog. Her name was Isa. She made coffee for us on an electric percolator while I received my instructions.

"Do you like to work with me?" the Bulgarian asked me.

"Yes," I smiled.

"I like to work with you, too. You are going to Scandinavia."

Two days I rummaged through the files of the Scandinavian countries, which were kept in a basement apartment in Berlin-Lankwitz, to gain background information on my new assignment. Without further delay I received my credentials, false passport and funds, and boarded the night express over Warnemuende-Gjedser to Copenhagen.

Controlling all Comintern operations in the north of Europe was Richard Jensen, a hulking oak of a man, a native of Denmark. Orders from Moscow were relayed to Jensen by way of Berlin, and Jensen forwarded them to the chiefs of the Central Party Committees—Aksel Larsen in Denmark, Sillen in Sweden, and Christiansen in Norway. This Dane was an extraordinary figure, a rough and domineering Viking, three hundred pounds of flesh and bone, capable of formidable cunning, yet addicted to gusts of rolling laughter. He was seven feet tall and he drank immensely. He drank beer before breakfast, beer was constantly on the desk in his office, and at night, in bed, he drank beer before he was ready to fall asleep. All who knew him, liked him. Others came and went like so many shadows over the Comintern scene, and disappeared, burnt out or discarded or killed—but Jensen endured through the years. He was a former workingman who liked to spend his money like a lord, and he was one of that small group of foreign Bolsheviks who seemed to enjoy Stalin's unflinching trust.

Four times each year Jensen journeyed to Moscow, occasionally to Berlin and Paris, but he liked best his home town, Copenhagen. His address, until I left the Soviet service in 1938, was the most constant and reliable of Comintern addresses: Vesterbrogade 70, some five minutes' walk from Copenhagen's Central Station and the Tivoli. The favorite amusement of this comrade consisted of having every visiting emissary—including the highest—drink himself senseless. It gave him a primeval pleasure to walk away in triumph while some self-important "man from Moscow" lay snoring on one of the thick rugs in his apartment. Richard Jensen's wife, colorless but incorruptible, an able woman in her forties and two heads shorter than her husband, was a member of the G.P.U. Jensen's son, Martin, also served in the Foreign Division of the G.P.U. While in Copenhagen, I was Jensen's guest. I found my host a master in the difficult art of combining boisterous hospitality with the exacting requirements of conspirative work.

The Communist Party of Denmark was small but sound. It had four newspapers and eleven thousand members. It commanded an efficient military organization, a number of units in the Danish navy, and an exceptionally active group of cultured fellow-travelers led by a well-known Copenhagen architect, Paul Henningsen. Denmark was not an industrial country. Without its merchant marine and without its export of dairy products, the country would fall on extremely evil days. So the waterfront workers were, from the communist standpoint, the decisive portion of Danish labor. To break the socialist influence in the ports and to gather sufficient strength to threaten the Danish government with an export blockade—and thus make it malleable to the wishes of Moscow—was the principal aim of Comintern efforts in Denmark. To wield the cudgel of an export blockade with success, capture of the marine workers' trade unions was essential. The Sailors' Union and the Firemen's Union of Denmark were rich and powerful organizations, affiliated with the Amsterdam Socialist International (ITF), under the fighting Dutchman Edo Fimmen. Their eventual capture by communist cells working from within and without was later hailed in Moscow as a classical example of how a foreign trade union must be conquered and harnessed to Soviet power.

The campaign was directed by Richard Jensen. Organized drives of character-assassination against the socialist leaders, bribery and blackmail of lesser employees, the installation of spies, caucus conspiracies, packed meetings, outright terror, the sending of delegations of union members to be feted in the Soviet Union, a ceaseless propaganda among Danish crews in foreign ports, free Soviet films, and smooth collaboration with the cultured elements, through the Danish Friends of the Soviet Union, were the familiar methods employed. The shipping industry in Copenhagen fell under communist control. Jensen saw to it that anti-Stalinist elements among the seamen were ousted from their berths. By the end of 1932, there was not one Danish ship which did not have a communist unit in its crew. Even the only two steamers plying regularly between Iceland and Hamburg, *Dettyfoss* and *Godafoss*, were manned by a majority of communists and served as courier ships for the G.P.U. At the next convention, Edo Fimmen flew to Copenhagen to save his union. He made a three-hour speech in German, and then Richard Jensen bribed Fimmen's translator to fall ill. No other translator was at hand. The Dutchman returned to Amsterdam, beaten. The Firemen's Union, its treasury of millions, and the buildings it owned in Copenhagen, became the virtual property of the Comintern, with Jensen in power, collarless and unshaven, but "more powerful than the King of Denmark."

My assignment consisted of a ten-day tour through the Danish ports to speak at union meetings as the "representative of the transport workers of the Soviet Union." Denmark was a most happy and liberal country. I traveled—as a "Russian delegate"—to Odense, Sonderburg, Aarhus, Esbjerg, Aalborg and some of the lesser harbor towns, hatching new schemes with the local groups, tearing down in my speeches Danish institutions, assaulting the trade union leaders and the socialist Stauning government, and not once was I bothered by the authorities! In all the Danish towns I found overnight quarters in the homes of charming people, communist sympathizers of the intellectual type. Outside of Copenhagen, the nimbus of a "man from Moscow" was so pronounced that the Party girls felt compelled to outrival each other in offering their favors to the visitor "sent by Stalin." In Sonderburg I marched down the main street behind a band of accordion players, followed by a cheering crowd, to the tune of the *Internationale*. Unfortunately, there was little time for such pleasant play. The meetings, three in each town, one for the leadership, another for the general membership, and the third an open meeting, had been prepared by organizers sent out in advance. After each day, Martin Jensen, who acted as my translator, dispatched a detailed report to his sire. Richard Jensen was satisfied with the results of my tour. "Next time I go to Moscow I'll give your name a good sound," he promised. Then, truculently: "Let's get some beer."

From Copenhagen I proceeded to Sweden. Jensen warned me of the efficiency of the Swedish police which reputedly exchanged reports on foreign agents with Scotland Yard.

The procedure by which to avoid passport control on entering Sweden was simple. I ferried across the sound to Malmo. The passport control station in Malmo had two gates. One was marked "For Scandinavians," the other "For Foreigners." At the latter gate each traveler had to submit his papers to inspection and fill out a printed questionnaire; at the gate marked "For Scandinavians," no examination whatever took place. A girl from Richard Jensen's *Apparat* accompanied me. She chattered loudly in Danish as we passed through the "Scandinavian" entrance into Sweden. I nodded at her chatter and laughed. The official on guard, hearing the banter, passed me without molestation. Eight hours later I was in Goeteborg, the chief seaport and second largest city of Sweden.

The liaison agent in Goeteborg had been advised of my coming. I was at once escorted to his snug apartment on Jaemtorgsgatan by his courier, a girl who had been waiting at the station. This G.P.U. man's name was Harold

Svensson. He was a suave man of about thirty-six, short, slight of figure, and blond. I had heard of him in Berlin, Hamburg and Copenhagen. His job was coastal espionage and contacts. The communist units he controlled aboard the largest Swedish liners, the *Gripsholm* and the *Kungsholm,* had at times been used by the Western Secretariat for the transmission of special material to and from New York. Harold Svensson was a Swedish customs official and a member of the harbor police of Goeteborg. He camouflaged his conspirative connections by holding a nominal function in the Swedish branch of the Friends of the Soviet Union. His wife, a rather chic brunette, also was in government employ. The seven days I spent in Goeteborg I lived in the home of one of Svensson's aides, an idealistic ruffian named Knut Bjoerk.

My duties in Sweden were of a distasteful nature. The Communist Party of Sweden had long been, and still was, the most independent among the seventy-six Parties affiliated with the Comintern. It was the only Communist Party which had achieved sound financial independence, an ability to carry out its tasks irrespective of whether subsidies from Moscow, *via* Berlin-Copenhagen, arrived in time or not. Now, Moscow disliked a state of financial independence among its foreign auxiliaries, for such independence deprived the Kremlin of its power to precipitate any recalcitrant organization into bankruptcy, prevent the appearance of its press and the payment of salaries to its leaders.

It was an unwritten but iron law in the Comintern that no central Party organ should enjoy complete financial independence, and that the wages of Central Committee members must be paid not out of money obtained from membership dues, but out of the regular monthly subsidy from the treasury at the disposal of Ossip Piatnitzky in Moscow. Surplus funds raised by communist activities outside of the Soviet Union were required to be placed, in one way or another, under control of one of the numerous Soviet institutions, and Moscow then decided how much of it should be used by the various organizations, and for what purpose. Financial serfdom of this sort was one of the main levers used to keep the doings of all Comintern Parties subservient to the interests of the Soviet Union.

The financial backbone of the Communist Party of Sweden was a chain of modern and well-administered workers' clubs, operating popular restaurants and doing a thriving' business in all the larger Swedish towns. The Comintern had decided to separate this lucrative source of income from the Swedish Party machine, to place it as a co-operative enterprise under G.P.U. supervision, or—in case of insurmountable opposition—to destroy it.

My chief collaborator in this drive was Gustav Holmberg, a former teacher at the Lenin School in Moscow, member of the Swedish Central Committee, and head of the G.P.U. in West Sweden. Comrade Holmberg had the mild and steadfast appearance of a successful American retail merchant, an appearance greatly valued by the G.P.U. chiefs in the selection of stationary agents. Holmberg decided which functionaries should be invited to attend the "restaurant conferences." The speeches I made were not my own product. They had been written in advance in Berlin by one of the managers of the

Muenzenberg press "trust." I delivered them with all the vigor of which I was capable, and the wrangling that followed continued until far into the nights. Holmberg was busy making notes. "Reading the barometer," he called it quietly, leaving me to harangue and to search for arguments with which to counter the many stubborn objections to the Comintern scheme.

It is one of the peculiarities of the communist movement that an emissary of the Comintern—though he be far less able than a local functionary—wields much greater authority than the latter when it comes to the job of "co-ordinating" the views of an assembly of lesser communists. To the average Party member, the visiting International Representative is a powerful and mysterious creature, a veritable Solomon of World Revolution. To safeguard his prestige, he must keep a distance between himself and the rank and file similar to that kept by any colonial official of the British Empire who seeks to maintain a divide between, his august personality and the natives.

After four days of obnoxious horse-trading, the Swedes gave in to me. Unanimously a resolution favoring the reorganization of the restaurant business as a "private" enterprise was adopted, and the delegates were pledged to secrecy. The road was now clear for official negotiations between Berlin and the Stockholm Central Committee. A long report, signed by Holmberg and myself, went off to Berlin. One Eiling, a business expert of the G.P.U, a man who incidentally had a great outward resemblance to-H. G. Wells, was sent to Sweden to complete the stealing of the profitable restaurant chain in the name of the "Bolshevization" of the Swedish Party. Before he arrived, I was already speeding northward in a sleeping compartment of the Copenhagen-Oslo night express.

All the Swedish workers' clubs were eventually liquidated. The management of the club in Goeteborg, the largest and most prosperous of all, occupying two floors of the Rialto Building, refused to surrender the business to the G.P.U. In the summer of 1933, after the G.P.U. had deliberately used this club as a base for a sensational kidnapping expedition, the police closed the establishment *"because of crimes committed on the premises."*

The Communist Party of Norway was the *enfant terrible* of the Comintern. Time and again it had been split and purged almost out of existence, but as soon as it recovered, its leading personnel slipped back into the ways of Sodom and Gomorrah. Most Norse Bolsheviks were sincere revolutionists, hardy "activists," but nevertheless they remained in essence a gang of chesty libertines. A few months before my arrival they had received a substantial subsidy with which to finance the communist penetration of the Norwegian whaling fleet; a week later the Party cashier had run off to Sweden, taking with him the money and the wife of a Toensberg contractor. At the last Party convention in Oslo, a discussion dealing with the creation of women's committees had ended in a violent altercation about the wife-swapping activities of the Party chief, Christiansen, the organization chief, Ottar Lie, and the rest of the Central Committee.

On Christmas night of 1932, one of the leading propagandists of the Party, Alfson Pedersen, stripped the Communist Party headquarters of its typewriters and mimeographs, sold them to a junk-dealer, who was also a Party member, and together with his cronies he staggered up Carl-Johann Street toward the King's Palace, all roaring the battle-song of the Soviet aviators.

Dimitrov, talking to me about Norway, had called the Norsemen "good fellows, but dissolute brigands." The Party contained more déclassé elements and black sheep from bourgeois cradles than bona fide workers. The only stable groups were those among the students of the universities of Oslo and Trondheim, and the Norwegian seamen's units which were scattered over all continents. Apart from a handful of professional men, the dynamos of the local Party groups were invariably students or sailors. In the many Norwegian towns I visited in the course of a five weeks' journey, the reception I received was always the same: I was invited to drink, and only after I had proven my ability to keep abreast of the sturdiest native guzzlers were the comrades ready to engage in a series of protracted palavers on Party matters.

The chief liaison agent between the Comintem-G.P.U. *Apparat* and the communist organizations of Norway was one of the best-known physicians in the Norwegian capital, Dr. Arne Halvorsen. He maintained a private residence in a fashionable settlement called "Summer's Joy," a clinic at 22 Aakebergsveien, and a secret political laboratory at Number 2 Carl-Johannsgade, a building overlooking the large square which fronts the Central Station of Oslo.

Dr. Halvorsen was a man of multitudinous contacts. The threads he held in his hands ran into universities, hospitals and technical schools, into shipyards, coast-defense establishments and the government's hydrographic office. His wife, Karin, a tall, dark, melancholy young woman, was an executive secretary in the offices of Wilhelmsen, the most important shipowner in Norway. Karin Halvorsen was, like her husband, a secret Party member. Her brother, also in Soviet service, held a position in the Norwegian State Police. Dr. Halvorsen himself had begun life as a street-car conductor, had worked himself through university and medical schools, and had become a government physician attached to the pilot service of the Atlantic coastline. During the Russian civil war Dr. Halvorsen had made his way to Moscow to offer his services to the Bolshevist cause. He won the confidence of Lenin and Dzerjinsky, and had become an intimate friend of Anatole Lunacharsky, the first Soviet Commissar of Education. After his return to Norway, the G.P.U. had claimed him as an extraordinary find. Dr. Halvorsen was a large man, apparently lazy, but with a face full of fleshy energy. He had keenly intelligent gray eyes and a sardonic cast of mind. Excessive drinking had brutalized him. Night after night he sat up until three, forcing his wife and his guests to follow his alcoholic pace, and then slept until eight, which was all the sleep he needed. Among his secret operatives were a number of girls—Party members—who had fallen under the doctor's domination after he had performed on them needed abortions. Smiling pleasantly, he once showed me in a backroom of his clinic long rows of glass jars containing human embryos in all visible stages of development. Each jar bore a label on which, neatly printed, was the name of a dead revolutionist.

"What's this?" I exclaimed, aghast.

Dr. Halvorsen gave a sardonic guffaw. "I showed them to Comrade Lunacharsky when he toured Norway last year. He almost fainted."

Karin Halvorsen, the doctor's wife, was the unhappiest woman I have ever met. She looked on, without uttering a word, when her husband lounged in a club-chair with his arms clamped around a younger Party belle, a barrel of beer on the living-room floor, and an assortment of stronger drinks in bottles on the tables. I saw Dr. Halvorsen invent new ways of torturing her every night I spent in his abode. She gave the impression of being a woman who had wept her last tear long ago, and was incapable of weeping more. But she was loyal to him, loyal to the death—or was it loyalty to the cause? Through her, copies of all important documents pertaining to Norwegian shipping reached the G.P.U., and often before they reached the offices of their legitimate recipients.

On the second day after my arrival in Oslo I tackled a meeting of the Central Committee, laying down the ideas of Dimitrov and Jensen on what the Communist Party of Norway should be and do. Norway, outside of its railways and public utilities, had only three really important industries: whaling, fisheries, and merchant shipping. But there was not one man in the Central Committee who knew much about maritime matters. The only department which really functioned was the *Apparat* controlled by Dr. Halvorsen, whose agents, spread over all important points from Christiansand to Narvik, engaged in military work and espionage, particularly in the country north of the sixty-eighth parallel, a region coveted by the Soviet Union as of strategic importance. To me fell the task of making the Central Committee ocean-minded. To befog the issue, Christiansen, the Party chief, made a long speech about the "political situation." Ottar Lie, his right-hand man, and others followed their chief's cue. They all sounded very earnest and very respectable. It was the usual defense put up by functionaries desiring to hide the concrete weakness in Party activities. To pierce their defense, by way of showing them that the Comintern knew more about their personal short-comings and vices, I jumped into the subject of wife-swapping. Christiansen jumped to his feet in blustering indignation.

"Our private affairs have no bearing on our political tasks," he shouted.

"They have a powerful bearing," I retorted.

I had brought with me excerpts from reports the Comintern had received from its inner-Party spies in Norway. I was able to cite seven occasions on which a Norwegian Communist leader, in his tours of Norway, had exchanged his wife for the wives and mistresses of other Central Committee members. Getting wind of this, the Party rank and file had drawn certain conclusions, one of which was that next to drinking tournaments, "free love" had become the chief occupation of the Oslo communists. Anyone desirous of an abundant supply of bed companions of the opposite sex simply had to join the Party, which, indeed, was often referred to as the "Red Harem." Besides, Dr. Halvorsen had warned me not to associate with any female Norwegian communist without first consulting him. "They blossom with venereal disease," he had explained.

Comrade Christiansen and his aides saw the point. Should they be called to Moscow, and should the G.P.U. supply the anti-Stalinist press of Norway with details of the organized promiscuity of their amours, their careers as professional revolutionists and "labor leaders" would be shattered. In such a situation fresh young comrades from the Moscow schools, coming to Norway as crusaders for "proletarian decency," would have a good chance of success in spite of their obscurity and inexperience. The Central Committee appeared temporarily cowed.

We proceeded to lay down a plan of action for the communist invasion of the whaling fleet, and for the progressive consolidation of Party positions in the ports and in shipping. The organization program I submitted, which had been formulated in Berlin, was unanimously accepted. But after the conference ended I was due for a typical Norwegian surprise. I had not noticed in the heat of argument that Ottar Lie had slipped out of the meeting. I noticed, however, that my overcoat had disappeared. It was a good new camel's-hair coat. Ottar Lie, the organization head of the Party, had sold it in a second-hand store. He appeared a little while later, a bottle of gin under each arm.

"What's the idea, Comrade Lie?" I demanded.

"Oh," he laughed, "I saw the fine coat in the hall and I couldn't figure out to whom it belonged, so I sold it. Let's have a drink, Comrade International Representative."

I saw the humor of the situation. We drank. After the gin had gone down the throats, Ottar Lie proposed:

"Now let's go out and sell my coat. It's pretty shabby, but it's a coat just the same."

My work in Norway began in earnest. Christiansen proposed that his niece should accompany me as secretary and interpreter on my Norwegian travels. I, of course, rejected his offer; she was the usual spy which Central Committees under investigation liked to place into the International *Apparat* to keep them informed on the activities—and the vulnerable spots—of "the man from Moscow." Instead I accepted a secretary of Dr. Halvorsen's choice, a secret Party member with a G.P.U. commission. She was Kitty Andresen, residing at 26 St. Hallvard, Oslo, an Amazon with ugly features and an irrepressible vitality. Between trips, on Saturdays, when no party work could be done because the Party was drunk, she loved to take me out to Oslo Fjord to swim among ice floes, or to hike and ski among the densely wooded mountains and lakes of Nordmarken. I was a bad hand at these exertions, but her sparkling glee in the face of my own exhaustion was ample recompense. Kitty was a graduate of Oslo University. She neither smoked nor drank, was adamant in Party matters, but could surrender herself to emotional convulsions over an American "Wild Western" motion picture, provided the shooting on the screen was mixed with plenty of sentimentality.

In the first week of my mission I concentrated on Oslo; in the second, I overhauled our organizations in the smaller but vital ports south of the capital—Fredrikstad, Toensberg and Sandefjord, the latter two places being the home bases for the bulk of the world's Antarctic whaling fleets. The third week I gave to the Bergen district; the fourth to Trondheim. Everywhere I found the same picture: a fundamentally sound rank and file, and a leadership of semi-intellectual libertines. I changed administrators where the material for new leadership was at hand. The district leaders of Fredrikstad and Bergen I sent off to Berlin, ostensibly to report to the Western Secretariat, in reality to have them out of the way while a reorganization of their districts took place. I arranged with Berlin that they should be kept hamstrung for at least one month; I do not know what became of them later.

In Oslo, I inaugurated a new International Club and established a permanent action committee among shipyard workers and dockers. In Toensberg and Sandefjord, I laid the groundwork for schools in which ship organizers were to be trained to build up communist units aboard the large vessels of the whaling fleet. In Bergen, I addressed membership meetings of several independent local trade unions to prepare them for affiliation with the Profintern in Moscow, but only met with partial success. At the same time I gathered all available communists on the spot into caucus sessions, with the aim of having them capture control of the local unions from within. In Trondheim, aside from some organizational work, I addressed the communist group of university students on subjects of their own choice on three successive evenings. The themes they chose were "The Program of the Comintern," "The Tasks of Communists in the Event of Imperialist War," and "State and Revolution." I gained the impression that the youth of Norway was far less firmly rooted in their native soil than the youth of, say, France or Holland. The youngsters of Trondheim took a perverse pride in tearing down their own country in favor of a cold-blooded internationalism. But in the Comintern "internationalism" and "Soviet power" are synonyms.

In Norway, as elsewhere, the most tragic figures in the communist movement were those whose lives were deliberately destroyed by the cause they had sworn themselves to serve. There was Arthur Samsing, a tough, blue-eyed, cheerful little man, who was hounded to exile and possibly physical destruction because of some remarks he had made about the "haves" and "have-nots" in the Communist International. I had known Comrade Samsing for years. He had worked for the Comintern in America, in Belgium and Germany, and in his native land, Norway. Samsing made the mistake of saying what he thought. Once he was sent on a dangerous assignment to Gdynia. Death was the almost inevitable lot of any Comintern man caught by the police on Polish soil. But no danger or hardship could deter Samsing. While he was active in Gdynia, his young wife, whom he had left together with two small children in Oslo, became desperately ill. A costly treatment was necessary to save her life. Samsing appealed to Georgi Dimitrov to advance him the necessary funds. He received an answer to the effect that the organization could do nothing for his wife, who was not a member of the Party. Samsing left Gdynia and journeyed to Berlin. He was told that the Comintern had no funds to spare and that Comrade Dimitrov was on vacation. Dimitrov was vacationing in Zoppot, a fashionable gambling resort near Danzig, a short jump from Gdynia! Arthur Samsing sped to Zoppot. He found his Bulgarian chief, far from the trenches of class war, sharing a suite in an elegant hotel with a beautiful dancer from Berlin. Samsing asked Dimitrov for money to save his wife. He had no other resources; his whole life had been spent in and for the movement. Dimitrov, resenting the fact that one of his frugally living "activists" had trapped him in the role of a *bon vivant,* became very angry. Samsing departed, penniless. He did not return to his post in Gdynia. He went to Oslo to stand by his wife who was then living with her children in an abandoned cottage in the woods beyond Oslo. The Comintern struck him off its payroll as a deserter. Samsing replied in an open letter, contrasting the economic well-being of the Comintern chiefs —the *Bonzen*—with the chronic distress of the majority of "activists" who faithfully carried on the perilous work, in the lower depth.

"*Der Samsing ist verrueckt,*" Dimitrov replied to the open challenge. "Samsing is crazy."

That happened in the summer of 1931. Samsing's wife continued to live. Samsing himself became exceedingly active in the Communist Party of Norway. For all that he remained jobless. Clad in cast-off rags, emaciated from hunger, his only quarters the tumbledown cottage in the woods, he continued to serve the Party as a volunteer. Repeatedly he was arrested and sent to jail. But to a revolutionist of his type a life outside of the movement was unthinkable. He was one of the few Norwegians who did not drink. The Comintern did not expel him; Samsing had worked too long in the Soviet service and he knew too many of its secrets. More and more, however, he became obsessed with the idea that his mission was to clean the Party and the International of its *Bonzen*—its parasitic and all-powerful bureaucracy. The Comintern decided that Arthur Samsing was ripe for "liquidation."

Invited, Samsing refused to go to the Soviet Union. "There are enough communists in Russia," he replied, "but not enough communists in Norway." In the fall of 1932, the Comintern proposed that Samsing should send his wife and children to the Soviet Union, the wife to be treated in a sanatorium, the children to be cared for in a children's home. To this Arthur Samsing agreed. He knew that his family would be held as hostages, that he would never see them again unless he went to Russia himself. All the same he thought they would have a better chance in life in the Soviet Union than in a continuance of their former hunger-ridden existence. The family went to Copenhagen, and Richard Jensen dispatched them to Leningrad. Samsing went on to serve the Party in Oslo.

I met Arthur Samsing again in January, 1933. His bitterness toward Dimitrov and his ilk had not downed his enthusiastic belief in the future of socialism. The Norwegian Central Committee, fearing his clean-cut energy and his ruthless honesty, liked to use Samsing for actions which were likely to result in his arrest. One such action to which he was assigned, during my presence in Oslo, was the breaking up of a session of the Storting, the National Parliament of Norway. Samsing, at the head of a band of determined assistants, entered the Storting and successfully disrupted the proceedings. Before the day was over, the whole police force of the capital was hunting for Arthur Samsing. Not many days later Dr. Halvorsen handed me a letter from the Western Secretariat. The letter contained orders not to employ Comrade Samsing in any action that would tend to increase his already uncomfortable popularity in the Norwegian Party. This was followed up with the suggestion that I should induce Samsing to go to Russia. Samsing gave a harsh laugh when I told him about the letter.

"Tell Dimitrov to leave me alone," he said. "To make war on the *Bonzen* is more important than to have a soft job in the Soviet Union. Tell Dimitrov that I'm not ready to be put on ice."

I left it at that, warning Samsing to tone down his challenge. "You stand alone," I told him. "A revolutionist who stands alone against the Comintern can never win. The Comintern always wins over the individual mutineer."

"Tell Comrade Dimitrov," he replied earnestly, "that Comrade Samsing thinks that for a Norwegian communist Norway must come first, and not the Soviet Union. A communist must fight for the liberation of his class brothers, not for the national ambitions of the Soviet Union."

"The Soviet Union is the symbol of communist strength and glory," I countered.

"Rubbish! And you know it."

"Without the Soviet Union, World Communism has no chance to survive."

"The emancipation of the workers can only be accomplished by the workers themselves," Samsing jeered. "We can do without the great big man with the stick."

I pleaded with the stubborn little Norwegian. The argument I used in an attempt to bring him back to the old slave-and-soldier loyalty was the same I had used in silent hours to defeat my own gnawing doubts. "Perhaps there is something true in what you assert," I said. "The Comintern is becoming the illegal arm of the *Narkomindel* (the Commissariat for Foreign Affairs) in Moscow. It is nevertheless the strongest revolutionary organization that ever existed. There is no substitute for the Comintern. If we honestly want revolution and socialism in the world, we can only win it with the Comintern, against it—never."

"Go on," Samsing laughed. "Or shall I finish the sermon for you? Here goes: 'A communist who puts himself into consistent opposition to Stalinist leadership will inevitably wind up in the camp of the bourgeoisie and the counter-revolution.' I was a blind man. But when I saw Comrade Dimitrov whoring around in Zoppot, I got my eyesight back. That fur-coated proletarian! I told him I belonged to Norway, not to Poland. 'Comrade Samsing,' he said, 'we've long observed your opportunist tendencies,' and I answered, 'Comrade Dimitrov, you are wearing such a fine suit. It's too big for me, but I can have it changed.' What did he say? *'Samsing, du bist verrueckt.* You need a rest.' "

"Maybe you do need a rest," I muttered.

"I told Comrade Dimitrov," Samsing went on, "I told him: 'If you chase away all the intelligent people who are not pliable, and keep only obedient idiots, then you will certainly ruin the Party.' That's not from Samsing. Comrade Lenin wrote that in a letter to Bukharin. Comrade Dimitrov looked at me as if he wanted to say: 'Samsing, if you were not crazy, you'd be ashamed of yourself.' Ha-ha-ha! Tell the *Bonzen* that Samsing is still going strong."

Samsing was doomed. It was only a matter of weeks. At the end of January, Samsing was called to Copenhagen for a conference with Richard Jensen. To the astonishment of the Copenhagen "activists," Samsing arrived stone-drunk. He did not return to Oslo. He disappeared.

To jump ahead of my narrative, the Samsing episode, as far as I was concerned, was closed a few months later. I went again on a mission to Norway in April, 1933. In *Aftenposten,* Norway's greatest newspaper, I saw a photograph of Arthur Samsing displayed over a question printed in large type, which ran: *"Where is this man?"*

The Oslo police waited long for an answer. One evening I asked Dr. Halvorsen, "What became of Comrade Samsing?"

"Oh, he's in Russia," he replied pleasantly.

On January 30, 1933, I was in Trondheim. A telegram arrived.

"Come back. Urgent. Firelei."

I felt strangely disturbed. I hastened to Oslo, an overnight journey by rail across snow-covered mountain land. In Oslo, I jumped into the express to Malmoe-Trelleborg, and arrived in German Stralsund early the following morning. During my last days in Trondheim I had been too busy with workaday details to follow the press. On the train I had read Ernest Hemingway's *A Farewell to Arms.* Firelei was awaiting me on the platform of the Stralsund. She was poised on her toes as the train pulled in. I leaned out of the window and called out her name. For a second or two a cloud of Nazi storm troopers obscured her from my view. The sounds of clanking heels and the smell of leather went by. Then we were together.

"Something sad has happened," Firelei said.

"Yes?"

"Your mother has died."

The impact was strong. A short assault of anguish mingled with a vague consciousness of guilt because of things I had left undone shook me. It was too late.

"Was she still alive when you sent me the telegram?" I asked.

"No. The Party ordered me to wire you."

The hissing of steam from the locomotive filled the air. I heard the gruff exclamations of the porters, the strident cries of sandwich men, fragments of desultory conversation. Firelei drew me aside. And then, quietly, she added:

"Hitler has just become Chancellor."

BOOK THREE

THE NIGHT OF LONG KNIVES

Chapter Twenty-six

STORM SIGNALS

Through the day the storm troopers marched, their eyes blazing with elation. They marched through the night with the flickering light of torches shining on fluttering swastika flags. The troopers sang:

*"Let Hitler banners fly from German towers,
"This is the dawn of German liberty..."*

We in the upper ranks of the Party had no illusions as to the terror that would soon be unleashed against us by the Hitler movement. We had no illusions about the overwhelming virility of the Nazi Party's military organization, and about the relative weakness of our own. A frontal assault would be nothing but mass suicide; we all knew that. The German workers were divided into antagonistic camps, their leaders unable to agree on united action. Our Party, taken by surprise, floundered in a cul de sac. We were strong. But Hitler was stronger. We knew that an armed insurrection at this point would result in the annihilation of our leadership corps. At this point our standing extremist slogan of World Revolution had become sheer nonsense. Ernst Thaelmann, blustering with emotion, refused to give the signal for an offensive that was doomed to failure in advance. He quoted Lenin's famous words: "A general who leads his army to certain defeat deserves to be shot."

But Moscow apparently shared none of our hesitations. The Western Secretariat of the Comintern received its orders promptly. Dimitrov relayed them to the German Party Executive. I participated in two stormy meetings, one in Hamburg, the other in Berlin, where the élite of the sub-leaders received instructions on how to translate the Moscow command into action. Moscow demanded a general offensive along the whole line, and precipitation of a general strike against the Hitler government. In the Hamburg conference a man named Westerman rose and shouted: "For what purpose?" The delegate of the Comintern, a Hungarian, answered sharply:

"To sweep away Hitler. We have broken the Putschist Kapp and the Monarchist Cuno by mass strikes. Mass strikes will also break Hitler."

"This is lunacy," challenged Westerman. "The comrade from the Comintern knows as well as I that the Party is not strong enough to carry out a general strike, much less a revolution. The Party will be wiped out!"

"Comrade Westerman must understand that when Hitler is allowed to consolidate his power, he will march against the Soviet Union," the Hungarian retorted. "Hitlerism means war! I speak in bloody earnest when I say that it is now more than ever our duty to protect our Socialist Fatherland. Without the Soviet Union, we will never have a Soviet Germany."

There was a short roar of assent.

Westerman's ruddy face turned an ashen gray. "I think of the fate of our German Party workers," he said in a low, vibrating voice. "Their influence over the masses is insufficient to make a general strike a success. They will fight alone. They will be exterminated. The rank and file will not fight if you tell them they must die to protect the Soviet Union. To make them fight you must lie to them, you must make them believe that there is hope of sweeping the Hitler government away. My conscience forbids me to lead my comrades, whose trust I enjoy, to certain destruction."

Westerman sagged into his chair. The assembly was silent. Mute contempt marked most faces. The delegate of the Comintern replied, virulently:

"Must we regard Comrade Westerman as an agent of the class enemy in our midst? Westerman is a conciliator."

There were cries: *"Raus mit Westerman!* Away with the traitor!"

Voluntarily Westerman left the conference. He was not permitted to leave the building before the meeting had broken up. A day later he was expelled from the Party. Two years later, arrested by the Gestapo in the spring of 1935, he committed suicide in a cell of Fuhlsbuettel concentration camp.

We accepted the *Parteibefehl*. In the first days and nights of February, 1933, we organized the distribution of millions of leaflets. They bore the headline: *"Workers of Germany! Down with Hitler! General Strike is the Call of the Hour!"*

Once more, ironically enough, the Comintern had furnished Hitler the last and immediate pretext for the impending National Socialist Revolution. Those among us who were in favor of quietly preparing for a long spell of "underground" opposition were overridden by the Comintern's command: "No retreat—but general offensive!" Our wild general strike call was a God-send to Hitler. It enabled him to proceed to the crushing even of liberal anti-Nazi forces under the cry, "Save Germany from Bolshevism and Civil War!" Hermann Goering, now a member of the government, concluded a speech to the Nazi formations with the cry, "We cannot finish our job without a Massacre of St. Bartholomew. National Socialists! No sentimentalities!"

The trade unions did not move, and the communist elements within them were unable to prod them into motion at such short notice. Hitler had dissolved the Reichstag and Germany was again in the throes of an election war.

The strikes petered out. Demoralization invaded the fringes of the Communist Party. Already the Party's prestige had been irremediably damaged. In flying meetings at the shipping offices and the gates of the shipyards I heard the workers say, *"Was willst du?*—We won't strike for Moscow!"

In the hour of decision the apathy of the majority of Germans was appalling. They succumbed to the Brown terror with barely a whimper. It was as if the leaders of liberalism and the socialist chiefs did not understand at all the nature of the tidal wave that was engulfing the land. Their policy was one of "wait and see." The Comintern went to the other extreme. The more apparent the failure, the madder became the slogans. Couriers with secret instructions followed each other in rapid succession. On some days I received three and four instruction sheets from headquarters, one countermanding or confusing the other, and all of them were headed by the sentence: *"Take note and return to bearer, or destroy."*

In the vast harbor of Hamburg we held our own. Never since 1930 had the docks been so free of Nazi uniforms. It was death for storm troopers to be met alone or in small groups on the waterfront. During one night I sent my whole force into the harbor in launches and boats; next morning our war-cry, *"Jagt den Hitler fort!—* Chase Hitler out!" and *"Werft Nazi Spitzel in den Hafen!*—Heave Nazi spies into the harbor!" blazed in painted letters from every ship and quayside. The police and customs guards stationed at the harbor entrances were soon reinforced to such an extent that it became increasingly difficult for us to smuggle large amounts of propaganda material into the harbor. Firelei proposed that we should install a secret printing press aboard one of the marooned steamers in the huge ships' graveyard of Waltershof, to enable us to produce our anti-Hitler publications inside the port zone. The plan was accepted. Among the watchmen who guarded the million tons of laid-up shipping in Waltershof were numerous communists. After an early morning reconnoitering trip, I chose the *Bochum,* a medium-sized old freighter of the Hamburg-America Line.

The transport of a new hand-press and two mimeographing machines through the cordon of harbor police was accomplished the same night. A Party member operating a harbor barge owned by a wrecking yard smuggled the machines into Waltershof. Three of my aides hoisted them aboard the *Bochum.* A large quantity of paper and several hundred tubes of ink followed in a later transport. We established the printing paraphernalia in the 'tween-deck under number three hatch.

I exercised utmost care in the selection of operators for our new "underground" plant. Two men were needed to operate the presses. A third was to serve as courier between myself and the *Bochum*, conveying the manuscripts scheduled for printing. A fourth comrade, also a courier, was required to relay the finished propaganda material from the *Bochum* to five "district couriers," who in turn delivered it to the thirty detachment messengers awaiting him at certain hours and certain spots within the shipping area. The detachment leaders would then divide the material into smaller batches for distribution by the "activists" of their respective groups. This was the system of conspirative organization which all units inside the Party were advised to adopt. In this manner all that a weakling apprehended by the police could give away under pressure were the four other comrades belonging to his group.

I chose Firelei to act as courier between headquarters and the *Bochum.* She was also made responsible for the effective artistic make-up of our propaganda matter. As the courier between the *Bochum* and the lower units I appointed a man named Julius Emmerich, a marine engineer with a long Party record. No one among us suspected at the time that Comrade Emmerich had been for months an agent for the intelligence service of Heinrich Himmler's Elite Guards. The technicians of our workshop aboard the *Bochum* consisted of a little silent Roumanian, an expert in secret work, and of a jobless tugboat captain—Willem—serving as his assistant. The Roumanian's name was Alexander Popovics.

Comrade Popovics was an extraordinary type. A man approaching forty, dark, with a strong, friendly face, and slow-moving, he had once been a member of the luckless Bandura's crew. The Comintern had sent him to its Leningrad school, and had subsequently employed him as organizer and political contrabandist in Bessarabia. As the head of a communist frontier column he had for many years directed the practical end of the smuggling of printed matter, arms, letters and funds across the Dniester River from Russia to Roumania. Popovics knew rivers. He had begun life as a riverman on the Danube. His chief helper in his frontier function had been a girl he had married in the Soviet Union.

Popovics' mind had been affected. In intervals between Party work he was wont to give himself up to gloomy meditation. One day I found him in such a mood.

"Comrade Alex," I said, "what is bothering you?"

From an inner pocket he pulled out a clipping from a Roumanian newspaper. The clipping was pasted on a thin piece of steel, the size of half a postcard.

"Listen," he said. He read, translating each sentence:

"January 11, 1932. The frontier guards surprised six persons who secretly crossed the Dniester River. After challenging them several times, the frontier guards opened fire. All six persons were killed. Among them was a girl. Five of them were active members of the Communist Youth organization; the sixth was a smuggler. This happened last night in Soroca, in northern Bessarabia."

"The girl was your wife?" I asked.

Popovics nodded.

"And I was the 'smuggler,' " he said bitterly. "They thought I was dead, so I escaped. All the other comrades were really dead, the good young comrades. But the report is untrue. The guards killed them, after we had been arrested, to appropriate the money we carried."

That was what had cracked Popovics' mind. He had become unfit for complicated assignments. But he remained as reliable as granite. In the summer of 1932, he had turned up in Hamburg, after being pushed across the Belgian border by gendarmes, and had become an "activist" in the division which carried communism on ships under the flags of Balkan countries. During the day Popovics slept on a cot in the lower hold of the *Bochum*. At night he made the clandestine presses thump. He was calm, without fear. Duty was the breath of his life. He belonged to the type who would rather hang himself or cut his veins than betray a trust.

The first material which flew off the presses under Popovics' expert hands was a fiery manifesto the text of which had been forwarded to all organizations by the Berlin Central Committee. It had been written in a language of which Ernst Wollweber was master, and ended with the call:

"Disarm the Storm Troops—Arms into the Hands of the Workers!"

Communists on ships entering Hamburg from Dutch and Belgian ports brought with them consignments of firearms for the Red Front Fighters' League. To my *Apparat* fell the task of carrying the guns safely ashore, to be handed over to the couriers of Edgar Andree, the chief of the Party's military formations. I saw much of the Red Front Fighters in these days. Payroll robberies to obtain money for arms, raids on arms stores, organized plundering of food shops, ambushes with intent to kill, and terrorization of policemen in outlying districts formed the bulk of their current tasks. The sounds of shooting from tenement roofs were heard in the city every night. As yet, not many of the snipers were apprehended.

Coming home late one night I found Edgar Andree in my apartment. Andree liked Firelei. She had at times designed new insignia for his armed columns, and had often painstakingly copied plans of police stations, *Reichswehr* barracks, railway yards and the like at his request. This time I beheld a strange scene: Edgar Andree lay back in a corner of a *chaise lounge,* his powerful frame relaxed, sipping coffee with the usual vaguely humorous expression on his bold dusky features. In front of him Firelei paraded. She wore a bathing suit. Above her knees, strapped with strong rubber bands, were several small automatic pistols of a Belgian make.

I laughed.

"What's this?" I said.

"Not a seduction," Andree chuckled. "I am experimenting. Since our boys have started to relieve careless Brownshirts of their guns, the Nazis have started something new. The storm troopers promenade around trying to look love-sick, and close by walk the Nazi girls with guns strapped to their thighs. It's easy to search a Fascist. Not everyone of the comrades has the nerve to dig his paws under the skirts of a strange woman. Clever!"

"And now?"

"For the first time Comrade Edgar steals an idea from the Nazis," Firelei said. "Why shouldn't our girls learn the technique? Policemen, too, hesitate to search women on the open street."

"Truth is," said Edgar Andree, "I came here for a peaceful cup of coffee."

A few days later the "new technique" was used by Andree's guards in an assault on a storm trooper stronghold, the Adler Hotel near the Central Station. The troopers, finding the unknown men who lounged in nearby doorways, unarmed, feared nothing. The girls, who came later, were not molested. At the shrill of a whistle, they handed the pistols they carried to the Red Front guards. An instant later a deadly fusillade was under way. The Adler Hotel was wrecked. Seven Brownshirts were shot. Two innocent passers-by, one a woman with four small children, fell dead in the hail of bullets.

In the third week of February Albert Walter, the Comintern's maritime chief, summoned me to his camouflaged offices on the Baumwall. The bronzed old sailor was in a towering rage. He pounded through the room, shouting at his typists. When he saw me, he stopped short.

"Excuse me, comrade," he grumbled. "But this miserable *va banque* play of the Thaelmann crowd makes one want to make *Kleinholz* (smash things up). Every man who's any good disappears from the scene for a cursed variety of 'special work.' As if we were a club of spies and bomb-throwers instead of an association of revolutionists."

"You're nervous, Comrade Walter," I said.

"I'm not nervous. I'm mad!" the old warrior thundered.

"What's my assignment?"

"Oh, yes," he said sarcastically. " 'Special work.'" Then, calmly: "Berlin sent money for you. Pick out a dozen of our friends, fellows who know how to handle boats, and go to Berlin. No delay. Report to the Karl Liebknecht House. Ask there for Kippenberger."

"What is it about?"

Albert Walter clasped both hands to the massive mahogany dome of his forehead. "Hell and damnation," he whispered angrily. "Did you ever hear of rats running off a doomed ship the night before she leaves her last anchorage?"

"Sure, but . . ."

"Well, here's your money. Pick your men and go to Berlin. The Western Secretariat is going to move to Copenhagen."

Nine hours later I was in Berlin. While my comrades waited in the homes of communists in the Wedding and Moabit districts, I proceeded to Party Headquarters on Buelowplatz.

I came too late to meet Kippenberger, the Party's expert on military affairs, industrial espionage and Central European communications. Workers milled on the large square like so many bewildered sheep. The windows in nearby communist bookshops were smashed. The Karl Liebknecht House itself, the central fortress of Bolshevism in Europe, was full of policemen. Police trucks lined the front of the building. Policemen came out of the building in a steady stream, all of them carrying bundles, stacks of books and papers, typewriters, mimeograph machines or parts taken from the powerful rotary presses to render them useless for future use. Pell-mell everything was dumped into trucks, which then pulled out toward police headquarters. Empty trucks rolled on to join the end of the line. I stood at the curb, dazed. The realization that hostile police were sacking the symbol of communist strength in Western Europe was overpowering.

A worker tapped me on the shoulder.

"Better step back in the crowd," he mumbled. "They might arrest you."

I stepped back.

"They are closing the Karl Liebknecht House," the worker said.

There was no resistance. The whole area around the Buelowplatz bristled with police, carbines, machine guns, armored cars. No Nazi uniform was in sight. Storm troopers on the Buelowplatz would have been torn to pieces by the workers who eddied about glumly, helplessly.

I jumped into a taxi. At the Hallesche Tor I paid off the driver and got out.

I walked along the Wilhelmstrasse toward the drab palaces where Adolf Hitler and his aides were now in power. Number 48. *Neuer Deutscher Verlag.* Ostensibly a publishing house. In reality it was one of the former branch offices of the Western Secretariat of the Comintern. The place was silent and deserted, except for a pretty young girl who had been left behind to direct callers at loose ends to other, safer contact addresses. The girl munched chocolates.

She gave me an address in the Gesundbunnen district, in the North East of Berlin.

"Go there," she said, 'and wait."

I waited in the home of a crippled war veteran and his wife while the hidden Party control stations checked up on the authenticity of my errand. In the evening, a girl courier arrived.

"I am looking for a sailor comrade from Hamburg," she said.

The war cripple indicated me.

"Please come with me, comrade," she said.

We agreed on what we should say if we should be accosted by police. When two suspects, questioned separately, gave the same innocent explanation for their being together, the police usually lost interest in harassing them further.

The girl took me to a modern apartment block in the Wilmersdorf suburb. "Is Comrade Kippenberger here?" I asked her. "No," she replied. "You will meet another comrade, one whom you know well."

She pressed a bell. Three short rings, and one long. From inside a man squinted through the spy-hole. He opened the door and let us pass.

"Is our friend in?" the girl asked.

The man nodded.

I passed a room in which a group of well-dressed young men and women of various ages lounged idly. I took them for either bodyguards or couriers. Further on, in a large room which had been equipped as an office, I met Ernst Wollweber.

He stood in the middle of the room, barely over five feet tall, a chunky, saturnine figure in worn-out blue. A cigarette dangled from his lips. His thick face remained immobile, but his little black eyes glinted through narrow slits, digging, searching, alert. With him was a tall, elegant girl, working over what seemed to be a draft of a new code, I knew her. She was Cilly, who had worked with me in England. She glanced at me, not giving a sign of recognition.

Wollweber spoke through cigarette smoke, his voice barely audible: "How many comrades have you brought from Hamburg?"

"With myself—thirteen."

"Thirteen!" The Silesian showed his small tobacco-stained teeth in a ghost of a grin. "And sailors, too!" Suddenly, with a forward thrust of his shoulders, he added: "What do you think of the situation?"

"If we don't come to real mass actions before March, it'll be too late," I said.

"Too late for what?"

"For an offensive."

Wollweber growled, "It is not too late. Too early, rather. We shall leave the initiative to Hitler. He will blunder and the masses will wake up. Nothing is stronger than the masses. The character of our slogans is offensive. Naturally. What we need are waves of small skirmishes to cover a tactical retreat. A retreat is not a defeat. Or is it?"

A devilish gleam was in his eyes.

"No," I said.

"A leader must sense what is in the masses," Wollweber went on. "Just now the masses won't fight. The best we can do in the circumstances is to whip fight into the masses. And to keep Hitler on his toes. By disruption. By sabotage. By shooting out of the dark. In the long run, that'll unnerve the cutthroats. We must inspire ourselves and all the comrades with a will to self-sacrifice. If not, we can't survive."

"No fear," I said. "Our *cadres* show their mettle."

"The *cadres* are good," Wollweber said sullenly. "How our Grand Moguls will stand punishment—that's another question. The fellows who hang on for the legendary money from Moscow will never be willing to sacrifice their lives. They are going to get the bum's rush."

Ernst Wollweber was a thorough German. He despised all internationalists who did not bring with them the background and the traditions of the Russian Bolsheviks. In Wollweber's mind, I suspected, the world consisted only of two worthwhile countries. One was the Soviet Union. The other was Germany. And the rest was rubbish.

"I was told to see Kippenberger," I said.

"You don't need him. He had to disappear. Count Helldorf wants him for murder." Count Helldorf was the chief of the Berlin storm troops. The murder referred to was the assassination of two officers, Schenck and Anlauf, civil war experts in the Berlin Police Department. Both were shot to death in front of the Karl Liebknecht House by agents of the Communist Espionage Defense. Count Helldorf later became police president of Berlin. Hans Kippenberger, who was a Reichstag deputy, was arrested by the G.P.U. in Moscow in 1936, and has disappeared like so many of his comrades.

Wollweber then came down to my immediate tasks. I was to go to an address in Charlottenburg, to Kuschinsky, on Luetzowerstrasse, where a large number of suitcases and traveling bags packed with confidential documents of the Central Committee and the Western Secretariat were ready for transportation to Copenhagen. The route of transport led over the German port of Flensburg to the Danish town of Sonderburg, across an arm of the Baltic Sea. The job was a simple smuggling enterprise, but of utmost importance.

Wollweber arranged for couriers to inform my scattered crew to assemble inconspicuously in the waiting room of the Charlottenburg railroad station. There I issued the necessary instructions, never to more than one man at a time. One by one we proceeded to the address on Luetzowerstrasse. There each man received two heavy suitcases, a sum of money, and a second class ticket to Flensburg. We traveled at night, all aboard the same train, but each man in a different compartment. As the train rumbled northward through the night, I could not help thinking that, should the police swoop down on us at the next station, they would make the greatest haul of incriminating material since the day the Comintern was born. Heaven knew what those suitcases contained! Patrolling the corridors of the coaches were several stocky individuals in ill-fitting clothes. In passing they peered into the compartments. At stations they jumped at once to the platform from where all doors of the train could be observed. When we changed trains in Hamburg, these men also changed trains. At first I took them for detectives or Nazi Party spies. But the fact that they passed each other in the train corridor without exchanging a word soon convinced me that they were members of our own Espionage Defense *Apparat*, assigned to look after the safety (or check on the reliability) of this extraordinary expedition of couriers.

We all arrived in Flensburg without mishap. Still each man for himself, we proceeded to a liaison address near the waterfront. It was a saloon with placards on the walls which said: "Drink till you burst, but don't talk politics." Our illegal cargo was deposited among the beer barrels in the cellar. A special liaison agent, a blue-eyed, pleasant-looking chap with credentials from Richard Jensen in Copenhagen, awaited me here. His name was Julius Vanman. I learned months later that he was on the payroll of the G.P.U. Vanman had a boat in readiness. While my fellow couriers slept through the rest of the day, I accompanied Vanman to the waterfront. The boat was a heavy ship's lifeboat, equipped with six oars. It belonged to the International Club in Flensburg; but local communist sailors, known to the Nazis of this frontier district, were ruled out from manning the craft for this particular transport.

The night was icy. Between eleven and midnight I roused my assistants. In great haste we carried our contraband into the boat, shoved off a rickety wharf, and manned the oars. Vanman squatted in the bows; he knew the waters of Flensburg Fjord. I had the helm. We showed no light and we forced ourselves not to smoke. We pulled through perfect darkness, through a short choppy sea, with a chill wind blowing in over the starboard bows. The shorelights were bright. Red and green, the running lights of small steamers passed through the night. Strips of burlap wrapped around the oars, where they toiled in the oarlocks, muffled the sounds of rowing. The thumping noises were then not louder than the hiss and wash of the sea and the rhythmic grunting of the rowers. The night was starry. A jumble of overcoats lay atop the layer of suitcases in the bottom of the boat. Only Vanman and I, not engaged in hard labor, remained swathed up to the ears.

In six hours my comrades rowed fifty miles. As we approached close to the Danish shore, we proceeded with caution. Only half of the men rowed now. The chugging sounds of fishermen's motors were about us. Toward dawn the sky became overcast, and the sea among the promontories had the smoothness and color of a sheet of steel. The shore was low, and rocky in places. A sprinkling of houses hove into sight. There were rows of trees lining a highway. It was still too early for the houses to show light. Vanman scanned the shore through nightglasses. There was a bright light high above the half-hidden roof, and another one, less bright below.

"Easy now," Vanman murmured. "There—pull inshore."

Only four men rowed now. The others crouched low behind the gunwales to keep themselves out of sight of possible watchers. Ahead was a landing, barely above the level of the water. As our boat drew alongside, two men stepped out from cover ashore. I breathed freer. The gray tension which assails men in the quieter hours of a perilous undertaking slipped away. Vanman was happy. He whistled a dance-hall tune: *"Das ist die Liebe der Matrosen ..."* The Germans lit cigarettes and relaxed. They left it to the comrades ashore to unload the mysterious cargo.

In the house behind the landing was Georg Hegener, Jensen's chief lieutenant, burly, cheerful, tough. He punched my ribs. "Now our boresome Denmark is getting a taste of *Kultur,"* he laughed, indicating the array of luggage.

Comrade Hegener had already prepared for the transport of the load to Copenhagen. The smuggling station at the edge of Sonderburg had only recently been established. Ours had been the third transport of Comintern documents from Berlin which had passed this backdoor to Denmark inside a week. It was only the beginning. Here, and on hidden spots along the frontier, the organization got ready for the great exodus of the army of Comintern officials who had pitched camp in Germany for nearly a decade and a half.

My band dispersed. Alone and in pairs we returned to German soil, some using the autobus line which followed the coast, others going by train. My comrades had a chance here to escape to safety, if they had wished to, instead of returning to the German powder barrel, but none of them deserted. Their loyalty was their honor.

The German election battle was in full swing. The usual communist mass rallies and demonstrations had long been outlawed. Thousands of smaller meetings were carried through instead. Many illegal demonstrations, staged behind an armed vanguard of the Red Front Guards, took place simultaneously in six or seven different parts of the city. In utmost secrecy numerous Party members were detailed to join the Nazi formations. All official Party bureaus were abandoned. Secret offices and courier centers sprang up in the tenements and the backrooms of retail stores, arms depots were moved to safer places, secret printing plants were established in attics and basements in ever-increasing numbers. The Foreign Division of the G.P.U. in Hamburg re-established itself behind the shield of a shoemaker's shop. And the Party's military organization headquarters took on the facade of the Prometheus Publishing Company.

There were spies and traitors in our midst. One of them was Joseph Bleser, who was a chauffeur in the central courier service. Agents of the Communist *S-Apparat*, working at the Berlin police headquarters, found that Bleser was a storm trooper in the pay of Dr. Diels, head of the political police in Prussia. But the spy was warned and vanished. There was a rumor that he had come to Hamburg. From Michel Avatin I received a photograph and description of the man together with orders to watch the Nazi shipping centers, for Bleser had once been a navy man. In the last days of February I received a note to stop the search. Bleser had been assassinated. By keeping his wife under surveillance, the German G.P.U. operatives had traced the spy to a room in the Hoechst district of Frankfurt-on-the-Main. At night they had followed him and shot him to death in the Kasinostrasse. He was only one of many who ended in this fashion.

In the waterfront districts of Hamburg, and in the industrial suburbs no uniformed Nazi showed his face. Red flags, with hammer and sickle, flew from hundreds of windows, often in a single street. Red banners crossed the streets from house to house. The inscriptions on the banners and countless posters on the housewalls shouted: *"Kommunisten in den Reichstag! Tod dent Faschismus!* Vote for Thaelmann, Pieck, Clara Zetkin, Wollweber, Heckert!" The National Socialist press carried in every headline a curse on Communism. "Death, death, death," was the eternal refrain. In Berlin, Captain Goering had been commissioned to set up a new type of secret police—the *Geheime Staatspolizei*—the Gestapo. What did it mean? I discussed it with Edgar Andree, who had called on Firelei to design for him the head of a new paper for the *Reichwehr* soldiers. Andree smiled grimly. "The devils are trying to imitate our own G.F.U.," he said.

The anti-Nazi masses ducked down like frightened dogs, heedless of our cries for action, waiting, waiting for the blow. One day after the announcement that the Gestapo had been formed, the government proclaimed that storm troopers, Elite Guards and the Steel Helmets had been given the status of auxiliary police. Our men in the Nazi Party reported that select bands of ruffians were being organized and armed under the designation *"Konmmados zur besonderen Verwendung"*—Squads for Special Purposes.

Yes, what did it mean? There followed two strangely quiet days. The atmosphere was heavy and menacing.

Then, two o'clock in the morning, I came out of the harbor after a busy night aboard the derelict *Bochum*, where the faithful Popovics was grinding out another flaming call to the masses. I strode toward the *Bunte Kuh* café in St. Pauli, to see one Lewandowsky who specialized in the distribution of counterfeit five-mark pieces for the Party. The many cabarets and dance-halls along the Reeperbahn were full of life and noise. Sailors cruised for pleasure. The prostitutes patrolled the pavements or stood bargaining on corners. Someone accosted me. It was a courier.

"What's new, comrade?" I inquired.

"*Parteibefehl*—all functionaries must change their quarters at once. Don't go home."

"Why?"

"The Reichstag is burning. Mass arrests all over Prussia."

I was not surprised.

"So, that's it," I said.

"Yes." The courier nodded. "The night of long knives is here."

I hastened away to find Firelei, and to contact someone from headquarters. On the Holstenwall, a detachment of storm troopers marched toward the center of the city. Their boots clanked on the asphalt. One-two, one-two. The troopers were singing the Horst Wessel hymn.

> "*Die Strasse frei,*
> "*Debraunen Battaillonen...*"

Chapter Twenty-seven

IN THE HURRICANE

More than 4,600 communist and socialist leaders were arrested in the night of the Reichstag Fire. Nazi raiding parties occupied all Communist Party buildings in Prussia. At dawn, our couriers sped out in all directions spreading the order to print and distribute large editions of leaflets headlined, "Nazi Goering Set Fire to the Reichstag." The Hitler version was that a half-naked Dutchman, Marinus van der Lubbe, had been seized in the burning building. He was branded a communist. We, of the inner circle of the Comintern and the Communist Party of Germany, had never heard of this man.

Communists were hunted down like mad dogs. Weaklings in our ranks capitulated. Spies stepped from obscurity. The majority of the Party's top-rank leaders had saved their own hides by bolting across the frontiers to neutral countries. But some were captured. Ernst Thaelmann, betrayed by one of his own couriers, was arrested in his secret abode. Edgar Andree was betrayed by Eiche Redzinsky, a graduate of the Lenin School, and was seized by the Gestapo aboard a train. In Berlin, Georgi Dimitrov, denounced by a waiter, was apprehended and carried off to jail. Torgler, the head of the Communist Caucus in the Reichstag, surrendered voluntarily to the Gestapo. Albert Walter rushed home in the gray of dawn to save his mother from the raiders, only to find them waiting for him in the old woman's bedroom.

Overnight the Communist Party had taken on the appearance of an antheap smashed by a sudden hail of sledge-hammer blows. On March 2, the new terror laws against the Communist Party were decreed. Hitler's technique of victory was simple: concentration of the whole ferocity of the National Socialist movement against one enemy at a time, while maneuvering the others into a false sense of security.

Each morning brought intelligence of new disaster. Still, under the hammering blows, the cells of our rank and file, the "activist" units and the Red Front Fighters' brigades continued to function. One Thursday night, in March, a concentration of storm troopers in the working-class quarters of Hamburg was ambushed by one of Edgar Andree's detachments. The invaders were driven out. Nine Brownshirts fell under communist bullets. On the same day the waterfront organization under my command distributed within one hour a hundred thousand leaflets urging the workers to drive the newly-appointed Nazi port commissars out of the harbor. On the morning of the next day a communist sabotage squad opened all valves in the refineries of the Hannover Canal harbor, and 200,000 liters of gasoline flooded the surrounding grounds.

Of the old leadership, only one man remained at his post—Ernst Wollweber, the head of the Party's organization bureau. He moved through the general confusion with a stony indifference to danger. He was in Berlin today, in Hamburg tomorrow, and a day later on the Rhine, appointing new leaders in the districts and jabbing his fingers into organizational wounds. He was curt, almost haughty now, and seething with a merciless contempt for all who shied from doing his bidding.

In the night of March 5 the Brown terror struck Hamburg. Here, as in Berlin and other large cities, the elections had left the National Socialists still in a minority. But the rabid enmity between the two great camps of labor, the socialists and communists, was too deep, having been fostered too zealously through the years, particularly from the communist side, to be bridged in this last hour of decision for the history of the world. I was that night at the International Club in Hamburg, speaking to an assembly of delegates from the ship and harbor action committees. In another hall of the building, Firelei was in charge of a cinema performance where a Soviet film—*Storm over Asia*—was shown to a packed auditorium. On the waterfront, the red flags still flew from many windows. Outside, in the streets, our armed detachments were on guard, and reconnoitering parties cruised through the city on their routine surveillance of Nazi headquarters, police stations and public buildings.

Not long before midnight a headquarters courier brought the news that storm troopers had arrived in masses at all railway stations. An hour later came the message that the Nazi formations had seized the City Hall and Police Headquarters in a lightning coup. At two in the morning a comrade in the anti-Nazi *Apparat* telephoned me that several storm trooper brigades were on the march against the International Club. At once I contacted a call station of the secret headquarters of the Communist Party. A tired voice answered.

"They are coming," I said. "Has an agreement been reached for united action with the socialists?"

"No, we stand alone," the voice answered.

I returned to the International Club and informed the restless crowd of seamen of the situation. They wanted to stay and defend the building. Many of them had guns, others knives. Quietly Firelei stepped up to me. She was pale. Her eyes flashed.

"Why provoke useless bloodshed?" she said. "Tell the comrades to go home."

Hundreds of expectant faces stared at me out of the half-darkened hall.

"Go back to your ships," I told them. "We will wage our struggle not with a mass that can be trapped, but from a thousand corners. Let every action committee and every unit be an anti-Fascist spearhead in itself. Let each group know that it does not fight alone, that thousands of other groups are in the fight, even though they cannot readily be seen. Comrades, do your duty! Long live the Communist Party!"

The crowd dispersed. Shortly after three o'clock in the morning the storm troopers closed in. They carried rifles, machine guns and gas-grenades. The few of our men who had refused to leave the building were beaten half to death and dragged away to jail.

The list of anti-Nazis scheduled for arrest had been prepared long in advance by Heinrich Himmler's machine. This became clear to me when our few operatives in the Elite Guards had reported that even the names of men who had died shortly before Hitler became Chancellor were still on these lists. In this respect, also, Himmler had imitated the methods of the G.P.U. We, too, had prepared lists of persons who were to be seized and shot, or kept as hostages, in the event of a communist insurrection. Like the G.P.U., the Nazi raiders came in the night. They took away prisoners, without informing their relatives whether the captured men were dead or still alive. They grabbed the wives and mothers and children of fugitives as hostages. Out of the overcrowded prisons filtered gruesome tales. Comrades whom I knew, and valued as friends, had leaped from windows to escape torture, or were found in parks with their throats cut, or fished out of the river—their smashed heads wrapped in burlap.

The terror tightened the ranks of the best among us. I saw it on Firelei. "We must fight on,' she said. "We have no time to weep."

At first, the Gestapo was raw. Its new personnel was largely recruited from the Elite Guards. There were some trained men among them, former officers, but the majority began with no other assets than a cruel fanaticism and a fierce will to triumph. The former Political Police, which had contained many socialists and a few secret members of the Communist Party, had efficiently jumbled the records before they finally abandoned their posts at the Police Department.

The first phase of the Gestapo raids consisted in the apprehension of all militants—as far as they could be found—whose names appeared on the "blood" lists. Many of the intended victims escaped capture by changing their quarters every night. But this became increasingly difficult. The number of available cover addresses decreased rapidly. The families in whose households the Gestapo found an active communist in hiding were doomed. Neighbors distrusted each other, and parents feared their children. After the first wave of arrests there was a lull. The "blood" lists were exhausted. We used the two-day lull to reorganize our shaken units, to re-establish several contacts, to discard unstable partisans, and to supply the Party's Espionage Defense with the names of known traitors.

Then the Gestapo sprang anew, and in a different manner. Every member of the Nazi Party was ordered to collaborate with the Secret Police. Informers were appointed to ferret out the secrets of every factory, every block, and every house. An avalanche of denunciations poured in. Nazi spies who had operated in the communist ranks for years came out into the open. They were put into motor-cars, together with a Gestapo squad. From dawn to dark, and all through the night, these cars criss-crossed the city. Whenever the spy saw a communist of his acquaintance on the street, he gave a signal, the car stopped, and the comrade was arrested. In a city like Hamburg, which harbored more than one hundred thousand communist followers, such tactics had devastating results. One spy alone—Kaiser, who had been the chief of the Communist Unemployed Organization—accounted for nearly eight hundred seizures of communists and members of their families. And there were many more like him.

The communist *S-Apparat*, one of whose chiefs was Michel Avatin, dressed certain sections of its operatives in stolen storm trooper uniforms, and the comrades so disguised became a veritable terror to the above-mentioned category of Nazi spies. It was the activity of these groups that gave rise in the early stages of the National Socialist Revolution to the strange rumors that Nazi murdered Nazi in desolate sections of Hamburg and Berlin. I remember cases where agents of the Communist Espionage Defense, working inside the Hitler movement, cast suspicion on communist traitors with such success that these informers for the Gestapo ended up themselves in the torture chambers after they had become useless to Hitler's Secret Police.

There was a third phase in the Gestapo raiding technique, against which there was no adequate defense. The method was as crude as it was effective. Without warning, several hundred Gestapo agents, aided by thousands of Elite Guards and storm troopers, swooped down on a certain section of the city. The storm troopers formed a dense cordon around many city blocks. No one was permitted to enter or to leave the surrounded area. A trooper was posted at the entrance of every house. No inhabitant was permitted to leave the house nor was anyone allowed to enter it. The Gestapo agents and elite Guards then searched each house from roof to cellar. No room, no bed or drawer or upholstery was spared. Walls and floors were tapped for hiding-places. Men, women and children were stripped and searched. All who could not identify themselves satisfactorily were herded into waiting caravans of trucks. The hauls were huge. Secret printing presses, stores of arms and explosives, depots of illegal literature, codes, documents, and hungry-looking fugitives without identification papers were brought to light in almost every block.

I knew that my name was known to the Gestapo. I had taken the usual precautions demanded by our rules of conspiracy. Since the night of the Reichstag Fire, I had not visited the apartment which I had shared with Firelei and which was the home of our son, who was then five months old. I slept in the quarters of obscure communist friends. I used cover addresses for my mail, and three separate courier stations for messages and liaison purposes. The clandestine meetings and conferences in which I participated never took place twice at the same place. Parks, monarchist restaurants, abandoned ships, crowded dance-halls, barges and boats were the places in which I met my comrades to make plans, to give and receive reports and instructions. We seldom used private houses; as the days passed and the intensity of terror grew, every house was liable to be a trap.

Before going to a meeting place, I would send an aide—usually a young boy or a very young girl—ahead to investigate whether the rendezvous was free from suspicious loiterers. I made myself as inconspicuous in appearance and behavior as I possibly could. In my pockets I carried a Belgian passport and a few harmless letters in Flemish, bearing post-marks of Ostend. Never did I carry confidential material on my person. I had learned to memorize long lists of names and addresses and a conglomeration of code words. Written material has ever been the most dangerous snag in conspirative organization. When notes had to be carried, a girl courier in possession of a Nazi Party card carried them for me in a secret pocket on the inside of her girdle. Necessary consultations with one or the other of my superiors were invariably made while walking leisurely through some suburban street. I never used empty or half-empty autobuses or tramcars; crowded means of transportation were always good hiding-places. I avoided all superfluous personal relations with my former friends; only Party relations counted. All inquisitive people had to be treated as suspect. It was a Party order that members who asked questions of other Party members, outside of their limited sphere of activities, must immediately be reported to the local G.P.U. *Apparat*. I used a different name for each different district in which I was active. More, in my dealings with comrades whom I did not know intimately, I never used the name given in my identification papers, nor the name under which I occasionally had registered in hotels, nor the names under which I had previously been arrested, nor any other name I had ever used before.

A man engaged in political underground work learns punctuality, no matter how small the importance of the undertaking at hand. Waiting people were apt to attract the attention of passers-by or of unseen watchers. A few minutes of waiting for someone often caused the questioning and arrest of those who waited. We never waited longer than one minute; when the expected comrade did not arrive at the end of that time, an often painfully maintained contact was disrupted. Comrades kept their residences secret from each other; only the all-important liaison men and couriers were in possession of the vital addresses. In my various secret quarters, I never received visitors. I took care not to attract the attention of neighbors by burning a light until late at night. I moved quietly, entering and leaving my quarters only after the street and all nearby windows had been scanned for watchers.

With the friends with whom I lived I agreed on signals and signs to indicate safety or the presence of danger. A flowerpot on the window sill meant: "You may come in; all is in good order." A disarranged curtain warned: "Keep away. Danger." When walking along the street, I always kept far to the right, thus making it more difficult for raiders speeding by in automobiles to discern my face. Before turning a corner or entering a house, I made sure that no shadowers dogged me. Schoolboys and young girls were used especially by the Gestapo for small-time spying. The wives and sweethearts of arrested men or of fugitives were completely isolated by the Party, for they were the favorite objects of Gestapo surveillance. I never accosted another comrade in the presence of strangers; unless we had arranged in advance to meet each other, we gave no sign of mutual recognition. Of the highest importance became the so-called "conspirative minute": two or more underground workers meeting clandestinely spent the first minute of their meeting on agreeing as to what was to be said to the police in case of a sudden raid. The drinking of alcoholic beverages became a strict taboo. A communist caught in a love affair with a girl who was not a Party member was inevitably expelled from our ranks. More than one mistress of Party officials had been unmasked as collaborators of the Gestapo.

Such were the fundamental rules of our underground existence. Recklessness, flightiness had no chance for survival. Bravery alone was not enough, neither was loyalty. Only crafty dissimulation, aggressive cunning and steady nerves could keep our staffs afloat, and in condition to strike out of the dark. The Gestapo attacked with wild, smashing blows. There was little cleverness in their initial methods. It took many months before this instrument of terror developed the patience and skill and deadly routine which made later underground assignments in Germany a ticket to certain annihilation.

Three days after the big man-hunt began in Hamburg, Julius Emmerich, who acted as courier between our secret press aboard the *Bochum* and the "activist" units in the harbor, did his Judas work. It happened shortly before dawn. The ship's watchman lay asleep in his cabin amidships. Willem, the tugboat captain, and Popovics, the steadfast Roumanian revolutionist, had just finished their night's work of printing an underground paper, the *Searchlight*. They were waiting for Julius Emmerich to take the printed matter to the waiting group leaders for distribution. Emmerich did not appear. Instead, Popovics, who had come on deck to look for the courier, saw five or six men crawling over the deck of a steamer which was moored alongside the *Bochum*. Popovics ran to rouse the watchman. The watchman came forward and challenged the intruders who had already leaped aboard the *Bochum*.

"Raise your hands," was the answer he received. "Stand still or we shoot."

Guns in hand, the raiders spread out over the decks. Popovics yelled through a ventilator into the hold.

"Flee! Gestapo!"

It was too late for Willem to escape. He made a pathetic attempt to heave overboard the packages containing the treasonous Searchlight. The invaders caught him. Popovics jumped into the harbor, with guns cracking behind him. While swimming, he stripped off his clothes. He got out of the reach of the guns by swimming behind a ship which was anchored in the middle of Waltershof Basin. He finally reached a Greek freighter, shouted for help, and someone lowered a bowline. The Greek sailors supplied Popovics with clothes and helped him ashore. The Roumanian repaired immediately to my apartment, where Firelei, who had never been arrested by the police, still lived with our baby. Firelei knew where to find me.

The Gestapo worked swiftly. Before noon, seventy-eight members of our "activist" brigades were rounded up. The watchman of the *Bochum* refused to answer the questions of the Gestapo; he escaped by jumping to his death from a fifth floor window of the Police Headquarters. Willem, after two hours of beating with chains, told the Nazis all he knew. By nightfall I had received detailed reports on these events, and ordered all comrades whose names and addresses were known by the captured men to change their quarters without delay—if they could. For most of the militants of the rank and file were already homeless and penniless.

During the night, with the help of Firelei and several couriers, I strove to rebuild the remnants of my organization. That was a difficult task, because the arrests continued all through the night, and there was the constant danger of blundering into a house at a time when it was being ransacked by the Gestapo. Every unknown face, and be it ever so friendly, gave rise to the question: "Who are you? Friend? Foe? Can I trust you or will you betray me?" By morning we were dead-tired. Physical exhaustion and nervous strain defied all stimulants.

"I feel like a walking corpse," Firelei told me, attempting a brave smile. "Where can we sleep?"

"I don't know," I said.

"Jan, what a shabby life we are leading. Sometimes I think that all our efforts have no purpose," Firelei said bitterly.

"You are tired."

"Yes, tired."

"I shall find a place where you can sleep," I promised.

"First I have to go and rescue our son," she said.

"Be careful."

"I will."

We agreed to meet in a small restaurant in the Barmbeck district. I arrived there at the fixed time. Firelei did not come. I waited hour after hour, half mad with anxiety. Firelei did not appear. I borrowed a bicycle and rode to the Schaarmarkt, where the apartment in which we had lived through so many happy hours was located. From the street I saw that the windows were open. Books and papers were being thrown through the windows. They were my books and my papers. Storm troopers in the street collected them and stowed them into the back-seat of a car. At a respectable distance from the house, groups of men and women and a few children stood gaping in silence. To them a house raid was already a familiar sight. It was seven o'clock in the morning.

From behind, a hand tapped me on the shoulder. I saw a familiar face. It belonged to a functionary of our street unit. He motioned me to follow him. We slipped away.

"Comrade Firelei is safe," the comrade said.

"Where is she? She came here to get the baby."

"Be calm. You'll see her."

He led me through several dingy streets and finally into a well-kept tenement house. I found Firelei in a small apartment where children romped noisily. She was sitting on a chair in the kitchen, holding a handkerchief against her lips. A robust, red-armed woman tried to comfort her.

"What happened?" I demanded. "Where is the child?" Haltingly, Firelei told me what had occurred. She told it in a tone of unbelief, almost of self-accusation.

She had gone to our apartment where she had found Jan, the child, peacefully sleeping in his cradle. For some time she had stood still and watched the little face, careful not to disturb him. She had been tired, dead-tired. She had put some milk on the range to warm, had taken a hot shower, and had lain down on the bed with the intention of resting for a few short minutes. Then, against her will, she had fallen asleep.

A sudden ring at the front door had awakened her. She had lain still and held her breath, fearful that the baby should wake up and cry.

"Open up!" a voice had barked outside.

Then the door crashed under a powerful blow. Someone moved cautiously through the vestibule. An instant later a thick-set young man in a gray overcoat and a gray hat stood in her bedroom. The man had a Mauser in his hand. He did not take off his hat.

"Good morning," he said. "My name is Teege. I wish to have a chat with your husband."

"He's not here. Who are you?"

"*Geheime Staatspolizei.*"

"I am alone," Firelei said. "My husband has gone away."

"Where to?"

"I don't know. To France, perhaps."

The Gestapo man looked around the room. Then he said: "I don't believe you. Get dressed."

"Why?"

"You are coming with me."

"Where?"

"You'll see. Now dress yourself."

Firelei thought quickly. "I have nothing on," she said to the invader. "I cannot dress when you're in the room. You must step into the next room until I'm ready."

Gestapo Agent Herrmann Teege hesitated. He was confronted with the choice of waiting in the adjoining living-room or of having to drag a naked young woman out of bed.

"*Wie Sie wollen,*" he said. He lifted the child out of the cradle. With the still sleeping baby in his arms, he stepped into the living-room. "I better take care of the little one till you are ready," he announced.

Firelei now acted in wild violation of her own nature. She leaped out of bed, slipped on shoes and a coat and tiptoed to the second bedroom door, which led into the vestibule. In the other room, the Gestapo man was telephoning a nearby storm trooper station, requesting the assistance of a house-searching detachment. Firelei reached the front door and bolted down the staircase. The streets were still empty, except for occasional dockers on their way to work. She reached a small tobacco shop, the owner of which was a friend.

The shopkeeper led her to the apartment in which I found her. There Firelei had collapsed. There, under the care of a robust mother of many children, she was consoled with maternal persistence.

"Don't worry, don't worry," the woman murmured. "They wouldn't harm a baby. Just wait. You just wait till they've finished searching the house, the *dreckigen Hunde*. And when they've gone away, why—I'll go there myself and get your baby back. I'd like to see who'd dare to stop me! Nobody'd stop a woman like me. I'd show them. Now, my girl, you just be still and wait."

The scene was typical, I felt, of what was happening that very instant all over the German land. We waited. A feeble sun was crawling over the grimy tenement walls. Toward eleven I sent a youngster from the street unit to investigate. He pinned a swastika badge to his coat-lapel and sauntered away. After many endless minutes he returned.

"They're now searching the whole house," he reported, "and the houses on both sides of it. There's one Gestapo *Schwein* and nine storm troopers who do the snooping, and a car full of Gestapo men around the corner, waiting for trouble."

I detailed the youngster and two others to keep the house and the raiders under observation. Then I hurried to a house on a dismal alley which bore the strange name *Herrlichkeit*. Here was the secret district headquarters of the Red Front Fighters' League. But for an elderly liaison-man and three couriers—a girl of perhaps seventeen and two boys of fourteen and fifteen— the house was empty.

I wanted ten men with guns to create a diversion, to lure the Gestapo away from the Schaarmarkt into one of the old side-streets, so that one of my friends could dash upstairs and take away the child. The young couriers were eager to help. But the grizzled liaison-man shook his head.

"Comrade, you know that we cannot take orders from anybody," he said stolidly. "Our orders come from the *Gauleitung*. Those are the only orders we follow."

"Where can I contact Fiete Schulz?" I demanded. Schulz was the military chief of the Gauleitung, the successor to Edgar Andree.

The liaison-man smiled. "That I cannot tell you. You don't belong to Comrade Fiete's *Apparat*."

All my further arguments proved futile. The Red Front League squads were busy elsewhere. They would not imperil one of their men to salvage a baby. In the underground, I found, small children were dangerous ballast.

It was afternoon before I returned to the apartment of the robust woman. Firelei was not there. The woman said she had found some odd clothes for Firelei, who had then disguised herself by wearing her hair high under an old-fashioned hat, and by putting on eye-glasses and rubbing her face with fine ashes, which made her look older. She had gone away with the young comrade from the street unit.

"You better hurry," the woman told me.

I cast caution to the winds. I rushed to Schaarmarkt. In the center of the cobbled square, a flight of stairs led down to a public lavatory. I descended several steps until my eyes were level with the ground. So hidden, I scanned the sidewalk. I saw Firelei. She was walking slowly past the house which held our apartment. The house was silent now. No Brownshirts were in sight. Swastika flags hung limply on scores of poles protruding from windows.

As Firelei walked past the house, her eyes were directed upward to the windows of our apartment. She continued to the next corner, paused restlessly, and then retraced her steps, again passing the house, again scanning the apparently silent windows. She walked fifty yards past the house and then suddenly entered a hallway. I strode up the steps and toward the same hallway, forcing myself to walk leisurely. At the bottom of a semi-dark staircase I saw Firelei speaking to my young helper.

"Go away from here," I said nervously. "This is madness."

"I have to get my child," Firelei said firmly. "He's lying on the window sill. He is crying."

"And who else is there?"

"I don't know. Everything else is so quiet."

"Where are our watchers? Did you see the Nazis leave?" I asked the young communist.

"Two troopers went away with the car. They had it packed high with things they took."

"And the others? The Gestapo man?"

"I don't know."

"Don't go into the house," I said. "They've set a trap. They're probably hiding in the rooms, waiting for us to come for the baby."

"They put him on the window sill. He's hungry. He cries!" Firelei muttered. She clenched her fists. *"The beasts, oh, the beasts!"*

She wanted to go into the house.

"Don't go," I pleaded. "They'll arrest you."

"They wouldn't allow you to have your baby in jail with you," the young comrade said.

We stood in the hallway, not knowing what to do. A man passed on his way upstairs. His clothes smelled of stale beer.

"He looked at us," the youngster whispered. "We can't stay here longer."

Firelei said through clenched teeth, "If I ever get my Jan back, I shall teach him how to hate."

These were terrible words to come from the tender lips of Firelei.

"The man looked at us," the young communist repeated. "I tell you, we can't stay here any longer."

"I stay," Firelei said. "He was only a workman."

I could not budge her. There were pressing matters to which I had to attend. Already I had lost the greater part of the day. I felt that nothing could be done about our child. If the Gestapo agents got tired of lurking behind the curtains, they would take our son with them. I had an appointment with a Party member, who was a photographer, about the installation of a new printing plant in his *atelier*.

"I must go," I said painfully.

"Well, then go."

"You promise me to do nothing foolish?"

"I promise," Firelei said.

"This neighborhood is dangerous. Never forget that too many people know you here."

"I know. I shall do nothing foolish."

I gave Firelei most of the money I carried in my pockets. We agreed on a place where we could contact one another—the reading room of the City Museum, any day between two and three. We parted, not knowing whether we should ever see each other again.

I resolved to organize the new printing establishment of our harbor units on a basis of utmost decentralization, as the best safeguard against catastrophes-to-come. Each phase in the production of propaganda material had to be worked out in a separate place. There was one for the writing of copy, another for paper storage, a third for the typewriters, a fourth for the printing paraphernalia and a fifth as a depot for printed material awaiting distribution. No comrade working in one shop was to know the location of the other stations, and each two stations required a separate courier service. I forced my thoughts away from my personal troubles. Even so small a task as the purchase of a hundred thousand sheets of paper was fraught with danger and claimed total attention. All paper stores were under Gestapo surveillance, and the merchants had been instructed to report the names and addresses of all quantity purchasers of paper. It was exceptionally hard to find a man inconspicuous and courageous enough to go to a dealer to buy paper. But after much diligent and cautious searching I found Jan Templin, a foreman in the stevedoring firm *Einheit*—Unity—which handled the discharging and loading of Soviet ships.

Templin was a fine figure of a man, gray-eyed, blond-haired, and as sound as a full grown oak. Together we walked down a lonely street, a courier preceding us, and another following to warn us in time against the sudden appearance of a raiding squad. Jan Templin rumbled with discontent.

"By the grave of Karl Liebknecht," he swore, "I've three apartments crowded with big Comintern uncles, and I don't know what to do with them. They came scuttling from Berlin and now they want me to smuggle them out on Russian ships. The lot of 'em is so scared they'll dirty their pants when they see a brown shirt fluttering from a line."

I laughed. His wrath was funny, I thought.

"Who are they?" I could not help asking. Templin growled: "Never mind the names. If I only could put the whole lot in a sack and drown them. What do the bastards think? Can I shake Soviet steamers out of my sleeves?"

"That's your problem," I said. "My problem is paper."

"Paper!"

"Yes. Where can I buy it without being grabbed on the spot?"

"Buy it?"

"What else? Have you paper to give away?"

"Any amount," Jan Templin said.

"A hundred thousand sheets?"

"Sure."

He had forgotten his own problem. His eyes shone. His eyes shone because his imagination told him that the paper he could give me would be used to print appeals of resistance and sabotage and would soon find its way into cargo sheds, forecastles and hiring-halls. The *Einheit* was more than a stevedoring firm; it was a pillar of revolutionary conspiracy disguised as a commercial enterprise. Longshoremen who were not communists could find no employment in the *Einheit*. The firm's work gangs had long been organized along military lines. Often they were employed in all manner of perilous work as the price they had to pay for the privilege of earning their pay on Soviet ships. From Jan Templin I learned that the *Einheit* crew had successfully plundered a paper warehouse in the free-port zone. He spoke the truth when he said that he had "any amount" of paper at hand. The paper had been smuggled ashore past the customs after Templin's men had hidden it in the coal bunkers of tugboats manned by communists.

I received the needed consignment of paper, and found a storeroom for it in a basement under a baker's shop. I hired a pushcart to transport the paper. The contraband, once aboard the vehicle, was covered with three hundred pounds of potatoes, and two of my assistants pushed it to its destination. The same potatoes I used the following day to camouflage the transport of an electrically driven multigraph machine. The machine had previously been the property of a Party unit of white-collar workers, all of whom had been arrested. I mounted the machine in a dark room, adjoining a photographer's *atelier* on the top floor of a building on the Reeperbahn. This seemed an ideal spot for a secret printing plant. The *atelier* had two entrances. The front stairs led to the Reeperbahn, the back stairs into a courtyard opening on a sidestreet. I saw to it that an electric button was installed in the photographer's apartment, connecting it to a buzzer in the dark room. The men engaged in printing could thus be warned by the photographer should raiders enter the latter's apartment. I again appointed Alexander Popovics as head printer. He caressed the almost new machine as if it were his own child.

"Now we are ready again," he said happily. "You write—I print."

Of Firelei and the child I heard and saw nothing for two days. The reorganization of my propaganda *Apparat* had been accomplished without further arrests. All the old addresses, as far as they were known by the captured comrades, had been abandoned. New contact stations had been established, new meeting-places and passwords fixed, new cover addresses found for communication with the hundreds of communist ship units—strongholds which had remained practically untouched by the Gestapo drives. The first large edition of a new leaflet, entitled "The Hooked Cross is a Hunger Cross," was being launched under Popovics' tireless hands. And still there was no word from Firelei.

I met her again on the fourth day after the invasion of our former home by the Gestapo. I saw her sitting at a reading-room table in the City Museum, turning the pages of a large book containing reproductions of Albrecht Dürer's paintings. Her face looked drawn, but her hands were steady and her eyes serene. That she was there, safe for the moment, was like a miracle. That instant I pledged myself never to leave her alone again.

"You see," she smiled. "I can take care. I have done nothing foolish."

"Tell me."

She had roused a dozen people, who were not members of the Party, a grocer, a seamstress, a truck driver, a tailor's daughter, and others who had learned to like Firelei from previous association and were willing to do her a favor. Every few hours she had found someone else, and her request had always been the same: "My child is up there in the house. Please go and take him to your home until I call for him." One after another those friendly people had tramped up to the second floor, where our little Jan had last been seen squirming on the window sill. And none of the merciful rescuers returned.

"Our apartment was like a hungry maw," Firelei said. "Many people went in—none came out. The Gestapo just kept them there, and hoped that one of us would come in the end."

After three days of waiting the man hunters had tired. They had slashed the beds, broken the furniture, torn pictures off the walls. All my books, photographs and manuscripts they had carried away with them, together with a radio and other objects of value. They had found nothing. I had taken good care to clear my rooms of all incriminating matter. The people Firelei had sent into the house were then set free after each had submitted to a parting kick. The Gestapo crew departed, leaving the wreckage, and announcing that they would send a city nurse for the child.

The seamstress, a plucky girl named Lieschen, had then returned to our apartment and escaped with the baby.

"I gave Lieschen my last money," Firelei said, "to take our son to my relatives in Hannover."

She could not hide how hard it was for her to part from the child. I pretended not to notice her anguish. I spoke of work that was to be done. She listened as if nothing else existed for her. "You are my comrade," I said.

"Aye," she nodded. "Back to the trenches."

Chapter Twenty-eight

DEAD MEN ON FURLOUGH

I was called to Berlin. Walter Duddins, the swarthy Rhinelander who had succeeded the too-well-known Reichstag deputy, Herrmann Schubert, as the political chief of the Hamburg Party organization, conveyed the order to me. I had met him for a seemingly innocent stroll through the dark Stadtpark. He gave me a password, an address in Berlin-Neukoelln, and told me where and when a motorcycle courier would be waiting to take me along. Of course, I received no inkling as to the nature of my mission.

"And Firelei?" I wanted to ask. I remembered the promise I had given myself.

The question, to communist ears, had too absurd a sound to be uttered aloud. The Party needed Firelei in Hamburg. If she left her post, she would be regarded as a deserter. And the new Party rule branded desertion as treason.

"All right," I said to Duddins.

"Hand over your *Apparat* to Comrade Otto. He has guts."

"Very well." Otto K. was my chief *aide-de-camp* in our maritime organization. He had won a reputation for engineering mutinies on German ships in American ports during the October strike of 1931.

"I warn you," Duddins concluded. "Not a word to anyone about what you will hear or see in Berlin."

I met the courier at noon. He was a young student who had abandoned the university to become a professional revolutionist. He wore the insignia of the monarchist Steel Helmets on his leather jacket.

"If we're stopped on the road," I instructed him, "we don't know a thing about each other. You picked me up at a gas station because I offered you ten marks to take me to Berlin."

"Very well."

Five minutes later we raced through the outskirts of Hamburg. Five hours later, without a stop, we entered Berlin. The student drove to a branch hostelry of the Y.M.C.A., where we dismounted in the courtyard.

"I'll stop off here for two days," the student said. "If you need me, ask for Herr Gerdes."

I chose crowded street-cars for my journey to Neukoelln, an industrial suburb known as the "barricade quarter." The city of Berlin itself was full of Hitler guards; their brown and black uniforms flashed up in every block. But out in the treeless, stone desert of Neukoelln, Nazi uniforms were rare. Here no storm trooper dared to walk alone. They marched in closed groups of six or more, keeping well in the middle of the street. Even policemen patrolled their beats in pairs, armed to the teeth and ready for instant action.

I entered a three-story house. Apartment 4, Meyerhoff. I was aware of a familiar tenseness. My heartbeat became quick and short. One never knew when one rang a bell whether a friend still lived behind the door, or whether the Gestapo lay in ambush there. 1 rang the bell. A little boy opened the door. Seeing a stranger, he slammed it immediately.

"Papa!" I heard him cry.

Heavier footsteps approached. I saw a short man with an unshaven chin. The man was in shirtsleeves. From a door, at the end of the corridor, a woman's face peered at me. The man switched on a bulb which left me standing in a brilliant light, while he himself remained in the half-dark.

"What do you want?"

I gave him the password, which ran: "I've read your ad. I'd like to look at the stamps you have for sale."

"You're a dealer?"

"No, an amateur."

"Come in!"

The man led me into a neatly furnished room. "Sit down," he said. Out of a locker he drew a folder. It contained a stamp collection. "When you hear the doorbell ring, appear to be studying the stamps,' he advised me. "Nowadays you never know. I'm going to shave."

After the man had shaved and dressed, he left the house alone. About an hour later he returned.

"Let's go," he said. "Don't walk together with me. Walk ten paces behind. Stop when you see me put my right hand in my pocket. You'll notice a young woman. When I put both hands in my pockets, don't wait—beat it! "

"All right."

We strode through many streets, turning many corners. Each time, before my guide rounded a corner, he pretended to be looking at a street-sign to make sure that no shadowers followed us. Finally he walked into a small *Konditorei*. A few seconds later he reappeared, continuing for ten paces. He halted to look at a shop window. Slowly his right hand went into his coat pocket. I stopped. I was standing in front of the little *Konditorei*. A tall girl, a complete stranger, stepped out of the café. She greeted me cheerfully. "Hallo, I've been waiting for you." She hooked her arm into mine. Together we crossed the street like old acquaintances. I glanced back over my shoulder. The man who had led me here had disappeared. His part in the devious mechanism of conspirative communication had ended.

Again we walked in circles. The girl was chatting animatedly about Marlene Dietrich. Abruptly she piloted me into a restaurant, where a bevy of streetcar conductors was at supper. After she had finished her coffee, she shook hands with me.

"Linger until someone you know gives you a sign," she said in parting, and vanished.

I was alone for a while. People came and went, and I briefly scanned each new face for a sign of recognition. Outside, the street lamps were switched on, a radio played, and from the kitchen came the clatter of dishes. Then a slender young woman in black stepped in. She moved with poise. Her face was cool and well chiseled, and she had shapely legs. She sat down at a table near the entrance and ordered salad and tea. I knew her. She was Cilly. The mission on which I had been called to Berlin became clear to me: I was to meet Ernst Wollweber.

Cilly ate leisurely. After she had lit a cigarette, she occupied herself with playfully building a tiny tower of the spice-containers on her table. A motion of her knee jarred the table, the tower collapsed. I watched every one of her motions. She made an apparently inadvertent gesture of mock despair in my direction. It was the signal. Soon she departed. I paid the waiter, got up and followed her.

It was quite dark now. We boarded a taxi, and changed to another one in the clangor of the Friedrichstrasse.

"You may sleep, if you wish to," Cilly said slowly. "We have a long ride."

Nothing more was said. The tenseness had left me. I lay back, watching the dim shape of the driver in front. At times my eyes wandered sideways to where Cilly relaxed, serene as if she were returning home from the theater. Streets rushed past. Trees and houses spun by. We were traveling south-west, toward Zehlendorf. At the edge of Zehlendorf, in front of a modern apartment house, the driver stopped.

Cilly paid the chauffeur and stepped through the portal. Again I followed her. She ushered me into a ground floor apartment. The furniture was simple, but new. The papered walls were bare and the kitchen was empty. There was nothing to indicate that anyone lived there.

"Please wait," Cilly said. "I must inform Comrade Ernst that you are here."

Again I was alone. After a while the front door clicked. An agile, powerfully-built man entered noiselessly. I had seen him before. He was one of the Berlin-Moscow couriers of the Western Secretariat, and his name was Max. In bygone years he had been an instructor in jiu-jitsu for the Berlin police. He saluted me vigorously.

"Our friend is downstairs," he said. "He doesn't like to talk between four walls. Remember this house; when you're done, come back here."

A burly figure was waiting in front of the house. Only the glow of a cigarette showed that it was alive. So I met Wollweber in the shadows of Berlin under Hitler. He grunted with pleasure. Side by side we walked toward Zehlendorf Forest and the Grunewald.

"Sometimes," Wollweber said in a low steady voice, "the best plans are wrecked by unexpected happenings. But that's no reason for becoming panicky. In the end, we're going to win. 'Nobody ever killed his successor.' Machiavelli said that, and he knew what he was talking about." And in a growl, he added: "Tell me what you know about Hamburg."

I told him all I knew. Wollweber listened, his eyes staring ahead into the blackness against which were silhouetted the naked trees. After I had given my report, he asked questions. His questions were precise, and they demanded precise answers. His grasp of detail always astonished me anew. His interest in a new printing device or a new technique of propaganda distribution was as intense as his interest in the central action committees and the newly created net of sabotage units. It was characteristic of Wollweber that he showed no anxiety at all about the fate of the frightened Comintern emissaries, who had evacuated Berlin post-haste to wait for Soviet ships in Jan Templin's relay stations in Hamburg.

"They were a nuisance anyway," Wollweber commented. "Today one good little comrade in Germany is worth ten big ones abroad." And he went on:

"Things are not as bad as they might have been. Anyone who knows the Nazis can't be surprised by their methods. 10,000 comrades are now in thirty-two concentration camps. Last week, 247 comrades were murdered in Berlin. That is terrible, but not bad—considering the size of our organization. There will be more. Certainly. The cost is always high when a mass party changes from a legal status to an illegal existence. On the other hand, the Gestapo could have shot or hanged the whole 30,000. We must never forget that! The greatest danger for the movement is not the Gestapo. The greatest danger is panic."

Ernst Wollweber had the calmness of a rock.

"And the greatest mistake we can make today," he continued, "is to imitate the illegal methods the Bolsheviki used before the Soviet victory. The Gestapo is not the Ochrana. The Czarist Black Hundreds were laggards in comparison to the Elite Guards we've got to deal with. As compared with the Gestapo terror, the Ochrana terror was a holiday. We must shake off imitation in our practical working methods. We must fight Hitler with modern methods, and, if necessary, we must change our methods from day to day. That is why I called you to Berlin. The comrades must be prepared until they reach the point where no sudden change of policy or method will surprise them. Stubborn heads will have to be broken." Wollweber talked on. After each sentence he paused for my assent. It was long before I realized that he was sounding me out about my attitude toward Party discipline in general, and my subservience to the dictatorship of Wollweber in particular. I did not question his motives. But I understood that he was possessed by an implacable distrust of all who had been part and parcel of the old leadership of the German Communist Party. Many of the old leaders had been arrested, most of those still at large had escaped from Germany, and overnight Ernst Wollweber had become the responsible commander and the leading organizer of the new underground movement. He was a man determined to refuse to co-operate with anyone in the Party who did not unconditionally do his bidding. More than ever he resembled a chunky, formidable caricature of Stalin. It was impossible to tell where political motives ended and the personal ones began in him. It was almost impossible to predict his plans until the very last moment before their realization. One thing was certain, a ship captained by Ernst Wollweber must be manned, from chief mate to cabin boy, by Wollweber's trusted creatures.

He wanted a change of leadership in the Hamburg Party organization, which was next in importance only to that of Berlin. Walter Duddins, he intimated, had to go; a man named John Scheer was to be his successor. The task for which Wollweber had singled me out was to contact Comrade Scheer with the key functionaries of the Hamburg *Apparat*, without the knowledge of their chief— Walter Duddins. Thus, after thorough preparation, Duddins could be isolated by one quick coup. Duddins, who had been a Reichstag member, had had an international education. He was respected for his fearlessness and his ability. But he regarded Wollweber as "a peasant." And the only explanation which the saturnine ex-mutineer ever gave for his antagonism to Duddins was a growled, "Comrade Walter is a reckless opportunist." Wollweber would go to Hamburg himself to install John Scheer at the head of a reshuffled leadership.

The grim conversation ended. My chief stood leaned against the trunk of a big tree, and his slit-eyes peered up at my face from behind the glow of his cigarette. For a moment we stood in silence.

Then Wollweber said raucously: "Have you heard the latest German joke?"

"No."

"Who is the most desirable woman in the Third Reich?"

"I don't know."

"The 'Aryan' grandmother," he guffawed.

We parted at the edge of the Grunewald. The woods were deserted, the night warm and pitch-black. As I strode away, Ernst Wollweber's mirthless guffaw still ringing in my ears, I was glad to be alone.

Very late I returned to the house in Zehlendorf. Max and two other men were there, all in pajamas, playing cards in a back room.

"You look glum," Max told me. "Anybody bite you?"

"I want to sleep," I answered. "I never thought the chief could walk for hours at a stretch."

"The chief can do many things." Max laughed. "The comrades who come here to have a talk with the chief go out into the woods like matadors, and back they come like pallbearers. Come on, I'll show you your bed."

He led me to a spacious bedroom. Like the other rooms I had seen, it showed no trace of having been inhabited, except for a faint scent which reminded me of wild roses.

"Take off your shoes," Max cautioned me. "The folks below us will think we're counterfeiters, tramping around like that in the night."

"What's this perfume?" I asked. "I've smelled it before."

"Cilly sleeps here sometimes when the chief is out of town," Max replied matter-of-factly.

We were on the train to Hamburg: Wollweber, John Scheer, Cilly and I. It was not the express I had used so often in safer times. Prudence forbade hunted men to show their faces at any central railway station. We traveled from Berlin to Spandau on the inter-urban railway, and in Spandau we had boarded a local train which would permit us to get off at Bergedorf, a suburb of Hamburg, and thus avoid the Gestapo blockade of the Hamburg terminal station. Wollweber and I were in different compartments of the same coach, while John Scheer and Cilly were in another coach at the rear end of the train. Wollweber and Cilly traveled on Danish passports, I posed as a Belgian, and Comrade Scheer carried the credentials of a merchant from Minneapolis. John Scheer was a distinguished-looking man of thirty-six, with sharply-cut features and clear eyes. Dressed in Nelson blue, he had the appearance of a naval officer in mufti.

The journey was tedious. The train was fairly crowded with local travelers, among them a number of storm troopers from the country districts, and every few miles it stopped at obscure Elb-country stations. In Berlin I had bought one of the Parisian metropolitan dailies. At every station, I used its comfortable size to shut myself from the view of passengers and officials on the platforms. Neither I nor, I am sure, any of my fellow voyagers, suspected that the Gestapo had just evolved a new wrinkle in raiding technique.

The train was approaching Ludwigslust, a small town eighty miles from Hamburg, and not far from Bismarck's tomb. The engine shrieked, slowed down, and the train stopped as it had done at all the other stations on the line. As before, I spread out my paper and raised it until its center was on a level with my eyes and waited, pretending to read, for the train to move on.

The train did not move. I was shocked by a petty-officer's voice barking in from the platform:

"Alles aussteigen! All passengers leave the train!"

There was a stir and a scraping of feet and excited whispers. I looked up.

The train was surrounded by Brownshirts. They wore around their sleeves the white band of Goering's auxiliary police. Their pistols half protruded from their holsters, and the storm bands of their caps were strapped tight under their chins. I saw my fellow travelers scramble out of the coaches. Some joked, others asked nervous questions, a few looked frankly aghast at the raiders. I shuddered inwardly. "What now?" I thought. *"Das Spiel ist aus!"*

I thought of a sad and beautiful song which Firelei liked to sing. "Farewell, green earth." That was its first line.

Once more came the strident command: "Passengers must leave the train!"

Ten feet away, Ernst Wollweber stood on the platform, black eyes blinking in the sunlight. He held a match to his cigarette, and his eyes followed a cloud of tobacco smoke as it dissolved in the clear morning.

I jumped out of the compartment. I jostled past Wollweber, and in doing so I stepped on his toes I raised my hat. *"Verzeihung,"* I said. "I beg your pardon."

"Keep your nerve," the chief muttered. "These fellows know nothing."

Then we drifted apart. I fell toward the rear of the train, hoping to discover a loophole. The ring of storm troopers was closed. Anyone foolish enough to break through it would go down under their bullets. Storm troopers stamped through the coaches, looked into the tool-rooms and the lavatories. At the far end of the train, Cilly stood chatting with a Brownshirt. Cilly had thrown her head back to show her long white throat, and the Nazi grinned appreciatively. John Scheer was striding briskly toward the locomotive, looking neither right nor left, putting as much distance between himself and Wollweber as he possibly could.

For no reason I followed John Scheer. I patted my chest where the good Belgian passport rested. It was as important to me now as a flimsy raft is to a castaway in midocean. Suddenly I knew why I was following John Scheer. The crazy idea had seized me that Comrade Scheer was a locomotive engineer, and that he was about to board the locomotive and give her full steam ahead. Of course, he did not do it. He planted himself beside the engineer's cab, crossed his hands behind his back, and stared haughtily over the heads of the Brownshirts. I turned. Ernst Wollweber's face was a sullen mask. He was lighting another cigarette. I had a curious thought, one which had nothing to do with the immediate danger. "Our aim is in a haze," I thought, "the movement is becoming an aim in itself."

A voice, sounding as if it came through a megaphone, announced: "All passengers line up! Produce identifications!"

A small table stood at the end of the platform. On the table lay what looked like a book of medium size. Sitting on chairs behind the table were two young men in civilian clothes—Gestapo agents. Strung out in a single file in front of the table was the line of passengers. Among the first ten was John Scheer. Five or six passengers stood between him and myself. Toward the end of the line stood Wollweber, and behind him, almost a head taller, Cilly. A small distance away from the table, overlooking the whole scene, stood a tall young man with flashing blue eyes and an air of arrogant superiority. He wore no uniform, but in his coat lapel was the officer's insignia of the Elite Guards. He was the official in charge of operations.

"Step forward!"

To confront the Gestapo in broad daylight is a far different experience than to thwart and combat it out of the dark. I had no urge to see what was happening to Wollweber and Cilly. All my effort was concentrated on appearing unperturbed, and my glance was fixed on the table in front.

The examination began. One by one the passengers stepped up to the table, showing identification papers and giving answers to curt questions. Meanwhile a detachment of storm troopers was going through the baggage which had been left in the compartments. Several travelers in front displayed membership cards of the Nazi Party. They were passed without molestation. Somewhere behind me a man collapsed. He was a Jew. Two troopers bent down to run their hands through his pockets. Then they led him back to the train. The Brownshirts were polite. They brought chairs from the waiting room and offered them to elderly women. The line grew shorter.

Now came John Scheer's turn. He flipped his American passport on the table and looked disinterestedly into the sky. One of the Gestapo a g e n t s scrutinized the passport; the other thumbed through the book which contained lists of names and occasional photographs.

"*Sprechen Sie Deutsch?*"

John Scheer shook his head. "I speak English," he said.

The Gestapo man asked in bad English: "Why are you traveling in Germany?"

"Tourist," said John Scheer.

"You travel alone?"

"Yes."

"What is your business in America?"

"I have a steam laundry."

"What do you intend to do in Hamburg?"

"Take ship for New York," John Scheer said.

"How much money have you?"

"Ninety marks."

"Oh, you have bought your steamer ticket?"

"Right."

"Please show it," the Gestapo man demanded.

"I do not have it here, a friend has it in Hamburg," Comrade Scheer explained.

"Give the name and address of your friend."

Scheer gave a name at random, and the name of a street which did not exist. The Gestapo agent who had been thumbing through the suspect list made a pencil note.

"Thank you," said John Scheer.

He stalked away. He had not progressed six steps toward the train when one of the Gestapo men called after him: *"Aber Sie haben etwas vergessen?"* (But you have forgotten something.) Comrade Scheer had left his American passport on the table. He whirled and came back, his arm outstretched. The Gestapo agent grabbed the passport.

"I thought you couldn't understand German?" he rasped.

John Scheer looked at his fingernails. "A little I understand," he said.

The Gestapo officer who had so far kept aloof from the proceedings intervened. *"Ist hier ein Nationalsozialist der Amerikanish sprechen kann?"* (Is there a National Socialist present who speaks "American"?) he called into the line of waiting travelers. There were two Nazis who could speak "American." John Scheer's body sagged visibly. His face grew stark. The Nazi travelers talked to him in English. He tried to answer.

"Dieser Herr ist bestimmt kein Amerikaner" (This gentleman is surely no American), one of the Nazis announced. John Scheer's English was bad, and without an American accent.

"Sorry, we must detain you. Any baggage?"

Two storm troopers escorted Comrade Scheer into the waiting-room. Again he walked erect. It was the last I saw of him. Months later came the news that he had been murdered. No one except his killers knew how he died.

The examination continued. Except for a dull ache in my eyes I had already forgotten John Scheer. It was my turn now. Two men and a woman were now the only people between myself and the table. My passport, I knew, had a flaw. If expert hands took the second page of the passport and held it up against the light, expert eyes could easily see a spot where the paper was thinner, where the old photograph had been washed off and the new, my own, had been fastened in its stead. The man in front of me was being questioned. Mechanically I listened to his answers. He was Austrian, on the way to visit his married sister in the old town of Lauenburg. Throughout the inquisition he shifted from one foot to the other.

"*Schoen,* you may go back to the train."

The Austrian departed with alacrity.

"Next!"

I stepped forward and handed my passport to the Gestapo man. The other, after a quick glance at my face, was again thumbing through the list of wanted men. A little way off their superior stood like a statue.

"*Sprechen Sie Deutsch?*"

"*Jawohl!*" I was calm now. The clammy fear had gone.

"Are you traveling alone?"

"Yes, sir."

"For what purpose are you in Germany?"

"I am a seaman. I left my ship in Danzig. I am on my way back to Belgium to find myself another ship."

The Gestapo agent looked up. "What was the name of your ship?"

"*Yser,* of Antwerp," I said. "A Belgian ship."

"Why is there no Polish transit visa in your passport?" His finger stabbed at a blank page of my document.

"The Belgian consul in Danzig sent me by ship to Stettin. There I took a train."

"Show your ticket!"

Luckily, on Wollweber's advice, I had bought a through ticket from Berlin to Hamburg *Hauptbahnhof.*

"Why are you going to Hamburg?"

"My consul in Hamburg will ship me to Antwerp. It is cheaper than going by train."

"Have you been in Germany before this?"

"Only aboard ships."

The Gestapo man seemed satisfied. He looked at his colleague who had closed the book and shook his head slightly. He had found nothing.

A question, shot at me all of a sudden, almost took me off guard. "Why are you using the local train to ride from Berlin to Hamburg?"

"It's cheaper," I said. "My consul would not pay the express train tax."

"How much money have you?"

"Forty-three marks."

"Where did you learn to speak German?"

"My mother was from Eupen. I lived there many years. The district was German before Versailles was signed."

"Ah, then you are almost a *Volksgenosse* (comrade)?"

"Yes, sir."

"Thank you, you may go back to the train."

It was over. I was afraid that I was walking too fast toward my compartment. I was afraid I would break into a run. I forced myself to walk slowly, in a manner I thought would look casual to sharp-eyed observers. Back on the train I thought of Ernst Wollweber. He would never pass. If anyone's photograph was in the suspect list on that table, it must be Wollweber's. I lowered the window of my compartment and glued my eyes to the chief. I held on to the sides of the window. The compressed excitement which filled me like liquid stone imparted to me the sensation of being in danger of floating off the floor of the coach.

Ernst Wollweber was smoking steadily. He gave no sign of agitation. His short, thick-set shape appeared harmless and insignificant between Cilly's tall elegance in the rear of him, and the large man in front of him, whose coarse face and heavy watch-chain conveyed the impression of a butter-and-egg man, or a horse-trader.

The line grew shorter. Two men who had no identification papers were led off to the waiting-room. An hour, perhaps, had passed since the train had been stopped. The Gestapo officer grew impatient. He marched down the length of the still waiting line of passengers, motioning the women and a few children to go back to the train. Among those who went was Cilly. She walked to her compartment gracefully, leisurely. A score of male travelers remained in the line. The last of them was Ernst Wollweber. His head had become restless on his chunky shoulders. His small feet fidgeted on the concrete. Death, to him, was fifty feet away.

The drab station and the blue sky, the trees and the houses and the locomotive—they all seemed to ask, "Comrade Ernst... What now?"

Then something astonishing happened. Ernst Wollweber limped out of line. His face was screwed into an apologetic grin. He limped straight toward the tall young Gestapo officer, bowed clumsily, handed him the light-gray Danish passport. An instant, the two were engaged in conversation. The Gestapo agents at the table, seeing the squat little passenger talking to their superior, did not bother to call him back into the line—nor did they dare to question him. I could not hear what was said. They talked animatedly, Wollweber with a strange show of respect, the Gestapo officer in a jovially patronizing manner. His gloved hand patted Wollweber's shoulder after it had handed the Danish passport back to him.

The examination of the remaining passengers was almost completed. The Gestapo officer escorted Wollweber to his compartment, chatting all the while. Moving over to the next window, I heard fragments of their talk.

"*Gruessen Sie unsere Blutsbrueder* (greetings to our blood-brothers) in Nord-Schleswig" he was saying. "The New Germany does not forget its sons beyond the frontier line. *Gute Reise! Gute Reise!* (happy journey.)"

A sergeant's voice barked: *"Alles fertig!* (all's ready.)"

The train began to move slowly. The Gestapo officer stood at attention. His right arm flew up in a straight line.

"*Auf Wiedersehen!* Heil Hitler!"
"Heil Hitler," Wollweber answered, without stirring a finger.

In a vegetarian restaurant in Bergedorf the chief ordered Cilly to return to Berlin immediately. Cover addresses, depots, illegal residences, liaison stations—all such cogs of the underground machine, as far as they were known to John Scheer, had to be changed without delay, before Comrade Scheer's resistance could be broken by the Gestapo.

Later, in Hamburg, I asked Wollweber: "How did you do it?"

"Do what?"

"On the train—in Ludwigslust?"

The Silesian gave one of his sardonic grins.

"I let him know I had gout," he said, "found it hard to stand so long in line. I told him I was a German Dane come south to convince myself that the atrocity tales in the foreign press were Jewish propaganda. The fellow was flattered. He swallowed it. He had pride, a pride as big as a house."

"If Comrade Scheer had had that idea," I observed, "they would have taken you."

Half in scorn, half mockingly, Ernst Wollweber muttered: "Why should they take me? ... You know, most fellows have a hidden crack in their head. You don't see it till it's too late. In one wrong moment they do the one wrong thing, and that ends the infernal *Mummenschanz* (masquerade)."

For the rest of the day he dismissed from his mind all the underground problems. He locked himself into the room I had procured for him in a worker's dwelling near the Hamburg airport. There, in solitude, he drank many bottles of Patzenhofer beer.

But Wollweber's presence in Hamburg soon electrified the Party and the Gestapo. The survivors of the old bureaucratic Party *Apparat*, trembling for their chance of honorable retirement in the Soviet Union, developed a sudden suicidal bravado in an effort to prove to their chief that Hamburg was still the Reddest town outside of Russia. The younger, and often hardier communists in the lower Party committees, who saw themselves as the heirs and the shock-brigadiers of the newly-formed underground movement, set out with elan to show Ernst Wollweber that the old leadership had been irretrievably outdistanced by events. Anyone outside of the Bolshevik movement would have regarded such rivalry for control of a doomed cause as a weird race for the privilege of dying painfully. To the cynic, it was nothing but evidence, written in blood, that even among the living dead the fight for meager rations is far fiercer than the battle for pots that are well filled.

The city of Hamburg echoed with communist demonstrations, and clouds of crimson leaflets descended from the housetops at hours when the streets below were most crowded. The Gestapo struck with lightning speed. From Police Headquarters reports filtered through that the masses of prisoners were made to suffer under the persistent accompaniment of the question: "Well, *du Kommunistenschwein*, are you ready to tell us now where Ernst Wollweber is?"

Hugo Marx, and Fritz Luchs, the heads of the Hamburg G.P.U. *Apparat*, were arrested. Walter Duddins was seized, and a thousand others. Marx hanged himself in his cell. Fritz Luchs was beaten to death. Duddins went to prison, convicted of treason. Wollweber survived. No one, except perhaps his superiors in the Comintern, and Max, the leader of his bodyguard, knew the sum total of his comings and goings. In the course of a single day, Ernst Wollweber conferred with a special "transport commission" of the Comintern press service, with a Russian who had come to Hamburg as a radio operator aboard a Soviet ship, and with a disagreeable ruffian named Rudolf Heitman, who was a Gestapo agent on the payroll of the G.P.U. Circulating among Party members was a new manifesto, issued by Wollweber, which began:

"Comrades! Our retreat has ended. Another offensive begins. A military command begins a war with an army ready at hand; the Party must create its army in the course of the struggle itself."

The new offensive, however, ended in Hitler's prison camps. To close one's eyes to the fact of defeat became the criterion of loyalty. It was not permitted to ask, "Why?" It was treason to intimate that there had been mistakes in the general policy of the past. We were, I suspect, more afraid of facing the truth and the doubts in our own hearts than of facing the might of the Hitler guards and the Gestapo.

Early one morning, toward the end of March, my secret printing plant in the photographer's dark room was raided. The story of this raid is a tribute to the devoted heroism of Alexander Popovics. I had given the Roumanian a batch of instructions but a few short hours before the raid took place. He had the aspect of a man who had lived for weeks without a bath or decent food. But he was indomitable.

"We are all dead men on furlough," he had told Firelei. "But we can't quit, we'd die of shame. We'd lie awake at night and see the faces of all those who have disappeared stare at us from behind barred windows."

In that conspirative dark room atop a gloomy apartment house Firelei cut a most incongruous figure. Black paint covered the panes of the one window in the room. Blankets had been spread over all the walls to stifle the sounds of the thumping machine. And there was an electric bulb around which Firelei had tied a handkerchief to soften the glare. Firelei was twenty-six. She was slender and desirable, and she still adored the bright colors of summer. She seemed an utter stranger in the bleakness of a life of constant menace. Not her enthusiasm for the cause, but her love for me, had compelled her to take the irrevocable step. She had fought hard to conquer the fine rebellious strain in her nature. She won. She had become one of us, and she had never lost the sincere intensity of her emotions. The machine thumped, and clean printed sheets leaped out like so many eager animals. When a hundred were ready to be tied into a harmless-looking package, Popovics would raise his shaggy head and say with pride: "Ho! Comrade Firelei, look! Now say, 'Travel far, you good little papers.' "

And Firelei, to please him, would say softly: "Yes, travel far, you good little papers," and the Roumanian would grunt with pleasure and bend over his machine with renewed ferocity.

So I had left them, not long before midnight, Firelei, Comrade Alexander, and a young courier.

The story of the raid, which was one of thousands, came to me in fragments, partly from Firelei, partly from later fellow-prisoners who had talked with Popovics before he went to his death, and partly from the testimony given in a high treason trial in which I was one of the accused.

Between three and four o'clock in the morning, the house-watcher of a tenement building on the Reeperbahn dialed Number 0-0001—the number of the Gestapo. He reported a suspicious noise in the building assigned to his supervision. An old woman tenant had complained that the noise, which seemed to come through the ceiling of her bedroom, disturbed her sleep.

It was a faintly thumping noise, the house-watcher reported. It sounded as if someone was beating an orange against the floor.

Half an hour later a car from Gestapo Headquarters halted in front of the tenement building. Two men leaped from the car. They spoke to the house-watcher, and then they all went in and mounted the stairs.

Popovics was the first to hear the footfalls of the raiders. Instantly he stopped the machine.

"What is it, Alexander?" Firelei asked.

The buzzer signal from the adjoining photographer's apartment sounded a warning simultaneously with a battering against the door of the rambling *atelier*. Firelei stood bewildered. Popovics grasped her wrist and drew her toward the hidden backdoor on the far side of the *atelier*. The lock had been oiled; it yielded at once.

It was as if Popovics did exactly what he had planned to do in such an emergency. He pushed Firelei out on the dark landing, and said, "Run."

"But you?" Firelei gasped.

"I have business," Popovics replied.

The young courier had already darted, down the backstairs. Firelei slipped out into the darkness. Behind her, Popovics locked the door. Firelei had taken off her shoes. As she was running down toward the yard, she heard the front door being splintered. Popovics drew the key out of the back door, opened the window, and threw the key into the night.

The Roumanian then snatched a list of coded distribution addresses from its hiding-place behind the rafter. He tore it into little pieces and put them into his mouth. Then he hoisted himself out through the window onto a ledge, which ran along the base of the roof. He closed the window behind him and crept away on the ledge. Was he inviting capture to detract the Gestapo from Firelei? Or was he thinking of his own words, "We can't quit, we'd die of shame"?

The Gestapo was ransacking the *atelier* and the dark room. The photographer and his family were placed under arrest. Popovics continued to crawl along the edge of the roof. The stone was smooth and made the crawling slow. A drain pipe ran down at the end of the ledge. If he could only—

A man leaned far out of the window. Popovics was caught in the beam of a flashlight. He flattened himself against the ledge and lay still.

"Come back!" the man shouted.

Popovics did not move.

"Come back—or I shoot!"

So Popovics became a prisoner of the Gestapo. One of many thousands.

For many weeks I did not see Firelei again. We were torn apart, as many lovers in the movement had been torn asunder before our turn came. The Party sent her to Berlin. She was forbidden to tell me where she lived or what her assignment was. There was not even a farewell.

A day or two later, the steamer *Beira* entered Hamburg harbor. She was a Danish freighter trading regularly from Copenhagen. A member of the strong communist unit in the crew of this ship was a courier between the Western Secretariat and the Central Committee of the German Party. He brought me the order to transport the confidential shipping-files of the Seamen's International—ISH—safely from Hamburg to Copenhagen. The files had been in the possession of Albert Walter, the imprisoned chief of the Comintern's Maritime Section.

Through a girl courier I contacted the old sailor's mother. She was a frail old woman, but her militant spirit was intact. Of course, she declared, I could have the files, which contained information accumulated in years of persistent work by the harbor brigades of many ports. The files were in a camphor chest. The chest was hidden in the basement of a trawlerman's home in Altona. Beyond that old Frau Walter talked of nothing but her son, Albert, who had been her only child.

I found the camphor chest, and I guarded it as if it were the apple of my eye. With the assistance of a ship-chandler's runner, I smuggled it aboard the *Beira*. I endeavored to inform Ernst Wollweber that I was escorting the consignment to Copenhagen. Wollweber could not be found on such short notice; each week he shifted his headquarters, and contact with it could only be established through a complicated system of relay stations.

The passage to Copenhagen was quiet. The sudden relief from the nightmare of Germany left in doubt, at times, whether I was awake or dreaming. The enormous bulk of Richard Jensen awaiting me on the quay in Copenhagen jolted me: I was really awake.

Chapter Twenty-nine

IN THE LANDS OF TWILIGHT

Richard Jensen rolled his celebrated corpulence into the driver's seat of his new Renault. He chuckled with satisfaction. "Now that the lights have gone out in Berlin," he said, "Copenhagen will be the first capital after Moscow."

Copenhagen bubbled with light and the joy of springtime. The crowds who drank and danced and ate with gusto in the many pleasure palaces around Tivoli Park had no inkling of the dark forces that invaded their cheerful little Kingdom since the flames had burst through the dome of the German Reichstag. They were, like the citizens of their brother countries in the North, and of the great democracies of the West, quaintly unprepared to cope with the onslaught of forces which spoke of the emancipation of mankind, but meant seizure of power. The broad undertow running from Moscow had been diverted from its main course— Germany—and for the first time struck with full force the countries north of the Baltic and west of the Rhine.

Jensen laughed, "My wife complains: 'All day long they ring our door bell. Tovarish here, tovarish there. They come from Moscow, from Leningrad, from Berlin and Hamburg. They don't speak one word of Danish. Comrade Jensen, they say, fix us up with Danish passports.' So it goes!"

"And the police?"

"The police are harmless," Jensen assured me.

We were driving to the provisional offices, which the Westbureau of the Comintern, routed from Berlin, had established in Copenhagen at 42, Vimmelskaftet, under the camouflage of a firm of lawyers headed by Otto Melchior. It was easy to see why Copenhagen had been chosen as the pivotal point of the Comintern executive center abroad. The old road over Berlin was blocked by the Gestapo. Paris was too distant from Moscow, and the routes of communication around Germany too circuitous to commute to France in comfort and safety. The journey Moscow-Leningrad-Helsinki-Copenhagen led through relatively harmless countries. By train and boat, it could be made in forty-eight hours. The communist positions in the Scandinavian merchant fleets were strong, particularly in Denmark, and this made Copenhagen a suitable center for a world-wide network of conspirative marine communication. Moreover, the Danes were one of the most hospitable and liberal peoples on earth, and the amiable laissez-faire spirit of the Danish police had long been proverbial among Comintern men.

In the pseudo-law firm on Vimmelskaftet I met Georgi Dimitrov's temporary successor. Of Czech nationality, he was known in the Comintern as Walter Ulrich, alias Ulbricht, Leo, Urvich and Sorensen. In 1923, in Germany, he had been the chief of staff in the organization bureau of the Red Hundreds. He had now with him a smart young Pole, an emissary of Kommissarenko in Moscow, entrusted with the reorganization of the International of Seamen and Harbor Workers, which had been deprived of its most able head through the capture of Albert Walter by the Gestapo. Comrade Ulrich was a short man, with broad shoulders and a broad yet ascetic face, slow-moving and dark-skinned. He had deep-set intelligent brown eyes.

"I don't think you will go back to Germany," Ulrich told me. "We need you elsewhere. We are moving toward a new policy, directed against the bourgeois democracies. Our investment of energy there is bound to bring us ten times greater results than in Germany. Hitler's coming has radically changed the world-political situation. The so-called democracies are rotting alive. They offer us opportunities of bold expansion that will more than make up for the losses in the German retreat. We'll lay a Red ring around Germany, and—in good time—strangle Nazi power to death."

"The German Party expects me to return," I said. 'The Central Committee gave me no leave of absence."

Jensen yawned resoundingly. "That's all right. Copenhagen is now tops. We will send Wollweber a German comrade from the Lenin School to take your place."

"You're going to Sweden," Ulrich said.

A great shipping strike had broken out in Sweden, the greatest in the class-war history of that country. The strike was led by the socialist-controlled Seamen's Union, whose leaders made every effort to keep the struggle within the limits of an economic dispute between the sailors and the shipowners. The Comintern, Ulrich explained, was not content with such a course. "We must convert this strike into an upheaval," he said. "We must give it the character of violent *political* conflict. We must create conditions which will result in collisions between workers and the government. The Swedish proletariat must learn that it is not enough to fight a wage-cut, but that Soviet power alone can achieve salvation from chronic distress. This is important. Remember that Sweden is only one step away from the gates of the Soviet Union."

There were some fine points in my assignment which Ulrich and Jensen took pains to make clear. One of these was an ingenious plan for the wrecking of the Swedish Seamen's Union. The agreement between this union and the Association of Shipowners contained a clause by which the seamen were bound to give seven days' notice before leaving their ships. It was part of my job to induce the ships' crews to disregard the legal clause and to abandon their vessels immediately upon their arrival in Swedish ports. Such action, the Comintern hoped, and the hopes were later substantiated, would result in scores of damage suits against the Seamen's Union for violations of contracts, and thus drain it of its financial resources.

Comrade Ulrich twisted his hands as if he were wringing somebody's neck. The growth of communist influence in Sweden, he explained, depended on the extent to which Swedish commerce could be disorganized, and Swedish state power weakened.

"When do I leave?" I asked.

"At once," said Ulrich.

Two Danish couriers were appointed to act as my liaison men between Sweden and Copenhagen. An action budget of $1,800 weekly was put at my disposal for the duration of the strike. Jensen supplied me with a Danish passport.

"A good passport," Jensen said. "The stamps are genuine. Right from my friends in the Fredriksberg police."

Richard Jensen drove to the Soviet Trade Mission to draw the necessary money. He brought it to a back room of Restaurant Helmerhus, where the currency was counted. Here a grotesque episode occurred. The money was spread out on a table. There were five-, ten- and twenty-dollar bills. Around the table, over glasses of beer, sat Ulrich, Jensen, the Pole and I. Suddenly there was a knock on the door, which had not been locked. Like birds of prey swooping down on their quarry, our eight fists shot out for the Comintern money. With monkey-like speed, Ulrich, the Pole and I stuffed bills into our pockets. Jensen unhooked his belt, opened his trousers, and with one sweep of his enormous arms he shoved the money which remained on the table inside his trousers. The man who knocked was the waiter.

"Telephone for Mr. Jensen," the waiter said.

Jensen got up and walked to the telephone, which was off the main dining-room. While walking, he held both paws pressed against his abdomen. The waiter watched the giant obliquely. The Pole pushed back his chair and followed Jensen like a suspicious tomcat. Sure enough, every two or three steps American banknotes slipped out from the bottom of Jensen's trouser legs. The Pole picked them up. The manager of Helmerhus came running, a puzzled expression on his face. Jensen proceeded on his course like a battleship, not paying the slightest attention to the others. Returning from the telephone, he waved away all suspicions with a laugh.

"Good God," he rumbled. "Now all Copenhagen will know that I have a lazy wife."

I took the express *via* Malmo to Goeteborg, the headquarters of the striking seamen. Harold Svensson, the Swedish customs officer in the G.P.U. service, received me cordially. Less than an hour after my arrival in Goeteborg, I was in conference with Gustav Holmberg, of the Swedish Central Committee. With him were two other men. One of them was Georg Hegener, Jensen's chief of staff. His thick body was no impediment to his mobility. He possessed a disarming smile, a liking for practical jokes, and years of experience in the Comintern service. The other was Bertil Berg, a native of Malmo, and the chief liaison man between the G.P.U. operatives and the Communist Party on the coast of South Sweden. He was young, and he was audacious. Cold, almost colorless eyes gave his handsome boyish features an appearance of disquieting cruelty. Both had been sent to Goeteborg two weeks earlier to execute a coup against the recalcitrant communist management of the thriving restaurant of the Goeteborg Workers' Club which occupied two floors of the Rialto Building, the largest edifice in town.

With helpers recruited from the military organization of the Swedish Party, the two emissaries had engineered an exploit which had thoroughly aroused the press in all the Scandinavian countries. The seamen's strike was under way, and Hegener and Berg seized the opportunity to combine a terrorist enterprise with a cunning incrimination of the Workers' Club. A steamer, the *Kjell*, had been manned by strikebreakers. The ship lay anchored in the outer harbor. One night Bertil Berg hired a motor launch, loaded it with Party guerrillas, and drew alongside the *Kjell*. The G.P.U. raiders boarded the ship and overpowered the crew. They selected five of their victims, tied them hand and foot, and flung them into the waiting launch. Once ashore, the kidnapped men were loaded into a motor-car and driven to the Rialto Building. Here, before a crowd of customers in the restaurant, they were brutally manhandled, quickly dumped into a small truck, and whisked away.

The Swedish authorities gave a general alarm. The police turned out in full force to scour the country for the missing quintet, without results. The Workers' Club was promptly raided and nearly two hundred persons who had had nothing to do with the affair were arrested. From Trondheim to Copenhagen, from Esbjerg to Stockholm, the front pages of the press described the kidnapping as the most sensational crime committed in Scandinavia for many years. Day after day, they screamed the question: *"Where are the men from the Kjell?"*

They were found five days after they had been abducted. Stripped of their clothing, bleeding and bruised, they came limping out of the woods far in the interior of Sweden. Not long afterward the Goeteborg Workers' Club was closed by the police. The G.P.U. had achieved its aim.

"Why?" the manager asked the Goeteborg chief of police.

"Because of the crimes committed here," the official replied.

Bertil Berg was arrested. He denied everything, and openly defied the court. He was convicted, not of kidnapping, but of sedition and sabotage. At a later stage of the strike, Richard Jensen, arriving in Sweden to speak at a national conference of strike committees, was arrested on the train by agents of the State Police. He was locked into the Goeteborg jail and charged with having been the originator of the *"Kjell"* affair." Jensen flatly denied that he had ever been connected with the Comintern; he was a trade union man, pure and simple. A number of Danish intellectuals from the organizational fringe of the Friends of the Soviet Union signed a petition corroborating Richard Jensen's declaration of innocence. The Swedish government released him with apologies.

The Swedish strike developed, from the communist point of view, into a grand success. For the first time in my career I became the virtual dictator of a violent mass movement. The orders I issued in the secret meetings of the communist caucus in the central strike committees were accepted as decrees against which there was no appeal. Communists acting as a disciplined bloc in the strike committees translated my commands into "majority decisions" of the rank and file. This method, copied from the Soviets, went under the flag of "proletarian democracy." It was also employed with success in the trade union conferences and in open mass meetings called to arouse public sympathy with the strikers.

I learned to understand the power which co-ordinated and centrally directed propaganda could exert on an excited mass of human beings. I learned with what ease a mass, once it was in motion, could be incited to concerted acts of violence. At an earlier period in Berlin, Georgi Dimitrov had once told me: "When you feel that you have a solid grip on the minds of the masses, never let go, never let the mass shift for itself; tell the masses what they must do morning and night; let them feel that there is a force behind them which knows the right way, and points it out untiringly." Proof of the correctness of this advice loomed high around me in the Swedish strike.

I smashed the Seamen's Union of Sweden, hitherto one of the best organized in Europe. Special strong-arm squads boarded the ships coming in from abroad and forced their crews to abandon their berths without regard for the seven-day notice agreement of their union. The shipowners responded with court actions, demanding seizure of the union's treasury. Attempts of the union leaders to counteract this turn of events gave me the opportunity to brand them, in daily manifestos printed on blood-red paper, as betrayers of the strike and lackeys of the shipowners. I dispatched the best comrades on hand to Stockholm and Lulea, to Karlskrona, Malmo and Helsingborg. In all ports, strike committees under communist control were created, and by ceaseless agitation they soon took the direction of the strike out of the hands of the accredited union representatives. Every official union meeting was captured by the communist storm brigades. In Goeteborg and Malmo, the strikers ousted the union leaders. The union organization in Stockholm was expelled for wholesale violations of the union constitution. The union was breaking up. A letter of instruction which I received from Ulrich ended with the remark:

"*Das hast du gut gemacht*"—Well done, comrade!

The union executive issued an appeal to its members: "Save your union from foreign criminals and wreckers!"

Three hours later I answered with a crimson poster, under the jeering headline: "Away with the traitors! Rotten wood will not float, neither can it be carved!" Democracy in the Swedish labor movement was losing a major battle.

Our terror campaign against strikebreakers and active anticommunists in the ranks of the strikers progressed concurrently with the assaults against the trade unions. In the harbor of Goeteborg lay anchored the *Lumplena*, a ship which served as a floating home for strikebreakers. Our picket fines made it impossible for the *Lumplena*'s denizens to go ashore. They were brought to Goeteborg in government launches, and they remained aboard the *Lumplena* until they were transferred to steamers tied up by strikes. At first I tried to frustrate the strikebreaking activities by smuggling a score of reliable comrades aboard the *Lumplena*, who shipped out with blackleg crews of non-seamen. At sea our men practiced the art of starting fires in the coal-bunkers, of treating the bearings of the propeller shafts with fine sand and ground glass, or, this failing, of denouncing their shipmates as strikebreakers to the communist brigades in foreign ports of call. But the Western Secretariat demanded more. Richard Jensen sent a courier, a certain Longfors, with orders that the *Lumplena* and her complement of scabs should be sunk in the Goeteborg harbor.

"New situations require new methods of combat," he explained. "Comrade Ulrich is nervous," Longfors reported to me. "The papers are full of rumors that Soviet agents are leading this strike. They say that Swedes could not invent such methods. We want you to be careful not to be caught. Ulrich is afraid there will be a terrible scandal if the police get hold of you."

I was not worried. I was flushed with triumph. My personal contacts in Goeteborg and Stockholm were limited to less than a dozen couriers and key men of the Swedish Party. The rank and file who executed my orders did not even know of my existence. When the fronts clashed and things happened, I took pains to remain far in the background.

I conferred with Gustav Holmberg on ways of doing away with the *Lumplena*. A sudden act of sabotage, particularly if lives were lost, would antagonize the general public, I felt. A preparatory campaign was imperative. Public opinion must be stirred up against the *Lumplena* before the ship could be sunk, so as to make the sinking appear as an act of spontaneous desperation. Comrade Holmberg agreed. A group of five men from the Red Front League was detailed to be in readiness to proceed against the ship when the psychological moment for the coup arrived. An opening of the sea-cocks or a fire in the hold, or both, would do the job. Meanwhile Holmberg mobilized the Young Communist League to prepare public opinion for the event.

Overnight the house walls, the sidewalks and quaysides of Goeteborg were plastered with painted slogans: "Away with the *Lumplena!*"... "Down with the pest-ship *Lumplena*"... "What is a scab?—A man who steals your children's bread!"

Newspaper cameramen photographed the slogans. The pictures appeared on the front pages of the Swedish press. "What does this mean?" asked the captions. "Where is our police?" The shipowners' association demanded police reinforcements to guard the harbor and the *Lumplena*. The plan to sink the strikebreaker ship was overshadowed by another event. The *Gripsholm*, the flagship of the Swedish merchant fleet, arrived in Goeteborg from New York. After landing passengers and mails, the liner was ordered to leave port at once. I sent my storm brigades into the harbor. The *Gripsholm* was detained by main force and stripped of her crew of hundreds. She was the hundredth ship paralyzed by the strike. One night I wrote a leaflet: "Sailors, form storm brigades!"

The storm brigades were formed. The next night I wrote another leaflet: "Sailors and Firemen! Storm the harbors! Yank the strikebreakers off the ships!"

The leaflets were printed at night on the Party presses. Motorcycle couriers carried them to the most distant ports of Sweden almost before the print had had time to dry. The results made Bolshevist hearts leap with joy. The seafaring masses were in motion, and, for lack of any other energetic leadership, they did exactly what the hidden communist command bade them do. Any attempts of the trade unions to apply the traditional and tedious democratic procedure of proposal, discussion and vote-taking were simply torn asunder by surprise actions of the iron-clad communist minority. It all showed me how ineffective democratic tactics are when pitted against a centrally led conspiracy at the helm of a frothing mob.

The men stormed the harbors and ransacked the blackleg ships. The mass of attackers did not consist of seamen only. The Communist Party was there, men, women and children, most of whom had never before been aboard a ship. This happened in Stockholm, in Malmo and in Goeteborg. Aboard the Swedish Lloyd steamer Gwalia, the storm brigades were not content with demolishing whatever came under their hands, but they also set fire to the vessel in several places. The assaults in the harbors took place at night. In Goeteborg, mounted policemen were dragged from their horses and disarmed. The police used tear gas, but being inexperienced, they released their bombs too early, and the strikers hurled the gas-containers back at the attackers.

News arrived from Hamburg that several shiploads of Nazi storm troopers had put to sea, bound for Stockholm to man and sail Swedish ships. This—though no one outside of the Nazi Foreign Division realized at the time—was the beginning of a systematic penetration of the merchant marines of the Scandinavian countries, and Holland and Belgium, by trained members of the Hitler movement. Once more, the Comintern had unwittingly opened the gates to the Fascists. But when the news came, it was water on the communist mill. It offered us the opportunity to accuse the Swedish Shipowners' Association of having entered into an alliance with the well-hated National Socialists.

Of the two shiploads of Brownshirts expected at Stockholm that week, only one arrived. The other had unloaded its passengers in Oscarshamn, Norrkoping and other small ports *en route*. I found the International Club crammed with mariners of various nationalities. They had armed themselves with hammers and axes, clubs, bottles full of sand, sandbags, knives, marlinespikes, brass knuckles and screw drivers. They formed themselves into squads, and their talk was bloodthirsty. Wild plans were afoot. They wanted to duplicate the *Kjell* abduction on a mass scale, with storm troopers as the victims. Loud arguments about methods of torture, one more fiendish than the other, were in progress. The minds of the female hangers-on were more inventive in this respect than the minds of the sailors. I marveled at the monumental hatred displayed by the normally placid Swedes.

The climax came like a chilling shower. The German steamer *Alster* entered port in the small hours. The larger portion of the Stockholm storm brigades lay asleep on the benches and floors of the International Club. The rest were in nearby apartments, waiting for the alarm. As soon as one of the harbor vigilantes had informed me that the Nazi ship was in, I hastened to the International Club. Couriers roused the sleepers in the apartments. "The Brown cut-throats are in," was their cry.

Had I been roused a minute earlier, I should have fallen into the hands of the Stockholm police. They had surrounded the Interclub. One after one, like dazed sheep, the members of the storm brigades emerged from the building to be disarmed. I stood in the shelter of a doorway not far off, watching the scene, gnashing my teeth. Our plan had been betrayed.

I telephoned the private home of Sillen, the Communist Party leader.

"We must at once issue a manifesto," I shouted into the mouthpiece, explaining the happenings of the night. "Run this headline: 'The Stockholm Chief of Police Is Servant of Hitler.'"

Sillen's voice answered like the creaking of a door: "What? In the middle of the night?"

"Don't you know there's a strike going on?"

"Who is that? Why do you ask such silly questions?"

"Well, get moving! My couriers will be at headquarters at nine." I hung up. The leaflet was printed and distributed in the harbor before noon. I still wanted to provoke an assault against the *Alster*. But the leaders of the harbor brigades had been arrested. Our forces had been scattered by the police raids. Only one recourse remained: guerrilla warfare. Party couriers mobilized all available able bodied communists. They gathered on street corners along the wide harbor front. I sent them in small units into the harbor, with instructions to trounce and push off the quays anyone who had come ashore from the *Alster*. One or two of the German refugees were detailed to each unit. They were assisted by the striking seamen of Stockholm.

The arrested comrades, after having spent the day in jail, were released in the evening. Despite the frustration of the planned mass raid, it had been a day of terror for the Nazis. It also was a day of surprise. A score or so of the storm troopers, on learning that they were to be used as strikebreakers, refused to budge from their ship. Moreover, eleven of the supposed Brownshirts marched to the International Club after dark, and reported themselves as anti-Nazis who had seized this chance of manning Swedish ships to escape from Germany. We welcomed them as brothers; the girls who the night before had reveled in mapping out torture devices now were frantic in their efforts to please the comrades from Hamburg.

Meanwhile the leaders of the Swedish Seamen's Union made every effort to salvage the battered remnants of their organization by making peace with the shipowners. They accepted the demanded decrease of the seamen's wages, and advised their followers to return to the ships. A telegram from Richard Jensen informed me of these secret negotiations to end the strike. The nature of my assignment was suddenly reversed. Instead of drawing more ships' crews into the strike, I had to endeavor to induce the communist sailors and their sympathizers to make a rush for the available berths! Gripped by the fever of the struggle, the comrades wanted to carry on at any price.

Another telegram arrived from Jensen:

"No nonsense. Our friends must re-embark."

If they did not, I knew, our socialist trade union rivals would take the jobs, and the communists would be left on the beach.

Party discipline carried the day. In mass meetings in all major ports the communist caucuses bludgeoned the seamen into an acceptance of the wage-cut. So, for the Swedish mariners the strike ended in defeat. But the Communist Party returned to the ships, more solidly entrenched than ever before. The Western Secretariat, the Comintern in Moscow, and the whole Comintern press characterized the strike as an important political victory.

I dispatched a courier to Copenhagen to submit a report and to ask for further instructions. Then I returned to Goeteborg, exhausted. My thoughts were in Germany. Where was Firelei? Where was my son? I had heard no more of them.

Harold Svensson had a letter of instruction for me. His uniform coat unbuttoned, he was letting his little son ride on his knees. He made neighing sounds, and the child squeaked with pleasure. I was reading my instructions.

Svensson stopped his play. "Well, comrade, where to?" he asked.

"Norway," I said. "Narvik."

Richard Jensen, who had advanced to the position of finance chief of the Westbureau, failed to send me funds. He had indicated that large sums were needed in America, where a drive for the official recognition of the Soviet government was in the making. So, because of the Comintern's abruptly mounting interest in the United States, I was compelled to travel beyond the Arctic Circle third-class, and on a daily budget of two dollars.

In Oslo, I went straight to Dr. Halvorsen's abode. I found him fortified behind a quart of whiskey, working over a massive report on the Norwegian State Railways. The material comprised many hundreds of pages, maps, photographs of tunnels and bridges, particularly of the line connecting the mountain-town of Honefoss with Bergen.

"Quite a piece of surgery, Comrade Arne," I commented.

"A hobby of mine," he countered, "a delightful hobby."

I dropped the subject. I had come to get from Dr. Halvorsen my credentials for the Narvik unit.

"I have a very good man up there," he said, "Martin Hjelmen. He's got a very active group among the fishermen all along the Northland coast, but the contacts with the Kiruna railway are bad. You see, he feels isolated up there. It will stimulate him to see that the International takes an interest in his work."

I was intrigued to discover that Dr. Halvorsen had his confidential organization files camouflaged under the medical designations. Correspondence and records concerning Narvik he produced from a locked metal box labeled, *"Epidemic Encephalitis—*the Sleeping Sickness." He selected a handful of papers.

"Study that to get your bearings."

Dr. Halvorsen telephoned Kitty Andresen, his girl courier. The tough-faced Amazon bounced into the room a bare half-hour later. Her superb physique rippled with anticipation.

"Hi, sailor!" she cried. "You are going north, I hear. Take me with you. I am bored to death."

"No money," I replied. "I'll have to go alone."

Kitty Andresen grimaced. Nothing, however, could quench her spirits.

"I must tell you," she bubbled. "I had a long chat with King Haakon of Norway."

"The King?"

"Certainly. It was in February. I was skiing in Nordmarken. All of a sudden a fellow who looked like an overgrown scarecrow was skiing behind me. He passed me downhill, so I got angry and shouted, 'Hey, stop!' He stopped and apologized for passing me. We sat in the snow and ate sandwiches, and he called me a 'brimming daughter of Norway.' I laughed and said, 'Friend, you're old enough to have a daughter of my age yourself. I've seen you somewhere before.' And Presto! 'Sure,' he said, 'I'm Haakon, the King.' Soon we talked politics. You know what he said? 'Our ships, they are our life and our might.' "

Dr. Halvorsen showed his most pleasant satanic grin. I guessed his thoughts. He was thinking of Karin, his wife, and the sleuthing she did in the offices of the shipping magnate Wilhelmsen.

I took the night train to Trondheim. No railway runs north from there as the country is too rocky and too wild. Save for the Kiruna railroad from Sweden, all travel to the Northland is carried on by ship along a rock-bound shore of pagan beauty. The steamer was small, but sturdy. As a third class voyager, I was obliged to make the journey on deck. Peasants, fishermen's wives, a weatherbeaten clergymen and a handful of railway workers and lighthouse guards were my travel companions. They were hardy, friendly people, who loved the clean sternness of their coast. They cursed the ships which in ever-increasing numbers hugged the shore on their course to Murmansk, Archangelsk and Kara Sea. These steamers spread oil on the sea, and the oil killed the fish.

Not far from the entrance to Saltjorden and the harbor of Bodoe, I saw what oil could do to seabirds: some passing tankship had pumped the dregs of her tanks and bilges into the sea, and the layer of oil on the water had clogged the feathers of swimming gulls. For miles a dismal sight insulted the eye—countless birds, encrusted in oil, dead or dying on the North Atlantic waters. It would be futile, I reflected, to tell the simple Norsemen of the wonders of the Five-Year-Plan, which spread oil on their doorsteps and killed the fish and the birds. On the third day, under a dull sky, the ship nosed into Ofot Fjord. Long-sloped black-brown mountains shut out the horizon, and the huge iron-ore pier, which made the steamers moored alongside it look like toys, towered on the starboard bow.

Were it not for the iron ore, Narvik would have remained a sleepy fishing village. Iron was the life of Narvik; the railway leading down from Kiruna to the ice-free coast had transformed the town into one of the foremost ore ports in the world. First in Narvik shipping were the flags of Great Britain and Germany, but the German flag was rapidly superseding the Union Jack. Narvik, like Murmansk, was a frontier town, full of virility and the clangor of toil, but without a trace of the crowded cheerless squalor of Murmansk.

My assignment in Narvik was closely linked to the policy of the Hitler government. The reports we had received about the acceleration of secret rearmament in Germany, the recent appointments of military attaches to all major German embassies, and the increase of German orders for iron by way of Narvik all pointed in one direction—long-view preparation for war. War against the Soviet Union, we believed. The iron ore without which Germany could not make war came chiefly from the Kiruna mines. There was no doubt in my mind that, when war came, the Red Army would not hesitate to push an iron wedge between the Norwegian ore ports and German shipping. To us, of the Comintern, fell the task of preparing the ground. My instructions from the Westbureau demanded that I should divert the communist forces of the Narvik area from their preoccupation with the fisheries and shipping toward the dockers of Narvik and the workers of the Kiruna railroad. In case of war, a general strike and revolt of the dockers and railwaymen would offer a fine pretext, especially if the Norwegian government intervened against the strikers, for the occupation of the Northland province by the Red Army and the Soviet Navy. Had not Stalin himself publicly declared that the Red Army was the army of world revolution?

The Communist Party organization of the Narvik area counted close to nine hundred dues-paying members. Party headquarters had been established in the building of the International Club, created by the luckless Arthur Samsing in the spring of 1931, and it existed since that date on a monthly subsidy of $400 from the Comintern treasury. A month before my arrival in Narvik, Knut Bjoerk, whom I had met in Sweden—and who was later killed in Spain—had been appointed the official leader of the Narvik district. But holding the threads behind the scenes was Dr. Halvorsen's man, Martin Hjelmen.

Hjelmen hailed from Oslo. He had had military training, and was a capable organizer. A man of medium size, with lively dark eyes, bold features and a mop of unruly brown hair, he was one of the rare Norwegian communists who were not drunk and useless for at least one day each week. He spoke English expertly and had toured America in earlier years. Collaboration with a man of Hjelmen's caliber was for me a high pleasure. He was honest to the core. As a Bolshevik, he saw Norway's only salvation in a close alliance with Soviet Russia. For that he worked.

In numerous conferences I primed the Party workers on the necessity of turning the harbor of Narvik and the Kiruna railway into a Stalinist stronghold. Together with Hjelmen and Bjoerk, I worked out a detailed plan covering the next six months of Party activities. We decided to publish a weekly paper for the Narvik dock workers, and another for the railwaymen. We also decided to establish permanent observation posts in the homes of comrades who lived along the Kiruna railroad. After five intensive days of reorganization, I felt that the future course of our Narvik units had been shaped. They were now able to continue alone. I made ready to leave. In a town like Narvik, a stranger who associated with known local communists could not for long escape observation by the Northland police.

Martin Hjelmen was excellently informed on Nazi activities in the Scandinavian countries. The first Nazi Party groups had been established more than a year before the Reichstag Fire. Already toward the end of March, 1933, the Gestapo had begun to branch out across the German frontiers, its agents masked as journalists, business men, or as anti-Hitler refugees. A nameless cruiser had been spooking around the Lofot Islands. An organization of local Germans, calling itself *Kulturverband*, had made its appearance in the North. Another organization, the *Deutsch-Schwedische Reichsvereinigung*, had bobbed up from nowhere on nearby Swedish soil. A certain Herr Haupt from Berlin had established himself as a freight-agent in Narvik, using his business connections ostensibly to suggest the expulsion of "non-Aryans" from Norwegian firms dealing with Germany. A burglary of Haupt's office by two of Comrade Hjelmen's aides had netted a number of *Schulungsbriefe*—Letters of Instruction—for members of the National Socialist Party. They had also obtained leaflets printed in the Norwegian language and issued by the *Fichtebund* in Hamburg, a camouflaged subsidiary of the Nazi Foreign Division. In these leaflets, the Hitler movement was praised as the protector of Norway from Bolshevist invasion. In the late spring of 1933, all this was startling information.

What Martin Hjelmen did not know was that Herr Haupt had his spies also in our International Club. Herr Haupt was a Gestapo official, and his couriers served as sailors on ore ships from Hamburg. Pretending to be rabid enemies of Hitler, they did not hesitate to participate in communist meetings in Narvik. One morning Knut Bjoerk was questioned by detectives on the whereabouts of a Comintern agent from Hamburg. The detectives mentioned a name. It was my name. It was clear that one of the Nazi spy-couriers had recognized me, and reported my presence in Narvik to Haupt who, in turn, had denounced me to the Norwegian police.

A wild chase began. The police were watching all steamers leaving Narvik harbor. Hjelmen conscripted the services of a fisherman to smuggle me out of Narvik. The fisherman's boat was thirty-two feet long, built of oak, and nearly ninety years old. It had a coughing motor of World War vintage. We slipped out of Ofot Fjord in the dead of night, the fisherman, his ten-year-old son, and I. A stiff nor'wester blew, and the surf roared menacingly against the pitch-black battlements of the shore. That night, on the cliff-infested wastes of Vestfjorden, we were close to losing our lives. I thought of the fisherman's wife. How she would curse me if her man and her son perished!

The fisherman, a squat, titanic figure on the heaving and pitching stern, steered. He chewed tobacco as if it were chocolate. About once each hour he roared for his son to bring him tea with rum. The boy nursed the refractory motor. I pumped, drenched to the skin, salt water burning in my eyes. We reached Bodoe, on the northwestern reach of Saltfjorden, the evening of the following day.

"I am sorry I cannot pay you now for your troubles," I told the fisherman. "But give me your address. And good wishes to you for the trip back to Narvik."

"I would not take your money," the fisherman said. "It's you who is most in need of good wishes!"

A steamer was due to sail for Trondheim in the morning. In a restaurant, I sold my new Continental portable typewriter to a lawyer's clerk. He gave me eighty kroner. Sixty hours later I was in Trondheim. I went to the International Club.

Comrade Birkland, the secretary, was surprised to see me.

"The police were here," he said in great agitation. "They were asking for you."

The poor fellow was anxious that I should leave. He was afraid the Comintern would hold him responsible if I were seized by police.

"Advance me fifty kroner," I said. "I'm going on to Oslo." Emerging from the Oslo station, I became aware that I was followed by plainclothesmen. I turned several corners in quick succession and then darted into the City Hotel. The detectives had broken into a run. They overtook me in the lobby. One put his hand on my shoulder. The other guarded the entrance.

"We are from the Alien Squad. Please come with us to headquarters."

They called a taxicab. Wedged in between my captors, I rode to police headquarters. In a spacious office, a calm-faced, broad-shouldered man sized me up minutely. He was the chief of the Alien Squad.

"Sit down," he said.

I sat, bracing myself for a defense of silence.

"Why do you violate Norwegian hospitality?" the man asked. "I don't know what you mean," I replied.

"You know! Do you know Samsing?"

"Who?"

"Arthur Samsing."

"No."

From a folder the official drew a photograph of Comrade Samsing.

"What did you have to do with the disappearance of this man? " he demanded. "Where is he?"

"I don't know the man," I said.

"What were you doing in Narvik?"

"I've never been in Narvik. I came from Trondheim."

"For what purpose did you come to Norway?"

"I came as a tourist. Norway is a beautiful country."

My questioner grew angry.

"I see it is of no use talking to you," he said irately. "However, let me tell you something. We know who you are. We know that you are wanted by the German State Police. You have come to Norway for unlawful purposes. We will have to deport you. If you talk frankly to us, we will send you to a country of your choice. If you persist in leading us around by the nose, then ..."

"Yes?"

"Then we'll deport you to Germany," the commissioner concluded. "What that means—you know better than I."

"Let's talk," I said.

"Good. Tell me why you came to Norway, tell me whom you have met here."

"I came here to see the country," I said. "But chiefly to see a girl I am in love with."

"Which girl?"

"Miss Kitty Andresen."

"Address?"

"26 St. Hallvard."

My examiner scoffed: "Oh, you didn't come here just for the sake of a girl. Who is this Miss Andresen?"

"A lady. I cannot give you more information. If she wishes, she will talk for herself."

"We'll see.... By the way, are you the instructor of the Communist International for the Scandinavian lands?"

"What?"

The inquisition dragged on for an hour, leading nowhere. In the end the chief of the Alien Police said in a quiet fury: "Enough! With you we must speak in another language!"

He summoned a detective. I was handcuffed and led into a gloomy corridor in the basement of the building. Ponderous iron doors led off to both sides. A door was opened.

"In here," the detective said.

A heavy lock snapped shut behind me. Except for a small aperture for air and a thin shaft of light there was only the iron door, the stone around me, above me and below. I began to pace up and down, trying to piece together the mosaic of events that had led to my capture. It was the thirteenth time in my life that I had blundered into the hands of the hated police. The thought that the

Norwegians would surrender me to the Gestapo was like the gnawing of a rat in my head. I began to search the cell for a razor blade left behind by a former inmate. "I'll never go to Germany," I thought, "not as a prisoner. Never!"

I was thinking of a way out, of the Gestapo, of death, of Firelei, of ships meandering over the oceans, thinking how different, how easy and joyous life could have been.

At seven in the evening, the key grated in the lock and a warder entered my cell. He was followed by a prisoner. The prisoner carried a large tray. The tray was covered by a snow-white napkin. He put the tray on the table, and looked at it with greedy eyes.

"Sir," the warder said respectfully. "A friend sent this dinner from the restaurant across the street."

Now I knew that Kitty Andresen had been questioned by the police, and that Kitty told Dr. Halvorsen of my arrest. I carefully probed each dish for a hidden note, and found it under the pudding. A typewritten message from Dr. Halvorsen. *"Dear Friend,"* the note read, *"eat everything. Kitty, the angel, will see you soon. A."*

I ate everything. Toward nine I was gripped by a violent fever. I realized that Dr. Halvorsen had "treated" my food. My head reeled, my eyes burned, and a painful lassitude invaded every muscle. I lay down on the low iron cot, waiting for the spell to pass. I tried to sleep, but sleep would not come. The darkness around me was in a slow gyration, and the sensation that my head was sagging downward in spite of anything I could do persisted.

Suddenly the light was switched on. The night warder appeared. Someone coming up behind pushed the warder aside. Dr. Halvorsen, carrying a small leather bag, barged into the cell. He was followed by Kitty. Dr. Halvorsen blustered abuse at the guard.

"What sort of cattle-brained administration runs this jail," he blurted out. "I told them this man was sick. The scandal will have consequences. Lock up a sick man, will you? Let a sick man die in a rheumatic hole like this, will you?"

His left eye closed, and with a diabolic grin on his ravaged face, Dr. Halvorsen bent over me. He tested my pulse. He inserted a thermometer in my mouth. He opened my shirt and applied a stethoscope.

"Take it easy," he murmured, "take it easy, old boy. I'll pull you through or my name isn't Arne Halvorsen." Turning to the guard he shouted: "Get me some water—ice cold!"

The guard hastened away.

Dr. Halvorsen pushed an ordinary matchbox under my blanket. "Can you understand what I say?" he whispered.

I merely nodded. My physical lethargy was genuine.

"Don't worry," the doctor was saying. "Don't be afraid. The stuff in the box ... take it tomorrow about six. You'll feel weak, you'll sweat. Pretend you're choking, can't get air, pain under the ribs."

The warder came back with the water. Dr. Halvorsen poured a powder, and then water into the glass.

"Drink. Drink slowly. It'll make you feel better."

I drank. Kitty, kneeling by the cot, held the glass to my lips. From her lips came endearing words, loud enough for the guard to hear. In the end, she kissed me. She left the cell, apparently weeping and blowing her nose.

"Leave this man quite alone," Dr. Halvorsen told the guard. "Alone do you hear? I'll talk to the jail physician before he makes his round tomorrow. Leave him alone. Alone, I said."

"Yes, sir," the warder muttered, looking at me as if he was seeing a ghost.

Next morning I felt curiously light, but fit. Nevertheless I stayed up to my ears under the blankets and refused to take a breakfast of coffee, black bread and butter. Shortly before noon, the warder again entered my cell.

"Can you walk?" he asked.

"I think so."

"Gentlemen upstairs want to see you."

I slipped into my pants and the warder supported my arm on the way down the gloomy corridor, through several steel doors, and up two flights of stairs. I feigned dizziness and pain. Several times I leaned against the wall, hunched my shoulders, pressed my hand to my chest, breathed with furious irregularity and emitted groans. The warder helped me into an office. I entered the room, a fair imitation of a man who stands with one foot in the grave, and sagged limply into a chair.

The chief of the Oslo Alien Squad confronted me.

"How do you feel?"

"Not too well," I said.

He shrugged, mumbling about the infirmary. With him was another man, young, athletic, with wide-awake gray eyes in a smooth boyish face.

The police commissioner said, "This gentleman has just come over from Stockholm to interview you. He is a representative of the Swedish State Police.,,

"But this is Norway," I vaguely protested.

"The police authorities of Norway, Sweden and Denmark operate in a close official alliance," the Norwegian explained. "My Swedish colleague has a proper right to question you, even though you are in Norway."

The Swede smiled. He offered me a cigarette. I declined. He settled himself at one end of the desk and drew a notebook.

"My government," he began, "is interested in having your opinion on certain recent occurrences in Sweden. Among other things, I have in mind the acts of vandalism in the harbors of Goeteborg and Stockholm. And also the abduction of Swedish citizens from the S.S. *Kjell*"

"I know nothing of Sweden," I grumbled.

"Perhaps not much. I know Sweden myself very well. I am now concerned with the activities *in* Sweden of certain agencies connected with the Soviet government. I have instructions to pay you liberally for any information of value to my superiors."

I had to force myself not to burst into laughter. Most Scandinavians were too honest, too fair-minded and devoid of trickery to make efficient policemen. I could not help reflecting how handicapped a man like this Swedish secret service operative was against such antagonists as Dr. Halvorsen, or Comrade Ulrich, or Richard Jensen.

"I am no seller of information," I said.

"But you have been in Sweden?"

"I have crossed Sweden on my trip to Norway, that's all."

"You have not lived secretly in Goeteborg?"

"No. Why should I live secretly?"

"Are you not an employee of the Communist International?"

"No."

The head of the Alien Squad intervened. "Of course you are," he shouted. "We have proof! In Germany you are wanted for high treason."

I had my answer ready:

"The public of free Norway will not be enthusiastic when it hears that its own police force co-operates with the Gestapo of the incendiary dope-fiend Goering."

The faces of my questioners did not change. "It is of no use to waste time with this man," the Norwegian said to his Swedish colleague. "We cannot use G.P.U. methods to make him talk, unfortunately not."

After another round of questioning the door was opened abruptly and Kitty Andresen entered. Her splendid body leaped forward; her homely face was screwed into a mask of compassion. Paying no attention at all to the officials, she whipped a chair alongside of mine, put her arms around my neck. "My poor boy . ... Can't they see how you are suffering? ... Here, let me have your hand ... So ..." In her eyes were tears. I was much amazed at the detectives.

The chief of the Alien Squad said to Kitty: "My dear young lady, I must warn you. This is a dangerous man. He will disappoint you. He will make you unhappy, and desert you cynically." He spoke in the Norwegian tongue, and in a stern fatherly manner.

Kitty produced a delightful peal of laughter. "Oh, sir, how comical you are!" Her words came like a waterfall. "I've known this boy for years. Dangerous! Indeed! He's sweeter than any boy I've set eyes on in Denmark, or Norway, or anywhere else. Only he's ill! Can't you see he's ill? Please let me telephone. I'm going to telephone the King. The King will tell you to go after the burglars and the murderers, and to leave alone the beloved of a Norwegian girl"

The officials were plainly embarrassed. They called the warder, ordering him to take me back to my cell. Kitty followed me down the stairs to the entrance of the gloomy basement corridor, bubbling words, and stroking my arms and face. I feigned exhaustion.

Kitty yelled at the warder: "Dare to keep this boy one day longer here! I shall make a horrible noise. I shall go to the newspapers. I shall—"

Silently the warder led me to my cell.

There was no infirmary in this police jail.

I undressed and buried myself under the blankets. After the guard had departed, I reached under the mattress where I had hidden the matchbox Dr. Halvorsen had given me surreptitiously. It contained a light grayish powder. I crept from my cot and filled a tin cup with water. I poured the drug into my mouth and gulped it down with the aid of water.

The effects were not tardy in coming. My head became clouded, I vomited cold slime, and squirmed and cursed in the most authentic misery. After a time sweat began to pour from all my pores and my breath came in rasping sounds. My feelings toward Dr. Halvorsen were most unfriendly.

However, he appeared punctually. I heard him clamoring outside in the corridor, demanding to be admitted. The door was opened. Dr. Halvorsen, after a rapid glance at me, peremptorily commanded the warder to telephone the prison physician. Until the latter arrived, Dr. Halvorsen stomped up and down the dungeon corridor, treating the officials on night duty as if he were the owner of the Oslo jail. At last the prison doctor arrived.

The examination of the patient began. It was conducted by Dr. Halvorsen who referred to me as his "valued client." The young prison doctor gave the older man a free hand. I moaned and writhed, let my breath come like the fitful gusts of the Doldrums, clutched my chest, doubled up and groaned, and showed symptoms of choking.

Dr. Halvorsen spoke earnestly and rapidly to his colleague. "Immediate removal," he boomed. And then: "The man must have special care. I give my pledge to be responsible for him."

Both rushed out. The prison doctor soon returned to administer a sedative, and left again. I waited, alone in my cell, producing unearthly noises for the benefit of the night warder outside.

Presently Dr. Halvorsen, the prison physician and two other men arrived. They helped me into my clothes, and with Dr. Halvorsen's assistance I crawled through the corridor, passed two gates, crossed a sidewalk and tottered into my rescuer's car. We drove to the outskirts of Oslo, to a small house occupied by Leif Foss, a taciturn bulldog of a man and a veteran of many international trade union congresses in Moscow. Dr. Halvorsen acted as if he had unexpectedly inherited a fortune.

"This accursed medicine," I asked. "What was it?"

"Ipecac," he said. "Useful stuff. The Spaniards got it from the South American *Indios*."

"And the sickness?"

"*Angina pectoris.* Maybe food poisoning. Maybe a touch of pleurisy. The mess was not quite clear."

"And now?"

Dr. Halvorsen laughed. "Norway, my friend, this is Norway! I am responsible for your safe delivery. That means you're going to clear out by sunrise. If you ever marry, catch a woman who's got a detective as a brother, like our good Karin. Take my advice. Take a stiff drink!"

"You're going to have trouble!"

"Leave it to me."

In the house of Leif Foss, Kitty Andresen was waiting. She had prepared a supper of roast duck. We ate and drank Tokay, and talked till far into the night. I could not keep the food; my stomach was still rebellious. Kitty was exuberant. Dr. Halvorsen, who had heard that I had at one time spent a few days in Hollywood, insisted that I talk of my experiences as a movie pirate. He confessed that he had had for years a consuming ambition to become a permanent denizen of the motion picture capital. Leif Foss alone was serious; he wanted to discuss the second Five-Year-Plan. His attempts came to naught.

In the early morning hours, Dr. Halvorsen drove me to a comrade who was a photographer. Here my picture was taken. I went back to Leif Foss' house alone. At dawn Dr. Halvorsen reappeared. Out of one pocket he drew a weatherbeaten Danish passport, from another he pulled a metal box containing certain chemicals in small glass bottles. It took Kitty Andresen barely twenty minutes to make some changes in the passport, to exchange the old photograph for one of myself, and to transfer the rubber stamp of the Danish police with the aid of a hard-boiled egg. She peeled the egg while hot and rolled it gently over the original imprint of the stamp until the latter had been transferred to the white of the egg. After she had affixed my photograph to the passport, she carefully rolled the cooling egg over its edge. As if by magic, the stamp was transferred back to the passport, a little paler than the original, but true to form.

At nine o'clock Dr. Halvorsen departed to buy a steamer passage to Antwerp. I took the passport and the steamer ticket—it was first class. Kitty escorted me to the harbor. We boarded a ship, the *Brabant*. Before Kitty Andresen went ashore, she demanded a kiss. This time it was a real kiss. The siren roared.

The S.S. *Brabant* steamed out through Oslo Fjord at eleven. Two days later I arrived in Antwerp. The local liaison agent, Comrade Anton, tall, cool and conservative, met me on the quay. Dr. Halvorsen had advised him of my coming.

"I have wired Copenhagen," said Anton. "Comrade Avatin is here. He might need you. Antwerp is infested with Gestapo spies." It was May.

Chapter Thirty

WEST OF THE RHINE

I had supper with Michel Avatin; he had slipped out of Germany but a few days before my arrest in Oslo. What he had seen and heard of the fate of many of our common friends was enough to chill anyone's blood. I asked him about Firelei.

"She is lucky," he said. "She is a courier for Comrade Kippenberger."

I could not suppress a shudder. Hans Kippenberger was the director of the Party's military intelligence *Apparat*. I knew Hermann Goering's new laws. For collaboration in the betrayal of military or industrial secrets, there was but one sentence in Germany: death.

We talked about the Gestapo. Avatin had been watching the growth, the methods and the habits of that force as an animal fancier might study the doings of his pet tiger. The Foreign Division of the Gestapo was branching out. Its corps of operatives abroad was composed of two distinct categories— the spies and the man-hunters. The spies usually arrived in the guise of political fugitives, brimful of fervor and anxious to win for themselves a place in organizations combating the Hitler movement. The man-hunters, however, were trained kidnapers and killers; they came in groups of three or five, commissioned to carry out abductions or assassinations of political antagonists after the latter had been spotted, identified and pointed out to them by the spies. In every large city in countries adjoining Germany, the director-in-chief of the Gestapo espionage and strong-arm units was in constant communication—by mail, telegraph, couriers, and through diplomatic channels—with the headquarters of the Secret Police in Berlin, and its Foreign Division in Hamburg. It was he who ordered and directed the *coups de main,* and who forwarded to Germany the information gathered by his spy brigades. A chance discovery by a Nazi spy in Paris or Basle or London often spelled sudden disaster for courageous conspirators at work within the German frontiers. Michel Avatin reported that there was a Gestapo observer aboard every German ship trading with foreign ports. But it was not a one-sided game; spies and counter-spies were active on both sides. And if one was caught, he was killed like a poisonous snake, without trial or mercy.

The chief organizer of Gestapo espionage in Flanders was a former Czarist officer, Ilia Raikoff, who, because of his enormous physical strength, was dubbed "The Ox" by those who knew him. The Ox had been betrayed to us by Rudolf Heitman, a G.P.U. operative in the Hamburg Gestapo, and Avatin had received the assignment to execute the Russian.

"The Ox is hard to catch," Avatin commented. More he would not say.

Before another month had gone by, our militants in the harbor of Antwerp were shocked by a sample of Ilia Raikoff's efficiency. The Hamburg-America liner *Caribia,* returning from the West Indies, had entered Antwerp. A crew member, Hans Lisser, who had served the Comintern as a courier to the West Indies since 1932, came ashore in Antwerp and requested that the Party send a trained comrade aboard to speak at a meeting of the liner's action committee. None of us knew at that time that Comrade Lisser had become a Gestapo spy and a cog in The Ox's machine.

An organizer was sent aboard. He was Ignace Aussinger, an experienced and fearless comrade who had not many days before escaped from the Gestapo in Cologne. Together with his girl, Paula, he had come downriver to Antwerp, hidden in the hold of a barge loaded with rails. Aussinger boarded the *Caribia* at eight in the evening, carrying with him a good quantity of anti-Hitler pamphlets. Several hours after midnight his girl, Paula, hammered against the doors of the Antwerp International Club. She roused the guards. The girl was so agitated that the guards found difficulty in understanding her incoherent babbling. But soon the truth dawned on them. Comrade Aussinger had not returned from the *Caribia.*

Paula shouted hysterically, "They've taken him. They've locked him up. You've got to help him . . ."

Three of the guards raced to the quay where the *Caribia* lay moored. Except for the gangway lights, they found the ship dark and quiet. Four youthful gangway watchmen, Elite Guards, barred the three nocturnal visitors from boarding the ship. The three German communists could not give the alarm themselves; they were illegally in Belgium, and liable to immediate arrest and deportation. They hastened to the headquarters of the Belgian Party and roused the male *concierge*. The *concierge* summoned two policemen. The policemen boarded the *Caribia.*

The Nazi guards stopped them at the head of the gangway. They spread the German national flag across the gangway.

"Now trample over our flag, if you dare," they told the policemen. "This is German territory."

The policemen hesitated.

"We have been told that you have a man in irons on your ship," one of them said. "We have come to investigate."

"He is a crew member. He struck the chief officer. That is why he was put in irons."

The Belgians demanded to speak to the captain. The captain was called. He corroborated the story of the Nazi guards: the man had been put in irons because of mutiny. The Belgian policemen did not suspect that the real master of a German ship was not its skipper, but the chief of the Nazi ship *Stuetzpunkt.*

At dawn came high tide. The *Caribia* steamed seaward, and Ignace Aussinger was a prisoner aboard her. By the time responsible Party leaders could be informed of the abduction, it was too late to save the comrade from Cologne. The legal methods of the Belgian authorities were singularly ineffective against the ruthlessly illegal methods of the Gestapo. In January, 1934, Ignace Aussinger was beheaded in Cologne. His girl, Paula, acted as if she had lost her reason. The Party could not use her. For a while she roamed Antwerp's sailortown like a vengeful specter. She took to drink. The Belgian police arrested her, and because she had no passport, they pushed her clandestinely across the frontier to Holland. The leader of the International Club in Rotterdam proposed to send her to the Soviet Union. But Paula was classed as mentally deficient. The Russian consul refused her a visa. She became a prostitute in The Ton, a music hall on Rotterdam's Schiedamsche Dyke.

At last my instructions arrived. They were conveyed to me from Denmark by a man named Dietlevsen, a courier who served as boatswain aboard the Danish steamship *P.A. Bemstorff*. Save for the air-line Copenhagen-Amsterdam-Paris, this ship, trading between Esbjerg, Antwerp and Dunkerque, had become the main bridge for conspirative communications between Copenhagen and the capitals of Western Europe. Railways had become taboo, since they crossed forbidden German soil. Dietlevsen also brought me funds. Among the money consignments was a thick envelope which I was ordered to forward to Roy Hudson, George Mink's successor on the American waterfront. A courier aboard the liner *Ilsenstein*, of the Bernstein Line, carried the consignment to New York, for delivery at 140 Broad Street, Comrade Hudson's headquarters.

My instructions demanded, as most Comintern instructions do, more than a common mortal could hope to fulfill in his allotted time. A man who is given a crowbar and the order to use it to shift the Matterhorn must have much the same emotions as a Comintern agent has when perusing a freshly arrived set of instructions.

"Where shall I start?" I asked Comrade Anton, who controlled the financial end of these schemes.

"Begin with what is nearest to your heart," he calmly replied.

Now, under Comintern instructions, I launched a general offensive against the swastika flag. For three consecutive days the harbors of Antwerp, Rotterdam, Ghent and Dunkerque were flooded with manifestos, all of which had as their central tenor: *"Down with the murder flag! Refuse to load or discharge ships that fly the ensign of Assassin Hitler! The Hooked Cross is a Hunger Cross."* The dockers rallied. Action Committees were formed. Nazi seamen encountered wearing the swastika badge on Dutch and Belgian waterfronts were beaten within an inch of their lives. Clinging precariously to the back seat of a very old motorcycle, I was whisked from Antwerp to Rotterdam, back to Antwerp, and on to Ghent and Dunkerque. Emotions ran high. The response of the workers was swift, for they had been well prepared by the intensive publicity which the Gestapo and storm trooper atrocities had received in the foreign press

My propaganda squads in the harbor of Antwerp scored the first success. Dunkerque followed, and then Rotterdam and Ghent. Five days after the campaign began, twenty-odd German ships lay paralyzed, besieged by a hostile mob in these ports alone. The dockers of other harbors, from Sydney to Seville, soon followed the example of the vanguard in Antwerp. As soon as a German steamer was moored, I sent a delegation of dockers aboard to ask for the captain. The dockers demanded that the swastika flag should be hauled down. The captain, of course, refused: arrest by the Gestapo would be his lot if he complied with the delegation's demand.

The answer of the dockers was: "As long as you fly the murder flag, we won't work your ship."

A cordon of pickets was thrown around the stricken ships. No German was allowed to go ashore. More action resulted when the officers aboard the steamers attempted to compel the German crews to work the cargoes. Communist and socialist crew members refused to obey this order. The ships' captains sounded the siren signals, "Mutiny aboard!" A sorry chapter in the police annals of the democratic nations began. Belgian and Dutch policemen seized the German seamen as mutineers. The mayor of Antwerp, M. Huysmans, arrived on the docks to induce the stevedores to labor while the swastika fluttered high above their heads. That happened at night, at about eleven. From the shadows of a cargo shed I watched the progress of the action.

"Who is that fat man talking to the action committee?" I asked one of the couriers on the scene of battle.

"Mayor Huysmans," he replied.

The Mayor was a socialist. I summoned a group of young "activists"—Letts, Germans, an Estonian and an Irishman—and sent them forward to push the interloper off the quay. He was, however, too far from the water's edge, and my comrades were content with giving the Mayor of Antwerp a trouncing.

"Serious trouble in the Harbor of Antwerp," reported the headlines of the following morning.

In Ghent and Dunkerque, the boycott of the swastika flag was so complete that German shipping companies canceled them from their list of ports of call.

The campaign, after two violent weeks, was abruptly throttled by an ingenious maneuver which probably emanated from the headquarters of Dr. Joseph Goebbels in Berlin. Manifestos appeared on the docks of Antwerp and elsewhere, signed by the "Communist Opposition," and asking the dockers why the swastika flag was not boycotted by Soviet stevedores in Russian harbors. The bottom of the leaflet showed photographs of Leninport, the harbor of Leningrad. There was a ship which flew the swastika banner, and not far off another which showed the hammer and sickle in red. The hatches of the German ships were open, and the figures of men at work could be discerned. "Stalin wishes you to strike against German ships," the leaflets concluded. "Now ask Stalin why he does not strike against the German ships in Russia." The question caught on. In the next rally of the strikers the dockers asked: "Why?"

The answer which I and my colleagues could give them was feeble. "German ships that sail to Russia," we explained, "carry goods which are necessary for the victorious construction of socialism. To strike against German ships in Soviet ports means to strike against the second Five-Year-Plan."

In one of these meetings, which I supervised, a man rose yelling, his arms outstretched in a gesture of accusation.

"Only lawyers talk that way," he yelled. "The Soviet Union has betrayed us!"

I had the sensation that this man's shout knocked the bottom out of our effort to drive Nazi shipping off the seas. I looked at his face. It was a pale, half-cynical, half-reckless face of a man of forty. He had blond hair, bold eyes and a stubborn chin. Who was he? His features seemed familiar to me. After the meeting ended I followed the man out on the street. And suddenly I recognized him. His name was Herrmann Knueffgen. I had first seen him in Hamburg, in the bleak spring of 1919. He stood in the middle of a band of mutinous longshoremen and had shouted: "The rich must die so that the poor may live." He was the man who had captured a trawler on the North Sea with which to carry the German delegation to the first congress of the Comintern in war-torn Russia, and who had later gone to prison for it, convicted of piracy on the high seas.

I overtook him near the *Steen*.

"Hello, bandit," he said. "You here?"

"Let's have a beer," I suggested.

"Oh, sure."

It was a strange meeting. Here was the man who had done much, indirectly, to push me into the tide of the communist movement; and here was I, a corpuscle in the bloodstream of the Comintern. And the man whose path I had decided to follow in my youth now sat three feet away, a bitter enemy of the cause. There was no hostility between us. We talked, I guardedly, he with frank cynicism. After years spent in German prisons, Herrmann Knueffgen had been amnestied by President von Hindenburg. For a time he had been detailed to the Scandinavian Bureau of the Comintern, and then been transferred to Leningrad to serve *Sovtorgflot*—as an organizing expert.

"I soon saw how things stood in Holy Russia," Knueffgen told me. "That was not socialism. That was not what I had fought for. What I saw was the carcass of a great nation; and who was in the bowels of the poor beast, gnawing lustily?—The lovely Bolshevist bureaucracy. That castrated *my* little dream. I was sorry I stole that trawler for them in 1919. I did some figuring: The trawler was worth half a million rubles; seven years in jail were worth seven million rubles. So I thought I'd better get my money back. Seven-and-a-half million rubles was just about what Mr. Stalin owed me. Well, I got my hands on a lot of rubles and started selling them wherever I could, two hundred rubles for one English pound. Until, one day, my friends from the G.P.U.—"

I knew the rest. Knueffgen had been seized as a speculator. There was a scandal that rocked *Sovtorgflot*. Knueffgen was condemned to death. Because of his record as a collaborator of Karl Liebknecht and Rosa Luxemburg, the Soviet government commuted the death sentence to ten years of hard labor.

After less than two years of toil in a Karelian prison camp, Herrmann Knueffgen escaped.

"Maybe a thousand poor devils tried it, and I'm the one in a thousand who got away alive," Knueffgen grinned.

"And now?"

"Now I'm here," he said.

"Doing the dirty counter-revolutionary work," I concluded. Knueffgen leaned back. His eyes followed the smoke of his cigar. "I never lived better than I do now," he said contentedly.

"I believe it."

"You are a God-damned fool. You fellows think you're wolves, but you're only puppies chasing the butterflies. Don't you realize that Joe Stalin and his *tovarishchi* have nothing but contempt for you foreign lickspittles?"

"Who are you working for? The Gestapo?" I asked in deadly earnest.

"Nonsense! The Gestapo pays too little."

"Who pays more?"

"Scotland Yard. You see, I've become a realist."

"Why did you oppose the boycott of German ships?"

Knueffgen laughed coldly. "I enjoy throwing clubs between the Comintern legs," he said, adding seriously: "All brands of politics are frauds. You know that as well as I do. Why not draw the consequences?"

"What consequences?"

"Keep alive and fit, paddle your own canoe, and have some fun."

"I am sorry for you."

"Ah, you still hold that 'right' and 'wrong' are two different things," Knueffgen said. "You are diseased with a conscience."

"Call it conscience."

"Enthrone conscience and you'll starve to death. You might also find a rope around your neck, some day."

We got nowhere. Before I left him, I warned the renegade: "Keep out of our campaigns, in future. Take some good advice."

"Nur kaltes Blut, mein Junge," Knueffgen drawled. "I am an old hand in the business. Tell my friends of the G.P.U. that Comrade Stalin owes me just about ten million rubles—in gold. You can't expect a man to let such an investment go, can you?"

We parted. Through Comrade Anton, I contacted Michel Avatin. I gave the Lett a report on Knueffgen. Avatin merely nodded. A fortnight later Willy Zcympanski, who had been my comrade in the Hamburg jail ten years earlier, arrived in Antwerp. Zcympanski had become an operative of the Soviet military intelligence, but the G.P.U. borrowed him at times from the military *Apparat* to use him for special assignments. Brusque and tight-lipped, he questioned me about Herrmann Knueffgen. I knew then that he had been sent to Antwerp to do away with the former "Captain Kidd" of the Comintern. He failed. Knueffgen is still alive. Zcympanski died by suicide, in the summer of 1937, after his capture by the Gestapo during an espionage mission in Germany.

The sporadic strikes against the Nazi flag had left many German seamen stranded in Antwerp. They were the militants who had struck, and who were subject to immediate arrest if they returned to German ports. To me, and to the Comintern, they were welcome reinforcements. Five of the most talented I gathered into a "press committee" for the publication of our new weekly newspaper, which I named Scheinwerfer—"The Searchlight." The first edition of twelve thousand was topped with the challenge, "We live, and we shall stay alive!" Two days after its appearance the bulk of the edition was already on the underground railway to

Germany, concealed in the coalbunkers of ships to Bremen, Hamburg and Stettin, and in the bellies of barges going up the Rhine.

Other stranded German militants I organized into sabotage groups. I established schooling circles where comrades from the German ships were instructed in the simple technique of doing great damage to ships and cargoes with the fewest possible means. A list of suggestions of maritime sabotage technique had been worked out by some expert in the Western Secretariat. It had been forwarded to me by Jensen's courier aboard the *P. A. Bemstorff*. A number of points in this training program for saboteurs follow:

The oldest and most effective method was that of commixing fine sand with the lubricants used in a steamer's engines, preferably for the bearings of the long and heavy propeller shafts. A handful of sand, judiciously applied, would be enough to cripple for days the largest craft afloat. Sand or grit could also be used on the cargo winches and the anchor windlass. Other methods were: Outright destruction of compasses and sextants; the disabling of compasses by removing or confusing the controlling magnets; bunker fires by pouring kerosene and water over coal, particularly in warm weather; the sawing through of rudder chains at sea; the lowering of temperatures in the holds of ships carrying tropical fruits, particularly bananas; the application of kerosene on cargoes of meat and other perishable foodstuffs; the sprinkling of cement and water over new machinery, motors, electric drills, pumps, presses and typewriters which Germany exported in great quantities to South America. Aimed directly at the wrecking and sinking of ships were the instructions which called for the soaking of grain and soya bean cargoes with water, either by drilling small holes into the side of the underwater portion of the vessel, or by fastening the nozzle of a firehose in the opening of an airshaft, or simply by turning the airshafts into the wind during rain or heavy weather, and under cover of darkness. Grain or soya beans, once wet, would expand to three times their normal size and burst the steel decks and flanks even of the best-built ship. Proposed as the culmination of the sabotage drive was the seizure of German ships by their crew in the event of war. Destruction of the wireless apparatus, imprisonment of officers as hostages, and a dash into a neutral or a Soviet port were the salient directions in this program.

The Comintern held the theory that German economy was weak, and that sabotage in industry and transport, lashed into a mass movement, would hasten the economic and therefore the political breakdown of Nazi power. The theory proved a fallacy. But the fact remained that no ponderous, and therefore highly vulnerable, organization was required for acts of sabotage. One trained man, working alone, was enough to disrupt the smooth functioning of a ship. That the sabotage units were not formed quite in vain was demonstrated by events in subsequent years. In Puerto Colombia, the North German Lloyd freighter *Helgoland* was set afire by members of her crew, and a mutiny followed. The stokers of the *Bahia Blanca*, a vessel of the Hamburg-South America Line, disabled their ship in the harbor of Rio de Janeiro. Near Pernambuco, an act of sabotage caused a fire in the bunkers of the *São Paulo*, of Hamburg. The fire raked the ship for five days. The Chinese seamen aboard the German wheat ships *Nienburg* and *Anatolia* mutinied off Buenos Aires. Aboard the Hamburg-America liner *Leuna*, where stokers and coalheavers were communists, the leader of the Nazi ship group vanished without a trace in the Indian Ocean.

In the first days of June, I was ordered to Paris to attend the World Congress against Fascism as "delegate of the workers of Hamburg" and as representative of the Seamen's International.

The train to Paris was crowded with delegates from many lands. They all had the same destination, but all of them pretended not to know each other until the express arrived in Lille, the first safe station after the crossing of the Franco-Belgian frontier. The *Gare du Nord* of Paris swarmed with the runners of Roger Walter Ginsburg, our central liaison agent in the Seine city. One of them escorted me to my quarters, 221 Rue Etienne Marcel in Montreuil, an eastern suburb. It was the home of Comrade Beaugrand, a member of the Chamber of Deputies and the chief of the communist military *Apparat* in France. He was a lean-bodied giant, and his trade had been that of a butcher in a municipal abattoir. His apartment was cluttered with the souvenirs of many journeys to Russia, Red Army mementos and photographs of Soviet leaders. His wife, a chunky, lively woman, held a position in the administration of the Les Halles, the pivotal point in the distribution of the Paris food supply.

One of my jobs now was to organize surveillance over all seamen, dockers, river workers and fishermen among the foreign delegates. Another was to act as interpreter in conferences between Comintern executives and the heads of the various deputations. These meetings took place either in the "architect's studio" of Walter Ginsburg, on the Rue de Seine, or in the rambling offices which the Western Secretariat had established at 288 Rue Lafayette. The cream of the Comintern had come to town.

My chief, Ulrich, flew over from Copenhagen, together with Richard Jensen and a full score of their lieutenants. But the majority of the delegates were not communists. Workers and intellectuals, teachers, writers and professional men belonging to the liberal camp arrived in droves, anxious to give a hand in building a world movement against Hitler and what he stood for. Few of these guileless pilgrims, it seemed, had the faintest notion that the force which had organized and financed the World Congress, written all the resolutions and made all decisions in advance of its formal opening, was the Comintern. The hundreds of guards and interpreters, typists, stenographers, guides and couriers were all members of the Communist Party. The Congress convened in the *Salle Pleyel,* the famous concert hall not far from l'Etoile and the Arc de Triomphe. Outwardly it was one of the grandest international assemblies the world had ever witnessed. But the real convention took place, as usual, behind the scenes. The Congress elected a "World Committee against War and Fascism," and agreed unanimously to the communist proposal that corresponding "Leagues against War and Fascism" should be set up in every democratic country on earth.

On the third day of the Congress I spoke in the densely packed *Salle Pleyel.* Like other speakers who had come from "totalitarian" countries, I wore a mask, for the danger that Gestapo agents were among us was ever present. I exhorted the international delegates to make use of the thousands of ships of all flags which entered German harbors and rivers as battering rams to cleave a way for anti-Hitler propaganda and organization across the marine frontiers of the Third Reich. There was thunderous applause. My speech was translated into seven languages.

One of the personages who had been expected to turn up at the Congress was Ernst Wollweber. But the ex-mutineer had stuck to his post in Germany. Cilly, his secretary, arrived in his stead. Tall, lissome, smartly attired, she had lost none of her admirable poise.

But her face betrayed the strain of months of perilous underground work at Wollweber's side.

"I am glad I came out alive," she told me. "It is not simple death that shakes one; it's the horror, the feeling that all around you are teeth, murderous teeth, ready to snap at you and mangle you."

At a special conference of German communist leaders in Walter Ginsburg's *atelier* the name of Ernst Wollweber became the center of a dismal squabble. A diminutive but fierce-eyed Russian from the Comintern Secretariat in Moscow was present. The remnants of the old German leadership—Pieck, Koenen, Remmele and their satellites—were plainly afraid of Wollweber's rivalry. All of them were for leaving him in charge of our organization in Germany, a function which they hoped would, sooner or later, plunge him into the cellars of the Gestapo. Against this attitude the Russian emissary flared up in anger. He lashed out savagely. Ernst Wollweber, as the organizer of the new subterranean Comintern machine in Germany, had won a formidable reputation with the Soviet leaders. They were unwilling to sacrifice the most able of their German crew. The German leaders finally succumbed to the Russian's demand that a courier should be sent to Berlin to spirit Wollweber safely out of the country. They succumbed like men hearing the announcement of their own death sentence. They offered to send one of their own aides to Berlin. The Russian refused. Mutual distrust and dull hatred were in the air.

"Go and find Comrade Jensen," the Russian told me. "Tell him to be at *Metro Vavin,* eight o'clock sharp."

Jensen suggested that his *aide-de-camp*, Georg Hegener, should go to Germany to rescue Wollweber.

On the eve of Hegener's expedition to Germany I had a rendezvous with Cilly in a café near the Odeon. She was in a state of great agitation. Her habitual *sang-froid* had given way to chagrin, and gnashing helplessness. Over a glass of *pernod*, she clutched my arm, talking rapidly.

"This Wilhelm Pieck! He's so anxious to wear Ernst Thaelmann's boots that he considers everyone who comes out alive from Germany as a personal affront. He is afraid of having me work in the Central Committee. He thinks I'm a spy for Ernst (Wollweber). He's afraid I'll collect material against him for the day Ernst comes out of Germany."

Cilly loved Ernst Wollweber. Her mind was essentially unpolitical, but she was a communist, unquestioning and unflinching in the execution of her duties. Now I saw the woman in her break through the armor of discipline. Her dark eyes, her whole chic slimness was in a mutinous uproar. Like many other Comintern operatives, she had a vague but deep-rooted fear of a sudden call to Moscow; no one was ever sure whether such a call did not mean a final farewell to the stormy, yet pleasant, life abroad.

"I will speak to Comrade Jensen," I told her. "He can inform Moscow that he needs you for a temporary assignment."

"Do, please. I shall be grateful."

Jensen conferred with Ulrich. The *S-Apparat*—the Comintern's Espionage Defense department—was in need of capable female assistants. Cilly was detailed to the unit of Michel Avatin.

Among the delegates who had come from Germany was Bror Nystroem, a Swede by birth, but a citizen of the Soviet Union. He had worked in the industrial espionage *Apparat* of Hans Kippenberger, as a specialist for the Siemens Trust, the electrical and steel combine. From Nystroem I learned the whereabouts of Firelei. Once more she had become a fugitive from the Gestapo. From Berlin she had been transferred to Dresden, in Saxony, and from there, after a raid, she had fled to Stettin. Bror Nystroem gave me an address in Stettin.

"You may write her," he said. "It is a good address, as addresses go nowadays."

I wrote a few harmless lines on a postcard, giving the address of a French worker in Montreuil, and mailed the card. Four days I waited. They were days of cruel torture. Then the answer came, in the handwriting that was so familiar. It was a pitiful cry for help. I telegraphed Firelei all the money I had in my possession.

From the telegraph office I rushed to the branch headquarters of the Western Secretariat in the Rue Lafayette. An imperturbable secretary received me. I demanded to be contacted with one of our executives.

"Wait," she said.

I waited an hour, and another hour. Couriers came and went, bent on business of their own. Finally the secretary directed me to go to a foot-bridge which crossed the Seine in front of the Louvre. On the bridge stood a middle-aged man, immaculately dressed in gray. He was René, the Pole, leader of the newly-formed Comité Mondial—the general staff for the Leagues against War and Fascism the world over.

Immediately he began to talk to me about my next assignment. "You must go to Strasbourg and Basle," he said. "We must arrange facilities for a large-scale transportation of the *Rundschau* across the Rhine to Germany." The *Rundschau*, published in Basle, was the journal of the Comintern press service. I hardly listened. René talked on! "We are bringing out a Brown Book about the Reichstag Fire. It is highly important. A hundred thousand copies of a miniature edition must go to Germany. And Strasbourg—"

"Listen," I interposed, "I am troubled by another matter. My wife, Comrade Firelei, is in a desperate situation."

"Yes?"

I spoke. René was a good listener. I requested that the Party should help me get Firelei out of Germany. The look of curiosity on the Pole's face changed into a frozen little smile.

"Dear comrade," he said patiently, "I respect your sensibility. But the situation is too serious to allow us to jeopardize our *Apparat* in the solution of our comrades' private difficulties. Later, perhaps. We need you to build up a working bridgehead in Strasbourg. It is very pressing."

We parted, hostility between us. In that instant Firelei meant more to me than the sum of all political schemes and conspiracies. I went in search of Richard Jensen. But Jensen had left Paris. He had flown back to Copenhagen. I went to Ginsburg, the liaison man. I needed money and a reliable courier who was not known to the Gestapo. Ginsburg was sympathetic, but afraid. He would do nothing without exact instructions from his superiors. I was determined not to engage in any further assignments as long as Firelei was hunted and homeless in Germany.

I decided to return to the waterfront. The sailors would not hesitate to help me. Most of those who had been in Hamburg in bygone days knew Firelei and considered her as their pal. I wrote Firelei to hold herself ready to travel at a moment's notice. It was a reckless thing to do. If the letter fell into Gestapo hands all would be lost. I borrowed a hundred francs from Comrade Beaugrand. It was enough to pay my fare to Antwerp.

In the office of Comrade Anton in Antwerp I found a letter from the Western Secretariat, ordering me to proceed to Strasbourg without delay. I paid no heed. In the back room of Café Belgenland, I gathered about myself the hard-bitten élite of the Antwerp waterfront brigades. "Help me to rescue Firelei," was my appeal to them. They gave a subdued cheer. Their loyalty and enthusiasm brought tears to my eyes. Among them was Birzinsch, a young Lett. Under the latter's leadership, the "activists" went out next morning to raise the required money by collections aboard the ships. By nightfall nearly four hundred Belgas were in my hands.

"I need one volunteer to go with me to Germany," I said.

Birzinsch volunteered. We left Antwerp the same night, arriving in Verviers, a Belgian town facing the German frontier, at four in the morning. A guide from the local communist unit led us along smugglers' paths to the outskirts of Aachen, a five-hour march through dense woods. We reached German soil without encountering a single frontier guard.

In Aachen we parted. Birzinsch took the larger part of the collected money and entrained for Cologne and Berlin. From Berlin he would go to Stettin. I waited in Aachen. All day I wandered through the quiet, clean streets, avoiding the center of the town, turning into doorways at the approach of storm troopers, and during the night I lay hidden in the woods. I neither ate nor slept. The minutes crawled like malevolent and infinitely slow animals. The day went by, and the night, and another day and another night. I was tormented by many gnawing questions: "What had happened to Birzinsch? Would he find Firelei? Where were they? When would they come?" Countless times I asked myself these questions.

Each time a train arrived from Cologne, I hovered in the vicinity of a teamsters' restaurant where we had agreed to meet. And finally they came, Birzinsch with a look of immeasurable triumph on his stoic Baltic face, and walking at his side was Firelei, in a red-and-white summer dress and a gay handbag dangling from her wrist. I wanted to rush at them with a shout of joy, but I held still and let them pass. And then I followed them slowly until we had reached the edge of the woods.

Birzinsch wandered a little way off, pretending to look for mushrooms. We were alone in the dim twilight under the beeches. I looked into Firelei's eyes. They shone like stars.

"Now we are together again," she said softly. "I am so glad, so glad! I shall never let you go away alone again ... ."

All night we moved eastward through the black woods. Birzinsch took the lead. Toward morning he halted until we were abreast of him.

"Now you can have the good embrace," he said happily. "We are in Belgium."

Again life promised to be like a song. We reached Antwerp, and for a week we lived in a garret above a foundry, oblivious of the outside world. The insistent clamor made by the Western Secretariat ended our clandestine vacation.

"We are going to Paris," I announced.

"I have always wanted to see Paris again," Firelei said.

We journeyed to Paris, crossing the border afoot, for Firelei was still without a passport. In Paris, Walter Ginsburg procured for her a passport in the name of Jeanette Languinier, a native of St. Nazaire. Thus equipped, we traveled on to Strasbourg and Basle.

We were in Strasbourg when the news reached me that the chief of the Gestapo espionage in Flanders, Ilia Raikoff—The Ox—had at last been executed by Michel Avatin and his aides. I learned the details of this execution later, partly from Avatin himself, partly from Cilly who had helped him, but mainly from Comrade Anton, the Antwerp liaison-man, who had collected the reports.

Four had been assigned to do the job—Avatin, a Belgian named Rose, a tubby little Greek from Thessalonike, and then Cilly. They found that The Ox was hard to catch. He knocked about town in taxis and made his conferences in cafes flooded with light. Avatin and Rose kept on his heels. The tubby Greek prowled around the waterfront to watch those who walked in and out of The Ox's quarters. And Cilly, dressed in gowns that were like silk in the rain, sipped drinks in the cafes, doing her utmost to induce The Ox to ask her for a favor. After a week of this, Avatin became impatient.

He wanted Cilly to get The Ox drunk, then to take him for a nocturnal promenade along the river. But The Ox did not drink enough, and he never walked out of the reach of bright lights and policemen. So, when he took Cilly one night to a hotel, Avatin decided to change his plan.

Because Cilly disliked using a knife, the Greek went to a library to study up on poisons. He returned to report that a few drops of undiluted nicotine would be all right. All Cilly had to do was to mix the nicotine into The Ox's tea before he went to bed, and after that she could take a plane to Paris, and Comrade Ginsburg would arrange for a passport to prove that she'd been in Paris for a long time.

It was a promising scheme. During the next week, The Ox took Cilly to three different hotels. Nothing happened. Each following morning she came to report that The Ox was still alive. It seemed that Cilly was nursing scruples. On the third morning her face was so pale that her lips looked almost blood-red. When she said The Ox was a very unhappy man, Avatin gave her a ferocious sample of his mind. He sent a message to Copenhagen, proposing that Cilly be relegated to less serious work.

Then, all of a sudden, it happened.

Cilly did not poison the spy. Just before midnight she telephoned from a hotel on the Meir that The Ox was drunk and unbearable. She promised that she would take him out in a taxi, and dump him among the trees near the old fortress by the river.

Three hours Avatin, Rose, and the Greek, waited on the bench beneath the trees. Nothing was said. They listened to the charivari of voices that went up like steam from a club of beachcombers camping on a patch of grass.

Around half past two a taxi nosed in among the trees. They saw Cilly get out. Quickly she walked to the quay, pretending to look at a passing steamer. The Ox staggered out of the taxi half a minute later. He shouted for her to wait. Cilly turned. Just as he was reaching for her, she shoved him over a bench. Then she ran back to the taxi and told the driver to step on the gas. By the time The Ox had his bearings, the taxi was gone. The beachcombers brayed and guffawed. They had surrounded The Ox, showering mockery and consolations.

"Let's go," Avatin said quietly.

The clouds hung low over the towers of Antwerp. The lights on the other side of the river were bleary in the rain. One after another the beachcombers trudged away. Their obscure shapes moved over the wet pavement toward sheltering doorways.

Avatin stood in front of the Russian. He was calm, as always in the face of imminent action. The waterfront was deserted. The rain fell heavily now.

"Ox," said Avatin, "when one man puts a gun against another man's spine, what happens?"

"Nothing," The Ox said with contempt.

"And when he pulls the trigger?"

The Ox looked up. "One man is dead, one alive," he muttered.

They acted swiftly now. The Greek pressed the muzzle of a pistol against The Ox's spine.

"Stand up."

The Ox rose to his feet. He towered in the rain, bewildered.

"March," said the Greek.

The Ox marched. He marched toward the edge of the quay, Avatin on his right, Rose on his left, and behind him the tubby Greek with the gun.

"We're going to kill you," Avatin said.

The Ox seemed suddenly astonished.

"What ails you fellows?" he quavered.

"The Gestapo will be sorry to lose you," Avatin said.

Beneath their feet the black water of the river gurgled against the stones. The Ox stood on the edge of the quay as if he were thinking, and abruptly he whirled and struck at the Greek's face. In the same instant Avatin plunged his dagger into the spy's groin and ripped it sideways. Then he kicked him. The Ox grunted. Then he pitched into the river, and the current carried him away.

Chapter Thirty-one

"DEATH IS EASY"

For sixty days we journeyed through France, Belgium and Holland. From Strasbourg, Firelei and I proceeded to Basle, crossing the border at the rim of a village called St. Louis. From Basle we returned to Paris, and from Paris we went to Rouen, Le Havre, Boulogne-sur-Mer, Dunkerque, Ghent, Antwerp, Rotterdam and back to Antwerp, in that order. In all these ports it was my task to establish "underground" bases for the shipment of illegal printed matter to Germany, a task which I combined with the overhauling of the communist marine units along the rivers and coasts. In the second half of August it was my lot to play the role of one of the chief tacticians in the great strike of the rivermen and canal workers of the Paris area and Northern France.

We were in Le Havre, in the home of the liaison-agent, M. Cance and his gracious wife, when the news of the first official execution of communists in Germany was flashed around the world. On August 1, 1933, the heads of the workers Hermann Luetgens, Bruno Tesch, Wolff and Moeller fell under the executioner's ax in Hamburg-Altona. I had known them, and so had Firelei. Other death sentences had been pronounced by the Special Tribunals in Chemnitz and Breslau, in Berlin and Cologne. The effect of this butchery on our minds could not have been greater had we been told that our son had been murdered. First there was abysmal sorrow, then hatred, and a cry for revenge. In a fit of passion, Firelei drew a caricature of Hitler in the role of a headsman, the ax in his right hand, the lopped-off head of Comrade Luetgens raised high in his left hand, and the headless body sprawling between the victor's legs. Across this drawing she wrote the three familiar lines:

*"Verflucht, verflucht
Wer die sen Tag vergessen will,
Wer dieses Blut nicht raechen will."*

' (Accursed, accursed be he,
Who will forget this day,
Who will not avenge this blood.)

"Once I loved to draw beautiful things," Firelei said darkly. "But that is past and gone now."

I wrote an appeal for revenge, a violent emotional outcry in words, and had it printed on the Party presses against the background of Hitler the Headsman in an edition of twenty-five thousand. I had it shipped immediately to all ports where our units specialized in the smuggling of printed contraband to Germany. Firelei took about a hundred of these broadsides and left Cance's house, running down the hill as fast as her legs could carry her.

"Better look after her," Cance advised me. "She is terribly upset." I dropped my work to find out where Firelei was going. I could not see her. I rushed downhill and cruised aimlessly through the streets of Le Havre, without finding a sign of her. The truth dawned on me suddenly. There were two German ships in port, the *Gerolstein* and the *Bellona*. Firelei had gone into the harbor to distribute the leaflets among the German crews.

Nothing could be more dangerous. There was no German merchant ship afloat which did not have a Gestapo spy among her crew. A group of three or four Nazis a ship were powerful enough to terrorize a crew of fifty.

I raced to the *Gerolstein*, which had a communist unit.

"Yes," the gangway watchman told me, "there was a chit here who distributed some sort of wild papers."

"Did she leave?"

"Aye."

"When?"

"Oh, a good hour ago."

"Where's this ship bound for from here?"

"New York."

I hastened away. I rushed to the Bellow, which lay in another part of the harbor. The *Bellona*'s home port was Bremen. She had come from Spain, homeward bound, and was one of the few ships which was manned by a majority of organized Nazis. The gangway of the *Bellona* was guarded by two sailors who wore the storm troopers' insignia. I could not get aboard. A little distance away from the ship the quayside was littered with crumpled copies of our appeal for vengeance. Firelei had been here.

I asked a tallyman who was checking slings at the door of the cargo shed: "Have you seen a girl here, a young girl in a red and white dress, a blonde girl?"

"Une fille? ... Ah, la garçonne! Mais oui!"

Where?"

"In yonder freight-office."

It was the freight-office of the German Neptun Line, at the end of the shed. I hailed a group of longshoremen while I approached it. "What is the matter?"

"Au secours," I cried excitedly. *"Brigandage. Les Nazis."*

Four or five followed. The dockers of Le Havre were anarchists. They had not participated in the strikes against the swastika flag, which they considered as a meaningless rag, as they did all other national ensigns; but they hated the Hitler movement just the same. Without preliminaries, I burst into the German freight-office. The dockers followed. The office consisted of two rooms, a large front room and a smaller office in the rear. In the front room an officer from the *Bellona* was talking to two German clerks. "Here," the officer shouted, "where are you going?"

We shouldered past him and through the door of the rear office. Firelei was there. She sat at a table, confronted by a young man. The young man, who was no sailor, stepped back against the wall. Firelei gave a cry of surprise.

"What are you doing here?" I demanded.

She was out of her senses. She rose and advanced toward the young man, her fists clenched. "This little murderer," she muttered, "he wanted me to go to the ship with him. This interesting—" Men gathered in the outside office. The dockers stood awkwardly, not knowing what to do.

"Let's get out of here!"

I seized Firelei's arm and dragged her away. The Germans made room for us in silence. The dockers wanted to demolish the office. "No, no," I told them. "It was a mistake."

Firelei and I were illegally in France, unregistered, and with false passports. We could not risk questioning by police. Firelei chattered crazily. I helped her into a taxi and climbed in behind her. "Where to?"

"A bath-house."

I rented a shower room and forced Firelei to stand for ten consecutive minutes under the cold water.

"Are you recovered now?"

"Yes," she said timidly. "I don't know. I went mad."

"Now dress. We are going to Cance's. You'll stay in bed for a day, and read and see nothing."

She followed me like a tired child. In her sleep, she screamed. She screamed the names of the men who had been beheaded in Hamburg-Altona, and she called them her "little brothers."

I did not ask her what had happened on the quay in front of the *Bellona*. She told me of it herself, weeks afterward. She had distributed the leaflets, throwing them in little rolls over the steamer's rail so that they landed on deck. Then she had entered the freight-office to distribute some more. There two men refused to let her go out again.

"They wanted me to go with them aboard the *Bellona*," Firelei said. "But they waited, because I threatened to scream. And then you came."

On August 15 we were in Dunkerque. The strategic position of this port had long attracted the special attention of the Comintern. Communist trade unions monopolized the harbor and the connecting railroads. We knew that in the event of a war the country between Dunkerque and Lille would be the most vulnerable in France. The stationary agent of the G.P.U. in Dunkerque was Marcel Wegscheider, an engineer; and his chief aide was Gustave Huyge, the leader of the Dockers' Union. Both had their offices in one of the finest buildings in town, the *Salle d'Avenir*, 9 Rue l'Ecluse-de-Bergues.

With Wegscheider and Huyge I discussed the possibilities of a strike movement on the rivers and canals in Northern France. The campaign plan had been drawn up by the Western Secretariat. It aimed at nothing less than the throttling of the industries of the area by cutting off the raw-materials which they received over the river and canal systems linking Paris with Lorraine and the Channel coast. Already the C.G.T.U., the communist-controlled Confederation of Trade Unions, had prepared the ground in weeks of strike agitation. The outbreak of the *bataille des bateliers* was merely a matter of days. To the Dunkerque leadership of the Communist Party fell the task of supplying a staff of experts who could transform the impending strike into a real battle by blocking the waterways to Paris with—ship barricades.

It was an hitherto untried form of large-scale transport sabotage. Wegscheider, I and our band of assistants journeyed separately to Paris. We came together again in the C.G.T.U. headquarters, on the Rue des Granges aux Belles, for a conference with René and the French Party leaders.

Benoit Frachon, the strategist of Bolshevist enterprise in France, spread out a general staff map of the Paris area. Military garrisons and stations of the *Garde Mobile* were marked in blue. Marked in red were places of confluence and strategic canal junctions. Frachon, his voice meticulous and cold, pointed them out as the spots where ship barricades would be most effective, and where squads of Parisian militants already lay ready for action. Two motorcycle couriers were attached to each squad to maintain a steady contact with the central strike headquarters which, to give an appearance of independence, was established in St. Denis, far from the official buildings of the Communist Party. Appointed to act as "advisers" to the central strike committee were Jean Rigal, Emile Ramette, and one Mauvais, all veterans in the Comintern service, and I as representative of the International of Seamen and Harbor Workers, the Comintern's Maritime Section.

The strike began on August 19. As yet the French government did not suspect the scope of the plot. But at dawn, on August 20, our sabotage brigades swung into action.

The French river workers—the *bateliers*—followed the leadership of our units. On the Aisne River ten barges were tied side to side until they obstructed the river from one bank to the other. We stiffened this ship barricade by instructing the *bateliers* to bring out all available anchors. The barges on both flanks of the river blockade were then manned by squads of Red Front Fighters, whose task was to defend them against attacks from shore. The river was blocked. When daylight came, ship transports on their way from the region of Rheims to Paris were unable to proceed. Where the Aisne flows into the Oise, the tangle of held-up river shipping waxed worse from hour to hour.

Next we proceeded to block the Oise. The Oise was broader than the Aisne, and fourteen barges were needed to build a floating barricade. On the canals branching off toward the north and to Belgium three or four ships anchored and moored in a cluster at the entrance of the lock-gates formed efficient obstructions. By noon a total of twenty-two barricades had been constructed. Traffic on the rivers and waterways below Paris had come to a halt.

The French authorities were too surprised to act at once. In Lille and Amiens, at Dunkerque and Rouen, the *bateliers* followed suit. Shipping between France and Belgium and Holland ceased. The North closed, we threw all our forces toward the South and East. New ship barricades sprang up. The

Seine was blocked, and then the Marne. On August 22, the Paris government threatened to intervene. It issued an ultimatum, demanding that the barricades be cleared away.

To gain time, we sent delegations of striking *bateliers* to negotiate with the government. Ramette and Jean Rigal sped north to draw the workers of the mining and textile industries into the strike. I issued a manifesto: "Rivermen, defend your ship blockades!"

I was in a session with the strike committee at Conflans Ste. Honorine on the morning of August 23 when a sweating courier ran into the meeting.

"Take care," he shouted. "The *Garde Mobile* is coming, and police, and the Paris fire department."

The conference broke up. Arrachard, a leading Parisian communist, rushed to the nearby ship barricades to take charge of the defense. Detachments of *Garde Mobile* marched toward the river. I was hastening toward the courier center when a detachment leader stopped me.

"Halt! Where from? Where to?"

Doris Ginsburg, who acted as my interpreter, was with me. She produced a bewitching smile. I produced my Danish passport.

"He is a tourist," she explained. "I am his guide. We came to see the exciting ship blockades."

The *Garde Mobile* officer apologized. "Pass," he said. "You should know, *mademoiselle* that there are better things to see in France than this."

On the floating barricades the *bateliers* stood off attempts of the attackers to board the barges. They used clubs and boat hooks and streams of cold water from canvas hoses to keep the police boats at a distance. A flanking assault from ashore was also repelled. The government forces retired. Three hours later they renewed their attack, spurting high pressure jets of water from hoses of the Paris fire engines. Defenders were toppled over by the impact of the water. The *Garde Mobile* boarded the barges and cut the moorings. Turning slowly around themselves, the ships drifted downstream, some alone, others still clinging together. As soon as the *Garde Mobile* reassembled to tackle the next line of obstruction, Mauvais and I sent out the couriers with orders to re-establish the smashed barricade. This time we were not content with one blockade. Over a stretch of one mile we built three barricades with over forty ships.

The combined forces of the government now assaulted our barricades at all points at once, using the darkness of night to approach unobserved. We had received orders from the Comintern not to advocate the use of firearms, since the action had more the character of a dress rehearsal than of a decisive combat. To avoid an outright insurrection, the police and the *Garde Mobile*, the latter in steel helmets, also abstained from using their pistols. Bruises, broken heads and countless drenchings in river and canal water were the lot of both sides.

The general melee lasted four days and nights. It was the most adventurous strike play ever enacted on French soil. On the night of August 26, all key organizers were called to a consultation in St. Denis. Frachon informed us that the order had come to call off the strike at daybreak. Comrade Arrachard flew up in a rage. "Why," he protested, "the affair is going wonderfully. Why stop?"

"The comrades from the Comintern are satisfied," Frachon relayed. "We must not play all our cards. It has been an experiment, a successful experiment. We may now draw from it lessons of value for the greater battles of the future."

Several hundred *bateliers* had been arrested in the course of the "experiment." Thirty imported militants from Dunkerque were charged with rebellion. Not one of the real leaders of the strike was among them.

On a sultry day at the end of August, seemingly appearing from nowhere, Ernst Wollweber arrived in Paris.

Firelei met him in Comrade Ginsburg's *atelier* on the Rue de Seine. Wollweber was crouching over a map of Paris, and another one of Europe.

"Comrade Ernst," Firelei cried. "Welcome to Paris. We feared you had been taken."

"Feared?" The Silesian grinned. "Even the best can be replaced, though it happens at times that the dead come back to life."

The arrival of Wollweber in Paris was like the appearance of a hungry hawk over the chicken ranch. The numerous German communists who had installed themselves in comfortable offices since their flight from Germany feared for their positions and their budgets. They did everything in their power to isolate the dangerous newcomer, to head him off to Brussels or Moscow. For a week the Silesian quietly took his bearings. He recruited a train of devoted assistants from the rank and file of refugees. He dispatched private couriers to Copenhagen and the Soviet Union, and soon these dispatch-bearers returned with favorable answers. Conferences with delegates of the Western Secretariat followed. Ernst Wollweber's reputation as the organizer of the German "underground" was immense.

Wollweber's greatest asset was the fact that he was hardly known outside the German frontiers. He was a man of mystery, and he knew how to exploit that role. He moved through the streets of Paris, thick-set, silent, his iron forehead almost hidden under a too-large fedora hat, his saturnine eyes glinting into the hot Paris summer air.

He used a great number of names. At the *Comité Mondial*, they called him Schulz. In the refugee committees, he was known as Anderson. In the conferences of Party functionaries, he was introduced as Kurt Schmidt. Ernst Wolhveber seemed to take a sinister delight in using the names of men who had died in Gestapo dungeons. Firelei called him "The Cannibal," a name which he seemed to like, especially when it came from the lips of a likable girl. He would stop in his tracks then, and his black Mongol eyes would peer upward, as if they were studying a hidden code in the pattern of the kalsomine on the ceiling, and a grin would come to his tobacco-smeared lips, a grin to which Firelei's only answer was a rather comical "Ugh!"

One evening Firelei and I were with Wollweber in a café on the Champs Elysees. Wollweber drank soda water. We talked about Germany, about Paris, and the future. And suddenly he said:

"I've been looking around. This Paris is a treasure-chest. I've learned more here in one week, I tell you, than in three years in Germany. In Germany, our comrades either starve to death or are beaten to death. And here? The boulevard cafes are lousy with deserters!" At this point he broke into an ugly snarl. "I'm going to round them up," he growled, "one and all. I'm going to send them back to Germany where they belong."

Our café conference continued. Wollweber spoke of the Western Secretariat, the highest body of Comintern plenipotentiaries outside of the Moscow offices of Molotov and Piatnitzky. Ulrich he called a "lawyer scoundrel." Of the Pole René, the chief of the World League against Fascism, he spoke as a *Schlappschwanz*—a "dish rag."

"If I had René's powers," he growled, "I could make the world turn around the other way." We came to Henri Barbusse. Wollweber had never heard of him. "Who is this Barbusse fellow?" he queried.

"He wrote the book *Under Fire*," Firelei explained.

"He wouldn't last long under fire," Wollweber commented sardonically. "He's too tall and thin. Any fool of a detective could pick him out among a million others."

Firelei laughed. "Comrade Ernst, how about this fellow Goethe?"

"Goethe is dead," Wollweber said. "Goethe wrote *Faust*," Wollweber told me that he would shortly leave for Moscow. From Moscow he would go to Copenhagen. He aspired to create for himself an *Apparat* on which he could rely utterly. The names of prominent rivals—like Wilhelm Pieck and Muenzenberg—were anathema to him. He would not have them as collaborators. He would choose his own collaborators from the unspoiled rank and file. And abruptly he said to Firelei:

"You're going to Copenhagen with me."

Firelei recoiled. She would stay with me, she answered.

"Your man will follow shortly," Wollweber commented. "There are a lot of things I'm going to do in Copenhagen. The air is cleaner there than in Paris."

Three days later Firelei received her sailing orders from the Western Secretariat. She was needed in Copenhagen, and to Copenhagen she had to go. Expulsion from the Party for violation of Bolshevist discipline was the alternative. Wollweber went to Copenhagen by airplane. Firelei traveled aboard the *P. A. Bernstorff* from Dunkerque.

In Roger Walter Ginsburg's *atelier* I found a letter from the Western Secretariat, assigning me to direct a special conference of the Anglo-American delegations to the World Youth Congress against War which convened in Paris in September. The object of the special conference was the co-ordination of the work of communist organizations in the armament and shipping industries for purposes of military intelligence and the obstruction of arms shipments not approved by the Soviet government.

At the end of the World Youth Congress, in the offices of the Comintern Bureau for Railroads (*Internationales Kommittee der Eisenbahner*) on the Place de la République in Paris, I met the former Polish army officer whom the Kremlin had appointed, after the arrest of Albert Walter, to act as commissar for the Maritime Section of the Third International. This comrade informed me that he was about to be recalled to fill an administrative post in the Soviet Union, and that he had proposed to Molotov that I should be considered for the function of secretary-general of the Maritime Section.

"Nobody knows the international waterfront better than you," he said.

I was filled with a riotous elation. It was the highest office I could ever hope to attain in the service of the Communist International. Tonie, a girl of forty, husky and youngish, the chief of the Comintern Railroad Bureau, threw her arms around my neck and hugged me for no plausible reason.

"I want to go to bed with the chief of all the sailors," she crowed.

The Pole snickered, "Tonie, you'll have plenty of competition, but there's no hope for you girls to cut in on this comrade's budget."

Since the arrest of Albert Walter, the monthly subsidy which the International of Seamen and Harbor Workers (ISH) received from Moscow varied between twenty to forty-five thousand dollars, depending on the scope and importance of current actions and campaigns.

I repaired to the Comintern hotel, the Hotel d'Alsace, and packed my few belongings. I was to go to Copenhagen to receive a new set of passports from Richard Jensen, and to proceed then to Moscow for a conference with Ossip Piatnitzky, the organizational chief of the Comintern.

I bade farewell to my Paris friends and boarded the North Express to Amsterdam. One of the agents of the G.P.U. in Holland met me at the airport. His name was de Groot, and he had the appearance and the credentials of a coffee merchant. He handed me a package containing several dozen blank Netherlands passports for delivery to Richard Jensen in Copenhagen. The customs examination of air travelers was less stringent than the examination of voyagers arriving by train or boat. Soon the motors began to roar, dust flew astern, and my plane left the ground. The Frisian Islands slipped by below, the North Sea spread out in a panorama of green and white, with the hostile German coast to starboard, and the friendly coast of Jutland straight ahead.

Immediately on my arrival in Copenhagen I went to Richard Jensen's home on Vesterbrogade. There a girl secretary directed me to a secret office, 18 Toldbodgade, in the disreputable Nyhavn district. It was the home of the new passport forging center of the Comintern's Westbureau. I delivered the Dutch passports to Jensen, and requested him to arrange with the Soviet consul for the documents necessary for my journey to Moscow.

"You are not going to Moscow," Jensen told me. "Comrade Wollweber wants to see you."

"I have instructions to report to Piatnitzky," I countered.

"Never mind Piatnitzky. Comrades Kuusinen and Bela Kun are in Copenhagen now. Everything can be arranged here," Jensen advised me.

Three days passed before the Western Secretariat found time to attend to my future work. Meanwhile I saw Firelei. She had her quarters on Oeresundsvej, in a modern room overlooking a beautiful beach and the reaches of the Baltic Sea.

"Wollweber works day and night," she said. "He is like a steam-shovel in breeches, digging his way into the Westbureau."

Firelei suffered under the reports of unabating horrors in Germany. But she was happy in her work. Wollweber had put her in charge of the transport of communist literature from Denmark and South Sweden to Germany by maritime couriers. In addition to this function, it was her duty to remain each morning from five to eleven near the telephone in her room to note down the exact wording of each of numerous incoming messages. The texts of these messages were then transmitted by courier to the Western Secretariat. The bulk of the telephone messages were in code. Firelei neither knew their meaning, nor the identities of the callers. It did not matter. The dreams of her youth were gone. Her child was lost. She was resigned to serve the cause which had taken so much, and from which a return to a former manner of life—now so remote and strange—had become impossible.

On the morning of my fourth day in Copenhagen Jensen's son, Martin, who was a G.P.U. man handling the management of communist activities in the water, gas and electrical works of Copenhagen, called on me. It was a Sunday.

"We're going to the Westbureau," he said. "There's a fight on about you."

"What sort of fight?" I asked, somewhat startled.

While we journeyed by tramcar to the suburb of Charlottenlund, where Otto Wilhelm Kuusinen, the unofficial secretary of the Comintern maintained an office in the apartment of a woman G.P.U. operative, Martin Jensen gossiped in whispers. He was anxious to please me, for I knew of some of his indiscretions with Party belles, and Comrade Martin was afraid that his pretty wife, Inge, who loved him fanatically, would learn of his erotic escapades.

"It is a jurisdictional fight," he exclaimed. "The internationalists want you to boss the waterfront groups, and then Wollweber came and said, 'Nothing doing, I need this comrade in Germany!'"

"Has there been a decision?"

"No, they're still fighting."

"Who is stronger?"

"The German, I believe—Wollweber. He has the big patience. He sits and argues until the others are tired of the argument and go home."

We halted near the home of Kuusinen's hostess. Charlottenlund was a fashionable residential district. Old trees and comfortable benches lined the avenues. Martin Jensen entered a house, 173 Ordrupvej, and returned presently with a tall, rather bony woman of about forty. She had an intelligent face, and she walked with a lanky, peculiar gait which seemed to denote that she was unable to bend her left leg at the knee. The woman was Petra Petersen, a secret agent, and a veteran operator in the central telegraph exchange of the Danish capital. I came to know her better in later years when, for several weeks, I made my quarters in her apartment, sleeping in the same bed in which Kuusinen had slept during the early fall of 1933.

Martin Jensen departed. Petra Petersen put her arm into mine.

"A beautiful day," she casually observed. "Let's promenade." We walked through Charlottenlund Park until we came upon a beach. The sun glittered on the waters of Oeresund, and peaceful islands rose in the distant blue. At the south end of the beach lay an old fortress, now converted into a park, with a boat landing at its foot. Petra Petersen led me to a small trim motor launch. We boarded the craft. Aboard it were Kuusinen, the Finn; a small colorless man with a tautly angular face and sharp mouse-like eyes; and Ernst Wollweber, who appeared more dumpy than ever in light flannel trousers and a blue jacket. The launch was operated by Julius Vanman, who had become a member of the Espionage Defense.

While the boat cruised at low speed along the friendly shore, we conferred. When Kuusinen spoke, his voice rose barely above a rapid mutter. From his thin lips the sentences leaped jerkily. The decision, as far as I was concerned, had already been made. I was not going to Moscow. I was going to Germany. Wollweber watched me like a lynx. I took the news silently.

"For the present Comrade Ernst will take over the leadership of the Maritime Section himself," Kuusinen informed me.

Into my mind flashed the realization of the game that had been played behind the scenes, a game in which I was a pawn—one of many pawns. Ernst Wollweber had come to the conclusion that I would never be his obedient creature. My horizon was international. Wollweber saw only Germany. His one ambition—that of directing all available forces into the German struggle—not only embraced men, but also money. *I was being sent to Germany because Ernst Wollweber was determined not to leave the Kremlin's subsidy for the Maritime Division in the hands of a man whom he could not control at will.* "After all," Wollweber growled, "you are a member of the *German* Party, and therefore subject to the dispositions of the *German* executive."

"We have come to the conclusion that you are indispensable in Germany," Kuusinen seconded. "For a Bolshevik it is the greatest honor to do his revolutionary duty at the most dangerous post."

"Why, Comrade Kuusinen," I wanted to ask, "did you not return to Finland after the revolution there was drowned in blood?" Instead I nodded. Hitler was the most dangerous enemy of workers' rights, and of the Soviet Union. "Very well," I said, "I will go to Germany."

"Are you nervous?" Wollweber asked.

"No."

"We'll give you a week's vacation. And when you come back in six months or so, we'll celebrate the grand *Auf Wiedersehen.*"

"Don't try to fool me," I answered sullenly. "No illegal worker in Germany can hope to last six months. Not one in ten of our friends there ever comes back."

"In the Party we have no friends. In the Party we know only comrades," the Silesian observed. And in a slow growl he added: "We've all faced death. What of it? *Das Sterben ist nicht so schwer.* (Death is easy.) The difficult art is to keep alive."

"Death is easy!" There was a long silence.

"Let's get down to concrete tasks," Kuusinen suggested drily.

My week's 'vacation" passed like a gust of wind. The days were brimful with work. From Losovsky, in Moscow, came words of praise for my share in the great river and canal strike in the Paris area. "The sailor from Hamburg," he wrote, "der hat seine Sache ganz gut gemacht!" It added much to the reputation I had won in the Swedish strike. Losovsky requested that I write a short history of the latter campaign, and I spent two of my "vacation" nights on the report. It was published under the title, *The Lessons of the Swedish Shipping Strike*.

I also translated much confidential material dealing with the arrest of Georgi Dimitrov in Berlin and with the preparations for the Reichstag Fire Trial, which already then promised to develop into an international sensation. The heroism with which the world press has credited the former chief of the Western Secretariat and the present nominal leader of the Comintern in Moscow, because of his bold and clever sallies against the government's "witnesses," Hermann Goering and Joseph Goebbels, was only the result of a carefully and cunningly organized play. The confidential material which passed through my hands in the Vimmelskaftet offices of the Westbureau in Copenhagen contained data as far out of the reach of the ordinary news-hawk as the complicated codes devised by Piatnitzky's nameless *chiffre* experts.

Months before the famous Berlin trial began, secret negotiations were already under way between Moscow and Berlin to exchange Dimitrov and his two Bulgarian aides for three German officers who had been caught by the G.P.U. as spies on Soviet soil. Dimitrov had to be saved from being broken down by Gestapo torture, not for his own sake, but for the sake of the Soviet Secret Service and the Comintern, whose inside workings he knew too well.

Under duress, Dimitrov had proved himself less steadfast than many of the comrades under his command. He surrendered to the Gestapo the address of a couple who sheltered him; both man and wife sought escape in suicide when the Gestapo came for them. They cut their own veins, but were rushed in time to a hospital by the Nazi jailers. Dimitrov also surrendered to the Gestapo the name and address of his mistress, Annie Krueger. His wife died suddenly, under circumstances which remain a mystery to this day, in May, 1933, while Dimitrov was in prison, awaiting trial.

It was at this time that the G.P.U. stepped in with this threat to the Gestapo: "Leave Dimitrov alone. Whatever you do to him, we shall do to your spies in Moscow." Negotiations for an exchange of prisoners began through the medium of the Soviet consulate in Copenhagen, and through Georgi Dimitrov's sister, to whom the Gestapo, strangely enough, granted free passage in and out of Germany. The deal between Moscow and Berlin was concluded on the eve of the trial. But Dimitrov, for face-saving reasons, was kept in Germany until the end of the great Leipzig show. He, the star prisoner of the Gestapo, enjoyed jail privileges unattainable to the mass of more obscure captives. He was supplied with newspapers, allowed to smoke cigars in his cell, and to receive mail. The "little" comrades, meanwhile, received only beatings, and often bullets. In later years, I heard them speak bitterly in the concentration camps about Dimitrov and his rescue by Stalin. They felt themselves betrayed and abandoned by the cause they had served. Had *they* insulted General Goering in open court, as Dimitrov did so dramatically at Leipzig, they would have paid hideously, and paid with their lives for such an "heroic" gesture.

I was preparing to take the road to the land where "death is easy." The map of Germany was in my head—its cities, rivers, railroad schedules. I memorized a long string of names and cover names, addresses and cover addresses. Whenever Ernst Wollweber mentioned the name of one of my prospective collaborators, he would add: "Maybe the comrade is still at large or maybe he's caught or dead. You'll have to find that out."

I was to organize the distribution of large quantities of propaganda to the various district headquarters. The printed matter was smuggled into the port of Hamburg by maritime couriers, but the organization which had been created to relay the literary contraband from its depots in the harbor of Hamburg to the Party staff in the inland had broken down. My task was to rebuild it. Besides, there were other assignments, of a more limited nature, but no less important: the forwarding by ship couriers of confidential reports from Germany to Copenhagen. Some of these reports would come from Rudolf Heitman, the G.P.U. man in the Hamburg Gestapo; others would come from our spies in various Nazi organizations, among which the German Labor Front and the *Auslandsabteilung*—the Foreign Division of the Nazi Party— were the most important. Two of the best courier ships were reserved to carry such reports, the steamers *Beira* and *Jolantha,* Danish vessels trading between Copenhagen and Hamburg, and manned exclusively by Richard Jensen's men. All preparations for my illegal entry to Germany were surrounded with the utmost secrecy. From Jensen I received two carefully forged passports. One was of Danish origin; the other was British, issued in the name of Robert Williams, a journalist, and signed by Sir John Simon. From Jensen I also received the sum of $12,000, half of which was to be conveyed to the Berlin organization, while the other half was to cover my expenses for the first three months of "underground" activities. And finally Ernst Wollweber informed me that he had detailed a reliable girl comrade to act as my personal secretary and courier.

"Who is she?" I demanded.

"Cilly."

Since Wollweber's arrival in Paris, Cilly had married—*pro forma*—an elderly and obscure member of the Danish Communist Party. Such procedure was common with our female agents. Through her marriage Cilly had legally changed her name and had lawfully acquired Danish citizenship. The Dane, after he had played the role of husband as a Party duty, had been shipped to Russia and taken out of harm's way.

Came the day of leave-taking from Firelei.

A tear trickled over her cheek. "You'll never come back to me now," she said. "From Germany nobody ever returns." A little later she was brave again. We had a quiet supper, and then we went to Firelei's room which she had decorated with many flowers. She clung to me fiercely, tenderly, possessed by a gigantic determination to give me everything, the best she could give, the most any woman can give in a last embrace.

At ten o'clock Julius Vanman, the G.P.U. man from Jensen's cortege, arrived. For a time he waited quietly. Then he said:

"Time to go, comrade."

I tore myself free and followed the G.P.U. guide to the street. Firelei must stay. She was forbidden to know at what point I crossed the German border. She began to sing a folksong she loved. *"Fahre wohl, du gruene Erde . . ."* Farewell, green earth! After the first line her voice broke.

Julius Vanman led me to a back room of Café Helmerhus on the Raadhus Place. Ernst Wollweber was there. He was drunk. He had his arm around the neck of a young brunette, Lola, the wife of Walter Duddins, the former Hamburg Party leader whom Wollweber had wanted to replace with the luckless John Scheer. Duddins had been arrested in Germany and was awaiting trial on charges of high treason. Lola was but one of the growing army of "Party widows" who populated Copenhagen and Paris after their men had been sent to Germany and their doom.

Wollweber shook my hand vigorously. His thick face was full of wrinkles produced by a mirthless grin, and his eyes gleamed black.

"Hals und Beinbruch," he growled. "Do your job well. The Party won't forget its children."

Vanman had arranged for every detail of my passage. By train and ferry we crossed to Fredericia on the east coast of Jutland, and from there a train bore us south to Sonderburg. On the way I asked Vanman about Michel Avatin, whom I had not met in Copenhagen, although he was there.

"He was busy catching Nazi spies," Vanman said.

"Did he catch any?"

Vanman grinned, "Yes, if that'll cheer you up. The day you arrived from Paris he caught a fellow named Milenzer. This Gestapo rat had rented a room opposite Jensen's home. He had a film camera and was making pictures of all who went in and out of Jensen's house. Heitman in Hamburg tipped us off."

"What happened to Milenzer?"

"Our friends took him out on the Sound in a boat. They strangled him and sank him with a shackle fastened to each foot."

From Sonderburg a highway skirts the shores of Flensburg Fjord. We took the autobus until we were less than a mile from the German frontier. Then we struck inland over the grounds of a huge estate, across fields and through woods, until we reached a cottage situated on a country road. The trek had been so complicated that I had lost all sense of direction.

"Where are we?" I asked.

"In Germany," Vanman said. "Three miles from Flensburg."

In the cottage a frontier courier was waiting, a squat young man with an imperturbable temperament. Julius Vanman bade me good-by. "Keep the flag flying," he said simply. The frontier courier, whistling cheerfully, drew two bicycles out of a nearby shed.

"Nothing like a morning ride to whet the appetite for breakfast," he drawled.

He led the way. I followed. Through the cold morning mists we rode into the town of Flensburg. At a tavern near the station we stopped for coffee. After he had emptied his cup, the courier gave me a nod, and sauntered off. I waited until he had disappeared down the street. Then I also left the tavern. I walked into the station, inwardly tense as I passed the storm troopers on guard, and bought a ticket to Ahrensburg, a suburb of Hamburg. It was the tenth of October.

Chapter Thirty-two

CAPTURED

On November 30, 1933, the Gestapo seized me.

The seven weeks that followed my arrival in Germany were one continuous nightmare, filled with darkness and treacherous swamps, with crouching shapes ready to spring and tear, with cautious advances, reckless leaps, a wide-awake fatalism, fatuous fervor, with comedians of invincibility and the death-cries of the lost. No longer did the Gestapo strike with wild, haphazard blows. It had learned the deadly value of subtlety and patience. The mass raids of the great man hunt of the preceding spring had given way to methods of precision. The man hunt had slowed down, but it had become more cruel, less noisy, and hence more nerve-racking and destructive than ever.

From Hamburg, the central gateway for contraband from abroad, I made trips to Berlin and Bremen, to Luebeck, Emden, and Duisburg on the Rhine. Most of the names and addresses of subleaders in the propaganda distribution *Apparat*, which Wollweber had designated as my collaborators, had gone out of existence. The bearers of those names were either in dungeons or already in their graves, or they had simply disappeared and their former homes had become traps for those who would come to pick up the broken threads and build the secret network anew. With the liaison *Apparat* between the lower Party units and the leadership all but wiped out, I was compelled to feel my way toward the unknown comrades at the bottom of the battered "underground" machine to re-establish disrupted contacts and to select new staffs from the rank and file. This was a most perilous undertaking: to find a man or a woman of whom I had not heard for months in the depths of a large city, to maneuver with infinite caution for an interview in the night, while wondering during each of scores of such approaches whether the man or the girl was still loyal, or had turned traitor to the cause and former friends.

My nerves had become so mutinous that I felt I would burst if I did not force myself to be on the move. Each week of conspirative work had been like a minute and a century. At times I thought a man was lucky if he had the privilege of dying before a firing squad. To die in such a quick and gentle manner seemed better, by far, than to slink through interminable days pregnant with hate and fear, with a hectic courage, with disquieting schemes and convulsive action—and with a constant promise of disaster which made one marvel at each new dawn that one was still alive.

I prided myself on having no illusions. I fought because I hated. Beyond that nothing seemed to bear importance. I was miserable in contemplation.

It was action that made me quietly and fanatically happy. I knew I was a member of a suicide brigade attacking in the face of insurmountable odds. I knew that a captured communist— particularly if the Gestapo considered him a communist leader— was treated with greater ferocity than any murderer for material gain. I had seen the crimson posters blaze the news that the heads of comrades, found guilty of high treason, had fallen under the executioner's ax.

There was, for instance, the problem of finding a place where a man could sleep. Most of my assistants had themselves been driven from their abodes. Each house had its watcher, every stranger was reported to the police. It was a stark invitation to disaster to rent a private room or to register at a hotel. Fear and distrust leered from every doorway. It had become high treason to give an enemy of the state a place to sleep. Informers infested the streets, the railway stations and cafes, the factories, the docks and the ships. They formed an army of volunteer spies, whose existence and activities alone accounted for the phenomenal successes of the Gestapo. The raiders were most active between midnight and dawn. The rush of traffic through the seven portals of Gestapo headquarters reached its height in hours when the normal traffic of the city was at its lowest.

During these seven weeks I hardly ever slept twice in the same bed. The hours of daylight were the hours of rest. My workday began late in the afternoon, when dusk began to settle, and rarely ended before five or six in the morning. The all-important contacts were established at night. There were conferences with Party instructors and couriers, with comrades in charge of propaganda consignments to inland destinations, with tugboat men, barge skippers and ships-chandlers' runners, who smuggled newly-arrived batches of printed matter from the ships to the depots ashore, past harbor police and the cordon of customs guards. Nothing is static in "underground" work. The scenes shift constantly, and so do the faces, and only the distant consciousness of danger is ever-present. Toward morning I scouted for a place in which to rest. Sometimes it was the home of an unknown Party member, sometimes a cellar or the dusty floor of a storeroom, sometimes a room in a fly-by-night hostelry rented by the hour to surreptitious lovers, and occasionally it was a church. The safest places, however, were the lairs of prostitutes. They hated the Nazi troopers, who came most often and paid the lowest prices.

Once each week I met Rudolf Heitman, our operative in the Gestapo. Heitman was a broad-shouldered man of medium height. He had a heavy, but inconspicuous face, almost expressionless blue eyes, and a reserved manner. His hair, cut in Prussian fashion, was graying at the temples. He had been a member of the Political Police in the times of the Weimar Republic, and when Hitler became Chancellor, Rudolf Heitman had joined the National Socialist Party on instructions from the G.P.U. He was no real revolutionist. He sold information for money. The Gestapo had taken him over and assigned him to a minor desk in the railroad-control department. From this obscure observation post he collected data on persons wanted by the Gestapo, on the behavior and fate of comrades who had been arrested, on local spies who had been promoted to specialized work in the Gestapo's Foreign Division. His data which, at best, covered but a tiny fraction of the Gestapo's doings, then came into the hands of the Western Secretariat. Communist operatives inside the Gestapo were worth to us their weight in gold. There were not many, not more than a dozen in all of Germany. Among other material, Richard Jensen's weekly courier aboard the Beira brought me each week an envelope containing money for Rudolf Heitman, whom I met the same night, in a basement cabaret in the St. Georg district. We sat at separate tables, pretending not to notice one another until I gave Heitman a signal to follow me to the lavatory. Here I exchanged my money envelope for the information he had gathered. He was ingenious in finding methods of camouflage. One week his report would be concealed in the text of a penny-dreadful novel, the next it was typewritten on sheets of thin paper which had then been baked into a raisin bun, and on a third occasion it was pasted into the lining of a cheap wallet crammed with postcard pictures of horses, movie stars and Nazi leaders.

My chief aide was Karl Burmeister. He was a native of the North Sea coast, tall, angular, fair-haired and blue-eyed, a graduate of Moscow's University of the West. He was a cautious and reliable worker, capable of exercising great patience, of long periods of watchful waiting, but when he clearly saw his course, he could act with swift and ruthless efficiency. He was in charge of our courier network among the rivermen of the Elbe, the lower Rhine and the middle German canals which connect the Rhine and Elbe with the Berlin area. Upon his loyalty and his memory rested the safety of several hundred ship couriers and other comrades engaged in the secret transport *Apparat*. Karl Burmeister's young wife had been arrested as a hostage. The Gestapo had announced that they would hold her until her man was in their hands. It was he who had succeeded in maneuvering a number of young communists into the Foreign Division of the Nazi Party. Burmeister's unit there did excellent work. It furnished us—and we relayed the information to Copenhagen and the G.P.U.—the names of most Gestapo operatives on German merchant vessels, of Gestapo liaison-men in foreign ports, and complete lists of Nazi seamen who had been trained in photography and equipped with cameras to photograph strategic strips of coastline and every foreign harbor entered by German ships. The last was a routine form of mass espionage which the Gestapo had copied from the G.P.U.

Burmeister was curiously sensitive, but fearless. He had a high sense of duty. He was like a good officer who is always ready to strike out alone behind the enemy lines to recruit his followers in enemy country. Once, laughing, he compared himself with one of those Jesuit emissaries who carried out secret missions in Elizabethan England. "Only I wish we had as easy a time as the Jesuits," he remarked. He was a master in the art of bolstering the morale of the shaken by imparting to them the conviction that our "underground" organization was much stronger and better organized than it could possibly be in reality.

Contacts, often lost by unexpected enemy interference, were at times recovered by a quirk of circumstance. For a fortnight I had been hunting for Otto K., the central liaison-man for our units aboard the Hamburg-America liners, whom I had lost after a

Gestapo raid in the harbor. I searched doggedly for him, without results. He had not slept at his home for more than half a year. His wife, a flaxen-haired peasant girl, had given birth to a son whom Otto had never seen. About four o'clock one morning, after a hard night's work, I sat brooding over a glass of beer in an outlying waterfront tavern. The last customers were staggering out and the waiters were counting their night's tips. I was weary, pondering where I should go to snatch a few hours of sleep, when a broad-faced, thick-hipped girl accosted me.

"What's the matter," she said brusquely. "You sit all alone so long behind one small glass of beer."

"I like it," I answered. "Besides, it's none of your business."

"I know you," said the girl.

"Know me?"

At once I was alert, ready to strike or escape. The girl sat down beside me, clasping her hands and leaning them on my shoulder.

"You are a sailor," she said. "You came in with an English ship, oh—maybe nine years ago. You came to Café Rheingold and drank cherry brandy with me. Plenty of cherry brandy, so funny, that's why I remember you. Three nights you loved me. Then your ship went out. Remember?"

"Your name is Berta," I said. "You were a salesgirl."

"Now my name is Marie."

"Marie?"

"Yes. What ship are you on?"

"I have no ship. It's tough to find a ship nowadays."

"Let's celebrate our meeting again," she said.

"No, I'm tired."

"Are you tired?"

"Yes, let me sleep with you," I asked.

"Oh, you have no place to sleep?"

"No, and no money to pay you."

"But listen," she whispered, "I'm sick."

"I won't touch you."

I went with her to a house populated by prostitutes, unemployed dockers and waterfront scavengers. She was kind, and she had a good bed. On a worn-out divan sat a teddy-bear with green glass eyes. He had his right paw raised in the fascist salute. Above Marie's bed, flanked by obscene photographs, hung a lithograph of Adolf Hitler. On a small table beneath the portrait lay a weather-beaten briefcase. The cracked brown leather caught my attention. A piece of rope took the place of the leather hand-strap. I recognized it immediately. It was Otto's.

"Where is Otto?" I asked, pointing to the briefcase.

"Who?" Marie faltered. "I don't know what you are talking about. It's mine."

I grasped her arm and shook her, and repeated the question. The girl was frightened.

"He is with Emmie," she blubbered, "a girl three doors down the corridor."

So I found the comrade whom I had lost, for whom I had feared the worst.

In a far different manner ended my quest for Jan Templin, the harbor foreman for Soviet shipping in Hamburg, who, a half-year earlier, had so generously supplied me with a store of paper for the illegal printing plant under my command. Templin was a man of innumerable connections of long standing. But shortly before the November "election" of the new Nazi Reichstag, when storm troopers patrolled the streets with posters showing a man hanging from a gallows over the inscription, "'He has voted against the New Germany," Jan Templin mysteriously disappeared from his old haunts. His former home was occupied by an Elite Guard officer. My search was fraught with danger; when one seeks a man who has gone, one has to ask questions. In all such cases, the first assumption is that the man is in hiding, the second that he has fled abroad, the third that he has been arrested. My search ended when a frightened wisp of a girl in the Neustadt district told Cilly that Jan Templin had been seized by the Gestapo.

Jan Templin knew much about our contacts aboard Russian ships. I prepared a note of warning, which I intended to dispatch by the *Beira* courier. However, by the time the Beira arrived from Copenhagen events had overtaken the contents of my note. Jan Templin was dead. With him he had taken the secrets of the Soviet ships. My tenseness relaxed. He hanged himself in his cell, the Gestapo press bureau reported.

Olga Templin, his wife, received a note from the police informing her of the time and place of her husband's burial. Observers of the Party *Apparat* attended the ceremony. The corpse of Jan Templin was carted to the grave under a Gestapo escort. The coffin was sealed. Olga Templin was not permitted to take a last glance at her dead mate's face. The coffin was covered with seven feet of earth, and when the ground above the grave was level, the Gestapo agents departed.

My comrade, Karl Burmeister, had certain suspicions. "Suppose," he reasoned, "Jan Templin is not dead at all, but alive. Suppose the Gestapo has buried an empty coffin, or another dead man, to make our comrades believe that Templin is dead. What will other arrested men be likely to do to save themselves? They will think that a dead Jan Templin can't suffer more, and so they will incriminate him to lighten the lot of others who are still alive. Suppose now that is just what the Gestapo wants. Jan Templin is alive and incriminated by his own comrades, and the Gestapo can stage an open trial and have him condemned for high treason."

What Burmeister said had happened before. Tony Taube, of the Hamburg Party Committee, decided to ascertain that Templin was really dead. That night a silent group of communists marched to Jan Templin's grave. They carried shovels. While some stood guard, others opened the grave and pried the lid off the coffin. They found a corpse. They put the corpse into a canvas sailor's bag and carried it to the home of a Party member not far from the edge of the cemetery. Then they called Burmeister.

The dead man was Jan Templin. But he had not died by hanging. His face was crushed, as if it had been struck by heavy boots. His right wrist and a number of ribs had been broken. The body was covered with welts. The legs were bruised. The sexual organs showed signs of having been burned with the ends of cigarettes. The corpse was photographed. The comrades, some weeping openly, stood around Jan Templin and hummed the funeral march of the revolution.

Burmeister reported to me in the morning.

"If ever I get caught," he said stonily, "I won't give them time to do this—do such things to me. I'll find a way out. A quick one, and a sure one."

To shake off the bad spell, we had coffee in a tavern. After that we walked along peaceful streets, talking of the work that lay ahead.

Cilly's versatility and her quick grasp of vital detail had made her indispensable to me in my clandestine crusade against Nazi power. She had an agile mind, and a genius for picking up apparently lost contacts and for making total strangers feel sympathetic and at ease. Intuitively, it seemed, she could sense whether a man or woman was sincere, or wavering, or capable of treachery. She was as yet unknown to the Nazi police and had little to fear. She lived in fashionable hotels and wore smart clothes, and in duty and pleasure alike she retained a nonchalance as if she still had a hundred years to live. A hundred years of youth. She lacked the hatred and the bitterness so prevalent in our ranks. She was eager to please me, eager to show her mettle. Her beautiful face, the straight simplicity with which she attended to her tasks, and her tall, cool body reminded me always anew of a Diana I had seen in the Louvre in Paris. Often I wondered why Cilly, who was Ernst Wollweber's mate, had been sent to Germany. Once, talking to me about herself, she gave me the answer.

"I have been banished," she said.

"Why?"

"When Comrade Ernst was in Paris, he had a love affair with a Polish girl. Later, when we were together again in Copenhagen, Ernst received letters. The letters were perfumed and the writing was feminine. They were written in Polish, which I could not read. I was mad with jealousy. Ernst laughed. He told me the perfume was merely camouflage for organization letters. I knew he lied, and I was hurt. I stole the letters and had them translated. They were the love letters of a half-crazy girl. I was foolish enough to make a scene."

"And so Wollweber sent you to Germany?"

"He sent me to Germany," Cilly said defiantly. "He expected me to refuse, to cringe, to beg him to let me stay with him in Copenhagen. He was mistaken. I went to Germany."

"The end is bound to be unpleasant," I said.

"Pleasant things can happen, too," she answered.

"Don't fool yourself, Cil."

It was evening. We sat in a corner of the Vaterland Bar. Cilly leaned forward over the table, an unwonted liquid warmth in her eyes. Vehemently she said:

"I don't fool myself. I know where I stand. We are prisoners, intellectually and bodily. Our minds and our bodies are confined in a narrow alley with high windowless walls on both sides. The alley has a name. The name is 'Party Discipline,' the most beastly thing that's ever been invented."

"It's necessary. Without it, the Party could not live."

Cilly raised her glass. "Long live the Party," she whispered, tears in her eyes. "I also want to live. Any animal wants to live. And here, as—*Tote auf Urlaub*—we should live as if each day on earth would be our last."

"All right," I said, "I must go now. I have a meeting at ten."

"Will you see me tonight?" Cilly asked quietly.

"Not before twelve."

"Be sure to come. Hotel Mau, room sixteen."

It would be rank folly for me to enter any large hotel. "What is the matter with Cilly?" I asked myself, departing. "Is she cracking up?"

The man I sought that night was Martin Holstein, a militant whom Wollweber had recommended to me as one of the best. For weeks already I had striven to establish contact with this man. I knew Martin Holstein as one of the most reckless fighters in the movement. He was a man of twenty-nine or thirty, with thin lips, pale green eyes and a cadaverous face. He was no organizer, but he had proved himself useful in assignments which required personal courage and the ability to strike with lightning speed.

No one in our ranks suspected Martin Holstein. Many of my collaborators had been delivered to the Gestapo by some unknown traitor. Hugo Gill, the head of our units on the overseas quays and the oil docks, had disappeared one night with thirty-two of his assistants. Alfred Feddersen had been betrayed and was beaten to death in the central prison of Hamburg. Two weeks later Karl Rattai and Matthias Thesen had been seized by the Gestapo; Rattai went mad under torture, and Comrade Thesen opened his veins with glass from a broken window. There were many more who had gone the same way. Burmeister and I and Cilly, assisted by a special unit of the Espionage Defense, had considered every member of our organization in order to determine who could be the hidden traitor among us. Certain comrades were put under G.P.U. surveillance. But no one suspected Martin Holstein, who had served the Party for years in Germany, in America and the Soviet Union. I remembered Wollweber's words: "Comrade Holstein is there somewhere. Use him for liaison work, or in the smuggling units or the sabotage groups. Holstein is good!" Diligently I had searched for Holstein. Cilly contacted him through a courier on November 29, and arranged with him to meet me the following night in the Botanical Gardens.

The night of November 30 was dark. A cold northwester blew in from the North Sea. Cilly was with me. At three minutes to eight we entered the Botanical Gardens. A conference with Burmeister and Otto was scheduled for eight o'clock. The steamer *Jolantha* had come in that morning from Copenhagen with fresh instructions from the Western Secretariat. At half past eight I was to meet Martin Holstein.

The paths were muddy. The cold struck into our faces. Our eyes were wide in the darkness. Overhead the wind screeched through the tops of naked trees. Cilly, wrapped in a long fur coat, stepped gingerly over the puddles. We skirted the shore of a little lake, counting the benches as we went along: "One, two, three, four. On the fifth they must be waiting."

Someone huddled on the bench, shoulders hunched and head stuck forward, shielding with cupped hands the tiny glow of a cigarette. We stopped. Cilly whistled the first notes of a Nazi battle song. The man rose from the bench and approached us with slow steps. Inside the pocket of my trenchcoat my fist lay tightly around Firelei's little gun. I was determined to shoot it out if things looked wrong.

In front towered the shape of Karl Burmeister. He grunted as we shook hands.

"Where's Otto?" I demanded.

"Arrested."

Such news is like an oaken truncheon coming down on the top of your head. For a second it makes you stop in your tracks. You stare like a man who is caught in a dense fog. Then your lips tighten and it is as if you toss your head. Burmeister spoke in a low, solid voice:

"They took him this morning."

"Where?"

"At his home."

"He went to see his Anja?"

Anja was Otto's wife.

Karl Burmeister nodded. "Maybe he wanted to see his son, too. He was so damned hungry and felt ill and thought he would have just one good night's sleep. The Gestapo had his house watched all the time." Mournfully Burmeister added: "A revolutionist has no business having a family."

"Where's Anja?"

"Arrested."

"We must shift all addresses and depots that were known to Otto," I said.

"I've seen to that," Burmeister replied. "I've had Otto's paraphernalia brought to a girl in a flower shop until we can fix up other places."

"A girl?"

"Some girls are all right."

"I hope so."

"Damned handy sometimes," Burmeister muttered.

We walked to and fro under the trees, scanning the road in front and behind us. Ghostly patches of gray sailed over the black sky.

"How is your wife?" I asked Burmeister.

"I wish I knew."

Then we talked of our work, of ships, propaganda consignments, relay stations, methods and plans and the maze of technical details inherent in conspirative organization. Suddenly Karl Burmeister squared his shoulders.

"Somebody is following us," he said calmly.

Twenty paces behind us a man was smoking a cigarette.

"Probably Holstein."

"Damn him."

The man behind us sauntered leisurely from tree to tree. He was Martin Holstein. He wore neither hat nor overcoat.

"Hello, Martin."

"I got cold sitting on the bench," Holstein drawled. "Let me in on the devil dance."

Our conversation lasted another hour. I was glad that I had found Holstein. His enthusiasm was contagious. After the latest reports had been discussed and analyzed, and an outline for the next day's campaign laid down, we parted, walking away from one another in different directions.

I left the gardens and strode along a street which followed the old City Moat. I thought of going to the rooms Burmeister had obtained for me but two days earlier to decode a message a courier had brought that afternoon from Berlin, and to draft notes for the relay stations to pick up the packages of printed matter which our harbor couriers had deposited in the baggage rooms of railway stations around Hamburg. I thought of Cilly and her pathetic hunger for other than political companionship. I also thought of Firelei and her loneliness, her kindness and courage and her shattered dreams.

The sky was covered with sullen clouds. Under the yellow light of lanterns, patches of pavement swam like circular islands in the dark. Ahead of me a couple, arms linked together, swayed around a corner. A broad-hipped woman scuttled through the cold and disappeared in a doorway. Empty sidewalks are likely to make any hunted man feel apprehensive. Jammed in a crowd a man feels safer. I saw the headlights of a car flash their beams along the street. I wondered why the car slowed down as it came up behind me. I thought of turning quickly into a doorway to let the car pass by. But then I thought, "Oh, nerves!" And I took care not to quicken my stride.

It was not a trick of my imagination. The car slowed down. I heard the sudden scream of brakes.

"Raus!" snapped a voice. *"Auf ihn!"*

I jerked around and dived toward the entrance of a house. In the pocket of my overcoat the little automatic pistol which Firelei, my wife, had given me when I had said farewell to her in Copenhagen, was tangled with a glove. In this moment of emergency I knew exactly what I wanted to do, what I had been instructed to do when overtaken in the street. I wanted to run into the house, race to the top floor, escape over the roofs, shooting to cover my retreat. More than once this technique had been tested.

The door was locked. The pursuers were around me in a second. They were three young men who had jumped from the car. They had guns in their hands. They jabbed their guns into my face and against my body, and snarled:

"Up with your hands!"

"One move and we plug you!"

I raised my arms and stood still. One Gestapo agent pressed the barrel of his pistol against my teeth. His eyes were curiously bright, and he growled like a dog. The hands of the other ran over my shoulders and down my arms and legs, feeling over every inch of my body and sweeping into pockets. All they found they stuffed into their overcoats.

I heard their panting breath. After they had snapped handcuffs around my wrists the tenseness in their faces gave way to expressions of boyish triumph. I felt like a man who sees the ground under his feet burst wide open and rush up high on all sides.

They brought me to a police station in St. Pauli, Hamburg's Coney Island. As they led me through the streets, shackled, people assembled from nowhere and stared. A grunted command from a Gestapo man sufficed to disperse them.

At the station they pushed me into a chair. Two prostitutes who had been brought in before me were hustled into a backroom. Several uniformed policemen regarded me silently from behind their desks. Their faces were mask-like, noncommittal. The three Gestapo agents joked and beamed. They took off their overcoats. They took their guns from their overcoat pockets and shoved them into their hip pockets. Then all three lounged on desks and lit cigarettes. Their clothes were shabby; the lines in their faces signaled lack of sleep.

A strange numbness had taken hold of my mind. I noticed every detail, but I could not think. I knew what was going to happen in the next hours. Somehow, it was not I to whom this was happening. It was someone else. In the circle of my colleagues in the international Comintern service we had often discussed what a comrade was up against when he fell into the hands of the Gestapo. Shoulder shrugs could only feebly disguise the mute horror most of us felt deep inside when headquarters received the intelligence that one of our friends had become the prey of Heinrich Himmler's guards.

Friends? Crouched on a chair under the glaring lights of St. Pauli police station I remembered Ernst Wollweber's scowling face as he had growled, "The Party knows no friends—the Party knows only comrades," and had added with a derisive grin: "Keep calm. Death is easy."

One of my captors was a powerful man with a dark skin and jutting cheekbones. The others were slender and blond. All three completely ignored the uniformed policemen in the room.

"Ha, got you after all," said one who caught my glance.

Another chuckled as he slowly drew his forefinger across his throat. "Your beard is bound to come off," he drawled.

The dark-skinned man, after a minute scrutiny of my passport, said with an air of immense self-satisfaction, "If you hadn't come back to Germany, we'd have brought you back from Copenhagen or Paris dead or alive. Had you gone to China, we'd have trapped you, too."

One of the other agents had picked up my passport.

"Nice passport you had," he said. "Where'd you get it?"

I gave him no answer.

"Have it your way," the other said lazily. "We'll find out— pretty soon."

I tried hard to think. I tried hard to think of what they might know about me and what I'd have to say. In the democratic countries the communist rule for arrested comrades is to say nothing. If you say nothing here, I thought, they'll beat you to death. In the long run, you'll break or die. Even the strongest are broken if they do not die. Flesh and blood can be broken. Spirits can be broken. If they took care to give a man no opportunity for suicide, that man could be broken. They knew I had been in Copenhagen and Paris. They knew I had used a false passport. They knew I had carried an automatic pistol of Belgian make for which I had no official license. They knew more; much more. No prisoner knows upon arrest how much his captors know about the deeds he committed in violation of the law of the land.

My brain was capable only of a single conclusion: "Tell them nothing! A coolie in a den full of hungry tigers would probably fare better; he would at least die quickly. I must look for a chance to destroy myself. Until then, I must tell them nothing. Nothing! There is not a trace of hope. But there is still a purpose. Every day, in all the world, men fall for the cause. But the cause survives. The cause is invincible. Tell them nothing! Cut away your limbs, one by one, rather than do a thing that could harm the cause."

"Want a smoke?"

I nodded.

The dark-skinned man put a cigarette between my lips. My lips were dry, without feeling. I could not feel that I had a cigarette between my lips. The Gestapo man then struck a match and lit the cigarette. Greedily I drew the smoke into my lungs. I felt the bite of smoke in my eyes, and impulsively I tugged at the shackles around my wrists to take the cigarette out of my mouth. The dark-skinned man saw that. He took the cigarette from my mouth and laid it on the edge of a desk. And a few seconds later he shoved it back between my lips.

"You see," he said, "we treat you fair and square."

The other two grinned. The policemen stared stupidly.

I wondered what could have happened to Karl Burmeister, Cilly, Comrade Holstein. My arrest had been no haphazard affair. When they pounced on me, the Gestapo knew who I was. I could not explain it. We had been careful in the extreme. We had adhered to all the complicated rules of conspirative work. We were too alert, too well trained not to recognize at once when we were trailed. We were no tyros in illegal work. What if Karl Burmeister had been taken? Or Cilly? Or Holstein? I refused to believe it. Cilly would come to my quarters at midnight, and find me gone. She'd guess the truth. She knew that I had hidden a list of courier addresses in my bedroom. She would find them and take them away and warn the others.

All this was absurd.

The formulation at which my brain rebelled was this: "Among your aides is a spy. All big Gestapo coups are brought about through spies. Were it not for spies, Gestapo work would be limited to a sterile bureaucratic routine."

I fought against the realization. It made me violently ill. Who was the spy? What did he know? I groped in vain.

"You're a fool," the dark-skinned Gestapo man said. "I'd have recognized your face in a thousand. Don't you remember me?"

"No."

"Haven't you seen me ride beside you in the subway in Berlin?"

"I don't remember."

"Didn't you see me in the meeting in Antwerp where you told the docker delegates to boycott all German ships that came to Belgian ports? Do you remember that?"

"I never talked in such a meeting," I said.

"We're going to thaw up your memory, my boy." The big man laughed. "Where's your home, boy?"

"I was born in the Rhineland."

"Ah, I know it well. Is it not beautiful, your home?"

"Yes, it's beautiful," I said.

The Gestapo agent thrust his fist within an inch of my eyes. "And you sell out your beautiful home to Moscow!" he snarled. "What do you suppose should be done with a scoundrel who betrays his country to the Muscovites, hey?"

I said nothing. One of the big man's colleagues, leaning back on the desk, spat into my face.

"Soon you'll lose your beard," he said, without moving his lips. "Shooting is too good for anyone who works against his own country."

"I didn't work against my country," I protested.

"Shut your mouth! Anyone who wants to destroy Hitler wants to destroy Germany. Hitler is Germany and Germany is Hitler."

I was silent.

The dark-skinned man eyed me with cold hostility. "One thing I'm sorry for," he said. "I'm sorry you can't see your own head roll off your carcass."

The telephone rang. A policeman took the receiver.

"Herr Magnus," he addressed the dark-skinned agent. "A message for you. St. Georg station speaking."

Magnus stamped over to the telephone.

I strained to catch every word he said.

"Herr Magnus . . . Oh, yes, a perfect evening ... You have the lady? Good. Very good. Excellent! Call *Stadthaus* for instructions. ... Yes, yes . .. Heil Hitler!"

Immediately he dialed another number. I watched his forefinger move, 0-000-1, that was the number of Gestapo headquarters. I knew it because I had called that number many times to give the Gestapo misleading information.

Then Magnus' rumbling voice: "Inspector Kraus? ... Sure, we got him. He walked away pretty fast, but we got him ... No ... no, he acted quite civilized.

Had a shooting iron, though. One of the little ones from Belgium. Didn't give him a chance to use it. ... Yes, quite civilized. ... Bring him up right away? Very good. *Wird gemacht.* Heil Hitler!"

The other two leaped from their desks. The chair was kicked from under me. The uniformed officers leaped to attention.

"Off we go."

At the curb a car waited, a burly chauffeur at the wheel. The chauffeur had a gray muffler wrapped around his neck and a greasy cap pulled down to his eyebrows. As we boarded the car, passers-by gazed at us with vacant faces, and hastened on their way.

I was pushed into the back of the car, wedged between two Gestapo men.

"Don't move and don't talk!"

Each of the men held the muzzle of his gun against my ribs. Magnus, in front beside the chauffeur, turned his head.

"Did you ever have a bloody behind?" he asked.

"No, sir."

"Well, you'll have it damn soon."

The chauffeur yawned. Then the car began to move ahead.

We sped through dismal streets toward police headquarters. Shadows flew by, and lights. People moved along the houserows. In a doorway, a boy strained to draw a laughing girl into the house. At another spot, the sounds of an electric piano pounded through a dimly-lit window.

The car slowed down because a dog was leisurely crossing the street. Magnus roared wildly at a truck driver who did not keep far enough to the right. The truck driver waved his arm with disdain, but then he recognized the police car and pulled quietly out of the way. The deep droning of a ship's siren came in from the river. The man on my left prodded me with his gun.

"Hear the steamer calling?"

"Yes, sir."

"You'll never hear another steamer calling," he muttered. "You'll never have another girl. You'll never have another glass of beer. How do you like that?"

They knew I'd had to do with shipping, I realized.

"I don't think I'll like it," I said.

"I don't blame you," he growled. "It's nice to make a steamer trip and have a beer with a girl." He tapped my head with his fist. "Next time I have one, I'll think of you," he chuckled.

My own calmness astonished me. Things were so simple, after all.

Now we were in the center of the city. The car lunged across a short bridge, and then the towering bulk of police headquarters dominated the street.

Sentries in the uniforms of the Black Corps threw up their arms in the Hitler salute as the car veered through an arched gateway and clashed to a halt in a gloomy yard. The yard was cluttered with motor cars. Massive walls towered in the dark. Light flooded from high windows. I heard the clanging of the great bell from the St. Michael Cathedral. It was eleven.

The Gestapo men jumped from the car. The chauffeur stretched his arms and yawned.

"The devil," he grumbled, "a man needs sleep."

"All right—get out."

One of my captors brought his lips close to my ear.

"Now your beard will come off," he growled menacingly.

"Tell them nothing," I thought. "Whatever happens, tell them nothing. The Comintern recognizes but a single crime: Betrayal of the Party. All else is merely a matter of expediency. Thousands have already gone the way I am about to go."

"Smart now! Get going!"

One led the way. The others followed closely on my heels.

We marched down a murky hall. Our steps echoed from dust-covered walls. An Elite Guard passed with a ringing stride. His hand held the end of a chain which was twisted around the wrist of a bedraggled prisoner. They passed without giving us a glance.

At a rapid pace we traversed a labyrinth of corridors, up broad stairways, past armed guards and large rooms full of clattering noise. Doors were unlocked at a signal from Magnus, and locked again after we had passed. In leaps and bounds two manacled men came down the stairs. They were chained together. Behind them was a young trooper. The trooper swung a rubber truncheon.

"Faster," he yelled. "Run faster!"

On the next landing a score of men stood facing the wall. Guards shouted names. One guard, a youngster, had seized the scraggy neck of an elderly worker and amused himself with banging the worker's head against the wall. Where the file of male prisoners ended, two Elite Guards stood over a plump girl. The girl's face was white as death. She threw herself to the stone floor and scrambled back on her feet. A trooper swung his arms and barked commands:

"Up—down! Up—down! Up—down! We'll make you eat dirt, you bitch. Up—down! Up—down ..."

Hideous shouting came from the end of the corridor. A well-dressed man was down on hands and knees. Astride him sat a grinning trooper. The man was screaming at the top of his voice: "I'm a Jew, a stinking Jew! I'm a Jew, a stinking Jew!"

We were on the sixth floor. The hallway was silent as a graveyard. Carpets covered the floor. The walls were clean and the smell of paint was in the air. On a bench sat a dejected-looking woman. She clasped a cardboard box on her knees, and her head hung forward.

"Halt."

I stood in front of a heavy door. It was guarded by two armed troopers who wore black uniforms and the silver skull and crossbones on their peaked caps. The sign on the door said: *Inspektion 6—Zutritt Verboten.*

The troopers grinned broadly.

"*Hallo,* who is that?"

"A traitor," Magnus said curtly.

He pressed an electric button. The door opened. I was pushed into the room with such violence that I pitched headlong to the floor.

A roar went up. It was a large, bare room. At first I was stunned by the blinding glare of cluster lights. Then I saw knots of plainclothesmen around me, and all of them looked at me and roared. Maps and posters covered the walls. Clouds of tobacco smoke swirled under the ceiling.

A whiplike voice cut through the bedlam. "Up on your feet!"

Slowly I rose from the floor.

Chapter Thirty-three

THE GESTAPO QUESTIONS ME

About me hostile faces and threatening voices whirled thickly. A swimmer at sea attacked by a shark cannot be more alone than is an enemy of Nazi power in a stronghold of the Gestapo. Yet, it was just what I had been told to expect. I was not a victim of persecution. I was not an innocent man jerked out of his bed before dawn because of an anonymous denunciation. I had fought the Hitler regime with all the means and wiles at my disposal. I had fought for a proletarian revolution in which I still believed somehow.

A fist crashed into my face. Kicks from the rear sent me sprawling. Hands tore me up from the floor and pushed me against a wall. A bald-headed man butted his knee into my abdomen. Another hit me on the head with handcuffs. I was strong, but I fell. It was Magnus who dragged me back into the middle of the room and told me to stand upright. He motioned the others to stand aside.

"Leave him alone," he ordered.

A short, broad-shouldered man entered the room through the door of an adjoining office. He had dark, deep-set eyes and his face was strongly lined. He wore a well-pressed suit and had rings on his hands. An aroma of pine needles came from his glistening hair.

"Good evening," he said.

The men stood back. They were silent. Someone brought a chair. The short man sat down two yards in front of me and eyed me placidly. At his side stood an Elite Guard with a six-foot leather whip in his hand, and a girl holding a stenographer's pad. Both had followed the short man from the adjoining room.

"We are going to cut belts out of your skin," the short man said.

The girl smiled. She had fine teeth. She was large, with wide blue eyes and a thick flaxen mane. Her arms were folded beneath her heavy breasts. I recognized the girl. Her name was Hertha Jens. She was the daughter of a wealthy peasant in the marshlands. She smiled at me and said, "My, you look fine."

Less than a year before Hertha Jens had still been the confidante of Herrmann Schubert, a Reichstag member, and one of the leaders of the Communist Party. She had had access to confidential files and had taken part in conspirative meetings. Because of her, printing plants had been raided and hundreds of comrades had gone into the dungeons. Many of us had liked Hertha Jens; she had seemed so reliable and so generous. And then we learned of her treason, and the *S-Apparat* had for some time regarded her as overdue for execution. Some maintained that she had been Hitler's spy for years. Others thought that she became a traitress to the cause when Hermann Schubert abandoned her and fled to Paris. In the end, that did not matter. Since May already, Hertha's name had been on the G.P.U. list of traitors scheduled for "liquidation."

Hertha Jens saw my stare. Her smile became a jeer.

The sunken eyes of the short man in front of me lit up as if he had switched on an electric bulb inside his head. He spoke quietly.

"I know of many things I can do with you," he said. "It is not often that we catch a fish like you. Berlin will be delighted."

A snicker rose in the circle of the man hunters about me. Their faces were taut with expectancy. The smoke from their cigarettes curled upward in many sinuous columns. The Elite Guard with the whip went to a table by the window. He raised the whip until its tip touched the ceiling. Then he crashed it down on the table. The impact sounded like a rifle shot. I winced.

"I am Inspector Kraus," the short man said languidly.

Again the trooper smashed his whip on the table.

"This is Inspection 6," Inspector Kraus continued "the anti-Comintern division of the *Geheime Staatspolizei*. Among your friends in Moscow this Inspection has a rather bad reputation." A Gestapo man guffawed. The others nodded vigorously. Hertha Jens thrust her lips forward until they looked broad and soft. Inspector Kraus regarded me steadily.

"Will you be sensible?"

"Yes."

"Remember this—if you lie, you won't live. Is that clear to you?"

"That is clear to me."

"Whom did you meet tonight at the Botanical Gardens?"

"I met no one," I said. "I took a walk."

"Who sent you to Germany?"

"I came on my own initiative."

"Where are your living quarters?"

"I arrived in Hamburg this afternoon, and I was about to take a room in a hotel."

"Three questions," the Inspector said, "and three answers. All your three answers were lies."

I was silent. My knees were trembling. I wanted to stop the trembling, but I found it impossible to do so. Inspector Kraus demanded:

"Who taught you to lie?"

"Nobody."

"Did your mother teach you how to lie?"

"No, sir."

"Do you lie because you think that'll save your hide?"

"I don't lie,' I said thickly.

"You lie to save your organization from being blown sky-high?"

"No."

"Tell me, my friend, where is Ernst Wollweber?"

"I don't know."

"You do not know Ernst Wollweber?"

"I know him by name, but I never met him personally."

"Who gave you the Danish passport we found in your pockets?"

"The consul in Antwerp refused to give me a German passport," I explained. "I had no papers. So I bought the passport from a stranded Dane."

"Who are your fellow-conspirators? What are their addresses?"

"I have no fellow-conspirators."

"Where are Hans Kippenberger, Heinz Neumann, Bela Kun? Where are Herrmann Schubert, Adolf Deter, Max Ulrich, Kommissarenko and the whole lot of other international scoundrels who infested this country? Where are they? Where do they live? Under which names?"

"I don't know."

"Where is Kuusinen? Where is Remmele? Where is Willy Aiuenzenberg?"

"I don't know."

Sullenly Inspector Kraus said, "I can make you wish you were dead. However, I shall first ask you a few things I hope you do know."

He sent Hertha Jens into the adjoining office to get some papers. A young man who had come into the room spoke to Inspector Kraus in whispers. Kraus nodded. The young man hastened away. My interlocutor took the sheaf of papers which were handed to him by Hertha Jens.

"Now then," he said, "you are a member of the Communist Party?"

"No, sir."

"You *were* a member?"

"Yes, sir."

"How long?"

"From 1923 until the National Revolution—until the Reichstag Fire."

"And you dropped out after Hitler came to power?"

"Yes, I dropped out."

"Were you such a weakling that you deserted your Party after the situation became dangerous?"

"I dropped out," I said. "I went abroad to find a berth on some foreign ship."

Inspector Kraus curved his lips in contempt. "Oh, you're such a harmless, such a lovable creature. But so are we, to be sure. Now listen: I have here some excerpts from your dossier. Let's see if you're the gentle lamb you'd like to be in the present situation. You have been a ship's officer?"

"I have a ship's officer's ticket."

"At one time you engaged in building up a communist ship officers' organization, and edited a weekly sheet called *The Bridge*. Is that correct?"

"That's correct."

"In 1923 you took an active part in an armed insurrection against the government of the German republic. You were then a detachment leader in the second proletarian hundred of the Red Marines. You were arrested, but you escaped. Is that right?"

"Yes," I admitted.

Inspector Kraus went on: "There's a gap of a few years. But now we come to 1926. In 1926 you murdered a man in California."

"I have never murdered a man," I interrupted vehemently.

"Oh, no? ... I have here," Inspector Kraus said, "an official report, checked by the German consul in New York. This report states that you were sentenced by a superior court in Los Angeles to ten years of penal servitude for a crime which involved the use of a deadly weapon."

Waves of ice and fire shot through my body. Out of the ring of watchers sounded a low whistling sound. The room seemed to reel about me and the shapes of men were blurred.

Inspector Kraus purred sardonically, *"Ja, mein Freund,* the ghosts of the past can be damned disagreeable at times, *nicht wahr?"*

There was nothing I could answer. An animal caught in a trap and seeing the hunter approach must feel as I felt then. In a dead-calm tone Inspector Kraus inquired:

"Have you ever been in the employ of the Russian OGPU?"

"No, sir. Never."

"You probably have. I shall find out later. We now come to 1929. In December, 1929, you were in charge of the French alien police, yes? You broke jail in Le Havre and escaped. The French authorities sent a report about you to the German embassy in Paris. So I take this jailbreak as a fact."

I nodded. My mouth was dry. I wanted to ask for water, but I could not formulate the words.

Inspector Kraus smiled. "In the next four years the ghosts come thick as thunder," he continued. "In 1931 you were wanted by the German police for incitement to mutiny, but you vanished. Here is also a report from England. The British government protested against the smuggling of treasonable propaganda to British colonies —as culprits in this affair were named one Losovsky in Moscow, a certain James Ford from New York, another negro, and you. In the summer of 1932, you were arrested and deported from London by Scotland Yard. In the spring of 1933, you were wanted in Sweden for the riots and kidnappings you engineered in the course of a seamen's strike. A month later you were arrested and held for deportation in Norway, but again you escaped. Two months later the French Surete was looking for you in Paris and Strasbourg. So were the police departments of Holland and Belgium. In all these places you used false passports. You took your orders and your money from the Communist International in Moscow. And now we have you here. This time you won't escape. The charge against you is high treason."

Inspector Kraus leaned back. In a rapid succession of blows, the Elite Guard slammed his whip on the table by the window.

I wanted to speak. My voice came as a hoarse croak.

"Shut up!" a Gestapo man snapped.

"You could tell us volumes," the inspector muttered. "So why not be sensible? Life can be so smooth, my friend. I implore you: are you going to be sensible?"

"Yes," I said.

Inspector Kraus jerked to an upright position. "Now we come to brass tacks," he said. "Do you think you can fool me?"

"No," I answered.

"Who is the young woman you ran around town with?"

"Which young woman?"

"You know—a tall girl, brunette, very chic."

"I don't know such a girl," I said.

"Are you sure?"

"Yes."

The inspector turned toward Hertha Jens.

"Bring the lady in," he commanded.

Hertha Jens left the room, whistling a tune, and half a minute later she returned with Cilly. Cilly's face was pale and set, and her eyes were wide, and she looked as if she had not slept for three nights. Inspector Kraus grinned quietly.

"She's a trim specimen," he said. "I must acknowledge your good taste."

Cilly stared at me with unbelieving eyes. The red from her lips was gone and they twitched at their corners. Behind her, Hertha Jens smiled brightly.

Cilly stood so close to me that I could have touched her. We stared at one another without a sign of recognition.

"Do you know her now?" Inspector Kraus demanded harshly. "No, sir," I said.

"Look well," he snarled. "She'll be a rotten old hag before we're through with her."

Cilly's lips had become a thin, straight line. Her dark blue dress was rumpled. Her amber bracelets were gone. Her youthful slenderness contrasted strangely with her weary face. She pressed her lips together until they were white. Her lips were eloquent. "Tell them nothing," they said.

Inspector Kraus got up and grasped her arm.

"Do you know this man?"

Cilly replied steadily, "I've never seen him before."

Inspector Kraus reached out. Five, six times his hands struck viciously at Cilly's face. She gave a little shrieking gasp.

"Do you know this man now?" the Inspector snarled.

"No," she said dully. "I do not know him."

"That'll do. Take her away."

Hertha Jens clutched Cilly's wrist and escorted her into an adjoining room. When Hertha Jens returned, I saw through the open door that a lanky Gestapo man pushed Cilly into a chair. A look of unforgettable utter desolation was on her face.

All fireside talk of heroism is rot. If it were possible for a man to creep into himself and hide, hide physically, I should have done it. In front of me stood Inspector Kraus, a short dog-whip in his hand. The whip had been soaked in water. Wet leather cuts deeper. A drop of water glistened at the end of the whip. I watched it fall to the floor.

"Who is the girl?" asked the inspector.

Dismally, I looked away. I did not answer.

Then the whip slashed across my face like liquid fire.

It was followed by a peal of melodious laughter.

"That's nice," Hertha Jens said.

"Who is the girl?" said the inspector.

"I—don't—know."

Again the whip ripped at me. It ripped from ear to ear. At first a whining sound, as it cut the air, and then a sudden burst of pain that blinded the eyes and pierced the brain with slow-moving daggers. I know that I moaned and staggered backward.

"Will you tell us now what the name of that girl is?"

"I can't... I don't know..."

The inspector's face froze in a cold fury. The whip cut into my face. It bit across my throat, was torn free, and bit again with bewildering speed. I tugged at my shackles to clasp protecting hands in front of my face. I tugged at my shackles and screamed.

"Will you please tell us now who this woman is?"

I was crazed with pain. I lunged toward the wall. Hands grasped me and pushed me back into the circle.

"Who is the girl? What's her name?"

"She ... she ..."

"Well? Out with it!"

I hesitated. A moment of blind, unthinking hesitation.

A Gestapo man seized my arm at the elbow and wrist. I shrieked. I thought the arm would snap.

"Who is this woman?" growled Inspector Kraus close by. "We'll break your bones if you don't talk."

"I met her on the train," I gasped.

"Which train?"

"The train from Copenhagen."

The Gestapo man let go of my arm.

"Now we're going places," Inspector Kraus said. "So you came from Copenhagen?"

"Yes," I admitted, "from Copenhagen."

"And she was on the same train? The Comintern assigned her to help you?"

"She was on the train. She had nothing to do with the Comintern."

"But you had?"

"No, sir."

"Take down the fellow's pants," someone burst out impatiently. "Now tell us how you met her," Kraus demanded.

"On the train. She sat opposite me in the compartment. She asked me for a cigarette and we got acquainted. After that I thought we could be friends."

"When was that?"

"Yesterday."

"What's her name? "

"I don't know. I did not ask her."

"What did you do with her in the Botanical Gardens?"

"We took a walk."

"All this is a fairy tale you two have prearranged," Inspector Kraus said calmly. "You did not come yesterday. You arrived in Germany months ago. You've been under surveillance in Berlin and Hamburg for the last two weeks. There was a third person with you in the Botanical Gardens. There was a whole bunch of you scheming and slinking to sabotage the New Germany, to fabricate discontent, to plant your spies, to disseminate high treason. We have reports about you. Sufficient reports to bury you for life."

I said nothing.

"Is Ernst Wollweber in Copenhagen?"

"I don't know. I don't know Wollweber."

"What orders did Wollweber give you in Copenhagen? What was your mission in Germany?"

"Wollweber gave me no orders. I don't know Wollweber."

"Would you like to smoke a cigarette?"

"Yes, sir."

Inspector Kraus gave me a cigarette. While I smoked, he laid his hand on my shoulder. His face changed abruptly into a friendly mask.

"Listen," he said, "we two can make a bargain. You're finished, absolutely finished, you know that. All right. There're two ways 'in which a man can grow old once we've got our hands on him— a peaceful way, and a painful way. The painful way is gratis. The price for the peaceful way is to tell us all you know about your organization. All the names, all the addresses, all the crimes you know of and who committed them.

"You are one. Your love in the next room makes two. We also have the third man. But who was the fourth? Who were the dozens of others who made up your conspirative *Apparat*? Where are the print-shops? What are the codes? Which points are used for crossing the frontiers? Who brings the money? Who fakes the passports? We know you've been in Comintern service. We know you came to Germany on Comintern business. Tell us what part of the Stalin machine you handled here and who your helpers were. You'll never be sorry if you do. You'll suffer if you don't."

I was glad of the cigarette. It gave me time to think. The shifting glint in the deep-set eyes of Inspector Kraus told me he realized that he had made a mistake when he allowed me to smoke. I was too much a part of the Comintern to think of myself. The individual was nothing. The Party was all! If I held out through this night, the comrades outside would have time to change their residences, meeting-places and depots. They would change their lines of communication, change their codes and even change their names. The "underground" organization had learned to maneuver fast, to abandon quickly all points endangered by the arrest of some of its members, to occupy new points and use new routes of which the comrades who had been seized knew nothing. The Gestapo men watched me like wolves. They knew: if they could make me talk that night, a series of raids and mass arrests would be the result.

They'd make a big haul. They'd be praised by Goering and Himmler. I was resolved to tell them nothing. I'd rather die horribly than betray the Party. I was a soldier of the Comintern. No pain could be greater than a comrade's accusation—"He allowed himself to be broken; he betrayed the cause to escape destruction." Hertha Jens raised her skirt and scratched her thick white thigh. "What are we waiting for?" she grimaced.

Inspector Kraus said to me, "Have you thought it over?"

"I cannot give you information on matters I know nothing about," I explained. "I left Party work after Hitler came to power." Instantly the dog-whip slashed across my face.

"Who sent you to Germany? Who gave you the money? What were you instructed to do?"

"No one sent me."

"And still you came. You knew you were wanted for high treason and still you entered Germany with a doctored passport. Why?"

"I came to find my son. He disappeared after my wife's apartment in Hamburg was raided by the secret police. I came to Germany to find his whereabouts."

"Ah! A Bolshevik developing an interest in his family, what? When was the apartment raided?"

"This year in March," I said.

"What for?"

"My wife was to be arrested."

"She escaped, I believe?"

"Yes. She returned later to look for the baby. Our son was just six months old. When she returned, the baby had disappeared. I wanted to find him. That is why I came to Germany."

Hertha Jens laughed.

"Your son is in good care," she said. "Your wife will never see the baby again unless she comes to give herself up."

"Hold your tongue," Inspector Kraus cautioned her. Then, turning to me, "So you wanted to smuggle your child out of Germany?"

"Yes, sir."

"I don't believe it. Who sent you to Germany? What were your instructions?"

"I came to find my son."

"Nonsense," he barked. "What role did Karl Burmeister play?"

The question struck me like a hammer blow.

"Burmeister?"

"Yes, Burmeister. What was Burmeister's function in your high treason outfit? Don't be a fool—heroism is a farce."

I did not believe it when they told me that Karl Burmeister had been captured. He was the coolest, most reliable militant in the "underground."

Inspector Kraus said, "Burmeister has told us everything."

"I have not seen Burmeister for six months," I said.

"No? Your comrade Burmeister says that he's received money and instructions from you a few hours ago in the Botanical Gardens."

"That's impossible."

"Nothing is impossible." Inspector Kraus walked out into the corridor. A minute passed. The Gestapo men showered me with taunts and curses. Hertha Jens sat on the chair and showed me her teeth. "Times have changed," she said. "I'm really glad to see you again."

The door from the corridor banged open. Karl Burmeister was hurled into the room. He stumbled to his feet. His massive chest heaved up and down, and rasping noises came from his throat. Behind him Inspector Kraus and two Gestapo agents in shirtsleeves stamped in. They pushed Karl Burmeister against the wall.

"Now, Karl, don't say one single word," Inspector Kraus said precisely. "I shall ask you a question, All you do is nod your head or shake it."

Burmeister was stripped to the waist. His face was bruised. His body was covered with livid streaks; his sides and back showed patches of blood. Blood was on his trousers and shoes.

"Tell me," Inspector Kraus, pointing at me, demanded, "is this the man who gave you the directions in the Botanical Gardens?" Burmeister was silent.

"I only want to confirm what you've already told the gentlemen who questioned you."

All of a sudden, with an inhuman roar, Karl Burmeister threw himself on the nearest Gestapo man.

"You dogs," he roared. "You goddamn lousy dogs."

One of the men in shirt-sleeves sprang forward.

He shouted wildly: "Hold him! The son-of-a-bitch!"

Then they were on top of him.

"Take him out," the inspector ordered. "Make him sing."

Karl Burmeister fought like a lion. He fought with his head, his knees, his teeth, his feet, his shackled arms. He fought and cursed and his breath came like the breath of a strong woman in childbirth. One of the police agents leveled his pistol. Inspector Kraus waved him off. Burmeister was still struggling after four men pinned him to the floor. Only when one of them crushed his shoe against Karl Burmeister's throat, did he become quiet. The eternal smile had gone from Hertha Jens' face. With a catlike alertness Inspector Kraus watched the struggle. In the clutch of a Gestapo man, I stood there like a helpless, fascinated idiot.

They raised Karl Burmeister from the floor and dragged him toward the door. Halfway to the door, he opened his eyes and with one tremendous effort he tore himself free. He ran across the room and threw the whole weight of his body against the window. The glass splintered. Karl Burmeister pitched out into the night.

Silence.

Several Gestapo men walked over to the window and looked into the courtyard six stories below. The man in shirt-sleeves, who had drawn his pistol, raged.

"*Dieser dreckige Hoellenhund!*" (The dirty bastard.)

Inspector Kraus was calm. "Two of you go down and clear away the hash," he directed. "Hertha, please telephone the canteen for coffee and sandwiches."

Hertha Jens telephoned.

A young storm trooper brought up a steaming jug of coffee and a huge tray loaded with cups and sandwiches. Soon every Gestapo man had a cup of coffee in one hand and a sandwich in the other.

Someone grumbled: "Confound these irregular hours; nowadays a man loses all conception of time . . . Can't even get a decent night's sleep!"

The telephone rang.

Hertha Jens listened. While she listened, her body stiffened, and her face assumed an aspect of intense concentration. All eyes glued themselves to her Junoesque shape.

She turned. "*Blockwart* (house-watcher) Number 1— is calling. Reports a detachment of civilians distributing propaganda stuff in the Grossneumarkt District." Her words came like the burst of a machine gun.

Half a dozen Gestapo men reached for their overcoats. They took their guns from their hip pockets and put them into their overcoats. The clock on the wall beneath the giant portrait of Adolf Hitler showed half past one.

"Mobilize Special Detachment Number Eight," Inspector Kraus snapped. "Surround the district. Should the streets be empty, conduct a house-to-house search.'

Again Hertha Jens telephoned. She rapped out instructions to someone of the Special Detachment of the Grossneumarkt District. The Gestapo men rushed out. I heard them pounding along the hallway and down the stairs. Besides myself, only Hertha Jens, the Elite Guard, Inspector Kraus and two of his aides remained in the room. From the adjoining room, where Cilly was being questioned, came the sound of muffled voices.

The Inspector munched a sandwich. "Let's proceed," he said coolly. "Don't get the idea now to blame Burmeister for the things you're guilty of. You fellows usually wait till somebody is dead to shove all responsibility on a corpse. Either on corpses or on comrades who're safe in Moscow. Am I right?"

I thought of Karl Burmeister. Not long ago we had talked of the spirit of self-abnegation, the will of a revolutionist to persevere through all suffering; the Leninist attitude of mind which we had defined as one of selflessness and determination; of a revolutionist's duty to save his life for the cause if he could do so without betraying the movement. Karl Burmeister had agreed that we should not endeavor to die for the revolution, but to live for it. Still, he had anticipated his fate. I remembered his words: "When I feel I can hold out no longer, I shall find a way to get killed, or to kill myself before you can spell the word Traitor."

"Traitor—it is the ugliest word in the world," I thought. "Where is your wife?" Inspector Kraus shot at me. "Did she come to Germany with you?"

"No, sir, she's in Paris," I replied.

"She is not in Copenhagen?"

"No, she's in Paris."

"You're mistaken. Our agents have photographed her in Copenhagen. We've a picture of her walking on the street. We've another one showing her on a station platform. Both were taken in Copenhagen."

"She's in Copenhagen," I admitted.

"Her name is Firelei, that right?"

"Yes, sir."

"Russian girl?"

"No—Flemish."

"But she has been trained in Russia? Attended a school where they teach treason and murder?"

"No, sir."

"What does Firelei do in Copenhagen?"

"She lives as a refugee. She is not engaged in any sort of political work."

"Oh, no? She's an artist? Attended art schools?"

"Yes, sir."

"Then wouldn't it be a pity for the Comintern not to use her in one of the passport faking bureaus?"

"She's through with the Communist Party. When I quit, she quit as well."

"Stop lying!" Inspector Kraus' eyes glinted dangerously. "Tell me exactly what Firelei has been doing since she escaped when we raided her rooms."

"I was in Sweden when the raid took place," I said. "Firelei went to Berlin. From Berlin she went to Munich. She was alone and she had no place to live and no money. So she made her way to Cologne."

"By train?"

"No, along the highways."

"Who gave her shelter in Berlin, Munich, Cologne? What were her Party connections in these cities?"

"I don't know. I had arranged an address in Paris. She wrote me to Paris, and I answered her poste restante."

"Which address in Paris?"

I invented an address. Hertha Jens noted it down, together with some of my other answers.

"How did your wife get out of Germany?"

"I was in Strasbourg when Firelei was in Cologne. I wrote her to come to Kehl, opposite Strasbourg, on the Rhine. I crossed the Rhine in a boat and brought Firelei to France."

"At night?"

"Yes, at night."

"Illegally?"

"Yes, she had no passport."

"You knew that Firelei was wanted for political crimes. In spite of that, you smuggled her out of Germany?"

"She belonged to me," I said. "She was my wife."

"Bolsheviks and wives! That seditious prostitute! She was guilty of treason. You admit having smuggled a fugitive from justice out of Germany?"

"I admit that."

"How many other traitors did you smuggle out of Germany?"

"None."

"What did you do in Strasbourg?"

"I was looking for a job on some Rhineship."

"Just looked for a job, eh? And as a sideline you organized strikes and smuggled Muscovite pamphlets into Germany, is that it?"

"No, sir. All I wanted was to find a job and a home for Firelei."

"She's got a knack for painting?"

"Yes."

"She could draw caricatures and posters?"

"She had the ability," I admitted.

"Caricatures ridiculing the leaders of the Third Reich?"

"She never did that."

"Posters calling upon the workers to fight us tooth and claw?"

"No."

"I'll show you some, perhaps?"

"There are none."

"No?" There was pride and contempt in the inspector's smile. "Our agents photographed them. In Antwerp, in Paris, in Copenhagen, in New York."

"Firelei did nothing of the sort."

"She did, I assure you. . . . The trouble is she can't hide her style. It's got distinction. I could recognize it if I saw one of her posters in China.—What happened to Firelei after you smuggled her to Strasbourg?"

"She went to Paris."

"What did she do in Paris?"

"She tried to earn her livelihood by drawing."

"And after that?"

"She traveled through France with a side-show."

"And you with her?"

"No, I went back to Antwerp," I said.

"On subversive business?"

"To look for a ship. I wanted to go back to sea."

"Firelei came to Le Havre with her circus?"

"Yes."

"What happened to her in Le Havre?" demanded the inspector. I saw the Mona Lisa smile on the full red lips of Hertha Jens, and I knew its significance.

"She was seized for abduction to Germany," I answered. "Firelei was seized for abduction?"

"Yes."

"Who seized her?"

"Unknown men."

"Men from the Gestapo?"
"From the Gestapo."
"Not some of your own friends?"
"No."
"And?"
"They tried to spirit her aboard a ship going to Germany."
"Which ship?"
"The *Bellona*."

"Now please tell us how she managed to escape. Who were the men who helped her? How was it done?"

"I don't know," I replied.
"She did not tell you."
"She only told me that she got away."
"She joined you in Antwerp after that?"
"Joined me in Antwerp."
"What did Firelei do in Antwerp?"
"Nothing."
"She did not work against the New Germany?"
"No."
"Did not commit high treason?"
"No."
"Did not edit the *Searchlight?*"
"No."
"You lie like a newspaper!" Inspector Kraus snarled.
"No."

"Did not your friend Ernst Wollweber come to Antwerp to send Firelei to Copenhagen to take charge of the stuff smuggled from Scandinavian countries? "

"No. I don't know Ernst Wollweber."
"Who sent Firelei to Copenhagen?"
"I did."
"And why?"
"To live there with a friend. She had no other means of existence."
"What's the name of that friend?"
"I don't remember."
"Was Ernst Wollweber that friend?"
"No, I don't know him at all."
"You don't know your boss?"
"He was not my boss."
"Who, then, was your boss?"
"No one. I was unemployed. I had no boss."
"How did Firelei get into Denmark without a passport?"
"She went as a stowaway."
"On which ship?"
"On the *Brabant* to Oslo."
"And from Oslo to Copenhagen?"

"On the highway to south Sweden."

"And from Sweden to Denmark?"

"She crossed the Sound in a boat."

"She stole a boat and crossed the Sound?"

"No, a fisherman took her across."

"At night?"

"At night."

"So she was smuggled into Denmark. Where does Firelei live in Copenhagen?"

"I don't know."

"What! You've lived with her before you came back to Germany, slept with her, and you can't tell us her address?"

"She was about to change her address when I saw her last," I explained.

"She changes her address often," said the inspector, "because she fears that the Gestapo will bring her to justice?"

I did not answer.

"What does Firelei do in Copenhagen?"

"She was trying to find work when I left her," I said. "Since then I don't know what she's doing."

"I'll tell you what she does," Inspector Kraus said drily: "She's got a crew of cut-throats under her command. She sends these cutthroats aboard German ships as they come into Scandinavian ports. The cut-throats invite the German seamen to have fun ashore, and then Firelei meets them in some café and tries to seduce them into smuggling subversive propaganda into Germany. Our agents have watched her and brought us some of this material. She's not the innocent angel you say she is."

"Firelei is no revolutionist," I persisted.

"Then why doesn't she return to Germany? Nothing will happen to her here. What kind of a mother is she to desert her baby? The lowest sort of animal demonstrates more decent loyalty than that."

"That's why I came to Germany," I said. "I came to find the child."

"Rot! Where does your wife live in Copenhagen?"

"I don't know."

The whip came into my face like the swift stroke of a red-hot knife.

"Tell us Firelei's address in Copenhagen!"

"No ... I don't know."

Again the whip. There is a pain that is worse than death. I sagged to my knees, groaning, and then my head was on the floor. I heard the whip sing and bite around the back of my neck.

"Get up."

I remained on the floor, eyes closed, refusing to believe that I was still alive.

A man grasped the thumb of my left hand, bending it backward. I felt the bone of my thumb snap ... I jumped straight up. The man who had broken my thumb, leaped back; he seemed startled by my unearthly howl. In the same second, the whip came slashing once more into my face. My lips were devoid of feeling. The front of my shirt and coat were full of blood. I know I swayed to and fro like a drunken man, wondering why I did not fall.

"Go easy," Inspector Kraus commanded. "I don't want this specimen to lose consciousness."

"All right," a voice muttered.

"Will you tell us now what Firelei's address was?"

I mentioned a street in Copenhagen. "Venedigvej," I said.

"What number?" snapped the inspector.

"Number eighty-three," I answered.

"We'll check up on that... Now repeat this: Firelei is a whore."

"Firelei ... is ... a ... . whore."

"She stinks to the heavens."

"She . ... stinks to the heavens."

"My wife is a whore who stinks to high heaven."

"My wife is a whore who stinks to high heaven."

"He's learning nicely," Hertha Jens smiled. "Only his wife should be here to listen to him."

Inspector Kraus was pacing up and down the room. A Gestapo man sat on the window-sill, smoking. He sat there to prevent me from taking the same road that Karl Burmeister had chosen. The Elite Guard had brought a pail of water from the lavatory and was soaking his long whip in the water. After that, he took a jar of vaseline from a shelf and began greasing his whip. Rapid talk came from the room where Cilly was being pressed for information. A young man came from that room, and whispered into the ear of Inspector Kraus. I could not understand the words, but I knew that they were comparing notes. Hertha Jens flopped down on the table, her back against the wall, yawning and puffing smoke toward the ceiling. As I stood there, much more resembling a tortured beast than a human being, a thought crawling through my brains kept telling me how pleasant it would be to burn gaping wounds into Hertha's insolent flesh and to see her writhe in unspeakable agony.

I was in a fever. The stocky figure of Kraus and the voluptuous figure of the traitress assumed the outlines of unreal monstrosities. On the wall the portrait of Adolf Hitler seemed to break into a gleeful chuckle. Nothing was left for me to hold on to except my hatred. A hatred which fills the veins and lungs and the head, a hatred which is stronger even than unconditional devotion to the cause. In Gestapo headquarters at night, a man's strength depends upon the measure of black hatred he is capable of raising in himself. It was as if Inspector Kraus had read my mind.

"Tell me," he said, "what would you have done with us if Bolshevism had come to power in Germany?"

I gave him no answer.

"You'd have murdered the whole lot of us," he concluded. "Communists are not sadists," I muttered.

"Neither are we," said the inspector. "We don't like to hurt any man. But when a man is in possession of information we need, and refuses to give it—*all* means are justified to make him talk. We find that a high plane of sustained horror is often convenient for reasons of state. Do you understand that?"

"Yes, sir."

"I'm glad you do. Where did you live? What were your hideouts in Berlin and Hamburg?"

"I had no steady place," I said. "I went to hotels. I went to a different hotel each night."

"Give the names of the hotels."

"They were small hotels in side-streets on the *Alster* and in Barmbeck."

"Their names!"

"I don't remember their names."

"No? Where did you sleep last night?"

"I picked up a prostitute. She took me to a small hotel."

"What was her name?"

"Emma."

"Emma—what?"

"I don't know. I did not ask."

"Do you want to have all your fingers broken? One at a time? One for each lie you tell us?"

"No, sir."

"What did you do in Antwerp?"

"I tried to find a berth aboard a ship. It was difficult because I had no papers."

Inspector Kraus stepped up to me. His voice became ominous, barely audible.

"Antwerp, you say? Many crimes were committed in Antwerp around that time. For example: Who organized the gangs who came aboard German ships to tear down the Hitler flags?"

"I don't know."

"Who printed the newspaper *Searchlight* and had it smuggled to Germany from Antwerp?"

"I don't know."

"What do you know? Do you know Ilia Raikoff?"

"No, sir."

"You look as if that name made you very uncomfortable. Maybe you know him as The Ox?"

"No, sir."

"What happened to Ilia Raikoff? Was he abducted to Russia? Was he murdered by the G.P.U.?"

"I don't know. I don't know who Ilia Raikoff is."

Inspector Kraus drew back his lips. "I am famed for my patience," he said. "But my patience is limited. I am a mortal. I know of several hundred gentlemen in this building whose fingers itch to make you howl till you scramble up sheer walls. It's their way of turning stubborn customers into pliable customers. Do you know Edgar Andree?"

"I have heard of him."

"Edgar Andree was a hard man," Inspector Kraus said with a grim smile.

"He was one of the hardest men alive. He's responsible for the murder of dozens of storm troopers, yes?"

"I don't know."

"We know! He thought he was made of granite," the inspector went on sardonically, "but after my young men got through with him he was like butter in the sun. Until his head comes off, he's glad to eat out of our hands."

"Please give me a glass of water," I begged.

Hertha Jens flashed a smile. "Certainly," she drawled. "You can have wine."

The Gestapo agents guffawed. From the corridor sounded angry voices and the tramping of feet.

"Water?" Inspector Kraus growled. "We'll put pepper into your carcass when it bursts open." His thin lips curled and tightened. "Will you tell us now on what business the Comintern sent you to Germany?"

"No one sent me. I came to find my son."

Inspector Kraus said quietly: "That'll do. Give him *Kaschumbo*. Thirty to start with."

Hands in his pockets, he walked out of the room. Hertha Jens followed him. She smiled over her shoulder and swayed her hips. In my mind stood a single weary thought.

"In a few minutes you will be a cripple," I thought. "They are going to smash your kidneys. Pray that you fall unconscious before you tell them what they should not know."

I was not nervous. I was calm. The inevitable had come.

A tall young man with sandy hair took command. He took the shackles off my wrists. He ordered me to push the table from the window to the center of the room. Then he ordered me to take off my clothes.

"Take your time," he said. "Don't hurry."

Two Gestapo men took my clothes and proceeded to inspect them closely. They ripped open the seams, and they ripped the lining out of my coat and overcoat and out of my hat. The Death Head guard slapped his whip tentatively across my back.

I was naked. They grabbed me and threw me across the table, face down. They pulled more handcuffs out of their overcoat pockets and shackled my wrists to the table legs. With leather straps they tied my ankles to the other table legs. Then they spread a wet towel over my back.

"Give us the names and addresses of five of your accomplices," one of the agents demanded.

I said nothing.

"Just five names and addresses between you and hell," he continued. "Think it over. I give you ten seconds to think it over."

"Refuse to think!" I thought. "Switch off every accursed nerve inside of you and refuse to think!"

The tall young man with the sandy hair gave a signal. My head hanging sideways over the edge of the table, I saw the Elite Guard raise the whip high over his head. I heard the whip whistle through the air and I closed my eyes.

The spurt of pain made me groan and jerk upward.

"Shut up," growled the trooper.

"One," counted the man with the sandy hair.

I opened my eyes and pressed my head downward. Through the space, between the table legs, I saw the black-booted legs of the Elite Guard spread out wide, feet firmly on the grimy floor. The whip sang through the air and struck, and with each blow the world was blotted out. The strokes did not come fast enough to make the blackness last. My senses crawled back into place just in time to be aware that the next stroke was ripping down from the height of the ceiling. The measured ferocity of that flogging filled me at first with a murderous and impotent rage, and then with screaming despair. The screaming gave way to a moan. I heard myself moan in a dull, continuous whine and I heard the crashing impacts of the whip and I felt its stab and bite, and the pain was so great that I thought my brains were oozing out through nose and eyes.

A voice, sonorous and lazy, was counting in the distance. "Sixteen ... seventeen ... eighteen ..."

Was this the end?

The whip came in a rhythm. Back. Buttock. Thighs. Then the back again. Unbearable was the agony when the whip cut twice into the same strip of flesh. I could not see. The legs of the trooper, the table, the floor and my arms and hands dissolved into red and black spots, flowing and ebbing, sinuous, dancing and whirling, widening and shrinking and milling about.

"Twenty-two ... twenty-three ..."

I was sinking away into a bottomless hole and I struggled because I did not want to die.

I was floating in a dusk. Something that stung in my nostrils made me open my eyes. There were voices and the tramping of feet and a blinding light. Cold water was poured over my head. I tried to raise my head because the blood hammered hard into my brain. A door was opened and Inspector Kraus returned. Hertha Jens followed him, carrying a typewriter pressed against her body. Inspector Kraus walked slowly around the table.

"Your spread-eagled carcass is no object of beauty," he said mildly. "How do you feel?"

"All right," I said after a while.

"I hope you've taken this preliminary caress to heart. If you haven't there's more to come, much more, I assure you. For the time being, we'll leave you hugging that table."

A man brought a small collapsible table. Hertha Jens put the typewriter on this table and sat down behind it.

"I'm ready," she said.

Inspector Kraus dictated. The typewriter began to clatter. Name, date and place of birth, family history, youth, arrests and other details already known to the Gestapo went down on the paper.

Paul Kraus continued to dictate: "The accused, arrested on the night of November 30, 1933, in the vicinity of the Botanical Gardens under suspicion of high treason committed while he was in the employ of the Communist International in Moscow, states of his own free will—"

"Now what?" the inspector snapped. "Will you talk?"

"Yes, sir."

Hertha Jens, sitting less than two feet in front of me, smiled. Her fingers ran nimbly over the keys of her typewriter.

"When did the Comintern send you to Germany and what was your mission?"

Inspector Kraus had taken the whip out of the hands of the trooper. With every word he said he tapped my back with the butt of the whip.

I said, "The Comintern did not send me. I came to . ."

"The accused," Paul Kraus dictated, "stubbornly denies the well-known fact that he has been an active agent of the Comintern, sent to Germany to prepare the violent overthrow of the Hitler government. His attitude is typical of that of a confirmed and hardened enemy of the New Germany." The inspector paused. "The court will like that," he added.

The whip sang in the air. Then it bit viciously.

"Where are your illegal quarters in Hamburg?"

"I changed quarters every night. I lived in hotels."

"You lying hound!"

Again the whip slashed down on me.

"Where was your hide-out?"

After every evasive answer I gave, Paul Kraus struck me mercilessly. And after each stroke, he repeated the one question:

"Where were your illegal quarters?"

I had heard that men could end their lives by sheer force of will. Just close their eyes and wish hard: "Death come!" It was a futile thing. Each time Inspector Kraus waited long enough to be sure that my eyes were open and that my body was able to squirm— before he swung the whip back over his shoulder to strike again.

"You're a fool," he said. "Do you imagine that one of your chiefs—Kuusinen or Piatnitzky or Wollweber or any one of the other blackguards—that if one of your chiefs were strapped to this table instead of you—do you imagine that they'd hesitate a minute before they'd sell you out and a thousand others with you if they thought that'd help them?"

I said nothing. I was more dead than alive. Beneath me blood and sweat were sticky on the table. My left hand had swollen to twice its normal size.

Inspector Kraus' voice came calmly: "We have a high respect for heroism. We have a big contempt for traitors. Our experience has shown us that the biggest bosses in your movement are the most cringing cowards once they're in our hands. Whenever we catch a big shot, we roll up his whole organization. All you have to do is follow this precedent and you'll be perfectly comfortable. Are you going to tell us something real now?"

"Yes, sir."

"You know damn well I can have you shredded to pieces inch by inch, and the most mangy cock on earth wouldn't crow in sympathy with you. You know that. If you decide to stop leading us around by the nose, we might come to terms. Suppose you tell us all you know, suppose you help us pull off a big scoop, catch a lot of subversive fish—then we could recommend you to the judge. You might get away with a life sentence."

"Yes, sir."

"There're several thousand questions I want to ask you. Thousands of questions to which you know the interesting answers. What I want you to know is that we have no time to fight with you an hour or two for each answer. Should you persist in wasting our time in such fashion, we'll be compelled to consider you guilty of sabotaging the necessary work of the Gestapo. You know what that means, don't you?"

"Yes, sir."

"Very well, tell us now where you had your illegal quarters." I gave no answer.

"Give him *Kaschumbo*" said the inspector. "Fifteen on the legs to limber up his memory."

Fifteen strokes across the thighs eat up the skin. Under the whip, raw flesh burns like fire. Each stroke jolts through every inch of body and brain like a fiery hammer. A man groans until every cell in him groans, and then it is as if he loses his mind.

"Shoot me,' I groaned. "Shoot me."

"Why should we shoot you?" a derisive voice sounded. "Who do you think we are?"

"Shoot me."

I do not know how many times I said it.

"Where did you have your illegal quarters?"

Now the whip came down in the small of my back.

Paul Kraus growled: "By-and-by you'll piss blood." Then, "Will you answer my question now?"

I could not answer. A stabbing pain was in my right ear. Someone had kicked the side of my head.

"His ear is bleeding," said Hertha Jens.

"Where did you have your illegal quarters? Will you tell us that now?"

Somebody poured water over me.

"This is your last chance," growled Paul Kraus. "We'll put a hose in your behind and fill it with boiling water if you don't answer. Before we do that, we'll put salt all over you. Will make you feel fine. Salt is a noble stuff."

The whip came whistling through the air.

"Where did you have your illegal quarters?"

There was a long silence and the smell of freshly-lit cigarettes. "Give him *Kaschumbo*," Paul Kraus ordered. "Twelve on the kidneys."

Did you ever have the feeling of having your insides filled with pointed rocks which grow bigger and bigger and move into your lungs and your throat and take your breath away? A flogging on the kidneys, with half an eternity between each stroke of the whip, are preparation for a thousand nights of agony to come.

In the end I told them the address. "Martin Holstein is still free," I thought.

"He'll tell the couriers to strike the address from their lists."

"Venusberg," I said.

"Speak louder!"

"Venusberg."

"What number?"

Each question was followed by the bite of the lash.

"Number seventeen."

"The names of the people?"

"Baumgarten."

"Jewish?"

"No."

"A couple? Do they have children?"

"No."

Inspector Kraus telephoned. *"Fahndungskommando? ...* Good! Send a car down to Venusberg number seventeen. The name is Baumgarten. Search the apartment. Arrest and run in whoever lives there. Leave two men in the place for the next three days. Seize and run in all visitors for Baumgarten. Thank you. Heil Hitler!" The inspector turned back to me.

"Are you going to be sensible now?"

"Yes, sir."

He ordered his helpers to take me off the table. They brought a chair and I sagged into the chair, and then I sagged to the floor and lay on my stomach because I was too wounded to sit. Hertha Jens gave me a glass of water. I raised myself to the elbows and drank the water. Inspector Kraus gave me a cigarette. While I smoked, the side of my face on the floor, he dictated and the typewriter clattered.

"The accused," the inspector dictated, "after having been confronted with irrefutable evidence, admits that he took illegal residence with one Baumgarten at Venusberg 17 in Hamburg after his secret arrival in this city to engage in unlawful communist activities."

"Mrs. Baumgarten is pregnant," I said.

"A pregnant woman?"

"Yes, sir."

Inspector Kraus made a grimace.

"Oh, well," Hertha Jens assured him. "We can bring her in anyway."

"Are the Baumgartens communists?" demanded the inspector. "Did you give them instructions?"

"No, sir," I said.

"How did you get their address?"

"By chance. I heard they had a room for rent."

"Now you are lying again. You got their address in Copenhagen. You got their address from the Comintern."

"No, sir. They were not communists."

"We'll see Baumgarten about that. We'll put Baumgarten on the table and make him give you the lie. You see, my friend, the plot thickens."

I did not answer. The Baumgartens were simple comrades. They knew little that could harm the movement. And I had arranged with them that they should say, when questioned, that they had taken me to be a foreign journalist.

"You have said A," Paul Kraus observed. "Now let us come to B, and proceed down the alphabet. What was your business in Germany?"

"I came to find my son."

"I ask once more: What did Comintern headquarters instruct you to do in Germany?"

"I was not sent by the Comintern."

"You were sent by the G.P.U.?"

"No, sir."

Inspector Kraus bent down and struck the cigarette out of my face.

"Get some salt," he said curtly. He walked into the next room. The Elite Guard prodded my ribs with his boots. Inspector Kraus returned and showed me a photograph. It was the photograph of a stocky man, taken as that man was getting off a street car. Hertha Jens went down on her knees and held a magnifying glass over the face of the photograph. I blinked my eyes and wanted to look sharply. I could not. My vision was blurred. It was as if the pain shooting from my right ear had somehow paralyzed my ability to see clearly.

"Who is this man?"

"I don't know. I can't see."

"Is this Michel Avatin?"

"I can't see."

"Do you know Avatin?"

"No, sir."

"In Copenhagen you were seen together with Avatin. Avatin was in Antwerp the week Ilia Raikoff was murdered. So were you. Did Avatin send you to Germany?"

"No, sir. I don't..."

"Is Avatin in Germany?"

"I don't know."

"What was your business with Avatin in Antwerp and Copenhagen?"

"I don't know Avatin."

'Who was Avatin's lady-love in Hamburg?"

"I don't know."

"Did you get her address when you were in Copenhagen?"

"No, sir."

"What were your lines of communication from Hamburg to Copenhagen? How did you send your reports? How did you get your money?"

"I came to find my child."

"On what mission did the Comintern send you to Germany?"

"I did not work for the Comintern."

"What assignment did the G.P.U. give you?"

"I never worked for the G.P.U."

"What was your illegal business in Germany?"

"I wanted to bring my son out of Germany."

"Why did you carry a gun?"

I was silent.

Inspector Kraus said, "Give him *Kaschumbo*. Take care he won't fall asleep."

I was not dragged back across the table. They left me lying on the floor and the Death Head guard snapped the whip in his hands, and after that he struck savagely and I crumpled up and tried in vain to bite the floor with my teeth. After the third stroke he stepped aside.

"Are you going to tell us now what your job in Germany was?" Inspector Kraus shouted.

Even had I wanted to tell him, I was unable to bring forth the words.

"Give him *Kaschumbo*," the inspector ordered.

The night dragged on, an endless crawling through a hellish morass. There came a moment when the brain could still register the impacts of the whip, but the nerves ceased to respond to pain. There was another moment when the room was suddenly filled with people—returning Gestapo men who shouted and cursed and threatened—and young workers and frightened girls who stumbled about and were pushed face foremost against the walls and were roared at to tell who gave them the leaflets they had distributed that night. At times the telephone rang. And once Hertha Jens' melodious laughter burst into the reeling blackness.

Later I was aware of daylight, and of a smell of something somebody had smeared over my back and face. I was aware that I lay on a narrow cot and that light came through a small barred window high in the wall. I was also aware that I was naked, that I lay on my stomach, that my wrists and my ankles were chained to the iron sides of the cot, and that waves of heat steamed up from under the cot. I could feel nothing. I could hear nothing. My left hand lay in a stiff bandage. I did not know whether this was death, or whether I was still alive. I tried to raise my head, and all of a sudden it was as if I was falling through space. And then I knew nothing more.

Chapter Thirty-four

HELL

One hundred and one days the inquisition continued. All these weeks and months I fought like a wounded beast in a trap. They were one hundred and one days of bloodstained blackness teeming with merciless fiends. Except for one week, I was alone all this time when not in the company of my torturers. For two months I lay in chains, in solitary confinement. For three months I did not see a piece of soap nor was I given a chance to bathe and shave. I wrote no letters and received none. The outside world had ceased to exist. And all around me was despair and death and madness, and manifestations of a mute and futile courage, ghostly faces and others full of harsh insolence, and the enemy's will to break me or to kill me.

The hope and expectation of a swift death were as pleasant as the prospects of a bridal night. When I was led to the bleak top floors of Gestapo headquarters for questioning and more questioning, my eyes searched for an unguarded window and my brain yearned for the opportunity of an unguarded moment in which I could hurl myself through the glass and out into space. But invariably on such excursions my wrists were chained and the end of the chain was in the grip of a Death Head Guard. Only two other, slower and less certain, means of suicide remained: a man could bite open his veins, or slash his wrists with a piece of glass broken from the cell window; or he could hang himself, if anything could be found to take the place of a rope. Many attempted to escape in this manner, but hardly one out of ten succeeded in winning the coveted death. Most prisoners were chained to their cots at night, and during the day their arms were shackled together on their backs.

On two occasions, despite this impediment, I tried to hang myself with strips torn from my reeking blanket. I strove for hours to adjust their ends to a waterpipe above the battered toilet, and finally I succeeded.

In my mind was only the dull determination: "Finish it! Finish it!" The urge to die was like a thirsty man's urge for water. I stood on the seat of the toilet, and with circular motions of my head I wrapped the lower portion of my improvised rope around my neck, and clamped the end between my teeth. "God-damned, finish it before they come again," I muttered to myself, and without a thought for anyone I let my feet slip sideways. I hung. There was no pain. The sensations were pleasant. I had expected that I should struggle painfully for air; instead I was aware that the clutch of the blanket strips around my neck cut off blood circulation from my head. I had a feeling of dizziness, and then the walls reeled about me, and my legs and arms were jerking spasmodically as if a recalcitrant motor inside of them had suddenly and inexplicably sputtered into action. The blanket strips parted. Regaining my senses I found myself on the floor, on hands and knees, and shaking my head like a dazed dog. I tried again two nights later, when the escape of a fellow-prisoner in another part of the concentration camp had caused so much excitement that the night guard had forgotten to chain me to my cot. Again I failed. In a sullen fury I lunged through the length of my cell and smashed my head against the wall. But I only lost consciousness, and my head throbbed for days afterward.

Spells of fitful sleep brought on maddening dreams. The dreams were always the same. A fine new rope hung from the bars of my cell window, with a noose tied expertly; I struggled forward with all my might to reach the rope, and to use it, but it was as if unseen hands reaching out from behind me clutched my ankles and knees, and all my struggles did not bring me one foot ahead.

I was in Concentration Camp Fuhlsbuettel, on the northern outskirts of Hamburg. Nearby was the airport, and the droning of airplanes could be heard day and night behind the rust-brown walls. Camp Fuhlsbuettel was no "camp," but a cluster of old prisons which the Ministry of Justice had ordered demolished but a few days before the Nazi triumph. For years these prisons had been out of use. But the sudden overcrowding of more modern jails with political prisoners had caused the Gestapo to halt the process of demolishing the condemned buildings. Almost overnight the once deserted dungeons became populated with thousands of men and women. There were four huge cell blocks, built of brick, thick-walled, and four stories high. They were surrounded by a number of naked yards, and the yards in turn were surrounded by guard posts and high brick walls. Along the inside of the walls ran a tall fence of barbed wire. The wire was charged. In the space between the barbed-wire fence and the outer walls black-uniformed Elite Guards, in steel helmets and armed to the teeth, were on duty. Two of the main buildings contained only solitary cells, while the remaining two were fitted with common halls for those who had "confessed."

The cells were ten feet long and five wide. Beyond a low iron cot and a battered toilet seat, they contained nothing. Heavy steel doors opened on narrow tiers. Each cell had a small barred window, seven feet above the floor, and the glass of most of the window-panes was broken, for the young Elite Guards in the yards amused themselves at all hours of the day and night with shooting at random through the windows into the cells. Rifle shots and the sounds of splintering glass were almost as common as the roar of arriving and departing planes. Most of the guards were young, from eighteen to twenty-three years old. They were the same men who had been our antagonists in the guerrilla warfare of the past years. And now that they found themselves in the position of victors, with their hated adversaries unconditionally at their mercy, they reveled in the role of avengers. Fanatical, trained to cruel ruthlessness, they regarded themselves with pride as the exterminators of the "Marxist" pestilence. Aside from the special treatment which the Gestapo prescribed to break down the resistance of certain prisoners so as to make them surrender names and addresses of comrades, the camp guards devised horror-shows of their own. Such enterprises ranged from the forcing of prisoners to perform exhausting physical "exercises" in the yards to artfully organized murder.

One day, when I marched back to my cell after a round of "exercise" in the yard, I saw the guards bring in a Jew. He was a small man of about forty, with a fat round face and astonished eyes. They made him run along the hallway on hands and knees. Two guards with rubber truncheons in their hands kicked him into cell 27, opposite mine. The troopers were too preoccupied to pay attention to me as I stood in front of my cell door, waiting to be locked in. Since the Jew was a newcomer, still wearing his civilian clothes, I cocked my eyes and ears to find out who he might be. What I saw made my blood run cold.

In cell 27 the guards told the Jew to take off his pants and drawers. He complied, trembling like a leaf. Suddenly one of the troopers put his arm around the Jew's throat and held him in a half-hanging, half-standing position. The other guard, swinging his rubber truncheon, began to strike well-aimed blows at the Jew's genitals. With a horrible groan, the Jew's body surged upward, and after the third blow between his legs he sagged limply, as if every bone in his body had been broken. The guard who held the Jew relaxed his grip. The Jew fell to the floor. He had both hands clasped to his genitals and was writhing feebly. Both troopers spat into the Jew's face, and then they left cell 27, locking the door.

One of the two, a blond, keen-eyed boy of twenty-two locked me into my cell.

"Did you see what happened to the Hebrew?" he asked excitedly.

"Yes, I saw it."

"That slimy swine ... Can you imagine what he did?"

"No. What'd he do?"

"He wanted to rape a Hitler girl. Lured her into his apartment and tried to make her. The hound! The abominable cur!"

Indignation blazed in the guard's face.

All afternoon I crouched as near to the door as I could get, and half the night as well, almost forgetting the pain in my wounded wrists. Hour after hour men stamped in and out of cell 27. It was as if every guard in Camp Fuhlsbuettel had come to visit the Jew. Curses, blows, cruel laughter and spells of hoarse whimpering came from cell 27. And off and on a voice that sounded like the crack of a whip:

"Ist das Arschloch noch lebendig?"

During the night the victim died.

At nine o'clock next morning I was ordered from my cell.

Out in the yard, in a sickly winter sunshine, the Jewish prisoners of Camp Fuhlsbuettel were digging a deep hole in the ground. Lined up against the wall were about sixty prisoners who were not Jewish. In twos and threes still other prisoners were marched out of the building.

"Stand against the wall," a guard ordered. "Don't talk and don't move till you're told to."

In double-quick I reached the wall and lined up with the other non-Jewish prisoners. All around the yard were guards in steel helmets, their rifles ready to fire. Toussaint, the lanky, martial-looking adjutant of the camp commander looked into the hole the Jews had dug.

"Deep enough," he said. "Stand back!"

The Jews fell back, their heads hanging forward and their faces ashen with fear. Another group of men approached from the prison. They carried a stretcher, and they were escorted by a trooper in a doctor's garb. All eyes stared. Except for the shouts of cruising gulls the yard was silent.

On the stretcher lay the mangled corpse of the Jew who had been murdered at night. His abdomen was a smear of dried blood and a clump of bloody rubbish was where his genitals had been. His face was convulsed and his eyes, wide open, were twisted upward in a glassy stare. The guard in the doctor's garb led the stretcher crew past the lined-up prisoners, and all of us stared silently at the dead man. The corpse was naked and the gulls cruised close and screamed. At a command, the stretcher-bearers dumped their burden on the ground close to the rim of the hole.

Several of the Jews who were standing around the hole clasped their hands in front of their faces. Two others collapsed. They were cuffed and beaten until they stood straight again.

"Pants down," commanded Toussaint.

The row of Jews lowered their pants. They were not men any more. They were animals without a will. They were stiff with fear.

"Now masturbate," commanded Toussaint.

A few of the Jews reached for their genitals. Guards ran along their file and struck the others in their faces.

"Masturbate, I said," Toussaint roared. "Masturbate, you swine!"

The Jews obeyed. They feebly went through the motions that were demanded of them and many of the guards wore broad grins.

"Faster," Toussaint shouted. "You desert bandits! You lustful reptiles! Show us how you do it in your cells at night!"

The Jews pretended to masturbate faster. They knew they would be beaten if they did not. They knew they could not afford to collapse.

Toussaint turned to us who were lined up against the wall.

"You sing!" he commanded. "Sing the Three Lilies on the Grave!"

We sang, low at first, and then we sang at the top of our voices.

"Drei Lilien, drei Lilien,

"Die pflanzt ich auf ein Grab, jufalleraaa ..."

"Look at the devils," snarled Toussaint. "They spent all their virility on Aryan virgins, and now they can't—"

One of the Jewish prisoners, a mere boy, seemed to have gone mad. He danced out of the file and croaked. He croaked like a crow. "Kra ... kra ... kra."

The sound of his voice was enough to make any man weep. It was so pitiful, so utterly desolate. "Kra ... kra ..." Our eyes had forgotten how to bring forth tears. The dead Jew on the ground looked ugly. The others kept masturbating, all but the young one. Some of us stopped singing, and then we all stopped.

"Kra ... kra ... kra."

The guards had pounced on him and Toussaint said: "Off with him!" And after that Toussaint barked. "Masturbation squad— halt!"

The crazy Jew was led away. Two troopers rolled the dead Jew over the ground with their boots until he flopped into the hole. Each of the other Jews was ordered to step forward and shout three times: "I am a race polluter." After shouting this three times, each Jew in turn was pushed into the hole atop the dead Jew. After he had shouted again, "I am a race polluter," he was allowed to climb out of the hole. Several had to be dragged out of the hole because they had suddenly become too weak. After all the Jews had finished shouting and falling on top of the corpse, the dead Jew was dragged out of the hole, and the others were forced to roll him from one side of the yard to the other, shouting all the time, "We—are—race polluters!"

In the end, the Jews were formed into a column. They had to march around the corpse and sing anti-Semitic songs. The mournful chorus filled the yard like fog:

"Wenn's Judenblut vom Messer spritzt,
Dann geht's nochmal so gut... dann geht's nochmal so gut..."
(When Jewish blood squirts under the knives,
Then all is well, then all is well ...)

And,

"Armer Jude Kohn, kleiner Jude Kohn,
Hast ja keine Heimat mehr..."
(Poor Jew Kohn, little Jew Kohn,
You have no home any more ...)

They sang until their voices were hoarse. To satisfy Toussaint and the guards, they sang as loud as they could. They sang despairingly, without a trace of that murderous fighting spirit which we others worked hard to keep alive within us. We looked forward to the day when men like Toussaint would fall by the thousand under the machine-gun bullets of the revolutionary workers. That was what kept us struggling and scheming; that was what we looked forward to. But the Jews, they had nothing like that to keep them up.

As the guards grew tired of the game, they, too, fell to singing, and all we other prisoners sang as well.

"Um den Juden auszuroden,
Schneide man ihm ab die Hoden—
Und den weiblichen Semiten,
Sollte man das Ding vernieten..."

Then we marched back to the cells, and the scavengers carried the corpse to the furnace in the cellar.

A day in Camp Fuhlsbuettel began at six in the morning with the loud clanging of a bell. A minute later I would hear the rattling of keys in ponderous locks, the crashing of doors, the banging of the troopers' boots, and angry shouts. The instant the door of my cell swung open, I rose from the cot as far as my chains allowed me to rise, to report my presence to the guard on duty. At the top of my voice I would shout my name, and add: "... red pig in chains for high treason!"

"Louder!" the trooper would snarl. "What are you?"

"I am a red pig in chains for high treason!"

"Louder! Shout it fifteen times!"

While I shouted, the trooper stood over me, his rubber truncheon poised, and slamming it down on my chest if I paused too long to catch my breath. Then he unlocked my chains. I leaped from the cot and reached for my pants and an undershirt. I was not permitted to wear other articles of clothing. While I slipped into my rags, the trooper rummaged through my cell and shouted: "Faster! You move like a sack of flour! Faster, *du Lumpenhund!*"

Then he threw the "night chains" out on the tier, shackled my wrists together with "day irons," and clattered out to repeat the procedure in the adjoining cage. For an hour I was alone. At seven o'clock a hunk of black bread was thrown into my cell. Breakfast.

Ten minutes later began the assembling of prisoners who were scheduled for questioning at Gestapo headquarters. With curses and kicks I was summoned from my cell and herded into the yard. There I stood, face to the wall, until my name was called. I jumped toward the prison truck. At the door of the truck stood two young Elite Guards with chains in their hands. Each prisoner, before he was pushed into the truck, was struck across the back with the chains.

The prison lorry had steel walls and a steel roof. There were no windows. Its interior was divided into a number of steel lockers in which a man could neither stand upright nor sit. It was like being crouched in a short steel coffin. There was such "room" for twenty prisoners in one lorry, and there were four such lorries shuttling every day between the concentration camp and Gestapo headquarters in the heart of Hamburg. About me was utter darkness. The rumbling of wheels and the distant purr of the motor told me that the transport was under way. When the truck stopped about forty minutes later, it was in the gray stone-yard of the Gestapo headquarters.

A man's thoughts on such a journey to a new torture session are gloomy. If he is determined to fight, his mind is permeated with a dull stoicism, or he is frantically anticipating the questions and answers of the hellish hours ahead. I lost count of the number of journeys I had made between Camp Fuhlsbuettel and the Gestapo; but I made that trip scores of times. Around me were darkness and suffocating emptiness, a desolation accentuated by the knowledge that I was rolling through crowded streets, that only a few yards away men and women were bent on workaday errands, people who still were lucky enough to have a piece of soap for themselves and a place where they could chat and rest. Each day such prison transports rolled through every German town. Eyes stared into the darkness, and minds struggled to meet the horrors to come.

In the court-yard of Gestapo headquarters the prisoners formed a column. Then came a barked command: *"Vorwaerts, marsch!"* Surrounded by Death Head guards, we broke into a run. Those among us who could not keep the pace were beaten mercilessly. We ran through the court-yard, through corridors and up three flights of stairs until we came to a halt in front of a door which bore the sign, *Wartezimmer.* The door was unlocked and we were herded into a long room.

"Noses and toes against the wall! Absolute silence! He who speaks will be lynched!"

When dealing with political prisoners, the Elite Guards displayed cold savagery in every word and every gesture of theirs. We lined up against the walls, stood rigid and kept still. Troopers with clubs in their hands patrolled continuously behind our backs. Intermittently a telephone rang. The Elite Guard officer at the desk received the calls. They were calls from the various Gestapo departments—the Passport Division, the Explosives Division, the Bureau of Firearms, the Anti-Communist and Anti-Socialist Division, the Foreign Division, the Bureau of Identification, the Counter-Espionage Department, and others—calls requesting that certain prisoners should be escorted to certain rooms for questioning. Each ring of the telephone brought a terrible tenseness into the mask-like faces of waiting prisoners; the ringing stabbed through heads and hearts and jangled in the marrows of our bones; and there was always the thought: "Now they have called for me!" There were old men among us, motherly women, and girls. Once in a while, someone collapsed—and was doused with cold water and showered with abuse.

One day, in the waiting room, a thin-faced girl named Martha Helm, who had been a member of the communist organization in Kiel, seized a penknife from the Elite Guard officer's desk. Without saying a word, she slashed her left wrist. Then she sat down on the floor, while her blood sprayed over the white-washed wall in front of her. Two troopers picked her up and carried her hastily out of the room. She cried faintly for help then. The remaining troopers raged like wild beasts. "Eyes to the wall, you Red bastards! Don't move, you curs!" There was a hail of curses and kicks. The mask-like faces of the prisoners hardly changed.

My name was called and an Elite Guard put a chain around my wrist and led me to the offices of the Foreign Division. Inspector Paul Kraus conducted the questioning, assisted by Hertha Jens and a group of assistants. The method was always the same: Questions —threats—beatings; questions and beatings; promises of peace and luxury if I would give them the desired answers; threats and questions, questions and beatings. Maledictions and yells and whimpers floating through the walls from other rooms showed me that I was not alone in the grinding mill. At times Inspector Kraus would repeat the same question thirty times or more, and each evasive answer was followed by a spell of slashing pain. Often the inquisition lasted until I was too battered to understand the meaning of words. But sometimes it was cut short by a wave of new arrests which claimed Inspector Kraus' attention. The

Gestapo was overworked. The agents of the Foreign Division looked as if they had not slept for days. Their irritation made them more vicious. Only Hertha Jens was always the same. She relished the agony of those who had once called her "comrade." She lounged on tables, showing her thick white thighs and puffing smoke through her cherry-red lips. I hated her to the point of insanity. Her insolent presence gave me strength to delay the final, inevitable surrender.

"Hello, *mein Junge*" she once asked me. "Do you know Karl Lesch?"

I knew him. I gave her no answer.

"Our young men whipped him to death yesterday afternoon, unfortunately," she drawled.

Inspector Kraus gave her a snarl: *"Diese Weiber!"*

After each turn of questioning, two Elite Guards dragged me to a room on the fifth floor, which was known as the "Repair Shop." A young Nazi doctor was in attendance, and two male nurses in the Brownshirt uniform. Their one and only treatment was the smearing of vaseline over the backs and legs of tortured men. The Brownshirt nurses worked silently. The doctor would walk around me, rubbing his hands and beaming, "Remarkable, remarkable."

Toward four in the afternoon we were assembled for the return transport to the concentration camp. By five, we were again locked in the cells. Those who had not had their midday meal were now given a liter of thick soup—of potatoes or peas or cabbage or beans; the rest received again a hunk of dry black bread. Even the manner in which the food was handed out was designed to break the nerves of prisoners who met the Gestapo assaults with stubborn passive resistance. The soup given me was boiling hot. The time allowed me to consume it was one minute. After the minute had passed, I was again handcuffed. The first few times I miserably burned my mouth and throat. But as time passed I developed the technique of gobbling a liter of soup in a minute. As soon as it arrived and my hands were unshackled, I dumped half of the soup into the toilet of my cell. Then I filled the bowl with cold water. The remainder of the soup, thus diluted and cooled, I drank down in fast gulps.

When the prisoners returned from questioning from Gestapo headquarters, they found the concentration camp in an uproar. Driven by guards, prisoners ran in circles around the yards; others were made to race on all fours up and down the grimy stairways; others again stood facing the wall and shouting abuse at themselves. Once I saw Albert Walter. He was naked. The bronze color of his skin had changed to a sodden gray. At the command of two troopers, he was turning somersaults through one of the ground-floor corridors of the cell-block. Whenever his head was poised on the concrete floor, the troopers slammed their rubber clubs on the old sailor's hams. He also saw me. His eyes were sunken and glassy. Neither of us gave a sign of recognition.

The "lights out" signal came at seven, and then the night. In this winter of 1933-1934, each night in Camp Fuhlsbuettel was a night of horrors. Each night men died. Most died by suicide, some were deliberately murdered on Gestapo orders, and others died "accidentally" under the hands of marauding night guards. Most of those who died were communists. The aim of the Gestapo was to obtain convictions of their prisoners for high treason. Incriminating evidence was required to stage public high treason trials. "Confess, so that we may convict you—or die!" was the order of the day. Nine-tenths of all political prisoners "confessed." The Special Tribunals condemned them to death or prison. Until the end of 1936, there was not a day in Hamburg on which men and women were not condemned for high treason. Often a hundred or more accused were sentenced in a single trial. Once—in the *Lemke Prozess* in Hamburg—1,200 communists were sent to prison after one common mass trial before the Special Tribunal. For such trials the nights in Fuhlsbuettel prepared the ground. The horrors were calculated to bring each individual captive to the point where he would "confess" and go to prison gladly—only to get away from the clubs and the boots of the Death Head guards. On Christmas Night of 1933, twenty-four communists died in Camp Fuhlsbuettel. The guards burst into the cells and handed ropes to the doomed.

"If you don't hang in five minutes, w will hang you," they announced.

There was a great noise each time a corpse was dragged through the corridors. An Elite Guard alone was more or less a human being; but when a crowd of Elite Guards were together they strove to outdo one another in smart cruelty, for the highest ambition of each of these youngsters was promotion into the Gestapo. On Christmas Night a brewery supplied the Death Head guards with free beer. Pandemonium reigned in Camp Fuhlsbuettel. Each time a corpse was dragged to the prison morgue the troopers sang:

> *"Ja, sowas das ist herrlich,*
> *Ja, sowas das ist schoen,*
> *Ja, sowas hat man lange nicht*
> *In Ko-La-Fu gesehen."*

"Ko-La-Fu" was the official abbreviation for *Konzentrations Lager Fuhlsbuettel.*

Uncounted times I was awakened from fitful sleep by my own groaning. Dreams harassed me with persistent malevolence. Inadvertently I tossed from side to side, a curse on my lips, and the chains brought my motions to a sudden and painful halt. The faint rattling of those chains often roused me to a blazing fury. I jerked and tore at them, and moaned. Then I lay still. My thoughts wandered. The past was a jumble of colors and faces and irremediable mistakes, and the future was a toothless hag grinning out of black fog. Faint noises scurried through the walls. Other chained men lay in the cells to my right and left, above me and below me. Off and on, an insane yell stabbed through the night. Out in the yard the searchlights blazed, fingering over the long window rows of the cell blocks.

I thought of Cilly, of Otto, of many others I had known. What had become of them? I thought of Firelei. "Where are you?" I asked. "What are they doing to you?" And I would hear a whisper, Firelei's voice drifting close beside me, saying words that were kind and sweet and meaningless, until they were swallowed up by sounds from other sources: a night guard barking commands at a column of newly-arriving prisoners, or the voice of Arthur Ewert growling out of the gloom: "I tell you, we are making a horrible mistake!", or the lusty voice of Comrade Cance of Le Havre crackling, *"Buvez du vin, et vivez joyeux!",* or the cordelia voice of Mariette, the whore with the noble soul, reiterating, "Up the stairs, and down the stairs, oh-lala." And there was always the droning of airplanes.

Toward one o'clock in the morning the Command for Special Purposes arrived in Camp Fuhlsbuettel. They were young Elite

Guards, a hand-picked lot of Gestapo apprentices. Invariably they arrived on a sputtering motor lorry. When the lorry arrived in the yard, its driver blew the horn to announce the commencement of the nocturnal horrors. It began with the ringing of boots on the concrete tiers, and the banging of doors. A loud voice read off a list of names. Troopers entered the cells. Hoarse whispers: "Hello, hello, you'll be shot at sunrise." The door closed. Sometime later it was opened again. The outline of a Death Head guard stood against the corridor lights. "Hey!" he yelled. Then he emptied his revolver into the walls and ceiling of the cell. A period of silence followed, until the banging of doors began anew. Chained men were beaten in the night. I could hear the banging doors, the tramping boots, the wild howls of the beaten. They came nearer, nearer. Then the turning of a key in the lock of my cell door. Three troopers barged in. They stripped away the faded blanket and their rubber truncheons hailed on me indiscriminately. A prisoner who did not yell was beaten until he yelled, to satisfy the guards, and to terrify the comrades in adjoining cells, whose turn would be next. I awaited them, shivering as if under an attack of malaria, and after they had done their work, I lay still, too stupefied to listen to the howling of the others. Three cells away from me lay the Jewish editor of the socialist paper in Luebeck. His name, I believe, was Sollmitz. His voice was high, almost like that of a woman. One night, when the Command for Special Purposes invaded his cell, he yelled: "Protest! Protest!"

A trooper cried triumphantly: "Listen to the Jew! The Jew complains!"

The Death Head guards assembled in this man's cell. Sollmitz was beaten to death. It lasted until dawn, when a guard banged against the cell doors of other prisoners, shouting: "Extra! Extra! *Will jemand einen krepierten Juden sehen?"* The days dragged on. The future stared at you with gray, implacable hostility. You lay awake. You stared and stared and searched for a way out. You stared and searched, and pain and fear and hatred were your constant companions.

Sometime in the middle of February I was transferred to the infirmary. I prayed and begged for death, but death would not come. The bed was clean, and the food plentiful—white bread, milk, eggs. Elite Guards sat silently between the beds to see to it that no prisoner could speak to another. The grizzled doctor, whose face was disfigured by saber scars, did not permit the

Gestapo to enter his wards. On the same corridor, already for weeks in a water bed, lay Edgar Andree. The Elite Guards made bets from day to day as to whether Comrade Andree would live or die. They showed an undisguised admiration for his fortitude. The prisoners in the infirmary were men whom the Gestapo considered too valuable to let them die without the propagandistic show of a high treason trial. On the ninth day I was discharged from the infirmary. I still felt a dull pain in the right side of my head. My ear had been smashed; I was half deaf. My kidneys were damaged; my urine came with blood. I had received an abdominal injury that was beyond repair. Before I left the infirmary, the doctor shook my hand.

"Well, my boy, times have changed," he said.

A Gestapo agent escorted me to the railway station. We rode in an open car. The sights and sounds of traffic, the shop-windows, the people in the streets—they all seemed to belong to a far-away world. They sailed over my line of vision like marionettes in a distant and uninteresting show. Only the outstretched arm of a girl wiping the pane of a window fixed itself indelibly into my mind; a small, firm hand, and a half-bared arm moving swiftly over the smooth surface. Long after it had disappeared, I still saw it move in front of my eyes.

"Where are we going to?" I asked the Gestapo man.

"To Berlin."

We had a third-class compartment to ourselves. My guard was a man of twenty-eight, with a long head, a narrow face and a whiplike body. "We have respect for fellows who don't cringe," he told me, after the train had pulled out of Hamburg *Hauptbahnhof.* "But it is our duty to break them, make them harmless once and for all, in the interest of the New Germany." In the course of the journey, he told me his life story, and I smoked his cigarettes. He had been the son of a *gymnasium* teacher and became a member of the Nazi Party when he studied chemistry at the University of Hamburg. He had to give up his studies for lack of money and became a ditch-digger for the government relief organization—the *Wohlfahrt.* At the job, he was often manhandled by communists and socialists among the laborers because he insisted on wearing the swastika badge while he swung the pick. After he had received a particularly severe beating, he gave up the job of ditch-digging, and the *Wohlfahrt* struck him off the relief lists for "refusal to work." He then enrolled with the storm troops, lived in barracks and hardened in continuous street warfare. Twice he was wounded in nightly skirmishes. In December, 1932, he was selected for service in the Elite Guards, and his dash and intelligence won him a *staffelfuehrer's* honors just before Hitler became Chancellor. After the Reichstag Fire, he was detailed to a Command for Special Purposes, and three months later he was recommended for services in the Gestapo. He had a fierce pride, a limitless belief in the mission of Adolf Hitler, and the hard conviction that traitors had forfeited for all time their right to freedom and life. A "traitor," of course, was anyone who actively opposed National Socialist rule.

I saw nothing of Berlin, for my journeys through the capital were made in closed police trucks. Two nights I spent in the deep dungeons beneath Police Headquarters on the Alexanderplatz. The dungeons were overcrowded with all manner of people, and there was a constant coming and going of prisoner transports. Locked into a small, vault-like cubicle, the front of which was open except for steel bars I was given no opportunity to speak or signal to any of my fellow-prisoners. Once during the night a horde of prostitutes, young and old, was marched past my cell and down the corridor. Every few steps they shrieked in unison, "Heil Hitler! *Hoch das Bein, der Goering braucht Soldaten!*" Troopers bringing up the rear dealt out kicks. "Shut up!" they roared. "Shut up! Shut up!" And the prostitutes would shriek again: "Heil Hitler!"

For two days I was questioned by the Berlin Gestapo. They were less brutal than their colleagues of the Foreign Division in Hamburg, but the officials seemed better trained and more experienced in police work. Here I was subjected to a special form of torture: kneeling for hours at a stretch on a police carbine, and at another time on a shallow box filled with nails. The general atmosphere, however, was the same as in Hamburg—grimy corridors, offices furnished with Spartan simplicity, threats, kicks, troopers chasing chained men up and down the reaches of the building, shouting, rows of girls and women standing with their noses and toes against the walls, overflowing ashtrays, portraits of Hitler and his aides, the smell of coffee, smartly dressed girls working at high speed behind typewriters—girls seemingly indifferent to all the squalor and agony about them, stacks of confiscated publications, printing machines, books, and pictures, and Gestapo agents asleep on tables. The questioning of me got nowhere. Already I had become so experienced that I could formulate an answer to a question before it was asked. My answers were either evasive, or misleading. Not to answer at all is—in Gestapo headquarters—always a fatal course.

"We give you three days to think it over," I was told.

A police truck whisked me past the Stettiner Bahnhof, across the Havel River and out on a road which leads toward Straslund. There were perhaps thirty prisoners in the truck, a sullen and dejected-looking crew. Elite Guards stood between the rows of prisoners to keep us from communicating with one another. After a couple of hours we arrived at Concentration Camp Oranienburg. I saw factory buildings, long barbed-wire fences, low barracks and a large paved court-yard. Again I was singled out for solitary confinement. A damp little compartment in the basement of an old brewery became my temporary home. Outside was a driving rain. I received no cot and no blankets, but two burlap sacks stuffed full of ill-smelling rags. I shivered dismally. One of the troopers on duty amused himself by poking his head into my cage every two hours or so saying gravely, "Blankets are coming." On the second day, the cold became unbearable. I pounded against the door with both fists. A Death Head guard appeared.

"*Du Schwein,* why all the noise?"

"I am freezing to death here," I said.

"You're freezing? All right. Step out. I'll warm you up!"

In quickstep he chased me out into a yard. "Faster! Faster! You run like an old woman in the seventh month! Faster, I said!" There were other prisoners in the yard, undergoing a perverted form of military drill. The Elite Guard chased me to the edge of a mud hole. The hole was ten feet deep and about twenty-five feet wide. Across it led a narrow plank, which sagged downward in the middle. The plank was worn off by many feet.

"Walk the plank!" the guard commanded, brandishing his club.

I staggered out on the plank. After ten lurching steps, the trooper jumped with both feet on the end of the plank. I lost my balance and toppled into the mud.

"Get out of the hole "

I scrambled back to the level of the yard.

"Do you feel warm now?"

"Yes, *Herr Wachtmeister.*"

"Comfortably warm?"

"Yes, sir."

"Good! Back to your boudoir! Run, *du Sauhund!*" Down came the club. "One-two-three-four, one-two-three-four! Faster! Faster!"

On the morning of the fourth day, I was brought back to Berlin. Two hours of questioning followed. A Gestapo inspector showed me a map of the western border districts of Germany and demanded that I should draw in the location of Comintern frontier relay stations. Then he showed me a series of photographs for identification. After that followed questions about the names and addresses of communists in countries adjoining Germany. Again, all this led to nothing.

"I see now where we stand," the Gestapo man said coldly. *"Wir werden andere Saiten aufziehen.* With you we must play a different tune."

I expected to be strapped over a table. Instead, chained to a dozen other prisoners, I was led to an inner court-yard. I was pushed aboard a police lorry and into a steel box. Soon the lorry was speeding over roads I could not see. Around me was complete darkness. Hour after hour passed. My body grew stiff and numb.

"Where to?" I asked myself.

The journey lasted all through the night. Finally the truck stopped. Outside keys grated in locks. "All out!"

I stood in the dim light of morning. Snow was falling. Death Head guards in steel helmets snapped orders. A little way off stood the lanky shape of Toussaint. The holster on his belt was open and his fist rested on the butt of his Mauser.

"Welcome," he brayed.

Overhead the crows cried bleakly: "Krah—krah—krah!" I was back in Camp Fuhlsbuettel, the murder camp.

All day I watched the wind drive snowflakes through the naked trees at the edge of the yard. Toward evening the wind died down, and night came dark and still, interrupted only by the droning of distant airplanes. I did not feel so well. I had thought much about the black, humiliating defeat of the Communist Party of Germany, and I could not find a satisfying answer. The brain is restless, insatiable in its anguished boring. Had we become so accustomed to fighting for an unattainable ideal that fighting became an end itself? In the best of times the ideal was hardly more than a ghost. Besides, my back still burned from half-healed lacerations, and a leaden pain was in my bones.

They were out to break me and I refused to be broken.

I was a piece of the Party. They could kill me, but they could never, never kill the Party.

The old snarl was in my throat. It leaped to my throat even though I did not call it.

"Do your worst, you bastards! I'll tell you nothing!"

The lights were out and I lay on the iron network which was my bed, shackled hand and foot. I was about to blow cool air on my right wrist which had been chafed raw by the handcuffs when I heard pounding steps approach along the tier. Were they coming for me? If they came for someone else, I should soon know by the banging of a door, by groans and yells and the muffled cursing of the guards.

No. It was for me. From outside a hand I could not see switched on the light. A key rattled in the lock. The door swung open. I stiffened to attention. Under my wounded nakedness the cot gave little metallic creaks.

Two guards entered the cell. Under the black steel helmets their faces were pale. Young, thin faces with grayish eyes and colorless lips. Each of them carried a rifle, a bayonet, a pistol, a belt with cartridges and a rubber truncheon. They were not guards from the tier. They were sentries from the yard. One of them reached over and unlocked my shackles. Mutely I wondered what deviltry they

I stood under the window now, still naked, and swaying queerly to and fro.

"Do you want to piss?"

"Jawohl, Herr Wachtmeister," I rapped out.

"Here." He handed me a rusty cup, "Piss in that."

I urinated into the cup.

"Now drink it!"

I held the warm cup in both hands and hesitated.

"Verfluchtes Schwein," the guard snapped. "Drink it! Quick or I'm going to piss in your mouth."

I drank. Urine tastes stale and salty. There are worse things a man can do than drink his own urine. The cup clattered to the floor and I vomited.

The guards laughed.

"Sissy, sissy," said one.

"Get dressed," commanded the other.

At top speed I slipped into my patched blue pants and the shapeless tiger-striped jacket.

A guard growled: "You move like a sack of flour. Hurry up!"

I put on the stinking, hobnailed boots and the little black round cap. For months I had seen neither underwear nor socks.

"This guy looks like Gandhi," one of the troopers said.
"He looks like an ape after a bridal night," said the other.
"What do you look like?"
"Like Gandhi," I said.
"Hell, no, not Gandhi."
"Like an ape."
The trooper kicked me hard. "What sort of an ape, hey?" he yelled.
"Like an ape after a bridal night," I said.
"Like a she-ape after a regimental rape," the trooper said.

I stared straight ahead, wondering what they were up to. Had there been one, a man could have talked. Talked sensibly. But when they came in a pair or more, one was ashamed of the other; each wanted to be the smartest, most ruthless of the crew. A guard jabbed his fist into my stomach.

"Say: I am a dissipated she-ape," he ordered.
"I am a dissipated she-ape," I said.
"Louder!"
"I am a dissipated she-ape!"
Ten times I roared, "I am a dissipated she-ape." The troopers watched me, fascinated.
"Step out!"

I stepped out. The tier was empty. Here and there a guard squinted through the spy-hole of a cell. I marched down the stairs through a gloomy hall and toward the yard. I crossed the yard and the snow crunched under my feet. The cold night air sang in my lungs and mounted into my head like wine. Behind me, the trooper counted the steps—

"Links! Links! Links, zwei, drei, vier . . ."

Every twelve steps his rubber club came down on the back of my neck.

The guard at the gate raised his hand in the Hitler salute and let us pass. We marched through the darkness of another yard and on the soft earth the snow made little swishing noises about our boots. At times the beams of searchlights leaped up and down the walls like animals who have lost their way. Along the outer walls I saw the immobile shapes of sentries in black greatcoats and under black steel helmets. Their hands buried, they held their rifles in the hollows of their arms, and when they passed the lantern at the outer gate, I saw that there were hand-grenades in their belts. The outer gates, gray and huge, blocked the way.

I had begun to cultivate the habit of forcing my thought into neutral channels. Just then I was mumbling to myself, "Green birches remind me of young girls . . . The waters of the Rio de la Plata are yellow with floating mud . . ."

"Halt," a trooper ordered.

A whispered conversation took place between the guards at the outer gate and those who had taken me from my cell. From the trooper's kitchen drifted the aroma of pea soup and fried onions. Heavily a crow flopped overhead. One of the sentries pushed his face close to mine.

"Oh, it's you," he said softly. "That's good. Did you ever have a busted spine? No? . . . Well, good-by, darling."

A portion of the heavy gate clanked open. I looked into a dark road lined with trees. The road led away among gardens, patches of empty ground and a few cottages with feeble streaks of light.

The night was immense. The great Outside leaped at me, engulfed me, and the first sensation was one of suffocation. In those distant houses lived men who were free and who did not know the value of freedom. Free to walk down any street they chose; free to walk into a restaurant for coffee; free to crawl into bed and put their arms around their women; free to sing, to open doors, to switch on and off their lights! My head reeled and I heard my heart pound and my senses clamor. And then I asked myself again: What do they want? Why this excursion in the dead of the night?

"Step out."

I stepped through the gate.

"Keep to the middle of the road.—March!"

I marched along the middle of the road, the sweet smell of manure in my nostrils. Somewhere nearby must have been a barn with horses and cows. Far off a locomotive shrieked. It was a fearful thing to think of a locomotive speeding through the night. Going to Cologne, to Amsterdam, to Paris or Turin. To the left, silent orchards floated away in impenetrable darkness. The man behind me stopped hitting me every twelve steps. Snow fell. To the right, the prison hulked like a giant geometric shape against the sky.

"Where are you taking me?" I asked.

"We're going to shoot you," was the curt reply.

"They're going to shoot me," I thought. "What of it!" When the lead-filled whips come biting into a man's carcass, he thinks of being shot as a festival. One single slash of a whip is more painful than a slug in the head, he thinks. So death by shooting can become a final, merciful caress.

Beyond the colossal outlines of the prison the searchlights from the flying-field played like avid fingers in the night. I listened to the thunder of a plane which was circling to land. It was a night like any other night. A night full of discord and danger. Gradually I realized that I did not want to die. Death would put an end to the dancing whips, the shivering nights, an end to pain and degradation and hope that had no right to exist. A man is ready to die, but when death is ready to spring, he discovers that the privilege to breathe the good clean air alone is abundant compensation for all the hellish whips can do. Three paces behind me the troopers' boots crunched on the road. Their rifles, I knew, were pointed at the small of my back.

"Oh, it's you! . . . Did you ever have a busted spine?"

Somewhere Firelei was still alive. If she knew, I thought, she'd weep. Maybe she wept. Or maybe she was now sleeping with a comrade bound to go to Germany and to his doom. "Firelei, farewell," I thought.

"Do your worst, you bastards! It hurts to admit that Hitler has won. It is hard, so hard to imagine that Hitler could be defeated without you, yourself, being alive to help in this defeat. Hate! Hate hard!

"What if I ran, took a chance in a thousand? If I ran, I'd be shot. I'd probably be dead on the spot. It would be like a swift sledgehammer blow against the spine, a sudden piercing gust of pain, a ridiculous attempt to breathe and clutch the air, and then nothing more. Except, perhaps, the butt of a rifle crashing down on the top of my head. Such an end would not be bad. It would be easy."

I did not want to die. I wanted to live.

If I ran, and they did not shoot me, but caught me alive . . . My brain revolted against the thought!

No. Don't run.

The guards behind me had suddenly stopped marching. The sounds made by their boots had stopped as if the men had frozen or sunken into the earth. Instinctively, after two more paces, I also stopped. We all stood silently in the dark.

I did not dare to turn my head. A rubber club would smash across my face if I looked around. I just stood in the snow and felt the cold gnaw at my skin and did nothing.

"March!" a trooper said angrily.

I did not move.

"March, *gottverdammter Hund!*"

I marched two further paces, but then I halted again because I could not hear the boots of the guards march three paces behind me. Snowflakes sailed across my face. Slowly, an inch at a time, I turned my head to the right, straining my eyes. Indistinctly I saw the guards. Pinpoints of light gleamed on their helmets and on the barrels of their guns. I was astonished to find how plainly their silhouettes stood out against the snow. If I made one more step away from them, they'd shoot me through my back. "Shot while trying to escape."

Five yards behind me the troopers stood in the night. I did not budge.

In a hoarse whisper a guard snarled:

"March!"

I did not march. I stood rooted to the ground and felt nothing. There is something inside of every man that is much stronger than the will to die. When death looms close, this something is right beside you, inside you, above and around you to prevent you from taking the step that would make death a quick victor.

A trooper came up to me and looked into my face.

"Are you crazy?" he demanded.

"No, sir," I said.

"Then why don't you march?"

"You'd shoot me down like a dog."

"Damn right we would," said the trooper.

A figure came shambling down the desolate road. A worker smoking a pipe. His overcoat flapped like the wings of a bat. He shambled toward us, swinging his arms.

"March! " said the trooper.

I did not march. I stood in the snow, motionless, my lungs working like volcanoes. I could turn now and say, "Look here, my friends. I'm tired of this. Bring me to the Gestapo and I'll tell them all I know, all the names, all the addresses, and then I'll sign a confession, any confession you'll give me to sign." If I did that, everything would be all right. I'd get cigarettes and a steak and a real mattress to sleep on. The worker had stopped beside a tree and was watching me silently.

The trooper said sullenly, "March, you red hound!"

I did not march. Maybe they had orders to shoot me so that I did not die. Shatter my knee, or shoot off the genitals. Such things had been done before. A man with a shattered right knee would rather sign a confession than have his left knee shattered as well. An ax slicing through the neck, with a judge in a top hat looking on gravely, and Gestapo witnesses smirking their self-satisfaction is less painful than a shattered knee. The worker knocked out his pipe against the trunk of the tree and moved on with uneasy steps.

"Heil Hitler," he said as he passed the guards.

"The whore won't march," said one of the troopers.

"We'll make the bloody whore march," said the other.

One of them kicked me. I pitched forward into the snow. Boots struck my side and the butt of a rifle came down on my back..

"Get up! Who in hell's name told you to lie down?"

I stood up. Hard and cold the barrel of a pistol pressed into the back of my neck.

"Now, march!"

I marched. I counted the steps because I did not want to think of the pistol pressing the back of the neck. Thirty ... thirty-seven, forty-one...

"My hands get cold," the trooper muttered. I felt him take the pistol barrel away from my skin. "Keep marching," he added.

I marched. Three paces behind me marched the guards.

"Sing," one of them commanded. "Sing the Horst Wessel song!"

I sang. I sang at the top of my voice.

*"Dann wehen Hitlerfalmen ueber allen Strassen,
Dann bricht der Tag der deutschen Freiheit an ..."*

The melody is one of a revolutionary song. I had heard it sung by workers' demonstrations, surge up from a hundred thousand throats. The tramp of militant proletarian columns in hostile streets was the highest music I knew. My mouth brayed the Nazi words, but in my heart other words welled up in a pounding rhythm—

*"Hoch ivehen Sovietfahren ueber Barrikaden,
So bricht der Tag der roten Freiheit an ..."*

Once more the guards stopped marching. Immediately I halted, treading the spot, still singing. The prison walls heaved hollow echoes.

"March!" a trooper snapped.

"I won't march unless you follow," I said.

"Oh, you won't march?"

"No," I answered.

"All right, stand still then till you're blue in the face."

The troopers had a consultation while I stood still.

"If you don't march, we'll give you a beating," one of them said.

"March!" commanded the other.

I did not march.

"We'll beat you till you hear the angels' hallelujah."

I said nothing. I stood still.

"March!" said the trooper.

I did not march.

"You're a stubborn chunk o' shit, all right," one of them muttered. "Take off your pants."

I unloosened my belt and let the pants slip down to my knees. The guards laid their rifles in the snow. One of them grasped his rubber truncheon. The other held his pistol cocked. They led me to the side of the road and pushed my face against a tree.

"Bend over! Clasp your arms around the tree and bend over!"

From the prison yard came the shot of a rifle and the sound of splintering glass. That happened often. The searchlight had spotted a prisoner looking out of the window and the sentry in the yard had shot at the window. They hardly ever hit a man that way, but the window was shattered and the cell became a pneumonia trap.

Bending over, I threw my arms around the tree. A trooper grunted.

"Bend down farther."

They beat me till I sagged into the snow. They stretched me out on the ground and beat me more. Then they took off their shoulder straps and with them they struck me in the face. When the headlights of a car came near, they stopped beating.

"Stand up! Get behind that tree and fasten your pants."

After the car had passed we marched back. At times I staggered and the guards stood aside and gave me a chance to rest. The sentry at the gate seized my throat and shook me to and fro.

"Ah, darling," he muttered. "You don't know how lucky you are."

One of the troopers who had taken me out brought me back to my cell. When he turned on the light I saw that he had the face of a youngster who needed, above all, ten hours of sleep.

"Well, how do you feel?" he queried.

"Very well, *Herr Wachtmeister*."

"Here. Take a cigarette. That'll make you feel better."

He gave me a cigarette and then he struck a match and lit it.

"If they know I gave you a cigarette, it'll be daylight out for me," he grinned.

He turned off the light and locked the door of my cell. I smoked as if nothing else had ever mattered. While I smoked, the guard stood in front of my cell. When the last tiny fragment of my cigarette had gone out between my lips I heard him walk away down the tier. His heels rang on the concrete, became fainter and then they clattered down an iron stairway.

Sleep would not come. The live pain in my flesh was like the digging of many teeth. Feverish, shivering, abysmal nights. Nights without end. They were wearing me down. Down. All night that word was in my head. Down, down. They were wearing me down.

Four times in ten days they took me for walks in the night. Each time the walk began with a promise of execution, and ended in sleepless exhaustion.

Chapter Thirty-five

I SIGN A CONFESSION

The Gestapo broke me on March 11, 1934. That day, at nine in the morning, I heard a ringing stride approach along the tier.

"An Elite Guard is marching down the line."

The boots of a prisoner creak dismally, the walk of a jailer makes soft swishing sounds, but the steps of the Death Head guards ring. A key rattled in the door of my cell. I sprang to attention. The door opened abruptly.

The trooper eyed me with cold hostility. He wore a black uniform and a steel helmet. There was a bayonet and a pistol in his belt. A thick rubber truncheon swung from his hips. In his hands he held a carbine.

"Come out!" he said.

I stepped out of the cell. The trooper ran searching hands over my chest, back, sides, legs. There was a feeling of emptiness in my belly and a fog of hate and apprehension in my brain. I could not think. I was like a beast under the whip of a keeper: watchful and powerless.

"March!" he said.

I marched along the tier and down the steps.

Two paces behind me marched the trooper, the end of his carbine pressed against the small of my back. We marched across the prison yard. Iron gates were opened by silent guards with upturned coat collars. We marched through more yards, marching across crunching snow. From the naked trees came hoarse cries of crows. In the still cold my breath showed white.

In the yard three troopers made a skinny prisoner roll in the snow. The prisoner was naked. I recognized him. He was Horst Witzel, a tug-boat engineer who had a wife and three small children. He stared at me out of the snow without a sign of recognition. A trooper struck his rubber truncheon across the skinny man's flanks and made him get up and run through the yard. A wolfhound sat on his haunches, watching the naked man run.

The guard stroked the dog's head.

"Get him, Nero!" said the guard.

The dog bounded away in great leaps. Horst Witzel fell into the snow, shrieking, the animal atop of him and snarling, and the troopers laughed.

"Laugh, damn you!" commanded one of them.

I laughed.

"Ha—ha—ha!"

"Once more! Louder!"

"Ha—ha—ha!"

It sounded like a cart going over cobbles.

Then we marched on. We marched into a gloomy hall flanked by many grimy cell doors. A trooper moved stealthily from door to door, squinting through the spy-holes.

"Against the wall! Nose and toes against the wall!"

That's not easy. Put the tips of your toes and the tip of your nose against the wall, with your hands shackled behind your back, and stand straight. After you stand so for an hour your eyes bulge out of their caves and you feel as if huge rocks are pressing in on you from both sides. I stood there for three hours. I saw men who fainted after an hour. I also saw men who began ramming their heads against the walls, howling like lunatics until they crumpled up under the butt of a carbine. In a long line they stood nose and toes against the wall, a score of workers, and here and there a desolate Jew.

Only those can stand three hours and longer who down all thought and pump themselves full of hatred. ... At first they think, but then they go down, or they hate, and their hate keeps them alive.

You can't stand there in peace. Every few minutes a passing trooper bangs your head against the wall with a sudden blow from behind. Others kick you. Still others bring the butts of their carbines down hard on your toes. . . . They sneak up silently and then suddenly smash your toes. That makes you jump. If you raise your foot and moan, or if you jump, they turn you around, back to wall, and hit you with rubber truncheons.

One small blond ruffian made me take off my shoes. He put a cartridge shell in each shoe and made me put them on again and stand nose and toes against the wall. All the time the clanking boots of Death Head guards passed behind my back, bringing in new prisoners, and taking others away I knew not where. I listened to groans, commands, abuse. So three hours went by.

I was grasped from behind and dragged into an open cell. Then the door was closed and locked.

I was not alone. Four Elite Guards under black steel helmets sat on chairs. Their faces were cocked expectantly. Stretched out on a filthy cot lay a Gestapo man in shirt-sleeves. Blood spots were on the mattress. The Gestapo man had a thick round face and a big mouth and gray-green eyes. He eyed me coldly.

"Do you know who I am?" he drawled.

"No, sir."

"I am Inspector Radam. Your comrades wish I'd burn alive in hell. I'm the best friend of Prosecutor Jauch of the Special Tribunal." Radam grinned broadly. Then he added: "Do you know what you are here for?"

"No, sir."

"Oh—ho! He doesn't know what he is here for. Let the bastard have it!"

The troopers cuffed me into a corner. They used their rubber clubs until the Gestapo agent bade them to stop.

"Do you know now what you are here for?" Radam drawled.

"Yes, sir."

"Well?"

"As an enemy of the Third Reich," I said.

"Nice going," Radam commented. "Suppose we have a little chat? Suppose you tell me all about the crimes you committed in 1932?"

"Crimes?"

"Sure. Tell me about the crimes."

"I was in England and Holland," I said. "I don't know what you mean."

"I'm not interested in the horses you stole in England and Holland. Let's stick to the good brown German earth. In 1932, you were a communist. Is that right?"

"Yes, sir."

"You believed in the slogan 'Strike the Fascist wherever you meet him.' Is that right?"

"The Party has always rejected the theory of individual terror," I answered. "We believed in winning over an antagonist by discussion."

"Ah," Radam said, "the famous 'ideological weapons!' About two hundred of our brave boys were slaughtered in 1932. Do you mean to say they died of discussions? Or of old age?"

From a shoe-box at the end of the cot Radam drew a sheaf of photographs. He handed them to a trooper. One after another the trooper held them in front of my eyes. They were the pictures of the corpses of murdered storm troopers.

"All these boys succumbed to 'ideological weapons,' " Radam said sarcastically.

I was silent. It dawned upon me gradually that the Gestapo had decided to link me with one of the murderous affrays of the days before the Reichstag Fire.

"I don't want to know what you did in Timbuctoo,' Radam snarled. "I only want you to help me clear up a few facts about blood spilled right here in Hamburg. I've looked over the fairy tales you told to Inspector Kraus. Herr Kraus is a gentleman. I am not. You can't get away with squirming like an eel. Your measure is full! With me it's *biegen oder brechen* (bend or break)." He paused for breath. The faces of the troopers about me seemed to close in. "Tell me all you know about the acts of terrorism committed in 1932," Radam concluded.

"I am no terrorist," I said quickly.

Radam turned to the Death Head guards. "Limber this bastard's memory," he drawled.

The troopers pulled me out into the corridor. They forced me to perform what was known in the camps as the "bear dance." It consisted of running and frog-leaping while carrying a pail full of water in manacled hands. While I ran and jumped, the troopers ran beside like gleeful youngsters, kicking at the pail. Each time water slopped over the rim of the bucket, I received a kick or a blow with a rubber truncheon. The torture went on until my legs gave way. The guards allowed me a minute's rest. Then they pushed me back into the cell where Radam was waiting. The Gestapo man gave me a quizzical stare.

"Why are you breathing so hard, hey?"

"I don't know."

"Has anybody hurt you?"

"No, sir'."

The troopers grinned. Inspector Radam sat erect on the paillasse and stared at me.

"Was Jan Templin your friend?" he demanded.

"Yes."

"What happened to him?"

"He's dead."

"He died after we arrested him?"

"I believe so."

"And Fritz Lux, where's he?"

"Also dead."

"That's right. And Hellmann?"

"Dead, too."

"And Wildinger?"

"I don't know."

"He's dead," said Inspector Radam, a sardonic smile on his lips. "Dead and gone."

He pulled out a pack of cigarettes and passed them around. All the guards were smoking now. Radam stood up and pushed his face into mine.

"Tell me all about the murders you committed," he said with sudden ferocity.

"I've committed no murders."

"Don't talk like a lawyer."

"I'm no murderer."

"Clout the bastard," said Radam. "Take off his pants and clout him." The troopers ripped away my trousers and shackled my hands to the bars of the window. Then they hit me until a trickle of blood ran down my legs. At first I moaned. I gritted my teeth and tried to think how big my hatred was, but the moaning came anyway. The blows were like the strokes of a whipsaw biting deeper and deeper into the flesh.

Things began to whirl around my head. The walls, the bars of the window, the cot, Radam, my manacled hands. The floor rushed up and gyrated in a jumble of black and red clouds.

"Everything is going to hell," I thought. The nearness of oblivion gave me a remote feeling of happiness. But then I heard a distant voice:

"Stop!"

A basin of water was dumped over my head like a steel helmet. They unshackled me. Again I stood in the center of the cell. From the hips down I was naked. The blood between my toes was getting sticky.

"The murders," said Radam.

"Yes?"

"Tell me about the murders."

"I don't understand. No, no murders."

Radam rose to his feet and poked a stubby finger at my throat. "Listen," he said, "you think you're tough. I can tell you the names of the toughest comrades in the land and how they got soft, oh, so soft and tractable. Thought they were tough, but they were not. Those who don't get soft, are dead, you see? Do you think you're tough, hey?"

"No, I'm not tough."

"Well, then don't lie like a newspaper, tell us the truth."

"I'm telling the truth."

"That's fine. Did you ever hang from a ceiling—heels up and head down?"

"No."

"It makes honest men out of liars. Do you recall the nineteenth of May? Do you remember the murder? The one you planned? The murder you're responsible for?"

"I don't remember. There was no murder."

Inspector Radam bared his teeth. "We'll boil you," he drawled. "You are a fanatic. Look how he grits his jaw. It'll take a bit longer than usual, but we'll boil you. That's certain."

He blew the smoke of his cigarette into my face. His gray-green eyes shone hard and bright.

He continued quietly. "Here's your choice. Either you confess. Then your head will come off. One stroke with the big ax. Ssst! Like that. Quick! But till then you've peace. Or you don't confess. Then we'll take the meat off your bones, inch by inch, gently, and you'll howl, and you'll die anyhow."

Alone in such a cell a man does not think. I had no thought and no conscious will to keep alive. There was only a dark, overpowering urge inside—hate. "Hate him or you're lost!"

"Roll in the phonograph," Radam ordered.

Two troopers brought a phonograph and some records. For thirty seconds the door of the cell was open and I saw the faces of Elite Guards peer in at me from the gloomy hallway. Harsh commands rang in from the yard. *"Lauf, du Drecksack!* Run faster!"

Radam grasped my hair and jerked my head backward. "Head up. In five more minutes you'll be a cripple." Then, turning to the troopers: "What are you playing?"

"The Blue Danube."

"Not loud enough," said Radam. "Better play a good, loud march. Play the Fredericus Rex."

"All right."

Radam pushed his knee into my abdomen. "We're gentle souls," he muttered. "We don't like to hurt anybody, unless we have to. When we think a man knows something and won't talk—what else shall we do, what? I am going to give you one more chance. You know what crushed kidneys are like? They make you piss blood to the end of your days. You know, it's hard luck to piss blood all the time. So I think you'll tell me now how you organized that murder."

"I've organized no murder."

"Are you sure?"

"I'm sure."

"Don't be funny. I'm going to make you wish you'd never been born. After that you can join the gents in the cool earth." Radam tapped the concrete floor with his toes. "A select company! Some got broken necks and the others have no heads."

The troopers laughed.

Radam said: "This bastard is sullen. Clout him. Clout the holy ghost out of him."

"The phonograph is busted," a trooper reported. "They'll hear him scream."

"Then tie a towel round his head," Radam directed, "and jam a steel helmet over his face, and then all you fellows sing. Let him yell to his heart's content."

They tied a dirty towel around my head and clapped a steel helmet over my face and threw me to the floor, face down. Radam bent down. "Tell me about the murder," he growled.

I shouted something. I do not know what I shouted.

"Clout the bastard. Put a wet towel over him and clout him!" I heard them soak a towel under the faucet. They stretched the towel taut over my back. Then the troopers sang.

>"Am Brunnen vor dem Tore,
>Da steht ein Lindenbaum;
>Ich traeumt in seinem Schatten
>So manchen sue-ssen Traum..."

The whips started to crash and waves of fire curled and slashed through every muscle. At first a man squirms and tries to sink his teeth into anything they can get hold of. Then he howls into the helmet and the shrieks pound back like thunder into his own ears. And after that he can't scream any more. He groans ... a long groaning intermingled with sharp gasps for air. A sonorous voice counted,.. seventeen ... eighteen ... nineteen ..."

The troopers were singing a different song now. Their voices were slow, deep, mournful.

>"Morgen-roo-ot, Morgen-roo-ot,
>Leuchtest mir zum fruehen Too-od."

Things went red and black again. "Twenty-four ... twenty-five ..." It did not hurt any more. Only my legs were out of control and kicking wildly in the air. The singing voices receded as if they belonged to a detachment marching way down a long street.

A dash of cold water came ripping into the silence. My eyes were open again. First thing they saw were boots to right and left, and in between the bright yellow oxfords of Inspector Radam.

I was naked and utterly weary. The brain hammered: "Tell them nothing." The blood was pounding everywhere close under my skin and my whole body seemed studded with pieces of hot iron. The electric light was turned on. Through the window I saw that it was getting dark outside. Again I stood in the center of the cell. In a corner sat a young girl behind a small table. On the table was a typewriter.

"What happened to you?" asked Radam.

"Nothing," I said.

"Did anybody hurt you?"

"No."

"Nobody?"

"Nobody."

"So nobody hurt you?"

"Nobody hurt me."

"All right," said Radam, turning to the typist. "Write: Everything I am saying now I offer voluntarily and of my own accord. I am making this confession freely, without compulsion of any sort." The typewriter clattered.

"Is that right?" asked Radam.

"That's right," I said.

"And you don't remember the murder?"

"No."

"I shall assist you in refreshing your memory."

"Yes."

"On the nineteenth of May you were present at a conference of the leaders of the Party units of the harbor district. The leaders of detachment three of the Red Front League were also present. This conference discussed an assault against the newly-established storm troopers' headquarters on the Schaarmarkt. This assault took place the next morning, shortly after midnight. The storm trooper Heinzelmann was stabbed to death, six others were seriously wounded. During the conference in question, you proposed that a Nazi had to be murdered in order to frighten off further attempts of the National Socialist Party to gain a foothold in the harbor districts. Right?"

"No."

The typewriter clattered while Radam spoke. It recorded question and answer.

"You were a leader of the seamen's union?"

"Yes."

"You've fought the growing Nazi influence on the ships and on the docks?"

With each question came a swift hail of blows and kicks. "Yes."

"Told your followers to heave overboard any Nazi who might board a German ship?"

"No, I fought them in the press, by leaflets, in meetings."

"In demonstrations?"

"Yes, also in demonstrations."

"With guns and knives?"

"That's not right."

"You've never shot or stabbed a storm trooper?"

"Never."

"You were wise. You preferred to have your rank and file do the shooting and stabbing. You sat back in the dark, pulling the wires, and now you're afraid of punishment, and you deny it. That's right, yes?"

"No, I do not believe in terrorism."

"You believe in revolution?"

"Yes."

"Strike? Armed uprising? Revolution? "

"Yes."

"You were present at the meeting where it was decided to murder storm troopers?"

"No."

"Your comrades say you were."

"That's impossible."

"Would you like some more beatings?"

"No."

"Nobody hurt you up to now?"

"No."

"Will you tell the truth?"

"Yes."

"Who was at the meeting besides you?"

"I don't know."

"So you admit you were at the meeting where a murder was planned?"

"I was not there."

"Liar! . . . You've organized strikes?"

"Yes, I have."

"The strike in Sweden last year?"

"Yes."

"The strike of rivermen in France? The seizure of German ships abroad? Strikes against the swastika flag in Antwerp? In Marseilles? In Le Havre?"

"Yes . . . no."

"Were any people killed in those strikes?"

"There was some fighting with police and scabs."

Radam approached me closely. He stretched out a finger and traced a swastika in the slime of sweat, dust and blood which covered my belly.

"Some strikebreakers were killed, yes? And some workers, yes? And some policemen in Hamburg, yes? Who killed them?"

"I don't know," I said.

"You murdered them!" snarled Radam.

"No."

"You are intellectually responsible for those murders. You're more guilty than those who did the direct killing. You said at that meeting that storm troopers had to be murdered. That that would drive the Nazis out of the workers' quarters. Right?"

"That's not right."

"So you organized the strikes, but you did not do the actual killing?"

I did not answer.

"The accused is silent," said Radam. Then: "Do you believe in the thesis: 'Kill the Nazi wherever you meet him?' "

"No."

"Your comrades Wollweber and Neumann originated this slogan?"

"I believe so. It was a wrong slogan."

"Why?"

"I believed that many Nazis could have been won over by friendly discussion, that individual violence was harmful."

"Wollweber was a communist?"

"Yes."

"And Neumann?"

"Yes."

"And you?"

"Yes."

"And Wollweber and Neumann propagated murder?"

I did not answer.

"You wanted to win over Nazis by discussions?"

"I did."

"And those who could not be convinced had to be murdered; that was your conviction, yes?"

"No."

"Are you a pacifist?"

"No."

"So you're a man who believes in violence. It'll cost you your head, friend." Radam turned toward the troopers: "Take this bastard out for exercise and bring me Dettmer, Wehrenberg, Hoppe and Koopmann."

Two Elite Guards took me out into the dark yard. I was naked. They kicked me and told me to run. I ran across the yard and the Elite Guards ran beside me, and hit me with their rubber clubs, shouting: "Run faster! Faster!"

After that I stood still in the cold, with arms raised. Five minutes, ten, sixty—I do not know. I had ceased to be a man. I was a living chunk of meat without ambition, hope, will. I did what I was told to do, and only once did I fall into the snow and cry: "Finish it!

Shoot me, shoot!" A shot in the back of the neck would have been sudden paradise. The troopers laughed. They slapped my face with belts. Then they made me run around the yard on all four. After that, they brought another naked man out into the snow, and stood him up, facing me.

"Do you see this fellow?" a trooper asked.

"Yes," I said.

"That's Mr. Adam," the trooper said. "Adam and Eve."

The others laughed.

"Hit him!" said the trooper.

I did not move. I could not see the features of the man in front of me. All I could see in the dark was his nakedness and his trembling knees.

"Damn you, hit him!"

I reached out and slapped the man's face. Not hard.

An Elite Guard jumped between us and struck me violently.

"That's how I want you to hit him," he said. "Hit him!"

I did not move. A trooper kicked me from behind.

"Hit him!"

I could hear the breathing of the naked man with the trembling knees. His head was bent slightly forward, like the head of a hanged man. I felt the sudden impact of a rubber bludgeon across my abdomen and I doubled up with pain.

"Take it easy," said a trooper. "Stand straight."

I stood straight.

"Hit him!" he commanded.

I reached out and hit the naked man in front of me. He sank to his knees and shook his head. This monstrous thing was repeated again and again, and then it was his turn to hit. He hit me many times, lightly at first, but then with astonishing force. The night was calm and the skeleton arms of the trees reached weirdly into the starlit sky. A dog barked in the distance; muffled sounds of torment and madness pranced from the hulking flank of the prison and subsided in interminable groans; the bell of the prison church rang a melancholy midnight, and a breath of air stirred the tip of the swastika flag in the beam of searchlights on the outer walls. Two naked men stood in the yard and hit each other, and from somewhere drifted the aroma of steak.

From a window sounded Radam's voice: "Bring the bastard back!"

In the four corners of the cell stood four men, noses and toes against the wall, and beneath the window stood a fifth. As I entered the cell, they twisted their faces sideways to see. Their faces were gray and hollow and crusted with dirt and bristly beards. They had had no chance to wash or shave in months. I knew they were comrades. I knew that I knew them, that they were workers who had gone with me through battle and distress, and yet I was not able to recognize a single face, so much had they changed.

"Hoppe! " called Radam.

One of the men turned around. He was the harbor worker Arthur Hoppe, who had been married three weeks before the Gestapo took him between midnight and three in the morning.

"Hoppe," said Radam, pointing at me, "was this man at the meeting where the murder of Heinzelmann was planned?"

The typewriter clattered. Hoppe looked at me out of great sunken eyes.

"Yes," he mumbled, "he was there."

"Did he incite to violence?"

"I can't remember?"

"Well think! Did he?"

"He did."

Hoppe turned his face back to the wall and his shoulders drooped.

"Wehrenberg!" Radam commanded.

A man in another corner turned around. He was the ship's stoker Alfred Wehrenberg, a strong, tall man of thirty-five, who had been the organization chief of the Red Marines.

"Wehrenberg," Radam said, "you were at a conference where the killing of storm troopers was discussed?"

Wehrenberg nodded.

"Was this man there, too?" Radam continued, pointing at me.

Again Wehrenberg nodded.

To me the situation was monstrous and incomprehensible. Before Radam mentioned it, I had never heard of the conference. I had had nothing to do with the massacre of storm troopers on the morning of May 20, 1932, for it had been the day of the opening of the World Congress of Seamen, and I had been fully occupied with the preparations for the convention during the days preceding its opening. The four comrades who confronted me in the torture-cell were not traitors. I had known them as staunch and reliable fighters, though they had been at no time under my direct jurisdiction. All four had been functionaries of the military department of the Party.

"Wehrenberg," Radam said, "did this man say that storm troopers had to be killed?"

I looked straight into Wehrenberg's face. He did not seem to see me. He was like a man in a trance. Slowly he nodded.

"Koopmann!" Radam commanded.

Comrade Koopmann also acknowledged that I had been at the murder conference.

"Now, Dettmer," Radam barked.

I looked into the face of Johnny Dettmer, the political leader of the Red Marines, who had been my comrade in the gun-running enterprises and the barricade battles of 1923. I had known him as a bold-eyed stalwart, a reckless man of action who had always laughed at those who paused to count the cost. Comrade Johnny was bent forward as if his chest had been bashed in. A filthy reddish beard covered his face. Where his right eye had been, there was now a bluish-red hole. He did not wait for Radam's question.

"No, no, no, no," he coughed. "This comrade was not at the meeting. He had nothing to do with it. And even if he had, I wouldn't have taken my orders from *him*. That's all I have to say, Commissar Radam! "

Radam pursed his thick lips. He signaled to the guards to seize Dettmer. "Limber up the bastard's memory," he drawled.

The troopers pushed Johnny Dettmer out of the cell. They were absent many minutes. Finally returning, they carried Dettmer between them.

"Do you remember now that you friend here was at the murder conference?" Radam asked.

Dettmer's breath whistled painfully. "Have it your way," he gasped. "Damn you, Commissar Radam!"

"Was he there?" Radam grinned like a hunter who sees his game in line with the barrel of his gun. "Was he there?"

"All right, he was there," Dettmer growled.

"A—ha!"

A long silence followed. My four unwilling accusers stood in their corners like mummies propped upright by a joker's hand. More troopers crowded into the cell. About me was a ring of grim young faces under black steel helmets. Painted in white on each helmet was a skeleton head and two crossed bones. The silence was broken by the clatter of the typewriter. Inspector Radam dictated: "The accused, confronted by the *Schutzhaftgefangenen* Dettmer, Wehrenberg, Koopmann and Hoppe still persists that he had nothing to do with the assassination of Storm Trooper Heinzelmann. The four above-mentioned prisoners, however, stated voluntarily and in the presence of witnesses that the accused has played a leading role in the meeting in which the plan to murder National Socialists was hatched." Turning to me, Radam said quietly: "What do you say now? Are these four not your good comrades? Are you coward enough to let them take the sole blame for a crime in which you were a partner?"

"I had nothing to do with street murders," I replied dully. Radam went on: "With the evidence of four of your accomplices against you, do you think the Special Tribunal will believe one word of what you say?"

"I had nothing to do with it," I repeated, almost too weak to formulate the words.

About me the troopers grumbled. Ice-cold menace was in Radam's voice, as he drawled, "This is the last chance I am giving you. *Das Spiel ist aus.* The last chance, do you hear?"

"I had nothing to do with it," I said, incapable of any other thought.

"Enough!"

The four other prisoners were led away. Again my wrists were shackled to the bars of the window. From under the cot one of the Death Head guards extracted a length of chain. He doubled it into a bight and wrapped the loose ends around his right fist. "Ready," he said.

"Clout him," Radam ordered, "clout him to death."

Jan Templin had been beaten to death with chains. I closed my eyes and waited. I was going down, down.

"Clout him," Radam said.

In that instant I gave up the hopeless fight. I was not conscious of a decision or a definite act of will. I had suffered more than most of my comrades. I had fought with all the skill, all the tenacity, all the loyalty and hatred that was in me. I could do no more. A strange voice said clearly: "All right, I was at the meeting." A moment later I realized that it had been my own voice.

"A—ha!" Radam grunted. "So you were at the meeting?"

"Yes," I said.

My shackles were unlocked. Death Head guards placed me gently on the cot. Someone handed me a cup of strong coffee. Someone else stuck a cigarette between my lips and struck a match. I smoked ravenously; nothing else mattered.

Inspector Radam dictated in a subdued voice and the typewriter rattled at high speed. I could not hear what he said. I heard him mention my name repeatedly, but that was all. A trooper asked me if I wanted a sandwich. Another trooper inquired whether I wished to write a letter. I did not answer them. I smoked cigarette after cigarette, drank coffee and cold water, and rested. The noise of the typewriter ceased suddenly.

"Please step over here," Radam said.

He thrust a pen into my hand and indicated several typewritten sheets on the table.

"Sign your name under each sheet, please."

I was unable to read the text of the "confession" I was signing. The letters danced and the lines swirled toward me and receded. I took the pen and signed. In a last futile gesture of resistance I strove to make my handwriting as different from my usual signature as I possibly could. When I was about to sign the last sheet, Radam intervened.

"Wait a minute," he said, "this is the end of your statement. Write: 'I have read this myself and have found the contents correct.' Then sign your full name."

I wrote: *"Selbst gelesen und fuer richtig bejunden."*

"Now sign your name."

I signed.

Radam grabbed my hand and shook it vigorously. "Now, there's a sensible fellow," he rumbled. "Any time you want to tell me more, just ask the guard on duty to telephone."

I was led back to my cell. The first pale light of dawn welled up in the eastern sky. I was not put in irons. I received clean sheets and clean blankets and a package of tobacco.

"Sleep as long as you like," the tier guard said. "When you've slept enough, bang on the door. We'll give you a bath and a haircut, and a shave, too."

Sleep would not come.

Chapter Thirty-six

OF COMRADES AND THE HEADSMAN

Ten days after my night of defeat I was transferred from Camp Fuhlsbuettel to Camp Papenburg in the moorlands near the Dutch frontier. Fuhlsbuettel was so overcrowded with men and women who were being broken by the Gestapo that prisoners were forced to camp in the corridors of the cell-blocks. The Papenburg camps—there were five in all, with about eight thousand inmates—were filled with political prisoners who had "confessed" and were awaiting trial before the Special Tribunals.

The Gestapo had more prisoners to transport than it could accommodate in the available prison trains. On the way to Papenburg, the human freight of my train was lodged for one night in a camp near Worpswede, and another night in Oslebshausen, the central prison of the Weser country. More than half of the prisoners in Camp Worpswede, in the Heath of Lueneburg, were Nazi storm troopers, adherents of Captain Roehm's program of a "second revolution." I spoke to some of these troopers, at night, in a crowded barrack. They represented the most radical and brutal element in the Hitler movement. Unauthorized looting of shops and other violations of discipline had landed them in protective custody. Rough-housing among themselves and the practice of homosexuality seemed to be their favorite occupations. After three days of traveling, I and about a hundred other prisoners arrived at Papenburg, a small town on the lower course of the River Ems.

The country around Papenburg is perhaps the loneliest and most desolate in Germany. A dreary expanse of moorlands stretched away to the horizon. The ground was soggy, the houses of the poor peat peasants crouched low over the ground, as if they were ashamed of their dismal existence. Everywhere black swamps abounded. As our train pulled in, the station swarmed with Death Head guards.

"All out!"

We lined up on the station platform. The guards received us with jeers and kicks. Anyone who was better dressed than the run of unfortunates became the object of particular cruelty.

"March!"

We marched through the streets of Papenburg to the hooting of the local Nazis. Among us were workers, professional men, a few white-collar workers, and a brigade of sailors carrying their sea bags over their shoulders. Soon we struck out through open moorlands. After three hours of uninterrupted marching, we arrived at the camp: a conglomeration of long, low barracks behind a triple fence of barbed wire. The prisoners were counted. Names were called. Each man, after receiving an introductory kick, was given a pick and a shovel, and assigned a place in one of the barracks.

Life in Camp Papenburg gave me little time to think. We were roused at five in the morning, and an hour later, in company formation, we marched out to work. We dug ditches to drain the swamps. We worked from seven until five, with an hour for lunch from the field kitchen. By six in the evening we were back in the barracks, dirty, exhausted, and longing for sleep. At night, after the evening count, we were left in peace. The proximity of the Dutch frontier caused many prisoners to attempt escape. Few succeeded. On the flat terrain the majority fell under the bullets of the sentries. Each week an average of three prisoners were shot while trying to escape. The names of the dead were read to us at the morning roll call. Those who were caught alive received thirty strokes with the *Nilpferdpeitsche*. The floggings took place in the mornings, before breakfast, in the open court-yard, with all prisoners mustered to witness the punishment.

The Sundays, on which we remained idle in the camp, were frightening. The Death Head guards were bored with their routine. They cursed the lack of amusements and girls, and they blamed us—the prisoners—for their deprivations. On Sunday morning the guards had military practice. They were instructed in sharpshooting, bayonet attacks, defense against bombing, tank assaults, and a series of civil war maneuvers. The latter included: "How to stop a railway train,"

"How to disperse a rebellious mob," "House raid," "Arrest of an action committee," "Transport of prisoners," "How to storm a barricade," and others. Invariably prisoners were summoned to play the role of the suffering parties. These maneuvers ended at noon. And by three o'clock in the afternoon every Death Head guard in the camp was drunk enough to embark on a private rampage. Their best-liked Sunday afternoon play included the staging of tournaments between the prisoners and vicious dogs, and the forcing of prisoners to cover their genitals with black shoe polish. A special pastime was to force a prisoner to sit on a small barrel which the guards then endeavored to shoot from under him.

During my stay in Papenburg two bestial murders were committed by the guards, probably on orders from the Gestapo. One night a middle-aged Jew, a physician from Bielefeld, was called out of the barrack. We all liked him, because he was an excellent chess player, though he never talked about himself or the cause of his arrest. Hours passed; the doctor did not return. Next morning the *Sturmfuehrer* informed us in his barking voice that the Jew had been found hanging from a rafter in the latrine. Cynically, he detailed two men to clean the latrine. The latrine had no rafters, because it had no roof. But the comrades who cleaned it found the rough wooden walls spattered with blood. The doctor from Bielefeld had not committed suicide.

The second murder was committed in broad daylight, while we were at work. The victim was a former police official of Altona, a Social Democrat named Heinrich Kessel. He was accused of having shot and killed a storm trooper while he, Kessel, was still in the service of the police. The leading

Death Head guard of the *Arbeitskommando* made Kessel stand on a mound of earth and shout a hundred times: "I am a murderer!" Then Kessel was chased around a wide circle of guards. In front of each guard he stopped, lowering his pants. Each guard gave Kessel three strokes with his rubber club. Following this, the chief of the guards ordered the tortured man to "run toward Holland." Kessel was too battered, too frightened to think. He ran. Before he had run fifty yards, an Elite Guard raised his carbine and shot the running man through the back of the head.

One morning, in the second week of April, the camp commander's clerk shouted my name. I sprang to attention.

"Get ready to leave," I was told. "You're going to Hamburg for trial."

"The hour of the verdict is at hand," I told myself, and was glad of it.

I was brought to the vast courthouse prison on Hamburg's Sievekingsplatz. There I was assigned to a cell on the ground floor, on the *Totenreihe*—"Dead Men's Row—which harbored the Gestapo's candidates for death. The walls of the cell bore the scribblings of men who had been there before me, men who now lay in their graves, or in the dungeons, condemned to many years of hard labor. "We never die!" one inscription read, and another: "We are *still* the architects of the future. Red Front!"

"Dead Men's Row" was closely guarded. Every few minutes the eyes of a guard appeared at the little spy-hole in my cell door. The cells on the *Totenreihe* all bore the sign: *"Sachen herausnehmen. Nachtlicht."* All night the electric lights were left burning. Every evening all my clothes were taken away from me for the night.

The trial before the Special Tribunal began the morning after my arrival in Hamburg. There were fifty-three in my party of defendants. All of them, except myself, were former functionaries of the Red Marines of the Hamburg area, accused of many specific counts of terrorism against the storm troops and the Hitler Youth. We sat huddled on benches, row on row, in the center of the large court room. A Death Head guard sat between each pair of prisoners. To the left, in a separate enclosure, were the lawyers' benches; one Nazi lawyer had been appointed to "defend" each group of five prisoners. To the right of us sat an array of Nazi officials, some in civilian clothes, the majority in glittering uniforms. Among them I recognized Fiebelkom, the supreme chief of the Hamburg storm troops; Karl Kaufmann, Hitler's special commissar for the Hamburg district; Wilhelm Bohle, the head of the Foreign Division of the Nazi Party, and many others: Elite Guard chieftains, Gestapo men, police officers, a representative of the *Reichswehr*, Inspector Radam and Hertha Jens. Behind us, the court room was packed with the wives of Nazi functionaries and the relatives of slain storm troopers. Lining the walls, Elite Guards stood shoulder to shoulder, all of them heavily armed. In front was the judges' bench. Above it hung a portrait of Adolf Hitler against the background of a huge swastika flag.

There was a sudden commotion. All around us the Nazis rose to their feet, their arms outstretched in the Hitler salute. The guards on the prisoners' benches prodded the ribs of their charges. "On your feet, you murderers!" We rose slowly. Through a carved oaken side door three judges filed in. They wore the swastika insignia on their black robes. They faced the assembly, raised their arms stiffly, and then sat down. Not one of the prisoners had given the Nazi salute. The trial began. Court attendants spread a large accumulation of weapons over two large tables. They were the arms which had been confiscated from the arsenal of the Red Marines, pistols of all makes and calibers, a dozen service carbines, an assortment of knives and daggers, thirteen hand-grenades and two light army machine guns.

The trial dragged on for weeks. Day after day we sat on the prisoners' benches, a cadaverous crew of outcasts surrounded by all the symbols of Hitler power. The Prosecuting Attorney, a tall, thin pale-faced man named Jauch, dominated the hearings. His hatred for us was undisguised. His eyes flashed and his colorless lips drew back in snarls as he demanded death, and nothing but death. Each day the Nazi press blew into the same horn. The headlines dubbed us the "choicest band of assassins" that ever populated a German court room. Epithets like "sadists," "Asiatic killers," "bloodthirsty wire-pullers," "traitorous vermin," and many others were hurled into our faces day after day. The witnesses, of course, were nearly all Gestapo agents and storm troopers. The fathers and mothers of the slain Nazis made speeches clamoring for the blood of the slayers of their sons.

Johnny Dettmer fought like a Berserker. "If I had two guns in my hands," he declared on one occasion, "I'd be the Red judge at this trial, and the accused would be you, the Brown Pest!" The stoker Wehrenberg accused Gestapo witnesses of perjury. A comrade named Arthur Schmidt, the young adopted son of Edgar Andree, shouted at the judges: "Here is the worker Arthur Schmidt. You can kill him, but you cannot kill his spirit!" The answer of the court to such disturbances was always the same: "Hold your tongue! Don't forget your place. The Dimitrov method will not work here!"

The sensation of the trial, for me, was the moment when Dettmer, Wehrenberg, Hoppe and Koopmann retracted their statements that I had been present at the fateful leaders' conference of the Red Marines. They accused Inspector Radam of having compelled them, under threat of death, to incriminate me in the planning of terrorist acts. Two of the few witnesses who were not

Nazis, my former chief, Albert Walter, and a trade union militant named Erich K., swore that I had been fully occupied with the Seamen's Congress during the nineteenth day of May, 1932, the date of the "murder conference." Nevertheless, Prosecuting Attorney Jauch demanded for me, as for many others, the penalty of death.

Came the day on which sentence was pronounced. The court room was crammed with the Nazi élite. The faces of the prisoners were pale and tense. The curtain was ready to fall. Life was at an end. We rose in sullen silence as the judges marched to their fauteuils. We remained standing while the sentences were read. First came the death sentences. I held my breath. There were nine. My name was not among them. Then came the convictions to imprisonment for life, to fifteen years, fourteen years, thirteen years, twelve years, eleven years. ... As yet the president of the Special Court had not mentioned my name. Then it came. "Found guilty of conspiring to halt by violence the progress of the German Revolution—ten years of hard labor: *Zuchthaus.*" A string of lesser sentences followed. Nine of my comrades had been condemned to death. Seven had received life sentences. One prisoner had died during the trial. Another had been transferred to a lunatic asylum. The rest of us shared together 350 years of imprisonment.

The trial had ended. The Death Head guards clamped irons over our wrists. The Nazi womenfolk in the rear cheered merrily. Prosecuting Attorney Jauch beamed amidst a group of reporters. The stoker Alfred Wehrenberg climbed on a bench. "Farewell, comrades!" he cried. He was among the nine whose heads would fall under the ax. Young Arthur Schmidt, also condemned to death, raised his right fist. "We shall be avenged!" he shouted hoarsely. "Our children will play under red banners while Hitler will rot to feed the worms. Red Front! Red Front! Red—"

The fist of a Death Head guard smashed squarely into comrade Schmidt's face.

A few days after the termination of the trial, which went down in history as the *Rote Marine Prozess* or the *Prozess Adler Hotel* (the name of one of the scenes of terrorist assaults) I was awakened by a guard at dawn. It was the nineteenth of May, 1934, the day preceding Whitsunday. I was led into the yard.

"What's up?" I asked the guard.

"Don't ask questions," he retorted curtly.

I marched through the yard to a fairly broad alley which ran between the outer wall and the prison hospital. There, lined up against the wall, I saw about forty of my comrades who had been convicted in the trial of the Red Marines. Their faces were stony, their eyes wide open and staring. They stood motionless, under heavy guard.

"Stand in this line," I was ordered, "and don't move."

I stood in line. My eyes wandered. I was trying to find a reason for this early morning excursion. Suddenly my eyes struck something that made me freeze with horror. Halfway down the alley stood a low scaffold. It was painted a light green. Beside the scaffold stood four long baskets the size of coffins, and a large bin filled with sawdust. A thick layer of sawdust was distributed around the scaffold. I knew then that this was execution day. The air was clear and the sky was clear. Birds twittered in the fresh green of the trees outside the walls. The first rays of the rising sun sparkled on the roofs of the prison buildings. From the top of the highest tower floated a great swastika flag. We stood in silence. Death Head guards came and went. Minutes passed, and to me each minute was an hour. The countenances of my fellow-prisoners, which had seemed at first devoid of all expression, now expressed disbelief, stifled rage, anxiety and gnawing fear.

A mass of people tramped through the yard. There were the judges of the Special Tribunal and Prosecutor Jauch, all wearing cutaways and top hats. There was Inspector Racam, grinning nervously and chatting with colleagues from the Gestapo. They were followed by a long train of storm troop officers and Elite Guards. The youngsters were plainly concerned with giving their faces a martial cast; but apprehension and curiosity showed through their grim masks. Then another straggling group crossed the yard—the fathers and brothers of storm troopers who had fallen in the skirmishes for power. All these people took up positions in the alley, on both sides of the light green scaffold.

Last to come was the headsman, a chunky individual with a big-boned face and dull brown eyes. He showed complete emotional indifference to the task ahead of him. He, too, wore a stiff white shirt, striped trousers, a cutaway and a top hat. In a barely audible voice he issued orders to his four assistants. One of them darted into a side door of the prison hospital. Several seconds later he emerged with the ax. Formerly a guillotine had been used to chop off heads, but Hitler had discarded the guillotine as a French invention. The hand-ax had again come into its right. It had a handle of polished wood, perhaps four feet long. The ax was broad and heavy. Its back was a solid square of shining steel. The headsman's assistant placed it into a rack of metal and leather, a yard away from the scaffold. Prosecutor Jauch produced papers from a briefcase. The row of prisoners along the wall seemed to sway; but, perhaps, it was only my eyes which swayed. The headsman was ready now.

The first to be led from his cell was Johnny Dettmer. Marching between two guards, he wore the striped convict garb. He looked at the sky, at the treetops, and he swung his legs as if he enjoyed the morning saunter. They brought him to a halt in front of the Prosecutor. Jauch mumbled, hardly glancing up from his paper. I saw then for the first time that a clergyman was in the assembly. The clergyman was a little man in black, wearing the swastika badge.

"Go to hell,' Dettmer told him in a loud voice.

Cries came from the many cell windows: "Good-by, Johnny!" —"Long live the revolution!"—*"Nieder mit Hitler!"* Cries of rage and cries of terror. When the headsman's assistant seized Johnny Dettmer, our comrade fought wildly. He fought silently, with all his strength. But his hands were shackled on his back. Guards tied his ankles together and strapped him in upright position to a board. The board was swung to a horizontal position. Johnny's head protruded over the edge of the board. Beneath the head was a basket half full of sawdust.

"Farewell, Johnny," I thought. "Don't fight any more. Please stop. Try to die easily. You were a good fighter. Good-by, Johnny, good-by, good-by," Most eyes were tearless. They were wide open and dry and staring. Before I could realize what was happening, the headsman raised his ax over Comrade Dettmer's head. He did not strike. He simply let it fall on Johnny's neck. Then, with an easy motion, he drew the blade toward him, and stepped back.

Johnny Dettmer's head fell into the basket.

For a second or two the headless body twitched. Blood ran into the sawdust. The watchers were silent. The headsman's assistants unstrapped the corpse and threw it into one of the basket coffins. Others washed the board and swung it back again to an upright position. The clergyman mumbled a prayer. The headsman picked up the lifeless head and placed it gently between the thighs of the headless body. Then four guards carried the basket into the basement of the prison hospital. The attendants had hardly covered the blood with a new layer of sawdust when the next man was led out from "Dead Men's Row."

He was Herrman Fischer, a short, taciturn, courageous man, who, in the 1923 barricade-fighting in Hamburg, had been the leader of the First Red Hundred. Fischer looked neither to right nor left. He pushed the clergyman aside and walked straight up to the scaffold. When the headsman raised the ax, Fischer shrugged his shoulders.

"What a theater!" were his last words.

Fred Wehrenberg, the stoker, was the third. He walked ahead of the guards, singing in his ringing voice:

"Brueder, zur Sonne, zur Freiheit . . ." (Brothers, toward sunshine, toward freedom . . .)

Confronting the Prosecutor, he stopped his singing. As Dr. Jauch read out the sentence, Fred Wehrenberg roared into his face: "Long live the Soviet Union! Long live Soviet Germany!" He roared until the headsman's steel cut through his voice. In the row of watching prisoners, two men had collapsed. Guards dragged them back to their cells. From one of the barred little windows a high voice shouted continuously: "Revenge! Revenge!"

Last to die of this group was Arthur Schmidt. As he walked across the yard, it seemed as if he would break down. His knees wobbled, and the guards reached out to support him. In front of Arthur Schmidt, the blood showed through the now foot-thick layer of sawdust. He saw the blackish-red patches, he saw the one remaining basket coffin, the wet scaffold and the blinking ax, and he halted abruptly.

"The others are dead?" he asked.

No one answered him.

"Your head will roll, too," he said to Prosecutor Jauch, straightening in sudden defiance. Then they strapped him to the board.

Arthur Schmidt was talking to himself: "All men must die sometime ... I die for the proletariat.... They can kill the worker Arthur Schmidt, but they can't kill his spirit . . ." At the last moment, he shouted, *"Mutter, mutter!"* (mother, mother.)

The ax fell. It was too much. The wall reared up and the building plunged before my eyes. I heard an Elite Guard reading off the names of murdered storm troopers. As he called out each name of the dead, the assembly of Nazis in the prison yard answered it in a staccato roar.

"Storm Trooper Heinzelmann?"

"Here!" the guards roared in unison.

I reeled and fell. When I awoke, I was back in my cell.

Six weeks after the death and imprisonment of the Red Marines I still lay in solitary confinement in the courthouse jail. May passed, June went by, and the yards sweltered in the heat of July. "Why did they not transfer me to a penitentiary?" I wondered. I was alone in my cell. I was given no work. I could write no letters and received none. I had nothing to read. I heard next to nothing of what was going on in the outside world. I heard prison sounds, the banging of doors, the rapid footsteps of running men, and the cursing of the guards. Day and night the dripping faucet in my cell seemed to snicker derision. The green of the trees became darker, and the birds had ceased their morning concerts. On several mornings, lying awake on my cot, I heard the now familiar sounds of executions—the cries of defiance, the yells from the cell windows, and the raucous chorus of the Death Head guards.

On the night of June 30, and during the two following nights, the yards were in an uproar. Motor lorries thundered, barked commands ripped through the darkness, and in the early mornings the whole prison reverberated with the noise made by firing squads. I wondered what the meaning of these fusillades could be. The guillotine and the ax were more silent and discreet. It was as if I had been forgotten. To pass the long hours, I did gymnastics, I analyzed my past, tried to remember all the books I had read, and carried on imaginary conversations in German and English, and at times in Spanish and French. There were hours in which I saw my whole past life as one gigantic and miserable mistake, but I shied away from such insight, and defeated it deliberately by intoxicating myself with the concepts of Bolshevist duty and pride. At night, I had the feeling of being buried alive. Dreams continued to harass me; they were dreams of struggle and escape, and the struggles ended in defeat and escapes in deadly frustration. As a rule, a man in prison makes plans for the future: plans of glory and adventure and delights to come. I forced myself to build no castles in the air. There was no future.

One afternoon, early in July, I had an unexpected visitor. The key in the door rattled, the bolts were pushed back, and I jumped to attention. Rudolf Heitman, the G.P.U. operative in the Gestapo, entered my cell. An elderly guard was on duty. Heitman sent him away.

"Sit down," Heitman told me, "take it easy. Should anyone come into the cell, remember: I am here to have you identify a certain photograph."

I fought the urge to throw my arms around Heitman's neck.

"Tell me," I gasped. "What is new?"

"The same old routine," muttered Heitman. "Hitler is here for good. As for revolution—who believes in it? Perhaps we will have to come to terms with the Brown Pest."

"What was all the shooting in the yards some nights ago?" I asked.

"Forty storm troop officers were sent to Walhalla. *Brigadefuehrer* Fiebelkorn and his crowd. Roehm and Heines were shot in Munich. General Schleicher and Karl Ernst and a lot of others were massacred in Berlin. A first-rank mass liquidation of the 'second revolution' boys. No, Hitler has the rudder firmly in hand. Himmler supervised the slaughter. The whole Elite Guard and the Gestapo lay ready with machine guns, in case the Brownshirts would get the idea to start something. You fellows in the prisons are lucky."

"Lucky—why?"

"If Roehm and Heines had taken the cake," Heitman said "they'd have lined you all up against the walls and mowed you down with machine guns. Dead men cost no money."

"Through whom was I captured?" I demanded. "Who was the spy?"

Heitman shrugged his square shoulders. "That's just what I wanted to ask you," he muttered. "I'm not close enough to the Foreign Division to see the light. Copenhagen is raising hell—close to nine hundred arrests in the harbor in nine months. Our courier ships are searched, our depots raided. We've unmasked a lot of spies, but not the one responsible for that fiasco. I've heard that you had a bitter time in Fuhlsbuettel. Inspector Kraus has standing orders from Berlin to exterminate communism from shipping. Lucky for you that Kraus is so busy. He's the worst of the hellions —he and that man-eating bitch of his."

"Why is Hertha Jens still alive?"

"Ask me! She practically lives in Gestapo headquarters. But our good friends are working on the problem. She'll have her vacation in August. Should she spend it abroad..." Rudolf Heitman drew his stubby forefinger across his throat. "Lights out for Hertha," he added. "Who is on the job?"

"I don't know," Heitman said.

"Avatin?"

"Don't worry. Paul Kraus' bitch-baby will get what's coming to her."

"What happened to Cilly?"

"She played a high-class comedy," Heitman chuckled. "She gave away nothing. She said you hypnotized her and seduced her, and after that she was in your power. Don't forget the item. Don't spoil her game when you come to trial."

"Trial?"

"Yes, you're going to have another trial. High treason. Kraus suspects a lot, but there's very little he really knows. You're lucky he's so busy; works day and night. He's sending spies out wholesale. The Foreign Division opened a special spy school right after Christmas. They teach their boys everything, from safe-cracking to Oxford English. But never mind that. Just keep tight."

Heitman pulled out his service automatic. With it he scratched his scalp. "Get me pencil and paper," I suggested. "I want to put a report through to Copenhagen."

"Good you mentioned it first," Heitman said. "I was waiting for it. It's what I came for. I'll leave you writing material here. Write it tonight. Can you write in the dark?"

"Yes."

"No handwriting. Print your letters."

"All right."

Heitman handed me a block of note-paper and three pencil stubs, which I secreted in the inside of my reeking paillasse. I noticed that he was getting somewhat nervous. Heitman worked for money. He was regarded as reliable because he knew that his life was at the mercy of the Comintern.

"Never fear," I calmed him. "If anything goes wrong, they'll never learn who gave me the pencils."

We had spoken in whispers. Once in a while, for the benefit of the guards in the corridors, Heitman broke out in vile abuse. Equally often he produced a flask and gulped cognac.

"I have to keep drinking all the time," he said. "If I don't, I'll go loony."

Soon he departed. I was as excited as if I had pumped myself full of absinthe. Cilly had told them nothing. Hertha Jens was, perhaps, going to her doom, going the way Ilia Raikoff—The Ox—had gone. Martin Holstein.... At the thought of his name, I winced. Holstein had not been taken. Was Holstein the spy? I brushed the suspicion aside. I had known Holstein too long to doubt his loyalty. Roehm was dead. Heines was dead. Fiebelkom and many others of the Brown brigands were dead. I was hot with a grim satisfaction. "Ha-ha-ha," I laughed inwardly. "They are dead and you are still alive."

Late that night, when all was still, I wrote my report for the Western Secretariat. I wrote feverishly, wary to catch the footsteps of approaching night guards. They had a custom of sneaking along the tiers on rubber soles, and of suddenly switching on the light and bursting into a cell. Next morning Rudolf Heitman came again. He remained only a few seconds, long enough for me to give him my report. I was happy then. I had broken the ring of isolation. I had pierced the wall of loneliness and suffocation which had been around me for two hundred interminable days. I remembered Wollweber's parting growl: "The Party does not forget its children." It was true! The Comintern had found its way into my solitary confinement to shake my hand.

Only at the end of the day did I recall with a dismal feeling that I had forgotten to ask Heitman about Firelei; I could have included a letter for her in my report. I cursed myself for a disloyal idiot. It had seemed to me that Firelei was unattainably far away—as far away as Sirius. "Perhaps," I thought, "she has found a good comrade to be her lover." We had granted each other that freedom when we parted. I revolted at my own thought. Firelei was somehow not far away any more. She was close to me. All night I could not sleep. I thought of Firelei. In the darkness, between the stifling wall, I saw her many moods. At the very last she sang the beautiful, the sad song, "Fahrewohl, du gruene Erde..A jeering clangor interrupted her. It was the morning bell. Daylight hovered in the cell, and a small square of sunlight crossed by black lines crawled over the wall near the ceiling.

At the end of July I was haled again before a Special Tribunal. This time it was the court which dealt with high treason cases.

Instead of three judges, there were five. I saw Cilly again. She sat on the *Suenderbank* three yards away from me. She looked as cool and elegant as ever, but pale and a little thinner. But as soon as the judges entered the court room, she played the role of a frightened girl that had been debauched and misused by a Bolshevist emissary who had made her believe that he was the journalist Williams from London. She played her comedy superbly. I admitted that I had induced Cilly to become my willing tool. On all other questions I refused to give answers. The trial lasted four hours. The reporters of the Nazi press almost ignored me; their interest was concentrated on the "woman in the case." One of the witnesses of the defense was the Danish consul in Hamburg. I guessed that he had been drafted by Richard Jensen. He testified that Cilly, who had been his secretary in earlier years, had never had the slightest contact with the Comintern. Another witness, summoned by the Prosecutor, was the consul-general of the Soviet Union. He was a comrade and a friend. He sauntered into the court room with his hands in his pockets. The Nazi judges were irked by the Russian's casual behavior.

"Are you the Russian consul?" the presiding judge, Dr. Roth, snapped.

"No," said the consul.

"Well, who are you?"

"I am the consul-general of the Soviet Union," he replied.

The judge produced several photographs. They showed German communists, including myself, saluting the Soviet banner. The pictures had been taken in Leningrad during the German shipping strike of 1931.

"Can you identify any of the men who are standing here under the Red rag?" the judge asked.

"Der rote Lappen?" (The Red Rag?) the consul said slowly. "I regret."

Without a further word, he turned on his heel and walked out of the court room.

The judges deliberated for two hours. They had not sufficient proof to sentence me under the new high treason laws, and I had admitted nothing of a political nature. Nevertheless they sentenced me—not under the Nazi laws, but under the *Republikschutzgesetz*, the "law for the protection of the Weimar Republic!" I received three years in prison—the maximum sentence under the old law— for "preparation of treasonable enterprise." Mechanically I thought: "Three plus ten make thirteen." The presiding judge regretted that the Gestapo had not supplied sufficient incriminating material to warrant a death sentence for high treason. In his concluding speech, he branded me as an "exceptionally dangerous enemy of the New Germany." I was jubilant.

My terrible battles in Gestapo headquarters and in Camp Fuhlsbuettel had not been fought in vain. Cilly had succeeded in duping the five judges of the Special Tribunal; through her marriage, she had acquired Danish citizenship, and her release was vigorously demanded by the Danish press and the government in Copenhagen. They gave her seven months for "perhaps unconsciously assisting in the preparation of a treasonable enterprise."

After the trial, we were led back to prison. At the barred steel gate which separated the women's ward from the section for male prisoners, I suddenly turned and grasped Cilly's hand.

"When you are released, give Firelei my greetings," I said.

Tears were in Cilly's eyes. "Be sure I will," she answered.

I wanted to say more, but the guards tore us apart.

Shortly after my second trial I was transferred to the Hamburg penitentiary, a modern prison adjoining Camp Fuhlsbuettel. I was stripped naked and my body was examined, first by a prison official, who searched for hidden contraband, and then by a physician. The doctor decreed that I should remain for one month in the prison hospital to recuperate. I left the hospital at the end of August, greatly restored. I received the regular prison clothing—a black cotton uniform, a neck cloth and a pair of old boots. No prisoner received socks. No heavier garments were issued for the winter months. Political prisoners wore a yellow stripe around their right sleeve; those convicted of criminal offenses wore a green stripe, and those who had been sterilized or castrated wore a blue stripe. Again I was in solitary confinement.

During the first months, I attempted to keep track of time. But more and more I followed a natural craving to forget the meaning of time. Time had ceased to have significance. Time was a fraud. I detested the Sundays, for then the church-bells rang with malevolent insistence, as if to mark time. Twenty minutes each day I was taken into the yard for exercise. Then I and thirty-odd other prisoners from my tier ran around the yard in single file, keeping a distance of twenty feet between each other. Speaking was prohibited. The remaining one thousand four hundred and twenty minutes of each day I lived in the solitude of my cell. Breakfast and supper consisted of two slices of dry black bread; the midday meal consisted of a liter of soup. I ate in my cell. The food was thrust through a small aperture in the steel door. I was always hungry. I had known the meaning of hunger before, but never had I hungered like this. Occasionally strange-looking foods were handed to me, and I was ordered to eat them. They were Ersatz, food substitutes which were tried out on prisoners before they were offered to the population outside.

Ten hours each weekday I worked, plucking hunks of old rope into oakum. First the ropes had to be separated into strands. The strands had to be beaten against the stone floor to loosen the rope-yarns. Then each rope-yarn was plucked apart by hand. The dust flew thickly. At the end of a day's work, the whole cell was covered with a layer of dust. Three kilos of oakum were the day's task. The prisoner who was unable to produce them received half-rations of bread for breakfast and supper. I had books to read. Every Sunday morning I received a book. The books were distributed by the prison pastor, who was a Nazi of the Prussian school. It was he who decided what each prisoner should read. For reasons of his own, he persisted in plying me with ancient historical romances.

Every fortnight I was allowed to bathe. A bath lasted exactly two minutes. Undressing, hot water, soaping, cold water, towel use, and dressing—each of these performances was measured in seconds, and their execution was commanded by the guard on duty. Once each month I received a change of underwear, once a week I was shaved, and once in four weeks my hair was cut. Smoking and newspapers were taboo. Had a continent exploded, I should not have known it, unless it had been Central Europe. I was not permitted to receive visitors. Once in sixty days I was allowed to write a letter, and once each week—to receive one. The letters I was permitted could not be longer than twelve lines—and half of them were scissored away by the prison censor. But I received letters. They came from Firelei. They were beautiful letters, alive with kindness and love and courage. "You are not alone," she wrote me. "I am with you. Don't you see? I am in your cell. I put my hand on your shoulder and I walk with you. Four steps. Turn. Four steps back. I chat with you about the. unforgettable hours we have shared. I am thankful for such hours. No, no, you are not alone."

Life in solitary confinement is hard. Compared with the German prisons, San Quentin had been a pleasure resort. Sometimes I was near despair. I tried to overcome the gloomy hours by being brutal to myself. "They make life hard for you," I thought. "Very well, make it still harder yourself!" I threw bread out of the window. I produced more oakum than I was required to produce. I forced myself to stand for many minutes in painful positions. I disciplined my body and my mind. That was my triumph. Self-imposed hardships made prison hardships appear as the natural ingredients of an easy life. My greatest pleasure was to lie awake at night to let my imagination produce majestic music. I heard Carmen and Lohengrin. When the music would not come to sweep through my brain, I hummed songs for hours on end, all the folk songs I could remember, and all the battle songs of the Comintern.

I also explored my own resources. I discovered undreamt-of lands. I was never idle. I always had something to do. I could play chess with myself in the dark and without board or pieces; or I could force my mind to take me to China or Arabia or back to the ages of Alexander or Napoleon; I could resurrect the men and women I had known as if they were in the cell, live flesh and blood and voice; and I could take a dull book and spend a long Sunday translating portions of it into English or French, or training my memory by learning the dullest passages by heart. I came to the conclusion that man was a wonderful animal. I was content with my chores and explorations. As time went on, I thought less and less of the outside world. It did not exist. It was an illusion. The prison cell was the world, and the prison yard the universe.

November, 1934, brought me suffering and restlessness. Firelei's letters had stopped coming. Each morning, when footsteps approached on the tier, I thought eagerly, "Now, there is a letter from Firelei." But the steps passed. "What has happened to her?"

I asked myself. "Has she forgotten? Has she grown tired? Has she been sent away on some illegal mission? Has the Party forbidden her to write? Has she died?" I could not find an answer. The winter passed, and the spring of 1935. And no letter came. I was so lonely that I talked to the drowsy flies in my cell. "Where is Firelei?" I asked them. One day in June a butterfly meandered into my cell. I shielded it like a great treasure. "Have you come from Firelei?" I asked. It fluttered through the clouds of dust and beat its wings to shreds against the walls.

Chapter Thirty-seven

MAN-CAGE MAGIC

The captain of the guards was a dark, thin little man with a hatchet face. Walking, he bore a great resemblance to a broken broomstick. His face was yellow, his nose hooked, his lips thin, his eyes black and piercing. The prisoners called him "Marabou." This man's job was to harass guards and prisoners alike. It was he who determined the punishment to be inflicted for infractions of the rigid prison rules. Punishment ranged from depriving a prisoner of his privilege to write letters, or of his mattress, to the shortening of food rations and confinement in the dark-dungeons. For long periods at a time, "Marabou" would stand silently in front of a cell, watching the prisoner through the spyhole, searching for some irregularity, for a chance to inflict punishment.

If some restless soul paced his cell during work hours, "Marabou" called it "passive resistance." If someone saved a piece of bread from his breakfast to consume it with his soup at noon, "Marabou" termed it "hoarding of supplies for a planned escape." If, in the heat of summer, a prisoner loosened his neck cloth, "Marabou" was there to avenge the violation of discipline. If a prisoner's tin cup or his spoon lay an inch away from the spot designated for it in the printed prison regulations—that was "organized obstruction" to "Marabou." When he found a pencil stub hidden beneath a convict's mattress, "Marabou" called it a "conspiracy to write communist pamphlets or homosexual love notes." He was always stealthy and alert and merciless. The prisoners hated him. But "Marabou" never entered a cell alone, and was always protected by a vanguard of two husky warders. At times he appeared in the yard when we were out for our exercise. "Attention!" the guards on duty would yell, and we would all stop like rocks in our tracks. "Marabou" would slink from one man to the next, searching for faults. If a button on a prisoner's uniform was open, he would pull out a penknife and cut off the offending button and all other buttons as well. His favorite yard punishment was to have prisoners jump in and out of a huge barrel. Then his voice would crackle: "Into the barrel—out of the barrel! Into the barrel—out of the barrel!" Once each week he would surprise us and order us to strip. One crew of guards then searched our naked bodies, and another gang would go over every inch of our garments and shoes. Repeated attempts by maddened convicts to kill "Marabou" came to naught. Several of the would-be assassins were kept in chains in the cellar dungeons. Prison rumor, tapped through the walls and whispered at night from window to window, had it that these unfortunates were flogged each night by "Marabou" in person.

One day in June two guards shouldered into my cell. They were followed by "Marabou." I sprang to attention, shouting my name and number and the reason for my conviction. "Marabou" walked around me, sizing me up from all sides. His yellow hands were clasped behind his back. He was so near that I could have reached out to break his scraggy neck. I stood motionless. "Marabou" scrutinized my neck cloth. It was faultless. He squinted at my boots. They were shiny. Carefully he looked over my jacket. No button was open, no seam torn. His quick black eyes darted into every corner of my cell. He rubbed his forefinger over the floor behind the lavatory. He then looked at his finger. No dust. He ordered me to turn over my mattress, to show my eating utensils, to lower my pants to prove that I had nothing illegal hidden between my legs. Finally he said in his creaking voice: "How are you getting along?"

"Excellently, sir," I replied.

"Are you still a *Kommunist?*"

"No, sir."

"Well," he commented peevishly, "I can't see what's going on inside your head. But that's no reason why I should believe you. I have some pictures here for you."

Out of his pocket he drew a few snapshots. They were photographs of Firelei. I lunged forward, my hand outstretched. "Marabou" snarled:

"Don't move! Keep your fingertips glued to the seams of your pants when I speak to you."

"The pictures, sir," I said.

"They came with the letters from your wife. Nice letters she wrote you, very nice letters."

"Yes, sir."

"I cannot let you have the pictures," he said drily. The specter of a grin crept over his face. "You'll get them when you are released. In—in how many years?"

"In twelve years," I said steadily.

"It'll be nice to see then what your wife looked like twelve years ago," "Marabou" cackled. "People have the habit of getting older, you know. The joints get stiff and the skin flabby, and the face gets a good many lines. The lines of old age, I dare say. What did you do in the communist movement?"

"My duty, sir—as I thought it right at that time."

"Duty—aye! We all do our duty," he said.

"Yes, sir."

It gave me a wild pleasure to face him, and not to show the weakness which he craved to discern.

"Do you like solitary confinement?" "Marabou" inquired. "Yes, sir."

"Why?"

"I like to be alone."

"You like it better here than in the common hall?"

"I believe I do, sir."

"Why?" he demanded harshly.

"Because it's monotonous," I replied. "A man loses track of time, and so time flies faster."

"You live too well," "Marabou" said finally. He turned to one of the guards. "Here, take this man to Hall Nine."

"Marabou" walked off. He wore rubber soles, and it was impossible to hear him come or go. The guard ordered me to roll up my blanket and to follow him to Hall Nine.

I marched down the tier, past long rows of cell doors. The locks shone. The floor was polished. The whole prison was kept scrupulously clean. The silence was appalling; it seemed to belie the fact that nearly two thousand human beings lived behind those mute steel doors. The central hall was cool and gloomy, and there was no sign of life except the slowly floating shapes of the guards. One of them was cleaning a gun. Others paused to squint through spy-holes. The wings of the prison which harbored the solitary cells resembled more a half-dark tomb than a place full of incarcerated men, men who were month after month alone with their thoughts.

Over a narrow iron stairway I descended to the ground floor of the building. Convicts stood in long rows, their faces to the wall. There was no noise, and apparently no motion. But as I passed them I saw eyes glance furtively sideways. I saw a fair-haired boy whom I had last seen crouched on the roof of a tenement in Altona, sniping at marauding Brownshirts in the street. His shoulders twitched a salute; his hands jerked a signal: "Fifteen years." Then I passed the visitors' room. A young woman emerged. She was neatly dressed, but her eyes were reddened; with each hand she led a child, little girls with bewildered faces.

I passed the center of the prison. Here, on a raised platform, sat two guards behind a machine gun. They were so posted that they could send streams of lead—without even rising from their seats—into any one of the five radiating wings of the prison. Ironically, the gun platform had the shape of a five-pointed star.

I passed the great bell which boomed the commands to rise, to begin work, to stop work, to eat, to undress. Ten times daily it boomed; thirty-six thousand five hundred times it would boom in ten years; and each time its booming was like a contemptuous voice and a rattling of chains. It also was the only music—outside of the prison church—that had reached my ears since the day of farewell from Cilly. At first the persistent clanging of this bell had made me wince, but later I had fallen into the habit of answering the metallic clangor with a perfunctory, "Yell, you bell, and be damned."

We crossed a yard and swung into the largest wing of an older part of the prison. In it were the common halls. It had three broad tiers. Each tier had seven broad steel doors, and each door led into a hall. This part of the prison was filled with a continuous dull roar of a distant surf, a roar which began in the morning and did not cease until the "lights-out" signal was given at seven-thirty in the evening, a roar that was like the sound of unquenchable life and motion, the sound of a thousand human voices coming from beyond the gray steel doors.

"Hall Nine—stop here," the guard commanded.

The door swung open. My blanket roll jammed under my arm, I entered. From under the low, grimy ceiling a crazy cataract of sounds and motion sprang at me. I stood still, stunned by the mass of moving and talking shapes. I was shocked by the existence of so much life. And suddenly two firm hands reached up from behind me and covered my eyes.

"Ha—got you!" a voice triumphed.

I freed myself. In front of me stood Salomon, who had been my right-hand man in earlier years. He shook my hand until I nearly swayed off my feet. His grizzled face was twisted with joy.

"Welcome," he said. "By God! You're here! There were reports that they had killed and buried you."

Hall Nine was about forty feet long and thirty feet wide. It had three barred windows facing the yard, and two smaller windows which faced the tier to permit the guards outside to keep the hall under surveillance without running the hazard of entering it. The entire length of the other walls was obscured by clumsy wooden scaffolds which rose in two tiers, like enormous shelves. Each of these shelves was thirty feet long and six feet wide, and on them lay rows of burlap bags thinly stuffed with straw. These bags were our mattresses. No space separated one paillasse from the next, and there were fifteen paillasses on each platform. Thus, the sleeping space allowed each inmate of Hall Nine was twelve square feet. Five long tables occupied the central portion of the hall. Jammed in between the tables were crude wooden benches. The tables, the sleeping scaffolds, the concrete floor—every available space in Hall Nine—were littered with bulky bundles of brightly-colored bast.

About sixty men in convict uniforms squatted on the benches, shoulder to shoulder and back against back. With swift, mechanical movements they drew threads of bast out of the bundles and knotted them together to lengths of a thousand yards or more. The knotted bast was then smoothed and wound up into the shapes of huge eggs. In the basement workshops and in the solitary cells, the bast was then woven into mats, handbags, sandals, and the like.

A steady uproar of voices filled the turbid air. The men spoke and shouted at one another across the tables, their voices loud so as to be heard in the general bedlam. I caught a few words—"pea soup ... chess tournament... Schiller's *Glocke*... surplus value ... a tart with breasts like puddings... Litvinov ... sixteen apple trees ... letter from the wife ..." Some of the men squatted in silence, and their aspect was either one of dejection, dreaming, or of sullen ferocity. Sixty men worked and slept, ate and argued and washed and fought their great and small battles in Hall Nine. And there were eighteen such halls in the prison. Thirty minutes of goose-stepping in the yard each day was their only respite from life in a space of which each man's share was two square yards—month after month, and year after year. They rose at six and went to bed at half-past seven. Ten hours a day they worked. They stood in line in front of the single latrine, and they ate their food with spoons, for a fork was already considered a dangerous weapon. At night the windows were closed, and the air in Hall Nine became a suffocating stench in which dust settled slowly. It became clear to me from the beginning that such an accumulation of unruly temperaments in so small a space was fraught with promises of antagonisms and outbursts of helpless savagery. Men fought for a piece of soap, a crust of bread, a place by the window—and for more important prizes. One-third of the population of Hall Nine consisted of genuine crooks—forgers, thieves, burglars, robbers, marriage swindlers, knife-artists and pimps. Most troubles in the common halls were caused by the aggressive individualists in this category. The other two-thirds of the convicts were political prisoners. There were two or three socialists, editors and trade union officials, but the bulk of political captives was made up of members of the Communist Party. The name which the guards applied to a common hall was "devil's kitchen." They were afraid to enter it alone, preferring to invade it in squads.

Comrade Salomon whispered a warning. "Be careful whom you talk to," he said. "The Gestapo has its spies in every hall. Some only sit and listen; others are forever trying to recruit more spies. A careless word here may bring about the arrest of our friends who are still outside."

I asked for news. Much had happened during my long months of solitary confinement. An insurrection of the workers in Vienna had been drowned in blood by Chancellor Dollfuss, who, in his turn, had been shot to death by Nazi assassins. The King of the Belgians had fallen off a cliff and died. American shipping had been rocked by the violent San Francisco general strike. President von Hindenburg had gone to his grave and Hitler had stepped into the senile veteran's boots; and Fascist legions had gone to war in Ethiopia. The Saar district had been returned to the Reich, a revolution had taken place in Greece, and a near-revolution in France. In Marseilles the King of Yugoslavia and the Foreign Minister of France had died from the bullets of a Bulgarian conspirator. Of all these events, which the busy and tormented world had already half forgotten, I now heard for the first time.

"Do you get newspapers?" I asked.

"We have a way of smuggling them in," Salomon said. "We are kept well informed. We are in constant touch with the Party."

"You have a way to send out uncensored letters?"

"Sure. The comrades in all the halls co-operate. We have a tobacco line. We have a letter line, an intelligence service, and we also have the Communist Manifesto and the latest brochure by Comrade Dimitrov. The Comintern policy has been modified. Now it's *Front Populaire*. We defend democracy because democracy gives us the best chance of organizing the armed insurrection. An important tactical maneuver, though many of the comrades here are bitter about having gone to prison for a policy that's now declared erroneous by Moscow. You'll learn much. But caution! The halls are infested with unstable elements."

I received perhaps the greatest shock of my life when Salomon told me that

Albert Walter, the former chief of the Comintern's Maritime Division, had entered the Gestapo service.

"How is that possible?" I stuttered.

"A demonstration of human insufficiency," Salomon observed. "There are fellows who look as strong and tough as a tugboat, and who crack under the first thirty blows. A lot of our top leaders turned out to be figureheads of clay. At the same time, the little comrades you hardly noticed before show the grit of real devils. Indomitable! As to Albert Walter—his old mother was worth more to him than the revolution, or his honor as a revolutionist."

Albert Walter a Gestapo man! It sounded as grotesque to me as the assertion that Captain Goering was an agent of the G.P.U. The comrades in Hall Nine were, however, accurately informed, partly through the intermediaries of Rudolf Heitman, and partly through our own *Nachrichtendienst*. Albert Walter had been the key man of Stalin's power on the seven seas. The Gestapo knew that, and the Gestapo knew that if they broke Walter, they would gain access to the ramifications of the Comintern empire in international shipping. They had tortured him horribly. But a warrior of Albert Walter's caliber could not be broken by physical torture.

The old sailor's Achilles Heel was his deep love for his aged mother, who had catered to her fifty-year-old son's needs as though he were still an infant; who had lived with him through the stormy years, and who had fought fearlessly to lighten the lot of her son after his capture by the Gestapo. Inspector Kraus had seized old Mrs. Walter and kept her on water and bread in a solitary cell. He had brought Albert Walter to the women's section of Camp Fuhlsbuettel and had permitted him to peer through the spy-hole of the cell in which his mother languished. And then Inspector Kraus served this ultimatum:

"Walter, either you work with us, the Gestapo, or your mother will die in Ko-La-Fu."

The price Albert Walter paid for the liberation of his mother was treason to the cause he had served all his life. Both Mrs. Walter and her son were released, and Albert became a collaborator of the Gestapo, a *Ratgeber* (counselor) in maritime affairs. The Western Secretariat of the Comintern had then dispatched Georg Hegener, Jensen's trusted *aide-de-camp*, to Germany with orders to spirit Albert Walter out of Hitler's reach. Comrade Hegener's formidable brain was an arsenal of G.P.U. methods; but Walter, his former superior and now his quarry, also knew all the tricks and rules of foul play. One night, in 1934, Georg Hegener, armed with a false passport and a Colt, invaded Walter's home in the Pestalozzi Strasse in Hamburg. The conversation between the two must have been one of the grimmest and weirdest episodes in the history of the two grimmest and weirdest revolutionary movements of our time. Hegener retreated in the battle of wits and, perhaps, guns. For all his cunning and courage, he was no match for "Davy Jones' Great Uncle," as Walter was called by his intimates.

Next morning the Gestapo was informed of Hegener's presence in Hamburg. The Nazis did not arrest him. They aimed at bigger game. When Georg

Hegener left Germany clandestinely, he was shadowed by operatives of the Gestapo's Foreign Division. He led his shadowers straight to the offices of Kuusinen and Wollweber in Copenhagen. Inspector Kraus' emissaries rented a villa in the suburb of Charlottenlund, and a week later Inspector Kraus himself, using the name and the passport of a Hamburg master-baker, established temporary headquarters in Copenhagen. Another week passed. The headlines of the Danish press shrieked: "Gestapo Bandits in Copenhagen . . . Nazi Kidnapers at Work." Ernst Wollweber and a man named Vogel—whom the Gestapo raiders mistook for Kuusinen— had been slugged in a street and thrown into a waiting car. They had been brought to the villa in Charlottenlund to await being transported secretly to Germany. But the villa had already been under G.P.U. supervision. Men from the communist Espionage Defense, then directed by Leo Haikiss, went into action. Inspector Kraus and his aides fled. Wollweber and Vogel were rescued. Shortly afterward, Ernst Wollweber was taken into custody by the Copenhagen police, but Richard Jensen negotiated his release, and won it under the pretext that Wollweber—"Schmidt" to the Danish detectives—would leave at once for Russia.

"And Walter is still at large?"

"Yes," Salomon said quietly. "I'm unspeakably sorry for his militant old mother. And for him! Imagine living as a traitor! When Hitler falls, Walter will die before a firing squad. A pity if he'd have to share the same mass grave with Hertha Jens."

Each common hall was a seething hole of intrigues and a ruthless struggle for hegemony. The prison administration deliberately saw to it that the composition of the prisoners in each hall should allow for no mass solidarity. The most conflicting elements were crammed together between four narrow walls. The administration invited spying, denunciations and mutual frustration of conspirative endeavors. The prison officials themselves, responsible for the maintenance of political sterility of the prison inmates, lived in constant fear of the Gestapo. They left nothing untried to render it impossible for the vast numbers of political prisoners to embark on mass conspiracies. The task of administration spies and Gestapo creatures in the common halls was to sow strife and distrust, and to ferret out evidence which would lead to additional convictions and prolongations of sentences already imposed. Moreover, the Gestapo was always on the alert to recruit additional informers from the ranks of political convicts. The authorities encouraged the criminal prisoners to maintain a permanent state of dissent and enmity in the halls. Invariably, the criminal prisoners were banded together in numerous small cliques, each clique following the orders of a strong-arm leader, and all of them saturated with a spirit of hatred and fear for the majority of political convicts.

As the days went by, I learned that the Hamburg penitentiary was virtually ruled by a secret organization of communist prisoners. The Party existed and was active behind prison walls. In the Hamburg prison it had roughly eleven hundred members. The structure and discipline of this organization of convicts followed the standard communist pattern. The comrades in each hall were organized in groups of five. No one, except the unit leader, was permitted to have political associations outside of his own five-man nucleus. Each group leader followed the commands of, and was responsible to, the Hall Committee of three. All Hall Committees worked under the direction of a Spitzengruppe—the Central Committee, which had its headquarters in Hall Eleven, and which maintained, through prisoners who went "on transport," a secret courier service with other prisons.

Each newly arrived communist prisoner was inevitably drawn into this organization, except when he had proven himself a weakling or a traitor. The Central Committee had also created its own *Apparat*, a sort of prison Tcheka, which operated against and under the noses of the prison spies of the Gestapo. Underlying this whole prison organization was the principle: "Even in hell a Bolshevik must remain a Bolshevik; we must keep the Party together and sharpen its weapons for coming struggles; the greatest crime is to permit the Party to die." The comrade in the *Fuenfergruppe*—the group of five—knew little of the tentacles of this organization. He knew the members of his own group and its leader. The leaders were appointed by the Hall Committee, and the members of the Hall Committees were appointed by the Central Committee, which exercised, of necessity, a most stringent dictatorship. The contact between the Central Committee in Hall Eleven and the seventeen other Hall Committees was maintained by a special staff of liaison agents—trusties, food-carriers, and prisoners detailed to transport the bales of bast from the storage rooms to the various halls.

The organization, though dominant, was practically invisible to an outsider. It was intangible to the eyes and hands of strangers. But it was there. Behind the walls its arm could be felt every day and every hour, and most of all at night. The reckless desperadoes, who had been the natural overlords of all the convicts in bygone years, had found that their hitherto effective methods of leadership had become completely worthless.

Buried away in solitary confinement, I had already half forgotten the Party and the Comintern. Now, in Hall Nine, I was surrounded by communist militants whose minds were dominated by but one thought: "The Party comes first!" It was unique. Such a thing, I felt, had never before existed in any prison at any time. I felt the power of the Party. It gave me a wild sense of pride. In me the old revolutionary enthusiasm awoke with might.

My transfer to Hall Nine was quickly reported to the Central Committee in Hall Eleven by a convict courier who in his capacity as food-carrier served four halls during meal times. Communications between prisoners in different halls were forbidden, and severely punished by the prison administration. But the method we used to convey messages was nearly fool-proof: printed on a tiny piece of paper, the message was glued to the bottom of a soup pail and delivered at noon, together with the soup, while the guard on duty looked on unsuspectingly. Several days later the Central Committee sent back instructions that I should prepare for my transfer to Hall Eleven, which we jocularly called the "Kremlin of the Hamburg Big House."

"How the devil can I get to Hall Eleven?" I asked Salomon, who was the political leader of Hall Nine.

"Do nothing," he said. "Leave it to Tonio."

"Tonio" was the political chief of the whole prison. I had met him long before my arrest. He was a powerfully-built man of thirty-two, light-haired and blue-eyed, and as dauntless as he was cheerful. Resourceful and just, he had a driving personality, but, like Michel Avatin, he never demanded anything of other comrades which he would not do himself. Tonio was a Teutonic image of Avatin. He had been one of the Comintern's experts for the mining industries, and after the arrest of Walter Duddins, he had become the Party chief of the North Sea districts—the office in which Wollweber had planned to install John Scheer. Seized by the Gestapo, Tonio had been sentenced for high treason. His young wife had subsequently been sent to the Lenin School in Moscow for special training. I soon came to feel Tonio's power and ability even in a Nazi prison.

An elderly guard summoned me out on the corridor.

"Would you like to be shifted to Hall Eleven?" he asked.

"Yes, sir," I replied smartly.

"All right. Roll up your blankets."

Five minutes later I was in Hall Eleven. The guard was one of the older prison officials, who had been members of the Social Democratic Party before the advent of Hitler. When Hitler came to power, they had—to save their jobs and their pensions—joined the Nazi Party in a great hurry. Usually they "Heil-Hitlered" louder and fiercer than any of the genuine storm troopers. But the arrival of communists in the prisons plunged these former socialists into a dire dilemma. The communist convicts often knew of the Marxist past of their jailers, and the threat of denouncing them to the Gestapo for having entered the Nazi Party fraudulently turned these prison guards into helpless pawns in the hands of their communist charges. There were six or seven of them in the Hamburg prison. A single command from Tonio could make them jump like frightened bell-boys. It was a grim business. But all prisons are grim, and Hitler's prisons are the grimmest of all.

When Tonio saw me, he pranced across the hall like an exuberant colt. His rough playfulness was the best possible camouflage for the unflinching and ruthless determination which had its home behind Tonio's flashing eyes. He and three of his aides grabbed me and carried me to the lavatory in a corner of Hall Eleven. I received a thorough dousing with cold water. Tonio made a speech which drew laughter even from the most sullen criminals in our midst. I received a name—"Longsplice." After the noisy introduction, he drew me aside.

"We need you in the *Spitzengruppe*," he said. "The third man is Frederic, a young teacher. One thing you must always remember: *We* are the Party behind these walls. We must transform this jailhouse into a university of revolution. By that we turn the purpose of this prison into its opposite. Our attention must not overlook the most obscure comrades. The Gestapo puts them here to be broken. *We* are here to make them stronger and more loyal to the cause. Savvy?"

"Savvy."

"Good—let's get busy!"

I was a denizen of Hall Eleven and a member of the prison Central Committee for fourteen months. They belonged to the most crowded months in my life. They showed me that even in hopeless defeat men can retain their morale as long as the conviction that they are fighting for a worthy cause is alive in their brains. The individual may give up the struggle and sink away in despair, but banded together with other castaways for a common purpose, he sees his place, feels his strength, and salvages his belief that life still has a meaning. The inarticulate rank and file had greater fortitude in the face of crushing obstacles than the general run of the intellectually superior. The average communist militant, even in prison and facing an implacable future, would have jumped into a kettle full of molten copper, had his chiefs commanded him to jump. The tenet that men fight only for material gains was given the lie by the nameless "activists" in felon's garb. Obsessed by a faith, a human being fights longer and fiercer than his brothers and sisters whose foremost inspiration is shoddily disguised avarice.

With a pathetic *élan* and considerable cunning we transformed the prison into a "university of revolution." We supervised the lives of our comrades, and we organized their time with greater severity and detail than my own time had been organized when I had been a student at the Communist University of Leningrad. A frightened guard supplied us regularly with the latest pamphlets and resolutions of the Comintern. The decisions of the Seventh World Congress of the Comintern, which ushered in the era of Popular Front movements, were in our hands even before they were commented upon by the German press. In Hall Eleven, in whispered discussions, which sometimes lasted all through a night, we worked out the texts for revolutionary-political courses. "Imperialism," "Strike Tactics," "Sabotage," "Propaganda in the Army," "Marxian Dialectics," "Strategy of Civil War," and dozens of similar themes were elaborated and written down in the clearest possible and most concise form. Our paper and pencils were stolen for us by comrades working in the offices of the administration; the fountain pens we used were smuggled in by guards. A special group of "agit-prop" men—agitator propagandists—in Hall Eleven then copied the original tracts in neatly printed letters. They wrote at night. The copies were then circulated in all the other halls of the prison. Trusties and food-carriers acted as couriers between the various tiers and cell blocks. They delivered the written material to the political leaders of the various halls. The political leaders then pressed it into the heads of the other members of their group. The conferences were carried on at night, and in whispers, while as often as not a Gestapo spy lay only a few paillasses away. Our machine functioned smoothly, from Tonio down to the meanest comrade. Some day the majority of those we trained would be released; they would, we hoped, continue their "underground" work outside as firmer Bolsheviks than they had been on the day of their first arrest by the Gestapo.

Every Sunday morning the Central Committee met in conference with the political leaders of the halls. Reports were rendered, and the plan of action for the coming week laid down. These sessions took place in the prison church. Church attendance was compulsory. The prison pastor was an arrogant young Elite Guard officer. His sermons were a potpourri extracted from the Bible, German mythology and Adolf Hitler's *Mein Kampf*. There was little opportunity for surreptitious communications among the mass of prisoners in the nave. Our organization conferences were held in the choir, which was situated on a high gallery on the far end of the church. The choir master was a kindly old man who was always ready to do the prisoners a favor. The organist was a former social democrat. The Sexton was a fanatic Catholic who hated the Hitler movement. But all three wore the swastika badge and were members of the Nazi Party. The choir master employed only such singers who volunteered from among the convicts in the halls. Among others, Tonio and Frederic and I, the members of the *Spitzengruppe*, volunteered; so did, upon our instructions, the political leaders of all the other common halls. While the minor choristers roared hymns at the top of their voices, the political leaders retreated to the background of the choir, and there, out of sight of the guards in the nave below, conspiracies took their course.

Our intelligence service, the prison *Nachrichtendienst*, was well organized. It worked with thoroughness, and, of necessity, with utmost caution. The intelligence level of political prisoners was much higher than that of the run of criminal convicts. With much wary maneuvering we succeeded in placing communists in all key jobs open to convicts. The clerks in the offices of the administration were Party members. The attendants in the prison bathrooms were comrades; they were of great importance to us because their job brought them into contact with every prisoner in the course of each week. The majority of the trusties were communists, as were the foremen in the various industrial departments of the penitentiary. Those of our comrades who had slipped into the jobs of "con-bosses" took great care to accelerate production efficiency, at the same time using all means to keep the guards ignorant of production technique. Increased production won for the "con-bosses" a good reputation with the administration, and the guards' ignorance of production technique enabled the "con-bosses" to say: "To fill this vacancy, I need Convict X." And invariably "Convict X" was a seasoned Party member. The prison librarians and the book-binders were also Party members. Their function in our *Apparat* consisted in pasting pages from the Communist Manifesto and the latest speeches of Stalin and Dimitrov into such books as *The Count of Monte Cristo, Ivanhoe*, and Bismarck's *Gedanken und Erinnerungen*. Of course, the comrade librarians took care that such "doctored" books only reached reliable political prisoners. When men convicted of political offenses entered the prison, they invariably found themselves at first completely isolated by our organization. The political leader of the respective hall reported the new arrival to the Central Committee. The Central Committee then sent a note of inquiry to the comrades in the offices of the prison director, *Oberinspektor* Bruhns. The communists in the administration offices then lurked for a chance to peruse the official dossier of the newly-arrived prisoner. They gathered all available data and sent it to the Central Committee in Hall Eleven. Within a week we knew the past history of every new convict, the crime for which he had been sentenced, his behavior before the Gestapo and the Special Tribunal, and his political affiliations. We knew as much about him as the Gestapo did, and often more. Was he considered reliable, we informed the respective Hall Committee of the fact, and the newcomer was then drawn into our organization as an active member. Much of the information we gathered from the constant flow of political captives we collected into long reports, which were then smuggled out by our aides among the guards and forwarded by Rudolf Heitman to the Western Secretariat and the G.P.U. in Copenhagen. These reports contained information on new Gestapo plans and methods, on Nazi spies and traitors in our own ranks, and also industrial and military secrets in the possession of arrested comrades.

Our most important and effective method to keep control of the criminal element in the prison population was the organized distribution of tobacco. Smoking is prohibited in all German prisons. But certain prisoners, upon recommendation by the prison authorities or the police, were permitted to receive a weekly allowance of chewing tobacco—*Priem*. These privileged prisoners wielded great power among their underprivileged colleagues, and the possession of tobacco by a few select gave rise to the most vicious aspects of convict "politics." I saw men who were ready to murder each other for a stick of chewing tobacco. I saw others who were prepared to do the most sordid deed if they were offered an inch of *Priem* in payment.

"We must streamline the tobacco question," Tonio said to me one day. "As conditions are now, a tobacco knifing might bring the Gestapo swooping down for a wholesale investigation. The tobacco fiends would be only too glad to sell us out."

We turned tobacco into a political weapon, and did it in the following manner: Every two weeks Tonio ordered a consignment of good smoking tobacco to be bought from the funds which the International Red Aid had established for the relief of relatives of important political prisoners. An unknown Party comrade outside got the money and bought the tobacco, which was then smuggled in piecemeal by three former socialists among the guards. They delivered the contraband in Hall Three, and from there it filtered to Hall Eleven. The tobacco was then distributed equally among all prisoners, together with fire-stones and tiny pieces of steel. In this manner, criminal and political prisoners alike shared, in groups of five—called "tobacco groups,"— at least two cigarettes each day. This broke the power of the chewing tobacco monopolists, who comprised the most vicious cut-throats in the prison; they were, in the end, glad to be admitted to one of the disciplined "tobacco groups."

The harshest punishment that could befall a prisoner was to be ostracized by his own comrades. There could be no more cruel treatment than to live in a crowded hall and to be shunned by all hall mates. But the price of comradeship was co-operation in our political schemes. One of the political convicts who refused to co-operate was Comrade Nickel. He was the same Nickel who, as a Party leader in Bremen, had tried to impose his blustering will upon me on the eve of my voyage to Murmansk aboard the *Pioner*. The Gestapo had captured Nickel and over ninety of his aides in a single raid in the summer of 1933. Nickel was sent to prison for high treason. There he refused to accept Tonio's leadership. The answer of the *Spitzengruppe* was: "Nickel must be isolated!" And Nickel's isolation was complete. No one wanted to be his neighbor during meals or on the sleeping scaffolds. No one spoke to him. Comrades edged away from him as if he were a leper. Nickel fell into the habit of brooding alone in a corner of the hall. After nine months of such treatment he gradually became like a man who has lost his reason. "Speak to me," he would moan, "oh, why doesn't somebody speak to me."

And he would receive the contemptuous answer: "Croak—you saboteur!"

Our prison organization did not even relinquish its hold on a comrade after his release. Many, after serving their sentences, were not released; if the Gestapo considered them still dangerous, it sent them from prison straight to another concentration camp—*bis auf Weiteres*—"until further notice." The Estewege Camps in Western Germany and Camp Sachsenhausen near Berlin were the mammoth places of detention for anti-Nazis who had finished their term in prison. However, two prisoners out of three were actually released after they had served their sentence. It was this category on which we concentrated our interest. Such comrades, after their last day in the penitentiary had passed, were brought to Gestapo headquarters. There, as the inescapable condition for their release, they were required to sign a statement to the effect that they would henceforth collaborate with the Gestapo. The Gestapo procured jobs for them. In return, the comrades were pledged to send to the Gestapo weekly confidential reports about the actions, associations and conversations of their fellow workers and their neighbors. If such reports were not forthcoming, or if the Gestapo considered them unsatisfactory, the respective "informers" were promptly seized for another term in a concentration camp. So, theoretically, every anti-Nazi released from prison was a Gestapo spy. Those who refused to sign the spy-pledge were not released.

In the Hamburg prison we began to evolve a plan to turn this system of mass espionage into an asset for the Communist Party. We instructed all reliable comrades who were due for release in the art of concocting misinformation in reports which the Gestapo would nevertheless find "satisfactory." It was a dangerous game, but one calculated to divert the Gestapo's attention from the communist cells in the shops by furnishing them with information on Nazis who criticized the Nazi regime. Repressive actions of the Gestapo against rebellious Nazis would tend to increase the already existing anti-Gestapo sentiment in the Nazi rank and file. Before a comrade was released from prison, his name and the date of his release were transmitted by us to the secretly operating liaison committee of the Communist Party. The released comrade was then contacted and given his place in the "underground" Party machine. Each released communist was also entrusted with a *Patenschaft* (patronage) over three comrades who were still in prison. Once "free," his task was to maintain contact with the three prisoners assigned to his care and with their families, and also to keep them supplied with information and cover addresses to which they could report when they themselves would be released.

The months flew by. Summer passed. The trees in the yards became golden brown, and the sky was filled with storm clouds. The leaves fell, winter covered the land with snow, and thousands of gulls came screaming in from the frozen coasts. The sun rose higher and vanquished the winter, and it was spring again, and summer, the summer of 1936. King George of England had died, Hitler's armies had marched into the Rhineland, General Franco had raised the banner of civil war in Spain. And in the Soviet Union, the Great Purge initiated by Stalin after the assassination of Sergei Kirov, the Leningrad Party chief, brought countless members of the Old Bolshevik Guard before the firing squads. No letter had come from Firelei. It was as if the earth had swallowed her. Thirty-two months had passed since I had seen her last.

"Dear girl," I wondered. "Where are you? What are you doing?"

I received the answer at the end of July. A young comrade from Hall Eleven had been taken to Gestapo headquarters for questioning. He had spent the better part of the day in the office of Inspector Radam, who was then preparing the material for the trial of Edgar Andree for treason and murder. Late in the afternoon the comrade had been brought to the *Wartezimmer* to await his return to the penitentiary. There he had had an opportunity to scrutinize the faces of a number of other waiting prisoners.

"Five girls were sitting faces to the wall," he told me. "One of them wore convict dress. She was your wife, Comrade Firelei."

My voice trembled. "Are you sure this girl was Firelei?" I asked.

"I am certain. She, too, recognized me. We were too far from each other to whisper. But she smiled."

I meandered through Hall Eleven like a man who is struck by sudden blindness. Firelei in the hands of the Gestapo! When was she captured? Of what did they convict her? Was she abducted from abroad? Did she return to Germany herself? Did she come on a secret mission? Did she come because she wanted to rescue her child?

All night the questions rushed through my brain. It was a new kind of agony. Firelei captured by the Gestapo! Firelei condemned by the Special Tribunal! Did they beat her? Did they keep her in solitary confinement? How many months already has she been in the dungeons? I felt the urge to cry. I forced back the tears because I was ashamed of the comrades whose bodies pushed against me from right and left. I was seized by an insane hatred against all the world, and a hatred against myself.

I cursed myself. "Your fault! Your fault!" I muttered. "You drew her into the bloody morass! Had you never spoken to her— she would be happy now, and free!" I gnashed my teeth. Bitter self-accusations cut through my mind like sinuous knives and tormenting spirals. Toward morning, when the first gray light trickled through the barred windows, I grew calmer. "I must do something," I decided.

I wrote a letter to the Gestapo, requesting permission for a brief meeting with my wife. Permission was quickly refused. "Marabou," the captain of the guards, read to me the contents of the Gestapo's reply: *"Communication between confirmed enemies of New Germany is not permissible. Heil Hitler!"* I wrote again— and received no answer. Then I wrote another letter, this time to the President of the Special Tribunal, asking for information about the reasons for Firelei's conviction and the length of her sentence. The curt answer read:

"Your wife has been sentenced to six years of penal servitude for preparation of a treasonable undertaking. She is serving her sentence in the Women's Prison in Luebeck.

Signed: Dr. Roth.

Immediately I set the intelligence *Apparat* of the *Spitzengruppe* in motion to inquire into the details of Firelei's arrest and conviction. Recently arrested communists in Camp Fuhlsbuettel, who had been sent to Germany from Copenhagen and who subsequently had been questioned about Firelei by the Gestapo, were able to supply fragments of information. By piecing these fragments together with minute care, Tonio and I came to the following conclusion:

Firelei had continued to work for the Comintern in Copenhagen until October, 1934, eleven months after my arrest in Hamburg. After my capture by the Gestapo, she had, in a flurry of despair, accused Ernst Wollweber of being responsible for my arrest. In the spring of 1934, the Western Secretariat had received a report from Berlin that I had died in Camp Fuhlsbuettel. Half out of her mind with anguish Firelei had written a letter and addressed it to Ossip Piatnitzky at the Comintern headquarters in Moscow, for she knew that Piatnitzky had a high opinion of me as a maritime organizer. She wrote in this letter that Ernst Wollweber had dispatched me to Germany for no other reason than that of getting the ISH (International of Seamen and Harbor Workers) subsidies under his personal control. She had entrusted the letter to a Belgian comrade who was passing through Copenhagen on his way to the Soviet Union. Whether this letter ever reached Moscow, or whether the Belgian turned it over to someone in the Westbureau, I did not know. I learned many months later that the Belgian had surrendered it to Richard Jensen, and Jensen to Wollweber.

The fact remains that Wollweber, shortly after the letter had been written, sent Firelei on a secret mission to Germany. On her journey to Germany, Firelei was accompanied by another courier of the Western Secretariat, one Kurt Bailich, a former leader of the Party organization in Altona. I knew Kurt Bailich. He was a dapper, smooth-faced young man, an able conspirator and a master of three languages. But Bailich was also one of the most clever foreign agents of the Gestapo. Late in November, three weeks after her clandestine arrival in Germany, Firelei was arrested by the Gestapo in Bremen and transferred to Hamburg for questioning by Inspector Kraus. Nine months after her capture, she was sentenced to six years of penal labor at a secret session of the Special Tribunal in Hamburg.

"Two men who are responsible must suffer for this," I said grimly. "One is Wollweber, the other Kurt Bailich."

Tonio fixed his blue eyes at me for a long time. Finally he said: "You are upset. Let at least one night pass. Never forget that you are a member of our *Spitzengruppe. Wir sind Blutstropfen im Herzen der Partei!* (We are drops of blood in the heart of the Party.) Never forget that, my comrade."

"It had been proven that Bailich is a spy."

"I'll advise Copenhagen," Tonio said. "He'll be hunted down."

A man in prison, crowded in on all sides by fellow-prisoners who once were active in all the tentacles of the communist octopus, gains a far better insight into inner-organizational secrets and intrigues than the comrade who is still active and "free," and who, therefore, learns little beyond the doings of his own limited *Apparat*. I had heard much and I had kept silent. *And I knew that nearly every one of the many comrades whom Ernst Wollweber had sent on secret missions into Germany had fallen prey to the Gestapo 'within a month or two after he or she had crossed the German frontier.*

"Wollweber is a murderer," I said quietly.

Tonio stared at me in silence.

"Wollweber is the destroyer of our best staff workers," I added.

Tonio crossed his arms over his chest. His indomitable face looked down. "Comrade Ernst is the most consistent Bolshevik in the German Party," he answered slowly.

All through the following night I thought of Firelei. I shall not attempt to describe my thoughts and emotions. On the paillasse beside mine, Tonio snored in militant unconcern. He always slept soundly. He had even deliberately fallen asleep during his trial for high treason.

Dawn came.

All day Tonio argued with me. He argued with all the persistence and sincerity of a man defending his own naked life. "The Party is our life," he said. "Without the Party, we cannot live. Look at me! Should the Party take the life of my own mother, I will still say: I'm a Bolshevik! I shall remain a Bolshevik!"

Inside of me voices raged:

"Firelei is in prison!"

"Prison will not daunt her," Tonio said.

He won. Late at night, we shook hands. On our sacks of straw we lay so close together that we could feel each other's pulse-beat.

"Never say die," Tonio whispered with a wild elation. "In my next report to Copenhagen, I am going to recommend you as the best Bolshevik I have met since the Gestapo took me."

The *S-Apparat* of the Comintern eventually received all the data we had collected on the spy Kurt Bailich. The G.P.U. hunted the traitor through four European countries. But Bailich escaped to Germany, and for eighteen months he disappeared from my ken.

In 1938, his presence was reported in New Orleans. Bailich had been transferred in December, 1935, to the Gestapo's North American division.

However, another Gestapo spy, more important and more dangerous than Kurt Bailich, did not escape our vengeance. He was Martin Holstein, who had betrayed me, and hundreds of other comrades to Hitler's secret police. Until the beginning of 1936 no one among us had seriously suspected Holstein of being a traitor. He had been too cautious, too clever, and he knew well how to play the role of a fanatical revolutionist. His ultimate discovery was due to a coincidence. The political leader in Hall Seven had been summoned to the Gestapo for questioning. While he was being grilled in one of Inspector Kraus' torture-chambers, the door was opened abruptly and a smartly-dressed man burst into the room. The intruder was Martin Holstein. The recognition between him and our comrade from Hall Seven was quick and mutual. Holstein, without uttering a word, had turned and rushed out of the room.

"Who was that man?" the Gestapo agent who was questioning the communist from Hall Seven asked suspiciously.

"I don't know," the comrade answered.

Returning to the prison that night, the comrade reported to Tonio that he had seen Holstein move freely in the headquarters of the Gestapo. Such proof was conclusive: Holstein was the traitor for whom we had searched through the years. The fact was communicated to the *S-Apparat* in Copenhagen. The hunt for Martin Holstein began.

One day in September a corpse was fished out of the Rhine below the harbor of Duisburg. It was the corpse of a man whose throat had been slashed from ear to ear. The dead man was identified as Martin Holstein, the traitor.

The late summer of 1936 brought a grim end to our magic life in Hall Eleven. It was a scorching day in August. The men from Hall Eleven marched through the yard in closed formation. Sixty sweating men swung their legs and arms in a cloud of yellow dust. We marched, as always, closely packed, with not more than a foot of space between the back of one and the front of another.

In the first row marched Tonio. He was one of the tallest. He held his bold head high and his eyes glittered alertly. He crammed a maximum of physical motion into his goose-step, and his deep chest expanded visibly with every breath. His eyes roamed across the yard, and upward along the walls of the cell blocks, sharply scanning the small squares of the windows for familiar faces, always ready with an encouraging smile, always ready to strengthen purpose and defiance. Well I knew the warming grin that invaded the face of this or that comrade in his solitary cell when he caught the flashing salute and the dauntless smile of Tonio. All day that comrade would be a stronger man. "I have seen Tonio," he would think, "and he has told me to carry on."

In the middle of the sweating column marched Gottlieb, the theorist of Hall Eleven, white-haired and smooth, and always scheming to raise a little cheer. I heard his voice, subdued so as not to reach the ears of patrolling guards, for speaking in the yards was forbidden.

"Tell me," said Gottlieb, "what would you prefer in this furnace weather: a glass of iced beer, a roast duck, or a pretty girl?"

There were chuckles in front and behind him as the question was passed from man to man. "Beer," most of us said. "Duck," sighed Albers, the banker. "The girl," croaked an old convict named Udje. "The girl, just once more before I die." At the head of the column Tonio turned his head. "The world is ours," he proclaimed. "Down your modesty! First the duck and the beer, and then the girl."

Soft laughter passed down the length of the marching column, down to the very end, where a safe-cracker whom we called Tarzan shambled through the dust, short and immensely broad, and scowling through streams of perspiration.

Only one man showed no mirth. The laughter of the others seemed to hurt him. He was a youngster, barely twenty-two, with a handsome face that seemed to suffer under unbearable gloom. His name was Oswald. The others shunned him as a traitor. He had been a member of a terrorist group in the Party's *S-Apparat*, and had taken part in the assassination of a police officer in Hamburg. Arrested, he had given away the names of the comrades in his unit; the leader, a young communist named Lindau, had died under the Nazi ax, and his accomplices had been sentenced to prison for life. For Oswald, life behind the walls and bars became an intolerable hell. He was isolated by his comrades, despised, left alone with his own bleak thoughts. He could not live without the Party. He hungered to atone for his betrayal. "Kick me," he screamed, "kill me if you like, punish me! Do something! Anything! But don't leave me so alone!" A contemptuous silence had been the answer of the communists in Hall Eleven. Now, in the yard, Oswald danced abruptly out of the line. He lurched crazily, hurling vituperation at the guards. The guards came at a run.

"Beat me up!" Oswald howled. *"Lieber Herr Wachtmeister,* beat me up! Beat me hard! Let everybody see how you beat me! Beat me!"

One of the guards, a burly young roughneck, brandished his club.

"A beating you want?" he growled. "Any amount! I'll give you a beating!"

While Oswald was cruelly beaten, "Marabou," the captain of the guards, appeared in the yard.

"Attention!" a guard barked.

We all stopped in our tracks. "Marabou" inquired into what had happened. The guards stood sheepishly. "I wanted a beating," Oswald explained piteously, "because I have betrayed my friends." "Marabou" spoke to him soothingly. Then he turned toward us. His voice rang like a pistol shot.

"Fiends! Scoundrels!"

He ordered all prisoners to line up in single file and strip naked. Then he blew his whistle, and additional guards hastened from the cell blocks. We stood in the sunlight, naked, our hands raised above our heads.

"Search the lot of them," "Marabou" ordered the guards. "Search the carcasses and search the clothing."

The search lasted all of two hours. The guards found knives, illegal pencils, tobacco and several fire-stones. One of them drew a strip of paper from the pants of a prisoner. He stared at it, then handed it to "Marabou," who scrutinized the paper. His face tightened dangerously.

"Ten Commands for Young Communists in the Hitler Youth," he read aloud, adding: "Interesting, exceedingly interesting."

The comrade in whose clothes the paper had been found was one of our couriers in Hall Eleven. "Marabou" had him step forward, and slapped his face.

"Did you write this?" he snapped.

"Yes, sir," the comrade answered.

"What's your trade?"

"Laborer."

"This epistle is very neatly written. Could a common laborer write like that?" "Marabou" observed. He drew a notebook and a fountain pen from his breast pocket and handed them to the prisoner. "Now show me how you write," he commanded. "Write: 'Hitler Youth.'"

The comrade wrote in a clumsy scrawl. "Marabou's" eyes narrowed.

"Now tell me who wrote this sheet of instructions," he said softly.

"I wrote it," the comrade answered. His loyalty was superb.

"Marabou" ordered him to dress. "We are going to send you to the Gestapo," he said. "They'll loosen your tongue there." And, facing the column of naked men he hissed: "The whole lot of you will stand here naked in the yard until I know who has written this treasonable stuff."

Until nightfall we stood in the dust. No one had volunteered any information. The comrade on whom the incriminating paper had been found did not return from the Gestapo. But others, coming back from rounds of questioning, reported that the Gestapo had charged the courier with high treason committed while in prison. We never heard of him again. But several days after his transport to the Gestapo, a sinister newcomer was lodged in Hall Eleven.

The newcomer's name was Ludwig Grauer. He was a man approaching his fifties, with a massive body, gorilla-like arms and a ruthless nutcracker face, a man of action and one of the most formidable crooks in the Hamburg prison. One day after Grauer's arrival in Hall Eleven, "Marabou" appointed him as foreman of the hall. Again a day later Grauer received a trusty assistant, a tall, well-knit, red-headed man named Willy Kronenberg. Kronenberg had been, until the spring of 1933, the organization chief of the Anti-Fascist Guards; for money he had sold out his organization to the Gestapo. But the Gestapo's chiefs, after squeezing and buying the last scrap of information from Kronenberg, sent him to prison as a marriage-swindler. Kronenberg had served in the French Foreign Legion. He was an adventurous, unscrupulous type whom one could imagine even going to the gallows without losing his mercenary poise. We discovered that, in Hall Eleven, Kronenberg took his orders from Grauer. They had their paillasses side by side in the most sheltered corner of the hall. The watchers appointed found that Kronenberg and Grauer engaged in lengthy surreptitious conversations night after night. This caused Tonio to request his aides in the administration offices to look over Grauer's dossier. The data they gathered verified our suspicions.

During the World War, when he served as a gunner's mate in the Kaiser's navy, he was already a political spy for the reactionary' officer camarilla, informing on the revolutionary sailors in the fleet. During 1923, the year of the Ruhr occupation, he had spied against Germany for the French general staff. In 1927, he had been sent to prison for selling another man's Rhine ship to Holland. Released in 1931, he had gone into the banking business, and by 1934 he had become the director of a fraudulent enterprise—the *Zwecksparkassen*—which involved several million marks of poor people's savings. Grauer was tried and sentenced to eight years in prison. His dossier in the prison office contained a note from the Gestapo requesting the administration to dispense, in his case, with severe solitary confinement. Grauer, the pirate and bank-director, was a Gestapo spy.

"A fine pair they sent us here," Tonio grumbled. "Grauer and Kronenberg. *Die Gestapo wittert Morgenluft!* They smell a rat." With two seasoned spies among us, the political work in Hall Eleven was practically paralyzed. We exhausted all our contacts and influence to have them removed to another hall. The fact that we did not succeed was sufficient proof that the Gestapo had ordered Grauer and Kronenberg to keep Hall Eleven under constant surveillance. Repeatedly fist fights broke out between maddened communists and the two spies; but the latter two showed themselves to be fearless fighters.

"We had better come to terms with the cut-throats," Tonio advised. "Cultivate them, incriminate them, neutralize them."

Late the same night someone came crawling in the darkness to the window corner where Tonio and I had our sleeping sacks. The nocturnal visitor was Oswald, the traitor.

"Listen," he said tremulously. "You think I am a traitor. That's not true. I am a comrade. I will prove it."

"What's on your mind?" Tonio asked him.

"I am going to kill Grauer," Oswald whispered. "I am going to kill Kronenberg."

"Nonsense," I muttered. "We can't get away from this hall. We'd all pay for it a hundredfold."

"I am going to kill them both," Oswald said happily.

Tonio shook him by the shoulders. "You're crazy! Get back to your paillasse and leave us alone!"

Oswald patted Tonio's chest. He did not say another word, but crept away among the sleeping forms as silently as he had come. "Is he perhaps co-operating with Grauer?" I asked Tonio.

"Oswald is no provocateur," Tonio replied. "We can do nothing. He is crazy."

I fell asleep. Between three and four o'clock in the morning a hoarse scream roused everyone in Hall Eleven. Sounds of struggle came from the inky blackness of the lower sleeping platform. Then yells again, hoarse and wild, yells for help. Somehow everybody knew that the yells came from Grauer's throat. No one rose to help him, not even Kronenberg. By the time the night guards burst into the hall, the yells had subsided into spells of protracted moaning. The electric lights blazed. Grauer lay on the stone floor, his face and chest spattered with blood. Oswald was not in sight. The guards found him in the lavatory, giggling to himself. He had slashed Grauer's face and neck with a pair of scissors, such as were used by the bast weavers.

The rest of the night we all stood lined up in the corridor, our arms raised, clad in nothing but our shirts. There was a constant running and shouting of the guards, and an inquiry was on. At nine o'clock in the morning, a detachment of Gestapo men swooped down on the prison. The seventeen best-known communists in Hall Eleven, Tonio and I among them, were transferred from the prison to solitary cells in Concentration Camp Fuhlsbuettel. The whole prison was ransacked by the Gestapo. Batches of prisoners from other halls were sent away to Oranienburg, to Buchenwalde, to Dachau.

Again I lay in the house of horrors. The days passed with mocking slowness; and the memory of life in Hall Eleven was like the memory of some distant, unattainable paradise.

Chapter Thirty-eight

MY BATTLE FOR MEIN KAMPF

The twenty-ninth of September began like any other day in Camp Fuhlsbuettel. The night had been loud with the arrival of new loads of prisoners, with curses and commands that came like pistol shots, with the wakeful moans of the chained, the banging of doors and the roar of airplanes. The bell rang at six-thirty, and ten minutes later the guard entered my cell, took the shackles off my ankles and my left wrist to allow me to put my cot in order, to visit the toilet and sweep up the imaginary dust on the floor. Then he shackled my hands together on my back and threw a chunk of black bread into my cell. And I lay down on the floor and gnawed away at the bread.

Until about ten nothing further happened, except that I paced the cell, oblivious of time, occupied in making a mental list of all zoological terms I had encountered in my previous reading. When the key suddenly rattled in the lock and the door swung open I sprang under the window and yelled out my name, my number, and the charge of which I had been convicted. The guard stepped aside. Into my cell walked Rudolf Heitman, broad-shouldered, blue-jowled, thin-lipped, a pale double-chin resting on a lily-white collar.

Heitman nodded to the guard. *"Sist in Ordnung,"* he said. "You can lock me in."

The trooper locked the door behind Heitman—the G.P.U. man in the Gestapo. An instant later I saw that the guard had raised the small metal shield from the spy-hole in the door and was peering in through the glass disk. Under such circumstances, I could not greet Heitman. I continued to stand at attention.

Heitman pushed me rudely against the wall.

"You look too damned contented," he shouted. "Guys like you ought to be hung with barbed wire."

I regained my balance. Heitman reached out and struck the side of my head, and now I let myself fall to the ground. The pale blue eye of the guard outside was still glued to the spy-hole.

Heitman roared: "Stand on your feet! Who gave you permission to lie down?"

I raised myself and faced him squarely. Heitman's teeth were bared and his thin mouth curved down at the corners.

"Are you going to tell me the truth?" he bellowed.

"Yes, sir."

Heitman produced a photograph. Holding it in the palm of his hand, he brought it close to my eyes. It was a passport photo of a blond young man.

"Do you know this fellow?" Heitman demanded.

"No, sir."

Instantly his left fist hit my nose. It began to bleed.

"Do you know the man in this picture?"

"I don't know him," I said, tensely aware that the purpose of his visit had nothing to do with the question he asked.

At the spy-hole the guard's eye blinked.

"Shall I call in the boys to give you a whipping?" Heitman asked.

"No, sir," I said.

"Then tell me all you know about this man," he roared.

I was silent.

Again Heitman brought the hand with the photograph close to my eyes. He crouched in front of me as if ready to spring; his face was contracted, his small eyes gleamed.

"Look at this picture," he said softly, "and tell me what you know about this man."

I stared at the photograph. Now it was a photograph of Ernst Wollweber which Heitman had in his hand, a small photostatic copy of a picture of Wollweber which had appeared years before in the *Arbeiter Illustrierte Zeitung*.

"Look well," Heitman growled. "Think it over."

Slowly, with an almost imperceptible motion of his thumb, he turned the picture around in the palm of his hand, his broad back turned stonily upon the guard at the spy-hole. A short message had been printed on the reverse side of the photograph. My eyes absorbed letter after letter, memorizing each word as it slid along:

"Attempt entry into *PP-Apparat*. Situation favorable. Talk with caution."

"Was this man known to Ernst Wollweber?" Heitman barked.

"I think he was," I said quietly.

"You think, do you? Was he, or was he not?"

"He was."

Heitman shoved the photograph back into his pocket. He threw his head back and his throat bulged forward.

"So you saw him take orders from Wollweber?"

"Yes, sir."

"What kind of orders?"

"Police work, I believe," I said.

Heitman grunted. "Aha!" Peevishly he added, "You could have told me that at once."

He turned and pounded on the door of the cell. The trooper outside opened it at once.

"You may go about your duties," Heitman told him. "Our friend here is becoming tractable."

The Death Head guard was satisfied with what he had heard. He locked the door again, and then his departing footfalls rang on the floor of the corridor. We were alone now. Heitman relaxed. He pulled out a flask and drank. My mind was on the message. *PP-Apparat* was the communist designation for undercover work inside an enemy police force. I had no fear of Heitman. I knew enough about him to send him to a tryst with the headsman. Heitman was aware of this. He would never try to plunge me into a trap.

"Well, I am waiting," I said quietly.

He spoke in low tones. Instead of "Westbureau" we used "firm" and in place of *PP-Apparat* we substituted "our competitor."

"I've spoken with a man from the head office," Heitman said. "The firm has received Tonio's estimate of your qualities. You should try to join our competitor. The firm wants more men on the inside to tell them when and where to strike—for increased sales."

I understood the significance of the message. The Western Secretariat had appointed me to maneuver myself into the Gestapo. Such assignments had been given before. But, with two or three exceptions, the comrades who had tried to carry them out came to grief, and sudden death.

"Impossible," I said. "I am too discredited."

Heitman shook his head. "You will find the ground prepared," he murmured. "You will have co-operation. Our competitor is always on the lookout for bright young men. It'll take time—and patience. And cool blood."

"How?"

"The point is not to make an outright offer. Nothing that's clumsy or suspicious. The problem is to bring the competitors to a point where they'll come and invite you: 'Brother, how about it?' Understand?"

I crouched near the door, my left ear against the steel, listening for the steps of approaching guards.

"But..."

I showed Rudolf Heitman the document I had received after my transfer from the penitentiary to the concentration camp. Printed on blood-red paper was the legend:

ORDER FOR PROTECTIVE CUSTODY

The bearer, prisoner......, has been returned to Ko-La-Fu because he endangered the peace and order of the State Penitentiary.

(For the Gestapo): Paul Kraus.

"There you are," I said, "solitary confinement...chains..."

"That's fine," Heitman countered. "A man in chains is likely to do anything to get rid of the shackles. You have rummaged for years. You have given up the old ideas. You are ready to capitulate. That'll be your line. It's not so hard to fool people who think they're all-powerful."

"What would be the procedure?" I asked.

Heitman shrugged his shoulders. "It's your comedy," he muttered, "not mine. I can tell you only the beginning of the first act. After that you'll have to sail alone."

"Sail into the grave," I grinned.

"Or to freedom," Heitman said vaguely.

"All right. What's the beginning?"

"Ask for permission to read *Mein Kampf*. That's always safe. Then appear to be shocked by the mass shootings in Russia. Since Kirov bit the pavement, thousands have been shot, all ages, all nationalities. Let them know, somehow, that you're shocked. Bring yourself in conflict with the firm. Then wait for results. You'll win if you're lucky. How long have you been in the bunker?"

"Nearly three years," I said.

"Long enough to make any man break with his past," Heitman growled. "The thing is to be lucky. Luck counts for more than mathematics."

"I'll think it over."

"Look at me," Heitman smiled glumly. "I'm in it for years. And I'm alive just the same." He said it, I felt, more to reassure himself than to urge me on. A few minutes later he shouted for the guard.

Heitman departed with a curt "Heil Hitler!" The guard clicked his heels. He put the irons back on my wrists. Then I was alone again.

I paced the cell all afternoon. Night came, and I did not sleep a wink. I was oblivious of hunger and cold. Every inch of me was in fever and uproar. From the beginning I knew: this would be an ugly business, the most dangerous, the most difficult, the most deadly assignment of my career. I did not think a successful termination of this mission within the scope of possibility. I was firmly convinced that by embarking on it I was bound for certain death. I asked myself: 'Are you still a good Bolshevik?" Half the night I fought with myself to arrive at an affirmative answer. The faint aroma of a cigarette smoked by a night guard on the tier disturbed me in this battle.

But before the next morning bell sounded, I decided to go ahead. I felt myself a lone wanderer, surrounded by desolation, with nothing to rely upon except myself.

I asked the guard on duty for permission to read Adolf Hitler's *Mein Kampf*.

This guard was new on the tier. Guards were changed every few weeks to prevent them from becoming friendly with the prisoners. He flatly refused my request.

I let two days go by. Of course, I had read the book before, but, for two reasons, it was essential for me now to get it. One was that the Gestapo kept a close record of each prisoner's correspondence and reading matter; imprisoned men who seemed to spend much of their time over official Nazi literature were generally considered as being at odds with their former *Weltanschauung*. The second reason was that I wanted to acquire a thorough knowledge of National Socialist conceptions and phraseology in order to be able to meet the Gestapo chieftains on their own ground at some date to come.

On the third morning I asked to be led before the *Lagerkommandant*.

"For what reason?" the guard demanded.

"I wish to make a statement," I said.

"A personal statement? Nothing doing."

"A political statement, *Herr Wachtmeister.*"

The guard was impressed. He went off with clanking boots, and ten minutes later he returned and took off my manacles.

"Step out. The *Kommandant* wants to see you."

The commander of Camp Fuhlsbuettel lounged behind a battered desk. His office was overheated and cluttered with files and papers. Portraits of Nazi leaders lined the walls. The *Kommandant* was a slender, graying man with soldierly features. He wore the black uniform of the Elite Guard. A saber scar ran from his temple down to his mouth, a souvenir of a duel, or of the World War, or of his years in the French Foreign Legion. When I entered the office, clicking my heels and reporting in the sharp customary manner, he waved several clerks—also members of the Elite Guard—out of the room. For some time he looked me over. I stared at the pale blue eyes of the man under whose regime in Camp Fuhlsbuettel so many of my comrades had perished. Finally he snapped:

"Why are you here?"

"I wish to ask—"

"I don't want to know what you wish," he interrupted. "Why are you in protective custody?"

"I was accused of stirring up unrest in prison."

I saw that the *Kommandant* liked my frank answer.

"Is the accusation true?"

"In part—yes," I admitted.

"Why did you do it?"

"I saw the futility of the old ideas," I replied. "I despaired. To avoid facing the truth, I struck out in the opposite direction."

"That seemed easier than facing the truth?" he asked shrewdly. "Yes, sir. It seemed—for a time."

"Why were you sent to prison?"

"For illegal work against the Third Reich."

"How much?"

"Thirteen years."

"You were lucky. Had I been judge, you'd have been shot." Silence. He scanned me minutely. I looked straight into his face. His type had no love for servile skulkers.

"Why are you kept in irons?" he asked.

"I attempted suicide."

"All that I know," the *Kommandant* drawled lazily. "But you came to make a political statement. Now, out with it."

"I'd like permission to read *Mein Kampf*," I said.

At first he scowled. He had probably expected something else. Then he smoked thoughtfully. After a while he said: "Why should a traitor like you want to read the *Fuehrer's* book?"

"When a man is much alone, he starts to think, *Herr Kommandant*," I explained. "I said I had to make a political statement. I desire to read the book. That, to me, is a political statement, *Herr Kommandant*?

The *Kommandant* leaned forward. "You are not turning Nazi, are you?" he asked ironically.

"No, sir."

"You are still a communist?"

"I thought I was. But communism in Germany is dead, sir."

"That's tough luck, nicht wahr?"

I nodded. I continued to stand as rigidly as I possibly could. In the presence of the camp commander, no gesture was permitted a prisoner.

"The hardships of camp life are not conducive to communist morale, are they?" the *Kommandant* went on.

"I don't mind the hardships, sir," I answered.

"Hardships make men. Those who crumble under hardships are not worth bothering about. Just what put the idea in your head to read *Mein Kampf*?"

"My life has been irretrievably destroyed, *Herr Kommandant* " I said. "I've no intentions of becoming a *Nationalsozialist*. I cannot. It is too late. But I know that I've belonged to an army which has been beaten—definitely beaten."

"Beaten? . . . Annihilated," the *Kommandant* said. "Go on."

"Annihilated," I admitted. "It was a strong army and it has been annihilated by the Hitler movement. That is why I want to read *Mein Kampf, Herr Kommandant*. I am curious and anxious to understand what gives National Socialism such annihilating strength."

"You should have done that in 1930," the Kommandant observed.

"At that time I was blind, sir."

"And you are still blind?"

"No, sir."

"I don't believe you. You seem to me a Kerl who'd bash his head against a stone wall rather than admit that you were wrong. You shouldn't start crawling."

"I do not crawl, Herr *Kommandant*."

The Kommandant tapped his desk. He spoke crisply: "You find yourself in a situation where honesty is the foe of loyalty, my friend. The Communist Party is rotten from top to bottom. Always was rotten. The fact that very few communists stick to their guns even in hell proves it."

"I cannot profess loyalty to a cause which has ceased to exist," I countered.

"So you wish to read Hitler's book?"

"Yes, sir."

"Request refused. I'll have you chased twenty-five times around the yard instead."

The *Kommandant* pressed a button. A trooper clanked in, stood at attention. The *Kommandant* issued an order.

That ended the interview. I was taken out into the yard by two guards who made me run twenty-five times around the inside of the surrounding walls. The guards ran in a smaller circle. "Faster!" they shouted. "Faster!" If I did not run fast enough, they tripped me and beat me with their truncheons. Two rounds were nearly a kilometer. While I ran I saw the *Kommandant's* slight figure leaning against the barred window of his office. I ran for two hours. Then I sagged to the ground, was dragged back to my cell and handcuffed.

There was a special telephone line directly connecting the *Kommandant's* office with the headquarters of the secret police. I knew that over this wire my petition to obtain *Mein Kampf* had been communicated to the Gestapo. After several eventless days, I was again called to the *Kommandant's* office. With all the resources I could muster I continued the comedy on which I had embarked. To my astonishment, the *Kommandant,* when we were alone, told me to sit down.

He asked me about Cilly who had been his prisoner during the months between our arrest and trial. Her clever defiance, together with her rather exotic charms, had interested him. He seemed to derive some pleasure when I willingly answered a string of questions pertaining to Cilly's personal affairs and her erotic qualities. Finally he asked me point-blank:

"Have you had sexual intercourse with this girl?"

When I nodded, he almost leaped out of his chair.

"Is that true?"

"Yes, sir."

He rose and I saw him work himself up into an unconvincing rage.

He blustered, "You should be ashamed of yourself. A married man, aren't you? And with such a fine wife. I've had a few long talks with your wife. You—don't you feel any shame at all?"

"No, sir," I said.

The *Kommandant* guffawed. "I know all too well how it is . . . in the War . . . any day we might be blown to smithereens . . . anything that smelled of she-flesh we used to squeeze dry before it was too late. This—how'd she call herself?—this Cilly was a good-looking bitch. And you did have a lot of fun with her, did you?"

"Yes, sir," I said.

The *Kommandant* pressed me for details. I invented them for him. In that hour at least Cilly's skill as a mistress fascinated the *Kommandant* more than all the theories of Rosenberg and Hitler.

I felt the ice thaw. Our talk consumed hours. I forged ahead eagerly. The *Kommandant* was irritated whenever the telephone rang or when a guard knocked to ask for instructions regarding the *ordre du jour.*

From Cilly's role as an international voluptuary the conversation shifted to the moral corruptness of leading Bolsheviks in general and to the sexual degeneration of Dimitrov, Wollweber and Heinz Neumann in particular. I told the *Kommandant* weird tales about mass rapes during Stalinist jamborees in Moscow and Paris. Because communists were the culprits, he believed them. The next theme was prostitution in the Soviet Union. From there we jumped to the prices of prostitutes in various zones and climates.

"The greatest fault of the German is his narrowness," the *Kommandant* suddenly declared. "I, too, have seen much of the world."

I endeavored to flatter his pride until he, who was at best a scullion of the Gestapo, found it hard to conceal his pride at being regarded as a man of the world.

"First of all, I serve my country," he said.

I said respectfully, *"Ja. Sie sind Soldat, Herr Kommandant."*

"What you have told me today," the *Kommandant* mused, "all these details about the cesspool beneath the communist belt line—*verdammt*, they'd be worth an article in the *Voelkischer Beobachter."*

There was a short silence. The *Kommandant's* communicative mood tempted me to ask him about Firelei. I realized instantly that I had made a mistake. My vague question regarding my wife's health jerked him back into his customary brusqueness.

"Your wife got what she deserved," he snapped. "No more, no less."

"She never was a confirmed communist," I interjected.

"I know her case," the *Kommandant* said. "She deserted her child rather than face responsibility for the crimes she committed. Abhorrent, that! Worse than a beast. The lowest female beast takes care of her young ones, defends them, dies for them. Shooting is too good for such a one."

I hung in my chair, my arms dangling limp.

"Dismissed," the *Kommandant* barked.

A trooper entered.

"Take him back to his cell."

"Irons, *Herr Kommandant?"*

"Most certainly!"

The rest of that day and the following night remain a hellish memory in my mind. I let another day go by. The next morning I resumed the bitter offensive.

The guard on my tier that morning was a phlegmatic, apple-cheeked fellow whom the prisoners judged the most easy-going in Camp Fuhlsbuettel. When he entered my cell for the daily inspection I told him I wanted to write a letter to the Gestapo.

"What sort of a letter?"

"A confession, *Herr Wachtmeister."*

"Long or short?"

"A long one, *Herr Wachtmeister."*

"Very well."

Each prisoner, no matter how isolated, is always allowed to write to the Gestapo. The Gestapo welcomes letters from prisoners. The more they write, the more they bare themselves, the deeper— usually—do they become entangled in the thousand-and-one snares laid out for enemies of the New Germany. The prisoner may cover any number of sheets with his writing; the only condition is that he delivers to his guard as many sheets as he has received.

The guard brought me three sheets, and pen and ink. He also brought me a piece of board which was to serve as a table. Then he unlocked the irons from my left wrist, leaving them to dangle from my right, and left me. A quick glance at the spy-hole showed me that the trooper kept observing me from the outside. He merely followed camp regulations; many a prisoner, having his hands freed under the pretext of wanting to write to the Gestapo, seized the opportunity to commit suicide.

One sheet I addressed to *Regierungsrat* Schreckenbach, the chief of the Foreign Division of the Gestapo. I wrote a flaming denunciation of communism. I declared that I herewith severed all my connections with the communist cause. I concluded this letter with the sentence, "I am a German. I realize that he who embraces communism accepts the betrayal of his fatherland as a pan of his duty to Moscow." I added that I agreed to the publication of this declaration in the Nazi press. The Gestapo liked to publish such declarations, most of which were obtained under torture, on the assumption that they would do much toward demoralizing the remnants of the "underground" opposition.

The two remaining sheets I filled with notes about real and invented acts of profligacy of communist chieftains who had been more or less in the headlines of the German press since 1933. Over this slush I affixed the title "So live the would-be wreckers of the German family." This expose I addressed to the *Kommandant* of Camp Fuhlsbuettel.

The guard who received the two letters for dispatch grinned broadly. "I know what it means when a former *Staatsfeind* writes to the Gestapo," he said. "The inner struggle.... Oh, yes—solitary confinement and the inner struggle." He went away chuckling.

Nothing happened for a week. The monotony, the routine brutality, the food gobbled up from the floor, the banging doors and angry shouts and the screams of beaten men, the constantly gnawing pain in my wounded wrists—all that remained the same. Different only was the manner in which I occupied my brain. I had succeeded in forcing myself not to think of Firelei. I had abandoned my usual grind of mechanical mental exercises. My brain was filled—even in its dreams—with but one train of thought: "How can you best carry out the command of the Comintern?" This central problem gave birth to uncounted silent questions and a multitude of equally silent answers. I had been stripped of most illusions; I saw the Comintern for what it was. But I clutched at the task. I was afraid of emptiness. Regardless of how it ended, it seemed to bring a purpose into my life again. At the end of the week I wrote another letter to the Gestapo. I humbly asked for permission to study *Mein Kampf* by Adolf Hitler.

Early next morning, under supervision of two troopers, I was shaved by a tight-lipped, elderly Jewish prisoner.

"You are going to the Gestapo," a trooper informed me with a parting kick.

I was marched to the ground floor of the old prison, and stood nose and toes against the wall for several hours. To my right and left a long line of prisoners also stood nose and toes against the wall, waiting. At last I was herded into the prison van. As usual, it was overcrowded. But while the lorry rumbled through the streets toward the Gestapo headquarters I realized that the prisoners who were being carried to torture sessions in the latter part of 1936 were different types than the militants of the first three years of Hitler power. There were more Jews, professional men, Catholic priests, small merchants and others who never had belonged to the Party or the proletariat. I tried to draw one or the other of them into a discussion. But they were too frightened to speak, it seemed. My thoughts turned to my own problems. "Why are you being called to the Gestapo?" I asked myself. My whole future hinged on the answer to that question.

The truck veered into the yard of Gestapo headquarters, the yard in which Karl Burmeister had died a thousand days earlier. I was not driven into the waiting-room of the Gestapo. I was led into the basement dungeons and locked into a closet which barely provided standing room. There was a small grill in the closet door. Through it I smelled the wondrous aroma of pea soup. Imprisoned prostitutes ran around freely in the corridor, bearing brooms and mops and stacks of tin bowls. At last I was called. "Keep calm, now," I told myself.

A young Elite Guard handed me a book. It was *Mein Kampf*.

"When you have read it," he said, "give it to the prison library in Ploetzensee."

I was startled. "Ploetzensee?" I asked.

"Yes, you're going to Ploetzensee Prison," the trooper said.

I was marched through filthy corridors to another part of the cellar dungeons. Here a long line of men in crumpled civilian suits, most of them carrying cardboard boxes under their arms, was assembled.

"Step into line," I was told.

A chief guard barked: "Prisoner transport to Berlin-Ploetzensee—listen: Whoever attempts to escape during the transport will be shot! *Links um! Abteilung, marsch!*"

We tramped along gloomy corridors into the yard, where the vans were waiting. They brought us to the station.

"Ploetzensee!" I thought. "What does it mean?"

Ploetzensee was Hitler's central slaughterhouse. All anti-Nazis condemned to death by the so-called People's Courts were brought to Berlin from all parts of Germany to be beheaded in the yard of Ploetzensee Prison.

At the Hamburg *Hauptbahnhof* the prison train was waiting. The train was long. The coaches had no ordinary windows, but grilled air holes high in their sides. A narrow corridor ran through the length of the car. To the right and left of it were small compartments with steel walls and steel doors. Electric lights burned brightly. Some of the compartments had room for only one prisoner; others were fitted to accommodate two and four. Guards and prisoners alike called it the *Henkerszug*—the hangman's train. Together with three others I was herded into a four-man compartment. We waited a long time. New batches of prisoners arrived from various outlying prisons. Through the air hole I could see them march along the platform; there were men and women of all ages, political convicts bound for the numerous prisons in and around Berlin.

I soon got acquainted with my three companions. One, an elderly interior decorator, was a homosexual; one day he had become drunk and had walked through a crowded street, giving the Hitler salute and shouting, "Heil Captain Roehm!" For this he received three years. The other was a small merchant from Bremerhaven, a rotund Nether-Saxon who had assembled his friends to listen to anti-Hitler phonograph records which socialist sailors had smuggled in from England; one of the merchant's friends, after the police had raided a home adjoining his own, had become frightened, and betrayed the merchant to the Gestapo. He had received a sentence of eight years under the new terror laws of 1934. The third of my companions was a soldier, an exuberant and reckless youth. He had written a letter to a former schoolmate in Switzerland, telling him boastfully at what range he could kill a man with a newly-introduced machine gun. The former schoolmate's girl friend was a German and a Nazi. She had read the letter. She had had it photographed in a Nazi spy station in the Swiss town of Zug. The photostat had reached the Gestapo. The soldier was arrested and charged with betraying military secrets. The Special Tribunal, after a half-hour session, sentenced him to life imprisonment.

Toward evening the train began to move. It rolled through the night, crammed with a hapless human cargo. Every night, under cover of darkness, such prison trains rolled through the German land. The guards in the corridors were friendly. They brought us water when we asked for it, and they gave us tobacco and cigarette paper. They did not interfere when the soldier in our compartment began to tap against the steel partitions to communicate with prisoners in the adjoining boxes. The guards even allowed us to shout through the walls.

"Talk your fill," one of them said. "You won't do much talking in Ploetzensee, except to yourself."

Across the corridor from our compartment a man sat alone in his steel coffin. I could not see his face. But he had a deep, pleasant voice. He gave his name as Robert Gerdes, a communist, twenty-six years old.

"Where are you going?" I asked.

"Ploetzensee," said the voice.

"How many years? "

"Just a few days, comrade," he answered. "They're going to cut my head off."

There was a silence. The wheels hammered beneath us. Someone from another compartment asked:

"Death?"

"Death," Gerdes answered.

I gave him my name, the length of my sentence. "Tell me what you wish our friends outside to know," I said.

"I cannot tell you much," Gerdes said. "There are too many ears here. I was arrested in May, 1935. I ran a broadcasting station . . . on a ship . . . on the Baltic Sea. . . They came out with a subchaser and got me . . . never mind the consolations. Tell our friends I'm not sorry . . ."

The conversation lagged. In the cages around Gerdes the prisoners were depressed. The young soldier broke the spell. Two cages away from the condemned man was a girl. She had kept silent for a long time. She, too, was alone.

"Hello, *Puppe*" the soldier shouted. "Have a heart!"

The girl laughed. "I have a heart," she cried. "Wait a second. I'll make it bigger, big enough for you to come in."

"I'm twenty-one," the soldier crowed, "and five foot ten. How old are you?"

"Twenty-four," the girl called back. "What's your name?"

"Albrecht—and yours?"

"Gretchen."

"What did you do?"

"I was a smuggler—and you?"

"I betrayed military secrets," the soldier yelled. "I am a soldier." And then: "Hey Gretchen! What did you smuggle?"

"Other people's money and diamonds ... Cologne to Amsterdam."

"Why didn't you stay in Amsterdam?" the soldier yelled.

Again the girl gave a tinkling laugh. "I was too greedy," she said. "I came back to smuggle some more."

"What did they give you?"

"Four years for economic treason," she replied slowly.

"That's not bad," the soldier said. "I wish I had only four years. Then I'd meet you when I come out. I wish you were with me now. I'd do something to you, something nice."

"Oh, why can't I be with the soldier?" the girl wailed in mock despair. "Have you a good bayonet?"

"No—they took my arms away, silly!"

"A soldier without a bayonet isn't much good," the girl said.

In the corridor the guards laughed softly.

"Guard! Guard!" the girl cried suddenly.

"What do you want?"

"Ask the man two doors away ... Gerdes ... the one who's going to die ... ask him if he'd like to be with a girl."

The condemned comrade's voice said steadily: "I wouldn't mind."

"You would like it, wouldn't you?"

"Yes, I would like it, good girl."

The hammering of the wheels became slower. The locomotive shrieked. The girl pleaded with the guards.

"Be decent," she said. "You've once been young yourselves. Let me go to him. Let me be with him a short half hour."

The guards talked to each other. In the steel boxes the prisoners shouted: "Let Gerdes have Gretchen! Let him have her!"

"Shut up, you dogs!" a guard roared.

"Herr Wachtmeister..." the girl pleaded.

"Es geht nicht," the guard rumbled. "It's against the rules ... I'd get it in the neck ..."

"Gretchen!" Gerdes called her. "Never mind, Gretchen. Accept my thanks."

Gretchen beat her fists against the door.

"Now she's weeping," a guard said disgustedly.

Gray daylight seeped through the air holes. The train was approaching Berlin. The merchant sighed.

"I am troubled about my wife," he said drearily. "The business is going down... she'll have such a hard time... undeserved, undeserved..."

The soldier had become silent. Gerdes was singing one old German folksong after another. The train slowed down. It rolled into a station and stopped. The guards unlocked the doors of our steel cubicles.

"Good-by, Gerdes," Gretchen cried. "Good-by, boy."

"Step out! Single file! No talking, you dogs!"

No one among the prisoners spoke now. The soldier craned his brawny neck. Not far ahead of me walked the girl. She had a slight angular figure, and her face looked thin and serious. The platform was roped off by Elite Guards. Wide-awake eyes stared out of mask-like young faces under black steel helmets. From other platforms and from the windows of the waiting-rooms, scattered groups of civilians gaped in silence. The clocks showed eight-fifteen. The prisoners of each coach were marched off in separate formations. Now it was our turn. The girl and three other women were called out first. Before they went, Gretchen smiled faintly in the direction of Gerdes. Gerdes' taut face—the face of a man who had made self-discipline his god—showed no sign of response. I never saw Gretchen again.

There was the ringing of iron heels on the concrete, and a series of commands, curt and harsh, leaped along the lines of convicted men. One after one we descended from the train. Each two prisoners were handcuffed together. Then a chain was passed through the handcuffs the whole length of the column. So, each man became chained to seventeen others. A dense detachment of policemen surrounded our crew on all sides. A man complained; his handcuffs were too tight, his wrists were swelling rapidly.

"Tut's weh?" asked a policeman, "does it hurt?"

"Ja!"

"That's what I want... *Abteilung, marsch!"*

We marched through the station-hall which by that time was packed with people who stood in a solid mass on both sides of a lane cleared by the police. An old man whimpered; he shambled ahead of me like a decrepit ape. A marching Jew closed his eyes in a gesture of utter desolation. All the others marched erect, their heads high, as if they were proud of their fate, their eyes stony, or defiant, or glued briefly to the shape of young women in the front row of the watching multitude. The watchers stood immobile, staring mutely, some gloomy, some thrilled and curious, but most of them without a trace of expression.

Once outside of the station, we were herded into a grimy windowless truck. As we entered it, the chains which linked the column were taken off. Policemen were with us. Speaking was prohibited. At high speed the truck bounced and rattled through unseen streets. Twenty minutes went by. We stopped suddenly. There was the sound of voices outside, then the clanking of an iron gate. For a few yards the truck moved slowly over cobbles. It halted. Its door swung open. *"Alles raus!"* We were in the yard of Ploetzensee.

We stood in the sunlight with blinking eyes. Red brick buildings with hundreds of barred windows loomed all around. They were encircled by a patchwork of yards and gardens. A brick wall eighteen feet high shut off the grounds from the outside world. Guards in gray uniforms lined the inside of the wall at intervals of fifty yards. Each of them had an army carbine in his hands, a truncheon in a pocket fastened to his trouser leg, and bayonet and pistol in his belt. Low round machine-gun turrets topped the roof of each cell block. From a tall white mast in the front yard a monstrous swastika flag curved lazily in the breeze.

A stiff-backed lieutenant lined us up in the yard. As he called each newcomer's name the one addressed had to report his crime and his sentence. "Possessing fire-arms." ... "Attempted assassination" ... "High treason" ... "High treason" ... "High treason." So it went. "High treason" might have been anything from listening to Moscow radio broadcasts to running an underground printing press or dumping sand into the machinery of a tank factory. "Four years." ... "Ten years." ... "Fifteen years " ... "Life." ... "Death." The prisoners spoke without emotion. The lieutenant checked their reports as though he counted buttons.

In a rambling basement hall we were stripped naked. Each man was told to raise his arms, spread out his legs, and to bend over. Guards inspected every inch of our bodies for hidden contraband. A young physician raced past us and pronounced us healthy. Then we were given a cold shower and prison clothes. The clothes were handed out without regard to the individual's size, except shoes. Each man received a suit of woolen underwear, a pair of ancient gray socks, hobnailed shoes, a pair of shapeless mules, a blue handkerchief, a neck cloth, a black cotton uniform and a round black cap. The right sleeve of each jacket carried a bright yellow stripe. The prisoners who handed out the clothes worked like automatons. But for the snapped orders of the guards not a word was spoken. After each prisoner had been shorn of his hair, and had written a short history of his life, he was escorted to his cell by a taciturn guard.

Solitary confinement predominates in Ploetzensee. There are 1,800 solitary cells in four large cell blocks. The cells range in four tiers. Newly-strung wire nets between the tiers discourage suicide by diving head first to the ground floor. Each cell has a small window high in the wall which faces the yard, a steel door with a spyhole, an open toilet stand, a collapsible iron bed, a work table, a wooden stool, and a rack for wash bowl, plate and spoon. Knives and forks are taboo. There is steam heat, electric light and running water in each cell.

During his first week in Ploetzensee the prisoner is left alone. He sees no one. He has no books to read and no work to do. He does not leave his cell for exercise. Between seven A.M. and seven P.M. he is not permitted to sit down. During the other twelve hours he is not permitted to budge from his bed. Those who violate this rule are handcuffed to the bed, hands and feet; the window of their cell is closed and the steam heat turned on to the limit. In all the cells the radiators are installed beneath the beds. The latest handcuffs are of such construction that they tighten automatically with every accidental tug or jerk—and remain tightened. So the prisoner learns to be very quiet. After this first week, the prisoner enters the routine life of Ploetzensee. He is given work to do. All his work is done in the solitude of his cell. He may be given hunks of old rope to be plucked into oakum; he may be given worn-out army uniforms to be taken apart for re-utilization; or he may be given a store of paper and glue for the manufacture of paper bags. The making of paper bags is the best work available to the political convict in Ploetzensee. But most of them make oakum or take apart old uniforms, toiling from morning until night in a stinking cloud of dust and dirt. The prisoners are paid for their labor. Two pfennigs is an average day's wage.

For thirty minutes each day we were taken out into the yard for exercise. We were formed into columns of thirty men and went through those thirty minutes at an exhausting pace: running in circles, jumping on one foot, leaping like frogs with hands clasped in the back of our necks, galloping through the dust on hands and knees, diving into garbage pits, running backwards with heads stuck between our thighs, goose-stepping with pants lowered beneath the hips. There were many other variations. Each detail was commanded by the guard on duty, and each guard had his own set of ideas about exercise suitable for foes of the Nazi regime. There were, of course, decent men among the guards, mainly soldiers who had served their time in the army, but even they adhered to the man-breaking program in order not to forfeit their chances for promotion. The strongest among us forgot the degradation of this daily *Freistunde* ("free hour"), and even began to like the deadening prance, but for most it was an ordeal unmitigated by thousand-fold repetition. Those who rebelled were thrown into the dungeon, a basement hole of complete blackness, put on bread and water, arid often given nightly beatings. The *Pruegelmeister* (flogging master) wore a mask.

During the "free hour" conversation among prisoners was, as at any other time, severely punished. Nevertheless, each of those hours became a social event. The eternal militants among the inmates of Ploetzensee were experts at furtive contact and conspirative organization. Unnoticed by the guards they slipped information, exchanged the latest news, broadcast warnings about suspected traitors and spies, gave whispered instructions as to release. Their hawk-eyes watched the long rows of cell windows for familiar faces, flashed signals, smiles, and words and gestures of loyalty, encouragement and courage.

During one of these hours I saw two leading functionaries of the Communist Party sit side by side beneath an oak in the yard, munching acorns they picked up from the ground. They were permitted to do that because one had hobbled into the yard with a shattered knee, the other with his left foot swathed in a bloodstained bandage. That was the price they paid for the opportunity of thirty minutes of whispered conversation in the guise of munching acorns. Meanwhile, we others astounded the guards by marching like fiends.

In Nazi prisons, the time-honored method of tapping messages through the walls had gone out of fashion. Guards had ears, and codes could be deciphered. But there were other means of communication, all more or less known to the prison officials, but more difficult to check. The stealing of pencils from the doctor's or dentist's office and the passing of written notes at the end of broomsticks from window to window in the dead of the night; the use of the system of air-shafts which permitted verbal contact from tier to tier in a vertical direction; messages to the kitchen pasted on the bottom of dirty dishes, and messages from the kitchen hidden in a chunk of bread or a pail of cabbage soup. All this was extremely dangerous. Every newcomer among us was considered as a provocateur or an informer of the Gestapo until he had been identified by someone who knew his past or the circumstances of his arrest and conviction.

Once a week each prisoner received a book from the prison library. He had no choice of books: the teacher, a retired petty officer and a fanatical Nazi, decided what each man should read. So, with few exceptions, the literary diet consisted of super-patriotic propaganda, and of harmless scientific treatises, which as often as not, had been written and printed a hundred years ago.

All illustrations bearing any resemblance to a woman were removed before the respective books were given into circulation.

Church service in Ploetzensee prison was compulsory. I had barely entered my cell when a voice had hailed me through the window of the cell on my left.

"What are you?" the voice asked. "Political or criminal?"

"Political."

"When they come around to ask you about your religion, tell them you have become a Catholic!"

I followed this advice The Catholic Church in Germany had fallen on evil days. Adversity did much to cause it to regain its old, half-forgotten fighting spirit. Ploetzensee Prison was well populated by priests and monks from the South and the Rhineland. They had been convicted of all manner of sexual atrocities, but prisoners and guards alike knew that the charges of lewd conduct were merely a device invented by Dr. Joseph Goebbels and the Gestapo to screen the actual political and religious persecution of Catholic organizations and their militants. As a "Catholic" I was frequently visited by priests who attended the spiritual needs of the prisoners. I was surprised to find how close the minds and hearts of these soldiers of God were to the minds and hearts of the German masses. Not one of these priests ever gave me the impression that I was dealing with an opportunist or a hypocrite. I found in them keen-eyed, warm-hearted and understanding crusaders for human rights. Prudence and the watchfulness of the Gestapo forbid me to relate in greater detail my relations with these doughty representatives of religious internationalism, for they are still holding out at their difficult posts in Germany. Suffice it to say that during my sojourn in Ploetzensee Prison I succeeded, with their assistance, in exchanging short notes with Firelei, who continued to fight her own battle in the distant Women's Prison in Luebeck.

Once a week the prisoners of each tier were summoned to attend the prison school, the purpose of which was to impress the minds of the convicts with the glory and the achievements of the Hitler regime. One lesson consumed two hours; during the first hour the teacher would read a chapter from Rosenberg's *The Myth of the Twentieth Century,* or an editorial from Hitler's newspaper, *Voelkischer* Beobachter; in the second hour the prisoners were permitted to ask questions which the teacher then endeavored to answer. Some of our comrades kept the teacher busy with questions, while the rest of us settled down to a conspirative conference, speaking in the lowest of whispers. It often happened that a pointed question of some anti-Nazi convict effectively plunged the teacher into a dilemma. Some of the questions were: "What is the 'just wage' which Dr. Ley, the chief of the Nazi Labor Front, has promised the German worker?" Or: "Why did General Goering tell the people that cannon are more desirable than butter?" Or: "What is the origin of the First of May as a day of workers' parades, and why did Hitler proclaim it as a Nazi national holiday?" Once a communist asked: "What is imperialism?"

The teacher could not find a satisfactory answer. The comrade who had asked the question rose and quoted Lenin's interpretation of imperialism, without, of course, mentioning its author. "That was an excellent explanation of imperialism," the Nazi teacher beamed. "It hits the nail on the head."

Next day prisoners from another tier went to school. That night, back in their cells, they caused chuckles to travel from window to window. The teacher had begun the day's session by asking brightly: "Now, let's talk about imperialism. What is imperialism?"

After some discussion he had given the answer himself. To the prisoners' astonishment, the Nazi teacher gave them Lenin's interpretation of imperialism as his own.

But laughter was rare in Ploetzensee Prison. My cell was situated on the ground floor of Cell Block A. Another wing of this ground floor harbored Death Row. The cells of Death Row were never empty. We passed them daily when going to and returning from the yard. Inside the death cells the lights were kept burning all night, and the doomed inmates were not permitted to wear clothing. In front of each cell door, in a neat pile, lay the pants, the jacket and the boots of the condemned man inside. They only dressed for half an hour each day, when they went to exercise in the yard. Many times I saw them walking over the frozen earth. Every week, old faces vanished, and new faces took their place. The men walked briskly, their wrists shackled together behind their backs. Most of them seemed unconcerned; only a few looked strained or gloomy. Their heads fell at the rate of four to ten each week, and there were weeks when women, working girls and ladies of the nobility, convicted of treason or espionage, were among those who died at dawn. The laws of 1936 were far more savage than the laws of 1933.

Middle-aged men, young men, and mere boys of soldier age goose-stepped in this single file caravan of death. From all points of the compass they had been dragged to Ploetzensee to die. Here the hand-ax was not used. The executions were too numerous, and the guillotine had again come into commission.

Those among us who awoke early in the morning, waiting for the bell to command us to rise, soon learned to recognize the sounds accompanying an execution: the clatter of feet on Death Row at six in the morning, the creaking doors of the shed at the other end of the cobbled square facing Death Row—the shed where the guillotine stood hidden behind a canvas curtain; the sudden rattling of keys in ponderous doors, sometimes the sounds of a futile scuffle, roars of rage and screams for help, or a booming voice singing the *Internationale* and ending with a hoarse shout of farewell to the hundreds who lay listening in their cells, still alive. But most of them went quietly, without imprecation or audible complaint, and only the cries of solidarity, of hate and indignation from distant cell windows, perhaps imparted to the marcher the illusion that he did not die in vain.

In most cases we did not know the names of those who died. But toward noon, when we marched out for exercise, we would often see a heavy patch of sawdust on the cobbles. And we noticed that the guards were then less unfriendly than on other days.

On November 4, 1936, unknown to us who lay behind the thick walls of Ploetzensee, Edgar Andree's warrior head fell under the Nazi knife, after nearly four years of continuous torture. When the news of it was flashed through the prison some nights later, the walls reverberated as if by magic with the singing of the Russian revolutionary Death March. He had gone to his death with the defiant battle-cries of bygone years, a fighter to the last. But the guards who had been with him in his cell during the last moments had seen another Edgar Andree, and they spoke of him—much later—in whispers. When Andree had heard the footsteps of the headsman's assistants approach at dawn, he begged one of his guards to tell a joke.

"I have experienced everything that's good and noble in life," Andree had said. "Now I want to laugh once more before I go."

The guard had said that he knew no joke, but a Nazi lawyer among the attendants volunteered to make Andree laugh. He told a joke about a Jew. Andree was himself a Belgian of Jewish origin. By the time the other had finished telling his anecdote, the cell was filled with people. In addition to Comrade Andree, the guards and the lawyer, there were the headsman's aides, the prosecutor, Death Head troopers and Gestapo agents. All stood guffawing, Andree louder than any of the others.

"When I march out,' Andree told them, "my comrades will watch from the windows and say: 'Look, Andree is going to the guillotine!' They will all watch. They all want me to die as a real Bolshevik; to do that is my duty toward them. Not one of my boys will suspect that I am in truth nothing but a tired comedian of loyalty to a cause in which I have ceased to believe. Gentlemen, I am ready."

Andree died with the cry: "Death to Hitler! Long live the workers' revolution!" He died as revolutionists are expected to die by those who have followed their command. In his honor, the "Battalion Edgar Andree" was formed in Spain, and was counted among the shock troops of the International Brigade. Also, the Frenchmen and Belgians in the "Battalion Paris Commune" elected Edgar Andree as their honorary commander.

It was my fourth winter in Hitler's prisons. Around me men and women I had known toppled into their graves. Among those who died that winter was Franz Lauer, who had been my comrade in Hall Eleven; he attempted escape, and was riddled with bullets from the guns of the Death Head guards. News of his death filtered through the walls of Ploetzensee Prison. He was but one of many. Closing my eyes I saw the dead march through my cell in an endless and silent train. "Are they heroes?" I wondered. "Or are they no more than poor, betrayed wretches, who seem to me like heroes because my brain is blind and drunk and mad?" With savage efforts I fought down the forerunners of despair. By sheer will-power I could make myself hear the roar of guns in Spain, and the shouts of the forward-storming revolutionary volunteers.

"Shoot well, comrades," I would growl, gathering strength to fight my own dark and insidious battle: "Don't waste ammunition, comrades. For every slug—a dead Fascist! Roar, you guns in Spain! Give them the answer for workers' blood spilled in the horror camps. Give them the answer without fail and pity. Give them the answer they deserve. Roar, you guns in Spain! I am with you! We are all with you!"

Chapter Thirty-nine

DARK DUEL

In my cell I diligently studied Hitler's *Mein Kampf*. With a contraband pencil I copied whole sentences and paragraphs on scraps of toilet paper, added admiring comment to the quotations, and left them where they would be found by the guards during the next routine search of my cell. I knew that they would seize the notes, and the prison director would add them to my dossier. Occasionally I received letters from one of my brothers; I was permitted to have them for two hours before they were taken from me, also to be filed with my dossier. In these two hours I scribbled words of disillusionment between the lines. *"It is true,"* I wrote *"Hitler is Germany, and Germany is Hitler."* And: *"Communism is a heinous lie. One cannot be a communist and not be a traitor to the Fatherland."* The letters with such inscriptions, I hoped, would find their way to the Gestapo. They would be noticed, perhaps discussed, and the Gestapo would draw its conclusions—in one way or another. I worked patiently and cautiously, week after week, at this game.

A few days before Christmas, 1936, the majority of communist prisoners launched a secret campaign for a church strike on Christmas Eve. "Refuse to attend church! Let the Nazi pastor talk to empty benches! " were the main slogans of this drive. Deliberately I launched a counter-drive under the cry: "Down with the church boycott! Prisoners, refuse to be terrorized by the godless!" This caused some consternation in the ranks of the political convicts. I induced my cell-neighbor, a reliable comrade whom I had drawn into my confidence, to write a violent epistle against me, condemning me as a renegade, a counter-revolutionary, and a violator of Party discipline. This he did, under the headline: *"Down with the Trotskyist! Down with the lackey of the Church!"* He ended it with the exhortation: "READ—AND PASS ON." During the next exercise hour I dropped this broadside against myself in the yard. A guard picked it up. Before I was returned to my cell, I could see the guard striding toward the administration offices, the paper in his hand. A day later I was called before the prison director. He showed me the paper.

"I must say," he observed, "your communist friends have heaped a goodly load of maledictions on your head."

"They are not my friends," I answered stiffly. "I have broken with communism. If I knew of a way to fight communism, I'd do it."

"Who wrote this barrage?" the official inquired.

"I wish I knew, sir," I said. "I'd wring his neck."

"Oh, you would?"

"Yes, sir."

He nodded in a friendly way and sent me back to my cell.

I continued the grim comedy all through January. I avoided all contacts with other prisoners. When I knew that a guard was listening outside my cell, I hummed the Nazi anthem. I had come to the point where I resembled a man who stands with his head braced against a thick wall, determined to break it, or to crush his skull. And then the wall gave way. One day a guard came into my cell and told me to pack my things.

"Where am I going?" I asked.

"The Hamburg Gestapo wants to see you," the guard replied, glancing at the printed transport-order in his hand.

That night I was again aboard a prison train.

"The duel of darkness has begun," I told myself. "How will it end?"

An Elite Guard led me through the corridors of the Hamburg Gestapo headquarters. We entered a section of the building in which I had never been before. We passed through a door which bore the sign: *Auslandsabteilung*.

The armed sentries stood aside. We were in the offices of the Foreign Division of the Gestapo. The guard took off my handcuffs and ushered me into a thickly-carpeted reception room. In the distance, typewriters clattered, interrupted by the intermittent ringing of telephones. The room was large, light, and well-aired. The carpet was a rich pearl gray. On the wall, in solid black frames, were a map of Germany, regional maps, a map of Europe and another of the world. Behind a large, low desk lounged Hertha Jens. Curtly she signaled the guard to leave.

The years had not changed the traitress. Her clothes were smarter than they had been when I saw her last. On her wrist-watch flashed diamonds. Aside from her finery, she was still the pink-fleshed, large-breasted, capable traitress of 1933. Her blue eyes, in which the lights danced, were hard, and somehow naive. Her teeth were still superb. She nodded pleasantly, and gave me her best smile.

"How do you do?" she said. "We were expecting you." Then she spoke into a tube: "He's here!"

A short, rather grim-faced man came through one of the side doors. His eyes were deep in their caves, but intensely alert.

"Hello," he said briskly. "Glad to see you. You don't look as prosperous as you did when we first had you here."

"No," I said.

"Do you recognize me by any chance?"

"You are Inspector Kraus," I said.

He led me into a small office which adjoined the reception room. In contrast to the latter, it was furnished with studied simplicity. A desk by the window, two hard chairs, several steel lamps, a bookshelf, and a portrait of Hitler. On one side of the room a general staff map of Germany was fastened against the wall, on the other a map of Europe which reached from floor to ceiling.

"Sit down," Inspector Kraus said.

I sat. Facing me, he pushed a silver cigarette case across the desk. "Smoke?"

I took a gold-tipped cigarette. He struck a match and I thanked him. The thought that this was the man who had had me beaten within an inch of my life never left my consciousness. From a drawer he took the letters containing my repudiation of communism and my application for *Mein Kampf*.

"What," he inquired softly, "induced you to write this declaration?"

I feigned embarrassment. "The causes for it go back years," I said. "It is a long story, I fear."

"That's clear.—How long have you been imprisoned now?"

"Thirty-seven months. Since November, 1933."

"That was an unpleasant day. Your story goes back to that day?"

"Further," I said.

Inspector Kraus lit a cigarette. He had the expression of a very passionate smoker. *"Nun,"* he said, "go ahead. Get it off your chest. I am an excellent listener."

I talked, haltingly at first, and then in a continuous flow. At three Inspector Kraus ordered a lunch from a nearby restaurant and Hertha Jens joined us during the meal. I talked until five. Many of the things I said were not lies; they were conclusions I had arrived at in the self-searching and digging which many thousand lonely hours had invited. I used them now because they seemed to fit into my scheme. I was fully aware that the slightest slip of my tongue, a single wrong word or gesture under the experienced ears and eyes of Inspector Kraus, would plunge me to ultimate destruction. Inspector Kraus held the power of life and death. He could make life easy for men, could free men, could keep them incarcerated for life, could make them die fast, or die very slowly. A few times he interrupted me to murmur a question, but mostly he listened, his eyes following the eddies and spirals of tobacco smoke. The more I saw the expression of mingled curiosity and quiet triumph spread over his face, the greater my confidence became.

"What made you join the Muscovites in the first place?" Inspector Kraus asked, interrupting the flow of the blend that I was pouring out to him. "Didn't it strike you that they speak an alien language? That they are like pickpockets sporting a scientific vernacular?"

"To the worker the language of their 'theses' and 'resolutions' is like Chinese," I admitted. "But it was not so in the years following the World War. They seemed to offer a sound solution for a diseased and betrayed Germany. Our so-called democracy was a *Mummenschanz* from the start. I joined the Communist Party as a boy out of the same motives which brought other youths into the ranks of the Hitler movement. Germany was broken then, life had become intolerable, and a radical course away from the shame of Versailles became law to every German who longed for national freedom. I became a communist because I believed the revolutionary workers could build a better Germany. I fought the National Socialists in later years because I believed what my leaders— Thaelmann, Neumann, Wollweber—had told me: that the Nazi movement was neither 'national' nor 'social,' but a mercenary brigade organized by industrialists and bankers for the protection of their stranglehold on the German nation."

Kraus nodded. "Quite right," he said. "What is it that changed your opinion of the character of the Hitler movement? Prison is not likely to produce a cheerful state of mind toward us—or is it? " I had studied the psychology of the Nazi movement and of the Gestapo too long and too thoroughly to stumble over this snag. There was but one effective answer.

"Hitler's achievements changed my opinion of the Nazi movement," I said, and proceeded to give Inspector Kraus all the stereotyped explanations which the Nazi propaganda machine had been circulating for foreign consumption: "The new realization did not come overnight. I struggled against it for years, tooth and claw. But I am not foolish enough to persist calling a square after all the world has seen that it is a circle. Since 1933, there have been no wage cuts for the German workers. When Hitler came to power we had eight million jobless—and now we have almost none. No other government on earth has accomplished that. The workers have vacations with pay. They can make ocean trips to Norway and Madeira for very little money. Employers who pay less than the decreed minimum wage are sent to jail. Germany was weak and despised—now it is strong and respected. The roads which Hitler built—the *Autobahnen*—are the best in existence. Fellow prisoners have told me that the Hamburg slums have been torn down; new, modern houses with gardens were built in their place. Boys and girls who before were condemned to grow up in overcrowded hells and the gutter, are now in the Hitler Youth—they learn wood craft, they go camping, they have all that children should have to be happy. Before 1933 each winter hundreds froze and starved to death; today everyone knows that the Nazi Welfare's slogan, 'No one shall be cold or hungry,' has been translated into reality. Well, neither I nor my comrades expected that Hitler would do so much for the workers. I came to the conclusion that I had been mistaken. I came to the conclusion that the Hitler movement was *national* and *socialist* in the best sense. I came to the conclusion that I had made a ghastly mistake."

"I've said that already to many of the ex-Muscovites we've had up here," Inspector Kraus observed. "What did you fellows want here? Fight Hitler! Isn't it Hitler who has fulfilled many of the communist demands? Curbed capitalism? Broken the bourgeoisie? Cowed the church? Given security to the workers?

Refused to let Germany be bled white by the foreign bank sharks?"

"Hitler has done that," I said. "It was hard to admit, but it is the truth."

"Bitter, eh?"

"Yes, it was bitter," I said. "Bitter to find that one has been fighting on the wrong side."

"When did you begin to think that the Comintern was not so holy?" Kraus inquired suddenly. "Why did you stay with them so long?"

"The Hitler movement is built on the soldier ideal," I answered. "The Comintern is built up on military discipline. Hitlerism has an ideal. Communism rejected ideals—it recognized only historical materialism. What both had in common was the soldier attitude. I was a soldier. The soldier's highest virtue is loyalty."

I went on, for a long time, uninterruptedly, afraid to let Inspector Kraus listening brain slip from my grasp: Of course, by 1933 I had lost my brotherhood-of-man illusions; I recognized the Comintern as a mere instrument for the promotion of the imperialist aims of the Soviets, and its chiefs as a band of shyster lawyers and brigands. Yet I remained in the communist movement, a serf of Moscow, because I valued loyalty to a once chosen cause above all; because I despised the deserter; because I considered myself a soldier who fights with his army without asking whether his side is right or wrong. The decisive break developed during the years which followed my arrest by the Gestapo, which were years of painful inner struggle toward light. I heard what Hitler was doing for the German people. I recognized as falsehood everything the Jewish-Communist press printed about the New Germany. My own life, my home, my family had been wrecked, not by the Nazis, but by the communist leaders and their inhuman intrigues. I saw how I had been fooled. I had come to hate the leaders who had wrecked my chances for a decent existence. Allegiance to the Comintern was allegiance to the Kremlin, and equal to the crime of high treason. I had, at last, discovered that I was a German, that I belonged to Germany, that there was only one way in which I could atone for the crimes I had committed: to serve Germany by fighting its enemies, the communists, the overfed democracies, the emissaries of Judah! I hated the Jews. Was it not a Jew I had assaulted in California more than ten years ago?—All this had created in me the overwhelming urge to openly reject the communist creed. I wanted a clear break. I wanted all my former comrades to know that I was a communist no more. That is why I had written the declaration; I wanted it to be the tombstone of my ill-spent and futile past.

While I spoke, a number of Gestapo agents, single and in pairs, came into the office to report in whispers on the progress made in the questioning of various prisoners. A few of them put typewritten sheets on the inspector's desk. After receiving short comments or instructions, which their superior gave in a low, rapid voice, these agents departed. On one occasion Inspector Kraus placed, as if by chance, one of the typewritten pages on a spot directly under my eyes. My impulse was to throw a surreptitious glance at the writing. I controlled the impulse: the section of a report lying so close in front of me looked too much like a trap.

"When we first got you, you seemed a hard nut to crack," Inspector Kraus said, after I had finished. "Pity you didn't think then as you say you think now. You could have given us a lot of first-rate information at that time. Now, after years.... Anyway, you've traveled a long, long way."

Hertha Jens, ever-watchful under her placid exterior, interjected:

"Why, then, did you organize the communist training centers in the Hamburg and Berlin prisons? It doesn't seem to make sense!"

"You'll have to explain that," Inspector Kraus muttered.

I made my decision on the spur of the moment. Through my brain flashed the thought: "If you deny that you built up a schooling system, they won't believe you, they'll question the sincerity of what you've just told them; and if you admit that you did organize those training centers, you confess to a charge of high treason and lay yourself open to another trial and a possible death sentence." For a fraction of a second my whole plan hung in the balance. I told myself it was too late for retreat.

"I helped to set up the training centers in an attempt to kill the growing doubts in my own mind," I explained. "I faced communism with hostility, but I was afraid to admit this to myself. I was afraid of going mad. That's why I started this—to keep myself from thinking. Besides, in a prison full of communists, any comrade who does not do what is expected of him is likely to get hurt."

Strange as it may seem under the circumstances—I had spoken the truth. Though it was not fear of my comrades that had made me organize Stalinist courses in prison.

"Who was the head of the organization?" shot Hertha Jens.

"Lauer," I said.

Comrade Lauer was dead. I could not hurt him.

"And what were the roles of all the others we grabbed in that affair?"

I hesitated. "They were small fry," I said finally. "Please don't demand that I incriminate simple workers who have been made harmless already."

Inspector Kraus' face tightened. "For the time being," he said, "we shall not press you. There is bigger game than the few stinkers in prison."

"Let him tell us about them," Hertha Jens insisted.

"No," Inspector Kraus interrupted. "Why spoil a perfectly good day? We'll get the information when we want it." Facing me, he added slowly: "I am glad that you have written a renunciation of communism. Are you willing to see it published?"

"Yes," I replied steadily.

"I don't think we shall publish it," Inspector Kraus observed. "You still have a good name in the Party. Why spoil a useful reputation?"

He gathered up a handful of cigarettes and handed them to me. "Take them," he said. "I see you like to smoke. I'll phone the *Kommandant* to let you smoke."

I had broken through the first barrier. From now on I was moving in enemy country. "I must pretend that my friends are my foes, and that my foes are really my brothers," I thought. I loathed to take cigarettes from the man at whose hands thousands of my comrades had been tortured and degraded, at whose behest many of the best had been murdered in cold blood.

I took the cigarettes.

That night in Camp Fuhlsbuettel I was not handcuffed. I could move my arms as I liked to move them! I felt as free as a bird! During my absence someone had put a table into my cell. On the table were two books. One was a treatise on modern power politics by Professor Haushofer, the other was a brand new edition of *Mein Kampf*—a token from Inspector Kraus.

I did not read. I stretched out on my cot, intending to analyze the events of the day. But I was exhausted. Almost instantly I fell asleep.

An eventless day passed. The following morning a smooth-faced Gestapo man shouldered into my cell.

"Good morning," he said, "I come from Kraus."

He produced several sheets of drawing paper, pens and some india ink, and placed them on the table. Suddenly he asked me: "You've been connected with the Red Seamen's International, haven't you?"

"Yes," I said.

"Here," he drawled, pointing at the drawing utensils. ".My chief thought you would draw for him a schematic chart of the ISH network. The continents and harbors are traced on these papers. If you feel like it, Kraus thinks you can draw in the International Clubs, the names of the Red waterfront organizations, lines of communications and whatever else you know about the Muscovite grand admiralty for other countries' ships. We know most of the details. Your good friend Albert Walter gave them to us." He gave a crafty smile. "What the chief wants," he continued, "is a general outline, a picture of how these things hang together. Do you know anything about that?"

"A little."

"Fine! Here, the chief gave me some cigarettes for you. He wants me to tell you not to do anything if you don't like to do it. But if you're ready to do us a favor—well, go ahead. I'll tell the *Kommandant* to keep the light burning all night."

"All the information I have is over three years old,' I cautioned him.

"We know that," he said naively. "To the devil with information. Just now we're interested in your *attitude.*"

He departed, grinning.

At once I went to work. Midnight passed before the job was completed. The maze of lines and dots and tiny flags, and the array of foreign organization names with which I had covered the sheets looked complicated and impressive. I added membership figures, and across the top of each sheet I wrote: *Organization Plan of the International of Seamen and Harbor Workers in 1933.*

I did not state, however, that this International had ceased to function as an "independent" organization; nor that Moscow had decided early in 1936 to replace the ISH with a subtler and more secret form of marine organization.

Two days I waited. Again I felt that my fate hung by a thread. If the Gestapo's appraisal of the plans I had drawn was negative— the thread would part, once and for all.

On the third day another Gestapo agent called for me. He escorted me to a sleek gray motorcar. An instant later we were racing toward Gestapo headquarters. Again I was led to the office of Inspector Kraus. Hertha Jens served coffee and cake. Kraus, munching cake, looked at me for a long while.

"What would you do." he asked abruptly, "if we would let your wife free?"

"I'd do anything," I blurted out, taken off guard.

"We'll see," he said lightly. From a folder he took a number of typewritten sheets. "You have attended a communist school in Russia?" he inquired.

"Yes—years ago."

He pushed the typewritten sheets toward me. "It's the copy of a report of one of our men in the University of the West in Moscow," he said. "Read it over. Take your time, there's still plenty of good coffee. Read it over and tell me what you think of it. The boy who wrote it was once a fanatic Bolshevik. Now— he works for us."

I read the report. It was unquestionably authentic. It contained a description of life at school, of the study plan, the names of instructors and a long list of students' Party names. While I read, the telephone rang repeatedly. From the answers given by Inspector Kraus I gathered that the persons at the other end of the line were Gestapo agents engaged in shadowing a young woman. They were reporting on the movements of their quarry.

"Ah," Inspector Kraus would say, "she went into a restaurant? Whom is she meeting? Don't lose her, please."

I read on, bewildered by the revelation that a Gestapo operative had sent this report out of the innermost and exclusive training center of the Comintern, Again the telephone rang. Again I listened.

"Ah, she went into a movie?" Inspector Kraus drawled.

Hertha Jens was cursing. "Now she sits in the dark," she snarled. "And whom may she be talking to?" Inspector Kraus spoke into the telephone:

"Arrest the lady when she leaves the theater and bring her in." Turning to me, he smiled broadly: "Have you read the report? Do you find it interesting?"

"Very interesting," I muttered.

We talked about the report, going over it point by point. No significant detail, however small, seemed to escape the attention of Inspector Kraus. But he was vain. Whenever I said anything that implied respect and admiration for the efficiency of the Gestapo, pleasure spread over his half-suave, half-brutal face.

"How do you account for your phenomenal success in suppressing communism?" I asked.

"Our methods are a combination of enterprise, patience and the methodical application of workaday skill," he said, adding: "Communism was not suppressed; in Germany it was exterminated."

We came to a paragraph in the report from Moscow which mentioned the execution of nineteen German and Polish communists for alleged collaboration with the Gestapo. Kraus saw my questioning glance.

"Let them have their fun by killing off their own," he said quietly, indulgently. "They never shoot *our* men. We can have shot to order by the G.P.U. any man outside of the top-dozen in Moscow. All we have to do is to convey the word that he worked with us. Simple, what?"

I forced myself to remain calm. I was shocked and puzzled.

"I don't mean that all the damn-fool comrades who got a bullet in the neck were shot to our order," he laughed. "We aren't that bloodthirsty. With them, the problem of getting themselves killed is quite simple. Communists—the foreign ones—are rebels. When they go to Russia, they feel themselves at home. They think they have a right to criticize the breadlines. Presto! *Des So-*

viet Buergers hoechstes Glueck, ist eine Kugel ins Genick! (The Soviet citizen's highest bliss is a bullet in the neck.) Do *you* think that the Soviet mess is socialism?"

"No."

"What would you call it?"

"A form of imperialism camouflaged under a socialistic theory," I said quietly.

"And what do you think of the *theory?*"

"The theory has failed. Internationalism is an illusion."

"The methods of the Muscovites prove that their theory is wrong," Kraus remarked. "Stalin uses the ideas and the dictionary of Leninism to cover up his nationalistic aims. That makes every foreigner who works for Stalin a traitor to his own fatherland. Is that correct?"

"That is correct," I admitted.

"We are getting somewhere," Inspector Kraus smiled. "Things are different than they were when we arrested you. Moscow has abandoned all efforts to keep a Communist Party alive in Germany. Instead they've covered the country with a network of spies and sabotage groups. Most despicable and dangerous! What, in your opinion, should be the punishment of a German who sells out his nation to Stalin or the French finance hyenas?"

"Death," I said.

Abruptly he asked: "Would you like to see your wife? We could arrange that, you know."

I was silent.

"That would cost something," Inspector Kraus drawled.

"I realize that," I replied.

Now came the question for which I had been maneuvering for months.

"It is not enough to repudiate communism," Kraus said harshly. "One must fight it as long as there's fight left in the beast. Would you be ready for that?"

"Yes," I said boldly. "It has destroyed my life and I am ready to strike back."

Inspector Kraus relaxed. Hertha Jens folded back her skirt and scratched her thick white thigh.

"Would you consider working for us?" Kraus asked easily.

I pretended to deliberate. It would not do to accept the offer quickly; that would make them suspicious. With a tremendous effort of will I hypnotized myself into the role of a man who fights a hard inner struggle.

"We force no man." Inspector Kraus spoke in a placating manner. "We are simply logical. If you wish to reject my proposal, don't hesitate to do so. Nothing will happen to you. You will merely serve out the remaining ten years of your sentence."

"I will think it over," I said finally. "For me it is a monumental decision."

"Remember," Kraus said precisely, "working with us, you work with the winning side. No force on earth can keep Germany in the position of a second-rate power. As I have told you—times have changed."

"I shall give you my answer tomorrow," I replied

Leaving the headquarters of the Foreign Division, I ran into Rudolf Heitman. He passed me in the corridor. As he shambled by, his eyes struck my face—and glanced over it as if I had not been there.

Tomorrow came.

Between eight and nine in the morning the sleek gray car whisked me to the Gestapo center. A few minutes later I faced Inspector Kraus across his cluttered desk.

"Well," he cried cheerfully, "have you decided?"

"Yes," I said.

"You will work with us?"

"Yes, I will work with you—under two conditions."

"We, too, have our conditions," the Gestapo chieftain observed. "We will come to them later. What are yours?"

"First," I said, "the release of my wife. Second, I will not do any small-time spying in factories or city blocks. I have no grudge against the communist rank and file, against the poor suckers who do not even know whose wagon they are pulling. But when it comes to bringing the top conspirators to justice, the ones who scheme from neutral soil and send others to die in the trenches, the real wirepullers—I am at your service!"

"We don't want you for small-time spying," Inspector Kraus said matter-of-factly. "We have thousands to do that sort of work. We want you to slip into some central body of the enemy machine. We want you to get us a line on their sources of information, on their plans, their personnel, their movements. The world is big. We have, in most countries, an excellent *Apparat*. But the value of this machinery depends on the information furnished to it—and to us—by confidential collaborators in the inner circles of Germany's potential foes. That should not be difficult for you, if complete secrecy is maintained. You have traveled much. You have *Weltkenntniss*. And you will have our faithful and energetic assistance."

There was a pause. The Gestapo had put its cards on the table. In that instant I knew: If I did not succeed in winning their confidence, I would never be permitted to leave their prisons.

"The leaders of the Comintern know that I have been sentenced to thirteen years," I said. "I must have a plausible reason to account for an earlier release."

Inspector Kraus gave a mischievous grin. "We shall arrange for an 'escape,'" he said. "We'll let the enemy know in some inconspicuous way that you have escaped during a transport, and that we are looking for you, high and low. Among the anti-Nazis, a man who escapes from one of our 'sanatoriums' is always a hero. We have had experience. We have done that before. It has always worked."

"I understand," I inquired, "that you wish to employ me outside of Germany?"

"Of course."

"Where?"

"That depends on your own connections. Any European country, or Russia, or North America. South America is well covered. The Far East we leave to the Japanese."

"What guarantee have you," I asked slowly, "that I won't vanish once I am outside of Germany?"

"We are no children," Inspector Kraus said earnestly. "Any pact of value is a reciprocal affair. You will know what is good for you. Offhand, there are three guarantees: First, our own *Ueberwachungsdienst*—control-service—in foreign countries; as a rule, our boys abroad are trained and clever. Second, you will leave in our hands material which, should we choose to publish, will cause the G.P.U. to give you a one-way ticket to Valhalla. Third—"

"Yes?"

"Your wife and child will remain in Germany." Inspector Kraus, speaking in a gently menacing tone, accentuated each word carefully. "They will be free, but they will be under surveillance. You may come to see them as often as you like—in Germany. *Your* loyalty to us will be the best guarantee of *their* happiness."

"I see," I said.

"I am glad you do," Kraus remarked.

Hertha Jens smiled brightly. "You have a very nice wife, you know," she said in her most innocent manner.

Every few minutes the telephone rang. Gestapo business. Inspector Kraus made his decisions quickly. He seldom talked for longer than thirty seconds with each caller, except when the call came through from Berlin. Whenever Berlin telephoned, Kraus requested me to leave the office; I would stand in the reception room under the eyes of two Death Head guards. On more than one occasion I heard in what summary manner Inspector Kraus decided the fate of individual prisoners who had served out their terms. Hertha Jens would take the telephone and listen to the call. Then she would report to Kraus:

"Convict Meier, he has finished his sentence. They want to know what to do with him."

"Meier,... Meier," Inspector Kraus would then mumble. "Wait a minute ... what was he convicted of? ... Oh, yes, I remember. How did he behave?"

A few moments later he would make his decision:

"All right, let him go, he seems to have become sensible. Send him up here first to sign his declaration."

Or:

"Schultz? ... He was a stubborn customer. We'll send him to Sachsenhausen. Put him on ice for another year or so."

And the anti-Nazi's fate was decided ...

"Let's proceed," Inspector Kraus announced. Hertha Jens slipped behind a typewriter to take dictation.

PLEDGE

I herewith declare that I have become a devoted son of the Great German Fatherland. I declare that the enemies of the new Germany are also my enemies. I declare that I accept as my duty the tireless and consistent effort to aid in the destruction of my country's and Adolf Hitler's enemies. 1 declare my willingness to accept and execute to the best of my abilities all and any orders issued to me by the Secret State Police of Germany (Gestapo).

Hamburg, February 17, 1937

"Sign this," Inspector Kraus said.

I signed. My hand was steady. A photograph of myself, bearing the Gestapo seal, and my fingerprints were then affixed to the document. Inspector Kraus smiled broadly.

"We will celebrate this with a glass of cider," he said. "We are non-alcoholics here.... Hertha, please telephone the canteen .. ." Hertha Jens raised the receiver. Her whole Junoesque shape seemed to bubble and shiver.

"It is so very exciting," she giggled.

A trooper brought a bottle of cider and three glasses. We drank. "Anyone who still works against Germany today is shoveling his own grave," Kraus murmured. "We are not what we used to be." He had the disconcerting habit of staring at me silently, for minutes at a time. Not a flicker of emotion was in his sunken eyes. I survived these dangerous intervals by staring, in my turn, at the huge portrait of Hitler on the wall. After a while I would break the silence by quoting a sentence from *Mein Kampf*.

"The world does not exist for cowardly peoples."

"Oh, did the *Fuehrer* say that?" Kraus would murmur, thus ending the spell of acute danger—for me.

"Where would you like to work?" he asked me abruptly. "Where are your best contacts?"

"In Copenhagen," I said.

"We concur," Kraus drawled. "Wollweber is in Copenhagen. He's as hard to catch as a lame wolf. When wolves are old and lame, they become as wary as devils. Besides, ninety-five percent of the false passports on the fish we catch are produced in Copenhagen. Counterfeiter-in-chief is a fellow named Jensen. Old friend of yours, I believe."

"I know Jensen well," I admitted.

Hertha Jens whistled. "If we could have somebody in Jensen's lair, we'd be cocks in the chicken ranch," she chimed in.

"*Sei nicht so vorlaut,*" her chief warned her quickly. "Don't let your tongue run away with you." He telephoned the Bureau of Identification.

"Send me up a picture of Richard Jensen, Dane, Copenhagen, communist, passport forger."

A young Gestapo agent appeared. He brought a large collection of photographs. All of them showed Richard Jensen. There was Comrade Jensen speaking at a meeting in Moscow, Jensen at a congress in Paris, Jensen emerging from a railway-station, Jensen lolling on the sands of a beach, and many more: front view, sideviews, and snapshots taken by some shadowers in the rear of the giant Dane.

"Is this the Jensen you know so well?" Inspector Kraus inquired.

"Yes," I said.

"Would you come in friendly association with him if we sent you to Copenhagen?"

"I am sure of it. I'd probably live in one of his apartments. I've done so before."

"You see," Kraus explained, "we don't want Jensen. He can be a goldmine for us. We want Jensen hale and hearty, so as to furnish us a line on the passports and the men who use them, and where they use them."

"I understand."

"How well do you know Jensen? He is a great boozer. Do you know him well enough to have him buy beers for you?"

"Yes, I know him well enough for that," I answered.

Inspector Kraus deliberated.

"You will have to prove it," he said finally. "We'll give you a chance to prove it—if you can.'

Our conference lasted, with numerous interruptions, all through the day. Before I left to shuttle back to my cell in Camp Fuhlsbuettel, I clicked my heels and raised my right arm stiffly.

"Heil Hitler," I said.

"Heil Hitler," Kraus murmured, barely raising his fingers from his desk.

Chapter Forty

I JOIN THE GESTAPO

In the last days of February, 1937, the Gestapo engineered my "escape" from Camp Fuhlsbuettel.

While these arrangements were being made, I continued to languish in prison, and continued to wear the convict's uniform. The Gestapo worked with great secrecy, and equally great efficiency. Those were weird weeks. Even today I wake up at night, at times, and wonder how I pulled through them without losing my balance and my life. They were weeks in which my wits were pitted against all the craftiness of the Gestapo. I had ceased to be myself. I had become a cunning animal, battling in the dark, fighting a battle of despair.

A week after I had signed the "Pledge of Loyalty" to the Gestapo, I was transferred from the murder Camp Fuhlsbuettel to a small precinct jail in the heart of Hamburg—the Huetten Prison. The transfer took place in the dead of night. No prisoner could possibly know that I had left Camp Fuhlsbuettel. My new abode, a small jail which contained only a dozen cells, was almost empty. There were only two other convicts there—sexual criminals awaiting their official castration.

I spoke with one of them, an elderly machinist named August Austermann, who had misused his twelve-year-old daughter, and had continued to misuse her until she was fourteen. To keep her silent, he had bought her a piano. One night his wife had surprised him and denounced him to the police. Austermann was condemned to seven years in prison and to castration. His mind was deranged. He talked of cutting his wife's throat after his release. He wrote letters to lawyers, trying to find one who would institute a suit to regain the piano he had given to his daughter. Scores of times, in the course of a night, he mumbled, "They can't castrate a man like me!" On our second night together he showed me a rope which he carried next to the skin around his stomach. He sobbed and threatened to hang himself. I did not cherish the prospect of having the guards find a hanged man in a cell of which I was the second occupant. So I fought with August Austermann for the possession of the rope. I took the rope away from him and threw it out of the window. All night August Austermann kept me awake, complaining that I was his murderer, complaining that he was choking. Next morning they led him to the lazarette to be castrated.

In the meantime, the Gestapo staged a phony "escape" from Camp Fuhlsbuettel. One of Inspector Kraus' aides later told me how it had been done. An Elite Guard had been commissioned to saw through the bars of the cell window. Another guard had thrown a rope over one of the walls. The same night the high tension wires which ran parallel to the walls had been put out of commission by an "accident." At two in the morning, a night guard "discovered" that my cell was empty. He gave the alarm. A siren shrieked, flying squads of Death Head guards turned out, and the "hunt" was on. Of course, the supposed fugitive was not found—he sat securely in an obscure backwater jail. Only the Gestapo, the *Kommandant* of Camp Fuhlsbuettel, and two guards knew that the escape alarm had been a fake. The rest of the guards, some two hundred strong, and all of the prisoners, really believed that I had succeeded in making a successful getaway. Inspector Kraus calculated, correctly, that information would filter through to the Comintern that I had escaped. Even Rudolf Heitman was fooled by the trick; I later found that he had faithfully reported my extraordinary disappearance to his paymasters in Copenhagen.

Following this preparatory coup, I tackled the job of convincing Inspector Kraus of my connections with the Comintern Bureau in Copenhagen. It was a game which Richard Jensen and I played with marked cards, though we had not spoken or written to each other for more than three years. On its outcome depended, for me, life or death. Sitting in the office of the Gestapo's Foreign Division, I wrote a note to Richard Jensen. Inspector Kraus watched me lynx-eyed. Over my shoulder peered Hertha Jens.

"Dear Richard," I wrote. "Perhaps you will remember me. I am an old friend who needs your help urgently. I have just left the hospital after a long sickness, and I am in dire need of money to visit my Aunt Ernestine. Please help me!

"Williams."

"Williams" was the name of a British journalist under which I had illegally entered Germany in 1933. Jensen knew my handwriting; he would know. "Ernestine" was Ernst Wollweber. I added, at the instruction of Kraus, a general delivery address. Inspector Kraus had the letter photographed for the Gestapo files. The original he sent off to Copenhagen. I was returned to my jail cell, asking myself, "How will it end? If Jensen makes a blunder, you are as good as dead and gone!"

Two days I waited, seized by a mad restlessness, too excited to touch the coarse prison fare.

At the end of the second day, late at night, a Gestapo chauffeur called for me. We drove to headquarters, entering it through the door of another building which was connected with the Gestapo mansion by a short subterranean passage. Since my "escape" from Camp Fuhlsbuettel, my escort always used this passage to safeguard me against being seen by fellow-communists brought in for questioning. Hertha Jens received me. She was in high spirits. A letter, addressed *poste restante* to "Mr. Williams," had arrived from Copenhagen. It had not contained a single written word. Its contents were two new one-hundred-dollar bills in United States currency.

"Elegant!" she crooned. "It worked! They have fallen in the trap! Two hundred dollars—they show that the Muscovites still hold you in high esteem. I hoped they were counterfeit bills. But they are real." In my heart I fervently thanked Comrade Jensen. He had taken the one and only right road in this matter. Also, I was reassured in another respect: If the Comintern threw two hundred dollars into the maw of the Gestapo, they must consider the assignment which Rudolf Heitman had transmitted to me as one of considerable importance. Wollweber's words, "The Party does not forget its children," tingled in my brain. Hertha Jens called the inspector.

Inspector Kraus looked as if he had come straight from a torture session. His face was ashen, his eyes cruel, his mouth a thin gash. When he saw me, his features lit up.

"Well, you passed the test," he grinned. "I hope there will be no disappointments. I will take up the matter of your release with the Ministry of Justice—suspended sentence or something like that." In a sudden outburst of cold anger he added: "This fellow Jensen is a wily fox! The address on the letter was written by some woman. No usable fingerprints on the paper—well, it's time we do something!"

He hurried off.

"The chief is very busy tonight," Hertha Jens explained. "We caught a batch of Jesuits. The devils operate from Holland; codes, false passports and all. The religious hypocrites—they make me sick! "

I heard other Gestapo men talk of Catholic emissaries as the "Black Pest," and of the Pope as the "Black Devil." Inadvertently I thought of Bismarck's phrase: "Whoever feeds off the Catholic Center, will die of it."

Hertha Jens led me to another office. Here she handed me a thick mimeographed volume, and another, thinner one. "Go through them slowly," she suggested. "If you find acquaintances, mark down the names and all you may know about them."

The larger book bore the title, *Register of International Agents of the G.P.U. and the Comintern;* the other was the *List of Foreign Volunteers in the Armies of Red Spain.* The first contained approximately seven thousand names; the second, about nine hundred. Each name was followed by notes on the age, nationality, aliases, and the personal history of the suspect. Many hundreds of photographs had been pasted over as many names. The volumes had been produced by the *Gestapoamt* in Berlin. The names of men and women who had been apprehended by the Gestapo, or by the secret services of Italy and Japan, had blue-pencil marks.

For nine solid hours I pored over the volumes, straining my memory to retain data which might be of value to the Western Secretariat of the Comintern. It was curious to see my own name and picture, and Firelei's in the larger volume. Some fifteen pages were devoted to George Mink and other Americans. There were Joseph Djugashvili—alias Stalin, Meyer Wallach—alias Litvinov, Sobelsohn—alias Radek, and so on, down to Michael Appelman— alias Mike Pell, and Charles Krumbein—alias Albert Stewart, alias Dreazen. Much of the information I found to be alarmingly accurate. But in many cases the names and cover-names of many persons were tangled, and there were many names whose bearers had gone to their graves. Among the latter was "Bandura—leading G.P.U. agent in Greece." Him I selected, together with a score of others who were either dead or trapped in Russia, and augmented their records by adding "significant detail." Several hundred well-publicized Bolsheviks whose movements through many countries the Gestapo had recorded, I identified as men I had met "in Paris in 1933" or "in London in 1932." The Gestapo never tired of collecting details on the doings of suspects during years that seemed as far away as the Franco-Prussian war.

On March 15, when I was taken from my cell to Gestapo headquarters, I was not escorted to the offices of the Foreign Division. The Death Head guard led me to a small room on the third floor. No sooner had I stepped into the room than he closed and locked the door behind me. Except for a table, two chairs and a radiator in a corner, the room was bare.

Firelei rose from one of the chairs. Our eyes met. We had not seen each other in more than forty months of hardship and disaster. We looked at one another across the room, and it was as if each was afraid to take the first step forward. I put my forefinger to my lips to tell Firelei to be silent. I turned and looked at the door. There was no spy-hole. The walls and the ceiling were solid. The single window faced a large inner courtyard. There could be no watchers. I tiptoed around the room, scrutinizing the floor and the corners. At the radiator I stopped. There was a microphone, fastened between the radiator and the wall. Wires ran through the wall into an adjoining room. The little black-and-silver device seemed to grin at me out of the gloom and say, "Yes, I am here; you two had better be careful." I pointed it out to Firelei. Then I said:

"You—are you here?"

"Yes, I am here," she answered in a strange, somber voice.

"We shall begin a new life," I said sheepishly. "It is not too late."

"Why do you say that?" she asked slowly, the specter of a smile on her pale lips.

I did not know what to say. All that words could express seemed meaningless. "You should not have come back to Germany,' I said. "You should have discarded me and gone away."

Firelei stepped forward. Her gaze did not budge from mine.

"Let's not speak." Her voice was steady now. "I was afraid we would never see each other again. In Copenhagen they told me you were dead."

She was close to me. I held her lightly.

"Where is little Jan?" I asked.

"He is well. He is big. He will be five this year. I have not seen him, but I know."

"Your parents?"

"They hate you," Firelei said. "They have suffered terribly."

"Where are you?"

"In the Luebeck prison; they brought me here this morning."

"Are you alone?" I inquired.

"Two years I was alone. I am now with another woman. She is old and ugly, but she has a good heart."

A long silence followed. Words were futile. Neither joy nor sorrow was between us. Only a dull, brooding happiness. Firelei was not the same as she had been in earlier years. Her face was drawn, earnest, almost hard. There were lines in it which I had not seen before. The bitter years had wiped out her lust for mischief, her carefree laughter, her enthusiasm for life and her youthful enchantment. Her hands were still capable and firm. They were hard from manual work. Hard also was her slender body under the drab and shapeless prison garb.

"Yes," Firelei continued in a murmur, "I, too, am old and ugly. I know what you think—you think it is your fault that I have become hard and gray. You must not think that. Maybe I can be young again, if . . ."

". . . if—what?"

Firelei trembled under a sob that was half laughter. ". . . if I could feel the arms of our boy around my neck and hear his voice crow, 'Mama, give me . . .' "

"You will—soon," I said.

"I need no make-believe consolation," Firelei said harshly. "It's all over . . . the little girl dreams, the little girl softness . . . I could be content with lying down in the tall grass and sleep, sleep forever."

I do not know how long we were allowed to be together. Perhaps it was three hours, perhaps only one. We said little of what we had wanted to say. Mostly we were silent. At times we said things which were not parts of ourselves, words designed to lull the possible suspicions of the listeners on the other side of the wall. Firelei knew nothing of my assignment. When the Death Head guard came into the room to tell us that it was time to part, Firelei bade me good-by with the thought that it would be a good-by for many years. I could not tell her the truth then, without risking everything. That was the hardest of all. She had changed. We had both changed. We parted, inwardly disturbed, questing, and a little dazed. She returned to the Women's Prison in Luebeck; I— to the obscure little jail for men condemned to castration.

Each morning of the last two weeks in March I was whisked to Gestapo headquarters. Each night I was brought back, exhausted from the constant tightrope walking, to my cell in the Huetten jail. During this time I learned to find my bearings in the labyrinth of the Gestapo empire. I looked over thousands of photographs. I read hundreds of pages of reports from spies abroad, each bearing the signature of a letter and a number, instead of a name. I was questioned on the possibilities of recommending Gestapo agents as candidates for political schools in the Soviet Union; of organizing Nazi Vigilante Committees in foreign ports after the communist model; of placing Nazi agents in the International Brigade in Spain; of recruiting members of the crews of Belgian, Dutch, French, Polish, Russian and Scandinavian ships as paid auxiliaries of the Gestapo; and on the feasibility of many other schemes Each session with Inspector Kraus or his immediate aides was like a game of chess in which a single wrong move meant the loss of the game—the loss of my life.

The Gestapo's chief weakness was its fanatical eagerness to succeed. Its second weakness, as compared to the G.P.U., was its lack of foreign experts for work abroad. Ninety-nine percent of the Gestapo's foreign operations were carried on by German nationals, while the G.P U. had the nationals of fifty lands to draw upon. My knowledge of international shipping and of the workaday conditions in foreign ports evoked more than one exclamation of naive admiration not only from Hertha Jens, but also from her chief. The men who worked in the Foreign Division of the Gestapo were thoroughly German, and narrow. They specialized in one field, and of all that lay beyond their circumscribed horizon they knew little or nothing. Ruthless strength, tireless surveillance and gathering of details, and a vast army of half-trained spies, rather than a smaller number of experts, were their most valuable assets and the chief reason for their successes. The Gestapo was younger and more clean-cut than the G.P.U. Stalin's Secret Police were far craftier, better trained in conspiracy: Inspector Kraus spoke of the G.P.U. with respect. "We have much to learn from it," he added. "Each day we are learning something new."

I, also, learned. After weeks of concentrated maneuvering and observation, the framework of the Gestapo's Foreign Division lay before me like a picture-book. There was, for instance, one large office where a score of men and women did nothing but clip photographs of anti-Nazis of all shades and nationalities from foreign newspapers; faces on group pictures were scrutinized through powerful magnifying glasses and photographically enlarged. There was another office, lined with long galleries of files, which contained names and data on many thousands of Nazi foes in every civilized country on earth. Each of the countries bordering on Germany had a special room in the Foreign Division. There were Gestapo offices for German business firms abroad, for the Foreign Section of the German Press, the Hitler Youth, the Labor Front, the League of Germans Abroad, a Technical Division, a Cultural Division, a Maritime Section and another for the transport systems—rivers and railroads—of foreign countries. In all, there were twenty-five separate departments, each handling a special branch of the Gestapo's activities abroad. Geographically the Gestapo had divided the world into eight regions; Gestapo business pertaining to each region was handled through the respective Gestapo *Laenderamt*. The eight *Laenderaemter* were:

1. Scandinavian Countries, Finland and the Baltic.
2. Western Europe.
3. South-eastern Europe, including Turkey.
4. Italy, Switzerland, Austria, Czechoslovakia and Hungary.
5. Africa.
6. North America.

7. Latin America.
8. Great Britain, the Far East and Australia.

This *Apparat* functioned through 648 units in 45 countries (*Landeskreise*). The Maritime Division alone employed 1097 agents, scattered in the harbors and on ships. The offices of the Foreign Division of the Gestapo in Hamburg were manned, in 1935, by a staff of 170; by March, 1937, this staff had been increased to 710. In this gigantic machine of terror and espionage, Inspector Paul Kraus, for all his murderous power, was only a cog. He was the director of the Anti-Comintern Department. His chief was *Regierungsrat* Schreckenbach, the head of the Hamburg headquarters of the Foreign Division.

I met Schreckenbach toward the end of March. He was a well-knit man of thirty-eight or thirty-nine, of medium height and dressed in English tweeds. He had sharp gray eyes, smooth, dark-blond hair, and the tanned, healthy face of an outdoor sportsman. His mouth was straight, his nose strong and slightly hooked. Usually he appeared noncommittal, but when he talked, his words came in a tone which I immediately associated with that of a Prussian officer. During the World War, Schreckenbach had been a junior officer aboard a submarine; later he had commanded a submarine chaser, and after the demobilization he had entered the illegal naval intelligence service of the Weimar Republic. Discharged because of his allegiance to Adolf Hitler, Schreckenbach had become a commander of the Elite Guards, and after Hitler's Blood Purge in June, 1934, he had jumped into the leadership of the Gestapo. As I stood before him in his office, on the top floor of the Gestapo building, his eyes wandered slowly over my convict uniform and, for some reason not known to me, an expression of quiet amusement invaded his face.

"You were a fool," he said, "you should have come over to us in 1923."

"If men knew which army would win," I answered, "there would be no war, *Herr Regierungsrat*."

I could see that Schreckenbach liked my answer.

"I am glad that you don't pretend to have become a National Socialist," he said. "Or have you?"

It was a dangerous question. From behind his hand, which held a cigarette, Schreckenbach's eyes gleamed expectantly. Both a "yes" and a "no" would be equally wrong.

"I am a German," I said. "I prefer to fight with the winning army."

"Once German armies won the battles and lost the war," the Gestapo chief said pensively. Abruptly he added: "It shall never happen again, what?"

"No, sir."

"You have been a ship's officer?"

"I once officered a Russian vessel," I replied. "I was blacklisted in Germany."

"Blacklists are an invention of . . . Well, we have done away with them. What was your impression of the Russian Bear?"

"A rather unkempt beast, sir," I said.

"Bears can be trained," Schreckenbach observed. "Bears can be very docile. *Zuckerbrot und Peitsche* (sweets and the whip)—they will accomplish a lot under certain circumstances. Please sit down. Tell me in ten minutes what caused you to break with the Communist International."

For ten minutes I talked rapidly.

"Enough!" Schreckenbach said in his curtest manner.

My heart sank. I thought I had lost, after all.

He picked up a telephone.

"Inspection Six—Kraus. ... That you, Paul? ... I've talked with our friend ... . *Nein, keine Bedenken.* .... Next time you go to Berlin, take him along ... *Heil!*"

Schreckenbach rang for a guard.

"Take this prisoner back. Don't let him be seen by any of the traitors who're here for examination. I hold you personally responsible."

The Death Head guard slammed his heels together. His right arm flew up.

"*Zu Befehl!* Heil Hitler!' "

"Hitler," Schreckenbach muttered. I was led away.

More days at Gestapo headquarters followed. Warily I was threading my way through the maze of deadly snags. Each night between eight and ten I was shuttled back to jail. I had ceased to regard myself as a human being whose harmless privilege it is to meander, and to make occasional mistakes. Nothing counted but the thoughts and actions that would bring to an end, in one way or another, the insidious war in which I was at once general and meanest soldier. My ability to draw, by a simple request, two hundred dollars from one of the key figures in the *Apparat* of the Comintern, fascinated the chiefs of the Gestapo. Their respect for the G.P.U. in general, and for Richard Jensen in particular, caused them to see in me a find of rare value. And so I won my almost single-handed battle against all the cunning and the suspicions of the most dreaded police force in the world.

One morning early in April a long, low, open car halted in front of the Huetten jail. In the car were Inspector Kraus and two other Gestapo officials. Kraus entered my cell. Over his arm he carried a civilian overcoat.

"Here, put this over your jailhouse rags," he said. "You're going to Berlin with us."

Soon we were speeding out of Hamburg at a hundred kilometers an hour. Outside of Spandau, we stopped and the chauffeur distributed sandwiches and coffee, which we consumed at the roadside. At noon we arrived in Berlin. The car came to a stop in the courtyard of the *Gestapoamt,* the gigantic, newly-built nerve-center of Hitler's Secret Police. We passed three or four control-stations where Death Head guards examined the credentials of all who came to transact business in this citadel of terror. Inspector Kraus and his companions were required to deposit their identification cards and to sign their names before they were allowed to pass. Elevators whipped us upward.

Kraus led the way through a door, which bore a small sign: *Nachrichtendienst—Abteilung 16 F.* We passed a large room where men and girls sat behind many radio receiving sets, and crossed another where close to a hundred men sat behind as many small desks. Each desk was equipped with a telephone and a note pad. Sounds resembling the humming of many bees filled this room. We continued through a silent corridor until Inspector Kraus pushed open one of the side doors. A sign on this door said: *No Entrance.* We were in a small but comfortably furnished office. A middle-aged man with a quiet, friendly face sat in a leather armchair. He drank coffee. Without giving up his comfortable position, he shook hands with Inspector Kraus. After they had exchanged a few words, the man's eyes turned on me. They were uncanny eyes—cold, greenish. All of a sudden they smiled.

"Never betray a trust," he told me. "Whatever may happen, never betray our trust."

I nodded, facing him squarely.

"When you're abroad," he continued, "never take up connections with official agencies of the German Reich. Never go to an embassy, never to a consulate. That does not mean that you will work alone. Our eyes, our helpers are everywhere. Never betray our trust. Never go to an embassy or consulate. You know why; you are no greenhorn."

"Yes, sir," I said.

"We are taking a chance with you," the other went on. "We need not discuss the consequences of a violation of our trust. You know them. Do your duty as a German."

A pause followed.

"The details, *Herr Oberinspektor,*" Kraus murmured.

"Oh, yes." The Chief Inspector spoke slowly, almost haltingly:

"We are paying you three hundred marks monthly, in the currency of the country in which you will be at the beginning of each month. For every case when the information you send us results in the arrest of a traitor sent into Germany from abroad, we will pay you a bonus of one hundred marks. This is fair, I believe. Your first assignment will be to insinuate yourself into the counterfeiting *Apparat* of this man Jensen in Copenhagen. Concretely, we wish to know who uses false passports and under what names. We wish you to obtain samples of rubber and metal stamps used in the Comintern passport-forging center. Aside from that, send us everything you can lay your hands on: Printed matter, codes, correspondence, resolutions, photographs, handwriting samples, samples of writing from their typewriters, addresses, names, meeting-places, data on communication lines and on persons who may be willing to work for us—in short, everything you hear or see anywhere at any time that may be of interest to our office. Further concrete tasks will be given you as soon as you have established yourself. Schreckenbach in Hamburg will arrange with you the details of communication and — if required — supply you with seasoned assistants."

"I'll do my part to turn your game into a death-dance," I thought.

I clicked my heels. "Very well, sir," I said.

The conference ended soon afterward. Inspector Kraus led me to another part of the building. There a Death Head guard locked me into a small, empty, windowless room.

"Wait," I was told.

A pretty waitress brought me a meal on a black steel tray. I squatted on the floor and ate wolfishly. Later in the afternoon a tailor arrived to take my measurements. I was escorted to a bathroom, from there to a barber shop, and was then subjected to a medical examination. I was given clean underwear, new shoes, a hat, a shirt, two neckties, socks, a well-fitting civilian suit, a topcoat and a raincoat. Nearly three and a half years had passed since I had last worn civilian clothes. Inspector Kraus handed me fifty German marks and the two hundred dollars Richard Jensen had sent from Copenhagen.

"Keep them," he laughed. "Any time you can get money from the Bolsheviks, take it, and keep it." He looked me over from all sides. "The tailor brought you a good piece," he said. "Come on, now—Himmler wants to see you."

I made an effort not to show excitement or apprehension. Kraus strode briskly ahead. The men we passed did not recognize me as a convict; I walked without handcuffs and without a guard. I thought of Heinrich Himmler, the sixth important Nazi in the Reich and the supreme commander of the Nazi police, responsible only to Hitler himself. I had heard much of him during my years in prison. Gestapo agents called him, at times, "potato face." He had the reputation of being the most uncompromising and merciless man among Hitler's aides. He had bobbed up in the Nazi Party in 1924, in Munich, where he lived at that time as a student of experimental agriculture. He switched to police work two years later, when he became Hitler's master spy in Captain Roehm's unruly storm troops. In 1929, he was appointed as leader of the Elite Guards, created by Hitler to act as the Party police and his personal strong-arm brigade. Himmler, among the youngest of the Nazi chieftains, proved his mettle in the blood-night of June 29-30, 1934. He rose rapidly after that mass-slaughter of Nazi dissidents. Elite Guard commander, member of the Reichstag, Prussian State Councilor, Inspector General of the Gestapo, Heinrich Himmler became in 1936 the *Fuehrer* of all German police forces.

In the years which preceded Hitler's rise to chancellorship, I had come, in political mass meetings, face to face with most of the prominent Nazi leaders, including Hitler, But Heinrich Himmler I had never seen. He was neither a speaker, nor was he known as a fighter or a man of independent political initiative. In the prisons, Hitler, Goering, Goebbels, Dr. Ley and Walther Darre were hated as formidable foes, but for Himmler we had had only bitter contempt. I recalled all that as I followed Inspector Kraus through red-carpeted corridors, up a flight of stairs, past a barrage of Death Head guards and into a fairly large hall, in the center of which a large bronze eagle perched atop a marble swastika. Here we halted. Six doors opened on this hall, which had the form of a semi-circle. "Himmler is an overambitious brigand," I told myself. "To hell with him!" I felt my abdomen contract as if it were completely empty.

A door opened. A slender man in a dark-gray suit stepped out.

Inspector Kraus saluted. I jumped to attention. The man, walking toward us briskly, motioned us to stop our antics. The man was Himmler.

He had a sallow face, a pointed nose, an irregular chin, and his eyes were dull behind a prince-nez which gave him somehow the expression of a frightened teacher's pet. His body moved like a whip. His hands were gray and bony. He looked younger than Schreckenbach or Inspector Kraus. He spoke in a low, rather thick voice: *"So, da sind Sie?"*

"This is our new *"Vertrauensmann,"* Inspector Kraus announced, indicating me with a servile grin.

Himmler looked at me for a fraction of a second; after that, he seemed to gaze over my shoulder.

"You came late, but you *did* come," he said.

"Jawohl," I snapped.

"What was your motive?"

"I realized my mistake and drew the conclusions," I explained. "I thought once that the Hitler movement was the lackey of the rich. Hitler's achievements have shown me that I was wrong. I became determined to win for myself the right to live in the New Germany."

"He has become quite sensible, it seems," Inspector Kraus said.

Himmler stared past me toward the ceiling. *"Das freut mich,"* he said. "I am glad." He gave a short nod in the general direction of Kraus.

"Thank you," Kraus said. "Heil Hitler!"

"Heil Hitler," I echoed.

Himmler smiled thinly. *"Hals und Beinbruch!"* He turned and strode away.

"That's that," Kraus remarked contentedly, as we sauntered past the cordon of Death Head guards. "Now you can have two days to look around in Berlin. One of my young men will be with you. Acclimatize yourself. I'm going back to Hamburg tonight. I'll see that you and your wife get eight days' vacation before you start work. Good luck! Don't let me know what you are doing. Have a good time!"

Two days I roamed through Berlin, with a young Gestapo man as my "guide." I went to theaters, cabarets, a concert, good restaurants, and I got drunk. I felt no joy. I was homesick—homesick for Hall Eleven and for Tonio. After the two days had passed, I journeyed to Hamburg by train, still under guard.

I met Hertha Jens, who invited me to dinner. She instructed me to leave the following morning for Burhave, a small fishing village on the North Sea Coast, situated between the mouth of the Weser and Jade Bay. On this journey, too, I was accompanied by an unobtrusive, but watchful young man from Inspector Kraus' office.

We left the modest Burhave railway station and stepped into the sparkling morning. The land was flat, and the first young green thronged out of the earth. We walked along a country lane, past squat, low-walled and high-roofed peasant houses. Birds twittered. Cows dozed in the sunshine. Somewhere a dog barked joyously. A boy amused himself by jumping over hedges, whistling his prowess. A girl called him loudly, but he would not listen. All this, I reflected, had been here through the years. Cows had grazed and boys had jumped over hedges while elsewhere men and women had been bent upon hurting one another, had schemed and struggled, trembled in horror, won bleak triumph or gone to their death.

My young Gestapo companion walked with a springy step. His nostrils drank the flavor of the lowlands. "German earth," he said with simple pride. "Is it not beautiful?"

The road led toward the shore. The peasant houses gave way to the scattered dwellings of fishermen. The wind was tangy. The trees became smaller, twisted and storm-scarred. The smell of mud flats and fish was in the air. In front of us the broad green back of a dyke stretched away in the distance. I smelled the nearness of the sea.

"Someone is waiting for me here?" I asked.

The Gestapo man nodded. A grin spread over his face. "We'll be there in a couple minutes," he said. "Then you'll see her."

"I am going to see Firelei," I thought.

We climbed to the top of the dyke. I saw the sea. Low water had bared a strip of sand and a wide expanse of mud flats. Narrow channels criss-crossed the flats. Under the sun the mud gleamed, and crags and busy sea birds left their traces in the wet sand. From far out rolled the low mutter of the surf. We wandered along the dyke. Before us rose a white two-story house, incongruous among the low-crouched cottages of fishermen. It was a hotel, encircled by a garden and many old trees. In front of it, on the seaward side of the dyke, a narrow wharf jutted into the channel. Fishing craft lay moored at the end of the wharf, and brown nets were hoisted to dry in the sun.

"You go ahead alone, now," the Gestapo man said. "I'll just hang around. Don't mind me—I'm only doing what I'm ordered to do. Don't try to skip. I'd hate to shoot at a man in a place like this."

"Don't worry," I said. "I won't skip."

The Gestapo man threw himself into the grass. I strode ahead. I entered the hotel and stamped on the freshly scrubbed floor. A buxom young woman with a ruddy face and shining blonde hair came from the kitchen.

"Heil Hitler," she said pleasantly. "You are welcome."

"Heil Hitler," I replied, adding: "My wife is here, I believe?"

"*Ja! Und ein kleiner Junge!* He is a very beautiful child. I have given them the best room we have. You are the first guests I am having this year."

Firelei and our son, Jan, were not in their room. They had gone out to look for shells and to make a campfire of driftwood. I followed the dyke, toward the spot where the smoke from an open fire curved into the blue. I felt the longing to turn and to go away. I found myself wishing that the fire on the beach were still many miles off, far enough away to give me some hours to think. "Go," I told myself, "go forward. You have had years to think, and it availed you nothing." Now the fire was but a hundred paces away. I could see our son running around with great eagerness, collecting wood to feed the fire. Firelei sat by the fire; her gaze went out to the horizon where a passing steamer belched smoke. The smoke was black. Like a sinister flag it stood against the cleanness of the sky.

I halted. Jan, a piece of wood in each hand, was running toward the fire. He stopped suddenly, and peered in my direction. His little arm flew out, pointing. His voice sailed with the wind.

"Mama—there is a man!"

Firelei turned her head slowly. Her slender shape rose from the sand. The wind rippled through her hair and tugged at her coat. She put her right foot forward, and then her left, and I stood still and watched her coming toward me. Jan was running at her side.

"Mama, who is the man?"

"Why—that's your Papa," Firelei cried joyously.

The child was running ahead now. I gathered him up in my arms and his little face was full of curiosity and wonderment.

"Who am I?" I said hoarsely.

"You are my Papa," chirped Jan. "Have you come with a ship?"

"Yes—with a ship."

"From Africa?"

"Yes—from Africa."

"The lions live in Africa," Jan said importantly. "Mama said your ship might come today if the weather is good. Where is your ship?"

For minutes the highest happiness in the universe was to be at home on the weatherbeaten strip of sand between the dyke and the mud flats of Burhave. Jan clutched my left wrist with both hands. My right arm was around Firelei's shoulder. So we sauntered toward the crackling fire. Tears of joy were in Firelei's eyes. "It is so hard to believe that you are here," she said, "that we are all here . . . really here."

We sat in the sand and looked at each other, and then we talked until the fire had burned down. We searched one another, both intent on seeing not the ugliness of the vengeful and malevolent years, but on seeking to resurrect the beautiful hours, to rediscover the traits and nuances each had cherished in the other.

"You have become much quieter," Firelei told me. "Less wild. I must brush away that sadness."

"One cannot brush away all that has happened," I said.

"But one can draw a line—and build anew." Firelei's voice was gentle and insistent. "Build together," she added.

"Together!" The word slipped from me against my will. It was a gloomy, a bitter word.

"Are you tired? Or have I become an ugly old witch?" Firelei asked.

"You are the best and the most beautiful woman," I said.

"A very foolish woman," Firelei smiled. "But a happy woman. Can't you see?"

"He came from Africa!" Jan crowed lustily.

"Af-ri-ca," Firelei formed the syllables as if they were music. They reminded me of another day, long ago, but also so near the sea. There had been Firelei, young, bubbling with gayety, sparkling into the life which then had lain still ahead of her, and of whose hostility and viciousness she had known so little. On that day, Firelei had said: "Sumatra, Madagascar, Oran ... I like the names so much."

Not far away a man lolled on the slope of the dyke. I pretended not to see him. He was the watcher from Inspector Kraus' office.

Late at night, after the boy had fallen asleep I told Firelei the details of the campaign which had brought about her release, and mine. She listened, her face tense, her lips set in a hardness I had not encountered in her before. In her the soldier spirit of the fighting years had survived, despite all hardship and folly, despite all suffering and degradation. Nights of questioning, months of solitary confinement, and many more of hard labor in sunless halls had stifled her enthusiasm, but they had not strangled her will to live.

"We cannot give up," she said. "We can never give up! We would be people with empty hands and empty hearts. You can rely on me, and I will rely on you. I have learned that it is fruitless to dream of peace as long as one is alive."

The week passed swiftly. We made resolute efforts to play, and to laugh, but they petered out like artificial streams in a desert. We went on long walks along the dykes and over the meadows and the dunes. We talked of the past, of the prison years; we tried to untangle the present and to penetrate the uncertain and complicated roads of the future. Discreetly trailing us, at a distance of some fifty yards, sauntered Inspector Kraus' assistant. I could rely on Firelei's silence. She was sad and disillusioned, but she was neither broken, nor resigned. We spoke of the possibility of immediate flight—and rejected it. Germany was too well guarded; the frontiers were infested with watchers. We would not get far. We would be caught and destroyed.

"You must go out first," Firelei said steadily. "You have work to do. I am sure that you will find a way to bring Jan out, and me, after you have gained a foothold in the organization. Too much has changed. It would be insane to leap into the void before at least one of us had time to explore it."

"Keep silent, and do not lose your faith," I said. "I shall find a way to bring you out of this hellish land. I am sure I shall find a way."

"Why is the water blue?" The clean young voice of Jan, our son, prattled deliciously. "What do the sea-birds cry? Can the stars howl? Why are the fish so shiny? Can boats see? Do fishermen like to drink coffee?" Through many minutes he would stand still, his hands clasped behind him, his eyes, which were Firelei's eyes, watching men and women unload fish in baskets from a deeply-laden lugger.

The Gestapo ordered Firelei to make her quarters in Blumenthal, a little town on the lower course of the Weser River. Twice daily she was required to report at the local Gestapo office. She was not permitted to leave the town, unless a Gestapo agent accompanied her. She was not permitted to enter the railway station nor the waterfront, nor to send off letters to foreign addresses. We were not allowed to write each other directly; our letters were to pass through the censorship of the Gestapo. But she could be with her child.

Within the confines of the town she was allowed to move freely. She could draw, or work in a garden, or idle in the sunlight.

The week's respite ended. The abyss gaped.

Chapter Forty-one

FREEMAN ON A LEASH

I reported to *Regierungsrat* Schreckenbach in Hamburg. He gave me a regular German passport in my own name, and a special document, signed by Inspector Kraus, which bore my photograph, the official Gestapo seal, and the legend that I was the German engineer Emil Berg. These were to be my credentials in dealings with Gestapo units operating beyond the German frontiers.

"In hell or high water," Schreckenbach said, "never let these documents fall into enemy hands."

Next, Schreckfenbach's secretary explained to me the intricacies of a code which was based on the letters and numbers of squares on a chess board. I was to use it for the transmission of confidential names and addresses. Then I was introduced to two men who were to act as my couriers between Copenhagen and Hamburg; both were minor officials aboard international *Mitropa* express trains. Finally an agent from the Finance Department handed me my first month's pay, and Schreckenbach gave me a cover address in Hamburg for secret reports and other confidential material, and another address in Copenhagen which was to be used only in acute emergencies. The Hamburg address was *Miss Gertrud Schultheiss, 31, Wexstrasse;* the address of the Gestapo liaison station in Copenhagen was *Lily de Forte, Osterbrogade.*

Came the day of departure, the first week-end in May, 1937. I met Inspector Paul Kraus in a remote restaurant at the edge of the Hamburg Stadtpark. With Kraus, well-fed and obscenely content, was Hertha Jens.

"Remember this," Inspector Kraus said, an ominous rigidity in his sunken eyes: "The Gestapo has a long arm. Don't try to deceive us. You won't live long if you do. You may hide in China or in the Brazilian jungle. We'll find ways to bring you back. I warn you: the Gestapo never jokes."

We rose and shook hands.

Hertha Jens watched me silently, her lips half parted.

"Fair winds to you," Inspector Kraus smiled.

They were the same words my mother had used, eighteen years before, when I was hunting for my first outbound ship.

I dispatched a postcard to Richard Jensen, telling him of my coming to Copenhagen. A day later I entrained for Travemuerde, a seashore resort near Luebeck. I crossed the Baltic on one of the weekly excursion steamers to Copenhagen. As the ship approached the quay, I discerned the bulky shape of Richard Jensen among the mass of waiting people. Without a mishap I passed the Danish passport inspection. Jensen saw me. He turned and strode out of the harbor. I followed in his tracks. He walked to his car, which was parked on a quiet waterfront street. I jumped in beside him. The car leaped forward.

A tremendous grin spread over Jensen's titanic face.

"Damn it, you made it," he growled repeatedly, as if he did not trust his own eyes. "How does it feel to have climbed out of a tomb?"

"Not bad," I said.

I relaxed. I was overcome by an indescribable weariness. The high tension of my nerves gave way. I had only one desire—to rest and not to move.

"We will fix you up," Jensen said soothingly. "Very few ever come back from Germany. Damn it, you've made it . . ."

I fumbled through my pockets. I drew out my Nazi passport and the Gestapo document which bore the name of Engineer Berg. I handed both to Jensen.

"Keep them," I said. "I don't want to carry them around with me. It's better to pose as a simple refugee without papers."

Jensen perused the papers with interest.

"Very, very good," he growled.

We drove through Copenhagen to the suburb of Charlottenlund. The car turned into Ordrupvej and nosed into the gardens stretching across a colony of modern apartment houses.

"I am bringing you to Petra Petersen's place," Jensen explained. "You can live there. Keep away from the Party in Copenhagen. We want nobody to know that you are here. Do you know Petra?"

"Yes," I said. I had been at her address in 1933, when it was the temporary hideout of Otto Wilhelm Kuusinen, the leading Finn in the Comintern. Petra Petersen was a G.P.U. operative. She worked in the Copenhagen telegraph building. She was a tall, thin, intelligent, middle-aged woman. She had a peculiar limping gait; she could not bend her left leg at the knee. All these details I enumerated.

"Correct," Jensen said. "Tell me, how is your wife?"

"The Gestapo is holding her as a hostage. We must get her out without delay."

"We'll fix that," Jensen promised. "Can we still regard her as a good Party member?"

"Yes."

"We'll see," Jensen growled. "Nothing will happen to her as long as the Gestapo thinks that you're all right. Did they say anything about me?"

"Plenty!"

Jensen chuckled. "What?"

"Passport counterfeiter-in-chief. They want me to get them imprints of the stamps and seals you use, and the numbers of the passports you fix."

"I've a mind to have a special set of stamps made for them," Jensen remarked. "You could send them over, and we'll keep on using our old stamps. We'll see. Let's have a beer first."

He bought a case of beer, which we drank in Petra Petersen's apartment, while waiting for her return. I remember little of this drinking session.

"We must get Firelei out of Germany," I insisted repeatedly.

"We will fix everything, in time," he answered.

We talked about the astonishing successes of the new Popular Front policy of the Comintern in France, Spain, in the Scandinavian countries, in America and elsewhere. In 1933, at the time of my arrest by the Gestapo, the central slogan had been, "the Poor against the Rich"; now it was "Democracy against Fascism." Ostensibly, the Comintern had become respectable in the liberal sense, so respectable that broad strata of intellectuals, writers, artists, teachers, and rich men's wives had come to regard manifestations of sympathy with the Communist International and the Soviet Union as the badge of true liberalism. It had become a fashionable thing to "participate" in communist endeavors. "We are so respectable," Jensen chuckled, "that everything we do must be done underground; in the freest countries we must work with illegal methods, so as not to give away the show to the Boudoir Bolsheviks. But we will make them walk the plank in good time." Jensen told me many anecdotes. And then he spoke about the purge. Since the assassination of Sergei Kirov, the Leningrad Party leader and member of the supreme Politbureau in December, 1934, tens of thousands of communists had "walked the plank." By 1937, Stalin's purge had spread like wildfire from the Soviet Union into the branches of the Comintern; the majority of Communist Party heads abroad were called to Moscow like so many prisoners called by the jailer for questioning. Among many others was also Earl Browder, the American. Moscow probed their loyalty. The willingness of comrade to betray comrade constituted the test. All through the spring and summer of 1937, they passed through Copenhagen on their way to the Red Square, a rather taciturn, bedraggled, apprehensive lot of revolutionists. Those who returned were in high spirits; they had made the grade, they had passed the test, they were feted on their return through Copenhagen because they had convinced the G.P.U. that they believed that Stalin was really the wise and benign father of the oppressed on all continents.

"Everything is going fine," Comrade Jensen concluded, after reviewing the main events of the purge in Soviet Russia. "The Comintern has never been stronger than it is now."

Before Jensen departed, I had fallen asleep. I slept through the rest of the night and through most of the following day. The smell of coffee awoke me. Petra Petersen, home from her office, was stomping around in wine-red pajamas. When she saw that my eyes were open, she sat down at the edge of the couch and ran her firm cool hand over my forehead.

"Comrade how do you feel?" she said softly.

A day later I met Ernst Wollweber in the offices of the Western Secretariat. Of all the top-ranking German communists I had known, he was the only one who had survived. He had grown fat, and his head was almost bald. The clothes he wore, the restaurants he frequented, and the cars that were at his disposal bespoke his prosperity. But beneath the signs of opulence and good living, he was still the chunky, slow-moving, saturnine ex-mutineer I had known so well in bygone years. His small black eyes gleamed through clouds of cigarette smoke. From his thick lips the words rolled in a sullen growl.

"You have shown resource and skill," he said. "We have attached great importance to Comrade Tonio's judgment of you. Maybe it was a mistake that we sent you to Germany. You were too well known there—at least on the coast. I am glad you are back. Take a week off and write a report, a detailed report. Omit nothing."

I found my bearings slowly.

The secret headquarters of the Westbureau of the Comintern were situated in Vesterport, the largest and most modern office building in the heart of Copenhagen. They occupied a flight of seven rooms on the third floor. The atmosphere there was that of a prosperous engineering firm. A score of typists, guards and translators, in shifts, remained continuously on duty. The guards— Scandinavians, Letts and Poles—were armed with fountain pens filled with tear gas. A system of warning buzzers had been built into the walls. Conspicuous was only the complete absence of telephones. All messages were dispatched by courier. Aside from the front office, the home of the Westbureau was divided into six departments. Head of the Political Department was Kuusinen, who had been Lenin's personal friend, and who now divided his time between Moscow and the Comintern capital of the West. Chief of the pivotal Organization Department was Wollweber. The Espionage Defense *Apparat* was led by Michel Avatin, the Lett; and the treasury was in the hands of Richard Jensen, who had become a member of the Copenhagen City Council. In addition, there was attached to the Westbureau a number of Russians with ill-defined functions; one of them, the head of the North American Bureau, posed as a New Zealander named "Richard Rast." The name plate at the main entrance to the offices of the Westbureau bore the legend: *A. Selvo & Co., Architects and Engineers*. It was but one of nine offices which the Comintern and the G.P.U. maintained in Copenhagen.

May and June passed. The tension created in international communist ranks by the undiminished ferocity of Stalin's three-year purge was greatly increased by the bloody struggle between G.P.U. troops and Anarchists in Barcelona and other loyalist cities in Catalonia. Mutual distrust among comrades was apparent everywhere; it grew as the successes of the Popular Front policy increased. Old friends studiously shunned one another, and when they met, it was only on official business. Everyone collected "material" against everybody else. In this atmosphere I could not find my place. The Comintern was not what it had been in 1923, and neither was I the same youngster who had stormed police strongholds and fought behind barricades with a gun in my hand. Firelei now meant more to me than Joseph Stalin or the Soviet Constitution.

I had but little work to do. Three times each week I met one or the other of the Gestapo couriers from Hamburg; the reports and the material I handed him for delivery to Kraus and Schreckenbach came to me from Michel Avatin's department, which supplied me with cautiously assembled misinformation interspersed with morsels of industrial and military intelligence from the European hauls of the G.P.U. These morsels were designed to please the Gestapo without impairing Soviet interests. Moreover, the *S-Apparat* of the Comintern did not hesitate to keep the Gestapo informed of the movements and personnel changes in the rival organizations of the Socialist—or Second—International. By directing the Gestapo's attention toward the socialists, the Comintern diverted Nazi efforts from the communist machine. The bulk of the contents of the misinformation reports which I handed to the Gestapo couriers came directly from Moscow, brought by the regular weekly Soviet couriers to Copenhagen. The names and addresses of Gestapo agents and relay-stations which I had managed to obtain were put under G.P.U. surveillance. Avatin, his killer instinct aroused, burned to do away with them; but Wollweber cautioned him: Assassinations of Gestapo agents in the Scandinavian countries would inevitably lead to the disruption of the counter-espionage bridge which I had established.

Day and night I maneuvered for an opportunity to spirit my wife and child out of Germany. But the comrades whom I approached in this matter shied away. The fear of the Stalin purge filled their heads: it had killed initiative, and it had extinguished comradeship. The Comintern was now infested with a new species of spies. A careless word, spoken to a supposed friend, might be malevolently distorted and reported to the G.P.U.—with a sudden call to Moscow as the result. The G.P.U. held by the necks the communist leaders everywhere, and it was never at a loss to find a way, if need be, of drawing the noose around them.

At the end of June, in a conference with Wollweber, Jensen and Avatin, I requested point-blank that the Comintern courier organization operating in Germany should undertake to smuggle Firelei and our son out of the country.

"It is a small thing to you," I insisted. "It can be done by three or four determined comrades. And to me, this is a big thing." Almost at once Michel Avatin voiced his readiness for action. To him, every coup against the Gestapo was a feast. Jensen hesitated, waiting for Wollweber's opinion. The Silesian rejected my plea.

"We cannot afford to risk the liquidation of an excellent line of communication to the Gestapo," he said. "To the contrary. Our contacts must be built up. In the near future, we shall—through you—suggest to the Gestapo a number of reliable comrades as prospects for Gestapo service. The disappearance of Firelei would wreck our chances of planting our operatives there. If that is not clear to you, comrade, then you are no Bolshevik."

I flew up in a wild rage. Ernst Wollweber had married a Norwegian girl for whom, it seemed, he had a deep affection. Her name was Sylvia. She was the sister of Arthur Samsing, and a member of the G P.U. Arthur Samsing had been sent to Russia in 1933, and had not been heard of again. Wollweber's former mistress, Cilly, had also vanished after her release from a Nazi jail. I mentioned these facts.

"Comrade Wollweber," I shouted, "were Sylvia in Germany in Firelei's position, would you still say: 'She must stay there and perish so that a few spies can dig themselves in a little deeper'?"

"That's not the issue at hand," Wollweber muttered.

After this meeting, walking alone with Avatin through dark streets, I said to the Lett:

"Give me five hundred Danish crowns and a commission to go to Germany for one week."

Avatin halted. His bold head was silhouetted against the lurid light of a street lantern. "You may not come back alive, comrade," he said.

"I must go," I announced.

"You cannot go without Party orders."

"You are my superior," I said stubbornly. "Give me the orders."

"The Gestapo are no fools," Avatin warned.

"Remember Malka, your girl," I went on vehemently. "When she was arrested in Poland—what did you do? You flew to Poland, permission or no, to rescue her."

"Shut up!" Avatin cursed in Latvian. "Malka is dead. Don't speak of her."

"I must rescue Firelei!" I almost screamed.

For a while Avatin deliberated with himself. "I understand," he said finally. "Go to Germany. I shall give you something to deliver to the Gestapo—as protection, just in case of an emergency. Meet me tomorrow morning at six, at the Devil's Bridge."

We parted.

In a taxi I raced out to Charlottenlund to gather a few necessary things. Petra Petersen was in an amorous embrace with a boy from the Young Communist League; her man-hunger was immense.

"Where are you going?" she cried.

"To Sweden," I answered. "I shall be back in six days."

In the cool morning I met Avatin at the Devil's Bridge. He handed me money and a package containing the material for the Gestapo. "It is Russian," he said. "Crew lists of Soviet ships. Three years old. They can have them. *Bon voyage!*"

I boarded the Gjedser-Wamemuende day express. Seven hours later I was on German soil. I did not reach Blumenthal, where Firelei was living with our boy. I had been so excited that I did not realize that I was traveling without a passport until the railroad ferry across the Baltic was well under way. I cursed the laxity of the Danish officials in Gjedser: had they done their duty and demanded to see my passport, I should have been warned in time.

It was too late to turn about. When the ferry reached Sassnitz, the German terminal on the Island of Ruegen, the Gestapo agent on passport duty detained me. There was no other way for me to wriggle out of the situation than to request the agent to telephone Inspector Kraus of the Foreign Division. He telephoned. Hertha Jens was on the wire. She told the frontier agent to let me pass. I now had no choice but to proceed to Gestapo headquarters in

Hamburg. Had I not had Avatin's package to deliver, I would have been lost.

Inspector Kraus received me. I told him that I had been forced to travel without passports because the Danish frontier police were likely to have my name in their list of foreign suspects.

"Where do you keep your Gestapo credentials?" he demanded.

"I buried them in a safe place," I answered.

Kraus regarded the record of Soviet ship crews, which I brought him, as an important find. I told him that I had stolen them at the Soviet shipping office in Copenhagen. I did not tell him that they were three years old. He said he would have them translated and checked against the names on the Gestapo suspect lists of Soviet agents.

"Now that you have worked yourself in," he suggested, "we must come sooner or later to arrests. Perhaps I'll send a few of my young men over to help you in the next few months."

With this I pretended agreement. I was glad to get away from under his eyes.

On the way out, I ran into Magnus, one of the Gestapo men who had arrested me in 1933. He pounded my back and invited me for a drink. We spoke of recent arrests of Czech and Polish spies.

"By the way," he remarked, "we have caught a traitor in our own force. He was working for the Muscovites."

I felt the blood rush to my heart.

"Who?" I inquired, in a voice so low that I did not know whether the word had left my lips or whether it had only been a thought.

"Rudolf Heitman," Magnus said drily. "He worked in the Railroad Control Department. He says he's innocent, but it won't help him. We have evidence. We found photographs of certain communist prisoners in his apartment. He stole them from the files. Besides, he spent a lot more money than his salary allowed for. That's Heitman. He's going to lose his carrot."

Five days I was held up in Hamburg. They were filled with unbearable suspense. But Heitman betrayed nothing. Nevertheless, he was held for trial by a Special Tribunal.

On the sixth day I received permission to visit Firelei. I reported my defeat to her. The Gestapo knew that I was in Germany, which meant that flight, for the present, was out of question. Firelei was patient and courageous.

"We shall find a way," she said. "We must not lose hope."

A telegram from Inspector Kraus called me back to Hamburg.

A mysterious Russian who gave his name as Popoff, had been arrested aboard a train. From a Gestapo photograph I recognized in him a G.P.U. officer I had known as Schmidt.

"Do you know the man?" Schreckenbach asked me.

"No," I replied.

At the station, under the eyes of a Gestapo watcher, I kissed Firelei goodby. It was the last kiss. I did not know that I would never kiss her again.

I returned to Denmark disguised as a member of the crew of the German steamer *Jade*. The captain was a Nazi. The Gestapo had ordered him to sign me on, and to book me in his log-book as a deserter after I had vanished in Copenhagen. At once I reported the intelligence I had gathered to the Western Secretariat.

Wollweber was undisturbed at the news of Rudolf Heitman's arrest.

"Heitman was a questionable customer anyway," he remarked. "He had the old spy disease: he worked for both sides. Besides, he has cost us a small fortune."

But the Silesian was greatly perturbed when I told him of Popoff's arrest in Harburg, and of the suspicions and plans of Schreckenbach. He turned in his chair.

"Comrade Schmidt taken?" he exclaimed in a voice that was half-growl, half-snarl.

I had never seen him so agitated. He paced the office, a truculent and dismayed little man, bald, burly, his eyes glinting, his thumbs hooked in his belt, his teeth chewing an unlighted cigarette to shreds.

"We must do something," he growled. "We must do something. Of course they'll break him. Anybody can be broken. We'll have to recall a lot of men before Schmidt is made to tell their names. He should have guts enough to kill himself before he cracks."

"He can't," I said.

"Irons?"

"He's chained day and night."

I learned that Schmidt-Popoff had become since 1933 one of the most important agents of the Soviet military intelligence in Northern Germany. He had contacts in the navy yards, the railroad centers, the Labor Front, the Lueneburg army training camp, and aboard several German warships. Nine other trained operatives were working under Popoff's direction. Secret photographic *ateliers* in Stettin and Hanover were at his disposal. It had taken many months of painstaking effort to build up this organization. If Popoff talked, the whole Soviet espionage network north of Berlin would be blasted. If Popoff's aides were recalled, their lives would be saved, but it would mean the abandonment of important positions in Germany.

Wollweber muttered, "No, no, no! We cannot dissolve our German set-up without a stiff fight." Abruptly he added: "What guarantee have we that this comrade has not given things away already?"

"Popoff looked strong," I said. "But Schreckenbach will crush him. It'll take him weeks, but he'll crush him."

"Any comrade who falls asleep on a train ought to be shot." Wollweber crouched in a corner of his office, his thick neck thrust forward, pondering. "Get me Avatin," he finally ordered. "I want to see him at five. Tell Jensen to instruct all groups to suspend temporarily all communications with the North German *Apparat*. Notify Berlin, Hamburg, Prague, Basle, Strasbourg, Paris, Rotterdam, Amsterdam, Stockholm, Antwerp, Brussels and Danzig."

"All right."

By five o'clock that afternoon Richard Jensen had dispatched couriers to Berlin, Hamburg and Stettin, and coded messages to all other points. The head of the Foreign Division of the G.P.U. in Paris was informed. Through prearranged messages, Popoff's aides in Germany were warned to change their addresses and passports immediately, and to stop all operations until further notice, but to remain at their posts. A courier had been sent to Stockholm to recall the agent in charge of the Swedish section; this agent, a Russian of German extraction, was to go to Germany to prepare for the continuation of the work previously attended to by Popoff. At five o'clock Wollweber, Avatin, Jensen, I, and a smooth-looking man whom I now met for the first time, gathered in a private dining room of the Hotel d'Angleterre, opposite the Royal Opera House. Wollweber and Avatin had their plans already worked out.

The Silesian spoke with precision. He instructed me to report to the Gestapo that Popoff was only a minor courier, and that it would take me some days to collect more detailed information about the captured Russian. Furthermore, he indicated that a way had to be found to lure a man from Schreckenbach's corps out of Germany. Wollweber proposed to lure him either to France or Denmark, with the aid of a bait that would greatly whet the Gestapo's appetite. Once the Gestapo operative was outside of Germany, it would be Avatin's job to seize him and ship him, alive, to Leningrad—to be held as a hostage for Popoff.

"Once we have the scoundrel in our hands," Wollweber concluded, "we can telephone Schreckenbach and let him know that his agent will fare exactly as Popoff fares in Germany. They'll leave Popoff alone. Then we negotiate. We send him a passport to prove that he's Popoff. We'll agree to put Schreckenbach's man on a German ship in Leningrad, provided that Popoff is put aboard a Soviet steamer in Hamburg. We swap prisoners—and keep our German *Apparat* intact."

"Why not grab one of the Gestapo fellows who are in Copenhagen right now?" Jensen suggested.

"Small fry," Wollweber muttered. "We want a brigand from headquarters."

Avatin's eyes lit up. His willingness to help an important colleague equaled his cold hatred for policemen. He shrank from nothing. "Good," he said. "Let's go."

The fifth man in our council voiced hesitations. He was a member of the Soviet consulate in Copenhagen. He pointed out that an unforeseen mistake could cause trouble with the Danish authorities. It would not only endanger diplomatic relations, but also the whole Copenhagen *Apparat* of the G.P.U. and the Comintern. Wollweber, without uttering a word, stared the Russian into submission.

"We'll do it right here in Denmark," he said to the consular agent. *"You* will then be good enough to undertake the palaver with Schreckenbach. You will also request Leningrad to put the right boys on the next two or three ships that come here."

The vision of the tortured Popoff haunted me. The chance of aiding in the dispatch of a Gestapo agent to his doom was difficult to resist. But what of Firelei? I pointed out that the abduction of a Nazi in Copenhagen would probably disrupt my line of contact with the Gestapo. "Firelei, too, is a comrade," I said.

"We'll be careful," Wollweber promised. "It need not be Copenhagen. Why not Sonderburg?"

Jensen grinned. "Sonderburg is a good place," he said.

"The Party comes first." Avatin pressed the words through his teeth. "We must rescue Popoff before he goes to the dogs."

The Party comes first! Mountains of wrecked lives are buried beneath that epitaph! When a man belonged to the Party, he really *belonged* to it, body and spirit, without reserve. Despite the cynicism which grows in the hearts of men who have devoted their lives to the cause—we loved our Party, and we were proud of its power, proud of our own serfdom, because we had given it all our youth, all our hopes, all the enthusiasm and selflessness which we had once possessed.

Wollweber glowered. "Comrade Firelei is a Bolshevik, too," he said, giving my own words a sardonic and threatening twist. "It so happens that we cannot do without your help."

"I was thinking of that," I said sarcastically.

"Does that mean that you are ready to sacrifice Comrade Popoff and the *Apparat* to avert a hypothetical danger from your kin?"

I sensed the hidden menace in this sally.

"After all," Wollweber went on in a friendlier tone, "it is not at all certain that the Gestapo will connect you with the disappearance of one of their agents."

I replied, "You know better, Comrade Ernst. Schreckenbach is no fool."

Wollweber grinned. When he grinned, his masklike face became an ugly grimace. He was incapable of mirth which was not saturated with contempt.

"Are you afraid?" he growled.

"No."

"Then let's go ahead with the job."

The reports which I sent, under instructions from the Westbureau, to the headquarters of the *Auslandsabteilung* of the Gestapo of Hamburg contained misinformation calculated to throw the Gestapo off the tracks of Comintern and G.P.U. men actually working in Germany. The Nazi secret police received the names of known Communists who were at that time in the Soviet Union as the names of agents operating on German soil. Faked lists of German members of the International Brigade in Spain were given to Schreckenbach as copies of genuine recruiting files. When the Comintern concentrated its forces in the Rhineland, the Gestapo got a report that Bolshevist conspiracy was in the making in Silesia. Communists arrested in Germany were denounced as traitors by the Comintern to ease the lot of the imprisoned men. I sent the Gestapo false codes, carefully prepared bogus letters allegedly stolen from Comintern files, and old passports discarded by Richard Jensen as useless; false lists of shipping contacts, reports of the Moscow show trials, and many other items of supposedly secret character. Once in a while the Westbureau interlaced this maze of faked information with facts which would check with evidence known to be already in the possession of Schreckenbach and his aides. We invented meaningless terms, such as DUNS, REPS, etc., and imparted to them a mysterious significance. All this was done with greatest care, and the Gestapo seemed to swallow it all. But now I was to use our carefully-built up channel of misinformation to lure one of Hitler's man hunters across the frontier to Danish soil.

A special Nazi courier who maintained contact between myself and Schreckenbach operated under the guise of a sleeping-car porter on the night express Hamburg-Copenhagen. I met him every Tuesday and Friday morning in obscure little restaurants in the vicinity of Soederport. He brought me instructions and money and conveyed back to Schreckenbach whatever material I had to give him. This Gestapo courier, a slight man with a small black mustache and horn-rimmed glasses, used the name of Petersen. Occasionally he brought me in contact with other Gestapo agents active in Copenhagen and elsewhere.

Four days after I had met Wollweber and Avatin at the Hotel d'Angleterre, I contacted Petersen. He came out of the yard where the train by which he had arrived from Hamburg was being cleaned. He walked slowly ahead of me, and I followed him. After he had made sure that he was not observed by any third person, he slipped into a basement restaurant, where I joined him.

Petersen handed me a list of instructions from Schreckenbach. The Gestapo wanted me to investigate a number of persons in Danish and Swedish towns who had been anonymously denounced as having contact with anti-Nazi elements in Germany. He also showed me a number of photographs of men who had been caught smuggling a truckload of revolutionary pamphlets across the French-German border, wanting to know if I could identify any of the captured smugglers.

I handed him the usual report which had been concocted the previous day at the headquarters of the Western Secretariat. Then, following instructions from Wollweber, I said:

"Listen, I've got something much bigger. Wollweber is going tomorrow on a conference tour through Denmark. Sunday he'll be in Aarhus, Monday in Esbjerg, Tuesday in Sonderburg."

Petersen quietly made notes. "What of it?" he demanded. "What of it?" I repeated. "I said Wollweber will be in Sonderburg on Tuesday. Sonderburg is less than ten kilometers from the German frontier."

I could see the excitement mounting inside Petersen. His eyes shone bright, his face grew pale, and his hands became restless. He steadied his hands around the beer glass.

"Wollweber in Sonderburg," he mumbled.

"All Schreckenbach has to do is to send one or two of his young men to Sonderburg with a speedboat or a good car. Pounce on Wollweber and carry him off to hell."

"Is he going to be alone?" Petersen inquired cautiously.

"He'll have a translator with him, an old idiot. Tell Schreckenbach not to send too many men. Wollweber is an old wolf. He'll fly off at the slightest suspicion. Wollweber is short, thick, smokes too much. He can't fight. He can't run fast. He's a cinch."

"Where's the meeting?"

"Probably in Bork's tavern. Halfway between Sonderburg station and the waterfront."

Petersen emptied his beer. "Wollweber can be abducted," he announced calmly.

Petersen did not wait in Copenhagen for the departure of his train. Still in his *Mitropa* porter's uniform, he jumped into a taxi and took the first plane to Berlin.

By Tuesday morning Avatin had made his preparations. He had sent two of his men to Sonderburg immediately after Petersen's departure. They were to watch the station and the steamer landing for Gestapo arrivals. Most of the faces of men working in Schreckenbach's division were known to us. They had been photographed by G.P.U. men when entering and leaving their offices in Hamburg and Berlin. Comrades, released from German camps, had later identified many of the enlarged photos as pictures of Gestapo agents who had questioned them.

Tuesday morning Avatin himself, accompanied by men he had recalled from Sweden and Norway, proceeded to Sonderburg. The most reliable comrades of the Sonderburg Party local had been mobilized to aid the G.P.U. expedition. All of Avatin's aides were armed.

Of course, Ernst Wollweber did not budge from his Copenhagen abode. In his apartment on Oerensudsvej he discussed with Jensen, in my presence, the possibilities of shipping the prospective hostage to Russia. They had under consideration the Soviet steamer *Lena,* and the Danish steamers *E. M. Dalgas* and *Ask,* the crews of which had already shown their mettle in previous enterprises.

Hour after hour we waited for Avatin's message from Sonderburg, telling us that he had seized his man.

A half hour before midnight Avatin's message arrived. The telegram read: "Meat shipment delayed." It meant that no abduction had taken place.

I was vastly relieved. Jensen, who had been playing chess, cursed violently. He scattered his chessmen all over the floor. Wollweber stopped his pacing. He sat down at a table and began devising another scheme to kidnap a Gestapo man before Popoff would give up resistance in the Fuhlsbuettel dungeon.

Next morning I met Avatin at the Nordland Hotel on Vesterbrogade. I asked him what had happened in Sonderburg.

He gave a harsh laugh. "Nothing," he said. "Only Wollweber was much too big a fish to make a good decoy. Sonderburg was full of Gestapo men. All Flensburg Fjord was lined with storm troopers. The whole Hamburg *Rollkommando* was on the spot, a steamer, cars, a dozen motorcycles. Inspector Kraus was there. Everybody was there except Schreckenbach himself. Soon the Kingdom of Denmark is going to be a Nazi colony."

"That was to be expected," I observed. "They've had bad experiences with

Wollweber."

Avatin studied his hands. Ruefully he said, "Sorry I didn't take a couple of machine guns down to Sonderburg. In all the village just three policemen were on duty."

After a consultation with Wollweber, I sent a coded letter to Schreckenbach, explaining that the sudden influx of German stalwarts in the sleepy town of Sonderburg had caused the local Party committee to warn Wollweber that "something was rotten in Denmark."

At my next rendezvous with Petersen I was astonished to hear that Inspector Kraus of the Hamburg Gestapo, who had led the invasion of Sonderburg, had detailed two Nazi police agents to take permanent quarters in Copenhagen to track down a radio station maintained by the G.P.U. to receive information flashed by Soviet spies in Germany. I knew of no such radio station in Germany. But it struck me that Popoff must have known, and I feared that Popoff had begun to talk. Petersen refused to reveal the whereabouts of the two Gestapo operatives. We learned their names weeks later, through a waiter in Café Helmerhus, which the two Nazis frequented. They were Herrmann Teege and L. Brauch, both of Schreckenbach's *Inspektion 6*.

In accordance with a plan worked out by the Westbureau, I mentioned to Petersen that I had seen a package of forged passports in the apartment of a Party member, and that these passports were to be used by German communists within the next three months. Petersen duly reported this piece of news to Schreckenbach in Hamburg. A day later I received a short letter from Inspector Kraus, asking if the "children could be photographed." At once I informed Avatin that the Gestapo was anxious to have photostatic copies of the imaginary passports.

"Splendid! Tell the Gestapo to send one of their bandits with a camera." Avatin only showed his cruel little grin.

Came Friday. On the same night express with Petersen came a man whom Petersen introduced to me as Oskar. Oskar was tall, thin, blond, about thirty-six, elegantly dressed and apparently perfectly at ease. He was the agent Schreckenbach had sent to photograph the passports. From the minute he stepped out of the railway depot he was under surveillance of Avatin's guerrillas.

Oskar spoke briskly. He wanted me to bring the passports to the apartment of a young lady he said he knew, Lily de Korte, on the top floor of an apartment house on Osterbrogade. I replied that it was too risky to remove the passports from their present hiding-place, but that I would meet him after dark in the vicinity of the house in which the passports had been hidden. He could then photograph them in a hotel room. Oskar agreed. Before we parted, I asked him about Popoff. Oskar ran a finger around his neck.

"By and by his head will come off," he said.

I do not know if Popoff lost his life or not. The life of Firelei was worth more to me than the life of Popoff. I accused myself of allowing my love for my wife and child to make me waver in my life-long commitment to Stalin's cause. On that Friday in September I began to hate the movement I served, hate its hypocrisy, hate the brigands who led it. I could have warned Oskar, and could have betrayed Stalinism to save my luckless family. Yet I did not do it.

Between ten and eleven three G.P.U. men under Avatin slugged Oskar in one of the dark side streets which run off Holmbladsgade. They carried him into a taxicab, driven by a Party member, and brought him to one of the weekend houses which the Comintern maintains as emergency retreats in the outskirts of Copenhagen. There Oskar was kept a prisoner, chained hand and foot, as Popoff was chained in Fuhlsbuettel prison. On the night of October 10, Oskar again was slugged unconscious by his G.P.U. keepers and carried aboard the Soviet steamer *Kama* in the harbor of Copenhagen. On October 11, the *S.S. Kama* steamed seaward, bound for Archangelsk.

Chapter Forty-two

ABDUCTED

I was determined to sever all further connections with the Gestapo. But Firelei's perilous position in Germany compelled me to execute my plan with the utmost caution. Without first consulting the Westbureau, I let the Gestapo's regular couriers wait vainly for my appearance at our regular rendezvous. A week passed. Schreckenbach's messengers, unable to contact me in Copenhagen, returned to Hamburg empty-handed.

Schreckenbach, not hearing from his agent, Oskar, nor from me, dispatched a night letter to a cover address in Copenhagen, with which, at the advice of Jensen, I had supplied the Gestapo for use in emergencies. Unknown to the Gestapo, such letters went through Jensen's hands before they were given to me. Richard Jensen was disturbed. The Gestapo wanted to know why I had not met its regular couriers. It also wanted to know what had happened to Oskar.

I scribbled a hasty-looking note to the effect that I was on my way to the Soviet Union to attend a military school—aware of the Gestapo's keen interest in this field. This note I sent to Petrolevics, the Comintern liaison agent in Riga, with instructions to mail it to Schreckenbach's cover address in Hamburg. This gave the note the appearance of having been mailed *en route* to Moscow. The Gestapo would not expect me to write reports from Russia, and would understand my silence in the future. And Firelei, I calculated, would not have to fear retaliatory measures.

On a morning in October I was called to a conference with Wollweber and Kuusinen in a restaurant near the Thorvaldsen Museum. They ordered me to continue my work for the Comintern inside Hitler's Secret Police. Brusquely I told them that I had burned my bridges, that I was through with that assignment.

"I have told the Gestapo that I went to Russia," I explained. "As far as they are concerned, I have vanished."

Kuusinen smiled enigmatically.

"Well," he suggested, "after a few days you will write to the Gestapo that you have returned from Moscow and are now back in Copenhagen."

The next instant I stood in open mutiny against two of the most powerful figures in the Soviet Secret Service and the Comintern, both of which had by 1937 become thoroughly interlocked.

"Give me four men from Comrade Avatin's *Apparat* to maneuver my wife and child out of Germany," I demanded. "It has been done before; it can be done for me."

"You will not—"

"No," I interrupted. "I refuse!"

Kuusinen shrank back. He was frightened. He had always had the reputation of being a coward. My fists, after all, were still those of a sailor. He—Kuusinen—had never done an honest day's work since he had left the workers of Finland at the mercy of General Mannerheim, while he, their leader, had salvaged his skin by fleeing to Russia, to seek the Kremlin's forgiveness by writing documents of self-humiliation. Those were my thoughts.

Wollweber remarked that I sought to use the Westbureau as a means for the solution of my private difficulties.

"Private difficulties!" I snarled into Wollweber's face. "The thousands of comrades in the Nazi concentration camps would like to hear that! The ones who had their heads chopped off, the ones who were hanged, cut to pieces, beaten to death. The ones who died with the cry, 'Long live the Communist Party!' They all would like to hear that—the attitude of Comrade Wollweber, their leader, who sits on safe ground on a salary of six hundred dollars a month."

Kuusinen had jumped up and decamped during my tirade. Wollweber stood his ground.

"Calm yourself," he growled.

"I am calm."

"You are burned out; you need a rest."

"I am not burned out and I don't need a rest," I countered. "Only I'm disgusted at playing ball with the Gestapo. Give me the job of cutting the throat of one of the Nazi sadists, and I'll do it, even if it will cost me my life. Give me any other function, and I'll carry it out. But don't expect me to be the hangman of Comrade Firelei and my son."

Wollweber said stonily, "The Secretariat will consider your request."

I had made powerful enemies. From that day on I became in the eyes of Kuusinen and Wollweber and their legion of henchmen a Bolshevik in whom they no longer could place absolute trust. It was no secret in our ranks that Stalin's quiet method of eliminating —by intrigue, calumny and cold murder—all rivals and subalterns who still retained a spirit of independence had long been adopted also by his leading genuflectors throughout the Soviet network. Only those who succeeded in finding "wreckers" and "Trotskyite reptiles" among their closest friends could be sure of saving their jobs and budgets and lives. No longer as in the past, were antagonisms ironed out in stormy sessions. Straightforward talk was shunned like the pest. Instead, intrigues were spun, secret denunciations were written to influential friends in Moscow, G.P.U. terrorists were brought into play. Old, long-tested comrades were weeded out without apparent reason, and ruthless unknown newcomers took over the jobs of the purged. The bold revolutionary enthusiasm of bygone years had degenerated into sly cunning, cautious wriggling, snakelike assaults. No one in the higher Party circles believed that the "confessions" of the Bolshevik Old Guard in the Moscow show trials were true; yet everyone pretended to be convinced of the villainy of those who were once

Lenin's aides. The Comintern echoed the Kremlin's shouts: "Destroy the heretics! Shoot them down like mad dogs!"

I did not have to wait long. To Petra Petersen's apartment, where I had been isolated as if I had the cholera, came Richard Jensen's son, Martin, with orders from the Westbureau.

"Go to the Soviet consul to get your sailing papers for Russia!"

"I want to see Wollweber," I demanded.

"Comrade Wollweber has gone to Paris."

"Then I must see Kuusinen or Avatin."

"Kuusinen went to Moscow," Martin Jensen said. 'Avatin has business in Sweden."

"And what is my business in the Soviet Union?"

"A tour of inspection through the International Clubs—Leningrad, Black Sea ports, Vladivostok."

"All right. I can't go today; it's too late."

"Go early tomorrow."

For several days I deliberated on what I should do. "Is this the end?" I asked myself. "The miserable end?" Except Petra Petersen, I saw no one. My former friends shunned me. No one west of Leningrad, it seemed, dared to exchange a friendly word with one who had challenged Ernst Wollweber and his ilk. And Wollweber, I realized, feared me—for I was a spokesman for the multitude of silenced revolutionists who had been thrown into Hitler's maw for no good purpose. Faces trooped through my mind, the faces of men and women who had been sent in cold blood to prison and death because they were obstacles in the Silesian's path to total power. I decided to give battle. The chance for a counter-thrust came when I heard from Petra Petersen that an important emissary of the Soviet Government had come by plane from Paris to Copenhagen to discuss with Jensen the chartering of Scandinavian vessels to carry war supplies to the ports of Loyalist Spain. This emissary was Leo Haikiss. I accosted him, as if by chance, in the Soviet consulate.

Haikiss had been one of the founders of the Leningrad Tcheka in the initial stages of the Revolution. In the early twenties he had become the propaganda chief of the Comintern in Central Europe, operating from Berlin with Bela Kun and Karl Radek. Later he was attached to the Soviet embassy in Mexico, from which position he directed G.P.U. activities in Central and South America. He appeared in Spain in 1936, together with A. Vronsky, G.P.U. head of the so-called "motorized death" detachments in Madrid, and later became Soviet Ambassador there.

Haikiss, who had a brief glimpse of me in Berlin years before, began to ask me questions. He was particularly interested in Gestapo activities in Spain, the surrender of captured German anti-Nazis by General Franco to the Gestapo, and the doings of Comintern "activist" groups formed in German seaports to create sabotage acts and diversions against Nazi war shipments for the Spanish rebel army. We talked about the work of the Western Secretariat, and suddenly Haikiss astonished me with the remark: "Wollweber—hm, he is a bandit."

I told Haikiss that I had mutinied against Wollweber, and that I suspected Wollweber of having arranged for my trip to the Soviet Union for the purpose of getting me out of the way.

"This Wollweber," Leo Haikiss said slowly. "What is his background? Can you tell me of his private affairs? Or little opportunistic mistakes in his past? Manuilsky in Moscow is his good friend, and, to a lesser degree, Comrade Molotov. He will not deal with Dimitrov. Could it be that Wollweber is a secret friend of the Gestapo?"

Haikiss was a high official of the G.P.U. He was the superior of Avatin. The Western Secretariat had no jurisdiction over him. They were rivals. In Spain, I knew, the Comintern had fared badly at the hands of the G.P.U. Even such powerful figures as Heinz Neumann and Bela Kun had been carried off to Russia to face the firing squad. Haikiss, like all of his colleagues, collected "material" against all possible rivals. I felt that he had some hidden reason to break Wollweber. So had I.

"I know the names of nineteen comrades who were practically surrendered by Wollweber to the Gestapo," I said. "More than ten of them have been executed."

"How are the relations between Wollweber and Kuusinen?"

"Not of the best; they are too different, and they fear each other."

Haikiss regarded me out of narrowed eyes. His long yellow fingers were never at rest.

"And Avatin?" he inquired.

"Avatin is no intriguer. He is too much of a man of action."

"A very useful comrade," Haikiss observed. Briskly he went on: "Very well! You are not going to the Soviet Union. I will speak with an important comrade when I come to Moscow. Perhaps we shall need you in Spain. Why should you go to Russia when every able comrade is needed abroad?"

"I'd be happy if you will explain this to Comrade Wollweber," I said.

"Not Wollweber. ... I shall see Kuusinen and have a talk with Avatin."

"All right."

"Would you agree to have your family go to the Soviet Union?"

"Yes," I said. "Anything—to get them out of Germany."

"*Kharasho!* You can write me a report on Ernst Wollweber," Haikiss went on. "I do not want a diplomatic report. I want a report that comes from the heart. The comrades in Moscow distinguish between diplomatic reports and honest reports. Remember that Wollweber is a bandit. He drinks. He spends much money with women. In international questions he is a brazen nincompoop. Write in detail and sign your name. Retain no copy. I shall take the original to Moscow."

"Very well."

I wrote the report. Leo Haikiss took it with him to Moscow. I did not know then that he, too, was destined to vanish, like so many others, in Stalin's

Great Purge after the Spanish adventure had ended in dismal defeat.

Two eventless weeks passed. During this time I saw neither Wollweber nor any other member of the Western Secretariat. I was without papers and almost without money. I spent much of my time in writing a description of life in the German prisons. One night I surprised Petra Petersen as she rummaged through my writings. I asked her if she had been assigned to spy on me. She answered arrogantly. I was so wrought up that I threatened to give her a whipping. She broke down immediately. She explained that she had been ordered by Jensen to make copies of "my letters to Moscow."

However, the command that I should go to Russia seemed to have been dropped. Once each week Martin Jensen appeared, and paid me fifteen kroner as my allowance for food. On his second visit, he told me that a rumor had come from Germany that Schreckenbach had put me down on his casualty list. He believed, apparently, that I had blundered, and that I had been taken to Russia together with Oskar. "For the moment," I thought, "Firelei will be safe from Gestapo reprisals—provided that the Gestapo receives no report that I am still outside of the Soviet Union."

In November I received an order to proceed to Antwerp, to take charge of the Comintern communication bureau in that port. Jensen's workshop supplied me with a Swiss passport. Armed with this and a sum of money in American dollars, I boarded the westbound express to Esbjerg. I rejoiced. I believed that I had won at least my first round in my campaign against Wollweber. The Comintern was still mother, fatherland and home to me. I had traveled too far to turn back, to conceive of a life outside the Party. Moreover, as the head of the Antwerp *Apparat*, I felt sure that I would find a way of spiriting Firelei and Jan out of the talons of the Gestapo.

In Esbjerg, on the west coast of Jutland, I spoke to a young girl comrade who had escaped from Germany as stowaway in the chain locker of the steamship *Phoenix*. She betrayed the jumpy nerves of all those who have had a taste of Nazi concentration camp life; at the slightest unexpected noise she would leap from her chair and seemed to draw the air through her nostrils like a terrified animal sensing the nearness of the hunters. I gave her money to go to Copenhagen and report to Richard Jensen. Next day I boarded the steamer *P.A. Bemstorff* for France. In spite of the fact that I had passed through Esbjerg at other times with other passports, the state police in that port stamped without a murmur the new document I showed them.

There were other Comintern agents among the *P.A. Bernstorff's* passengers, bound for Paris, Marseilles, Spain—but all of us pretended not to know one another. The Gestapo knew that the *Bemstorff* was a Comintern ship, and we had to reckon with the eventuality that Schreckenbach had at least one spy among the passengers or crew.

A shadow was cast over my newly won though questionable freedom by the fate of the man whom I was to succeed as liaison chief in Antwerp. My predecessor's name was Franz Richter. He had been a servant of the cause since 1919, and a graduate of the Lenin School. Until the summer of 1931, he had been the secretary of the Hamburg International Club. He had had a wife and two children. He then served in the Leningrad Party machine, and was later appointed to the Antwerp post. The G.P.U. accused him of complicity with Piatakov, a leading Russian Bolshevik who was shot after a show trial in Moscow. Richter was lured aboard a Soviet vessel of the Smolny class—and disappeared. He never reached Leningrad; the ship on which he was held prisoner had to pass the Kiel Canal, where the Gestapo was on duty. Richter was either surrendered to the Nazi police, or he was murdered aboard the Russian vessel and buried in the North Sea.

I knew that the G.P.U. did not hesitate to deliver recalcitrant communists to the Gestapo. This practice bolstered the position of Soviet spies in Himmler's force. There was no more effective method of consolidating a G.P.U. spy's reputation in the Gestapo than to maneuver—through him—a wanted anti-Nazi into Hitler's dungeons; for the Gestapo chiefs based the value of a secret operative on the results he obtained. Promotion in the Nazi police would be his reward.

I left the *P.A. Bemstorff* in Dunkerque, and contacted Manautines, the resident liaison agent, an unkempt but able ruffian, who had his office in the Salle d'Avenir.

"How goes our drive in France?" I asked him.

"Superb," he replied, kissing his fingertips. "The *Front Populaire* has put the government of Paris at our mercy. Three more years of such progress and Red banners will flutter atop the Hotel de Ville."

Manautines escorted me to a seashore point near the border. A Party member living there put two bicycles at our disposal, and we entered Belgium by little-frequented paths, twice wading through shallow ditches. Once a frontier guard stopped us.

"Halt! Where are you going?"

"We are sick of French cigarettes," Manautines cried. "Your Belgian weed is better and cheaper."

The guard took us for smugglers. He grinned and waved us on. Tobacco smugglers were liked in the Flemish border villages. They boosted business, and they always had money to spend.

Manautines left me at Ostend. *"Bon brigandage,"* he laughed. "I have a girl here, a buxom Belgian mare. Also, I want to buy cigarettes. You know, a little money on the side in these times of decreasing budgets. *Au revoir.* I shall report to Copenhagen that you have passed here in prime condition."

From Ostend I took the train to Ghent. Avatin's representative in Ghent, an important post because this old city is a training center for the feared Belgian *gendarmerie* and also a center for Comintern contacts to England, was Verkeest, a grizzled fighter, consisting of little more than skin and bones, who had somehow managed to become a member of the town parliament and of the government harbor commission. Verkeest had trouble, however, with the police. Ever since the second officer of a British weekly tramp had been found mysteriously drowned in the harbor of Ghent, the police had harassed Comrade Verkeest.

"Wherever I move," he complained, "they follow me. But they are as stupid as they are dogged. They rent an apartment opposite from mine, and watch the door from the windows vis-a-vis. Every time I take a field glass and scrutinize the house on the other side of the street, I see a gendarme lurking behind the curtains."

"Why don't you disappear?" I suggested. "Have yourself replaced by a comrade not known in Ghent?"

Verkeest spat at the wall. He shook his meager body disdainfully.

"Every gendarme in this town is my personal enemy," he explained. "I am an old man. I have a head of iron. For twenty years I have fought the gendarmes of Ghent. I would be unhappy without gendarmes around me. Please do not report my quandary to Copenhagen."

I respected the old fighter's wish. A day later I arrived in Antwerp. I found the communist communications *Apparat* in hideous disorder. Since Comrade Richter's death voyage, our special units had been in the hands of Le Minter, a French Bolshevik of good intentions, but of bad habits and limited capabilities. Le Minter had lost the rest of Richter's budget in a card game in a Chinaman's den on Brouversvliet; an agent supposed to go to Freetown, Sierra Leone, had been shipped by Le Minter to Kingston, Jamaica. "I thought Kingston was on the West African coast, so I shipped the comrade there because I had no direct boat to Freetown," Le Minter explained. Propaganda in Malay language, printed in Leningrad and forwarded to Le Minter for transport to Singapore, had been dumped expeditiously into the oily waters of Siberia Dock. Besides, Le Minter collected commissions from a number of French and Flemish prostitutes for sending to them customers from incoming ships. The Comintern transport file, which listed the names of more than five hundred vessels, noted the political attitudes of their crews, contained the names of Party members aboard, etc., had been neglected for weeks.

"You can go to the devil," I told Le Minter. "I have a good mind to ship you off to Russia. You'd make a good pick-and-shovel man for the Tcheka mud-brigades on the White Sea Canal."

Le Minter grew shaky. The contortions on his sallow face showed how he squirmed inside. *"Mon dieu, camarade,"* he muttered. "I am a seasoned fox, but I am a stranger in this beastly northern country. Wine is prohibitive. Nothing but bock beer and potatoes. I am a child of the south. I have innumerable friends along the Mediterranean." Striking his chest, he concluded dramatically "I may even go to Spain. My life-blood, like yours, belongs to the world revolution."

I dispatched Le Minter to Marseilles to assume a minor function in the Comintern Bureau which, from 10 Rue Fauchier, directed communist activities on the North African coast and the Near East. I selected as my chief assistant, to succeed Le Minter, a certain Le Marec, a Frenchman who had become my friend during the French river strike of 1933. In a note sent to Maurice Thorez, the leader of the French Communist Party, I wrote: "I need Le Marec. Please free him from other work." Thorez replied immediately:

"Dear Friend, Le Marec is a devil. I am glad you are taking him off my hands. There are good devils and bad devils. Le Marec is a good devil." I found Le Marec a tireless worker, but he perfectly fitted the description of the ghoul who appears, I believe, in Dickens' *Tale of Two Cities*.

Among the various emissaries who came to Antwerp to be smuggled to various destinations by the maritime courier system of the Comintern was a young Japanese whose Party name was Hito. He had come from Moscow, equipped with proper credentials, and his destination was Honolulu, Hawaii.

"How much money have you?" I asked.

"Forty dollars," Hito replied.

"No budget?"

"Oh, yes! Got budget—but my travel allowance is forty dollars, no more."

It was a difficult order. No ships sailed directly between Continental ports and the Hawaiian Islands. I decided to ship Hito by way of the United States or Panama.

I had known him since 1932. He was the son of a well-to-do merchant in Yokohama. In 1930 his family had sent him to study at the Paris university. His father had granted him a liberal monthly allowance. While in Paris, Hito fell in with one of the Comintern talent scouts who combed the French and German universities for Japanese and Chinese students. As a result, Hito had studied in Moscow instead of Paris. Two years later, Dimitrov had sent him to Hamburg to set up propaganda nuclei aboard Japanese ships. Young Hito had brought with him the most complete Leninist library that could be found in Hamburg. He had taken quarters in the home of a Mrs. Renscher and her two daughters. By January, 1933, both Olga and Bianca Renscher were pregnant. Hitler came to power, and Hito decamped, abandoning his library and his girls. During all this time Hito's father in Yokohama had been left in the belief that his son was a student in Paris; with the regularity of a clock Hito's allowance had continued to arrive in Paris from Yokohama.

"Where have you been since 1933?" I inquired.

"I was very busy," Hito replied.

I finally shipped him out aboard the *Westernland*. It was the last service which I rendered to the Comintern and Stalin.

Once only did I write Firelei from Antwerp, using a cover address we had arranged during our last meeting.

Her answer was brief: *"Don't write—the danger is great."*

Another note followed. *"Wait,"* she wrote me. *"I shall tell you when the time is ripe."*

East of Antwerp lay Germany. More than ever my homeland resembled the jaws of a giant trap. Alone, I realized, I could do nothing. As long as I remained a part of the Comintern, there was hope for rescue.

Fate decided otherwise.

An old personal friend, the Marine Engineer Hans Krause, had been arrested by the G.P.U. in Spain. I received the intelligence through one of the recruiting agents for the International Brigade. Krause was a veteran in the service of the Profintern. He had conducted an arms shipment from Marseilles to Valencia, and had then volunteered for the front. He had been wounded in action. For reasons of its own, the G.P.U. had seized him in the hospital and thrown him into one of the private jails it maintained on Spanish soil. The accusation brought against Krause was the usual one: "Trotskyism and espionage in behalf of General Franco and the Gestapo." The charge was absurd. I knew that Hans Krause was no more a Gestapo spy than Stalin was an agent of the Bank of England. Krause's wife, a Flemish girl who worked in Antwerp in a secretarial position, showed me a letter from her husband which a fellow prisoner had smuggled out of jail. It was a bitter, heartbreaking letter.

"Do something," she pleaded.

Only one man I knew had the power to save Hans Krause. That man was Edo Fimmen, the Secretary General of the International Transport Workers' Federation. For a decade Moscow had struggled to conquer or to destroy Fimmen's organization of millions. Now, since the new policy of the Comintern required the simulation of friendship toward socialist leaders, Moscow might be glad, I calculated, to put Edo Fimmen under obligation by doing him a favor. He was too formidable a personality in the European labor movement to be ignored if he expressed an interest in the fate of Hans Krause. Fimmen, whose organizations in Germany had been smashed, had nevertheless many powerful friends in Holland, England, Belgium, Scandinavia and Spain.

I knew that Edo Fimmen came to Antwerp once each fortnight to confer with his Belgian assistants in a stronghold of the Belgian Social Democratic Party, the Transport House on the Paardemarkt. It was here that I met him. Fimmen, who made his headquarters in Amsterdam, was a Dutchman, robust of figure, cultured, ruddy and full of vitality in spite of his age, and his fine warrior head was topped by a thick white mane.

He promised to intervene in behalf of Hans Krause; he seemed to disregard the fact that Krause and I, as communists, had been his consistent enemies in earlier years. When I left Fimmen, he shook my hand vigorously.

"Some day, perhaps, we can all work together," he said, while an expectant smile played about his mouth.

Eventually, Hans Krause was saved from the G.P.U. firing squad.

Shortly after my meeting with Fimmen, I became aware that I was being watched. I recognized at once that my shadowers were not Belgian policemen. One evening, when one of them was again close upon my heels, I whirled around and confronted him.

"What are you—G.P.U. or Gestapo?" I snapped.

"I am a comrade," the man said sheepishly. It was an eloquent answer.

Two days later a courier conveyed to me the order to meet one of the leading agents of the Comintern in Paris. No one else was to be informed that I was going to France.

I took the train from Antwerp to Courtrai, changing cars at Ghent. From Courtrai I proceeded by tramcar to Menin, a Belgian village directly on the border. From Menin, led by a Party member stationed there to handle the clandestine border traffic, I crossed to the French village of Halluin. Because of the proximity of the Maginot Line extension, the French authorities kept a strict watch on strangers. However, all went well. From Halluin to Tourcoing I went by trolley. A local electric train brought me from Tourcoing to Lille. In Lille I boarded the North Express for Paris.

A courier met me at the *Gare du Nord*. In a taxi we sped down the Boulevard de Magenta, across the Place de la Republique, continuing along the Boulevard Voltaire. I wondered where we were going. My courier said nothing. One never knew in this year of purges from which side the insidious thrust would come.

The taxi stopped in front of an obscure little restaurant on the right bank of the Seine. At a corner table, behind a frugal French breakfast, sat a man I knew well. "Meet Monsieur Maurice," the courier mumbled before he vanished.

"Maurice" was really Adolf Deter, a former member of the Prussian Diet, and at one time head of Profintern operations in Germany; he had engineered the Berlin traffic strike which helped decisively to break the government of Chancellor von Papen, and later he had become a boss behind the huge strikes which brought France to the edge of civil war. Comrade Deter had grown paunchy in exile. A chill grin hovered on his fat round face.

"I have a message from Comrade Wollweber," Deter said softly. "It was better not to give it to you in writing. We need you for a special transaction."

"What is it?" I asked.

"We want to send a comrade to Germany, to Hamburg. We want to make absolutely sure that this comrade arrives in Hamburg. He will contact you in Antwerp. You will put him aboard a boat to Hamburg."

"All right," I said. "There are two good steamers each week."

Deter looked at me obliquely. His thick fingers toyed with the ash tray.

He spoke as if he considered every word as a valuable object. "I have said that this is a special business. I hope you will understand. This comrade who will call on you is not to go to Hamburg on one of our regular ships. He is not to come in contact with any of our confidential Antwerp addresses. He is not to be given any confidential addresses we might have in Germany. He has no passport except an old German document issued under his right name. As soon as he is on the way to Germany, you must send me a card giving the name of the ship and the date of its arrival in Hamburg. Is that clear to you?"

"Perfectly clear," I muttered. "In other words, this comrade is to be liquidated."

Deter winced. "I wish you'd be a little more diplomatic," he said peevishly.

"Why not tell him to go to Russia or Spain?"

"We need him in Germany," Deter said with an air of finality.

This, I reflected, was a case of delivering a communist functionary to the Gestapo. A comrade who for some reason had earned the enmity or the distrust of Deter, Wollweber and their higher-ups was about to be sold to Hitler's secret police to strengthen the precarious perch of Comintern and G.P.U. spies operating inside the Gestapo. One of the latter would undoubtedly deliver this comrade, I thought. A spy who caused the capture of a known communist agent would become, in the eyes of Schreckenbach, a most reliable spy.

"Who is the man?" I demanded.

"You know him: Karl Saar."

I controlled myself. Deter could not see what was in my head. I knew Karl Saar. He was short, blond, in his early thirties, agile as a panther and brimming with energy. He was a fanatic. In December, 1932, he had come from Moscow, a graduate of a Soviet military school. Less than a year later the Gestapo had captured him. Karl Saar was sent to prison. In March, 1936, on a prisoners' transport from Hamburg to Western Germany, he had seized a million-to-one chance, and escaped.

"What is wrong with Comrade Saar?" I demanded.

"He is a dangerous opportunist," Deter said vaguely, adding the warning: "We want no hitch in this. The affair must click. Saar is a danger to the Party."

"Is it a trap?" I thought. "Was all this merely devised as a test of my loyalty? Or do they really want me to send a comrade to his death?"

"All right," I said coldly.

I met Karl Saar in Antwerp. In a blue suit, much too large for him, he looked rather thin and emaciated, but his facial expression bore all the marks of his old determination. Had we met in prison, where speaking was prohibited, we should have connived to exchange views and tales of our experiences for hours; but now, with the whole world to move in, we were held back by a wall of utmost reserve. Above us both stood that great, intangible menace which makes men realize their utter *physical* insecurity from one day to the next.

"Listen, Karl," I told him. "Don't go to Germany."

"Have you received countermanding orders?"

"No."

"Well?"

"You haven't a chance to leave Germany alive, Karl."

He gave me an astonished look. "I know very well that nine out of ten who go never come back," he said.

"This is different," I warned him. "It's worse. Murder. A trap."

"What's the matter with you?"

The shabby furniture about us seemed to swing and reel. "I have instructions to send you to Germany in such a way that the Gestapo will stand on the wharf when your steamer arrives," I explained. "You're slated for liquidation."

"By whom?"

"I cannot tell you."

"Bah!"

After that exclamation, Karl Saar was silent for a whole minute. He shoved his hands under his belt and I could see that he was thinking. We stared at one another like two animals in a cage. Finally he said, "Why should they want to liquidate me?"

"I don't know, Karl."

Karl Saar said viciously: "What is *your* game?"

I pretended not to hear. "I can give you $100," I said. "You can go anywhere you like. There are ships to South America, to Mexico, to New York."

"I am not going to run away," Comrade Saar said.

"Were you a Nazi spy," I continued, "I'd drive a knife between your ribs and be done with it. It seems that most of us who come alive out of Germany, like you or I, are suspected of grubbing for the Nazis. I know what you think. You think that the worst a man can be called is that he is a coward. But this is not a question of courage or cowardice. It is a rotten game, Karl. From what I heard the Comintern considers you a political corpse. Why—I don't know. I won't ask. You're finished if you go to Germany. It's all I can tell you."

At this point Karl Saar laughed harshly:

"Do you still believe in world revolution?"

"No," I said.

"Neither do I," he echoed.

"Then why ..."

"We've chosen our side. The Party must live."

"Do you remember," I continued quietly, "how comrades bled to death in Camp Fuhlsbuettel? How spilled blood screamed from the mattresses? the walls? the floors and even the ceilings? How we sang the funeral march in the middle of the night from cell to cell? How you yelled from the window: 'High the banners! They died for the revolution!'? How the whole prison roared: *'Rache! Rache!'* ? How the guards started shooting at the windows?"

Karl Saar snarled. "Why do you tell me all this?"

I spoke for half an hour. I felt that it was not I who had spoken. It was Hans Krause speaking from the G.P.U. jail in Spain, comrades speaking from the cellars of the Lubianka in the heart of Moscow, comrades speaking from the bitter wastes of the Solovietsky Islands, comrades speaking from the bottom of the North Sea, speaking from countless graves in the Soviet Fatherland, in Germany, the Balkans, in Spain, in all the world—comrades betrayed and crushed by the cause whose loyal soldiers they had been.

"No, Karl," I said, "they did not die for the world revolution; they only thought they did; they died to gratify the lust for power of the Stalin clique; they died because they had been made to believe that it was more honorable to be a stinking corpse than a living thing outside the Party."

I sagged into a chair, exhausted.

Karl Saar looked like a ghost. A fanatic pride shone in his eyes.

"I am going to Germany," he said.

"Anything else I can do for you?"

He hesitated. "Tonight I'd like to sleep with a girl," he said.

Together we went out. I called up Adele, the young Jewess who helped me with the registration of ship movements. She knew that comrades who went to Germany almost never returned. She met Karl at the foot of Antwerp's lone skyscraper. Together they walked away, he seemingly unconcerned, she with a little self-satisfied sway of her body.

That night I went to Brussels Party headquarters. Comrade de Buck, the Belgian Party chief, was away. The best document the Party *Apparat* had on hand was a *carte d'identité* of a local communist who resembled Karl Saar. With such a paper I decided not to send Karl to Germany by ship. Through the Brussels Party machine I arranged for a guide who knew the border country. Next morning he and Karl Saar departed for the German frontier. I sent a telegram to Adolf Deter in Paris, informing him that Karl had left for Hamburg aboard the steamer *Adolph Kirsten*. Barely twenty-four hours later I received a telegram which called me to Copenhagen. Its contents were so worded as to make me think that it had been sent by Leo Haikiss.

Late in December, 1937, I took passage to Esbjerg. The towers of Antwerp sank away astern; the steamer pitched in the green North Sea.

It is less than a two-minute walk from the steamer-landing in Esbjerg to the North Sea terminal of the Copenhagen express. The passport inspection was carried out by officers I had not seen before. I avoided it by walking through the little gate marked "Scandinavians Only." I was halfway between the quay and the station-platform when a burly man in a thick gray sweater stopped me. "Follow me," he said. "I come from Jensen."

Quickly I gave Richard Jensen's password for December: "Does he have coffee?"

"Aye, the best coffee in Copenhagen," he growled in answer. At first I thought Jensen was waiting with special orders for me in one of the waterfront cafes. But the man in the sweater led me to a waiting car. It was an open car with Copenhagen license plates. In it sat two younger men whom I recognized as members of the *S-Apparat*.

"Step in," the sweatered man said.

"Where are we going to?"

"Copenhagen."

"Why not by train? The roads are bad in the winter."

One of the men in the car answered impatiently. "Why so much talk? Let's go. Our orders are to take you to Copenhagen in this automobile. Why? Detectives might be on the train."

That was a feeble excuse. It occurred to me that I was being taken by car to prevent me from communicating with someone on the train. The harbor of Esbjerg was no place to pick a fight. I was known to the Danish authorities as a Comintern agent. It was unwise to risk arrest with a false passport in my pocket. Something, I felt, had gone askew.

I slipped into the front seat. One of the young Danes drove. The other one sat in the back, both hands buried in his overcoat pockets. I tried to joke about their mysterious behavior. They were unresponsive. The burly man in the sweater saw us off.

We drove through the town, past farmhouses and fields, and out into the open heath-like country. The man behind me never took his hands out of his pockets. I turned on him abruptly.

"What have you got in your pockets? All the gold from Spain?" He said stolidly, "No, I have a gun in my pocket."

Halfway across Jutland we almost ran over an enormous hog which had blundered on the road. The car swerved wildly, ripping through a patch of low underbrush. It regained the road, gathering speed.

"You two are fools," I said. "You with your guns. I could just grab the wheel and wreck the car. Who told you to take guns? Comrade Jensen?"

The two were silent. The man behind me began to whistle the Soviet aviation march. When I started to sing the words, he stopped whistling. We drove for fourteen hours, leaving the car only twice for coffee and sandwiches on the Fredericia and Korsor ferries. At four in the morning we entered Copenhagen. Even at that hour the center of the city was filled with gayety and light. Prostitutes in fur coats huddled in the doorways of Vesterbrogade. The car squealed to a stop in front of Richard Jensen's home. In the passage, lined with show-windows, which led to Jensen's door, one of Avatin's men lounged. He jerked his head toward the stairway.

"They're waiting for you," he said.

"What's up?"

"I don't know. A palaver, I suppose, like many others."

Going up the stairway I stamped noisily over steps and landing. The sounds of my footfalls reverberated through the house. "I don't know what will happen up there," I thought, "but it cannot harm to let the other tenants know that men are tramping up to the Jensen apartment hours before dawn."

The guard behind me muttered, "You walk like an earthquake. Cut it out."

"Hold your tongue," I countered. "I walk as I like."

I was ushered into Jensen's study. Jensen, hair disheveled, his huge form wrapped in a dressing gown, nodded a greeting. We did not shake hands. His face was gray and grim under the electric lights. With him were four young men, a German, a Lett and two Scandinavians—G.P.U. aides on Avatin's force. They had been drinking beer. A thin fog of tobacco smoke eddied under the

"Sit down," I was told.

Jensen telephoned. He called the number of the Nordland Hotel, only a few houses away. His voice was a short, indistinct rumble. In a few minutes Jensen's son, Martin, appeared. On his heels, squat, dark, truculent, Ernst Wollweber walked into the apartment.

From the dining-room two guards brought in a large table. Wollweber sat down at one end of the table, I at the other. Between us, on both sides of the table, the guards took their place.

I knew now that I had to expect an inquisition. The old symptoms appeared. My stomach contracted, all muscles grew taut, I was ready to fight, and yet I sat very still, waiting. Jensen took a volume from his bookshelf and slid it toward me across the table. It was the official Soviet report of the Piatakov-Smirnov trial. I brushed it aside.

"Leave out the monkey-business," I said.

Wollweber reached into his pocket. Then he spoke. When Wollweber spoke, his lips were drawn back and he showed his tobacco-stained teeth. His eyes became narrow slits alive with black fire. He had the habit of throwing each word like a rock at his listeners, then jerking forth a rapid sentence or two to amplify what he had said. He was not the same Ernst Wollweber who, nineteen years before, had doused the fires and hoisted the first Red banner over the Kaiser's navy.

"Trotsky, Zinoviev, Bukharin and the other traitors," he said, "have always maintained that they were the staunchest supporters of Lenin. Yet, in every acute crisis they turned *against* Lenin. Such types may be of some use to the revolutionary movement, but in no circumstances can they be entrusted with key positions."

I agreed. Wollweber continued:

"Bitter experience has shown us that every former comrade who was caught conspiring against the Party must, as a matter of necessity, wind up in the camp of Fascism, an ally of Hitler and the counter-revolution."

"Concretely," I said, "what are the denunciations against me and who made them?"

"There are no denunciations," Wollweber growled. "There are charges. Comrade Dimitrov in Moscow is in possession of a report signed by you in which you accuse the Western Secretariat of the Communist International of having uselessly sacrificed able comrades on wild-goose chases in Germany."

"I did not accuse the Western Secretariat," I cried hotly. "I accused Comrade Ernst Wollweber. I maintain this accusation." Wollweber hunched his shoulders. Jensen leaned back with a sneer, half-incredulous, half-contemptuous.

"Names," Jensen rumbled.

"You have them. They are in my report to Moscow. The Comrades Walter Duddins, Funk, Fiete Dettman, Claus, Robert Stamm. The Swedish Comrades Persson and Mineur. The Reichstag Deputy Comrade Maddalena. The Comrades Saefkow and Hans Koschnik. The women Comrades Firelei, Cilly, Lilo Herrman. There are more. You have them on your list."

"You are too clever," Wollweber interrupted me. "None of the comrades you name are available to corroborate your statements."

"No, they are in prison. Claus, Stamm, Lilo had their heads cut off. They must have felt fine about being butchered! Before they went, they talked through the walls, through air shafts, in church, in notes pinned on broomsticks and handed from window to window. In the prison camps, the name of Ernst Wollweber smells of carrion."

"Rigmarole," growled Wollweber, "all this is open for later discussion. I have here another report. It comes from Holland. Here *you* are definitely accused of shady transactions with such counterrevolutionary wolves as the renegade Hans Krause, with the Socialist Fascist Edo Fimmen, with Franco spies, with a long gallery of other political adventurers."

I felt as if someone had hit me on the head with a hammer. "Comrade

Krause is no renegade," I said sullenly. "He went to Spain to demonstrate that the rumors against him were false. He was wounded at the front. I considered it my duty to—"

"Excuses!" Wollweber burst in. "True Bolsheviki have never grubbed around for excuses. They admit their mistakes, and let the Party decide."

"All right. I demand a hearing before the Control Commission."

"This is the Control Commission," Jensen said. "You will have time to talk later."

Then came the most shattering shock I had experienced in all my years of devotion to the Comintern.

"Finally," Wollweber said with great calmness, his outstretched arm pointing at me across the table, "the Party accuses you of having deliberately organized acts of sabotage against the *Apparat* in Hitler Germany."

"I think you are crazy," I shot at him.

Wollweber gave me a sardonic smile.

"Do you consider Comrade Karl Saar an unflinching Bolshevik?"

"I most certainly do."

"Here is a letter from Comrade Karl Saar," Ernst Wollweber spoke without emotion. "It is in code. Here is a decoded typewritten copy. A painful letter—a document! We learn that you have offered Karl Saar money to desert the Comintern. The money you offered was Comintern money."

There was a long silence. Jensen drew a geometric pattern on the fly-leaf of a book. Wollweber smoked. The guards sat immobile, but tensely attentive. I wondered what would happen if I simply stood up and walked out of Jensen's apartment. I could think of no place to go.

At six o'clock Avatin arrived, roughly clad as always, in a stiff brown suit of Russian manufacture. He flashed a smile of recognition at me. With Avatin a smile meant nothing. He could smile at a man one minute, and kill him the next. Accompanying Avatin was Inge, a stenographer, a handsome athletic blonde and the wife of Martin Jensen.

"You may now speak in your defense," Wollweber announced. "We give you half an hour."

I spoke of the stormy years of 1923 and of my part in the preparation and execution of the October uprising in Hamburg. I had done the hardest work that was required of the rank and file. I had fought for the revolution with arms in my hands. I spoke of my work for the Comintern in America, in Hawaii, in Belgium and Holland and France, in Switzerland and Norway, in Denmark, Sweden, Finland and Russia, in Singapore and Shanghai and England. I spoke of the jails and prisons, of the Nazi horror camps, where I had suffered and continued to fight for the Party, for the revolution, for seven years. Before I had said half of what I had intended to say, my time was up. Even in this situation I was too disciplined to break the rules made by those who had been my superiors. Inge, Martin Jensen's wife, had stenographed what I had said. Had I harangued a stone wall, I should have found no more response. Then I realized my mistake: I should not have defended myself—I should have attacked ... or bowed my head, proclaimed myself guilty, and cringed for mercy.

Then Wollweber spoke. No one in the room believed his accusations. Least of all did he believe them himself. His object was to make me crawl in self-abasement. He was not sure that I would crawl. Had he been sure, he would have chosen a larger audience.

"What are you going to do with me?" I interrupted him.

"We will send you to Spain or to the Soviet Union," he answered bluntly.

"To be shot?"

"We shoot no one without good cause," Wollweber growled.

"I know that," I replied.

Wollweber rose, and with a curt nod toward Avatin and Jensen, he left the room. I never saw him again. Richard Jensen offered me a bottle of beer. Avatin gave a signal to two of his helpers. They put on their overcoats and stepped up to me. One I did not know. The other was Ignace Schametzki, a native of Poland, a stocky man with a round stubborn face.

"You come with us now," he said.

"Where to?"

"Never mind!"

Avatin intervened. "We have been good friends," he said. "What I tell you is the truth: You will live in a country place. Until your case has been decided, you are relieved of all your duties."

"I am a prisoner?"

"Yes."

"You come with us now," Schametzki repeated softly.

It was morning. I followed the G.P.U. men's orders without resistance. I marched down the stairs into a waiting car. On my right sat Schametzki. On my left was a lanky Dane. Both had their pistols drawn. Martin Jensen drove. The car leaped forward. Large numbers of young men and girls were riding to work on their bicycles. Traffic grew thinner as the car neared the city limits. I felt like a man in a trance. I lit a cigarette and closed my eyes.

When I opened my eyes, I saw a stretch of open sea to the left.

We were speeding south.

Chapter Forty-three

FLIGHT

In the speeding car, my abductors felt ill at ease. Normally, they would have taken orders from me, and carried them out.

I did not quite know whether I should take these early-morning events as a melodramatic farce, or whether they heralded a bullet in the back of my head. I decided to wait. But as mile after mile of open countryside flew by, my apprehension grew.

"Danish beer is the best beer in the world," I said, for no apparent reason.

Martin Jensen stirred in his seat. "You asked for trouble," he grumbled. "And now you got it."

"Danish beer is good beer," Schametzki agreed.

"I think you boys are scared," I said. "You are wondering why I sit still and do nothing. Why should I? I've traveled clear around the world for the Comintern when you fellows were still thinking that Lenin was a bugbear."

"We're scared of nothing," Martin Jensen grumbled.

Ahead of us a policeman patrolled the sidewalk of a village street. As our car whisked past him, Schametzki pressed his gun into my side. The policeman did not even turn his head.

"You should be ashamed of yourself," I told Schametzki.

He did not answer. I thought of making a sudden grab for his pistol. If a fight broke out in the car, they would have to stop. They would never dare to shoot in broad daylight, with houses nearby. We would probably all be arrested and questioned; the press would get our pictures, and the Gestapo would learn that I had not gone to the Soviet Union. Schreckenbach and Kraus would not hesitate to take a swift revenge on me. And Firelei would be their first victim.

The road skirted Kjoege Bay. The roadhouses, full of light and gayety at night, lay dismal in the morning. The beaches, where bunting fluttered lustily over crowded tent colonies in the summer, were haunts of desolation. Clumps of frozen weed and patches of ice littered the shore. Where girls in sun-suits had romped and shouted, a broad-hipped woman in a man's greatcoat warmed her hands over a puny fire. Far out, a fisherman's craft crawled seaward. Gulls sailed over a fish wharf, screaming for loot.

No, it would not do to fight and run. I had no real urge to run away from the Comintern. Besides, strong as I was, Martin Jensen had the strength to strangle me with his bare hands. I decided to wait. "Will it be Spain or the Soviet Union?" I thought. Hitherto I had regarded every voyage to Russia as a glorious adventure. The news of the heroic defense of Madrid, and of the battle of Guadalajara, had filled me with a huge and savage joy. Now the fires had burned down. The Soviet Union had become to me a strangely sinister country. Emptiness, dull and painful emptiness, engulfed me.

The car rattled off the highway into a labyrinth of dirt roads, amid swampy meadows hard under the cold. It jolted, paused, and crawled on. Scattered over the level stretch of land were little wooden country-houses, tumbledown shacks, boats pulled up under the shelter of makeshift sheds. Ahead I saw a white flagpole protruding above a tall hedge. Coming nearer, I saw that the hedge concealed a fence, seven feet high. A moment later we had passed through a narrow gate to the inside of this fence.

There was a one-story cottage. Green paint was peeling from the outside timbers. On three sides old planks had been nailed over the windows. The fourth side fronted the Baltic Sea. On this side the surrounding fence was lower. There was a porch opening on an unkempt meadow. The meadow was littered with debris. A rickety boat landing jutted out at the far end. A mile offshore, a long low sandbank shouldered out of the sea.

"Here we are," Martin Jensen boomed. "Ho, Christiansen, here's a guest for you!"

A massive individual in dungarees and a leather jacket shambled out of the cottage. He had a barrel chest and a bristly face. He was Sven Christiansen, who had been a whaler in his youth and whom I had met several times when he helped Julius Vanman smuggle Comintern contraband, alive and otherwise, between Denmark and Sweden across Oeresund. Christiansen had also worked in South American mines. He had the reputation of being an expert in the handling of explosives. For this reason Avatin had selected him for the G.P.U. *Apparat*. Sven Christiansen was like a peasant—gruff, good-natured, patient—absolutely loyal, and unmerciful toward anyone whom he considered an enemy of the revolution.

"Good you come," Christiansen said, "a fellow gets so god-damn lonely out here."

I was hustled into the cottage.

"Hands up," Martin Jensen commanded. His enormous hands were feeling their way down my person, patting, searching.

"Keep your paws off," I protested. "Who do you think you are? Gestapo?"

"No," he grinned. "But just the same—hold still."

He took my watch, fountain pen, note paper and the two passports I carried. He even took away my penknife. He counted over the money he found, sixteen kroner, returned six to me, and kept ten.

"I don't like it," I said.

"I don't, either," he answered. "But Comrade Avatin holds me responsible for you."

"What are your orders?"

"Orders? To hold you here in good health till your business is cleared up in Moscow."

"Give me back my pen and paper."

"What for?" he demanded.

"I want to write a letter. I want Comrade Dimitrov to see both sides of this thing."

"I have to see Avatin about that," Martin Jensen said.

"Do you think I'm a Trotskyist? A Japanese spy? A Gestapo agent?"

Martin Jensen made a gesture of dismissal. "I think nothing," he said. "I know nothing. All I know is that you can become damned dangerous if what Comrade Wollweber said about you is true. All I tell you is that you'd better start no trouble."

"Do you think I couldn't break out of this dump if I had a mind to?"

Martin Jensen said stolidly, "Maybe you could."

"Well, what then?"

"We are all decent comrades here," Martin said.

Christiansen nodded. "Damn right we are."

"If you run, we might shoot," Martin Jensen continued. "First time you try a break, we're going to tie you up. After that you stay tied up, like it or not. Maybe Moscow says you're all right. If Moscow says you're all right, we'll all have a big celebration. We'll all laugh like hell."

Fire roared in the small cast-iron stove in the room which fronted the sea. It was the largest room in the cottage. Adjoining it was a kitchen and two smaller rooms. The windows of the smaller rooms were boarded up solidly. In the large front room lived Sven Christiansen and Martin Jensen. In the small room at the opposite end of the house lived Schametzki and the lanky, taciturn Dane. The small, connecting room was reserved for me. Each of its two doors opened thus on the quarters of my guards. But for kerosene lanterns dangling from rafters, the two smaller rooms would have been in permanent darkness.

My "prison cell" contained a camp bed, a collapsible table and a chair with broken legs. The blankets smelled of sweat and grime. Stacked up in a corner was a large pile of old newspapers and magazines. I saw that little spy-holes had been drilled through both doors, and that the doors could be secured from the outside with strong copper chains. The unpainted boards which shut off the window were covered with scribblings in pencil: "Red Front forever!", lines from the *Internationale*, a few unintelligible words in Latvian or Russian, "No pasaran," a love song, obscene drawings, a caricature of Hitler, "Max Jahnke"—a name, and half obliterated from scrapings with a knife, "Down with Stalin!"

The words "Max Jahnke" electrified me. They were followed by the figure "1936." I knew his story. Until 1931, Max Jahnke had been a leader of the Red Seamen's Union in Germany. He had been a grizzled and hard rebel, slow-moving, pig-headed, efficient. When the Comintern launched the international strike of German seamen in October, 1931, Max Jahnke came into deadly conflict with the Party high command. One of the most powerful figures in the Communist Party of Germany, Herrmann Schubert, Reichstag member, had demanded that Jahnke lead the striking seamen in Hamburg into clashes with the police. The Party needed corpses to give this strike a "political character." Jahnke had refused to spill the blood of German mariners; at a conference of seamen's delegates, he defended his standpoint and attacked Herrmann Schubert. At the next opportunity the Party stripped Jahnke of his power. Jahnke struck back in an unforgivable way: He supplied the socialist press with incriminating documents from secret Party files. A year later, the G.P.U. succeeded in luring him aboard a Russian ship under the pretext that *Sovtorgflot*—the Soviet Shipping Trust—had requested Jahnke's advice on a technical question, for the German had been a marine engineer of long experience. Jahnke was spirited to Russia, but managed to escape. He was recaptured by the G.P.U. in 1936. And in the spring of 1937 the staunch old trade unionist was turned over by the Soviet government to the Gestapo in exchange for one Eugen Priess, a captured Soviet spy.

A vast shame gripped me when I thought of Jahnke. My devotion to the Comintern had once made me view Jahnke as a danger to Party unity. When the howl went up: "Away with Max Jahnke!" I, too, had said: "Jahnke has become an enemy of the cause. He is a comrade no more."

The shadow of Max Jahnke haunted me for hours and days. In the confines of that evil-smelling room, he seemed to be walking silently at my side, to and fro, up and down, walking, walking, chuckling in his bearish fashion, "Well, my boy, what do you say now?" Mechanically I paid Max Jahnke a futile tribute. In his honor I began to hum the funeral march for those who had fallen for the revolution. The "revolution" had sold him to the Gestapo. Today, somewhere in Germany, he may still be alive, his heart a curse, mute and immense, against the treachery of Stalin and his hangmen.

This rotten old cottage, I felt, had many secrets. It was not an honest jail, like the blood-spattered cells of a *Gestapo Polizeigefaengnis*. It was dishonest, full of sham and stealthiness, creeping with the specters of comrade betrayed by comrade. I caught myself wondering how many hundreds of comrades in the Soviet prison camps had begun their journey from just such little houses as the one in which I now was held captive. No one, outside of the Kremlin or the Lubianka, would know their number. Not even Ernst Wollweber or Avatin.

I knew too much and had to be destroyed. To my ears, that phrase sounded silly. I knew what had happened to Richter and Bandura; to Bela Kun, Heinz Neumann, Hans Kippenberger, Dombal; to Schubert, Remmele, Max Hoelz, Samsing and many, many others. Dead, exiled, drowned, buried alive. I could not bring myself to believe that anything like that could happen to me.

I had no feud with the Comintern. But neither had the others I named. It was not only a feud between individual rebels and the International. It was, as often as not, a war between conscientious proletarian internationalists and the bureaucratic clique that followed Stalin. The clique always won. Its creed was the G.P.U. If Stalin commanded Dimitrov to hoist the swastika over the Comintern building in Moscow, Dimitrov would do it. If Stalin told Wollweber to publish a pamphlet proclaiming that Lenin was a pickpocket—Wollweber would do it. The years had utterly changed the Comintern. The revolutionary vanguard was now no more than a poisoned dagger in Stalin's hands.

I struggled with myself. I cursed myself as a weakling in a frantic search for excuses to justify my crumbling faith. At eighteen, I had felt like a giant. At twenty-one, it was simple: "Pitch the grenade into the face of the counter-revolution!" At twenty-two, I had circled the globe in Comintern service, gaunt, hungry, fierce—and proud of it! At twenty-nine, the police departments of half a dozen nations hunted me as the Comintern's chief troublemaker on the waterfronts of Europe. At thirty-one, I was at work transforming Hitler's prisons into schools of proletarian internationalism. And now, at thirty-three, I found myself asking: "Has all this been a falsehood, a fraud, a dismal spook?"

No man can strip himself of his skin.

In a desperate mood I turned to half-forgotten fundamentals. Marx, Engels, Lenin. Even Hegel. "Dialectic materialism is the philosophy of Marxism." "The history of mankind is a history of class war." "Revolutions are the locomotives of history." There was Karl Marx' law of accumulation of capital. ... "Capitalism in a *cul de sac*. ... Creates its own gravediggers. ... Proletarian dictatorship follows the complete destruction of the bourgeois state. ... The land to the peasants. ... The industries to the workers. ... Nothing to lose but chains, and a world to gain. ... A world of freedom, bread, dignity. ..." What was wrong with that?

"The triumph of socialism in the Soviet Union is the guarantee for the victory of socialism in the whole world."

Question: Who is the father of all the oppressed? Who is the greatest living statesman?

Answer: Comrade Stalin.

Three bloody words leered at me from the pine boards of my cell: "Down with Stalin!"

Somewhere in Germany was Firelei, living in insecurity from day to day, waiting, waiting for the moment when she could tell me: "Now, come, come quickly, they have relaxed their watchfulness!" Her message would go to Antwerp. It would never reach me. She would wait... wait in vain, abandoned, cheated, utterly betrayed. I remembered our first meeting on the wharves of Antwerp. She had drawn the stern of a barge, with a husky woman nursing her child, a string of fluttering laundry, and a barking dog. "A ship must have a name," I had told her. "It's *Oran*." We had been very happy together, and Firelei had built castles in the air.

I had destroyed those castles, one after another, until nothing had been left, nothing.... From the wintery reaches of the Baltic the wind came pounding in, whistling and wailing through the cracks of the fence. A voice was in the wind, the voice of Firelei.

"What have you done with me?" it asked me again and again.

My guards were optimistic. They sat in the overheated east room, which faced the Kjoege Bay, talking loudly. Martin Jensen's basso expounded the official version of the execution of Tukhachevsky and the other Soviet generals. The Red Army generalissimo was an agent of the German general staff! And Trotsky and Zinoviev had hired Dora Kaplan (who made her attempt in 1918) to shoot Lenin! With the traitors out of the way, Stalin's next job would be the liquidation of Hitlerism in Germany. A Soviet Germany would mean a Soviet Europe. The G.P.U. would machine-gun the Nazi leaders wholesale in their own prison camps. The rotten democracies of the West would fall like ripe corpses before the Stalinist hurricane. The workers would be free. They would build a workers' world under Stalin's guidance. Stalin, the dynamo of world revolution. Whoever opposed Stalin was plainly a lackey of Fascism, had forfeited even his right to breathe.

The hours were long. I began to sing every battle-song of the revolution I knew. I knew many. I sang until my voice was hoarse.

> "Forward, to sun and to freedom,
> Brothers, march on toward light...."

At the end I sang the *Internationale*, the national anthem of the Soviet Union, which is also the anthem of Communist Parties the world around. My guards were suddenly silent. I heard Schametzki's voice say: "Comrades—rise!"

I felt like a drowning man struggling toward land that was many miles away. The icy night air filtered through the boarded window. It was late at night. I stood in the middle of the dark room and howled like a melancholy wolf:

> "Death to hangmen, kings and traitors. . ."

Martin Jensen unlocked the door and his thick head appeared outlined against the yellow light of a kerosene lantern behind him.

"Now you better keep quiet," he said. "This is no insane asylum."

"You go to hell," I told him.

"If you start shouting in the night, I'll have to hit you on the head."

"Let me out of here."

Martin Jensen was irritated. "You are a real pest. I can't let you out till Comrade Avatin tells me you're all right."

I said derisively: "You're making the grade, Martin. By-and-by you'll get a job as a jailer in the Butirky. Four hundred rubles and padded shoes."

The faces of Christiansen and Schametzki bobbed up in the doorway.

"I don't want a goddamn jailer's job," Martin Jensen said sullenly.

Christiansen intervened. "Listen, comrade," he said to me, "I know how you feel. But this is not a very strong house. It can be wrecked with a few good kicks. I only want to tell you not to start wrecking the house. First thing you know you'll have handcuffs round your wrists and a towel round your mouth."

In a rage I picked up the chair and hurled it at Christiansen. He ducked, caught the chair and hurled it back at me. Pieces of wood flew about as it struck the wall. An instant later Martin Jensen had his arm around my throat and his knee in the small of my back.

"Leave him alone," Christiansen muttered.

Reluctantly, Martin Jensen let go.

"If you were a Gestapo man," he growled, "I'd put you in irons and dump a pail of ice water over you. Trouble with you is, you might be all right."

Christiansen laughed. "Nothing like ice water to make a man shut up. You know Oskar, the photographer guy? Well, every night around eleven he got the ice water cure."

The lanky Dane, whose name I did not know, swung his arms in an ape-like fashion. His mirthless half-smile told me that he was no tyro in Avatin's force. Such men were dead set on doing their duty. I knew their type. They were equally immune against terror and bribes.

"Get out, all of you," I said. "I want to sleep."

I did not sleep. Through the spy-hole in the door I watched Martin Jensen and Christiansen stretch out on their beds. Scharnetzki and the Dane kept watch. The Dane sat by the stove, smoking and reading, a pot of coffee at his side. Schametzki put on gloves, a muffler and a soldier's greatcoat and went out to patrol the space between the cottage and the fence. His crunching steps went around the house. At intervals he stopped, and I heard him flap his arms against his sides to warm up. Once he came in for coffee and to look into my room.

"Still here," he whispered.

"Chase yourself," I snarled back.

After two hours Schametzki sat by the stove and the Dane patrolled outside. The Dane hummed marching tunes. At times he cursed softly and broke into a trot. But he did not come in for coffee. Schametzki ate sandwiches. After that he cleaned his nails with a screwdriver. Later he pulled out a blue handkerchief and began to polish his gun. Whenever he heard me move, he was at my door with two quick strides, peering in.

"Ah, still here?" he would ask.

I could not sleep. Things came trooping into my head, happenings of the past, vague plans, faces of enemies and friends, some silent in unknown graves, others tottering as yet toward weary disillusion—or sudden destruction, and still others—the hard, cautious cynics, prowling for high rank and power.

I fingered over every inch of wall in my room. I tried to find a plank which could be lifted out of the floor. I climbed on a rafter and pushed hard against the roof. The wood was old, but solid. It would never give way without making a great noise. What if I broke out of the house? On one side was the Baltic Sea. On three sides was the fence. The gate in the fence was ramshackle enough, but it would be locked. They would be atop of me before I could climb the fence or kick in the gate.

I hoisted myself up on the window. There was a crack, almost an inch wide, between the casing and the topmost board. I could see the outside through this crack, the night, the silhouettes of other houses a little way off, dim light in a window or two. The discovery that people lived nearby astonished me.

The nearest house, I judged, was sixty yards away. Two hundred yards further on ran a highway. The headlight reflections of passing cars now and then streaked through the night.

A large house loomed in the distance, surrounded by strings of colored light bulbs. A roadhouse. Five hundred yards away, perhaps. What if I shouted? Shouted for people to hear? It was a ridiculous thing to shout for help. I had never shouted for help in all my life.

I fought the urge to escape. It would not be an escape from my proletarian guards. It would be an escape from the Comintern, an admission that I feared the Comintern, an admission of guilt. A miserable declaration of bankruptcy!

The window faced north. In the north lay Copenhagen. Above Copenhagen, the sky was a lurid glow, as though the city were on fire. The night was cold.

I heard the chain rattle on the other side of my door. Schametzki barged into the room. Around the house the Dane came running.

"Get down from that window," Schametzki said menacingly.

I got down quietly. "I can't sleep," I said. "The blankets stink."

"Nothing wrong with the blankets," Schametzki said.

The Dane stood glowering. From their cots Martin Jensen and Christiansen growled questions.

So passed my first night as a captive of the G.P.U.

Nearly three weeks I remained cooped up in my ludicrous prison, somewhere on the coast between Copenhagen and Kjoege. I waited for a decision, but no decision, it seemed, was made. More and more I came to the conclusion that Wollweber was determined to keep me here until spring and the breaking up of the ice in the harbor of Leningrad would herald the resumption of Soviet shipping on the Baltic Sea.

Each afternoon between four and six, Richard Jensen drove out from the city. Each afternoon he brought a case of beer and two hundred cigarettes. He was friendly enough. Sometimes, when I spoke to him, he seemed a bit ashamed. I could drink and smoke as much as I wanted.

Each evening, before he departed, Richard Jensen said to me: "Inside a week your troubles will be straightened out."

I demanded to see Wollweber.

"Wollweber has gone away," Jensen said.

It was a ruse, I knew. Wollweber lurked somewhere in Copenhagen, directing the show from behind the scenes.

"When I see Wollweber again," I said, "I'm going to punch his head off."

Jensen merely laughed, "Many have said that. Nobody's ever done it."

"I think you're scared of Wollweber," I told Jensen. "Wollweber is a very good comrade," Jensen said.

"Get me out of here," I demanded, during another of Jensen's visits. "Or give me some work to do. Translations, articles or something."

"You are too impatient," Jensen said. "Why don't you take a rest? Most comrades would be damn glad to have such a long rest."

"To hell with rest."

"All right, what can I get you?"

"Get me the latest *Runa* and the *Imprecorr*." (Respectively, the confidential and public news bulletins of the Comintern, published in Basle.)

"Orders are to give you no current material," Richard Jensen explained, adding soothingly: "I can get you good whiskey. A sailor comrade smuggled it for me from London."

"No," I said. "I don't want whiskey. But you can get me a girl. Your Tchekists out here are not very good company. They make me think of chained dogs."

Richard Jensen snapped, "Never call them Tchekists. The Party won't like it."

"All right: the Comrades from the *S-Apparat*."

"You want a girl?"

"Yes, I want a girl."

Late that night the gate in the fence creaked open, and a small car drove in. A woman entered the house. In a subdued voice, she spoke to my jailers. I recognized her by her footsteps. She was Petra Petersen, the G.P.U. operative in the Copenhagen telegraph building, and my former hostess. Without preliminaries she stomped into my room.

"I've taken a night off to give you company," she announced cheerily.

"You've come to do some more spying?" I countered.

Petra sat down on the cot. "Oh, forget this foolishness," she said. "I don't want to spy. What is there to spy? I just came back from my vacation. I have been in Moscow. I heard you were here, so I came to see you."

"For old friendship's sake?" I asked sarcastically.

She ignored the thrust. "When have you last been in the Soviet Union?" she inquired.

"Six years ago."

"You wouldn't recognize the country if you went there now," she continued amiably. "It has forged forward and upward. The people have become really modern in their ways of living. I have seen the new subway in Moscow. It is more beautiful even than the Paris *Métro*. And for the children the Soviet Union has become a veritable paradise."

"And the G.P.U. has become a veritable humane society," I added.

"You are ill," Petra Petersen said. "You should go to the Soviet Union to recover."

I stood in front of her and grasped her shoulders. "Listen," I whispered. "I want to write a letter to my wife. Get me paper and a pencil. I want you to take that letter out with you and mail it. Don't mail it from Copenhagen. Send it to Leningrad and have it mailed from there. Will you do that for me?"

"Of course."

Her response had come too quickly.

"Leave me alone," I said. "Go away. You make me sick."

"Why?"

"How can I trust you?"

"If you trust no one, you are lost," Petra said softly.

"Go away!"

She departed. The night was quiet. I thought of escape. I thought of a conversation I had once had with a group of exiled German comrades in Rotterdam. We had spoken of an anti-Fascist's ways of escape in the event of his abduction by Gestapo raiders outside of Germany. Most had spoken of suicide. But one had said:

"If they kept me aboard a ship or inside a house, I'd move heaven and earth to set the ship or the house afire."

The sentence became static in my mind. Fire. Smoke and flames attract other people and other ships. Fire exerts a strong fascination on the minds of men. When man first made a fire, and scurried to feed it and keep it alive, civilization began.

"I must make a fire," I thought. "Every castaway makes a fire, if he can, to attract the attention of passing ships.

"You are crazy," I told myself. "Perhaps everything will end all right. ... . Don't be like a hysterical old woman. Sleep!"

Sleep was far away. My brain continued to chew on the idea of making a fire. "When?" I thought. "Tonight?" I forced myself to lie still. "Not this night," I murmured to myself. "Wait. Wait until there is no other way."

Next morning I pretended to be calm. The house was old, and the timbers and planks were dry. I made my preparations quietly.

Early one morning in the last week of January, 1938, I heard a car drive up and stop outside of the fence. The gate creaked. A hand unfastened the chain from the front door of my room. In the doorway stood Richard Jensen.

"Good morning," he said. "Dress yourself."

"What's up?" I demanded.

"You are leaving today."

"Where for?"

"The Soviet Union."

I rose and slipped into my clothes. "So you are going to put me on ice?" I asked.

"That depends on yourself," Jensen answered. 'I only carry out instructions."

"Who gave the instructions?"

"The Control Commission."

"That is Wollweber?"

"The Control Commission," Jensen repeated stolidly.

"All right," I said.

I stepped out of the room. Martin Jensen had gone to town on the previous evening to have a night with Inge, his wife. He had not returned. Schametzki and Christiansen, both wearing hats and overcoats, stood on the porch.

"By what route am I going?" I demanded.

"By ship," Jensen said. "There is a steamer going out this afternoon'."

"You know as well as I that there are no ships in winter," I replied.

Jensen was silent.

"You better get ready," Schametzki said sullenly.

"Take your time," Jensen said in a conciliatory tone. "Go to Moscow and straighten things out with the Comintern. It is the best way for you."

"All right," I said. "I'm going to have a shave, first."

I stepped back into the half-darkness of my prison chamber. Every fiber, every nerve, every drop of blood in me was in a raging tumult. The tenseness seemed to lift me off the floor. I felt a monstrous strength, a deadly excitement which was far different from the emotion I had experienced in the early morning hours of a day in October, 1923, when the smashing of street fights gave the signal to storm the enemy forts, to annihilate and destroy, to kill and rage forward to victory. It was as if I were about to raise my fist, and with it a dagger, to drive it into the throat of my mother who had become a viper. "You Comintern. . . . You false mother. .. . You—you viper!" My heart was a mute snarl.

The kerosene container of the lamp which dangled from the ceiling was full. Two beer bottles filled with kerosene lay under my mattress. I drew them out. I took a cigarette and lit a match. Outside, Jensen was talking to the others. In quick succession I smashed the bottles on the floor. I dropped the brightly burning match into the spilled kerosene. A little yellow flame licked upward, crawled across one of the scarred boards, licked avidly, grew brighter, and was fringed with a ghostly blue. An instant later I was tearing the lamp from the ceiling. Someone was running toward my room. The flames blazed up now. While I bolted from the room, I hurled the lamp against the wall.

"Fire!" I yelled. "Fire! Fire! Fire!"

Jensen was cursing. The G.P.U. men ran out of the house. In two leaps I was among them. I plunged across the enclosure and out through the open gate. On the other side of the road stood a car.

"Fire!" I yelled at the top of my voice. "Fire! Fire! Fire! Fire!"

Schametzki was two paces away from me. He shouted something, his coarse face distorted.

"Fire!" I yelled. "Fire!"

Men came running out of the nearest houses—workers with disheveled hair, some still tightening their belts as they ran. A few women followed.

"Fire!" I yelled. "Fire!"

Thick smoke poured from the roof of Richard Jensen's cottage. Smoke curled through the boarded windows. On the porch the flames crackled lustily. People clustered on the road. Others ran to and fro. Someone was shouting for pails and water. Jensen staggered around the tall outside hedge, followed by the lanky Dane who seemed to ask his chief for advice. Near me stood Christiansen and Schametzki, watching me, but not daring to come closer. Through the commotion sounded Jensen's deep laughter. "Ah, it is an old shack, anyway," he exclaimed.

I turned and walked rapidly down the lane. I reached the concrete highway and turned north, toward Copenhagen. I passed the roadhouse whose colored lights I had seen night after night through the cracks of my boarded window. Its name was Jaegerkroen— Hunter's Resting Place. Some twenty paces behind me strode Schametzki and Christiansen. I entered the grounds of Jaegerkroen, as if I intended to walk into the inn. Schametzki paused on the highway. Christiansen turned and ran back toward the burning house. "I must move on," I thought. "He is going for the car."

I struck out toward Copenhagen on the middle of the highway. Each time a car approached, I halted and raised both hands. Two cars sped by, a third . . . fourth ... a fifth. The sixth car stopped and the door swung open. Its driver was an elderly man, going to work.

"Where are you going?"

"To Copenhagen," I said.

"There is a fire here?" he asked.

"Yes, a fire," I answered. "Sailors had a party there. They got drunk."

The man chuckled.

I did not remain in Copenhagen. I obeyed my urge to put the greatest possible distance between myself and the man hunters of Michel Avatin. He, who had been my friend for many years, would know no mercy now. I had six kroner. I entered a bathhouse and bathed. In a barber shop on the eastern outskirts of Copenhagen I stopped to be shaved and to have my hair cut. Then I bought a large breakfast. In a short street flanked by tenement houses I stole a bicycle which leaned against a wall near a doorway. With three kroner and eighty in my pockets I rode eastward along the highway which led to Roskilde and Korsoer. I had no passport nor any other document of identification.

I crossed the Large Belt with the aid of a comrade who was a sailor aboard the ferry. In seven hours I traversed the Island of Fyn. Another ferry carried me to Fredericia. A night I rested in the quarters of the Salvation Army. On the following day I rode across Jutland to the port Esbjerg. I arrived in Esbjerg with one kroner in my pocket.

The steamer *P. A. Bernstorff* lay at her pier. I boarded her and spoke to the leader of the communist ship unit. He knew me well from previous trips. He had, of course, no inkling of my real status.

"Comrade," I said. "You must arrange for my passage. I have official business in France."

The comrade was a sailor, and an honest revolutionist. He fed me and kept me hidden in his cabin, which he shared with another Party member. Thirty-six hours after the *P. A. Bemstorff* steamed out of the harbor of Esbjerg, I strode ashore in Dunkerque. I went to the Salle d'Avenir and spoke to Comrade Manautines, the liaison agent of the G.P.U. in Dunkerque.

"Comrade," I said. "I have urgent business in Paris."

Manautines lent me a hundred francs and saw me aboard a train to Paris. When I shook hands with him, I shook hands with the Comintern. Tears were in my eyes, and a lump in my throat.

"Au diable " said Manautines, "you are upset."

Ten hours later I picked my way through the surge and clangor of the *Gare du Nord* in Paris.

In Paris I wrote a letter to Richard Jensen, for transmission to his superiors in the Comintern. *"The Gestapo believes,"* I wrote, *"that I am in Russia; the lives of my wife and child depend on the continuance of this belief. I beg you to maintain silence as to my whereabouts, and I, also, shall maintain silence."*

I could not stay in Paris. The G.P.U. had spread the alarm. Men and women who had been my comrades were now duty-bound to hunt me down as an enemy of Stalin and his clique. One day I slipped away from two G.P.U. men who had shadowed me in the vicinity of the Place de Combat. The same night I left Paris.

I continued to wander from one country to another, alone now. In Antwerp I called on Edo Fimmen, the Dutchman, who had been my enemy, but had become my friend. He saw that I was ill, and in despair.

"Will you work in my organization?" he asked.

I declined. "If you will help," I said, "you may find me a ship. I am going back to sea, where I started."

Edo Fimmen was like a father to legions of sailors. Overnight he found me a ship, bound westward over the Atlantic to pack sugar from the West Indies. The G.P.U. had traced me from Paris to Antwerp; but by the time their man hunters arrived, I had already put out to sea. Once more I was a sailor before the mast. None of my shipmates knew whence I came, or where I was going. It was a sheer delight to walk again over a heaving deck, to sink my hands once more into a pot of tar. To Firelei I could not write. "It is best," I thought. "As time goes on, the Gestapo will believe that you have died somewhere in Russia, and then they will let Firelei go on her way."

But the G.P.U. and the Comintern gave me no peace anywhere. In the end, Ernst Wollweber had his revenge. Long after my flight from Copenhagen, a friend in Antwerp sent me a package. It contained copies of communist newspapers from various countries, ranging from the Pacific Coast to Scandinavia. I unfolded the papers. I was surprised to see a picture of myself on the front page of each publication. It was the same—the photograph that had appeared on my Gestapo credentials—which I had surrendered to Comrade Jensen upon my arrival in Copenhagen from Hitler's prisons. It bore the caption: *"On the watch! Gestapo!"*

I recognized, in a flash, the craftiness with which this betrayal had been engineered. I had eluded the G.P.U. assassins, had vanished from their horizon, and now they struck back in a most foul and underhanded manner. From the photographs of myself which they had in their files, they chose the one that would unfailingly render me and my family fair game for every totalitarian sleuth and man hunter on earth. The publication of this picture was a three-fold betrayal: It aspired to tar-and-feather me publicly in the eyes of labor leaders everywhere; it was calculated to prove to the Gestapo chiefs that I had deceived them; and it was designed to make the police departments of all countries do the work of the G.P.U.—to track me down and to deliver me to Germany, the Gestapo, and death.

The articles which accompanied my picture in the communist press vilified me as "one of the most important spies of the Gestapo." There was no word about my lifetime of service to the communist cause, no word about the years I had spent in the torture-chambers of the Gestapo. But there was word that I had just been "discovered in Paris." Thus the G.P.U. made it appear that it had not even heard of my existence before its agents "discovered" me fifteen years after I had entered the Soviet service

This treachery recalled other things to my mind. I remembered the day in Schreckenbach's office when he gave me the Gestapo credentials, and I remembered his words, "In hell or high water, never let these documents fall into enemy hands." I remembered the day when I had entrusted these same documents to Richard Jensen, and how he had perused them and growled, "Very, very good." And I also remembered Inspector Kraus' menacing voice saying: "Don't try to deceive us. You won't live long if you do. I warn you—the Gestapo never jokes."

This world-wide defamation in the Comintern press could have but one meaning. It was not just another call to Stalin's men to seek me out and to destroy me. No, this was more: These papers and that picture of me would find their way into the offices of every secret service. They would also come to Hamburg and Berlin. Hertha Jens and Inspector Kraus would scrutinize them, and so would Schreckenbach and Heinrich Himmler. They would know that I had surrendered their secrets to enemy hands. They would know that I had not perished in Russia. They would blame me for having had a hand in the disappearance of their agent, Oskar. They would know that I had duped them. They would realize what game I had played with them.

They did.

In July, 1938, I received the intelligence that Firelei had been seized and thrown into the Horror Camp Fuhlsbuettel.

In December, 1938, I received a message which told me that Firelei had died in prison. Did she, herself, put an end to her life? Was she murdered in cold blood? "The Gestapo never jokes!" Neither does it give explanations. Our son, Jan, became a ward of the Third Reich. I have not heard of him again.

END

WHO'S WHO

(To enable the reader to identify the more active individuals, generally unknown to the American public, as they appear in this narrative.)

ANDREE, EDGAR, a Belgian, leader of communist military units in Germany, symbol of terror to Hitler's storm troops until seized by the Gestapo—the Nazi secret police. He died heroically under the headsman's ax for a cause in which he had ceased to believe.

ANDRESEN, KITTY, Norwegian girl courier in the Soviet secret service, who exploited her acquaintance with King Haakon to rescue the author from jail.

AVATIN, MICHEL, alias Lambert, of Latvian origin. master-spy and executioner abroad for the Foreign Division of the G.P.U. (secret service) of the Soviet government. A fearless and incorruptible revolutionist, Avatin murdered in cold blood because of his fanatical loyalty to the communist cause and regime.

BANDURA, ALEXANDER, Ukrainian rebel and anarchist, king of the Antwerp waterfront, who waged single-handed war against capitalist and Soviet influences until kidnapped and spirited away to Russia by the G.P.U.

CANCE, M. and MME., resident agents of the G.P.U. at Le Havre for many years.

CILLY, Danish girl of striking appearance, who served as operative of the G.P.U. in England, France, Germany, Belgium and Denmark. She outwitted the Nazi secret police, severed all connections with Moscow, and retired from all political activity.

DETTMER, JOHNNY, German revolutionary buccaneer, gun-runner and leader of Red Assault Guards. Seized, broken and beheaded by the Nazis.

DIMITROV, GEORGI. Bulgarian revolutionist, now secretary-general of the Comintern (Communist International) in Moscow A central figure in the famous Reichstag Fire Trial, for years he was the director of the Comintern for Western Europe and the Americas, operating from Berlin under numerous aliases.

EWERT, ARTHUR, alias Berger, German communist, leading Comintern agent in Germany, France and in North and South America. Ostracized and abandoned by Stalin, Ewert has been in a Brazilian prison for years.

FIRELEI (pronounced Fee-re-lie), German art student who became the author's wife after embracing communism. Eventually the Nazi secret police took her life to avenge the author's escape.

GETSY, Russian agent in charge of G.P.U. operations on the Pacific Coast of the United States a decade ago.

GINSBURG, ROGER WALTER, general agent of the G.P.U. in Paris, France.

GOREV-SKOBLEVSKI, ranking Soviet general secretly stationed in Germany in the early twenties, in charge of preparations for a revolt, seized and condemned to death in Germany, but later released in exchange for German hostages held in Russia.

GUSHI, Russian girl operating under Getsy for the G.P.U. in California.

HALVORSEN, DR. ARNE, resident general agent of the G.P.U. in Norway.

HARDY, GEORGE, British agent of the Comintern who had carried out important missions in the United States, China, Germany and other parts of the world.

HEITMAN, RUDOLF, German agent of the G.P.U. who managed to become an official of the Gestapo upon orders from Moscow.

HOLSTEIN, MARTIN, Nazi spy in the leadership of the German Communist Party.

JENS, HERTHA, assistant and mistress to Inspector Paul Kraus of the Gestapo, a statuesque peasant girl who before Hitler s rise to power had been confidential secretary to communist leaders in Hamburg.

JENSEN, RICHARD, giant Dane, conspirator of the first rank, member of the City Council of Copenhagen, for years the chief agent of the Soviet secret service for all of Scandinavia.

KOMMISSARENKO, Russian agent and one of Stalin's most trusted deputies in all operations of the G.P.U. on the seven seas.

KRAUS, PAUL, Hamburg director of the Foreign Division of the Gestapo in charge of a world-wide network of agents and man hunters.

KUUSINEN, OTTO WILHELM, Finnish communist leader, secretary of the Comintern, director of its Western Bureau in Copenhagen. Stalin appointed him Premier of Finnish Soviet government when the invasion of Finland was launched.

LOSOVSKY, A. D., also S. A., chief of the Profintern (the Red International of Labor Unions) in Moscow, more recently Vice Commissar for Foreign Affairs.

MARX, HUGO, resident agent of the G.P.U. in Hamburg.

MINK, GEORGE, chieftain of the G.PU. on the American waterfront, with long record of operations in Germany, Spain and Denmark.

NEUMANN, HEINZ, son of a wealthy grain dealer in Berlin, favorite of Stalin, Reichstag deputy, organizer of revolts in Germany and China, executed in Moscow during the great purge.

POPOVICS, ALEXANDER, Roumanian revolutionist, operated underground printing plants in Germany until seized by the Gestapo.

RADAM, Inspector of the Nazi secret police in Hamburg, notorious as an extorter of confessions from Hitler's hardiest foes.

SCHRECKENBACH, head of the Foreign Division of the Nazi secret police and most trusted aide of Heinrich Himmler.

SVENSSON, HAROLD, Swedish customs officer who was in the secret service of the G.P.U. at Goeteborg, Sweden.

WALTER, ALBERT, German sailor who joined Lenin's forces early and became in time the chief of the maritime division of the Comintern, directing Moscow's operations in the navies and the merchant fleets of the world. For years Walter was the author's immediate superior. Deeply attached to his aged mother, Walter—to save her life—turned traitor to the Soviet cause when he was seized by the Nazis.

WEISS, ILJA, Hungarian terrorist and waterfront organizer for the Comintern in various ports of the Old World.

WOLLWEBER, ERNST, one of the most remarkable conspirators of our time, the son of a Silesian miner who became the ringleader of a mutiny in the Kaiser's navy at the end of the World War. One of the members of the inner circle ruling the Communist Party of Germany, Wollweber was later elected deputy of the Prussian Diet and of the German Reichstag, serving as one of Stalin's most powerful underground chieftains in Western Europe.

www.ingramcontent.com/pod-product-compliance
Lightning Source LLC
Chambersburg PA
CBHW071948110526
44592CB00012B/1029